SOUTH CAROLINA NATURALIZATIONS

1783-1850

SOUTH CAROLINA NATURALIZATIONS

1783-1850

Compiled by
BRENT H. HOLCOMB

CLEARFIELD

Reprinted for
Clearfield Company, Inc. by
Genealogical Publishing Co., Inc.
Baltimore, Maryland
1997, 2000

Library of Congress Catalogue Card Number 84-81868
International Standard Book Number 0-8063-1101-0
Made in the United States of America

INTRODUCTION

This volume is divided, of necessity, into several sections, as the naturalization records contained herein originate from a variety of sources. The first section of federal records (pp. 1-37) is a transcription of a volume from the Court of Admiralty for the District of South Carolina (National Archives Microfilm M1183, Roll 1). Spellings of names of persons, as well as cities and countries, are given as they are found in the original. The second section of federal records (pp.38-45) is composed of entries from the actual minute books or journals — entries which are missing in the first list. (Some duplication may have occurred here in an effort to avoid omissions.) Some of these entries are based on notices of intent to become citizens, while others are based on actual citizenship certificates. The volume numbers are those used by Marion R. Hemperley in "Federal Naturalization Oaths, Charleston, South Carolina, 1790-1860," which appeared in the *South Carolina Historical Magazine,* Vol. 66 (1965), pp. 112-124, 183-192, and 219-228. These are as follows:

No. 1 - Journal, Circuit Court, 1790-1809
No. 2 - Journal, Circuit Court, 1821-1836
No. 3 - Journal, District Court, 1789-1806
No. 4 - Journal, District Court, 1833-1849
No. 5 - Journal, District Court, 1806-1814
No. 6 - Journal, District Court, 1849-1860
No. 7 - Admiralty Journal, 1795-1806
No. 8 - Admiralty Journal, 1826-1842
No. 9 - Admiralty Journal, 1817-1826
No. 10 - Admiralty Journal, 1806-1814
No. 11 - Admiralty Journal, 1857-1861
No. 12 - Admiralty Journal, 1843-1857

Some numbers appear to apply to more than one volume; therefore, both volume numbers and years should be used in locating a particular record.

The first section of state records, the citizenship book (pp.46-67), comprises abstracts of certificates recorded in a book of that title, as well as a duplicate volume included in Miscellaneous Records (Columbia Series), Volume Q, at the South Carolina Archives. The second section of state records (pp.68-88) is comprised of abstracts of General Assembly (G.A.) petitions and committee reports from the legislature of South Carolina. The originals, from which these abstracts were made, are at the South Carolina Archives. The third section of state records (pp.89-117) comes from the two series of Miscellaneous Records at the South Carolina Archives. Fortunately for us, many of these entries are dual recordings of federal and county records, some of which are not otherwise extant.

The county records section (pp.118-226) is comprised of the records of the counties (actually districts at the time) of South Carolina, in alphabetical order. Some are merely surviving indexes, others are apparently complete runs of the naturalization records. For some counties no records are extant, or at least they have not yet been located. Brief notes on the records of each county are given at the beginning of the designated section.

Naturalization laws have changed fairly frequently in the history of our country. There were such laws for the colonies or provinces in America, but we are concerned here with post-Revolutionary naturalizations and citizenships for South Carolina. We could not begin to quote each statute relating to the subject, but, briefly, South Carolina passed a statute concerning naturalizations on March 26, 1784, and another on February 27, 1788. (See "Federal Naturalization Oaths, Charleston, South Carolina, 1790-1860," by Marion R. Hemperley, referred to above.) Congress passed a law on March 26, 1790, stating that "any alien being a free white person who shall have resided in the United States for two years may be admitted a citizen, on application to any common law court of record in any one of the states wherein he shall have resided for the term of one year at least." *(Public Statutes at Large of the United States of America,* Vol. I, pp. 103-4). Also, a law was passed April 14, 1802, stating that "any alien may be admitted to become a citizen . . . [if] he declares his intention in any court three years at least before his admission . . . resides in the United States at least five years, and at least one year in the state or territory . . ." *(Public Statutes at Large,* Vol. II, pp. 153-5). Therefore, records of naturalization are widely scattered. While it is not feasible to examine every court journal for every district and county in South Carolina, as well as the federal journals, an effort has been made to search the most likely sources. This volume is by no means complete, but as other naturalization records for South Carolina are found, they will be made available also. It is the hope of the author that this will be an aid for finding immigrant ancestors for many researchers.

Brent H. Holcomb, Certified Genealogist
Columbia, South Carolina

SOUTH CAROLINA NATURALIZATIONS

1783-1850

FEDERAL RECORDS

Names of Aliens	Age	Nation	Residence	Occupation	Admission
Adcock, John					15 Oct 1792
Adancourt, Francis		St. Dennis, France			12 Aug 1796
Alexander, George		Greece		Mariner	7 Nov 1796
Albouy, John B.		Martinique			20 Sep 1797
Anneley, George U.		London, England			24 Mar 1797
Allan, John		Edinburgh, Scotland			29 Nov 1797
Allan, William		Glasgow, Scotland		Merchant	16 Jan 1798
Anthony, Joseph		Tyrone, Ireland		Physician	22 May 1798
Alexander, Abraham		London, England		Merchant	4 Sep 1798
Abrahams, Moses		Friburgh, Germany		Shop Keeper	8 May 1799
Aveilhi, Jean B.	36	Gascoigne, France		Engineer	17 Jun 1799
Archbald, Robert		Dalyshire, Scotland		Cabinetmaker	17 Jun 1799
Affigne, Joseph		Bourdeaux, France		merchant, shoemaker	12 Dec 1803
Adams, John S.	24	Antrim, Ireland		Merchant	21 Apr 1804
Amsley, Alexander	28	Aberdeen, Scotland		Mariner	24 Jul 1804
Athroun, Samuel	21	Manchester, England		Mariner	15 Nov 1804
Andre, John	34	Havre de Grace, France		Merchant	27 Mar 1805
Anderson, William	37	Norway		Mariner	5 Apr 1805
Alexander, George	33	Londonderry, Ireland		Ship carpenter	25 May 1805
Alken, Martin	43	London, England		Merchant	27 Jul 1805
Adickes, Eggerick J.		Hanover		Merchant	8 Aug 1805
Austin, William	25	Tyrone, Ireland		Merchant	2 Oct 1805
Aitchison, William	25	Harwick, Scotland		Merchant	2 Jan 1806
Adair, Edward	27	Ireland		Merchant	7 Jan 1806
Adger, James	27	Antrim, Ireland		Merchant	10 Jun 1806
Arnold, Joseph Hayman	21	Burnham, Norfolk, England		Mariner	8 Dec 1806
Aspinall, Nicholas	24	London, Great Britain		Merchant	20 May 1807
Armstrong, Archibald	33	Dublin, Ireland		Merchant	28 Aug 1807
Agnew, James	25	Galway, Ireland		Mariner	29 Dec 1807
Anderson, John S.	31	Norfolk, England		Mariner	10 Aug 1808
Aiken, William	34	Antrim, Ireland	Charleston	Merchant	23 Sep 1811
Anone, Francesce	36	Milano, Italy	Beaufort	Merchant	22 Jul 1812
Adger, Robert	31	Antrim, Ireland	Charleston	Merchant	23 Aug 1813
Aitchison, Robert	29	Roxburghshire, North Britain	Charleston	Merchant	11 Dec 1813
Aberegg, John	35	Canton of Bern, Switzerland	Charleston	watch-maker	9 Jan 1816
Aymar, Sebastian		Piedmont, Sardenia	Charleston		13 Oct 1818
Alix, Charles Lucien		Paris, France	Charleston		13 Oct 1818
Albagnac, Pierre Anselme		Gavonne, France	Charleston		13 Oct 1818
Abbott, Samuel	75	Essex, England	Charleston	Scrivener	27 Aug 1823
Abrahams, Elias	37	London, Great Britain	Charleston	Merchant	5 Mar 1824
Almeda, De Antonio Robins	42	Oporto, Portugal	Charleston	Fruiterer	14 Jan 1830
Abraham, Alexander H.	29	Bremen, Germany	Charleston	Merchant	27 Feb 1830
Astair, Elizabet	50	Havre de Grace, France	Charleston		3 Jul 1830
Anderson, Edward K.	27	Gallowayshire, Scotland	Charleston		5 Aug 1830
Aarons, Moses	55	St. Domingo	Charleston		3 Aug 1831
Affansieffer, Daniel		Russia	Charleston		5 Aug 1831
Albert, Henry	22	Emden, Hanover	Charleston		23 Sep 1831
Allerding, Henry	32	Hambrugh	Charleston	Clerk	5 Oct 1831
Avery, James	26	England	Charleston	Lighterman	5 Oct 1831
Aendes, Frederick	32	Germany	Charleston	Grocer	5 Oct 1831
Ash, James E.	26	England	Charleston	Lighterman	8 Oct 1831
Antonio, Aires Dos Nevis		Lisbon, Portugal	Charleston		16 Sep 1834
Adams, Thomas	24	Bermuda, Island	Charleston	Mariner	27 Mar 1835
Aufderheide, Charles F.	34	Prussia	Charleston	Grocer	4 Aug 1835
Alsguth, C. B.	23	Hanover	Charleston	Grocer	18 Jul 1839
Allamong, Mary Teresa	37	Monaghan (Ireland)	Charleston	widow	5 Jul 1842
Amme, D. A.	25	Hanover	Charleston	Store-keeper	8 Apr 1847
Anderson, William	33	County Down, Ireland	Charleston	mariner	16 Aug 1847
Allan, Alexander	49	County Murray, Scotland	Charleston	House-carpenter	16 Aug 1847
Arndt, Henry L.	33	Rostock, Mecklenberg, Schwein	Charleston	Labourer	16 Aug 1847
Alquie, Jacques	36	Lyons, France	Do	silk-weaver	5 Oct 1860

Names of Aliens	Age	Nation	Residence	Occupation	Admission
Bell, Alexander		Great Britain			13 May 1790
Brodie, Alexander		North Britain			25 May 1792
Berry, Francis Hubert					17 Sep 1792
Bradford, Thomas					27 May 1794
Brailsford, Samuel					6 Jun 1794
Blair, James		North Britain			7 Jul 1794
Boate, Thomas					29 Sep 1795
Burch, Jeremiah		Bermudas		Mariner	18 Jan 1796
Brownlow, John		Bermudas		Mariner	16 May 1796
Bowen, William Jones		Ireland			20 Sep 1796
Booker, Anthony		Meath, Ireland			26 Sep 1796
Buckley, Philip		Kilkenny, Ireland		Mariner	28 Sep 1796
Branagan, John		Meath, Ireland		Grocer	8 Oct 1796
Bordezdes, Des Roy		Toulon, France			16 Jan 1797
Bailey, David		Yorkshire, England			17 Jan 1797
Bailey, Thomas		Yorkshire, England			17 Jan 1797
Bethell, David		Bermudas			11 Feb 1797
Blair, John		Paisley,Scotland			29 Nov 1797
Bladen, Thomas Dedimus		St. Eustalia			2 Feb 1798
Brown, Samuel S.		Scotland		Merchant	9 Mar 1798
Ballantine, David	26	Cambleton, Scotland		Mariner	21 Mar 1798
Bigam, William		Colerain, Ireland		Mariner	30 Mar 1798
Broadfoot, William		Galloway, Scotland		Merchant	2 Apr 1798
Budde, Marke	31	Droutem, Denmark		Mariner	19 Sep 1798
Burk, Walter		St. Croix		Mariner	25 Feb 1799
Bäck, John Mauritz		Stockholm, Sweden		Mariner	25 Feb 1799
Bailey, George Gibbs	35	Bristol, England		Merchant	28 Jul 1802
Bruckner, Daniel	35	Basil, Switzerland		Merchant	21 Sep 1802
Brown, John		Liverpool, England			28 Feb 1803
Blome, John	60	Triers, Germany		Physician	18 Jul 1803
Bell, Boaz	26	Bermudas		Mariner	7 Sep 1803
Bushell, John	22	St. Domingo		cabinet maker	19 Sep 1803
Bashford, Thomas Gunning	27	Belfast, Ireland		Merchant	28 Sep 1803
Bournois, Peter Louis	23	St. Domingo		Merchant	19 Mar 1803
Boyd, John	25	Tyrone, Ireland		Merchant	21 Apr 1804
Bannatyre, Thomas	31	Glasgow, Scotland		Mariner	6 Sep 1804
Brown, Adam	23	Edinburgh, Scotland		Mariner	11 Oct 1804
Burgoyne, William	22	London, England		Physician	11 Oct 1804
Barnwell, Edward	20	Dublin, Ireland		Mariner	5 Nov 1804
Backstrom, Jonas	27	Uma, Sweden		Mariner	11 Dec 1804
Butler, Peter	44	Kings County, Ireland		Mariner	16 Jan 1805
Baker, Thomas	30	Devonshire, England		Malster	8 Mar 1805
Bennet, Robert	44	Inverness, Scotland		Mariner	13 Apr 1805
Blanch, Martin	26	Volgast, Sweden		Mariner	13 Apr 1805
Buchanan, Hugh	32	Grenock, Scotland		Mariner	8 May 1805
Brebner, Archibald	35	Aberdeen, Scotland		Merchant Taylor	16 May 1805
Brooks, John	23	Yarmouth, England		Mariner	6 Jul 1805
Benoit, JohnBaptiste	58	Larochelle, France		Baker	23 Aug 1805
Bryce, Nichol	25	Edinburgh, Scotland		Merchant	16 Sep 1805
Butcher, Abraham	31	Norfolk, England		Mariner	19 Sep 1805
Barreyre, Peter	36	Bourdeaux, France		Baker	22 Oct 1805
Beckman, Adolph	37	Riga, Russia		Painter & Glazier	2 Jan 1806
Barrelli, John	31	Rouen, Italy		Mathematical Instrument maker	2 Jan 1806
Beckenerer, Peter C.	33	Louent, France		Mariner	14 Jan 1806
Bryce, Henry	23	Edinburgh, Scotland		Merchant	29 Jan 1806
Brescon, Jean	38	New Orleans		Merchant	18 Feb 1806
Bremar, Francis	22	Western Ocean		Mariner	19 Mar 1806
Burke, Thomas	28	Killala, Ireland		Mariner	14 Apr 1806
Brown, Thomas L.	37	Dartmouth, England		Mariner	14 Apr 1806
Butler, Daniel	34	Kilkenny, Ireland		Mariner	22 May 1806
Bradley, Peter	20	Campbeltown, Scotland		Mariner	10 Jun 1806
Bonthron, John	29	Edinburgh		Merchant	15 Sep 1806
Bernie, William	24	Aberdeen, North Britain		Merchant	29 Sep 1806
Blayney, Richard Stone		Cheshire, England		Merchant	29 Sep 1806
Beekman, John Frederick	38	Germany		Grocer	14 Oct 1806
Blanken, George	34	Germany		Grocer	14 Oct 1806
Brinan, Peter	37	Donnegal, Ireland		Carpenter	10 Apr 1807
Ball, James	35	London, Great Britain		Merchant	30 May 1807
Bowhav, Joseph P.	31	Devonshire, England		Butcher	13 Jul 1807
Brandon, David P.	45	Bourdeaux, France		Musician	13 Jul 1807
Bridie, Robert	23	Perth, North Britain		Cooper	13 Sep 1807
Belshaw, Robert	23	Antrim, Ireland		Merchant	11 Jan 1808
Beek, Samuel	31	Island of Bermudas		Mariner	21 Mar 1808
Brown, William	28	Londonderry, Ireland		Merchant	13 Sep 1808

FEDERAL RECORDS

Names of Aliens	Age	Nation	Residence	Occupation	Admission
Bourg, Pierre	53	Bourdeaux, France			17 Apr 1809
Blackwood, John	21	Down, Ireland		Merchant	26 May 1809
Bascome, Benjamin	24	Bermudas		Merchant	3 June1809
Bremar, Henry	28	London, England	Charleston	Dentist	5 Feb 1810
Blinn, John	33	Piempol, France		Mariner	2 May 1810
Black, Alexander	21	Cavan, Ireland	Charleston	Merchant	14 Nov 1811
Brown, Robert	37	Glasgow, North Britain	Charleston	Factor	29 Sep 1812
				admitted Denizen	22 Jul 1800
Battker, John Andrew	31	Mecklenburg	Charleston	Shopkeeper	24 Mar 1813
Bock, John	34	Rostock, Germany	Charleston	Mariner	7 May 1813
Bruchet, Joseph	36	Lyons, France	Charleston	Mariner	14 Jun 1813
Brown, Joseph	34	Limerick, Ireland	Charleston	Grocer	23 Aug 1813
Blain, Andrew	38	Gallowayshire, North Britain	Charleston	Wheelwright	27 Aug 1813
Braid, Mathew	34	Dunbartonshire, North Britain	Charleston	Carpenter	27 Aug 1813
Bradley, Charles	35	Tyrone, Ireland	Charleston	Printer	10 Sep 1813
Beswicke, John Brown	70	Hereford, England	Charleston	Lumber measurer	20 Sep 1813
Bell, Robert	40	Down, Ireland			13 Jun 1814
Blanc, Leonard	23	Cape Francois, Hispaniola	Charleston	Mariner	2 Aug 1814
Bock, Andrew	37	Ratisbon, Germany			11 Oct 1814
Barry, Peter	41	Christianstad, Sweden			11 Oct 1814
Bicais, Claude	52	Provence, France		cabinet maker	13 Jun 1815
Buisse, John Henry	25	Altona, Holstein, Denmark	Charleston	merchant	23 Oct 1815
				gave notice	5 Oct 1812
Berges, Louis	21	Bourdeaux, France	Charleston	mariner	25 Jan 1816
Ballund, Alexander	32	Stockholm, Sweden	Charleston		10 Apr 1816
Bonamy, Constantine Frederick	42	Nantz, France	Charleston		13 Apr 1816
Barbot, Anthony		Bourdeaux, France	Charleston	grocer	20 Jan 1817
Brown, William	37	Calmar, Sweden	Charleston	grocer	24 Sep 1818
				gave notice	6 Feb 1815
Birnie, George	29	Aberdeen, North Britain	Charleston	merchant	19 Oct 1818
				gave notice	4 Sep 1815
Blancke, Christian	35	Hamburg	Charleston		2 Apr 1822
				gave notice	19 Jan 1819
Bosch, Harman	51	Bremen, Germany	Charleston	grocer	14 May 1822
Boinest, Daniel	23	Harburg, Germany	Charleston		18 Dec 1823
Barker, James		London, Great Britain	Charleston		29 Dec 1823
Bery, Peter	48	Geneva, Italy	Charleston	confectioner	31 Mar 1824
Buerhaus, Herman D.	40	Delwig, Prussia	Charleston	Taylor	22 June 1824
Bull, William	32	Portsea, Hampshire, England	Charleston	Sc-----	22 June 1824
Bicaise, Peter Paul Alexander	23	St. Domingo	Charleston		4 Sep 1824
Bunell, William		Ireland	Charleston		4 Sep 1824
Bull, John	36	Hampshire, England	Charleston		8 Oct 1824
Black, James Campbell	22	Antrim, Ireland	Charleston	merchant	12 Oct 1824
Barelli, Joseph A.	25	Conis, Italy	Charleston	merchant	26 Oct 1825
Benjamin, Philip	44	Island of Nevis, Great Britain	Charleston		9 Jan 1826
Behrman, Charles	33	Hamburg	Charleston	grocer	13 Apr 1826
Bailey, Robert Smith	32	Yorkshire, England	Christ Church parish	Doctor of Medicine	5 Jul 1826
Brady, John	36	Cavan, Ireland			27 Sep 1826
Bermingham, John	27	Cork, Ireland	Charleston	School-master	28 Sep 1826
Bird, John S.	29	London, Great Britain	Charleston		7 May 1827
Boyle, Alexander Noe	27	Liverpool, Great Britain	Charleston	Mariner	19 May 1827
Bernard, Francis	27	Kenuffe	Charleston	Mariner	5 Nov 1827
Bull, Timothy	25	Portsmouth, England	Charleston	Mariner	17 Nov 1827
Brown, Edward	43	Norfolk, England	Charleston		15 Jan 1828
Blair, William	23	Kirkcudbright, North Britain	Charleston		21 Mar 1828
Brennan, Patrick N.	30	Waterford, Ireland	Charleston	Merchant	15 Apr 1828
Breithaupt, Christian E. O.	26	Saalfield, Sace Coburg	Charleston	Farmer & planter	15 Apr 1828
Bremer, Otto Peter Daniel		Holstein, Denmark	Charleston		29 Apr 1828
Black, William	34	Fifeshire, Scotland	Charleston		10 Oct 1828
Birnie, John	41	Aberdeenshire, North Britain	Charleston	Millwright	11 Oct 1828

FEDERAL RECORDS

Names of Aliens	Age	Nation	Residence	Occupation	Admission
Brenau, Charles	32	Sligo, Ireland			14 Apr 1829
Barry, John Revd.	30	Werford, Ireland		Clergyman	23 May 1829
Becker, Daniel	30	Denmark	Charleston	Grocer	22 Jun 1829
Burmester, Claus	22	Hanover	Charleston	Clerk	21 Sep 1829
Bohlen, John	28	Hanover	Charleston	Shopkeeper	25 Sep 1829
Breen, Anne, wife of Philip Breen		Ireland	Charleston		4 Jan 1830
" Elizabeth, their child a minor					
Barelli, Anthony M.	29	On the Lake Como, Italy	Charleston	Mariner	15 Mar 1830
Busing, John	34	Oldenburgh, Germany	Charleston	Grocer	7 Jul 1830
Buswell, Mathew	38	Sicily	Charleston	Grocer	14 Jul 1830
Boisseau, James E.	36	Island of Cape Breton	Charleston	Hardware merchant	21 Jul 1830
Bacon, Edward	34	Dorsetshire, England	Charleston	Merchant	29 Jul 1830
Blair, Hugh	22	Gallowayshire, Scotland	Charleston		5 Aug 1830
Ballantine, John	30	Ayrshire, Scotland	Charleston	House carpenter	26 Aug 1830
Brase, Peter	34	Bremen, Hanover	Charleston	Grocer	28 Aug 1830
Blondeau, Stephen	52	Paris, France	Charleston	Hatter	6 Oct 1830
Burnham, William	41	Kilkenny, Ireland	Charleston	Blacksmith & Locksmith	6 Oct 1830
Bringloe, Richard	35	Norwich, England	Charleston	Boat builder	15 Dec 1830
Baring, Charles	57	Exeter, Devonshire, England	Combahee	Planter	27 Jan 1831
Benseman, Frederick W.	36	Dantric, Prussia	Charleston	Mariner	6 Jul 1831
Bandrock, Charles	28	Statlin, Prussia	Charleston		3 Aug 1831
Buckan, Abraham	65	Switzerland	Charleston		3 Aug 1831
Brun, Ole Oleson	40	Norway	Charleston		3 Aug 1831
Bornes, Henry H.	24	Germany	Charleston	Clerk	5 Oct 1831
Bradley, James P.	29	Londonderry, Ireland	Charleston	Hostler	5 Oct 1831
Bruner, Peter	25	Germany	Charleston	Grocer	8 Oct 1831
Beck, Johann G.	21	Wirtemberg	Charleston		23 Jul 1832
Belnoux, John M.	25	France	Charleston	Sugarmaker	14 Aug 1832
Bicais, Frederick	28	Island St. Domingo	Charleston	House carpenter	14 Aug 1832
Black, John	22	Grenock, Scotland	Charleston	carpenter	31 Aug 1832
Bale, John	29	Canada	Charleston	Mariner	3 Sep 1832
Bums, James	27	Belfast, Ireland	Charleston	cutter	22 Sep 1832
Bissinger, Konrad	28	Mayhem, Germany	Charleston	clerk	3 Oct 1832
Bensen, Harman	21	Hanover	Charleston	shopkeeper	3 Oct 1832
Butler, John	30	Bristol, England	Charleston	clerk	4 Oct 1832
Bormbush, John H.	22	Hanover	Charleston	clerk	4 Oct 1832
Benson, Dierik H.	27	Hanover	Charleston	Sugarbaker	4 Oct 1832
Boag, WilliamS.	32	Stockport, England	Charleston	Druggist	4 Oct 1832
Bullwinkle, John		Hanover	Charleston		8 Oct 1832
Buck, Henry	26	Hanover	Charleston	shopkeeper	9 Oct 1832
Brophy, William	32	Nova Scotia			28 Nov 1832
Blumenberg, Frederick	50	Gross Kluger, Prussia	Charleston	Physician	7 Feb 1833
Becker, Hans	27	Denmark	Charleston		30 Aug 1834
Bullwinkle, George	34	Hanover	Charleston		30 Aug 1834
Burqu(?), Nicholas	47	Germany			14 Oct 1834
Bize, Daniel	57	Isl. St. Eustatia			14 Oct 1834
Bordenave, John	38	Province Gascony, France	Charleston	Hair-dresser	28 Feb 1835
Blake, Arthur Middleton	21	London, England		Planter	8 Apr 1835
Blake, Walter	29	Surry, England		Planter	14 May 1835
Brown, Henry	41	Finland, Sweden	Charleston	mariner	13 Apr 1836
Baker, Richard S.		Ireland	Charleston	Clergyman	7 Aug 1837
Bevans, David Clements	34	London, GB	Charleston	Mariner	25 Nov 1837
Bevan, Daniel	38	Wales, GB	Charleston	Storekeeper	19 Jul 1839
Betienman, Henry	22	Hanover	Charleston	Grocer	19 Jul 1839
Brunning, Henry	29	Hanover	Charelston	Grocer	9 Jan 1840
Brandt, John H.	23	Hanover	Charleston	Grocer	6 May 1840
Behling, Luder F.	24	Hanover	Charleston	Grocer	5 Jan 1841
Bohlen, Luder	22	Bremen, Germany	Charleston	Grocer	18 Mar 1841
Ban, James	30	Glasgow, Scotland	Charleston District	Planter	3 Feb 1842
Beecher, F.	29	Waldbroul, Prussia	Charleston	minister	22 Mar 1842
Bargmann, B.	32	Hanover	Charleston	grocer	14 Apr 1843
Burke, William	29	Ireland	Charleston	mirister	1 May 1832
Bulwinkle, Henry	31	Hanover	Charleston	grocer	6 Mar 1843
Brady, John	47	Ireland	Charleston	accountant	12 Jul 1843

Names of Aliens	Age	Nation	Residence	Occupation	Admission
Behling, Ernst F.	25	Hanover	Charleston	Grocer	1 Jul 1844
Borges, John H.	31	Germany	Charleston	Shopkeeper	1 Jul 1844
Birmingham, Timothy	43	Tipperary(Ireland)	Charleston	Clergyman	3 Jan 1846
Burke, John	29	Ireland	Charleston	Labourer	13 Jan 1847
Blase, C. L.	23	Prussia	Charleston	Grocer	14 Jan 1847
Blyden, Christopher	23	Island Sr. Martin West Indies	Charleston	Clerk	12 Feb 1847
Bischoff, Henry	25	Hanover	Charleston	Merchant	16 Apr 1847
Bensch, Charles	27	Poland (King of Prussia)	Charleston	Grocer	19 Jul 1847
Buerro, Emanuel	25	Genoa (King of Sardina)	Charleston	Clerk	6 Aug 1847
Bahntze, Henry	33	Marcullendorff, Hanover	Charleston	Store-keeper	16 Aug 1847
Buhre, J. Frederick	30	Lese, Hanover	Charleston	Grocer	10 Mar 1849
Brown, John	28	Dumfrieshire, Scotland	Charleston	Planter	5 Jul 1849
Bestmann, John	39	Holstein-Denmark	Charleston	mariner	24 Jan 1850
Buhre, Diedrich	34	Hanover	Charleston	Shop-keeper	4 Nov 1850
Behr, Heinrich	27	Hanover	Charleston	Clerk	14 May 1855
Brown, Alfred L.	31	Dublin, Ireland	Charleston	Watch-maker	1 Jun 1855
Bagly, James	44	Ireland	D^{o}		17 Mar 1857
Basvecchi, Pietro O.	29	Italy	Charleston	Professor of music	13 Mar 1858
Baruc, Bernard S.	29	Giesen, Germany	D^{o}	Merchant	22 Apr 1858
But, Jacob	35	Fume, Austria	D^{o}	Seaman	25 Nov 1859
Carroll, James Parsons		Ireland			12 Jun 1792
Crowly, Michael		Ireland			17 Sep 1792
Conyers, John		Bermudas			15 Mar 1795
Cameron, Samuel					10 Sep 1795
Coste, John Paul					17 Sep 1792
Campbell, John		North Britain		Mariner	19 Jan 1796
Charet, Prudent Brice		Nantz, Brittany			6 Jul 1796
Coleman, George		Dublin, Ireland		Mariner	17 Aug 1796
Corlett, Thomas		White Haven, England		Mariner	17 Jan 1797
Cooper, Peter		North Britain		Mariner	25 Mar 1797
Crawley, Elish		Middlesex, England			6 Jul 1797
Caruth, Peter		Gawonshire, Scotland			30 Nov 1797
Cooling, Thomas		Bristol, England		Mariner	26 Mar 1798
Craig, William		Carrickfergus, Ireland		Mariner	2 Apr 1798
Cocquereau, Charles		Rochelle, France			2 Apr 1798
Courtin, Francis	41	Paris, France		Merchant	17 Jun 1799
Curtius, Frederick	30	Brunswick, Germany		Merchant	17 Jun 1799
Caren, William		Waterford, Ireland		Mariner	17 Jun 1799
Chouler, Joseph	39	London, England		Physician	2 Aug 1802
Crovat, Peter	31	Vienna, Germany		Merchant	4 Sep 1802
Cormick, Thomas	30	Ireland			20 Sep 1802
Club, Alexander	35	Frazersberg, Scotland		Merchant	25 Sep 1802
Crow, John	30	Coleraine, Ireland		Bookbinder	15 Oct 1802
Carmichael, James	28	Glasgow, Scotland		Merchant	21 Mar 1803
Calder, Alexander	30	Edinburgh, Scotland		Cabiner maker	25 Mar 1803
Cott, Ramon	27	Mataxo, Spain		Mariner	4 Jul 1803
Canter, John	22	St. Croix, Danish Island		Limner	20 Jul 1803
Chazal, John Peter	22	Cape Francois		Mariner	6 Sep 1803
Coullion, John Lewis	31	Normouthie, France		Mariner	19 Sep 1803
Corrie, Alexander	27	Galloway, Scotland		Merchant	20 Sep 1803
Coates, William A.	29	Essex, England		Merchant	21 Sep 1802
Christopher, Constantine	33	Zantz, Venice		Mariner	14 Nov 1803
Crombie, Joseph	26	Belfast, Ireland		Merchant	23 Jan 1804
Crombie, Hugh	23	Belfast, Ireland		Merchant	23 Jan 1804
Claret, Joseph	28	Narbonne, France		Merchant	23 Feb 1804
Colman, John	34	Norfolk, England		Mariner	23 Feb 1804
Carson, Samuel	34	Belfast, Ireland		Merchant	23 Feb 1804
Catlin, Francis	30	Bermudas		Mariner	30 Apr 1804
Chirnside, George	32	Sunderland, England		Mariner	8 Jun 1804
Clineys, George	22	Liverpool, England		Mariner	20 Jun 1804
Cunningham, Robert W.	36	Waterford, Ireland		Mariner	17 Sep 1804
Cabos, Jean	47	Rochfort, France		Jeweller	11 Dec 1804
Connolly, Jeremiah	21	Kerry, Ireland		Mariner	15 Dec 1804
Champy, Alexander	22	Point Petre, Gaudoloupe		Physician	12 Jan 1805
Christian, Thomas	31	Douglas, Isle of Mann		Merchant	23 Apr 1805
Caruth, John	28	Galloway, Scotland		Mariner	17 Jul 1805
Cruckshanks, William	30	Murrayshire, Scotland		Shoemaker	15 Aug 1805
Coveney, Thomas	43	Cork, Ireland		Mariner	23 Aug 1805
Champey, Peter F.	18	Gaudoloupe		Apothecary	2 Oct 1805
Crout, John F.	30	London, England		Mariner	5 Oct 1805
Cashman, John	32	Waterford, Ireland		Shoemaker	16 Oct 1805

Names of Aliens	Age	Nation	Residence	Occupation	Admission
Conte, John	21	Martinique		Merchant	26 Oct 1805
Coudres, des Louis P.	26	Hesse Cassel, Germany		Merchant	2 Jan 1806
Craig, Robert	20	Grenock, Scotland		Mariner	19 Mar 1806
Chancognie, Simon Jude					14 Apr 1806
Coffill, Richard	22	Newry, Ireland		Mariner	14 Apr 1806
Chanet, Anthony	45	Valence, France		Merchant	7 Jul 1806
Corlett, William	23	Jamaica		Mariner	27 Aug 1806
Clark, Richard	22	Cambridge, England		Pilot	22 Sep 1807
Connell, Connor Thomas	27	Prescot, England		Mariner	25 Jan 1808
Coste, Loui	44	Montpellier, France		Merchant	9 Apr 1808
Clissey, Raymond	46	Bourdeaux, France		Coach maker	13 Sep 1808
Cobzy, Charlemagne	37	Aulnois, France		Taylor	19 Sep 1808
Chisolm, George	26	Edinburgh, Scotland		Mariner	20 Mar 1809
Campbell, Peter	32	Glasgow, Scotland		Mariner	16 Jun 1809
Colley, Thomas	39	Surry, England		Shopkeeper	20 Sep 1809
Crawford, John	40	Frenock, North Britain		Physician	20 Sep 1809
Carr, Dale	35	Durham, England		Mariner	20 Jul 1811
Caught, Thomas	56	Portsmouth, South-ampton, England	Charleston	Ship carpenter	26 Jun 1812
Charriol, Pierre	42	Libourne, France	Charleston	mariner	19 Nov 1812
Canneva, James	33	St. Malo, France	Charleston	mariner	20 Apr 1813
Cousins, Thomas	26	London, Gr. Br.	Charleston	Merchant	31 Aug 1813
Calder, James	23	Glasgow, North Britain	Charleston	Cabinet maker	1 Sep 1813
Cassin, Conly	22	Tipperary, Ireland	Charleston	Merchant	6 Oct 1813
Catherwood, John James	26	London, Great Britain	Charleston	Watchmaker	14 Oct 1813
Carnochan, Richard	30	Galloway, North Britain	Charleston	Merchant	16 Nov 1813
Caldwell, Robert	26	Tyrone, Ireland	Charleston		17 Nov 1813
			gave notice in Philadelphia		
Carvalho, Emanuel N.	45	London, Great Britain	Charleston	minister	23 Dec 1813
Caquet, John Mary	39	Department of Loire, France	Charleston	merchant & shopkeeper	11 Apr 1814
Clark, John	23	Suffolk, England	Charleston	mariner	7 Mar 1815
Craig, Thomas	33	Dublin, Ireland	Charleston	accomptant	21 Jun 1815
Caradeux, Jean Baptiste	30	Port au Prince, St. Domingo	Charleston		13 May 1816
Carmaud, Francis	28	Marmande, Giroude, France	Charleston	Merchant-Taylor	22 May 1816
Carivenc, Antoine Alexisandre	47	Toulouse, France	Charleston		2 Jul 1816
Cromwell, Samuel	43	Somersetshire, England		Bricklayer	9 Sep 1816
Coleman, Robert	23	Belfast, Ireland	Charleston	mariner	4 Jun 1818
			gave notice 10 Apr 1815		
Clark, Bartholomew		Armagh, Ireland	Charleston	merchant	13 Dec 1819
			gave notice 11 Dec 1816		
Carvalho, David N.	33	London, Great Britain	Charleston	Jeweller	11 Jan 1820
Chapeau, Marie Pauline		Island of St. Domingo	Charleston		19 Jul 1820
Cline, Jacob		Wirtemberg, Germany	Charleston		12 Dec 1820
Cathcart, Robert	27	Antrim, Ireland Great Britain	Winnsborough	merchant	21 Mar 1821
Corby, John	31	London, Great Britain	Charleston	Blacksmith	16 Jun 1823
Chapeau, John B.	43	Jeremie Island, St. Domingo	Charleston		23 Jul 1823
Cardoza, Joseph	37	Lisbon, Portugal	Charleston	Mariner	16 Sep 1823
Carmille, John	43	Champdotre, France	Charleston	Butcher	21 Oct 1823
Carson, William	31	Kirkcudbright, North Britain	Charleston	Merchant	6 Feb 1824
Changuion, Jean, Henry, Fedinand Louis	23	Brabaut, Holland	Charleston		5 Mar 1824
Corbet, Henry	29	Edinburgh, Scotland	Columbia		18 Nov 1824
Campbell, John	33	Glasgow, Scotland	Charleston	Merchant	17 May 1825
Clancy, John	31	Kilkenny, Ireland	Charleston		11 Dec 1826
Creber, William B.	26	London, Great Britain	Columbia (near)	wagon-maker	13 Dec 1826
Cohen, Lewin	37	London D^{o}	Charleston	watchmaker	19 Apr 1827
Cohen, Nathan A.	23	London	Charleston	Taylor	19 Oct 1827
Cassin, James	35	Tipperary, Ireland	Charleston		14 Nov 1827
Cross, Daniel	25	Denmark	Charleston	Grocer	1 Jul 1828

Names of Aliens	Age	Nation	Residence	Occupation	Admission
Christopherson, Chresten	34	Norway	Charleston		7 Jul 1828
Cox, George	42	Exeter, England	Charleston	Seedsman	7 Jul 1828
Christian, Martin	23	Mandell, Norway	Charleston	Grocer	10 Oct 1828
Crawford, Mathew	30	Donegall, Ireland	Columbia	Merchant	9 Dec 1828
Cassin, Mary	64	Donegall, Ireland	Charleston		22 Jun 1829
Cassady, Patrick	40	Mayo, Ireland	Charleston		21 Jul 1830
Cohen, Hartwig	40	Warta, Poland	Charleston	Merchant	26 Aug 1830
Cook, John A.	30	Hanover	Charleston	Grocer	26 Aug 1830
Cook, Otto	29	Hanover	Charleston	Grocer	26 Aug 1830
Calder, William	34	Paisley, North Britain	Charleston	Merchant	27 Jul 1831
Cowan, John	42	Ireland	Charleston		27 Jul 1831
Collin, Peter	29	France	Charleston		3 Aug 1831
Charmois, Denis	26	France	Charleston		26 Aug 1831
Classen, Harman W	33	Hamburgh	Charleston	Clerk	5 Oct 1831
Conally, Barnard	26	Dublin, Ireland	Charleston	Mariner	5 Oct 1831
Cleveringa, Bronno F	24	Rotterdam, Holland	Charleston	Grocer	5 Oct 1831
Chasteau, Rene Charles	71	Parthenai, France	Charleston	Physician	8 Oct 1831
Cassidy, George W.	29	Monaghan, Ireland	Charleston	Merchant	7 Jan 1832
Campbell, Henrietta	68	Scotland	Charleston		3 May 1832
Clement, Nicholas	30	Malta		Mariner	31 Aug 1832
Coffey, Bartholomew J.	30	Kerry, Ireland	Charleston	Shopkeeper	31 Aug 1832
Connolly, Richard	55	England	Charleston	Grocer	3 Sep 1832
Causse, Adolphe	42	St. Domingo	Charleston	Clerk	22 Sep 1832
Christiansen, Jasper	30	Denmark	Charleston	Clerk	22 Sep 1832
Clawson, John Christopher	37	Denmark	Charleston	Grocer	4 Oct 1832
Conlen, John	29	Antrim, Ireland	Charleston	Engineer	5 Oct 1832
Cunningham, Andrew	33	Dublin, Ireland	Charleston	Carpenter	5 Oct 1832
Cartey, Owen	40	Wexford, Ireland	Charleston	Labourer	9 Oct 1832
Curren, Daniel	34	Ireland		Blacksmith	11 Oct 1832
Clarken, Christopher	26	Ireland			14 Oct 1834
Clats, John or Klats	24	Dastrie, Prussia	Charleston	Shopkeeper	4 Aug 1835
Cay, John E.	35	Island St. Domingo	Charleston	Merchant	8 Feb 1837
Carsten, John Frederick	22	Hanover	Charleston		1 Aug 1837
Cohen, Henry S.	21	London	Charleston	Slopseller	12 Sep 1837
Cameron, George S.	23	Perthshire, Scotland	Charleston	Merchant	22 Dec 1838
Christofel, George	23	Roorhback, Bavaria		Miller	2 May 1839
Carey, Eugene M.	30	Westmeath, Ireland	Charleston	Druggist	18 Jul 1839
Collingwood, John	29	Glasgow, Scotland		Grocer	19 Jul 1839
Cohen, Samuel	22	London	Charleston	Slopseller	6 Jul 1840
Cohen, Aaron Nathan	64	London	Charleston	Shop-keeper	5 Jan 1841
Cohen, Husch Caspar	45	Prussia	Charleston	Merchant	5 Jan 1841
Cordes, Albrecht	51	Bremen	Charleston	Baker	28 May 1841
Clarke, Mary Jane	23	County Monaghan, Ireland	Charleston		2 Jun 1842
Cook, Jacob	23	Hanover	Charleston	Storekeeper	3 Jul 1843
Clarke, John	25	Cavan, Ireland	Charleston	Merchant	8 Nov 1844
Caldwell, John	49	Penny Cook, Scotland	Charleston	machinist	7 Apr 1847
Culbert, James	30	Donnegal, Ireland	Charleston	Merchant	6 Apr 1847
Chiesa, Antonio	23	Austria (Emporer of Austria)	Charleston	Mariner	6 Aug 1847
Conlen, John	35	Co. of Lond., Ireland	Charleston	Labourer	16 Apr 1849
Cameron, Archibald	35	Isld. Lesmore, Argyleshire, Scotland	Charleston	Machinist & Engineer	15 Apr 1850
Claussen, Fredk. Wm.	34	Oldenburg	Charleston	Baker	10 Jan 1856
Cantwell, James	30	Kilkenny, Ireland	Charleston	Clerk	3 Dec 1856
Corne, Thomas	35	Ireland	D°	Labourer	29 Sep 1857
Conlan, Owen	38	Ireland	D°	Labourer	14 Oct 1857
Cahill, John	37	Ireland	D°	Porter	10 Nov 1857
Cambatis, George	31	Spritzea, Greece	D°	mariner	27 Oct 1858
Collins, Daniel	23	Longfield, Ireland	D°	Brick-layer	2 Nov 1859
Cleary, Patrick	39	Tipperary, Ireland	D°	Labourer	3 Nov 1859
Cohen, Louis	28	Prussia	D°	Merchant	15 Feb 1860
Casey, Edmund	32	Limerick, Ireland	D°	Shoemaker	15 Oct 1860
Cook, Francis	28	Baden, Germany	D°	Gardener	17 Oct 1860
Dansie, Abraham					21 Jan 1794
Dalton, Peter		Waterford			19 Jan 1796
Downes, Jeremiah		Clyde, Scotland		Mariner	24 Mar 1796
Dawson, Thomas		Ireland			6 Jul 1796
Duffy, Henry		Tyrone, Ireland		Grocer	20 Sep 1796
Duffy, Barnard		Ireland			20 Sep 1796
Dowthwaite, Abraham		Keswick, England		Tallow-Chandler	23 Sep 1796

Names of Aliens	Age	Nation	Residence	Occupation	Admission
Dowthwaite, Robert		Keswick, England		Grocer	23 Sep 1796
Dennison, James		Orkneys, North Britain		Mariner	12 Dec 1796
Dupuy, Claude		Languedoc, France			14 Dec 1796
Desborder, Des Roy		Toulon, France			16 Jan 1797
Dickinson, John F.		Bermudas		Mariner	20 Mar 1797
Doran, William		Wexford, Ireland		Mariner	10 Aug 1797
Duffus, John		Great Britain			18 Nov 1797
Dubois, Charles Louis		Ath. in Ainault, Austria			2 Apr 1798
Drewais, Adam		Wismar, Sweden		Mariner	2 Apr 1798
Dunn, John		Cork, Ireland		Grocer	29 May 1799
Duffy, Patrick	22	Carrick McRoss, Ireland		Grocer	17 Jun 1799
Deishmann, Charles F.	24	Bassum, Lower Hessia		Merchant	13 Jun 1799
DeGrasse, Alexr. Frs. Augustua		Versailles, France		Engineer	17 Jun 1799
Dunn, John	25	Queen's County, Ireland		Mariner	17 Jun 1799
Duncan, George	29	Dundee, North Britain		Mariner	17 Jun 1799
Duglas, John	29	near Edinburgh, Scotland		Cabinet maker	24 Sep 1802
Denny, Thomas	30	Tyrone, Ireland		Physician	6 Oct 1802
Daken, Frederick	30	Minden, Prussia		Shopkeeper	23 Oct 1802
Delaval, Joseph	50	Rhone, France		Planter	8 Jul 1803
Depeau, Bertrand	24	Bayonne, France		Merchant	19 Mar 1804
Duboc, Peter John	45	Normandy, France		Merchant	21 Mar 1804
Durbec, Joseph	40	Normandy, France		Merchant	16 Apr 1804
Duluc, Christopher	35	Blaye, France		Merchant	11 Jun 1804
Dawson, John	45	Tyrone, Ireland		Merchant	11 Jun 1804
Dacqueny, John A.	26	Konfleur, Normandy		Printer	27 Aug 1804
Duboc, Francis Tite	34	Normandy, France		Baker	30 Aug 1804
Dupont, Joseph	47	Tours, France		Merchant	17 Sep 1804
Domu, Mark	50	Cape Francois		Merchant	12 Oct 1804
Douglass, James	32	Galloway, Scotland		Mariner	10 Dec 1804
Debon, Stephen				Merchant	20 Jul 1805
Dupony, John	29	Bearn, France		Merchant	15 Aug 1805
DeVilliers, Louis	40	Picardy, France		Musician	23 Aug 1805
Douglass, James	29	Lothran, Scotland		Turner	16 Oct 1805
DesCoudres, Louis P.	26	Hesse Cassel, Germany		Merchant	2 Jan 1806
Demisman, Joseph	19	Madeira		Mariner	16 Jan 1806
Dieckert, Jacob Gottfred	25	Bremen, Germany		Merchant	14 Oct 1806
Dalton, James	36	Bedfordshire, England		Physician	22 Oct 1806
Duffus, Alexander	23	Murray, Scotland		Merchant	15 Nov 1806
Daly, Richard	23	Waterford, Ireland		Mariner	26 Nov 1806
Davis, John	26	Antrim, Ireland		Merchant	31 Jan 1807
DeLisle, Thomas	30	Guernsey		Merchant	28 Mar 1807
Dile, Peter	28	Havre de Grace, France		Baker	19 Sep 1808
Duggan, John	32	Munster, Ireland		Bricklayer	3 Jun 1809
Duggan, Thomas	30	Linster, Ireland		Bricklayer	3 Jun 1809
Douben, Henry	28	Hamburgh, Germany		Mariner	27 Nov 1810
Drege, Pierre	23	Rochelle, France			9 Mar 1811
Deonua, Cenoile Deuse	51	Chamberry Savoy, France			27 Mar 1811
Dumont, Blaise	21	Cape Francois			31 Jul 1811
Diron, Dominique	44	Bas Pyronees, France		Mariner	20 May 1813
Dove, William Prichard	23	Cork, Ireland	Charleston	Ship Joiner	31 Aug 1813
Dempsey, Thomas	27	Kildare, Ireland	Charleston	Grocer	4 Oct 1813
Douglass, Campbell	31	Kirkcudbright-shire, North Britain	Charleston	Grocer	19 Oct 1813
Dignan, James	34	Meath, Ireland	Charleston	Bricklayer	19 Oct 1813
Doyle, Thomas	46	Dublin, Ireland	St. John's Berkley	Planter	22 Dec 1813
Davis, William	35	Devonshire, England	Charleston		28 Mar 1814
Donnally, Amherst	61	Halifax, Lower Canada	St. John's Parish	Planter	4 Oct 1814
Davis, George	27	Halifax, Nova Scotia L. C.	Charleston	Mariner	7 Mar 1815
Duquercion, Francis	32	Brittany, France	Charleston	Merchant	8 May 1815
Deguer, Peter Augustine	47	Nantz, Brittany, France	Charleston	Merchant	10 May 1815
Davis, Benjamin	31	Lesson, Prussia	Charleston	Broker	9 Jan 1816
Darras, Edme Jean Francois	22	Saint Valley sur Sounime, France			16 Sep 1816
Darras, Jean Lambert	30	Saint Valley sur Sounime, France			16 Sep 1816
Delchamp, Joseph	40	Liege, Netherlands	Charleston	Merchant	10 Feb 1818
DeJough, Joseph		Holland	Charleston	Planter gave notice 20 Mar 1815	22 Sep 1818
Durban, Ambrose		Gers, France	Charleston		12 Oct 1818
Deye, Benjamin	27	Oldenburg, Germany	Charleston		17 Mar 1819
Desbarreaux, Pellet	35	Toulouse, France	Charleston	Mariner	6 Aug 1819
Dias, John Joseph		Coimbra, Portugal	Charleston		21 Oct 1822

Names of Aliens	Age	Nation	Residence	Occupation	Admission
Dufort, Jean	45	Department Lalliere France	Charleston		1 Jul 1823
Dick, James	41	Birmingham, England	Charleston	Merchant	26 Aug 1823
Dursse, Laurent	35	Bourdeaux, France	Charleston		21 Oct 1823
DeLaVaux, Francis Padmore	44	London, Great Britain		Minister of the Gospel	21 Feb 1824
Deas, John	44	Middlesex,England	Charleston	Mariner	2 Nov 1824
Dreher, George Frederick Lewis	27	Rosenfeld, Wirtemberg	Charleston Neck	Tanner Wragsbo'	19 Jul 1825
Drummond, John	25	Sterling, North Britain	Charleston		17 Oct 1825
Dumont, Adelaide	70	Paris, France	Charleston		4 May 1826
Dempsey, Myles	43	Wexford, Ireland	Charleston	Keeper of a Hotel	3 Jul 1826
Dougherty, Joseph	44	Londonderry, Ireland	Charleston		5 Jul 1826
Durand, Victor	25	Nantz, France	Charleston	Merchant	5 Mar 1827
Dupont, Francis		Port au Prince			8 May 1827
Dempsey, Thomas	29	Kildare, Ireland	Charleston	Grocer	10 Oct 1828
Depras, Cesaire	30	Petit Goave, St. Domingo	Charleston	Merchants clerk	10 Oct 1828
Donegan, James	33	Cork, Ireland	Charleston	Boot & snoe. maker	5 Jan 1829
Davis, Rene Piere	50	France	Charleston		22 Jun 1829
Dumont, Maria Adelaide Rosignol	73	Paris, France	Charleston		28 Nov 1829
Dunn, John E.	24	Cork, Ireland	Charleston	Storekeeper	27 Feb 1830
Dunlap, William C.	26	Londonderry, Ireland	Charleston		29 Jul 1830
Davis, Henry		London, England	Charleston		26 Aug 1830
Delpina, Antonio Pena	44	Oporto, Portugal	Charleston	Grocer renew'd	13 Jul 1831 16 Apr 1833
Dufour, Augustus	35	Paris	Charleston		3 Aug 1831
Demasky, Martin	33	Danzic, Prussia	Charleston	Shopkeeper	5 Oct 1831
Donaly, Edward	29	Belfast, Ireland	Charleston	Coachman	8 Oct 1831
Dodey, Augustine	41	Genoa, Italy	Charleston		10 Feb 1832
Dutrieux, Cassimer	33	Nantz, France	Charleston	Baker	4 Oct 1832
Dabonville, Joseph	46	Cape Nichola Mole	Charleston	Carpenter	8 Oct 1832
Davidson, Wm. Jr.	35	Dumfries, County of, Scotland	Charleston	Merchant	6 May 1834
Dawson, John		Cork, Ireland	Charleston		20 Feb 1839
Duncan, James		County Elgin, Scotland	Charleston		23 Apr 1839
Dunn, George	33	Tyron, Ireland	Charleston	Factor	19 Jul 1839
Davis, Hannah	70	London	Charleston		18 Mar 1841
DeCottes, Laura	48	St. Domingo, W. Indies, France	Charleston	widow	23 Apr 1841
Durand,Joachim Victor	35	Brest, France	Charleston	clerk	21 Jul 1841
Dunn, Charles	22	Cork, Ireland	Charleston	Merchant	24 Sep 1841
Dunning, Patrick	28	Donegal county, Ireland	Charleston	Farmer	13 Dec 1844
Daly, Henry	38	Wexford county, Ireland	Charleston	Merchant	14 Jan 1847
Drake, Miles		Antrim county, Ireland	Charleston	Storekeeper	14 Jan 1847
Derily, Peter	26	Ireland	Charleston	Rigger	6 Aug 1847
Delaporte, Augustus	28	Havre, France	Charleston	Confectioner	6 Aug 1847
Dawson, Job	21	Cork, Ireland	Charleston	Clerk	16 Aug 1847
Dooly, John	35	Ireland	Charleston	Labourer	24 Sep 1849
Doran, Andrew	40	Ireland	D°	Carpenter	22 Sep 1857
Duane, Denis M.	27	Ireland	D°		22 Sep 1857
Dolan, Patrick	25	Ireland	D°	Porter	15 Apr 1858
Davies, John S.	49	So: Wales, G. Britain	D°	Bank-officer	17 Apr 1858
Douglas, Robert	48	Scotland	D°	Mail contractor	23 Apr 1858
Donaghu, John	30	Longford Co., Ireland	D°	Labourer	2 Nov 1859
Desmond, Jeremiah	23	Co. of Cork, Ireland	D°	Clerk	2 Jul 1860
East, Richard Sears					29 Apr 1795
Ehyrick, John Maths.		Hesse Cassel, Germany			25 Sep 1795
Eakins, David		Ireland		Mariner	23 Jan 1796
Ewing, Alexander		Colraine, Ireland			28 Oct 1797
Enerson, Anders	34	Swiner, Norway		Mariner	28 Sep 1803
Elsly, John	24	Liverpool, England		Mariner	2 Jul 1804
Elliott, Severd	27	Norway		Mariner	3 Jul 1804
Eason, Robert	25	Scotland		Merchant	11 Oct 1804

Names of Aliens	Age	Nation	Residence	Occupation	Admission
Edgar, John	23	Dumfries, Scotland		Mariner	7 May 1805
Eschausse, William		Languedoc, France			2 Jul 1806
Eiles, William	36	Breman		Mariner	30 Jun 1807
Ekstrom, Jacob	32	Sweden		Mariner	13 Dec 1806
Esnard, Peter	49	Dangoumois, France			15 Mar 1810
Edmondston, Charles	28	Shetland, Scotland		Merchant	26 Mar 1810
Establier, Louis Joseph	43	Hieres, France			9 Aug 1811
Ehrenpford, John Godfrey	26	Oldenburg, Germany	Charleston	cabinet maker	12 Oct 1812
Eckland, Oliver	36	Sundswall, Sewden	Charleston	Mariner	19 Oct 1812
Emerson, Jones	45	Christiana, Norway	Charleston	Grocer	22 Dec 1812
Eagar, Robert	24	Down, Ireland	Charleston	Merchant	23 Aug 1813
Eagar, George	24	Down, Ireland	Charleston	Bricklayer	23 Aug 1813
Evans, Leaycraft	45	Bermudas Island	Charleston	House Joiner	27 Aug 1813
Elliot, Walter	24	Roxburyshire, North Britain	Charleston		19 Oct 1813
Ellard, Michael	34	Tipperary, Ireland	Charleston	Carpenter	5 Jan 1816
Eckhoff, George Henry	31	Hamburgh	Charleston	Shop-Keeper	6 Jul 1821
Elford, James M.	52	Bristol, England	Charleston	Mathematician	2 Apr 1823
English, James	30	Dundalk, Ireland	Charleston	Shipwright	6 Feb 1824
Esswein, Theodore	28	Mainheim, Germany	Charleston		19 May 1824
England, John	39	Cork, Ireland	Charleston	Roman Catholic Bishop	6 Feb 1826
Egan, Henry John	29	Cork, Ireland	Charleston	Printer	12 Apr 1826
Eny, Francis	32	Island Madeira, Portugal	Charleston Inhabitant of East Florida at the Cession	mariner	19 Aug 1826
Eggart, John Jacob	52	Switzerland	Charleston	Grocer	8 Jul 1828
Eyman, Anthony	26	France	Charleston	Merchant	14 Jan 1830
Elder, James	48	West Linton, Scotland	Charleston neck	Tanner	6 Oct 1830
Ehlers, Carsten	49	Hanover	Charleston	Grocer	6 Oct 1830
Ellvell, Edmund	40	Ireland	Charleston		3 Aug 1831
Engle, Henry	42	Prussia	Charleston	Clerk	5 Oct 1832
Edwards, William	27	Devonshire, England		Mariner	28 Nov 1832
Eylman,Christian	33	Cronstadt, Russia		Mariner	14 Oct 1834
Eccles, Thomas J.	22	Armagh, Ireland			9 Oct 1838
Ewertson, Schwenn	45	Delt, Denmark	Charleston	Mariner	7 Oct 1845
Erickson, Christian	27	Naskon, Denmark	Charleston	House carpenter	20 Apr 1846
Epping, J. Peter M.	29	Campe, Oldenberg	Charleston	Druggist	14 Dec 1846
Englert, William	30	Grand Duchy of Baden	Charleston	Shoemaker	14 Jan 1847
Ellerhorst, Henry D.	29	Hanover	Ditto	Miller	16 Jan 1851
Ebberson, N.	35	Denmark	Ditto	Cabinet-maker	3 Nov 1851
Epstein, Phillip	23	Poland	Do	Jeweller	19 May 1858
Forrest, Michael		Ireland		Merchant	23 Sep 1791
Fraser, Alexander	32	Montrose, Scotland		Mariner	24 Jan 1792
Farquhar, Robert		Scotland		Mariner	1 Sep 1795
Foster, John Robert		Yorkshire, England		Mariner	23 Jan 1796
Findlater, William		Stone Eyre, Scotland		Mariner	18 Nov 1796
Fleury, Jean Baptiste		Rouen, France			11 May 1797
Farley, Hance		Antrim, Ireland		cabinet maker	4 Mar 1799
Fullerton, James	25	Rothsay, Scotland		Mariner	14 Jun 1799
Ferguson, Witney J.	21	Belfast, Ireland		Taylor	14 Jun 1799
Fair, Robert	30	Cavan, Ireland		Shoemaker	15 Oct 1802
Fyholl, John	34	Hessberg, Holland		Merchant	10 Nov 1803
Falls, John	38	Tyrone, Ireland		Merchant	25 May 1805
Flotard, John	30	Languedoc, France		Merchant	1 Jul 1805
Frost, Lawrence	34	Norway		Mariner	25 Jul 1805
Follin, Firmin	22	St. Domingo		Merchant	25 Jul 1805
Ferguson, John	25	WestPort, Ireland		Mariner	26 Oct 1805
Foster, John	38	Liverpool, Great Britain		Mariner	28 Jun 1806
Fayolle, Peter	38	Eione Gironde, France		Dancing master	14 Oct 1806
Faber, Christian Henry	30	Rosenfeld, Wirtemberg		Merchant	7 Jan 1807
			declared his intention		14 Nov 1803
Fair, Richard	25	Cavan, Ireland		Shoemaker	10 Jan 1807

FEDERAL RECORDS

Names of Aliens	Age	Nation	Residence	Occupation	Admission
Fraser, John	38	Inverness, Scotland		Merchant	16 Mar 1807
Farmer, Henry Tudor	20	London, Great Britain		Planter	17 Jul 1807
Fair, John	22	Cavan, Ireland		Mechanic	21 Sep 1807
Forbes, Alexander	24	Peterhead, Aberdeenshire, Scotland		Merchant	14 Dec 1807
Fitzpatrick, Peter	30	Cavan, Ireland		Taylor	2 Apr 1808
Fronty, Michael	52	Department of Lacreuse, France		Physician	27 May 1808
Fraser, John	25	Inverness, Scotland		Merchant	26 Feb 1810
Faber, Mathew F. C.	29	Rosenfeld, Wirtemberg, Germany	Charleston	minister of the Gospel	14 Jan 1811
		declared his intention 2 Jany 1808			
Fowler, James	34	Lancashire, Great Britain	Charleston	Lumber merchant	20 Jul 1811
Ferguson, John	26	Sutherland, North Britain	Charleston	Taylor	17 Nov 1813
Fitzpatrick, John	32	Tipperary, Ireland	Prince Williams Parish	Planter	14 Feb 1814
Fillette, Francis	25	Burgundy, France	Charleston	Jeweller	9 Jan 1816
Faber, Philip August	37	Glesen, Germany	Charleston	Doctor of medicine	10 Jun 1816
Feraud, Thomas	31	Paris, France	Charleston	Merchant	17 Feb 1817
Fraser, Hugh	48	Murrayshire, Scotland	Georgetown	Professor of Divinity	21 Feb 1817
Floderer, Johan	43	Vienna, Germany	Charleston	Grocer	31 Mar 1818
Fox, Patrick	34	Tyrone, Ireland	Charleston		11 Jan 1820
			declared his intention 30 Dec 1816		
Follin, John Charles Augustus	42	Cape Nicholas Mole, St. Domingo	Charleston	Merchant	13 Jun 1820
Fiche, Peter	41	London, Great Britain	Charleston	Carver & Gelder	10 Oct 1820
Flemming, Joseph S.	31	Monaghan County, Ireland	Charleston	Merchant	21 Feb 1824
Folingsby, Arthur G.	24	Dublin, Ireland	Charleston	Clerk	17 Jan 1825
Farley, John	33	Cavan, Ireland	Charelston	School master	16 Oct 1826
Francis, George	24	Portsmouth, England	Charleston	Pilot	5 Feb 1827
Fuldor, Fredk. C. L. A. W.		Imminghausen, Germany	Charleston		4 Jan 1830
Fechtman, John	31	Breman, Hanover	Charleston	Sugar baker	3 Sep 1830
Fourgeaud, Arnold		Dep. D'ordoque, France	Charleston	Baker	27 Jul 1831
Ferret, John F.	45	Cape Francois	Charleston		3 Aug 1831
Flouquet, Alexander	70	France	Charleston		3 Aug 1831
Fassmann, Henry	22	Hamburgh	Charleston	Grocer	14 Aug 1832
Florey, Andrew	37	St. Augustine, Florida	Charleston	Mariner	31 Aug 1832
Fetherberry, John A.	22	Liverpool, England		Clerk	31 Aug 1832
Forsyth, William S.	26	Derry, Ireland		Carpenter	14 Jan 1833
Flynn, William	36	Cork, Ireland	Charleston		7 Aug 1833
Finck, John Dederick	25	Hanover	Charleston	Grocer	1 Aug 1834
Francis, Edward	39	Wiltshire, England	Charleston	Keeper of Livery Stables	11 Oct 1834
Farrell, James	30	Meath, Ireland	Charleston	Laborer	17 Jul 1839
Fehrenback, Nicolas	34	Hanover	Charleston	Grocer	28 Oct 1840
Forrest, John	41	Edinburgh, Scotland	Charleston	minister of the Gospel	14 Dec 1840
Fourgeaud, Mary (wife of Arnold Fourgeaud)	49	Aux Cayes, St. Domingo	Charleston		21 Mar 1842
Flach, George W.	25	Hessen, Germany	Charleston	Jeweller	12 Jul 1843
Finkensteadt, George	34	Hanover	Charleston	Clerk	13 Dec 1844
Farrell, Daniel	39	Ireland	Charleston	Mason	13 Jan 1847
Ferrall, John J.	25	Longford County, Ireland	Charleston	Clerk	14 Jan 1847
Fink, Harmann	23	Hanover, Germany	Charleston	Blacksmith	5 Jul 1849
Finigan, George	37	County of Mead, Ireland	Charleston	Mariner	7 Jul 1851
Franke, Charles	31	Kurnick, Germany	Do	Coach blacksmith	25 Feb 1857
Flynn, Patrick	24	Ireland	Do	Watchman	22 Jul 1857
Fink, Boy H.	32	Denmark		Druggist	24 Jul 1857
Farrell, John C.	30	Longford Co., Ireland	Do	Tavern-keeper	6 Aug 1857

Names of Aliens	Age	Nation	Residence	Occupation	Admission
Flemming, James	37	Ireland	Charleston	labourer	22 Sep 1857
Fremder, Ludwig Charles	24	Diesel, Germany	Do	Clerk	10 Jun 1859
Floodey, Patrick	37	Maid, Ireland	Do	laborer	9 Nov 1859
Foot, Michael	27	Prussia	Do	Merchant	3 Oct 1860
Freese, Herman Friedk.	21	Hanover	Do	Machinist	31 Oct 1860
Geslain, Jacques Benjamin		Cul de Sac, St. Domingo			31 May 1793
Greenhoff, Jacob		Prussia		Mariner	20 May 1796
Grove, Samuel		Worcester, England		Mariner	20 Jul 1796
Gernon, William		Lowth, Ireland		Mariner	16 May 1797
Glaister, Robert		Cumberland, England			14 Nov 1797
Grochan, John		Bourdeaux, France			11 Dec 1797
Graham, John		Grenock, Scotland			29 Nov 1797
Goldie, Walter		Nithdale, Scotland			11 Dec 1797
Grehan, Edward		Dublin, Ireland		Mariner	15 Jan 1798
Greaser, Lewis A.		Bremen		Merchant	25 Jan 1798
Gibson, William		Moffat, North Britain		Merchant	2 Jan 1798
Gregorie(?), James		Glasgow, Scotland		Merchant	19 Oct 1803
Garnier, John	36	Rochefort, France		Merchant	23 Jan 1804
Girette, Peter Roger	40	Havre de Grace, France		Mariner	19 Mar 1804
Griots, Paul	34	France		Mariner	16 Apr 1804
Groning, Lewis	39	Bassum, Hesse Cassel		Merchant	16 Apr 1804
Godard, Rene	42	Nantz, France		Merchant	17 Sep 1804
Genery, Alexander	36	Waterford, Ireland		Mariner	22 May 1806
Grogen, William	36	Devonshire, England		Merchant	26 Jun 1806
Geiger, Valentine	45	Ittlingen, Baden		Merchant	10 Jan 1807
Guilbert, Eugenne	49	Madrid, Spain		Professor of Music	27 Jun 1807
Gordon, James	25	Monaghan, Ireland		Bricklayer	30 Jun 1807
Gordon, John	22	Monaghan, Ireland		Bricklayer	30 Jun 1807
Grant, Alexander	31	Bamshire, North Britain		Merchant	2 Nov 1807
Gyles, John	26	London, Great Britain		Goldsmith & Jeweller	13 Sep 1808
Gilliland, William H.	22	Antrim, Ireland		Taylor	7 Sep 1809
Gautier, William	36	St. Malo, France		Mariner	2 May 1810
God, Francis	33	New Orleans		Mariner	27 Nov 1810
Gilfert, Charles	26	Hesse Cassel, Germany		Musician	26 Jun 1812
Goldsmith, Morris	28	London, Great Britain	Charleston	Inspector of the Customes	15 Sep 1812
				Denizen, 4 Feb 1805	
Greniere, Francois	50	Peseuas, France	Charleston	Merchant	29 Mar 1813
Goldsmith, Abraham	59	Lynn, Norfolk, Great Britain	Charleston	Taylor	23 Aug 1813
Gordon, Charles Peate	28	Newry, Ireland	Charleston	Clerk	1 Oct 1813
				gave notice 9 Feb 1809	
Gray, William	33	Glasgow, North Britain	Charleston	Merchant	23 Oct 1813
Grady, James	33	Kildare, Ireland	Charleston	Grocer	15 Sep 1814
Goldsmith, Isaac M.	38	Rotterdam	Charleston	Shopkeeper	11 Oct 1814
Giraud, Francis	32	Bourdeaux	Charleston	Merchant	8 May 1815
Glendkamp, Henry	47	Westphalia	Charleston	Farmer	20 May 1815
Garnie, Joseph	42	Marseilles, France	Charleston		9 Jan 1816
Gaudouen, John	45	Richlieu, France	Charleston	Merchant	9 Jan 1816
Granados, Antonio	27	Havanna, Island of Cuba	Charleston	Merchant	9 Jan 1816
Green, Jacob P. N.	36	Stockholm, Sweden	Charleston	Ship carpenter	25 May 1818
Grille, Claude		France	Charleston		12 Oct 1818
Guien, Lewis Phillippe		St. Domingo	Charleston		13 Oct 1818
Gordon, Richard	80	London, Great Britain	Charleston		10 Jan 1820
Gaujan, Theodore	46	St. Domingo	Charleston	Merchant	1 Sep 1820
Gates, John	28	Sussex, England	Charleston	Butcher	10 Oct 1820
Gibson, Alexander	40	Ayrshire, No. Britain	Charleston	Merchant	20 Dec 1821
Galluchat, Joseph	33	Island of St. Domingo	Charleston	Minister of the Gospel	18 Feb 1822
Gyles, Charles	30	London, Great Britain	Charleston	Mariner	9 Dec 1822
Gunther, Frederick George Henry		Hamburgh	Charleston		11 Nov 1823
Gnash, Carls Daniel	33	Dantsix, Prussia	Charleston	Watchmaker	5 Mar 1824
error should have been Gnech, Charles Daniel					
Gordon, Alexander	24	Kirkcudbright, North Britain	Charleston	Merchant	20 Sep 1824
Gates, Thomas	26	Sussex, England	Charleston	Butcher	12 Apr 1825

Names of Aliens	Age	Nation	Residence	Occupation	Admission
Goldsmith, Henry	21	London, Great Britain	Charleston		12 Dec 1825
Gouldsmith, Richard	35	Sussex, England	Charleston	Cabinet maker	17 Dec 1825
Gonzales, Basilis	38	Havanna, Island of Cuba	Charleston	Merchant	18 Feb 1829
Gerard, Peter	32	L'orient, France	Charleston	Slopseller	17 Mar 1829
Graham, John Charles	25	Dantzic, Prussia	Charleston	Mariner	14 May 1829
Guerin, John A.	22	Havanna, Island of Cuba	Charleston		21 Sep 1829
Green, Christian Frederick	34	Hamburgh	Charleston	Grocer	25 Sep 1829
Guistelli, Michel	37	Italy	Charleston		27 Jul 1831
Gue, Victor A.	31	Island of Cuba	Charleston		27 Jul 1831
Gruvel, John	37	Lubeck	Charleston	Grocer	3 Aug 1831
Gianini, Jacob		lucca	Charleston		5 Aug 1831
Gecken, Christopher	35	Hanover	Charleston	Shopkeeper	23 Sep 1831
Grand, Nicholas	46	Isl. St. Domingo	Charleston	Merchant	8 Oct 1831
Geisl, Diederick	23	Hanover	Charleston	Grocer	31 Aug 1832
Graustein, George	36	Prussia	Charleston	Musician	8 Oct 1832
Glasen, von Albert Henry	31	Hanover	Charleston	Grocer	18 Mar 1833
Gaulthier, Felix		Bourges, France	Charleston	Teacher of French language	26 Feb 1835
Glennie, Alexander Revd.	30	Surry, England		minister of the Gospel	3 Mar 1835
Gerdts, Henry	29	Hanover			9 Oct 1838
Gilfillin, Robert	22	Belfast, Ireland	Charleston	Mariner	14 Dec 1839
Garcia, James R.	44	Dunkirk, France	Charleston	Professor of Music	16 Dec 1839
Gebkin, Ermer	25	Hanover	Charleston	Shopkeeper	13 Dec 1844
Gray, Andrew	44	Edinburg, Scotland	Charleston	Gardener	21 Apr 1845
Garbone, Geverd	30	Hanover	Charleston	Grocer	7 Jan 1847
Gannon, Michael	31	Longford County, Ireland	Charleston	Stone-cutter	14 Jan 1847
Gabedele, Antonio	38	Sardinia	Charleston	Rigger	6 Aug 1847
Graver, John H.	29	Bedecke, Hanover	Charleston	Clerk	16 Aug 1847
Gowan, Peter	51	Galloway shire, Scotland	Charleston	Watchmaker	5 Jul 1848
Gyles, Charles	32	England	Charleston	Farmer (late seaman)	18 Mar 1850
Gardener, Edward	32	Portsmouth, England	Do	Mariner	11 Mar 1857
Geerken, Jno: Henry	24	Bremen, Germany	Do	Shopkeeper	15 Apr 1857
Gahrs, Dederick	21	Hanover	Do	Clerk	20 May 1857
Given, Mrs. Martha	37	Londonderry, Ireland	Do	wife of Wm. Given	24 Jun 1858
Grube, John	26	Hanover	Do	Grocer	11 May 1859
Groverman, Fredk. L. (2 time)	34	Hanover	Do	Carpenter	4 Apr 1859
Hoban, James		Ireland		Architect	23 Sep 1791
Hammet, William Revd.		Ireland			29 May 1793
Hart, Daniel					26 May 1794
Hendricksen, Betze		Hanover, Germany			17 Sep 1794
Hands, John		Ireland		Mariner	29 Sep 1795
Harlow, Thomas					1 Oct 1795
Haslett, John		Ireland		Merchant	22 Jan 1796
			admitted by Judge Burke, Petition therefore delivered to N. W. S. Smith, Clerk of Court of Common Pleas 26 June		
Henry, Alexander		Stewart's Town, Ireland		Mariner	2 Mar 1796
Hutton, James	49	Fifeshire, North Britain		Factor	20 Apr 1796
Hunter, William		Antrim, Ireland			20 Sep 1796
Horn, Gustavus		Linkoping, Sweden		Mariner	23 Sep 1796
Hunter, James		Antrim, Ireland		Grocer	6 Oct 1796
Howard, Benjamin		Somersetshire			25 Oct 1796
Haasman, Jacob		Medenblik, Holland		Mariner	16 May 1797
Hamilton, James		Arran, Scotland		Mariner	24 Jul 1797
Hyndman, Robert Augustus		Ballymona, Ireland			25 Sep 1797
Hass, Francis		Louenberg, Prussia		Mariner	11 Dec 1797
Hoffman, Michael		Altona, Denmark		Mariner	11 Dec 1797
Hanly, James		Bristol, England			May 1798
Harrison, Samuel		Norfolk, England			8 May 1798
Hunter, John		Londonderry, Ireland			31 May 1798
Hattier, Henry	34	Port au Prince, Hispaniola		Merchant	27 Jul 1798
Hill, Alexander		Newry, Ireland		Mariner	13 Jun 1799

Names of Aliens	Age	Nation	Residence	Occupation	Admission
Hrabousky, John S.		London, England			20 May 1799
Henriques, Elijah	32	Bayonne, France		Merchant	20 Aug 1800 Admitted & Sworn in 8 June 1804 Registered
Hueston, Samuel	25	Carrickfergus, Ireland		Merchant	3 Sep 1802
Harper, John	36	Omagh, Ireland		Merchant	3 Sep 1802
Heron, Samuel	22	Galloway, Scotland		Merchant	4 Aug 1803
Harrison, Henry	21	Cheshire, England		Mariner	7 Sep 1803
Herbemont, Nicholas M. L.	36	Champaigne, France			28 Oct 1803
Hellerd, Ferdinand	21	Dover, England		Mariner	12 Dec 1803
Hall, William	29	Kelso, Scotland		Merchant	23 Jan 1804
Harrison, Hugh	33	Belfast, Ireland		Mariner	24 Jan 1804
Holmes, Andrew	24	Monaghan, Ireland		Merchant	21 Apr 1804
Hume, James	21	Antrim, Ireland		Weaver	11 Oct 1804
Humeau, Juhan P.	33	New Orleans, Louisiana		Merchant	11 Oct 1804
Hanby, John	24	Dumfrieshire, Scotland		Mariner	11 Oct 1804
Hancock, Richard	29	London, England		Mariner	16 Oct 1804
Holmes, Henry	33	Rotherham, England		Merchant	10 Dec 1804
Harper, James	31	Wiltshire, England		Baker	7 Feb 1805
Hueston, James	30	Hanamount, Ireland		Taylor	27 Mar 1805
Hayden, William	55	London, England		Merchant	7 May 1805
Hibbens, John	26	Liverpool, England		Iron founder	18 Jun 1806
Hart, Joseph	52	Manheim, Germany		Merchant	27 Aug 1806
Heulan, Jonathan	23	St. Domingo		Surgeon	29 Nov 1806
Happoldt, John M.	31	Wurtzburg, Braunspach, Germany		Butcher	7 Jan 1807 declared his intention 20 Sep 1802
Howell, Joseph	27	Chester, England		Merchant	18 May 1807
Hindley, Thomas Henry	25	Lancashire, Great Britain		Merchant	6 Jul 1807
Happoldt, John Philip	29	Germany		Butcher	17 Jul 1807
Hannah, Andrew	28	Gallowayshire, North Britain		Merchant	9 Nov 1807
Henwood, Samuel	26	London, England		Merchant	28 Jan 1808
Hammond, John	31	St. Johns, Denmark		Mariner	21 Mar 1808
Holahan, John	37	Cavan, Ireland		Artificer	5 Apr 1808
Hennon, Thomas	27	Down, Ireland		Gunsmith	19 Sep 1808
Heulan, John James	37	Cape Francois		Musician	4 Oct 1808
Hart, Nathan	27	Manheim, Germany		Merchant	12 Dec 1809
Henniquin, Jean Baptiste	70	Metz, Lorraine, France		Confectioner	30 Dec 1809
Hughes, John	32	Down, Ireland		Mariner	6 Mar 1810
Hedderly, William	42	Nottingham, England	Charleston	Bell hanger	5 Jun 1810
Hunter, James	28	Montrose, Augusshire, No. Britain	Charleston	Merchant	22 Aug 1810
Hughes, David	24	Liverpool, England		Mariner	16 Nov 1810
Hand, Martin William	30	Stettin, Prussia		Mariner	18 Mar 1810
Hall, George	32	Roxburghshire, North Britain	Charleston	Merchant	15 Jun 1812
Hinsen, Thomas	45	Tonderen, Denmark	Charleston	House carpenter	13 Oct 1812
Heyns, James	35	Laneck, North Britain	Charleston	Mariner	23 Aug 1813
Howe, Michael	32	Dublin, Ireland	Charleston	Stone Cutter	23 Aug 1813
Holland, John	47	Sussex, England	Sullivan's Island	Boatman	27 Aug 1813
Holwell, Thomas	34	Devonshire, England	Charleston	Boatman	27 Aug 1813
Hedley, John	45	Northumberland, England	Charleston	School-master	31 Aug 1813
Hall, James	36	Roslin, North Britain	Charleston	Stone Cutter	7 Sep 1813
Hewson, Thomas	30	London, Great Britain	Charleston	Merchant's clerk	5 Oct 1813
Hamilton, Marlborough Sterling	57	Dublin, Ireland	Charleston	School-master	7 Oct 1813
Hunter, Thomas	23	Glasgow, North Britain	Charleston	Blacksmith	8 Oct 1813
Hyams, Mordecai	28	London, Great Britain	Charleston	Storekeeper	22 Dec 1813
Hefferman, John	49	Tipperary, Ireland	Charleston	Cabinet maker	31 May 1814 gave notice 21 May 1811
Hassalback, John	32	Manheim, Germany			11 Oct 1814
Hancock, George	25	London, Great Britain	Charleston	Cabinet maker	9 Nov 1814
Huchet, Charles	33	St. Maloes, France	Charleston		28 Mar 1815

Names of Aliens	Age	Nation	Residence	Occupation	Admission
Hobrecker, John C.	38	Westphalia	Charleston	Blacksmith	20 May 1815
Haskett, Samuel	35	Tipperary, Ireland	Charleston	Sadler	5 Jan 1816
Huard, Stanislas	35	Feramp, France	Charleston	Apothecary	5 Jan 1816
Heydenfield, Jacob Moses Solomon		Ellrich, Prussia			9 Oct 1816
Happoldt, Christopher	33	Braunspach, Germany	Charleston declared his intention 14 Nov 1811	Butcher	13 Jan 1820
Hardey, John Jacob	40	Pillau, Prussia	Charleston		13 Apr 1820
Harbers, John R.	36	Oldenburg, Germany	Charleston declared his intention 12 Jan 1818	Shopkeeper	16 Jan 1821
How, Robert Nesbit	22	Berwick, Great Britain	Georgetown Dist., SC		8 Dec 1821
Haly, James	57	Cork, Ireland	Charleston	Stationer & Bookseller	17 Jan 1823
Hageman, John Frederick	42	Bremen, Germany	Charleston	Merchant's clerk	14 Apr 1823
Heery, Thomas		Cavan, Ireland	Charleston		27 Aug 1823
Hior, John	31	Amsterdam, Holland	Charleston	Mariner	10 Jul 1824
Hitchingham, Thomas	30	Wexford, Ireland	Charleston		4 Sep 1824
Henrick, John		Wexford, Ireland	Charleston		7 Oct 1824
Hopkins, David	45	Wales, England	Charleston		22 Feb 1825
Henry, George	27	Monaghan, Ireland	Charleston	Clerk	27 Jun 1825
Hogan, William	34	Limerick, Ireland	Charleston		18 Mar 1826
Hatfield, John	37	Leeds, Yorkshire, England	Charleston	Storekeeper	18 Apr 1826
Haslam, John	32	Lancastershire, England	Charleston	School-master	4 Aug 1826
Hartman, Justus	42	Gettingin, Hanover	Charleston	Shopkeeper	8 Sep 1826
Hanschildt, Peter	36	Hanover	Charleston	Grocer	13 Dec 1826
Halliday, Thomas A.	30	Tyrone, Ireland	Charleston	Grocer	17 Sep 1827
How, Thomas	26	Berwick, Great Britain		Planter	10 Jan 1828
Hannah, William	34	Belfast, Ireland	Charleston	Mariner	11 Mar 1828
Haslett, Roger	48	Cork, Ireland	Charleston	Paver	15 Sep 1828
Hamilton, John	21	Antrim, Ireland	Charleston	Clerk	13 Oct 1828
Herckemath, Leon J.	28	Amsterdam, Holland	Charleston	Merchant	11 Nov 1828
Hesler, John	27	Glarus, Switzerland	Charleston	Butcher	13 Feb 1829
Hall, James	33	Dublin, Ireland	Charleston		6 Jul 1829
Happoldt, Christian D.	40	Wirtemberg	Charleston	Butcher	7 May 1830
Henry, Bernard	37	Antrim, Ireland	Charleston	Storekeeper	24 May 1830
Hamye, Christopher Henry	32	Hanover	Charleston	Grocer	21 Jul 1830
Hashagen, Henry	29	Hanover	Charleston	Grocer	26 Aug 1830
Howard, James	45	Liverpool, England	Charleston	Mariner	20 Sep 1830
Hendricks, Frederick	41	Hanover	Charleston	Grocer	12 Oct 1830
Hertz, Jacob	52	Manheim, Germany	Charleston	Shopkeeper	14 Feb 1831
Henshaw, Vivion	56	Cheshire, England		Farmer	12 Apr 1831
Hyams, Catharine	44	London	Charleston		12 Apr 1831
Howell, Sidney S.	22	Island S. Martin, West Indies	Charleston		5 Aug 1831
Hantz, Charles	26	Switzerland	Charleston		26 Aug 1831
Heins, John Henry	30	Hanover	Charleston		23 Sep 1831
Hagena, John Peter	27	Hamburgh	Charleston	Clerk	5 Oct 1831
Holtge, Herman	24	Oldenburg	Charleston	Clerk	14 Aug 1832
Heimsath, Frederick	27	Hanover	Charleston	Grocer	31 Aug 1832
Hovde, Hans J.	40	Norway	Charleston	Shopkeeper	31 Aug 1832
Herbet, Michael	22	Bourdeaux, France	Charleston		31 Aug 1832
Hall, Thomas	40	Halifax, Nova Scotia		Carpenter & cabinet maker	14 Jan 1833
Hilson, John	37	Mimel, Prussia	Charleston	Grocer	13 Feb 1833
Hopley, George Augustus	31	Martinique	Charleston	Merchant	18 Mar 1833
Hannah, Alexander	29	Liverpool, England		Mariner	5 Sep 1833
Hencken, Henry	36	Hanover	Charleston	Grocer	30 Aug 1834
Hobson, Abraham	41	North Hampton, Great Britain	Charleston	Shoemaker	11 Oct 1834
Howard, Thomas M.		Tulla, County Clare, Ireland	Charleston		6 Jun 1837
Henesy, Thomas		Ireland	Charleston		25 Aug 1837
Hukamp, John		Hanover	Charleston	Grocer	12 Sep 1837
Hassett, Michael	21	Cork, Ireland	Charleston	Coachmaker	24 Apr 1838
Harvey, James E.	21	Ireland		Accountant	9 Oct 1838
Henrichson, Henry	22	Germany		Storekeeper	19 Jul 1839
Hughes, Thomas	39	Lancashire, England	Charleston	cabinet maker	23 Jul 1839
Hanek, Abraham	53	Stariska, Poland	Charleston	Jeweller	1 Apr 1840
Hiligen, Frederick	35	Oldenberg, Germany	Charleston	Grocer	30 May 1840
Heide, Henry C.	38	Hanover	Charleston		30 May 1840

Names of Aliens	Age	Nation	Residence	Occupation	Admission
Hudaff, Henry	41	Hanover	Charleston	Storekeeper	15 Jan 1841
Harms, Henry	23	Bremen, Germany	Charleston	Grocer	18 Mar 1841
Hamilton, Anna A.	35	Monahan, Ireland	Charleston	(widow)	5 Jul 1842
Hagan, Rosana	50	Tyrone County, Ireland	Charleston	(widow)	19 Sep 1842
Hanson, Joseph	23	Norway	Charleston	Mariner	19 Sep 1842
Hamilton, Wm. N.	33	Scotland	Charleston	Accountant	12 Apr 1843
Hagenon, Fredk. J.	21	France		Mariner	8 Apr 1843
Hanson, John S.	22	Scotland		Teacher	3 Feb 1845
Huikamp, Joanna M.	32	Duchy of Oldenberg	Charleston		17 Mar 1847
Henry, Mary	48	County of Tyrone, Ireland	Charleston		17 May 1847
Hora, Michael	26	County of Clare Ireland	Charleston	Drayman	6 Aug 1847
Hall, Wm. P.	27	Island of Cuba (Spain)	Charleston	Merchant	13 May 1853
Hill, James	27	Plymouth, England	Charleston	Mariner	16 Jan 1855
Hanratty, Ann Mrs.	46	Co. Kerry, Ireland	Charleston		22 May 1856
Hogan, Patrick	35	Kilkenny, Ireland	Charleston	Labourer	3 Dec 1856
Haesloop, J. H.	22	Hanover	Charleston		20 May 1857
Happoldt, Albert	54	Wirtemberg	Do	Butcher	23 Sep 1857
			special opinion that he is a citizen		
Hambruch, Wm. L.	30	Hanover	Do	Professor of music	4 Jan 1858
Hartnett, Thomas	35	Ireland	Do	Labourer	10 May 1859
Holgate, Harvy	21	England	Do	Chief mate	10 Jun 1859
Halpin, Maurice	41	Ireland	Do	Laborer	13 Feb 1860
Hollo, Herman	33	Hanover	Do	Professor of music	10 Oct 1860
Hollo, Charles	34	Hanover	Do	Professor of music	10 Oct 1860
Johnston, Robert				Mariner	22 Feb 1791
Johnson, Edward		Armagh, Ireland		Mariner	7 Oct 1795
Johnson, Thomas				Mariner	20 Oct 1795
Jaillet, Pierre		Switzerland		Merchant	24 Mar 1796
Johnston, Edward		Liverpool, England		Mariner	25 Mar 1797
Johnston, James		Monaghan, Ireland			14 Jul 1797
Innes, Daniel		Argyleshire, Scotland		Mariner	10 Aug 1797
Jeffords, Richard		Exeter, England		Mariner	21 Mar 1798
Jones, Joshua		Halifax, Yorkshire, England			5 May 1798
Johnston, Hugh		Belfast, Ireland		Grocer	1 Jun 1798
Joyce, Thomas	23	Connaught, Ireland		Mariner	17 Jun 1799
Josephs, Joseph	24	London,England		Merchant	17 Jun 1799
Jenny, John	46	Margravate, Baden		Baker	22 Sep 1802
Johnson, John		Longsound, Norway			6 Oct 1802
Ingram, Andrew	30	Eyemouth, Scotland		Shipcar-penter	12 Dec 1803
Javain, B. I. P.	30	Fort Dauphin, St. Domingo		Merchant	27 Jan 1804
Johnston, Barnard	23	Port au Prince , Hispaniola		Mariner	2 Jul 1804
James, William	27	Wales, England		Mariner	11 Oct 1804
Jackson, Jeremiah	26	Cumberland, England		Merchant	11 Oct 1804
Jost, John	39	Hesendarmstadt, Germany		Mariner	2 Nov 1804
Joseph, Francis	31	Lisbon, Portugal		Mariner	12 Nov 1804
Jacobs, Barnard	27	Saxony		Merchant	13 Apr 1805
Johnson, James	26	Cambridge, England		Mariner	15 Jul 1805
Johnson, John	29	Christiana, Norway		Mariner	16 Sep 1805
		a new certificate given to J. Johnson 18 Apr 1820			
Jacobs, Peter	23	Emden, Prussia		Mariner	19 Sep 1805
Johnson, John	20	Haverford, Wales E.		Mariner	26 Oct 1805
Jahan, Joseph	48	France		Planter	17 Mar 1806
Juntham, Joseph	23	Sicily		Mariner	27 May 1807
Jackson, Montague	29	London, England		Mariner	13 Jul 1807
Jones, Henry	48	Montgomeryshire, North Wales		Merchant	22 Oct 1807
Just, George	26	Fulde, Germany		Ship Carpenter	19 Sep 1808
Jantzen, Louis	34	Bourdeaux, France	Charleston	Mariner	19 Oct 1812
Johnston, Archibald S.	29	Port Glasgow, North Britain		Planter	23 Aug 1813
Johnston, James	49	Down, Ireland	Charleston	Soap Boiler	22 Jun 1814
Jamme, Jacque Joseph	23	Havre de Grace, France	Charleston	Goldsmith	9 Jan 1816
Jacoby, George	36	Prussia	Charleston	Grocer	29 Dec 1823
Johnson, Neils	26	near Carlscroon, Sweden	Charleston	Grocer	21 May 1825
Johnston, Archibald	27	Dumfrieshire, North Britain	Charleston		12 Dec 1825
Joseph, Calmenta	44	Lisbon, Portugal	Charleston	Mariner	21 Jun 1826
			inhabitant of Florida, admitted under Treaty		

Names of Aliens	Age	Nation	Residence	Occupation	Admission
Irving, John B.	26	Island of Jamaica	Charleston	Physician	4 Oct 1826
Johnson, Bennett	40	Gottenberg, Sweden	Charleston	Grocer	24 May 1827
Jones, Catharine (late Munro)	50	Fifeshire, North Britain	Charleston		21 Mar 1828
Ioost, Christoph	23	Border Kaise, Hanover	Charleston	Grocer	17 Jun 1828
Isemon, Peter Henry		Menden, Germany	Charleston	Grocer	11 Oct 1828
Jarcke, Nicholas	38	Hanover	Charleston		12 Jul 1830
Jacobs, Moses	31	London, Great Britain	Charleston	Shop keeper	26 Aug 1830
Joye, Peter S.	26	Copenhagen, Denmark	Charleston	Mariner	6 Oct 1830
James, Mildred alias Messer		Surry, England	Charleston		23 Mar 1831
Jenny, Robert	29	Dublin, Ireland	Charleston		3 Aug 1831
Johnson, Peter	24	Copenhagen, Denmark	Charleston		23 Sep 1831
Jordan, John	30	Kent, England	Charleston	Mariner	5 Oct 1831
Johnson, John	21	Sweden	Charleston	Mariner	5 Oct 1831
Johnson, Frederick	26	Prussia	Charleston	Shopkeeper	5 Oct 1831
Joseph,Francis	24	Lisbon, Portugal	Charleston	Rigger	14 Aug 1832
Joshua, Peter	48	Switzerland	Charleston	Shopkeeper	14 Aug 1832
Innes, John	50	New York while in possession of G. B.	Charleston	Sadler	31 Aug 1832
Johnston, Alexander	33	Scotland	Charleston	Shoemaker	5 Oct 1832
Immen, Johan	22	Hanover	Charleston	Farmer	9 Aug 1833
Jager, Hans	36	Holstein, Denmark	Charleston		9 Aug 1833
Jacinto, Ricardo	21	Madeira, Portugal		Clerk	9 Oct 1838
Jewis, Edward	23	England		Painter	9 Oct 1838
Johnson, Andrew	24	Norway		Mariner	19 Oct 1838
Johnson, Wm. C.	23	Liverpool, England		Painter	9 Oct 1838
Johnson, Benj.	39	Worcester, England	Charleston		17 Sep 1839
Jacob, Mathew	35	Austria	Charleston		26 Sep 1839
Joye, F. S.	28	Copenhagen, Denmark	"	Store-keeper	28 Oct 1840
Jacobs, Jacob Simon	48	Copenhagen, Denmark	Charleston	Shopkeeper	1 May 1843
Irving, Richard	33	London	Charleston	Clerk	6 Mar 1843
Jordan, Edward	40	City of Cork, Ireland	Charleston	Sail Maker	6 Aug 1847
Johnson, Thomas	22	Island of Fana, Denmark	Charleston	Mariner	16 Jan 1855
Jevis, L. F. J.	33	Oldenburg, Germany	Charleston	Tailor	15 Oct 1860
Kennedy, Andrew		Ireland			27 Mar 1794
Keptenius, Gustavus		Lapland, Sweden		Mariner	31 Aug 1796
King, James				Mariner	16 Jan 1797
Kennedey, Samuel		Belfast, Ireland		Mariner	11 Dec 1797
Kelly, Daniel		Monagan, Ireland		Mariner	19 Jun 1797
Kennedy, Peter	28	Curhindale, Ireland		Grocer	20 Sep 1802
Kelly, Michael	22	Lismore, Ireland			27 Sep 1803
King, Henry	40	Bermudas		Mariner	10 Nov 1803
Kelly, Christopher	22	Dublin, Ireland		Mariner	14 Apr 1804
Kennedy, Charles	18	Edinburgh, Scotland		Mariner	24 Jan 1805
Knust, Henry	27	Hanover		Merchant	22 Apr 1805
Kern, John Daniel		Hamburgh		Merchant	15 May 1805
Kirkpatrick, John	26	Galloway, Scotland		Merchant	8 Aug 1805
Kirk, Alexander	24	Sterlingshire, Scotland		Merchant	2 Jan 1806
Ker, John	27	Invernessshire, Scotland		Merchant	20 Jan 1806
Keinmeitz, Francis F.	33	Berlin, Prussia		Grocer	14 Oct 1806
Knox, Walter	36	Glasgow, Scotland		House Carpenter	14 Oct 1806
Kirkland, William	18	Belfast, Ireland		Mariner	17 Jul 1807
Ker, Ann Blair	21	Edinburgh, North Britain	Charleston		31 Oct 1810
King, Mitchell	27	Fifeshire, No Britain	Charleston	Lawyer	17 Nov 1810
Knieff, Francis	36	Bremen, Germany	Charleston	Grocer	6 Oct 1812
Kennedy, Rody	29	Tipperary, Ireland	Laurens District	Planter	30 Apr 1814
			gave notice 30 Jan 1811		
Ker, John Cessford	41	Inverness-shire, North Britain	Charleston	Merchant	11 Feb 1820
			gave notice & was registered as above 20 Jan 1806		
Kane, Francis H.	24	Tipperary, Ireland	Charleston	Clerk	2 Nov 1821
			gave notice & was registered 13 Mar 1816		
Kennedy, James P.	27	Dublin, Ireland	Charleston	Attorney at Law	2 Nov 1821
			gave notice & was registered 11 Mar 1816		
King, John Jr.	32	Armagh, Ireland	Charleston	Comission Merchant	27 May 1823
Kiall, Peter	38	Leghorn, Italy	Charleston	Mariner	16 Feb 1827
Keown, Robert	30	Liverpool, England	Charleston		17 Sep 1827
Knuth, John	31	Courland Russia	Charleston	Grocer	5 Nov 1827

Names of Aliens	Age	Nation	Residence	Occupation	Admission
Klenck, John	31	Holstein, Germany	Charleston		15 Jan 1828
Kohnke, Christian Frederick	26	Altona, Denmark	Charleston	Grocer	19 May 1828
Koster, Casper Jurgen	24	Loxstedt, Hanover	Charleston	Grocer	17 Jun 1828
King, John	43	Clare, Ireland			14 Apr 1829
Keller, Jacob	36	Bavaria	Charleston	Grocer	22 Jun 1829
Knee, Harmann	29	Hanover	Charleston	Grocer	6 Oct 1830
Knoop, Christopher	31	Hanover	Charleston	Grocer	3 Aug 1831
Kanapaux, William		Cape Nicola Mole	Charleston		5 Aug 1831
Kanapaux, Joseph		Cape Nicola Mole	Charleston		5 Aug 1831
Kitchell, John S.		St. Thomas (Island) Denmark	Charleston		5 Sep 1831
Kleysaat, Johan A.	35	Prussia	Charleston	Grocer	5 Oct 1831
Kellers, Cansten	23	Hanover	Charleston	Clerk	5 Oct 1831
Kleps, John G. E.	25	Germany	Charleston	Clerk	8 Oct 1831
Keamey, John	22	Newry, Ireland	Charleston	Storekeeper	4 Oct 1832
Korder, John P.		Germany	Charleston	Sugar refiner	8 Oct 1832
Kalb, George	26	Suabia, France	Charleston	Farmer	2 Oct 1834
Kalb, Jacob	29	Suabia, France	Charleston	Farmer	2 Oct 1834
Karck, Charles Theodore	23	Holstein, Denmark	Charleston	Accountant	11 Oct 1834
Keregan, John	24	Cork, Ireland	Charleston		11 Oct 1834
Kottmeyer, Ernst Henry	49	Minden, Germany	Charleston		19 Mar 1835
Klatz, John or Clatz	24	Dantzic, Prussia	Charleston	Shopkeeper	4 Aug 1835
Kohlman, John H.	40	Hanover	Charleston		25 Aug 1837
Koennecke, Albert	34	Breslaw, Prussia	Charleston	Shopkeeper	1 Apr 1840
Keifer, John	26	Bavaria	Charleston	Cabinet maker	5 Jan 1841
Kennedy, Simon	26	Ireland	Charleston	Labourer	5 Jan 1841
Kapmann, Jacob	22	Oldenberg, Germany	Charleston	Baker	10 May 1841
Kennan, John C.	22	Dublin, Ireland	Charleston	Clerk	4 Jun 1844
Keetz, Frederick H.	36	Hamburg	Charleston	Grocer	9 Apr 1845
Kelly, Ann Y.	67	Amsterdam, Holland	Charleston		10 Dec 1849
Kappelmann, Marcus Henry	47	Hanover	Charleston	Clerk	19 Jan 1850
Kennedy, John	32	Co. Tipperary, Ireland	Charleston	Labourer	13 Dec 1852
Knox, John	32	Ireland	Charleston	Merchant	12 Nov 1856
Kiencke, Francis D.		Oese, Hanover	Do		31 Mar 1857
Keely, Edmund	38	Ireland	Do	Carpenter	22 Sep 1857
Kelly, Thaddeus	32	Sligo Co: Ireland	Do	Merchant	5 Apr 1858
Kogan, John	28	Ireland	Do	Policeman	5 Oct 1859
Kennedy, Patk.	48	Waterford Co. Ireland	Do	Carter	1 Nov 1859
Koldewy, Frederick	36	Hanover	Do	Watchmaker	3 May 1860
Kühn, Robert	35	Saxony	Do	Mechanic	17 Sep 1860
Levi, Moses					20 Jun 1793
Laing, Peter				Mariner	15 Mar 1795
Lee, William					30 Mar 1795
Laughton, William		Orkneys, North Britain		Mariner	18 Jan 1796
Lewis, John					12 Apr 1796
Levy, Nathan		Amsterdam		Shopkeeper	23 Sep 1796
Lamonte, James		Antrim, Ireland			6 Oct 1796
Lane, Robert	31	Somerset, England			11 Dec 1797
Lamb, John		North Britain		Mariner	25 Mar 1797
Love, John		Westminster, England		Watchmaker	20 Mar 1798
Lecat, Francis		Laon, de la Loire, France		Musician	15 Aug 1798
LeSeigneur, Vincent	35	Cain, Normandy		Physician	17 Jun 1799
Lovely, William	38	London, England		Ship Carpenter	5 Jul 1802
Lewis, Alexander	27	London, England		Merchant	16 Aug 1802
Lewis, Isaac	28	London, England		Merchant	3 Sep 1802
Leonhardi, Henry Augustus	24	Worms, Germany		Cooper	8 Oct 1802
Lindsay, Thomas		Scotland	Columbia		30 Nov 1803
Leef, Benjamin	25	Malton, England		Merchant	24 Jan 1804
Lebourg, John James	55	Quellebeuf, Normandy, France		Mariner	19 Mar 1804
Lamb, John	43	Findhorn, Scotland		Mariner	19 Mar 1804
LeBourchier, John N.	28	Rouen, France		Mariner	19 Mar 1804
Lefevre, Etienne	71	Beauvais, France		Merchant	21 Mar 1804
Lafiante, Peter Frederick	29	Hamburgh		Merchant	16 Apr 1804
Laurans, Peter	43	Hiere, France		Merchant	16 Apr 1804
Lucas, Jonathan	51	Northumberland, England		Millwright	24 Jul 1804
Lydikins, Peter	17	London, England		Mariner	27 Jul 1804
Lorent, Paul E.	24	Hamburgh		Merchant	16 Aug 1805

Names of Aliens	Age	Nation	Residence	Occupation	Admission
Lowndes, John	25	Sterling, Scotland		Mariner	16 Oct 1805
LeQuesne, William	26	Guernsey, England		Mariner	23 Nov 1805
Laurence, Vincent	56	New Orleans		Merchant	7 Jan 1806
Lang, Bertrand	35	Bayonne, France		Merchant	2 Jan 1806
Lavelle, John M.	32	Canary Island		Merchant	14 Jan 1806
Leach, George	23	Portsmouth, England		Mariner	18 Mar 1806
Ladeveze, Joseph	53	Toulouse, Languedoc, France		Merchant	15 Sep 1806
Lynch, Thomas		Ireland		Bricklayer	29 Sep 1806
Lockless, Garret	21	Oldenburg, Germany		Mariner	28 Aug 1807
Lapieres, Bernard	33	Metz, Moselle, France		Cabinet maker	13 Nov 1807
Levis, John L.	37	St. Domingo		Merchant	22 Dec 1807
Lacey, John	21	Bristol, England		Pilot	15 Aug 1808
Lewis, John	29	Madeira, Portugal	Charleston	Shopkeeper	6 Oct 1810
Levins, James	25	East Cowes, Isle of Wight, England	Charleston	Pilot	31 May 1811
LeChartier, Placide	26	Moilaix, France	Charleston	Mariner	19 Nov 1812
LeSage, Jean	54	Nantz, France	Charleston	Carpenter	18 Dec 1812
Lameson, Pierre	31	New Orleans	Charleston	Mariner	26 May 1813
Lafite, Peter	36	Bourdeaux, France	Charleston	Mariner	21 Jun 1813
Lanneau, Peter	27	Liverpool, Halifax, No. America	Charleston	Mariner	24 Aug 1813
Livingston, Robert Y	34	London, Great Britain	Charleston	Accountant	27 Aug 1813
Livingston, Gordon	23	Monaghan, Ireland	Charleston	Shoe maker	13 Sep 1813
Lincoln, Horatio	41	Rotherhithe, Surry, England	St. James Santee	Schoolmaster	20 Sep 1813
Leghorn, George	27	Monaghan, Ireland	Charleston	Manufacturer	28 Sep 1813
Liston, Andrew	36	Perthshire, North Britain	St. John, Colleton	Millwright	16 Nov 1813
Lainhart, Ludwig	25	New Orleans	Charleston	Mariner	23 Nov 1813
Labat, Andrew	42	Bourdeaux, France	Charleston	Merchant	15 Dec 1813
Latta, Robert	30	Ireland (near) Londonderry	York Dist.	Merchant	7 Feb 1814
Lechais, Jacqueline F. P.	38	Port au Prince, St. Domingo	Charleston		5 Jan 1815
Loper, John	32	Galicia, Spain	Charleston	Grocer	9 Oct 1815
Lefevere, J. B.		Flanders	Charleston		9 Jan 1816
Lege, John M.		Paris, France	Charleston		25 Jun 1816
Loris, Henry	35	Brabant, Netherlands	Charleston	Merchant Jeweller	30 Dec 1816
Lavincendiere, Michell	36	St. Domingo	Charleston	Segar Manufactorer	26 Jan 1818
Lavincendiere, Jean Pierre	38	St. Domingo	Charleston	Segar Manufactorer	26 Jan 181-
Livingston, Hugh	40	Argyleshire, North Britain	Charleston	Mariner	12 May 1819
Leuder, Francoise	60	Paris, France	Charleston		15 Oct 1819
Loney, Thomas		Devonshire, England	Charleston		11 Jan 1820
Labaussay, Peter	58	Saintonge, France	Charleston	Baker	4 Apr 1820
LeBouteiller, Nicholas Florentine	30	Fecamp, France Territory of Lauxane	Charleston	Mariner	3 Aug 1820
Lowe, John		Middlewitch, England	Charleston		10 Oct 1820
LeChavalier, Oliver	29	Granville, Department La Mouche, France	Charleston	Surgeon gave notice in Massachusetts	14 Feb 1821
Lorent, George Jacob	40	Hamburgh	Charleston	Merchant	1 Aug 1823
Levin, Lewis	31	London, Great Britain	Charleston	Shop keeper	7 Jan 1824
Leprince, M. V. Charles Achille	41	Bastia, Island of Corsica	Charleston	Merchant	12 Oct 1824
Lafon, John	56	Bourdeaux, France	Charleston	Cooper	19 Apr 1826
Lockart, John		Frankfort, Austria	Charleston	Grocer	15 Dec 1826
Lovegreen, Andrew A.		Gottenburg, Sweden	Charleston	Merchant	10 Apr 1827
Levin, Emanuel	27	London, Great Britain	Charleston	Shop keeper	19 Apr 1827
Lordan, Patrick	39	Cork, Ireland	Charleston		15 Jan 1828
Land, O. Diederick	24	Hanover	Charleston	Grocer	17 Jul 1828
Lyon, George	42	London	Charleston	Watchmaker	10 Oct 1828
Lubken, Luden	31	Hanover	Charleston	Shop keeper	15 Jul 1829
Lieure, Peter	37	Bordeaux, France	Charleston	Merchant	26 Aug 1830
Lindbergh, Nicholas	32	Island of Curacai	Charleston		20 Sep 1830
Lund, Peter I.	58	Denmark	Charleston	Mariner	20 Sep 1830
Labaussay, Mary Catharine Coursol	66	Island of St. Domingo	Charleston		14 Apr 1831
Lafourcade, John B.	31	St. Sever, France	Charleston		3 Aug 1831

Names of Aliens	Age	Nation	Residence	Occupation	Admission
Lenobar, John	32	St. Augustine, East Florida	Charleston		3 Aug 1831
Larkin, Dennis	27	King's County, Ireland	Charleston		5 Sep 1831
LeBleux, Ferdinand	33	Bourgogne, France	Charleston	Dyer	28 Jan 1832
Laffiteau, Peter S.	42	St. Domingo	Charleston	Bookkeeper	14 Aug 1832
Landreth, Robert	31	Yorkshire, England	Charleston	Seedsman	17 Sep 1832
Lomer, William	30	Gosport, England	Charleston	Cabinet maker	5 Oct 1832
Lossan, Hans	34	Denmark	Charleston	Mariner	5 Oct 1832
Ladey, William	28	Prussia	Charleston	Grocer	8 Oct 1832
Lathers, Edward	21	Monaghan, Ireland	Charleston	Tailor	10 Nov 1832
Ludaca, Conrad	22	Hanover	Charleston	Clerk	11 Oct 1834
LeCaron, Charles	38	Rouen,France	Charleston	Merchant	12 Jan 1835
Landon, J. G.	25	Hereford, Great Britain	Charleston	Clerk	6 Sep 1836
LeCarpentier, Victor	30	Havre de Grace, France		Clerk	9 Oct 1838
Lenox, William	22	Ireland	Charleston	Clerk	18 Jul 1839
Lacoste, Emilie Gabriella		Paris France	Charleston	Feme sole Trader	19 Feb 1841
Levy, Levine L.	33	Plymouth, England	Charleston	Slop seller	16 Mar 1841
Langlois, Maria Zelis		St. Domingo, France	Charleston	Instructress	29 Mar 1841
Leckie, David	36	Forfar, Scotland	Charleston	Accountant	25 Apr 1843
Lins, Frederick	33	Hanover	Charleston	Grocer	12 Jul 1843
Lafrenz, Ernest C.	28	Denmark	Charleston	Miller	12 Jul 1843
Leon, Abraham	23	Mecklenberg (Schwein)	Charleston	Merchant	18 Dec 1843
Lege, Marie (widow)	53	St. Domingo	Charleston		17 Jan 1846
Lambert, Patrick	35	Wexford County, Ireland	Charleston	Artificer	14 Jan 1847
Lucas, Benjamin	30	Manchester, England	Charleston	Bricklayer	16 Aug 1847
Ligniez, Peter	39	Sandouis, Prussia	Charleston	Tavern-keeper	19 Mar 1849
Leonard, Thomas	30	Ireland	Do	Labourer	14 Oct 1857
LeHardy, Camille	43	Belgium	Do	Teacher of languages	10 Apr 1858
Lyons, Thomas	23	Ireland	Do	Printer	27 Oct 1858
Leddy, Patrick	30	Ireland	Do	labourer	28 Oct 1859
McKenzie, Andrew		Argyleshire, North Britain		Grocer	17 Jan 1792
McDonald, William		Ireland			26 May 1792
		This was an application to & order made by Honble J. F. Grimke, a Judge of the State Court, the record consequently belonged to the Office of the Clerk of the State Court and is accordingly delivered to him 8 June 1821 by J. J.			
Murphy, James		Ireland			15 Sep 1794
McCormick, William		Ireland			26 Mar 1795
Marshall, William				Mariner	7 Jul 1795
McIntosh, John				Mariner	30 Oct 1795
McCaul, William		North Britain			1 Apr 1796
McDowell, Alexander		Belfast, Ireland		Mariner	1 Apr 1796
Manson, John		London, England		Mariner	20 Apr 1796
Maclean, John		Isloy, North Britain		Mariner	20 Apr 1796
Miller, James		Eyreshire, North Britain		Mariner	17 Jun 1796
Maurice, George		Bristol, England			3 Sep 1796
McBlair, William		Down, Ireland		Merchant	20 Sep 1796
McCormick, William		Clare, Ireland			20 Sep 1796
McEvoy, James		Drogheda, Ireland			22 Sep 1796
Martin, Patrick		Newry, Ireland		Cooper	4 Oct 1796
Michau, John		Painbeuf, France			4 Oct 1796
Moore, Richard		Kildare, Ireland		Painter	4 Oct 1796
McDonald, Christopher		Louth, Ireland			8 Oct 1796
Maxwell, John		Down, Ireland		Mariner	6 Oct 1796
Merrieult, John Francis		Normandy, France			25 Oct 1796
Munroe, James		Fifeshire, Scotland		Mariner	7 Feb 1797
Morley, Mathew		Bristol, England		Mariner	20 Mar 1797
Miller, Francis		Eyreshire, Scotland		Mariner	13 Apr 1797
McWilliams, Archibald		Air, Scotland			3 Jul 1797
McCaw, Peter		Galloway, Scotland		Mariner	14 Nov 1797
Moran, Nicholas		Ireland		Mariner	29 Nov 1797
Molcomson, Samuel		Belfast, Ireland			16 Jan 1798
Myers, Michael	26	Sussex, England		Merchant	19 Jan 1798
Maureau, Lewis Francis		Cape Francois			2 Feb 1798

Names of Aliens	Age	Nation	Residence	Occupation	Admission
McFarlane, Alexander		Nova Scotia			8 Feb 1798
Martin, Frederick		Point Petre, Gaudoloupe			2 Apr 1798
Mair, Thomas		Shetland, Scotland		Merchant	27 May 1798
McKay, Mungo Campble		Sterling, Scotland		Merchant	31 May 1798
Morison, James		Glasgow, Scotland		Grocer	1 Jun 1798
McCay, Joseph Ringland	25	Down, Ulster, Ireland			26 Jul 1798
McMillan, Alexander	32	Campbleton, Scotland		Mariner	26 Jul 1798
McAffe, John	27	Larne, Ireland		Carpenter	13 Jun 1799
Mullen, Daniel		Liverpool, England		Mariner	13 Jun 1799
Mooney, Patrick		Linster, Ireland		Grocer	13 Jun 1799
Macadam, James	30	Dryman, Scotland		Merchant	17 Jun 1799
Munroe, David		Larne, Ireland		Mariner	17 Jun 1799
McGrath, Edward	26	Cork, Ireland		Carpenter	22 Sep 1802
Mulligan, John		Leinster, Ireland			23 Sep 1802
McKeirnan, James		Granard, Ireland			23 Sep 1802
Mulligan, Barnard		Westmeath, Ireland			24 Sep 1802
Miers, Jacob	30	Carlscrow, Germany		Mariner	23 Oct 1802
Muck, Philip	33	Bamberg, Franconia		Musician	4 Aug 1803
Marshall, Thomas	52	St. Clements, London, England		Comedian	4 Aug 1803
Manoel, Peter		LaSalle, Languedoc		Merchant	28 Oct 1803
McKenny, Christopher	23	Larne, Ireland		Merchant	4 Feb 1804
McEwing, John	30	Glasgow, Scotland		Mariner	9 Feb 1804
Macaire, Jacques Louis	39	Geneva			2 Jul 1804
Monies, James	28	Kirkudbright, Scotland		Mariner	23 Jul 1804
McBeth, Charles	34	New Castle, Tyne		Mariner	16 Aug 1804
McKean, James	23	Derry, Ireland		Merchant	16 Aug 1804
Mompoey, Honore	26	Gonaive		Grocer	16 Oct 1804
McClure, David	22	Antrim, Ireland		Mariner	12 Jan 1805
Marks, Joseph	33	Portugal		Mariner	26 Feb 1805
Monnar, Lewis	36	Nevirs, Germany		Hair dresser	18 Mar 1805
Mathiessen, Conrad F.	25	Altona, Denmark		Merchant	21 Mar 1805
McCartney, Samuel	25	Kirkudbright, Scotland		Merchant	24 Jun 1805
Munroe, William	36	Grenock, Scotland			6 Jul 1805
McKay, Malcom	36	Argyleshire, Scotland			8 Aug 1805
Mezger, George C.	44	Frankfort, Germany		Merchant	2 Jan 1806
McOwen, Patrick	25	Tipperary, Ireland		Merchant	13 Jan 1806
Milliken, Thomas	26	Belfast, Ireland		Merchant	14 Jan 1806
Murdock, John	34	Antrim, Ireland		Linen Manufacturer	14 Feb 1806
Mallaville, John	39	New Orleans		Mariner	4 Mar 1806
Mills, John	29	Liverpool, England		Mariner	19 Mar 1806
Martindale, James Cannan	22	Hexham, Northumberland, England		Merchant	5 Aug 1806
McKerns, Michael	32	Dorset Clare, Ireland		Mariner	14 Jun 1806
Monefeldt, Esaias	34	Copenhagen, Denmark		Merchant	5 Aug 1806
McNeill, Neill	25	Buchanan, Sterling, Great Britain		Grocer	14 Oct 1806
Maddock, Benjamin	47	Stockholm, Sweden		Mariner	17 Jan 1807
McConchie, Samuel	26	Galloway, Scotland		Merchant	2 Mar 1807
Morison, John	26	Fife, North Britain		Merchant	18 Mar 1807
Mabille, Adrian Francis	41	Valenciennes, France		Merchant	27 Apr 1807
Martini, Charles	28	Milan, Russia		Merchant	4 May 1807
Morton, Alexander	28	Leith, North Britain		Merchant	18 May 1807
Marten, Christian	39	Germany		Shipwright	23 May 1807
Millar, William	26	Montrose, Scotland		Baker	27 May 1807
McKenzie, William	36	Perthshire, Scotland	Georgetown	Farmer	27 May 1807
Miniere, John James Joseph	39	Cape Francois		Planter	27 May 1807
Maguire, James	39	Emiskellin, Ireland		Shoemaker	16 Jun 1807
McElmoyle, William	32	Moneycannon, Ireland		Grocer	16 Jun 1807
McDouall, James	55	Wigtownshire, North Britain		Merchant	21 Sep 1807
Mays, James	26	Epsom, Surry, England		Mariner	9 Nov 1807
Magrath, John	27	Waterford, Ireland		Merchant	13 Nov 1807
McAdam, John	34	Galloway, Scotland		Merchant	29 Dec 1807
McKenzie, John	23	Argyleshire, Scotland		Merchant	11 Jan 1808
Macnamara, John	24	Waterford, Ireland		Merchant	24 Mar 1808
McCall, John B.	31	Cork, Ireland		Grocer	2 Apr 1808
McCall, John	28	Argyleshire, North Britain		Grocer	19 Sep 1808
Moderen, James	32	North Britain		Mariner	19 Sep 1808
Moore, Newman	24	Derry, Ireland			11 Oct 1808
Madan, James		Surry, England		Lawyer	3 Jun 1809
Meeds, William	33	Kent, England		Tavernkeeper	20 Sep 1809
Moorhead, Thomas Campell	22			Merchant	8 Mar 1810

Names of Aliens	Age	Nation	Residence	Occupation	Admission
McIntosh, John	25	Edinburgh, Scotland		Mariner	11 Apr 1810
Mooney, James	30	Kings County, Ireland		Mariner	11 Apr 1810
McMillan, John	27	Newton Stewart, Galloway, Scotland		Merchant	11 May 1810
McDermot, Patrick	36	Longford, Ireland		House Carpenter	11 May 1810
McEachern, Angus	43	Argyleshire, Scotland		Mariner	24 May 1811
Moore, Henry H.	32	Kerry, Ireland	Charleston	School master	24 May 1811
Menude, John B. G.	29	Cape Francois, West Indies	Charleston	Planter	7 Oct 1811
Macfie, Dugald	42	Grenock, North Britain	Charleston	Merchant	25 Jun 1812
McNeel, Samuel	28	Whitehorne, Gallowayshire, No Britain	Charleston	Merchant	25 Jun 1812
Magwood, Robert	50	Monaghan County, Ireland	Charleston	Doctor of Medicine	22 Sep 1812
			admitted Denizen 21 Jan 1812		
Maillard, John M.	21	Island of St. Martins, West Indies	Charleston		12 Oct 1812
Michel, John	22	Port au Prince, St. Dominique	Charleston	Merchant	23 Nov 1812
Myers, Johan	35	Westphalia, Germany	Charleston	Mariner	5 Mar 1813
McDowell, Robert	23	Cavan, Ireland	Charleston	Shoemaker	23 Aug 1813
McGregor, Neil	40	Perthshire, North Britain	Charleston	Gardener	23 Aug 1813
McIntosh, John	42	Edinburgh, North Britain	Charleston	Cabinet maker	24 Aug 1813
Morgan, Benjamin	47	Bermudas Island	Charleston	Boatman	27 Aug 1813
Muirhead, James	21	Edinburgh, North Britain	Charleston	Accountant	27 Aug 1813
Marley, Peter	33	Northumberland, England	Charleston	Deputy Sheriff	1 Sep 1813
Morris, Simpson	40	London, Great Britain	Charleston	Merchant	3 Sep 1813
McGowan, Thomas	26	Ulster, Ireland	Charleston	Baker	10 Sep 1813
McLoughlin, Thomas	25	Antrim, Ireland	Charleston	Labourer	10 Sep 1813
Murrell, Samuel	40	Derry, Ireland		Planter	4 Oct 1813
McGuffie, Anthony	30	Gallowayshire, North Britain	Charleston	Clerk	19 Oct 1813
Monies, Hugh	22	Gallowayshire, North Britain	Charleston		19 Oct 1813
McLeod, Hector Chisolm	23	Sutherlandshire, North Britain	Charleston	Clerk	19 Oct 1813
McVicar, Archibald	22	Argyleshire, North Britain	Charleston	Butcher	19 Oct 1813
McFarlane, Malcolm	27	Perthshire, North Britain	Charleston	Merchant	23 Oct 1813
McNinch, John	48	Antrim, Ireland	Chester	Merchant	1 Dec 1813
			admitted at Columbia		
McDonald, Hugh	21	Monaghan, Ireland	Charleston		22 Dec 1813
		gave notice Nov 1810	Lancaster District		
Mordecai, Noah	36	London, Great Britain	Charleston	Storekeeper	22 Dec 1813
Murphy, Peter	31	Tipperary, Ireland	Charleston	Grocer	28 Dec 1813
Miot, Charles Henry	27	Kingston, Jamaica	Charleston	Carpenter	14 Jan 1814
Maguire, Hugh	47	Tyrone, Ireland	Charleston	Taylor	22 Jun 1814
			admitted a Denizen under act of Assembly		
McDermott, John	29	Donnegal, Ireland	Charleston	Sadler	11 Oct 1814
McCleran, Archibald	43	Glasgow, North Britain		Millwright	9 Nov 1814
Moore, John	49	St. Augustine	Charleston	Butcher	22 Jun 1815
Moisson, John Louis	40	France	Charleston	Gunsmith	25 Sep 1815
Myer, John	43	Hanover, Germany	Charleston	Merchant	11 Dec 1815
McDowall, Andrew		Gallowayshire, Scotland	Charleston	Merchant	3 Jan 1816
Manne, John	26	France	Charleston		9 Jan 1816
Maurel, Mayol	70	Marseilles, France	Charleston		9 Jan 1816
Maurel, J. N.	29	Jacquemel, Island St. Domingo	Charleston		9 Jan 1816
Marzoiceti, Eugenio Antonio	37	Bregnano, Milan, Italy	Charleston	Merchant	1 Jul 1816
Miller, Archibald Edward		Great Britain			15 Oct 1816
Motta, Judah Anas	38	Curracao	Charleston	Merchant	7 Jan 1817
McNamara, Dennis	35	Tipperary, Ireland	Charleston	Storekeeper	17 Feb 1817
Missroon, James	46	Londonderry, Ireland	Charleston	Merchant	21 Oct 1818

Names of Aliens	Age	Nation	Residence	Occupation	Admission
McCardell, John	41	Down, Ireland	Lancaster District	Farmer	27 Jan 1819
McDonald, Alexander		Monaghan, Ireland	Charleston		13 Dec 1819 gave notice 21 May 1816
Moffett, Andrew	25	Berwickshire, Dunde, North Britain	Charleston	Merchant	14 Feb 1820 gave notice 3 July 1816
Manson, Andrew	34	Ross Shire, North Britain	Charleston	Merchant	28 Feb 1820 gave notice 29 Jany 1816
Mitchell, William	60	Perthshire, North Britain	Charleston	Mariner	25 Jul 1820
Mohr, Henry	33	Grunendeisch, Hanover	Charleston		26 Jan 1821
Mill, John	38	London, Great Britain	Charleston	Bookseller	9 Jul 1821
McCormick, William	26	Gallowayshire, North Britain	Charleston	Grocer	6 Mar 1822
McDowell, Alexander	24	Cavan, Ireland	Charleston	Student of Medicine	14 Oct 1822
McGinn, Arthur	27	Tyrone, Ireland	Charleston		23 May 1823
Maynard, Richard	43	Oxfordshire, Great Britain	Charleston	Druggist	30 Aug 1823
Mills, Alexander	34	Leitrun, Ireland	Charleston		1 Sep 1823
Michel, Frederick	33	Port au Prince St. Domingo	Charleston		13 Nov 1823
Moore, John	24	Ireland	Charleston		19 Jan 1824
McVicar, Niel	30	Argyleshire, North Britain	Charleston	Butcher	29 Jan 1824
Martin, Patrick James	30	Lettecum, Ireland	Charleston	Grocer	29 Jan 1824
Magwood, James	29	Armagh, Ireland	Charleston	Merchant	21 Feb 1824
Memminger, Christopher Gustavus	21	Wirtemberg(Dutchy)	Charleston	Student of Law	22 Jun 1824
Mullings, John	33	Grenock	Charleston	Pilot	5 Jul 1824
Meinadier, Pascal Etienne		Montpellier, France			5 Aug 1824
Muggridge, Mathew	33	Sussex, England	Charleston		5 Aug 1824
McAnnally, John	32	Armagh, Ireland	Charleston		20 Sep 1824
McLean, James	23	Perthshire, North Britain	Charleston		6 Oct 1824
Mulloy, James	23	Roscommon, Ireland	Charleston		13 Dec 1824
Magson, Saul Joseph	34	Halifax, Yorkshire, England	Charleston	Merchant	17 Jan 1825
Maxton, John	38	Perthshire, Scotland	Charleston	Baker	4 Feb 1825
Mosimann, Jacob	72	Bern, Switzerland	Charleston	Watchmaker	7 Feb 1825
Murray, Robert	43	Sutherland, North Britain	Charleston	Taylor	8 Feb 1825
McKnight, Samuel	24	Galloway, Scotland	Charleston	Accountant	20 Apr 1825
Moses, Reuben	54	Amsterdam, Holland	Charleston	Shopkeeper	24 Jun 1825
McCready, William	27	Cavan, Ireland	Charleston	Sadler	29 May 1826
Middleton, Francis	27	London (lately an Inhabitant of Florida)	Charleston	Mariner admitted under Treaty	9 June 1826
McKenzie, James	33	Rosburghshire, North Britain	Charleston	Plaisterer	26 Sep 1826
Magee, John	40	Down, Ireland	Charleston	Boatman	27 Sep 1826
Mantrass, Francisco	27	St. Augustine, East Florida	Charleston	Mariner	19 Apr 1827
McGregor, Alexander	30	Denny, North Britain	Charleston	Merchant	29 Sep 1827
Mitchell, Thomas	22	Grenock, North Britain	Charleston	Mariner	29 Sep 1827
Miles, Edward	36	Down, Ireland	Charleston	Mariner	15 Jan 1828
McWhinnie, William	27	Galloway, Scotland	Charleston	Merchant	17 Mar 1828
Meyer, John Henry	23	Hanover	Charleston	Grocer	1 Jul 1828
Muller, Johan	23	Hanover	Charleston	Clerk	3 Jul 1828
Murray, John D.	35	Leitrim, Ireland	Geo; Town dist.	Planter	8 Jul 1828
Maynard, Gabriel	29	Oxford, England	Charleston	Baker	10 Oct 1828
Milling, David	30	Down, Ireland	Columbia		8 Dec 1828
Michel, Francis	45	Island of St. Domingo	Charleston		2 Jan 1829
Moorhead, James	30	Antrim, Ireland	Charleston		15 Jul 1829
McIntyre, John	29	Down, Ireland	Charleston		20 Jul 1829
Meyer, Jurgen Wilhelm	26	Oldenburg	Charleston		25 Sep 1829
Monk, Stephen Patrick	30	Ireland	Charleston		4 Jan 1830
Meacher, Thomas	35	London, Great Britain	Charleston	Corn merchant	17 Mar 1830
McLeod, George	34	Sutherlandshire, North Britain	Columbia	Tailor	13 Apr 1830
Morison, Simon	34	Fifeshire, North Britain	Charleston	Cabinet maker	13 Apr 1830

Names of Aliens	Age	Nation	Residence	Occupation	Admission
McHugh, Mary Q.		Ireland			26 May 1830
McCormick, John	23	Tyrone, Ireland	Charleston		29 Jul 1830
McDowall, John	23	Galloway, Scotland	Charleston		29 Jul 1830
McKinlay, Peter	27	Grenock, Scotland	Charleston	Carpenter	6 Oct 1830
Mead, Alfred	30	London	Charleston		6 Oct 1830
McIntosh, Donald	21	Inverness-shire, Scotland	Charleston		12 Oct 1830
Meislahn, Hans	42	Denmark	Charleston		12 Oct 1830
Michel, William	35	Port au Prince, Isl. St. Domingo	Charleston	Physician	23 Mar 1831
Messer, Mildred alias James		Surry, England	Charleston		23 Mar 1831
Mairs, Elizabeth		Prussia	Charleston		25 Apr 1831
Murray, Robert	46	Sutherlandshire, North Britain	Charleston	Taylor	15 Jul 1831
Mathev, Charles	23	Switzerland	Charleston		3 Aug 1831
Michel, Francis	25	Havre, France	Charleston		3 Aug 1831
Murphy, John	67	Ireland	Charleston		3 Aug 1831
Marshall, John	30	Lincolnshire, England	Charleston		5 Aug 1831
McAlister, James	44	Derry, Ireland	Charleston	Carpenter	5 Oct 1831
McKenzie, William		Edinburgh	Charleston		5 Oct 1831
Mauckens, Henry	33	Germany	Charleston	Shopkeeper	5 Oct 1831
McBride, Patrick	23	Armagh, Ireland	Charleston	Grocer	14 Aug 1832
Moreland, Andrew	36	Down, Ireland	Charleston	Lumber merchant	31 Aug 1832
Mignot, Reney	32	Granville, France	Charleston	Confectioner	31 Aug 1832
Martin, Francis	27	Kent, England	Charleston	Boarding House keeper	31 Aug 1832
McMillan, John	50	Dumfrieshire, Scotland	Charleston	Merchant	5 Oct 1832
Malone, Thomas W.	24	Island of Jamaica	Charleston	Student at Law	5 Oct 1832
Mercey, John	24	Bourdeaux, France	Charleston	Blacksmith	5 Oct 1832
Masterson, Michael	32	Cavan, Ireland	Charleston	Shop keeper	9 Oct 1832
Moffat, Peter	33	Scotland	Charleston	Blacksmith	9 Oct 1832
Metevier, Francis	52	St. Domingo	Charleston	Baker	9 Oct 1832
McIntosh, William	44	Navin, Scotland	Charleston		9 Dec 1833
Morgan, J. B.	27	Island of Bermuda		Mariner	10 Dec 1833
Mulloy, William	40	Mayo, Ireland	Charleston	Shoemaker	11 Oct 1834
McBurney, William	28	Monaghan, Ireland	Charleston		11 Oct 1834
McKenna, John	26	Down, Ireland		Mariner	14 Oct 1834
Meyer, Jacob	22	Oldenburg, Germany	Charleston	Grocer	14 Oct 1834
Mackie, Margaret	44	Fifeshire, Scotland	Charleston		29 Sep 1837
Mayer, Christian		Wirtemberg	Charleston		19 Mar 1838
Martin, Michal	26	Kilkenney, Ireland	Charleston	Mariner	24 Apr 1838
Meyer, Gottlieb	29	Wirtemburg	Charleston	Butcher	9 Oct 1838
Marshall, John T.	40	Scotland	Charleston	Baker	17 Jul 1839
McIntyre, Peter	48	Perth, North Britain		Keeper of a Hotel	18 Jul 1839
Meyer, Luder	40	Oldenburg, Germany		Storekeeper	19 Jul 1839
Mollet, Edward	27	Rouen, France	Charleston	Merchant	14 Dec 1840
McMillan, Thomas		Scotland	Charleston	Tailor	22 Dec 1840
Manck, John P.	29	Hanover	Charleston		15 Jan 1841
Morison, Thomas	38	Fifeshire, Scotland	Charleston	Cabinet-maker	15 Jan 1841
Meyer, John D.	28	Hanover	Charleston	Grocer	19 Apr 1841
Mintzing, John H.	23	Hanover	Charleston	Clerk	13 Dec 1841
Magee, Arthur	25	Belfast, Ireland	Charleston	Merchant	19 Feb 1842
McHugh, Patrick	27	Cavern, Ireland	Charleston	Clerk	12 Jul 1843
McCartney, Daniel	30	Ireland	Charleston	House Carpenter	15 Oct 1844
Mure, Robert	32	Scotland	Charleston	Merchant	3 Feb 1845
Miller, John	54	Copenhagen, Denmark	Charleston	Mariner	1 Jun 1846
McKenna, Thomas	32	Ireland	Charleston	Storekeeper	19 Jan 1846
McInnes, Benjamin	35	Perthshire, Scotland	Charleston	Black & White Smith	7 Jan 1847
McDonald, John	37	Ireland	Charleston	Laborer	6 Aug 1847
Maher, Michael	40	Ireland	Charleston	Porter	6 Aug 1847
Murry, James	36	City of Dublin, Ireland	Charleston	Boot Maker	6 Aug 1847
McKenzie, John	54	Invernesshire, Scotland	Charleston	Cabinet Maker	6 Aug 1847
McNolty, Henry	26	Toronto, Upper Canada	Charleston	Waiter	6 Aug 1847
McCasker, Edward	23	County Fermana, Ireland	Charleston	Boot Maker	6 Aug 1847

Names of Aliens	Age	Nation	Residence	Occupation	Admission
Meyer, Christopher J.	43	Markbeschoff, Bavaria	Charleston	Shoemaker	16 Aug 1847
Moore, Thomas	26	County Hary, Ireland	Charleston	Labourer	17 Aug 1847
McLarty, Edward	33	Argyleshire, Scotland	Charleston	Mariner	2 Oct 1847
Meyerhoff, Behrend	21	Beverstradt, Hanover	Charleston	Grocer	7 Jan 1850
Middleton, Francis	30	London	Charleston	Pilot	29 Oct 1850
McGarrty, Michael	30	County of Cavan, Ireland	Charleston	Labourer	6 Jun 1853
Martin, John Martin	24	Wirtemberg	Charleston	Brewer	2 Jul 1855
Morello, James	25	Gibraltar	Charleston	Fruiterer	10 Jan 1856
Maguire, John J.	23	Ireland	Charleston	Store keeper	1 Jul 1857
Melfi, Leonardo	32	Naples	Do	Musician	22 Jul 1857
Mackin, Patrick	27	Ireland	Do		29 Jul 1857
Malony, Thomas	32	Ireland	Do	Labourer	29 Sep 1857
Moran, John	29	Ireland	Charleston	labourer	14 Oct 1857
McLean, Wm	21	Antrim Co: Ireland	Do	Clerk	24 Jun 1858
Monahan, Wm	52	Roscommon Co. Ireland	Do	labourer	2 Nov 1859
Merker, Earnest	35	Brunswick, Germany	Do	Mechanic	17 Sep 1860
Morris, Richard	21	Wilkenney, Ireland	Do	Mechanic	2 Oct 1860
McPherson, John	25	Dunegal County, Ireland	Do	Policeman	31 Oct 1860
Nightingale, Henry					21 Sep 1792
Nobbs, Samuel	29	London, Great Britain		Hair Dresser	29 Mar 1796
Neill, William		Belfast, Ireland		Mariner	16 Jan 1797
Newton, William		Stockton, England			20 Sep 1802
Nicholson, Joseph	28	Cumberland, England		Carpenter	22 Sep 1802
Naylor, Wrench, Thomas	32	Middlewich, England		Merchant	22 Sep 1803
Naylor, Samuel	32	Middlewich, England		Mariner	8 Jun 1804
Nathan, Jacob	38	Loraine, France		Merchant	8 Jun 1804
Neal, John	22	Grenock, Scotland		Mariner	2 Jul 1804
Nelson, William	26	Copenhagen, Denmark		Mariner	2 Jan 1806
Newton, Anthony	28	Durham, England		Butcher	14 Oct 1806
		declared his intention 25 Sep 1802			
Niel, Julius	22	St. Domingo		Merchant	27 Jun 1807
Newman, Charles	27	Wexford, Ireland			13 Sep 1808
Napier, Thomas	35	Glasgow, North Britain	Charleston	Merchant	24 Aug 1813
			declared his intention 17 July 1800		
Nowell, Thomas S.	38	London, Great Britain	Charleston	Accountant	27 Aug 1813
Nevill, John	44	Waterford, Ireland	Charleston	Carpenter	3 Sep 1813
Nevill, Joshua	46	Queen's County, Ireland	Charleston	Cabinet maker	15 Sep 1814
Nehbe, John	42	Kanau, Germany			7 Jun 1816
Niolon, Jean Baptiste Marius		Marseilles, France	Charleston		13 Oct 1818
Nathan, Henry	33	Amsterdam, Holland	Charleston		2 Apr 1822
Newbold, Samuel	24	Island of Bermudas	Charleston	Mariner	5 Mar 1824
Nolan, John M.	26	Roscommon, Ireland	Charleston	Merchant Taylor	8 Jul 1824
Notta, Lewis T.	49	Flanders	Charleston		4 Sep 1824
Nesbit, Robert	25	Berwick upon Tweed			30 Mar 1825
Neve, William	30	Copenhagen, Denmark	Charleston	Grocer	19 Feb 1829
Newman, John A.	40	Dantzic, Prussia	Charleston	Butcher	3 Jul 1829
Norman, George A.	55	Scotland	Charleston	merchant	31 Aug 1832
Nicolai, Ludweg H. W.	23	Hanover	Charleston	Clerk	3 Oct 1832
Noel, Alphonse	21	Paris, France	Charleston	Clerk	2 Apr 1835
Nelson, William	28	Sweden	Charleston	Tavernkeeper	15 Jul 1839
Nicolai, John H.	32	Germany	Charleston	Grocer	8 Jul 1840
Nash, Michael	33	Limerick, Ireland	Charleston	Labourer	15 Oct 1844
Nevin, Patrick	29	Belfast, Ireland	Charleston	Butcher	2 Sep 1847
Niebuhr, John P.	30	Hamburg, Germany	Charleston	Druggist	13 Sep 1849
Nimitz, Chs. Henry	58	Hanover	Charleston	Tavernkeeper	7 Jan 1850
O'Hara, William		Antrim, Ireland		Mariner	7 Feb 1797
Olivers, Thomas		Cardiganshire, England			11 Aug 1797
O'Neale, Charles	21	London, Great Britain		Merchant	3 Sep 1802
O'Gallagner, Simon Felix	40	Dublin, Ireland			20 Sep 1802
O'Leary, John	25	Cork, Ireland		Merchant	21 Jun 1804
Osman, Joseph	22	Fayal, Portugal		Mariner	16 Nov 1805
Ohlweiller, Michael	31	Germany		Baker	14 Oct 1806
O'Neale, Richard	21	London, Great Britain		Merchant	20 Jul 1811

Names of Aliens	Age	Nation	Residence	Occupation	Admission
Ohring, Magnus	31	Calmar, Sweden	Charleston	Mariner	2 Jul 1812
Oates, John	48	Sligo, Ireland	Charleston	Weaver	6 Sep 1813
Orth, Augustus	31	Wissembourg, Department of Lower Rhine, France	Charleston	Baker	10 Sep 1813
O'Rawe, John	32	Antrim, Ireland	Charleston	Grocer	18 Sep 1815 Registered 22 May 1812
O'Brien, Mathew	42	Barony of Upper Ormond, Tipperary, Ireland	Charleston	Taylor	19 May 1821
O'Neill, Edmond	22	Antrim, Ireland	Charleston neck	Grocer	18 Feb 1822
O'Brien, James	23	Cork, Ireland	Charleston		6 Oct 1824
Osborn, Thomas	30	Tyrone, Ireland	Edisto Island	Clergyman	24 Jan 1825
Ordo, Joseph	32	Tunis, Barbary	Charleston	Trader	17 Dec 1827
Oppenheim, Hertz Wolf	40	Hanover	Charleston	Merchant	19 Dec 1828
Ohlescu, Johan Christian	28	Hanover	Charleston		20 Jul 1829
O'Neill, John	26	Antrim, Ireland	Charleston	Butcher	7 May 1830
O'Neill, Jeremiah F.	35	Kerry, Ireland	Charleston	Clergyman	24 May 1830
O'Brien, Stephen	39	Tiperary, Ireland	Charleston		29 Jul 1830
O'Neill, Patrick	35	Antrim, Ireland	Charleston	Butcher	21 Sep 1830
O'Neill, Bernard		Londonderry	Charleston	Baker	5 Oct 1831
Osterholtz, E. H.	31	Hanover	Charleston		30 Aug 1834
Otten, Frederick	33	Hanover	Charleston		30 Aug 1834
O'Neill, John F.	22	Moneghan Co. Ireland	Charleston	Merchant	5 Jan 1841
Ostendorff, John M.	26	Hanover	Charleston	Grocer	13 Jul 1841
Ohlendorff, William	30	Brunswick, Germany	Charleston	Tailor	8 Apr 1843
O'Mally, John	28	County of Mayo, Ireland	Charleston	Soldier	3 Jul 1843
O'Neill, Patrick Revd.	35	Ireland	Charleston	Minister of the Gospel	1 Jul 1844
Otten, Cord	22	Hanover	Charleston	Grocer	9 Dec 1844
Ogilvie, James T.	27	Bauff, North Britain	Charleston	Clerk	27 Jul 1846
O'Callaghan, Denis	26	Ireland	Charleston	Grocer	13 Jan 1847
Oates, George	57	Sheffield, England	Charleston	Book-seller	15 Mar 1847
Oates, George A.	26	Sheffield, England	Charleston		15 Mar 1847
Oates, Edward H.	22	Sheffield, England	Charleston		15 Mar 1847
Oates, Henry T.	24	Sheffield, England	Charleston		15 Mar 1847
O Sullivan, James	36	County of Kerry, Ireland	Charleston	Merchant	6 Aug 1847
O Neill, James	45	County of Kerry, Ireland	Charleston	Boot Maker	6 Aug 1847
Oland, Catharine	38	Hanover	Charleston	(wife of D. Oland)	20 Apr 1849
O'Brien, John	22	Ireland	Charleston	Conductor on Rail Road	24 Sep 1849
O'Brien, Ellen	45	County of Cork, Ireland	Charleston	(wife of Thos. OBrien)	14 Jul 1851
Ojemann, J. C.	27	Hanover	Charleston	Grocer	15 Jul 1851
O'meara, Cornelius	26	Tipperary, Ireland	Do	Clerk	28 Oct 1858
Ortman, Fredk. Wm.	22	Westphalia, Prussia	Do	Clerk	21 Mar 1860
Prince, Charles		Great Britain			17 Sep 1792
Peigne, Lewis					17 Sep 1792
Patterson, Hugh		London, Great Britain			17 Sep 1793
Pourie, Basil				Merchant	23 Jan 1794
Phillips, Benjamin					15 Sep 1794
Pogson, Milward		Great Britain			14 Dec 1795
Phepoe, Richard		Dublin, Ireland			20 Apr 1796
Petit, Peter		Picardy, France		Mariner	7 Nov 1796
Phillips, John		Great Britain			20 Mar 1797
Pearce, Charles		Pool, England		Mariner	22 Apr 1797
Parsons, Thomas		Dorcetshire, England			14 Nov 1797
Peters, Henry		Nantz, France		Mariner	11 Mar 1799
Powers, George		Dungarvon, Ireland		Grocer	29 May 1799
Pelletant, John Andre	45	Marines, France		Planter	17 Jun 1799
Poincignon, Peter Anthony	38	Lorraigne, France		Plate worker	25 Sep 1802
Parker, Thomas	25	Sheffield, England		Merchant	24 Mar 1804
Peterson, Laurens	39	Wordigberg, Denmark		Mariner	14 Apr 1804
Piere, Henry D.		St. Marc, St. Domingo			24 Jul 1804
Prebble, George	28	Devonshire, England		Mariner	7 Aug 1804
Perenchief, James	23	Bermudas		Mariner	7 Aug 1804
Perry, Isabella	40	Caithness, North Britain		Midwife	19 Mar 1805
Philip, John	22	New Orleans		Mariner	8 May 1805
Paul, Samuel	34	Norfolk, England		Mariner	10 Jun 1805

Names of Aliens	Age	Nation	Residence	Occupation	Admission
Prevost, Peter	20	Cape Francois, St. Domingo		Mariner	16 Oct 1805
Philips, Daniel	22	Hampton, No. Britain		Mariner	17 Mar 1806
		corrected Argyleshire, No Britain			
Pieckenpack, John	34	York, Hanover		Grocer	14 Apr 1806
Pyke, Thomas	30	Dorcestershire, Great Britain		Mariner	6 May 1806
Patterson, James	42	Ayrshire, Scotland		Mariner	8 May 1806
Pellissier, John B.	55	Vienne, Dauphiny, France		Merchant	14 May 1806
Powers, Edward	26	Waterford, Ireland		Merchant	24 Jun 1806
Pitray, Lewis A.	23	Bourdeaux, France		Merchant	27 Jun 1807
Phillips, John	34	Tipperary, Ireland		Painter	28 Aug 1807
Pinto, M.	24	Smyrna, Egypt		Merchant	22 Oct 1807
Patterson, Samuel	22	Coleraine, Ireland		Merchant	14 Dec 1807
Ponts, John	26	Minorca		Grocer	20 Jun 1808
Palmer, John	54	South Wales			19 Sep 1808
Poulnot, Nicholas	45	Tornay, France			19 Sep 1808
Paul, John	27	Kirkcudbrightshire, North Britain	Charleston	Grocer	15 Jun 1812
Peter, Vincent	32	Nantz, France	Charleston	Grocer	26 Jun 1812
Perrier, Augustus B.	24	Bourdeaux, France	Charleston	Merchant	7 Dec 1812
Pyne, John	46	Cork, Ireland	Charleston	Planter	20 Apr 1813
			admitted Denizen 3 April 1811		
Pierce, Edwards	67	Wiltshire, England	Charleston	Accountant	23 Aug 1813
Pringle, George	25	Monaghan, Ireland	Charleston	Merchant	23 Aug 1813
Peters, George	47	London, Great Britain	Charleston	School-master	24 Aug 1813
Pearce, Thomas	38	Ewel, Surry, Great Britain	Christ Church Parish	Miller	27 Sep 1813
Perot, George	49	Guadoloupe, West Indies	Charleston	Mariner	23 Oct 1813
			Gave notice 23 Sept 1809		
Phillips, John	39	Shrewsbury, Shropshire, England	Charleston	Mariner	21 Dec 1813
Pelzer, Anthony	31	Aix la Chapelle, Westphalia	Charleston	School-master	15 Aug 1814
			Gave notice 5 Aug 1811		
Printens, Antoine	40	Marseilles, France	Charleston	Instructor of the French language	12 Apr 1815
Pellissier, Jean Baptiste	23	Cape Nicholas Niole, St. Domingo	Charleston	Jeweller	17 Apr 1815
Petterson, John	49	Carlshaur, Sweden		Mariner	8 Jan 1816
Perrin, Philibert	23	Neufville, France	Charleston		9 Jan 1816
Phillp, Mathew	30	Stockholm, Sweden	Charleston	Mariner	12 Jan 1816
Plumeau, John Francis	21	Cape Francois	Charleston	Bookkeeper	30 Jan 1816
Peterson, John Edward	33	Stockholm, Sweden	Charleston	Grocer	16 Feb 1816
Pezant, Peter	30	Cape Nichola Mole, St. Domingo	Charleston	Jeweller	2 Jul 1816
Peire, Peter		Languedoc, France	Charleston		12 Oct 1818
Pellot, Onesin		Aunis, France	Charleston		12 Oct 1818
Penot, Charles		Bourdeaux, France	Charleston		13 Oct 1818
Prado, Manuel		Oporto, Portugal	Charleston		24 Jan 1820
Pezant, Louis	44	Cape Nicholas Mole, St. Domingo	Charleston	Mariner	19 Mar 1821
Paul, Dunbar	31	Kirkcudbright, North Britain	Charleston	Merchant	13 Sep 1821
Prowting, Charles	30	South Hampton, England	Charleston	Mariner	19 Oct 1824
Pellot, Andrew Peter Augustus	28	Mauze, France	Charleston neck	Merchant	6 Nov 1824
Pritchard, William	24	London, Great Britain	Columbia		18 Nov 1824
Pennal, Robert	32	Antrim, Ireland	Charleston	Merchant	2 Oct 1826
Pelmoine, Francis	39	Languedoc, France	Charleston	Barber	13 Dec 1826
Police, Francis	33	Ragouse, Italy	Charleston	Merchant	16 Feb 1827
Price, Thomas	48	Wales, Great Britain	Charleston		20 Mar 1827
Picault, Francis D.	22	Island of Cuba	Charleston		21 Sep 1829
Plane, William Ames	24	London, Great Britain	Charleston		21 Sep 1829
Praca, Domingo	40	Oporto, Portugal	Charleston		25 Sep 1829
Prendergast, Martin	24	County of Cork, Ireland	Charleston		25 Sep 1829
Pundt, John	29	Bremen, Germany	Charleston	Grocer	14 Jan 1830
Peterson, Hans Christian	31	Christiana, Norway	Charleston	Grocer	8 Apr 1830
Prele, John Frederic	24	St. Jago, Cuba	Charleston	Merchant's clerk	29 Jul 1830

Names of Aliens	Age	Nation	Residence	Occupation	Admission
Prigge, Claus (alias Sprigge)	27	Hanover	Charleston	Grocer	26 Aug 1830
Peyton, Ann	29	Belfast, Ireland	Charleston		21 Sep 1830
Passailaigue, Louis	41	Port au Prince	Charleston		5 Aug 1831
Pickenpack, Jacob	31	Hanover	Charleston		23 Sep 1831
Pausin, Joseph	21	France	Charleston	Cooper	8 Oct 1831
Pipard, Peter F.	28	Caen, France	Charleston		28 Jun 1832
Pregnall, Henry	22	London, England	Charleston	Carpenter	5 Oct 1832
Prendergast, Thomas	41	Tipperary, Ireland	Charleston	Gardener	9 Oct 1832
Pinard, Eugene	26	Troyes, France	Charleston	Merchant	8 May 1833
Perry, Stuart	32	Ulster, Ireland	Charleston	Merchant	21 Jun 1833
Paty, James	33	Down, Ireland	Charleston	Mariner	26 Aug 1834
Parkerson, John	51	Norwich, England	Charleston	Bellhanger	30 Aug 1834
Preston, John	.	West Meath, Ireland	Charleston		11 Oct 1834
Purves, William B.	23	Scotland	Charleston	Cabinet maker	14 Oct 1834
Papmeyer, Andrew B.		Denmark		Grocer	17 Jul 1839
Pritchard, Edward E.	47	Shropshire, England	Charleston	Accountant	18 Jul 1839
Peira, Emanuel	22	Island of Madeira	Charleston	Mariner	29 Oct 1840
Petit, Louis Florial	46	La Rochelle, France	Charleston	Confectioner	28 May 1841
Pezant, Sophie		St. Domingo(France)	Charleston		7 Sep 1841
Poincignon, Etienne	42	St. Domingo(France)	Charleston	Tin plate worker	9 Jul 1842
Prigge, Julianna C.	23	Rocktilz, Saxony	Charleston		13 Nov 1846
Phin, A. C.	36	Dundee, Scotland	Charleston	Druggist	13 Jan 1847
Plein, Jacob	21	Hagan, Hanover	Charleston	Clerk	14 Jan 1847
Peschke, Ernest	28	Berlin, Prussia	Do	Watchmaker	22 Apr 1857
Pyke, George	28	Liverpool	Do	Mariner	24 Jun 1857
Police, Joseph G.	23	Austria	Do	Engineer	21 Jul 1858
Pontz, Lawrence	47	Minorca (Spain)	Do	Mariner	6 Oct 1858
Posi, Geilio	38	Rome, Italy	Charleston	Teacher	10 Oct 1860
Pudigon, Augustus	31	Garchisy, Nieve, France	Charleston	Florist	29 Oct 1860
Quay, Alexander		Newry Down, Ireland			20 Sep 1796
Quay, John	40	Isle of Mann		Mariner	29 Aug 1806
Querard, Henry	33	Bayonne, France		Merchant	29 Nov 1806
Quin, Thomas	29	Limerick, Ireland		Grocer	5 Mar 1807
Quinlan, Michael	55	Ireland	Charleston	Storekeeper	19 Oct 1813
Quinlin, Mary		Ireland			26 May 1830
Quin, James	32	Ireland	Do		2 Jul 1855
Richards, William		Antigua			12 Mar 1791
Read, Robert		Ireland			21 Mar 1796
Rust, Peter		Bremen			19 May 1796
Rabb, John		Antrim, Ireland		Merchant	19 May 1796
Roberts, John		Bristol, England		Mariner	13 Apr 1797
Ross, James	21	Antrim, Ireland		Merchant	1 Jul 1797
Reardon, Dennis		Cork, Ireland			2 Apr 1798
Reilly, Charles		Carvan, Ireland		Merchant	3 Apr 1798
Reid, James		Ayrshire, North Britain		Mariner	3 Apr 1798
Reynoulds, David		St. Eustatia		Mariner	11 Dec 1798
Rolando, Henry	35	Cadiz, Spain			30 Feb 1798
Rodick, James		Annen, North Britain			4 May 1799
Robson, Caleb		New Castle, Tyne		Merchant	1 Jun 1799
Reilly, Thomas		Newry, Ireland		Physician	14 Jun 1799
Rose, Henry	35	Leipseg, Saxony		Merchant	17 Jun 1799
Reynoulds, Charles	32	Dublin, Ireland		Shoemaker	22 Sep 1802
Raine, Thomas	32	London, England		Law Stationer	6 Oct 1802
Richards, Samuel	42	Monmouth, England		Merchant	3 Nov 1802
Ross, William	32	Ayr, Scotland		Merchant	7 Sep 1803
Ross, Andrew	32	Gallowayshire, Scotland		Mariner	13 Dec 1803
Ramsay, John	31	Clackmanan, Scotland		Distiller	23 Jan 1804
Richards, Josiah	42	Wales, England		Mariner	19 Apr 1804
Richardson, Thomas	26	London, England		Merchant	23 May 1804
Russell, William	34	Ayrshire, Scotland		Merchant	24 May 1804
Rodick, Thomas	27	Richmond, England		Merchant	19 Jul 1804
Robinson, Thomas	21	Liverpool, England		Mariner	3 Jan 1805
Rodrigues, Abraham	37	Bourdeaux, France		Merchant	17 Mar 1805
Richards, William	40	Antrim, Ireland		Merchant	27 Jul 1805
Righton, William	30	Bermudas		Mariner	16 Sep 1805
Rosse, Paul	30	Leser Nowra, Italy		Cabinet maker	14 Jan 1806
Ralston, James	22	Argyleshire, Scotland		Wine merchant	9 Aug 1806
Rees, Loder Needham	24	Oxfordshire, Great Britain		Physician	27 Aug 1806
Roux, Francis	20	Jeremie, St. Domingo		Merchant	10 Nov 1806

Names of Aliens	Age	Nation	Residence	Occupation	Admission
Rhodes, Thomas	31	Shropshire, England		Planter	23 Jan 1808
Ricard, Francis	39	Department of Lot & Ganone, France		Grocer	10 Mar 1808
Reilley, James	27	Cavan, Ireland		Sadler	24 Mar 1808
Robinson, William	36	Dublin, Ireland			13 Sep 1808
Riondel, John Joseph	35	Samoens, Savoy, France		Merchant	28 Mar 1809
Rousset, Claude	20	Lyons, France		Mariner	15 Jun 1809
Ray, James	49	London, Great Britain		Merchant	1 Jan 1810
			declared his intention 16 Nov 1805		
Rabie, Louis Peter	21	Cape Francois		Merchant	11 Jan 1810
Ross, John	27	Lerwick, Shetland, North Britain	Charleston	Merchant	24 Aug 1810
Richelme, Louis Alexander	54	Daubagne, France	Charleston	Merchant	17 Sep 1810
Routledge, John	26	Westmoreland, England	Charleston	Merchant	30 Jan 1811
Remoussin, Arnold St. M.	29	St. Domingo	Charleston		1 Jul 1812
Ryan, Lawrence	26	Tipperary, Ireland	Charleston	Student of Law	23 Aug 1813
			declared intention 4th Monday March 1809		
Reilly, George	30	Cavan, Ireland	Charleston	Painter & Glazier	24 Aug 1813
Reid, Alexander	36	Edinburgh, North Britain	Charleston	Watchmaker	27 Sep 1813
Reilly, Daniel	26	Cavan, Ireland	Charleston	Sadler	8 Oct 1813
Ralston, Robert	30	Ayrshire, North Britain	Johns Island	Planter	23 Nov 1813
Reynaud, Louis Cabeuil	31	St. Domingo	Charleston	Taylor	28 Dec 1813
Rodrigues, Moses	47	Bourdeaux, France	Charleston		11 Oct 1814
Rabot, Laurence Maise	60	Dinan, France		Mariner	10 Jul 1815
Rodrigues, David		Bourdeaux, France	Charleston		6 Sep 1815
Romeo, Baptiste	50	Sicily	Charleston		9 Jan 1816
Rotta, Benjamin		France			15 Oct 1816
Raffin, Joseph	39	Nantz, France	Charleston	Merchant	30 Dec 1816
Roh, Jacob Frederick	43	Wirtemberg, Germany	Charleston	Blacksmith	15 Dec 1819
			Gave noitce 5 October 1812		
Renou, Louis Francois	46	Maurille, department Mayne et loire	Charleston	Shop keeper	30 Mar 1820
			resident New Orleans, La.		
Rantin, William	38	Newry, Ireland	Charleston	Baker	7 June 1820
Radcliffe, John W.		Great Britain	Charleston		9 Oct 1820
Robinson, Randal	36	Antrim, Ireland	Charleston	Merchant	22 Feb 1822
Robinson, Alexander	39	Antrim, Ireland	Charleston		27 Sep 1822
Ross, James	38	Shetland, North Britain	Charleston		25 Mar 1823
Robertson, James	27	Fifeshire, North Britain	Charleston	Merchant	5 Apr 1823
Roddy, Martin		Longford, Ireland	Charleston		27 Aug 1823
Roche, Edward L.	26	Cork, Ireland	Charleston	Taylor	14 Apr 1824
Ryan, Thomas	24	Limerick, Ireland	Charleston	Student of Law	22 Jun 1824
Reilly, James	32	Cavan, Ireland			19 Apr 1825
Roger, Thomas Joseph	26	Rouen, France	Charleston	Merchant	19 Oct 1825
Redmond, Mathew	33	Wexford, Ireland	Charleston		11 Mar 1826
Rose, John	36	Amsterdam, Holland	Charleston		18 Sep 1826
Rowan, Samuel	28	Armagh, Ireland	Charleston		10 Oct 1826
Reicke, Claus	30	Hanover	Charleston		14 Mar 1827
Ravina, Joseph Domingo	38	St. Sebastian, Spain	Charleston	Teacher of languages	13 Apr 1827
Ryan, Fergus	29	Dublin, Ireland	Charleston	Mariner	28 Apr 1828
Ricard, Jean		Gascony, France	Charleston	Farmer	20 Feb 1829
Richardson, Robert		London, England	Charleston	Bellhanger	18 Dec 1829
Rame, Claude		France	Charleston	Confectioner	18 Dec 1829
Redfern, John	36	Derbyshire, England	Charleston	Shoemaker	20 Feb 1830
Reedy, James	41	Tipperary, Ireland	Charleston	House carpenter	17 Mar 1830
Robb, James		Sterling, Scotland	Charleston		24 May 1830
Rosenberg, Francis	36	Prussia	Charleston	Grocer	21 Jul 1830
Rumpp, George Henry	35	Germany	Charleston	Storekeeper	6 Oct 1830
Riecke, Gerd	24	Hanover	Charleston	Grocer	12 Oct 1830
Recli, Carlo	68	Switzerland	Charleston		3 Aug 1831
Rivers, Joseph	32	Oporto, Portugal	Charleston		3 Aug 1831
Roumillat, Ulysses	34	Isl. of St. Domingo	Charleston		26 Aug 1831
Roach, Henry	32	Germany	Charleston	Grocer	5 Oct 1831
Rampel, George	23	Germany	Charleston	Clerk	8 Oct 1831
Ritchie, Euphan (Mr)	60	Edinburgh	Charleston		26 Jun 1832
Russe, Henry	25	Gremen	Charleston	Grocer	14 Aug 1832

Names of Aliens	Age	Nation	Residence	Occupation	Admission
Renauld, John	60	Rambouillet, France	Charleston	Gardener	21 Sep 1832
Reppenning, John	24	Denmark	Charleston	Clerk	5 Oct 1832
Redfern, Edward F.	28	Dublin, Ireland	Charleston	Saddler	8 Oct 1832
Ryan, William	23	Limerick, Ireland	Charleston	Grocer	24 May 1833
Reithmeyer, Johann	22	Hanover	Charleston	Mariner	3 Jul 1834
Rust, Luder	28	Hanover	Charleston	Sugar refiner	30 Aug 1834
Roberts, George	36	England		Mariner	13 Oct 1834
Robertson, James	43	Perthshire, Scotland		Grocer	13 Oct 1834
Reigne, Louisa	59	Is. St. Domingo	Charleston		13 Dec 1836
Rose, Wm. P.	26	Hull, England		Mariner	15 Jun 1838
Richardson, C. Y(?)	24	Surry, England		Engineer	9 Oct 1838
Rust, John C.	26	Hanover		Grocer	19 Jul 1839
Reid, John T.	33	Irvine, Scotland	Charleston	Clerk	14 Dec 1840
Rosenberg, Moses F.	42	Poland (Russia)	Charleston	Storekeeper	28 May 1841
Rinker, Charles F.	39	Hanover	Charleston		21 Jul 1841
Rice, Frederick	32	Wirtenberg (Austria)	Charleston	Blacksmith	16 Dec 1841
Renneker, John H.	23	Hanover	Charleston	Grocer	20 Sep 1842
Runcken, Siade J.	22	Wremen (Germany)	Charleston	Grocer	17 Jan 1843
Riecke, George	45	Hanover	Charleston	Grocer	12 Jul 1843
Rosenfeldt, Jacob	32	Duchy of Posen, Prussia	Charleston	Minister (of the Heb: Con:)	21 Dec 1846
Ramos, Eusebio F.	25	Havana, Cuba	Charleston	Segar-maker	16 Aug 1847
Rice, John W.	24	Ballyclair, Ireland	Charleston	Clerk	17 Aug 1847
Rohlfing, Heinrich	29	Hanover	Charleston	Bootmaker	13 Apr 1853
Rehkoff, George	30	Waldeck	Charleston	Merchant	28 Jan 1858
Rabuske, Bernard	32	Berlin, Prussia	Do	Merchant	24 Apr 1858
Riley, John	39	Mayo Co., Ireland	Do	Labourer	28 Oct 1859
Scott, William		Ireland			1 Jul 1793
Stephens, Samuel		Ireland			21 Aug 1793
Sweetman, M. C.		Ireland			6 Jun 1794
Shroudy, William					17 Jul 1794
Steedman, Charles					18 Sep 1794
Skrimsher, William		England			25 Sep 1794
Sanchez, Bernadine		St. Augustine			1 Nov 1794
Spinks, William					17 Mar 1795
Shroudy, William		Bermudas		Mariner	7 Jul 1795
Smith, William		Bermudas		Mariner	18 Jan 1796
Sangster, John		North Britain			8 Feb 1796
Scott, Thomas		Ireland			20 Apr 1796
Schepeler, George		Hanover, Germany			29 Apr 1796
Salgado, Joseph Raphel		Havanna, Cuba			14 Sep 1796
Sweeny, Bryan		Cork, Ireland			22 Sep 1796
Sergeant, John Payne		Wicklow, Ireland			29 Sep 1796
Slater, Thomas		Lancastershire, England		Mariner	25 Mar 1797
Sangster, William		Sterlingshire, Scotland		Mariner	27 Oct 1797
Smith, Francis		London			27 Oct 1797
Swart, John	38	Amsterdam			11 Dec 1797
Smith, James		Banffshire, Scotland			21 Jan 1799
Spies, JohnJacob		Amsterdam			21 Jan 1799
Sudermann, John		Konigsberg, Prussia			21 Jan 1799
Steinmetz, Jacob E. A.		Etzel, East Friesland		Merchant	13 Jun 1799
Schirmer, John Elias		Hamburgh			14 Jun 1799
Smith, William	26	Norway, Denmark		Mariner	17 Jun 1799
Schofield, Edmond	35	Yorkshire, England		Ship Carpenter	17 Jun 1799
Schute, David		Stellin, Prussia		Mariner	17 Jun 1799
Stevenson, James	35	Carrickfergus, Ireland		Carpenter	17 Jun 1799
Smilie, Andrew	26	Ballymony, Ireland		Merchant	7 Jul 1800
		application registered		Admitted & sowrn	1 Sep 1800
Samoy, Claudius Nichs	40	Paris, France		Merchant	25 Sep 1802
Sutherland, James	30	Elgin, Scotland		Merchant	21 Mar 1803
Sasportas, Abraham	25	St. Thomas		Mariner	20 Jul 1803
St. Martin, Auguste	24	St. Domingo		Merchant	28 Oct 1803
Strong, Lawrence	22	Shetland, Scotland		Mariner	27 Jan 1804
Sartoris, Peter	24	Geneva, Switzerland		Merchant	9 Feb 1804
Suau, Amant	36	Bourdeaux, France		Merchant	23 Feb 1804
Splenger, Frederick	32	Lenzburgh, Switzerland		Merchant	11 Dec 1804
Smith, John	38	Cork, Ireland		Mariner	22 Apr 1805
Sanders, John	33	Glasgow, Scotland		Merchant	16 May 1805
Sauvalle, Francis	23	St. Domingo		Merchant	10 Jun 1805
Solomon, Lewis	40	Nantz, France			26 Jun 1805
Smith, William	33	Bermudas		Ship Carpenter	26 Oct 1805
Spencer, Frederick G. S.	28	London, England		Mariner	28 Jan 1806
Smith, Peter	38	Cambletown, Scotland		Mariner	9 Jul 1806

Names of Aliens	Age	Nation	Residence	Occupation	Admission
Smith, Richard	35	Altona, Denmark		Mariner	5 Aug 1806
Sagory, Lewis M.	22	Nantz, France		Merchant	20 Mar 1807
Schultz, Andrew	23	Lubeck		Merchant	28 Mar 1807
Squiers, Jonathan	26	Liverpool, England		Mariner	30 Mar 1807
Smith, Henry	42	Cork, Ireland		Ship carpenter	20 Apr 1807
Segerstrom, John P.	37	Gothenborg, Sweden		Merchant	14 Sep 1807
Steele, John	29	Monaghan, Ireland		Mechanic	21 Sep 1807
Stanke, Christopher	46	Hanover, Germany		Mariner	26 Nov 1807
Stride, Samuel	36	Southampton, England		Mariner	20 Jun 1808
Saures, Jacob	34	Curracoa			13 Sep 1808
Saures, Isaac	62	Curracoa		Merchant	13 Sep 1808
Simons, John	26	Liverpool, England		Mariner	30 May 1810
Stevens, Clement William		Jamaica		Mariner	20 Jul 1811
Scott, William Junr.	25	Down, Ireland	Charleston	Merchant	29 Jul 1811
			Declared his intention 20 June 1808		
Scouler, Thomas	47	Haddington, North Britain	Charleston	Ship Carpenter	26 Jun 1812
Schrodar, John	37	Mecklenburgh, Germany	Charleston	Grocer	9 Oct 1812
Sicard, Pierre	32	New Orleans	Charleston	Mariner	19 Oct 1812
Sweeny, Patrick	38	Meath, Ireland	Charleston	Millwright	1 Sep 1813
Smith, George	29	Wicklow, Ireland	Charleston	Gardener	24 Sep 1813
Steele, William	22	Monaghan, Ireland	Charleston	Clerk	28 Sep 1813
Shiels, Henry	35	Fifeshire, North Britain	Charleston	Grocer	6 Oct 1813
Smith, James	32	Wicklow, Ireland	Charleston	Butcher	13 Oct 1813
Sun, John Caniedge	27	Manchester, England	Charleston		19 Oct 1813
Smith, John	28	Ayreshire, North Britain	Charleston		19 Oct 1813
Shields, James	38	Tyrone, Ireland	Charleston	Schoolmaster	23 Nov 1813
Shorton, John	31	Cork, Ireland	Charleston	Carpenter	21 Dec 1813
Smith, Andrew	52	Banff, North Britain	St. George's Dorchester	Farmer	7 Feb 1814
Sandford, John	34	Dublin, Ireland	Charleston	Grocer	20 Jul 1814
St. Amand, John A.	23	Cape Francois, West Indies	Charleston	Coach maker	11 Oct 1814
Schmidt, John W.	32	Emden, Prussia	Charleston	Doctor of medicine	2 Jan 1816
			gave notice 4 August 1812		
Smith, George E.	29	Cape Francois	Charleston	Carpenter	9 Jan 1816
Smith, William	40	Manchester, England	Charleston		8 Apr 1816
Schirer, John	42	Alsace, France	Charleston	Gunsmith	10 Jun 1816
Siau, Louis	40	Languedoc, France	Charleston	Merchant	2 Jan 1817
Swan, Johan	32	Calmar, Sweden	Charleston	Mariner	22 Jun 1818
Signias, John		Flanders	Charleston		13 Oct 1818
Sharpe, James	34	London, Great Britain	Beaufort District	Planter	26 Nov 1818
			gave notice Beaufort Dist. 14 Nov 1814		
Steele, Gordon	33	Grenock, North Britain			15 Mar 1819
Schutt, Henry	53	Hamburgh	Charleston	Mariner	24 Apr 1821
Schriener, John Henry	28	Hamburgh	Charleston		2 Apr 1822
				registered 19 Jany 1819	
Sluter, Jacob	44	Hanover, Germany	Charleston	Shopkeeper	15 Jul 1822
				registered 7 July 1819	
Silva, Domingo	33	Lisbon, Portugal		Mariner	29 Jul 1823
				registered 12 July 1820	
Sampson, Joseph	26	London, Great Britain	Charleston		21 Nov 1823
				registered 9 Aug 1820	
Schmock, John C.	30	Berlin, Prussia	Charleston		12 Feb 1824
Shegog, Joseph	33	Cavan County, Ireland	Charleston	Grocer	21 Feb 1824
Shegog, George	25	Cavan County, Ireland	Charleston	Grocer	21 Feb 1824
Schroder, Johan	32	Lubec, Hause Town, Holland	Charleston	Grocer	17 Apr 1824
Sassard, John	27	Bourdeaux, France	Charleston	Mariner	22 Sep 1824
Schaffner, Frederick	38	Mentz, Germany	Charleston	Shopkeeper	19 Oct 1824
Senet, Joseph	33	Port au Prince, St. Domingo	Charleston	Blacksmith	20 Oct 1824
Seigling, John	32	Erpert, Prussia	Charleston	Musical Instrument Maker	6 Dec 1824
Schipman, Harm Bernt	37	Poppenberg, Westphalia, Germany	St. Stephens Parish		23 May 1825
Smith, Eliza	42	Antrim, Ireland	Charleston		6 Jul 1826
Spring, Alexander T.	32	Kerry, Munster, Ireland	Charleston	Classical teacher	26 Sep 1826

Names of Aliens	Age	Nation	Residence	Occupation	Admission
Smith, John	24	Liverpool, G. Britain	Charleston	Mariner	10 Oct 1826
Stoppelbein, Lorenz	26	Dalmstadt, Germany	Charleston		13 Dec 1826
Selin, Peter	32	Dantzick, Prussia	Charleston	Merchant	17 Dec 1827
Seebeck, Conrad Diederick	23	Hanover	Charleston	Grocer	31 Dec 1827
Stephan, Christian	48	Prussia	Charleston	Merchant	25 Jul 1828
Schull, John Harman	34	Hanover	Charleston	Grocer	19 Dec 1828
Stall, Frederick	33	Memel, Prussia	Charleston	Butcher	5 Jan 1829
Smith, John Nielson	24	Copenhagen, Denmark	Charleston	Mariner	6 Jun 1829
Sielaff, Charles W.	41	Prussia	Charleston	Mariner	13 Nov 1829
Segelke, John Frederick	35	Hanover	Charleston		1 Jul 1830
Schroder, William Theodore	33	Hamburg	Charleston		29 Jul 1830
Smith, Daniel	43	Prussia	Charleston		6 Oct 1830
Schriver, Nicholas	37	St. Domingo	Charleston	Mariner	12 Oct 1830
Schröder, Wilhelm	27	Hanover	Charleston	Grocer	14 Apr 1831
Schlemt, George		Dantzic, Prussia	Charleston		31 May 1831
Santiny, Philip		France	Charleston		27 Jul 1831
Shinie, Alexander	49	Kincairnshire, North Britain	Charleston		27 Jul 1831
Storne, Joseph	38	Italy	Charleston		27 Jul 1831
Schultz, John Henry		Oznaburg, Hanover	Charleston		3 Aug 1831
Siddon, Joseph		Bermuda	Charleston		3 Aug 1831
Stillman, Thomas	30	Somersetshire, England	Charleston		3 Aug 1831
Shegog, William		Cavan, Ireland	Charleston		5 Aug 1831
Sturken, Henry		Hanover	Charleston		5 Aug 1831
Suran, Joseph	54	Cape Nichola Mole	Charleston	Shoemaker	5 Oct 1831
Stegeman, Johan H.	24	Oldenburg, Germany	Charleston	Mariner	5 Oct 1831
Stevenson, George	25	Hanover	Charleston	Mariner	5 Oct 1831
Stevens, Charles	26	Copenhagen, Denmark	Charleston	Mariner	5 Oct 1831
Smith, John	29	Hamburgh	Charleston	Clerk	5 Oct 1831
Stover, Albert	25	Bremen	Charleston	Clerk	5 Oct 1831
Sturken, John H.	25	Germany	Charleston	Grocer	5 Oct 1831
Salvo, Francis	21	Island of Malta	Charleston	Cabinet maker	14 Aug 1832
Scharenberg, Christian	40	Prussia	Charleston	Grocer	14 Aug 1832
Scott, Charles	43	Leghorn, Tuscany	Charleston	Cabinet maker	31 Aug 1832
Silver, Antonio	56	Portugal	Charleston	Mariner	31 Aug 1832
Siles, Michael	35	St. Augustine, Florida	Charleston	Mariner	31 Aug 1832
Schonboc, Frederick	22	Copenhagen, Denmark	Charleston	Mariner	31 Aug 1832
Schultz, Charles J.	21	Riga, Russia	Charleston	Mariner	31 Aug 1832
Stegman, John	35	Hanover	Charleston	Shop keeper	31 Aug 1832
Sege, Bartholomew	38	Florida	Charleston		3 Sep 1832
Shee, John	34	Kilkenny, Ireland	Charleston	Rice miller	21 Sep 1832
Schrage, Diederick	28	Oldenburg	Charleston		21 Sep 1832
Sarbst, Frederick	24	Hanover	Charleston	Grocer	22 Sep 1832
Shachte, John	22	Prussia	Charleston		3 Oct 1832
Stewart, Angus	40	Perthshire, Scotland	Charleston	Inn keeper	4 Oct 1832
Schnuck, John	27	Hanover	Charleston	Clerk	4 Oct 1832
Shultz, George	24	Hanover	Charleston	Clerk	5 Oct 1832
Simmers, Burcher	22	Hanover	Charleston	Mariner	8 Oct 1832
Sampson, Samuel	21	London,Great Britain	Charleston	Clerk	24 Jun 1834
Steinberg, Henry	28	Hanover	Charleston	Grocer	30 Aug 1834
Siemer, Herman A.	26	Hanover	Charleston	Weaver	30 Aug 1834
Stevenson, John	22	St. John's, New Brunswick	Charleston	Mariner	1 Oct 1834
Schabel, George	23	Hesse	Charleston	Grocer	1 Oct 1834
Steike, John	40	Dantzic,Prussia	Charleston	Salesman	11 Oct 1834
Saunders, William	26	Sweden		Mariner	11 Oct 1834
Schoehler, Jacob	23	Elsas, France		Stone cutter	11 Oct 1834
Street, Joseph	34	Portsmouth, England	Charleston		14 Oct 1834
Slyer, Claus	21	Bremen	Charleston	Carpenter	14 Oct 1834
Schroder, Jacob	27	Hanover	Charleston	Grocer	14 Oct 1834
Schrage, Gerhard	21	Oldenburg	Charleston	Mariner	10 Jan 1835
Smith, John D.		Stettin, Prussia			8 May 1835

Names of Aliens	Age	Nation	Residence	Occupation	Admission
Street, Angelique		Island of St. Domingo	Charleston		20 Jan 1836
Steen, Alexander		Great Britain	Columbia		28 Nov 1836
Symons, John		Northumberland, England	Charleston	Carpenter	29 Aug 1838
Silcox, Danl. H.	27	Wells County, England	Charleston		6 May 1840
Seaman, Henry D.	38	Hanover	Charleston	Grocer	12 Dec 1839
Schroder, Henrig	21	Gustendorf, Hanover	Charleston	Shop-keeper	21 Dec 1840
Schodel, George	23	Hanover	Charleston	Shop keeper	16 Apr 1841
Schulken, Henry	26	Hanover	Charleston	Grocer	13 Jul 1841
Samson, Joseph	27	Yorkshire, England	Charleston	Accountant	23 Jun 1842
Schmidt, Heinrich	23	Wremen, Hanover	Charleston	Grocer	17 Jan 1843
Sancken, Jacob	28	Hanover	Charleston	Grocer	5 Jul 1843
Schafesee, August	46	Hanover	Charleston	Grocer	12 Jul 1843
Smyth, Thomas D. D.	35	County of Antrim, Ireland	Charleston	Minister of the Gospel	2 May 1844
Schroder, Henry G.	22	Oldenberg	Charleston	Grocer	13 Dec 1844
Schroder, Jurgen	22	Oldenberg	Charleston	Grocer	12 Jan 1846
Strauss, Maurice	29	Frankfort on the Maine	Charleston	Merchant	18 Mar 1847
Scholle, Philip	25	Warberg, Prussia	Charleston	Engineer	6 Aug 1847
Schachte, William	30	Prussia	Charleston	Grocer	16 Aug 1847
Schumacker, Fredk.	30	Hanover	Charleston	Mariner	16 Aug 1847
Siemenson, Theodore	40	Hamburg, Germany	Charleston	Manufacturer	26 Mar 1849
Seevers, Henry	34	Amt. Siecke, Hanover	Charleston	Grocer	17 Sep 1849
Stints, Frederick	21	Lemwerden, Dukedom of Oldenberg	Charleston	Clerk	9 Jun 1851
Shaw, James	31	Abernethey, Scotland	Charleston	Store-keeper	5 Apr 1853
Sollee, Mrs. Elizabeth	55	Spain	Charleston	Teacher	21 Jan 1856
Salas, Ramon	36	Sabadell, Spain	Charleston	Merchant	14 Jan 1857
Seydel, Chas. A. J.	27	Hamburg, Germany	Do	Cabinet maker	4 Mar 1857
Seydel, J. A. A. H.	29	Hamburg Do	Do	Merchant	4 Mar 1857
Steinberg, Claus	22	Hanover	Do	Store keeper	22 Apr 1857
Scheuer, Simon	23	Hesse Darmstadt, Germany	Do	Merchant	22 Apr 1858
Siebert, Fritz	41	Bremen	Do	Carpenter	5 May 1859
Taylor, Alexander		Scotland			5 Feb 1793
Tate, James		England		Mariner	5 Sep 1795
Tate, John		Galloway, Scotland			9 Feb 1796
Toutain, Peter Nicholas		Rouen in Normandy			2 Dec 1796
Tombarel, John Francis		Canner, France			14 Dec 1796
Taylor, Alexander		Bricking, Scotland		Mariner	22 Feb 1797
Tromp, James		Venice		Mariner	27 Oct 1797
Thom, Robert		Lenarack, Scotland			1798
Truchelet, Joseph	29	Rehon		Baker	14 Aug 1798
Thorney, William		Selby, Yorkshire, England			14 Aug 1798
Taylor, John	32	Fifeshire, Scotland		Mariner	18 Mar 1799
Tovey, Henry		Somerset, England		Mast & Block maker	6 May 1799
Thompson, James	18	Perthshire, Scotland		Merchant	7 Jul 1800
Thebe, Peter	34	Parronne, France		Merchant	16 Jul 1803
Thomas, John James	43	London, England		Merchant	20 Jul 1803
Tavel, Frederick Francis	32	Peterlinguen, Switzerland		Merchant	4 Aug 1803
Thomas, John	32	Wales, England		Grocer	8 Sep 1803
Turnbull, James	32	Dublin, Ireland		Mariner	28 Oct 1803
Tooke, John	21	London, England		Mariner	11 Oct 1804
Toire, Charles D.	28	Rowana, Italy		Mathematical Instrument maker	20 Jan 1806
Troke, Thomas	22	Cumberland, England		Mariner	17 Mar 1806
Tyrrell, Walter	26	Dublin, Ireland		Surgeon & Apothecary	1 Nov 1806
Thomas, John	41	Saxony, Germany		Mariner	19 Sep 1808
Towle, Thomas		London, Great Britain		Lawyer	19 Sep 1808
Torre, Anthony Della	27	Milan, Italy		Optician	20 Mar 1809
Talvande, Andrew	22	Cape Francois, St.. Domingo		Merchant	3 Jul 1810
Tofel, John	37	Genoa, Italy		Confectioner	20 Jul 1810
Teuchelut, Joseph	42	Longuw", France	Charleston	Merchant	30 Jul 1811
Tart, James	36	Berwick upon Tweed, Great Britain	Charleston	Merchant	27 Aug 1813

Names of Aliens	Age	Nation	Residence	Occupation	Admission
Turner, William	35	Norfolk, England	James Island	Planter	20 Sep 1813
Tennant, Robert	26	Glasgow, North Britain	Charleston	Shop keeper	15 Oct 1813
Turnbull, Gavin	48	Berwickshire, North Britain	Charleston	Teacher	23 Oct 1813
Trenk, John P.	40	Fulde , Germany	Charleston		11 Oct 1814
Trescot, Joseph	27	Exeter, England	Charleston	Merchant	14 Mar 1815
Tirvert, Nicholas F.	38	Ypreville, Normandy, France		Merchant	10 May 1815
Thomassin, Francois	39	Nichola Mole, St. Domingo		Mariner	24 Sep 1817
Ture, Peter	35	Poligni, France	Charleston	Shopkeeper	3 Jan 1820
Thomas, John	44	Dublin, Ireland	Charleston		1 Mar 1820
Trapmann, John Peter Lewis	34	Frankfort, Germany	Charleston	Merchant	16 Jan 1821
Toole, John	29	Tipperary, Ireland	Charleston		6 Feb 1824
Thompson, Robert H.	21	Nassau, Bahama Island	Charleston	Clerk	5 Aug 1824
Trescot, Edward	28	Exeter, England	Charleston	Clerk	1 Oct 1824
Tjepkes, Albert	41	East Freeland, Prussia	Charleston	Mariner	9 Nov 1824
Thomson, John Blane	24	Kilmamock, Great Britain	Charleston		5 Nov 1827
Thomson, George		Kincardin, Scotland	Charleston	Ship Carpenter	15 Jan 1828
Tolck, John David	23	Hanover	Charleston	Grocer	16 Sep 1828
Thompson, John	36	London	Charleston	Whitesmith	11 Oct 1828
Trost, Christian Peterson	36	Sunderburg, Denmark	Charleston	Marine r	15 May 1829
Thorn, James D.	27	London	Charleston	Mariner	13 Nov 1829
Tanswell, William Nicholas	40	London	Charleston	Locksmith	26 Aug 1830
Turley, Michael F.		Down, Ireland	Charleston		3 Aug 1831
Thrane, George W.	24	Copenhagen, Denmark	Charleston		5 Aug 1831
Torlay, Peter	55	France	Charleston	Jeweller	14 Aug 1832
Trott, John W.	36	St. George's, Bermuda	Charleston	Marine r	31 Aug 1832
Thompson, William	27	Sweden	Charleston	Clerk	31 Aug 1832
Twistern, Von Christian	28	Hanover	Charleston	Clerk	22 Sep 1832
Thomlinson, Joseph	22	Oldtown, England	Charleston	Merchant	4 Oct 1832
Thompson, William		Devonshire, England	Charleston		5 Oct 1832
Thee, John H.	25	Hanover	Charleston		8 Oct 1832
Thetford, Andrew	34	Dublin, Ireland	Charleston		11 Oct 1834
Torrington, George	36	Bristol, England	Charleston	Storekeeper	11 Oct 1834
Tornland, Andrew	35	Sweden	Charleston		11 Oct 1834
Turner, William	43	Londonderry, Ireland	Charleston	Mariner	14 Oct 1834
Talle, Charles	30	Hesse Cassel	Charleston	Shopkeeper	14 Oct 1834
Talvande, Ann Marsan Neadame	40	Island St. Domingo	Charleston		4 Feb 1835
Talvande, Rose Madame		Island St. Domingo	Charleston		12 Nov 1835
Thee, Herman M.	31	Hanover	Charleston	Clerk	8 Mar 1836
Thomson, Andrew	33	Sweden		Mariner	9 Oct 1838
Tietzen, Hermann	38	Hanover	Charleston	Clerk	17 Jul 1839
Tietzen, Otto	25	Germany	Charleston	Storekeeper	18 Jul 1839
Tiedeman, John F.	21	Germany		Storekeeper	19 Jul 1839
Tweed, Robert L.	27	Ireland	Charleston	Engineer	20 Mar 1843
Tevlin, Patrick	25	Co Meath (Ireland)	Charleston	Storekeeper	19 Jan 1846
Topp, Charles Auguste	35	Denmark	Charleston	Clerk	17 Mar 1847
Vesey, Abraham		Bermudas		Mariner	11 Sep 1795
Villeneuve, John Baptiste		Tanagona, Spain		Merchant	16 May 1797
Verguin, Charles	25	Toulon, France		Merchant	12 Dec 1803
Vigan, James	39	Normandy, France		Merchant	21 Mar 1804
Vignier, Arnoldus R. M.	33	Port au Prince, Hispaniola		Planter	20 Jan 1806
Vidal, John	39	Montpellier, France		Grocer	23 Apr 1807
Vanderbusse, James	23	Ostend, Flanders		Mariner	22 Dec 1807
Verdier, Simon	37	Molieres , Lot, France			3 Apr 1811
Urquhart, Charles	29	Rosshire, North Britain	Charleston	Factor	30 Mar 1814
Villes, Peter		Languedoc, France	Charleston		13 Oct 1818
Valencia, Moses	62	Island of Curacao	Charleston		12 Dec 1820
Viel, Just		Charleval, Department L'eur, France	Charleston	Merchant	12 Jun 1821

Names of Aliens	Age	Nation	Residence	Occupation	Admission
Vonholten, Tennis	35	Hanover	Charleston	Merchant	15 Aug 1821
VanRhyn, John Martin	26	Amsterdam	Charleston	Merchant	14 Jan 1824
Vouderlippe, Frederick	33	Oldenberg, Germany	Charleston	Grocer	17 Jan 1825
VanRhyn, Lynch E.	33	Amsterdam	Charleston		29 May 1826
Vanroeven, Mary Elizabeth	48	Rotterdam	Charleston		23 Jun 1829
Vose, Caisten	23	Hanover	Charleston	Shopkeeper	31 Aug 1832
Von Glaher, Albert Henry	31	Hanover	Charleston	Grocer	18 Mar 1833
Valk, Sarah		London, England	Charleston		18 Jun 1835
VanCooth, J. A.	28	Amsterdam	Charleston	Merchant	11 Dec 1838
Vani, Niculis	51	Naples	Charleston	Boarding House Keeper	20 May 1839
Vielstich, Henry	24	Hanover	Charleston	Grocer	30 May 1840
Von Dohlen, Albert	25	Hanover	Charleston	Grocer	10 May 1841
Vanderlitte, John C.	23	Messelwarden (Hanover)	Charleston	Clerk	17 Jan 1843
Vonhollen, Henry W.	35	Hanover	Charleston	Grocer	13 Jan 1847
Von Glahn, Martin	26	Hanover	Charleston	Grocer	7 May 1849
Vidal, Marie	31	Toulon, France	Charleston		18 Dec 1854
Von Glahn, Christopher	22	Hanover	Charleston	Shop-keeper	12 Nov 1855
Vaughan, Patrick	32	Clara Co, Ireland	Charleston	labourer	2 Nov 1859
Vircetichi, Christo-phel	30	Ragusa, Austria	Do	Policeman	10 Jan 1860
Watson, Joseph		Ireland			19 Sep 1794
Williams, Cornelius		Bermudas		Mariner	18 Jan 1796
Wilson, William	29	Antrim, Ireland			19 Jan 1796
Williams, William		Worcestershire, England		Tinman	1 Feb 1796
Wilson, John		Donnegal, Ireland			21 Mar 1796
White, James		Derbyshire, England			2 Aug 1796
Walker, Thomas		Edinburgh, Scotland			20 Sep 1796
Walsh, Edmond		Waterford, Ireland			28 Sep 1796
Wilson, William		Yorkshire, England		Mariner	21 Jan 1797
Wade, William		Yorkshire, England		Merchant	22 Feb 1797
Wilkins, James		North Britain		Mariner	26 Mar 1797
Waller, Bayfeild		Yorkshire, Thirsk, Britain		Bookbinder	19 Jan 1798
Winkes, John Henry		Bremen		Mariner	10 May 1798
Wipon, Joseph	28	Sunderland, England			22 Oct 1798
Westbury, John		Stockholm			2 Jan 1799
Wurdeman, John George	31	Brocke, Hanover		Merchant	17 Jun 1799
Williamson, Thomas	33	London,England		Mariner	21 Dec 1802
Williams, John	41	Bristol, England		Mariner	29 Dec 1802
Ward, Henry	45	Nottinghamshire, England			18 Apr 1803
Williams, William		Rutland, England		School Master	21 May 1803
West, Thomas	42	Tercera, Portugal		Mariner	18 Jul 1803
Watt, Alexander	36	Carone, North Britain		Mariner	2 Nov 1803
Williamson, John	26	London, England		Merchant	23 Feb 1804
Wallace, David	36	Middlesex, England		Mariner	20 Mar 1804
Workman, James	32	Cavan, Ireland		Attorney at Law	21 May 1804
Wardrope, David		Edinburgh, Scotland		Mariner	2 Jul 1804
White, James	21	Liverpool, England		Mariner	7 Aug 1804
Witt, John	29	Holstein, Denmark		Merchant	26 Feb 1805
White, Peter	22	King's County, Ireland		Mariner	10 Jun 1805
Wilkinson, Abraham	37	Harley, England		Mariner	23 Sep 1805
Wilson, Hamilton	25	Down, Ireland		Merchant	23 Nov 1805
Wilson, James Junr	25	Angusshire, Scotland		Merchant	10 Dec 1805
Wilson, James	24	Dublin		Physician	19 Mar 1806
Welsh, Edward	28	Kilkenny, Ireland		Mariner	24 Jun 1806
Wylie, Thomas	21	Antrim, Ireland		Merchant	26 Jun 1806
Wilhelmi, John Philip	32	Bremen		Merchant	1 Sep 1806
		declared his intention 16 Sept 1805			
Witte, Martin Jacob	32	Hamburgh		Merchant	24 Nov 1806
Wulff, Jacob	27	Altona, Denmark		Merchant	2 Mar 1807
Watson, James	25	Fifeshire, North Britain		Mariner	16 Mar 1807
Westcott, Benjamin	22	Devonshire, England		Mariner	28 Mar 1807
Wileck, Charles	30	Memel, Prussia		Mariner	16 Jun 1807
Wilson, James	33	Leith, Scotland			13 Jul 1807
Whiting, John	35	Devonshire, England		Mechanic	13 Jul 1807
Welsman, James	24	Devonshire, England		Pilot	10 Aug 1808
Walker, William	29	Northumberland, England		Mariner	30 May 1810
Weapher, Andrew	22	Wicklow, Ireland		Boat Builder	28 Jul 1810

Names of Aliens	Age	Nation	Residence	Occupation	Admission
Ward, James	35	London, England		School-master	3 Oct 1810
Williams, John	30	Bristol, England		Mariner	27 Oct 1810
Wardleworth, Samuel	39	Kings County, Ireland		Millwright	19 Apr 1811
Whietenkamp, Charles	37	Saardam, Holland	Charleston	Mariner	7 Oct 1811
Waugh, Alexander Black	27	London, Great Britain	Charleston admitted Denizen 7 January 1808	Merchant	21 Sep 1812
Withart, Peter	37	Holland	Charleston	Grocer	7 Oct 1812
Wincey, James	46	Isle of Wight, England	Charleston	Blacksmith	29 Sep 1813
Wheeler, Josiah	23	Somersetshire, England	Charleston	Clerk	1 Oct 1813
Willson, John	50	Monaghan, Ireland		Physician	4 Oct 1813
Whyte, James	29	Newry, Ireland	Charleston	Accountant	19 Oct 1813
Wilson, William	25	Edinburgh, North Britain	Charleston	Butcher	23 Oct 1813
Wansley, Joseph	38	Cornwall, England	Charleston	Mariner	27 Oct 1813
Wadsworth, William	42	Yorkshire, England	Charleston	Shop keeper	16 Nov 1813
Whyte, Daniel	34	Argyleshire, Scotland	Charleston	Butcher	28 Dec 1813
Wilson, John	25	Lanarkshire, Scotland	Charleston	Engineer & Surveyor	7 May 1814
White, James	32	Cork, Ireland	Charleston gave notice 20 May 1811		31 May 1814
Wright, Robert	33	Litchfield, England	Charleston Jas. Isl	Millwright	9 Jan 1815
Winslow, Billings	35	Liverpool, England	Charleston	Mariner	25 Sep 1815
Walkington, John	35	Yorkshire, England	St. Bartholomew's Parish	Planter	24 May 1816
Wall, John	52	Waterford, Ireland	St. Stephen's Parish	Tutor	11 Feb 1817
Webber, Samuel	45	Devonshire, England	Charleston	Mariner	14 Jan 1819
Westendorff, Charles P. L.	31	Wittenburg, Germany	Charleston gave notice 24 June 1816	Merchant	12 Apr 1820
Wright, Thomas	59	Antrim, Ireland	District of York	Planter	20 Apr 1820
Williams, Thomas F.	38	Bridgewater, Great Britain	Columbia	Stone cutter	25 Apr 1820
Wienges, Conrad	37	Bremen, Germany	Charleston	Grocer	16 May 1820
Wienges, Jacob	43	Gremen, Germany	Charleston	Grocer	16 May 1820
West, Thomas	48	Middlesex, England	Charleston	Painter	29 Sep 1820
Ward, George		England	Charleston	Baker	9 Oct 1820
Willett, Samuel	34	Nova Scotia	Edisto Island	Merchant	17 May 1821
Walker, John Falls	23	Armagh, Ireland	Charleston		14 Oct 1822
Weyman, Francis Henry	39	Hesse Cassel	Charleston	Grocer	17 Dec 1823
Watson, Alexander	30	Fifeshire, North Britain		Planter	17 Oct 1825
Wallis, John	43	Cork, Ireland	Charleston	Grocer	29 May 1826
Wilson, George	23	Edinburgh, North Britain	Charleston	Pilot	19 Aug 1826
Wheeler, Daniel	22	Liverpool, England	Charleston	Clerk	4 Oct 1826
White,John	37	Edinburgh, No Britain	Charleston	Stonecutter	10 Oct 1826
Westman, William	45	Stockholm, Sweden	Charleston	Mariner	11 Dec 1826
Williams, Morris	34	North Wales, England	Charleston	Mariner	1 May 1827
Warren, James	41	Cork, Ireland	Charleston	Rigger	24 May 1827
Waithman, George Warren	28	St. Bartholomews, West Indies	Charleston	Mariner	8 Apr 1828
Wiley, Thomas	31	Antrim, Ireland	Charleston	Grocer	10 Oct 1828
Waddell, Robert	29	Donegall, Ireland	Charleston		8 Dec 1828
Wing, Sarah C.	54	Cork, Ireland	Charleston		16 Mar 1829
Weissinger, John	29	Wirtemberg, Germany	Charleston		20 Sep 1830
Whitaker, William		Ireland	Charleston		6 Oct 1830
Wotherspoon, Robert	36	Glasgow, Scotland	Charleston	Merchant	27 Jul 1831
Wenger, John	37	Switzerland	Charleston		3 Aug 1831
White, George	24	Edinburgh, Scotland	Charleston		3 Aug 1831
Wilson, Andrew	29	Norway	Charleston	Mariner	5 Oct 1831
Wiley, William	48	Antrim, Ireland	Charleston	Grocer	5 Oct 1831
Wulff, Andrew Henry	29	Hamburgh	Charleston	Clerk	5 Oct 1831
Wolf, Frederick	24	Germany	Charleston	Grocer	5 Oct 1831
Wilkinson, John	37	Cumberland, England	Charleston		8 Oct 1831
Wood, Daniel	30	London, England	Charleston	Mariner	3 Sep 1832
Weber, Hermann	25	Bremen	Charleston	Clerk	22 Sep 1832

Names of Aliens	Age	Nation	Residence	Occupation	Admission
Wise, Edward	26	London, England	Charleston	Innkeeper	5 Oct 1832
Weymann, Dederick	24	Hanover	Charleston	Grocer	7 Jul 1834
Wanless, Archibald	36	Roxburyshire, Scotland	Charleston	Sadler	11 Oct 1834
Worthmann, Henrick	24	Russia		Mariner	11 Oct 1834
Worsoe, Cecilius	25	Denmark			11 Oct 1834
Waddell, John		Ireland	Columbia		28 Nov 1836
Williamson, John	21	Denmark		Fireman	9 Oct 1838
Wagener, George	21	Hanover	Charleston	Distiller	2 Jul 1839
Wogal, Michael	24	Germany		Baker	17 Jul 1839
Willis, James	23	Ireland		Livery Stable keeper	19 Jul 1839
Wade, John M.	23	England	Charleston	Merchant	9 Dec 1839
Werner, Christopher	35	Prussia	Charleston	Blacksmith	10 Dec 1839
Werdehoff, Henry	30	Prussia	Charleston	Merchant	7 Jan 1841
Watson, Thomas	30	Argy, Scotland	Charleston	Mariner	16 Aug 1841
Wehlert, Jacob C.	31	Denmark	Charleston	Grocer	11 Jun 1842
Wittpen, Joanna D.	43	Hanover	Charleston	Florist	6 Mar 1843
Wear, John S.	30	Glostershire, England	Charleston	Druggist	7 Jul 1843
Westerton, Charles F.	27	Finland, Russia	Charleston	Mariner	15 Oct 1844
Walker, H. Pinckney	28	Norfolk, England	Charleston	Attorney at Law	4 Nov 1844
Wilson, William	38	Tyrone, Ireland	Charleston	House Carpenter	8 Jul 1846
Wilson, William A.	23	Liverpool, England	Charleston	Watchmaker	14 Jan 1847
Weylie, John L.	25	Hanover	Charleston	Shopkeeper	11 Dec 1848
Wickenberg, Fabian R.	35	Sweden	Charleston	Storekeeper	19 Feb 1849
Wienholz, Augusta	22	Hanover	Charleston	(wife of J. P. Wienholz)	7 Jan 1850
Webb, Mary	60	Liverpool	Charleston	(wife of Michl. Webb)	1 May 1855
Waid, Eliza Ann	35	Liverpool	Charleston		1 May 1855
Walsh, Patrick	30	Ireland	Do		22 Jul 1857
Walsh, James	30	Ireland	Do		13 Oct 1857
Wulbern, John	23	Hanover	Do	Grocer	10 Mar 1858
Wilson, Frances L. Mrs	38	Liverpool	Do	Milliner	15 Mar 1859
Wright, Charles E.	35	Co Clare, Ireland	Do	Clerk	22 Apr 1860
Young, John Tatem	26	Bermudas		Mariner	1 Nov 1802
Young, James	31	Liverpool, England	Charleston	Mariner	19 Oct 1813
Young, William	31	Galloway, Scotland	Charleston		6 Oct 1830
Young, Joseph Henderson	21	London, Great Britain	Charleston	Merchant	6 Oct 1830
Yates, John	21	England	Charleston	Clerk	5 Oct 1831
Yon, George	61	Elsnitz, Saxony		Planter	29 Dec 1837
Yates, Thomas Hall	24	Liverpool, England		Carpenter	9 Oct 1838

Names	Place of birth	Date	Volume & page
Abrahams, Elias	London	28 Feb 1821	9 138
Adler, Fanny	Frankfort on the Maine	13 Dec 1844	4 225
Ahrens, C. Diedrech	Hanover	18 Sep 1843	4 190
Allen, James	Ireland	21 Apr 1827	2 243
Alura(?), William	China	9 Jan 1826	9 410
Anderson, Hugh	Glasgow, North Britain	11 May 1821	9 164
Andler, Charles	Wirtemberg, Germany	6 Jan 1844	12 21
Apfel, J. Conrad	Germany	23 Jul 1839	4 70
Aufderhide, Charles F.	Prussia	12 Oct 1830	8 81
Bacon, Edward	North Britain	5 Apr 1823	9 290
Baina, John H. F. W.	Prussia	31 Dec 1827	8 37
Ballantine, John	Scotland	21 Apr 1827	2 243
Bandrick, Charles	Prussia	15 Dec 1826	8 2
Barelli, Joseph A.	Como, Italy	1 Jul 1823	9 301
Bargmann, B.	Hanover	28 Jan 1841	8 358
Barnes, Thomas	England	30 Apr 1827	2 249
Barr, James	Scotland	10 Jan 1840	8 278
Barre, Vincent		17 Jan 1823	2 94
Barry, Edmund	Ireland	16 Jan 1827	8 3
Barry, John	Ireland	2 Mar 1826	9 415
Becker, Daniel	Denmark	13 Feb 1827	8 5
Beeker, Hans	Denmark	14 Apr 1829	2 293
Behling, Luder F.	Germany	21 Jul 1838	8 255
Behrman, Charles	Hamburg	26 Aug 1823	9 308
Benningham, John	Cork, Ireland	11 Mar 1822	9 223
Beusse, John Henry	Attena, Denmark	5 Oct 1812	5 27
Bicaise, Peter Paul Alexander	St. Domingo	20 May 1822	9 233
Bieba, Charles G.	Prussia	2 Aug 1826	9 427
Biemann, Diedrich	Dukedom of Brunswick	12 Jan 1846	4 253
Biggs, Henry Seymom	England	24 Oct 1820	9 98
Bird, John	Great Britain	18 Jan 1822	9 212
Bischoff, Albert	Hanover	18 Mar 1841	4 112
Bischoff, Henry	Hanover	13 Dec 1844	4 226
Black, James C.	Ireland	7 Sep 1821	9 179
Blackhall, Gerald	Ireland	27 Aug 1823	9 309
Blake, Daniel Jr.	London	16 Jan 1827	8 3
Blake, Francis	Great Britain	31 Dec 1839	8 276
Blum, Frederick		7 Dec 1820	9 112
Blumenberg, Frederick	Prussia	23 Mar 1826	9 419
Boag, William S.	Cheshire, England	21 Nov 1822	2 52
Bohlen, John	Hanover	23 Jul 1827	8 24
Bohles, Lue E.	Bremen	13 Sep 1837	8 236
Bold, William		2 Aug 1813	10 12
"by virtue of the naturalization of his father in South Carolina, 26 May 1788...he was five or six years of age."			
Borges, John H.	Oldenburg (Germany)	15 Mar 1841	4 110
Boyle, Cunningham	Belfast, Ireland	22 Apr 1821	9 154
Brady, Hugh	Ireland	16 Oct 1822	9 265
Brady, John	Ireland	27 Sep 1826	9 433
Brady, John	Ireland	28 Jan 1841	8 358
Braidy, James	North Britain	14 May 1822	9 231
Brandes, Henry	Hanover	10 Mar 1849	12 194
Brase, Peter	Bremen, Hanover	10 May 1828	2 275
Brennan, Edward	Ireland	21 Jul 1830	8 74
Bright, Robert	England	20 May 1829	2 299
Brinham, William	Ireland	6 Oct 1830	8 80
Brodermann, Andrew	Hamburgh	17 Oct 1820	9 97
Broner, Diederick H.	Hanover	22 Jun 1829	2 305
Brown, Edward	Norfolk, England	26 Mar 1826	9 384
Brown, Henry	Sweden	13 Apr 1826	2 442
Brown, Henry	Finland	9 Apr 1833	2 387
Brown, Jacob	Scotland	5 Jul 1849	4 362
Brun, Ole Oleson	Norway	5 Jan 1829	8 56
Brunning, Henry	Hanover	19 Sep 1837	4 40
Buerhas, Herman D.	Prussia	26 Sep 1822	9 257
Bull, William	Hampshire, England	2 Nov 1821	9 195
Bullwinkel, George	Hanover	23 Jun 1831	8 97
Burger, Nicholas	Germany	14 Oct 1834	4 12
Burghauser, John	Prussia	1 Jul 1844	4 212
Burke, Francis		26 Jan 1821	9 124
Burke, Joseph	Ireland	2 Aug 1826	9 427
Burke, Martin	Ireland	4 Aug 1826	9 428
Burns, Charles D.	Scotland	28 May 1824	9 348
Burrell, Henry	Ireland	2 Apr 1822	9 227
Burrell, William	Ireland	2 Apr 1822	9 227
Burrell, William	Ireland	12 Aug 1824	9 354
Bush, Davis	Prussia	15 Mar 1841	4 110

Names	Place of birth	Date	Volume & page
Bush, Philip	Prussia	15 Mar 1841	4 110
Busing, John D.	Germany	28 Apr 1828	2 266
Buttman, C. T.	Hanover	22 Sep 1835	4 25
Caldwell, John Jr.	Ireland	30 Oct 1824	9 363
Campbell, Cunningham	Ireland	19 Mar 1849	4 354
Campbell, James	Argyleshire, North Britain	22 Aug 1810	10 74
Campbell, John	Glasgow, North Britain	1 Nov 1821	9 194
Campbell, Pat	Ireland	3 Apr 1822	9 227
Carey, E. M.	England	18 Jul 1839	4 67
Carnochan, Richard	Gallowayshire, North Britain	15 Nov 1813	10 47
Cartwell, Patrick	Ireland	14 Jun 1823	9 296
Carty, Daniel	Grenock	20 Oct 1824	9 362
Cassidy, George W.	Ireland	16 Jun 1823	9 298
Chapeau, J. B.		19 Jul 1820	9 78
Charriol, Pierre	Lebonne, France	19 Nov 1812	10 4
Chisolm, George	Edinburgh, Scotland	20 Mar 1809	5 48
Chouler, Jos. Dr.		2 Aug 1802	3 258
Christian, Martin	Norway	15 Apr 1825	2 265
Clarke, John	Ireland	3 Aug 1840	8 327
Clatz, John	Prussia	23 Jun 1831	8 97
Clausheide, H.		20 Jan 1836	4 27
Clauson,Christopher	Denmark	13 Aug 1828	8 50
Clauson, J. C.	Denmark	4 Oct 1832	8 119
Close, Langford P. H.	Ireland	13 Dec 1844	4 225
Cloth, Borje	Sweden	14 Jan 1824	9 324
Coby, Richard	Germany	8 Apr 1824	9 341
Cohen, Heartwig	Poland	7 Jan 1824	9 323
Cohen, Lewis	London	12 Apr 1825	2 162
Cohen, Samuel	London	12 Sep 1837	8 235
Cohrs, Henry	Hamlen, Hanover	13 Jul 1831	2 347
Conlen, John	Ireland	16 Apr 1849	4 355
Cook, John A.	Hanover	13 Aug 1828	8 50
Cook, Otto	Hanover	13 Aug 1828	8 50
Cordes, Albrecht	Bremen	19 Sep 1837	4 40
Cordes, Jacob	Hanover	16 Sep 1834	4 11
Costelo, Patrick	Ireland	20 Apr 1825	9 391
Cotes, Christopher	Yorkshire (England)	12 Jan 1836	4 252
Couie, Alexander		20 Sep 1803	3 315
Coulan, John	Ireland	28 Apr 1845	4 237
Crawford, George	Scotland	5 Jul 1844	4 213
Creber, William	London	20 Apr 1824	2 141
Cullen, Thomas	Ireland	19 May 1828	8 44
Cullion, John Lewis		19 Sep 1803	3 314
Cunningham, James	Ireland	6 Feb 1824	9 326
Das Nevis, Aries Antonio	Portugal	16 Sep 1834	4 11
Davis, Henry	England	28 Jan 1824	9 325
Davis, Rene P.	France	21 Jun 1826	9 424
De Almeida, Antonio Robin	Portugal	14 Jan 1830	8 65
Delpina, Antonio Peria	Portugal	13 Jul 1831	2 347
Dempsey, Thomas	Ireland	2 Aug 1826	9 427
Dempsey, Thomas	Kildare, Ireland	10 Oct 1828	8 52
Dick, James	Birmingham, England	12 Apr 1820	9 56
Dickson, Joseph Dr.	Ireland	25 Jun 1823	9 299
Dieckman, J. H.	Hanover	12 Oct 1830	8 81
Digner, Francis	Ireland	16 Oct 1822	9 265
Dile, Peter		19 Sep 1808	5 38
Dircks, Henry	Hanover	1 Oct 1834	2 411
Dirhsen, Gerhard	Prussia	18 May 1848	4 313
Dougherty, James	Ireland	16 Oct 1822	9 265
Dougherty, Joseph	Ireland	3 Dec 1822	2 62
Donagan, James	Ireland	4 Jun 1824	9 349
Douglas, Campbell	Kukcudbrightshire	10 Oct 1813	10 42
Douglas, John		24 Sep 1802	3 272
Drake, Miles	Ireland	13 Dec 1844	4 225
Dreher, George Frederick Lewis	Wirtemberg	10 Oct 1822	9 262
Dreyer, John	Hanover	15 Sep 1845	4 247
Duff, Martin	Ireland	29 Apr 1828	2 267
Dunn, John Jr.	Ireland	26 Jan 1826	9 411
Dunn, William	Ireland	10 Feb 1832	8 107
Dunning, Patrick	Ireland	13 Dec 1844	4 224
Dutrieux, L. F.	Nantz	1 Aug 1823	9 305
Dutrieux, R. C.	Nantz	1 Aug 1823	9 305
Edwards, William	England	9 Jan 1826	9 410
Egan, Henry I.	Ireland	12 Apr 1826	2 209

Names	Place of birth	Date	Volume & page
Ekstrom, Jacob		13 Dec 1806	10 16
Ellison, Tyler	Hamburgh	6 Feb 1824	9 326
Empson, John	England	18 Sep 1837	4 40
England, John Rev.	Ireland	21 Oct 1822	9 266
		6 Feb 1826	9 412
Erickson, Christian	Denmark	18 Sep 1843	4 189
Esswein, Theodore	Germany	30 Jan 1821	9 125
Eude, Louis	France	26 Feb 1835	8 183
Evans, William G.	"of Plymouth"	7 Oct 1820	9 95
Fehrenback, N.	Hanover	17 Sep 1838	4 53
Ferguson, Daniel	Scotland	10 Oct 1826	9 436
Ferguson, Hugh W.	North Britain	22 Feb 1822	9 220
Fielde, Frederick W.	Germany	20 Nov 1827	8 34
Finck, John D.	Hanover	1 Aug 1834	8 174
Finkensteadt, George	Hanover	15 Mar 1841	4 110
Fisher, William	Liverpool	15 Jan 1838	8 242
Fleming, James	Antrim, Ireland	3 Nov 1831	8 102
Fleming, John	Glasgow, North Britain	19 Feb 1810	10 45
Fleming, Joseph S.	Ireland	14 Feb 1821	9 328
Flint, James	Germany	27 Jul 1821	8 99
Floderer, Johan	Vienna, Austria	5 Oct 1812	5 27
Flonacher, Isaac	Germany	5 Jul 1849	4 362
Flynn, Martin	Ireland	1 Jul 1844	4 242
Fox, John	Dungannon, Ireland	14 Mar 1820	9 51
Francis, George	England	17 Dec 1823	9 322
Frederick, Joseph	Poland	13 Oct 1812	10 66
Friedlender, M. E.	Friedland	4 Mar 1836	8 205
Frost, Christian Peterson	Denmark	15 May 1829	2 297
Fryer, George	England	4 May 1843	4 170
Gaffy, Hugh	Ireland	14 Apr 1824	9 341
Gallagher, Michael	Ireland	23 Aug 1821	9 174
Galliott, Alexis	France	20 Apr 1835	2 432
Gates, Thomas		11 Mar 1823	9 275
Gebken, Eimer	Hanover	20 Sep 1842	4 153
Geikon, Christopher	Hanover	3 Jul 1828	8 47
Goldstein, Kalmes	Prussia	15 Mar 1841	4 110
Gonzales, Basilio	Havanna	13 Feb 1827	8 5
Gordon, Charles P.		9 Nov 1809	10 10
Gouldsmith, Richard	Sussex, England	10 Oct 1821	9 191
Graham, John Charles	Prussia	29 May 1826	9 420
Grahame, Archibald	Glasgow, Scotland	26 Dec 1809	10 26
Gravel, John	Ireland	13 Oct 1828	8 52
Greer, Benjamin	Antrim, Ireland	14 Nov 1821	9 197
Greniere, Francois	Persenas, France	29 Mar 1813	10 51
Grest, Valentine	Switzerland	27 May 1830	2 336
Grogriet, Louis Isidore	France	26 Aug 1823	9 308
Guin, James	Ireland	9 Oct 1838	4 54
Gunderman, Anton		20 Jan 1836	4 27
Gunther, Paul F.		21 Mar 1808	5 29
Gunther, Paul Frederick		21 Mar 1808	10 5
Gyles, Charles	England	18 Mar 1850	6 43
Hacket, John	Ireland	12 Mar 1824	9 331
Hackete, Patrick	Ireland	2 Aug 1826	9 427
Haharst, Cord	Brenen	16 Mar 1827	8 7
Halliday, Samuel	Dublin	1 Jan 1810	10 28
Hamilton, William N.	Ireland	28 Jan 1841	8 361
Hammarskold, Peter Hjalmar	Sweden	5 Nov 1849	6 7
Hamye, Christopher	Hanover	1 Jul 1828	8 46
Hamye, James H.	Hanover	21 Jul 1830	8 74
Hand, Martin William	Steltin in Prussia	18 Mar 1811	5 5
Hannah, William	Belfast, Ireland	11 Mar 1828	8 42
Hanschildt, Peter	Hanover	13 Mar 1824	9 332
Hapers, Heinrich	Bremen	1 Jul 1844	4 212
Happoldt, C. D.	Germany	28 Apr 1838	2 266
Happoldt, John M.		7 Jan 1807	10 22
Harbers, Claus H.	Hanover	15 Dec 1835	4 26
Harkamp, John	Hanover	8 Dec 1834	4 14
Harmon, Peter H.	Germany	8 Apr 1824	9 341
Harper, Peter	Ireland	12 Mar 1824	9 331
Harris, Abraham	Poland	19 Mar 1838	4 46
Hart, Joseph		27 Aug 1806	7 76
Hartman, Justus	Hanover	19 Aug 1823	9 308
Haslam, John	Lancastershire, Great Britain	23 Nov 1822	2 56
Hawes, James	Ireland	19 Jan 1824	9 324
Heevy, Thomas	Ireland	14 Aug 1820	9 86

Names	Place of birth	Date	Volume & page
Heins, John Henry	Hanover	23 May 1829	2 304
Heitman, John P.	Germany	3 Dec 1823	9 320
Hencken, Henry	Hanover	24 Jun 1831	8 97
Henderson, Francis Junr		24 Apr 1821	9 156
Hendricks, Frederick	Hanover	10 May 1828	2 275
Henry, Edward	Ireland	4 Aug 1826	9 428
Henry, George	Ireland	14 Jun 1823	9 296
Henry, Morris	Prussia	21 Oct 1823	9 316
Herckenrath, Leon I.	Amsterdam	21 Feb 1824	9 328
		11 Nov 1828	8 53
Hesler, John	Switzerland	15 Dec 1826	8 57
Hewson, Thomas		5 Oct1813	5 50
Heyus, James	Laneck, Scotland	23 Aug 1813	10 17
Hilderbrand, Charles	Germany	12 Feb 1824	9 327
Hilgen, Frederick		20 Jan 1836	4 27
Hior, John	Amsterdam	15 Jun 1822	9 241
Hitchingham, Thomas	Wexford, Ireland	7 Sep 1821	9 179
Hoffman, David	France	14 Jun 1836	8 216
Hollings, Benjn.	Hanover	10 Dec 1849	6 18
Holt(?), John	Sussex	27 Aug 1813	10 20
Holwell, Thomas	"of Devonshire"	27 Aug 1813	10 20
Hopley, George	Martinique	14 Mar 1831	8 91
Horde, Hans Jacob	Norway	24 May 1830	2 332
Hou, Robert Nesbit	Great Britain	6 Dec 1821	2 13
How, Thomas	Scotland	21 Oct 1822	9 266
Howe, Michael	Dublin, Ireland	23 Aug 1813	10 17
Huch, John	Hamburg, Germany	6 Jan 1844	12 21
Hudaff, Henry	Hanover	16 Nov 1835	8 201
Hughes, James		14 Dec 1838	4 56
Humburg, Henry	Bremen	20 Mar 1838	4 47
Hurtz, Jacob	Germany	8 Sep 1826	9 431
Irving, John B.	Jamaica physician	13 Nov 1823	9 317
Irving, Richard	London	12 Sep 1837	8 235
Jackson, Richard	Great Britain	20 Mar1840	4 82
Jacob, Mathew	Austria	19 Sep 1837	4 40
Jacobs, Philip Simon	Denmark	6 Feb 1841	8 364
Jenney, Henry	Dublin	11 Mar 1822	9 223
Johnson, Alexander	Scotland	6 Oct 1830	8 80
Johnson, Bennett	Gottenburg	12 Apr 1825	2 162
Johnson, Niels		15 Mar 1823	9 277
Jones, Thomas	China	26 Jan 1826	9 411
Joost, Christopher	Hanover	31 Dec 1827	8 37
Joshua, Peter	Switzerland	14 Jul 1830	8 73
Joy, Peter	Denmark	13 Feb 1827	8 5
Kahl, Henry	Saxony	26 Aug 1830	8 76
Keller, Jacob	Bavaria	23 May 1827	8 15
Kelso, Mathew	Grenock, North Britain	22 Feb 1821	9 137
Kennedy, Rody	Tipperary, Ireland	20 Jan 1811	10 24
Kennedy, Simon	Ireland	9 Oct 1838	4 54
Kenny, James	Ireland	16 Aug 1847	12 118
Kenyick, Daniel	Ireland	2 Aug 1826	9 427
Kidd, Charles	Ireland	5 Aug 1824	9 353
Kiefer, John	Bavaria	13 Oct 1838	8 256
King, John	Ireland	14 Apr 1829	2 294
King, John Junr.	Ireland	17 May 1820	9 61
King, Mitchell	Fifeshire, Scotland	26 Dec 1809	10 26
Kinsley, Stephen	Kilkenny, Ireland	11 Feb 1820	9 43
Klinck, John	Germany	19 Jan 1824	9 324
Klint, Nicholas	Sweden	13 Jun 1820	9 67
Knack, Carsten	Hanover	15 Mar 1841	4 110
Knee, Harmon	Hanover	1 Jul 1828	8 46
Knoof, Christopher	Hanover	13 Aug 1828	8 50
Knuth, John	Russia	27 May 1827	9 399
Koehler, Jacob	Germany	14 Mar 1827	8 7
Koenig, Henry Ernest	Germany	18 Jan 1813	10 22
Koeunecke, Albert	Prussia	13 Sep 1837	8 236
Kohlman, John H.	Hanover grocer	23 May 1835	8 196
Kornahrens, John H.	Hanover	12 Nov 1835	8 200
Kohuke, Christian I.	Denmark	11 Mar 1826	9 417
Kottmeyer, Ernest Henry	Germany	19 Mar 1835	8 70
Kuhtmann, H. W.	Germany	14 Feb 1849	12 187
Lafite, Peter	Bourdeaux	14 Jun 1813	10 78
Lafon, John	Bourdeaux	15 Jan 1822	9 210
Lafrentz, E. C.	Denmark	24 Apr 1837	8 229
Lambert, Patrick	Ireland	8 Nov 1844	4 219
Lanckeman, John H.	Hanover	23 Jul 1827	8 24
Larsen, Carl	Germany	31 Jan 1854	6 123
LeBleux, Ferdinand	France	7 May 1827	2 252

Names	Place of birth	Date	Volume & page	
Lecky, Alexander	Ireland	19 Mar 1849	4	354
Lecky, William	Ireland	19 Mar 1849	4	354
Lectner, E. F. L. Dr.	Germany	8 Jan 1835	8	181
Legerstrom, John G.		14 Sep 1807	1	322
LePrice, Marie V. Charles Achille	Island of Corsica	24 Aug 1821	9	175
Levin, Lewis	London	13 Dec 1820	9	115
Levy, Levine L.	England	19 Sep 1837	4	40
Lieure, Peter	France	12 Mar 1824	9	331
Lindsey, John		30 Nov 1803	1	218
Lockhart, John	Austria	13 Nov 1820	9	105
Lohman, JohnD.	Hanover	23 Dec 1834	4	15
Lomas, Edward	England	24 Mar 1824	9	338
Lowther, Thomas	Ireland	2 Aug 1826	9	427
Lovegreen, Andrew A.	Sweden	28 Mar 1823	9	286
Lubkin, Albert	Hanover	11 Jul 1827	8	22
Lyon, George	London	3 Nov 1824	9	364
McAllister, James	Ireland	24 Jul 1826	2	226
McCaffey, Hugh		11 Mar 1823	9	275
McCartney, Daniel	Ireland	20 Sep 1841	4	123
McCormick, John	Ireland	2 Aug 1826	9	427
McCormick, Richard		17 May 1808	10	27
McCready, William	Ireland	29 May 1826	9	420
McCullough, William	Ireland	10 Mar 1824	9	330
McDonald, John	Ireland	6 Aug 1847	4	303
McDowall, Andrew	Gallowayshire, Scotland	23 Dec 1813	10	59
McEmcore(?), John Rev.	Ireland	21 Oct 1822	9	266
McEncroe, William	Ireland	14 Jun 1823	9	296
McFeetus, Andrew	Ireland	5 Aug 1830	8	75
McGlenchy, Michael	Ireland	15 Jul 1850	12	223
McGregor, Alexander	Scotland	12 Apr 1825	2	163
McGuire, Bernard	Ireland	19 Jan 1824	9	324
McInnes, Benjamin	Scotland	12 Jul 1843	4	185
McIntosh, McDonald	Scotland	13 Feb 1827	8	5
McIntosh, William	Scotland	21 Oct 1822	9	266
McIntyre, John	Ireland	21 Mar 1824	9	331
McIntyre, Paul	Scotland	18 Dec 1833	8	143
McIver, John E.		28 Mar 1814	5	66
McKegan, Daniel	Ireland	21 Apr 1827	2	243
McKegan, John	Ireland	2 Oct 1826	9	435
McKeigan, Neil	Ireland	1 Oct 1834	2	411
McKenzie, James	Scotland	27 Aug 1823	9	309
McKenzie, John	Scotland	6 Aug 1847	4	301
McLean, James	North Britain	19 Jan 1824	9	324
McLeod, George	Scotland	14 Dec 1826	2	234
McLoughlin, James	Cavan, Ireland	25 Oct 1822	9	267
McMahon, Thomas	Ireland	16 Oct 1822	9	265
McMaster, John	Ireland	21 Dec 1836	8	225
McMillan, Daniel	Sussex, England	4 Apr 1820	9	54
McMillan, Thomas	Scotland	18 Sep 1837	4	40
McNicol, Daniel	North Britain	22 Feb 1825	9	378
McVicar, Neil	North Britain	29 Jan 1824	9	326
McWilliam, William	Scotland	27 Jan 1825	9	376
Macully, Robert Ferguson	Ireland	9 Dec 1822	2	63
Maginnis, John	Ireland	2 Mar 1826	9	415
Man, J. F.	Hanover	22 Sep 1835	4	25
Marshall, Andrew	Scotland	2 Oct 1826	9	435
Martin, Patrick James		26 Jan 1821	9	124
Martinia, Joseph	Oporto, Portugal	11 Feb 1820	9	45
Martins, Frederick	Hanover	18 Dec 1836	4	33
Mathews, Richard	Coleraine, Ireland	15 Nov 1819	9	29
Mayas(?), Charles	Prussia	12 Apr 1831	2	344
Mayer, C. A.		20 Jan 1836	4	27
Maynard, Gabriel	England	26 Sep 1826	9	433
Maynard, John	England	27 Sep 1826	9	433
Maynard, Richard	England	3 Aug 1820	9	82
Meeds, William		28 Sep 1809	5	58
Menninger, Christopher Gustavus	Wirtemburg	22 Jun 1824	9	352
Meyer, G. A.	Hanover	15 Dec 1835	4	26
Meyer, Gottlieb	Wirtemberg	22 Sep 1835	4	25
Meyer, H. H.	Hanover	13 Jun 1837	8	231
Mieslahm, Hans	Denmark	1 Jul 1828	8	46
Mignot, Henry	France	28 Aug 1830	8	77
Miller, John	Denmark	24 Sep 1831	4	126
Miller, John D.	England	15 Mar 1841	4	111
Monnar, Lewis		11 Dec 1804	3	358
Moore, John	Ireland	16 May 1820	9	60

Names	Place of birth	Date	Volume & page	
Moorehead, James	Ireland	17 Apr 1824	9	342
Moreland, Andrew	Ireland	29 Jul 1830	8	75
Morgan, John B.	Bermuda	19 May 1831	8	94
Morison, Simon	Scotland	4 Oct 1826	9	436
Morse, Abraham		14 Jan 1824	9	324
Moss, Joseph	England	12 Apr 1831	2	344
Mosy, Reuben	Holland	7 Mar 1823	9	274
Mudie, George	Arbroath, North Britain	10 Apr 1820	9	56
Mulligan, James	Ireland	13 Mar 1822	9	224
Muggridge, Mathew	England	5 Aug 1824	9	353
Mulloy, James	Ireland	9 Dec 1822	2	63
Murhard, Gustavus	Germany	10 Mar 1849	12	195
Murphy, Laughlin	Ireland	21 Apr 1827	2	243
Murphy, Patrick	Kilkenny, Ireland	22 Apr 1825	2	172
Napier, Thomas	Glasgow, North Britain merchant	17 Jul 1800	7	205
Nathan, Myer	Prussia	15 Mar 1841	4	110
Neal, John		2 Jul 1804	3	335
Neilson, Robert	Armagh, Ireland	17 Jan 1831	8	85
Nerdehoff, Henry	Prussia	7 Jan 1841	8	353
Nesbitt, James	Edinburgh, North Britain	18 Jun 1812	10	79
Neve, William	Denmark	11 Mar 1826	9	417
Newbold, Samuel	Bermudas	22 Feb 1821	9	137
Newman, John A.	Dantzic in Prussia	25 Jun 1827	8	21
Newton, Anthony	Stockton, County of Durham, England aged 24 years	25 Sep 1802	3	274
Nicolai, John H.	Oldenburg	19 Sep 1837	4	40
Niebuhr, J. P.	Hamburg, Germany	16 Aug 1847	12	117
Nolan, John	Ireland	12 Mar 1824	9	331
Nugent, Richard	Ireland	13 Feb 1843	4	162
Nunan, John C.	Limerick, Ireland	6 Aug 1821	9	172
O'Brien, James	Cork, Ireland	11 Mar 1822	9	223
O'Callaghan, Denis	Ireland	13 Jan 1847	4	282
O'Callaghan, Patrick	Armagh, Ireland	27 Aug 1821	9	176
Ochman, Frederick Wm.		21 Mar 1860	11	374
O'Connor, James	Wexford, Ireland	7 Jan 1831	8	353
O'Connor, Patrick	Ireland	16 Jun 1823	9	298
O'Hanlon, Charles	Ireland	1 oct 1834	2	411
Ojemann, John C.		13 Dec. 1847	4	308
Oland, Diederick	Hanover	17 Jul 1828	8	49
O'Neill, Hugh	Ireland	6 Aug 1847	4	301
O'Neill, James	Ireland	6 Aug 1847	4	301
O'Neill, T. F.	Ireland	2 Mar 1826	9	415
O'Reilly, Michael D.	Ireland	2 Mar 1826	9	415
Ostendorff, J. M.		2 Jul 1839	4	65
Osterholtz, Ehler H.	Hanover	23 May 1829	2	304
Osterholt, E. H.		30 Aug 1834	4	9
Ottea, Frederick	Hanover	30 Aug 1834	8	176
Otten, Cord	Hanover	9 Dec 1844	4	223
Otten, Henry	Hanover	22 Jun 1829	2	305
Pania, David Jopia	Mogadore	13 Aug 1828	8	50
Pelmoine, Francis	France	21 Nov 1823	2	107
		13 Nov 1826	8	1
Pennal, Robert		29 Apr 1824	9	343
Peterson, Bonnick	Denmark	15 Oct 1844	4	218
Peterson, Hans C.	Norway	10 Oct 1828	8	52
Petska, David	Poland	2 May 1848	12	176
Petit, L. F.	France	12 Dec 1835	8	202
Peyton, Miss Ann	Ireland	13 Nov 1826	8	1
Phillippe, Odet	France	3 Dec 1822	2	62
Phillips, Joseph	Bavaria	21 May 1827	8	14
Phin, Alexander C.	Scotland	12 Dec 1842	4	158
Picard, Samuel	France	15 Aug 1833	8	135
Pillot, Peter	Maune, France	2 Nov 1821	9	195
Plane, Madam Benoite	Savay, France widow	27 May 1811	10	51
Plane, William A.	London	21 Apr 1827	2	243
Police, Francis	Italy	12 Mar 1824	9	331
Pratt, William	Hanover	12 Sep 1837	8	235
Prendergast, Edward	Ireland	19 Jan 1824	9	324
Printz, Charles	SoHampton, England	2 Nov 1824	9	195
Pult, Francis	Prussia	14 Jan 1828	8	38
Pundt, John	Bremen	14 Jan 1828	8	38
Pyne, John	Cork in Ireland	3 Mar 1810	10	49
Quinn, Ornea	Ireland	16 Oct 1822	9	265
Rade, John C.	Germany	26 Mar 1813	10	50
Rapallo, Anthony	Genoa	17 Mar 1813	5	40
Rasne, Claude	France	22 Aug 1827	8	26
Redfern, John	Derbyshire, England	22 Apr 1825	2	172

Names	Place of birth	Date	Volume & Page	
Redman, Mathew	Ireland	14 Jun 1820	9	68
Reedy, James	Ireland	4 Nov 1827	8	32
Reicke, Claus	Hanover	12 Aug 1823	9	306
Reickes, Charles	Hanover	16 Mar 1827	8	7
Reittemeyer, Johanna	Hanover	25 Jun 1832	2	371
Rice, Frederick	Austria	12 Dec 1839	4	77
Riecke, George	Hanover	16 Nov 1835	8	201
Richard, Auguste		17 Jan 1823	2	94
Richardson, Robert	England	8 Oct 1827	8	29
Richey, Claus	Hanover	10 Oct 1828	8	52
Riondel, John Joseph	Savoy in France	9 Mar 1809	5	49
Ritchey, John P. C.	Hanover	23 Jun 1827	8	20
Roberts, Francis	Germany	24 Aug 1841	8	386
Robb, James	North Britain	28 Apr 1828	2	266
Roddy, Martin	Ireland	14 Aug 1820	9	86
Roh, John Frederick	Altenburg, Germany	5 Oct 1812	5	27
Rohdman, Gottlieb		11 Mar 1823	9	275
Rosenbalm, John Henry	Hanover	27 Aug 1829	8	51
Rosenberg, Frances	Prussia	1 Jul 1828	8	46
Rosenfeldt, Jacob	Prussia	13 Dec 1844	4	225
Rowan, Samuel	Armagh, Ireland	11 Oct 1822	9	263
Rowe, George	England	14 Oct 1834	4	12
Rumph, George Henry	Germany	3 Jun 1823	9	294
Rust, J. C.	Hanover	22 Mar 1836	4	28
Ryan, Elizabeth wife of Paul Ryan	England	16 Mar 1846	4	257
Ryan, Farquis	Dublin	13 Apr 1826	2	210
Ryan, Lawrence	Tipperary, Ireland	23 Aug 1813	10	17
Ryan, Paul	England	16 Mar 1846	4	257
Ryan, William	Ireland	13 Apr 1830	2	328
Sahlman, Rudolph		20 Jan 1836	4	27
Sampson, Henry		11 Mar 1823	9	275
Sampson, Joseph	England	9 Aug 1820	9	84
Sampson, Samuel	England	7 Nov 1848	4	325
Sarm, Samuel	Germany	16 Aug 1847	12	118
Sarse, Claus	Hanover	11 Nov 1834	8	179
Schaffner, Frederick	Mentz, Germany	5 Oct 1821	9	190
Schazenberg, Christian	Prussia	16 Jun 1830	8	71
Schepsian, Harrn B.	Germany	23 May 1823	9	292
Schevater, George M.	Hamburgh	28 Mar 1823	9	286
Schilph, George H. F.	Prussia	2 Aug 1826	9	427
Schirer, John	Alsae, France	6 Oct 1812	5	29
Schmelser, Christian	Germany	29 Jul 1830	8	75
Schmidt, Joseph W. Dr.	Emden in Prussia	4 Aug 1812	10	16
Schneider, Johann	Oldenburg	4 Mar 1836	8	205
Schnider, Wilhelm	Hanover	1 Jul 1828	8	46
Schroder, Henry (Henrig)	Hanover	21 Dec 1840	4	101
Schroder, John	Lubec	28 Apr 1824	9	342
Schroder, William	Hamburg	4 Jun 1824	9	349
Schroeder, C.	Hanover	15 Sep 1834	4	10
Schroeder, Jurgen	Oldenberg	13 Dec 1844	4	225
Schulher, Henry		2 Jul 1839	4	65
Schulte, J. H.	Hanover	19 Nov 1828	8	53
Schutt, Touses	Hanover	6 Jan 1835	8	181
Scott, Matthew	Ireland	18 Feb 1820	9	46
Seaman, Dirck	Hanover	25 Jul 1828	8	49
Seamurel, John Jr.	Ireland	26 Oct 1822	9	268
Seebeck, Carsten	Hanover	15 Mar 1841	4	110
Seigling, John	Eifurt, Germany	23 Aug 1821	9	174
Senet, Joseph	Island of St. Domingo	7 Sep 1821	9	179
Service, John	England	31 Mar 1824	9	339
Shand, Peter I.		14 Jan 1824	9	324
Sharkey, James	Ireland	6 Feb 1824	9	326
Shaw, Mathew	Isle of Bute, North Britain	4 Apr 1820	9	54
Shee, John	Ireland	21 Jul 1830	8	74
Sheehan, Godfrey	Ireland	13 Feb 1827	8	5
Shegog, George		26 Jan 1821	9	124
Shegog, Joseph		26 Jan 1831	9	124
Shegog, William	Ireland	14 Jun 1823	9	296
Sheridan, John Joseph	Ireland	14 Apr 1824	9	341
Short, William	"of Plymouth"	7 Oct 1820	9	95
Shrerin, Frances	Ireland	26 May 1830	2	335
Sicard, Peter	"late of New Orleans"	19 Oct 1812	10	73
Sielaff, Charles W.	Prussia	28 Apr 1828	2	266
		1 Jul 1830	8	72
Silberston, Morris	Prussia	15 Mar 1841	4	110

FEDERAL RECORDS

Names	Place of birth	Date	Volume & page
Simpson, John	Orkney, Ireland	10 Jun 1823	9 295
Sims, Frederick	Hanover	6 Jul 1840	4 88
		12 Jul 1843	4 184
Sinclair, William James	Scotland	4 Nov 1827	8 32
Slimp, George	Prussia	14 May 1829	2 296
Smith, Daniel	Prussia	30 Apr 1828	2 269
Smith, Edward M.	Holland	13 Nov 1829	8 65
Smith, John	Liverpool	30 Apr 1824	9 344
Smith, John D.	Prussia	8 May 1835	8 194
Smylie, Andrew		1 Sep 1806	7 79
Sprigge, Claus	Hanover	1 Jul 1828	8 46
Spring, Alexander T.	Ireland	12 Mar 1824	9 331
Steel, Richard		15 Mar 1823	9 277
Steeling, Frederick	Germany	13 Mar 1822	9 224
Steiffatter, Andrew	Baden, Germany	15 Mar 1841	4 111
Stieffatter, Jan	Baden, Germany	15 Mar 1841	4 111
Stieffatter,Martin	Baden, Germany	15 Mar 1841	4 111
Steinberg, Henry	Hanover	30 Aug 1834	8 176
Stinton, Hugh	Ireland	13 Oct 1834	4 12
Stocks, Henry	Prussia	18 Jul 1834	8 172
Stokes, Jos. Rev.	Ireland	25 May 1825	9 399
Stoppelbein, Lorena	Germany	1 Dec 1823	9 319
Strauss, Maurice	Frankfort on the Main	13 Dec 1844	4 225
Street, Joseph	England	29 Jan 1824	9 326
Strong, David	Scotland	21 Apr 1827	2 243
Tanswell, William N.	London	27 Jun 1825	9 401
Techeney, Antoine	France	20 Nov 1827	8 34
Tennant, Robert	Glasgow, North Britain	15 Oct 1813	5 78
Tevlin, Patrick	Ireland	19 Jan 1846	12 57
Thompson, John	England	10 Oct 1826	9 436
Thomson, George	Scotland	8 Apr 1824	9 341
Thomson, John Glane	Kilmarnock	4 Nov 1822	9 270
Thorn, James D.	London	21 Apr 1837	2 243
Tolk, C.	Hanover	4 Jun 1836	8 214
Tolnic, John		15 Mar 1823	9 277
Tongaman, John	Hanover	7 May 1830	8 70
Topp, Charles A.	Denmark	9 Dec 1844	4 223
Treaner, Owen	Ireland	27 Jan 1825	9 376
Trescot, Edward	England	31 Mar 1826	9 339
Trescot, William	England	31 Mar 1826	9 339
Turnbull, Joseph	North Britain	14 Jun 1823	9 296
Urban, Joseph	France	27 May 1823	9 293
Van Cooth, J. A.	Amsterdam	8 Aug 1836	8 220
Varne, Nickolas	Naples	1 Mar 1834	8 146
Vion, V.	France	19 Aug 1826	9 430
Vonallunden, Claus	Hanover	23 May 1825	9 398
Von Glahn, Christopher	Hanover	12 Nov 1855	6 157
Vonhagen, John	Rotterdam, Holland	11 Oct 1821	9 192
Wagner, Peter C.	Norway	17 Jan 1831	8 85
Wallis, John	Cork, Ireland	23 Nov 1821	2 2
Wallman, John Henry	Hanover	12 Apr 1836	2 441
Walsh, John	Tipperary, Ireland	6 Aug 1821	9 172
Walsh, Lewis	Longford, Ireland	20 May 1822	9 233
Ward, George	England	9 Oct 1820	9 95
Wardrope, David		2 Jul 1804	3 335
Watson, Alexander	Scotland	28 May 1822	9 238
Weinand, Joseph	Germany	30 May 1827	8 17
Welsh, Patrick	Ireland	6 Feb 1824	9 326
Westman, William	Stockholm, Sweden	24 Sep 1821	9 184
Weylie, Frederick William	Hanover	22 Feb 1845	12 33
Wheeler, Daniel	England	8 Sep 1823	9 312
Whitaker, William	Ireland	25 Apr 1827	2 245
White, John	Edinburgh	29 Aug 1823	9 310
Whiting, William Joseph	England	7 Nov 1848	4 325
Whyte, Joseph	Scotland	15 Sep 1845	4 246
Wiebens, Henry	Hanover	15 Sep 1845	4 246
Wiley, William	Antrim, Ireland	13 Feb 1829	8 57
Wilkinson, John	England	21 Oct 1822	9 266
Williams, Morris		29 Apr 1824	9 343
Wilson, John	Lanarkshire, North Britain	25 Mar 1811	10 50
Wilson, John	North Britain	15 Aug 1820	9 86
Wotherspoon, Robert	Scotland	2 Oct 1826	9 435
Wylie, John	Dumfries, Scotland	28 May 1810	10 64
Wynne, Patrick	Ireland	21 May 1827	8 14
Young, Edward	Lincolnshire, England	4 Apr 1820	9 54
Zerbt, Henry	Hanover	16 Oct 1843	4 191

Page 1: Andrew Kerr, Gentleman, late a Subject of the King of Great Britain is become a citizen...11 July 1787.

James Anderson, late a Subject of his Britannic Majesty, is become a citizen...9 June 1784.

Charleston, 17th April 1784. Adam Tunno is a Citizen of this State, he having before me taken the oath of allegiance.
Aedanus Burke

Thomas Stewart is a Citizen of this State...20 April 1784. So Carolina Chaston.

Page 2: South Carolina) John Potter, Gent., late a Subject of Charleston) the King of Great Britain is become a citizen...16 April 1787.

South Carolina) Jacob Cantor Junior, late a Subject of the Charleston) United Netherlands, is become a citizen...15 July 1784.

South Carolina) Isaac Benedix, Gent., late a Citizen of the Charleston) United Provinces of Holland, is become a citizen...1 June 1787.

Page 3: South Carolina) Jacob Eckhard, late a Subject of the Charleston) Prince of Hesse, is become a citizen... 18 March 1788.

Mr. Abraham Newton (Newson?) was admitted a citizen of this State by the Honble the Privy Council, 10 April 1783, took the oath of allegiance.

Page 4: South Carolina) Dominick Geoghegan is become a citizen Charleston) of this state...11 Oct 1784.

This 27th day of April 1784 appeared David Lamb and took the oath of allegiance & fidelity to this State by which according to Law he is entitled to citizenship.

Charlestown, April 9th 1783. Mr. Ralph Dawes hath this day taken and subscribed the oath of allegiance, abjuration, and Fidelity to the state of South Carolina.

South Carolina, Charleston. William White is become a citizen of this state, he having taken the oath of allegiance...16 Feb 1785.

Page 5: South Carolina) George Nelson, late a Subject of His Charleston) Britannic Majesty is become a Citizen of this State...11 June 1784.

South Carolina) William Fiddy, late a Subject of Great Britain, Charleston) is become a citizen of this state...9 Aug 1784.

South Carolina) John Macqueen is become a citizen of this Charleston) state, he having taken the oath of allegiance... 15 Sept 1787.

Page 6: South Carolina) William Kennedy, Gentleman, late a Charleston) Subject of the King of Great Britain, is become a citizen of this state...30 Dec 1784.

Charleston, Nover. 4th 1785. Conrad Gable hath taken this day the oath of allegiance...

South Carolina, Charleston. George Taylor Esqr., late a Subject of the Kingdom of Great Britain, is become a Citizen of this State...11 Aug 1784.

South Carolina) O Brian Smith, late a Subject of Ireland, is
Charleston) become a citizen of this state...31 July 1784

Page 7: South Carolina) Luke Breen is become a citizen of this
Charleston) state...24 Sept 1784.

South Carolina) John Price, Gentn., late a Subject of the King
Charleston) of Great Britain, is become a citizen of this state...5 Oct 1787.

South Carolina) Alexander Newall, Gentn., late a Subject of the
Charleston) King of Great Britain, is become a Citizen of this state...12 April 1787.

South Carolina) William Mowbray is become a citizen of this
Charleston) state...20 Dec 1786.

Page 8: Maurice Lahiffe is become a citizen of this state...11 Oct 1786.

South Carolina, Charleston. Thomas Montgomerie, late a Subject of the King of Great Britain, is become a citizen of this state. 25 May 1787.

South Carolina, Charleston. Francis Roux, Gentn., late a Citizen of Switzerland, is become a citizen of this state...12 April 1788.

South Carolina, Charleston. David Denoon is become a citizen of this state...22 Sept 1784.

Page 9: South Carolina, Charleston. James Graham is become a citizen of this state...6 Sept 1784.

South Carolina) John Jenkins, Gentn., late a Subject of the
Charleston) King of Great Britain, is become a Citizen of this state...24 May 1787.

Charleston, April 17th 1784. Edward Penman is a Citizen he having resided in this State upwards of twelve months and taken the oath of allegiance.

South Carolina, Charleston. John Black, late a Subject of Great Britain, is become a citizen of this state...24 May 1784.

Page 10: South Carolina) George Frederick Newman, Gen., late
Charleston) a Subject of the King of Prussia, is become a citizen of this state...11 April 1788.

Charleston, April 10th 1783
Mr. Laurence Campbell hath this day taken the oath of allegiance.

South Carolina) Arthur Harper, Gentn., late a Subject of the
Charleston) King of Great Britain, is become a citizen...19 May 1787.

South Carolina) Charles Banks, Gent., late a Subject of the King
Charleston) of Great Britain, is become a citizen...2 April 1788.

Page 11: South Carolina) James Jaffreys, late a Subject of the
Charleston) King of Great Britain, is become a Citizen...1 April 1788.

South Carolina) Gilbert Neyle, Esqr., late a Subject of the
Charleston) King of Great Britain, is become a citizen... 25 April 1788.

South Carolina, Charleston. Bernard Moll, Gentleman, late a Subject of the Emperor of Germany, is become a Citizen...23 May 1785.

Gilbert Davidson this day took the oath prescribed by Law to qualify him to be a citizen of the State of South Carolina. 20 March 1786.

Page 12: South Carolina) Mr. Cochran McClure, late a Subject
Charleston) of the King of Great Britain, is become a citizen...20 Feb 1786.

This certifieth that William McLure of Charleston, Merchant, is a Citizen of the State of South Carolina, he having taken and subscribed the oath of allegiance...18 June 1787.
So Carolina)
Charleston)

South Carolina) William Stephens, late a Subject of the King
Charleston) of Great Britain, is become a Citizen...15 Feb 1787.

South Carolina) Henry Lanchester, Gentn., late a Subject of
Charleston) the King of Great Britain, is become a Citizen of this state...15 Nov 1785.

Page 13: Charlestown, April 10th 1783. Mr. Daniel O'Hara hath this day taken and subscribed the Oath of Allegiance....

South Carolina, Charleston. John Wray, Gentleman, late a Subject of the King of Great Britain, is become a citizen...19 Feb 1787.

South Carolina, Charleston. George Parker, Gentleman, late a Subject of the King of Great Britain, is become a Citizen of this State...25 May 1787.

South Carolina) Alexander McCormick, Gentn., late a Subject of
Charleston) the King of Great Britain, is become a citizen ...9 May 1788.

Page 14: South Carolina) Michael Galway, Gent., late a Subject
Charleston) of this King of Great Britain, is become a Citizen...9 May 1788.

South Carolina) Archibald Campbell is become a Citizen of this
Charleston) State...22 Sept 1784.

State of South Carolina. In the House of Representatives, March 3rd 1783, the report of the committee to whom the petition of sundry persons who have applied to become citizens....Mr. James Gregorie Merchant...recommend them to be admitted citizens. It appears from the Journals of the privy Council, Wednesday, March 26, 1783, that James Gregorie was admitted as a citizen.

Page 15: Bennet Taylor is a Citizen of this State, he having this day complied with an Act of Assembly...taking the oath of allegiance...19 April 1784.

Charleston, State of South Carolina, March 29th 1784. Mr. William Thompson became a citizen of this state....

William Greenwood has taken the oath of allegiance & supremacy ...12 April 1784.

Pp. 15-16: South Carolina, Charleston. George Watson is become a citizen of this state...3 March 1787.

Charlestown, April 10th 1783. Mr. John Clark hath this day taken and subscribed the oath of allegiance....

City of New York. At a Court of Record held for the City and County of New York on Tuesday the 7th day of June 1785, James Wilson was in Pursuance of an act of the legislature of the sd. state to naturalize....

Page 17: South Carolina, Charleston. Francis Ley is become a citizen of this state, he having taken the oath of allegiance...21 July 1784.

South Carolina, Charleston. Lewis Rogers, late a Subject of the King of Great Britain, is become a Citizen of this state...29 June 1787.

Charlestown, April 9th 1783. Mr. Nicholas Primrose hath this day taken the oath of allegiance....

South Carolina. John Simpson did this day taken the oath of allegiance...30 April 1788.

South Carolina, Charleston. Nathaniel Douglass, late a Subject of the King of Great Britain, is become a Citizen of this state... 12 Feb 1788.

Page 18: South Carolina, Charleston. John Lee is become a Citizen of this State...20 May 1788.

Henry Ellison having resided twelve months in this state has taken the oath of allegiance...Charleston, 6th April 1784.

Page 19: South Carolina) Lyon Levi, late a Subject of the King
Charleston) of Great Britain, is become a Citizen
...25 Sept 1786.

South Carolina) Joshua Jonas, Gentn., late a Subject of the King
Charleston) of Great Britain, is become a Citizen of this
State...5 Dec 1786.

Page 20: William Cam is a citizen of South Carolina he having resided in this state one year and taken the oath of allegiance...22 April 1784.

South Carolina, Charleston. Isaac Teasdale, Gent., late a Subject of the King of Great Britain, is become a citizen...3 Nov 1785.

South Carolina, Charleston. George Lockie Esqr., late a Subject of the Kingdom of Great Britain, is become a citizen...26 June 1784.

Page 21: Henry Stuerman, Gentn., late a Subject of the United Province of Holland, is become a citizen of this state ...23 Sept 1784.

Charleston, March 30th 1784. John Ferrie has resided in this state for more than twelve months past has taken an oath of allegiance....

South Carolina, Charleston. Henry Maine Stromer, Gent., late a Subject of the King of Prussia, is become a citizen of this state...23 Sept 1784.

It appears in the Journals of the privy council that Robert Squibb was admitted a citizen of this state on the 26th day of March 1783.

Page 22: South Carolina) James Jacks of Charleston is become
Charleston) a citizen of this state...12 Sept 1787.

South Carolina) Benjamin Mordicai is become a citizen of this
Charleston) State...15 March 1785.

South Carolina) John Barron, Gentleman, late a Subject of the
Charleston) King of Great Britain, is become a citizen...30 May 1787.

South Carolina) James Madan is become a citizen...21 Feb 1786
Charleston)

South Carolina) Robert Brown late a Subject of the King of Great
Charleston) Britain is become a citizen...23 May 1788.

Page 23: South Carolina, Charleston. Charles Hubert, Gent., late a Subject of the United Provinces of Holland, is become a citizen...23 Sept 1784.

South Carolina) Edmond Haworth, Gent., late a Subject of the
Charleston) King of Great Britain, is become a citizen of this state...31 Aug 1784.

South Carolina) John Berry is become a citizen of this State
Charleston) ...13 March 1786.

Page 24: South Carolina) Thomas Abernethie is become a citizen
Charleston) of this State...13 March 1786.

South Carolina) Joseph Peppin is become a citizen of this state...
Charleston) 16 July 1784.

South Carolina, Charleston. Alexander Grant is become a citizen of this state...7 March 1787.

South Carolina, Charleston. John Woddrop is become a citizen of this state...5 July 1785.

Page 25: South Carolina, Charleston. John Munro, Gent., late a Subject of the King of Great Britain is become a Citizen of this state...10 Sept 1787.

South Carolina, Charleston. Adam Ewing, late a Subject of his Britannic Majesty, is become a citizen of this state...21 June 1784.

South Carolina, Charleston. Robert Ewing, late a Subject of the King of Great Britain, is become a citizen...24 May 1787.

South Carolina, Charleston. James Muirhead, Gentn., late a Subject of the King of Great Britain, is become a citizen...17 Sept 1787.

Page 26: South Carolina, Charleston. David Campbell is become a citizen of this state...21 Feb 1785.

South Carolina, Charleston. Hector McMillon is become a citizen of this state...24 May 1788.

South Carolina, Charleston. James Himeli, Gentn., late a Citizen of Switzerland, is become a Citizen of this state...26 Dec 1786.

John McDowin hath this day taken the oath of allegiance...25 May 1788.

Page 27: South Carolina, Charleston. George Forrest is become a citizen of this state...31 Aug 1784.

South Carolina, Charleston. John Moncrief, late a Subject of Great Britain, is become a citizen of this state...23 Aug 1784.

South Carolina, Charleston. James Hamilton, late a Subject of Great Britain, is become a citizen of this state...24 May 1784.

John Bold hath this day taken the oath of allegiance...23 May 1788.

Page 28: South Carolina, Charleston. James Charles is become a citizen of this state...7 March 1787.

South Carolina, Charleston. Samuel Watson Junr. Esqr., a Justice of the Peace for York County, hath taken the oath of office and Fideilty...22 Nov 1787.

South Carolina, Charleston. Christopher Fitzsimmons, late a subject of Great Britain is become a citizen...23 Aug 1784.

South Carolina, Charleston. William Trenholm is become a citizen...22 March 1787.

Page 29: South Carolina Charleston. James Scot is become a citizen...26 May 1788.

South Carolina, Charleston. John Aikens, Gentn., late a Subject of the King of Great Britain, is become a citizen of this state... 5 Oct 1784.

South Carolina, Charleston. John Teasdale, Gentn., late a subject of the King of Great Britain, is become a citizen of this state...31 Aug 1784.

Page 30: South Carolina, Charleston. James Brown is become a citizen...24 May 1788.

South Carolina, Charleston. John David Vale, Gentn., late a subject of the King of Great Britain, is become a citizen...23 July 1785.

South Carolina, Charleston. Willm. Eales, late a subject of Great Britain, is become a citizen of this state...11 May 1784.

South Carolina, Charleston. Andrew Westermyer, late a subject of the King of Great Britain, is become a citizen...17 Oct 1787.

Page 31: South Carolina, Charleston. Edward Shield, late a subject of the King of Great Britain, is become a citizen of this state...19 June 1784.

South Carolina) Thomas Bass is become a citizen of this state...
Charleston) 27 May 1788.

Charleston, April 10th 1783
Mr. John Wilson hath this day taken the oath of allegiance.

Charleston, So Carolina 20th April 1784
William Tunno is a citizen of this state he having resided here upwards of twelve months and taken the oath of allegiance...

Page 32: South Carolina, Charleston. Ralph Dodsworth, late a subject of Great Britain, is become a citizen of this state...24 May 1788.

South Carolina, Charleston. John Press Smith, Gentn., late a subject of the King of Great Britain, is become a citizen of this state...30 Oct 1787.

South Carolina, Charleston. Peter Zylstra, Gentn., late a citizen of the United Province of Holland, is become a citizen of this state...22 May 1788.

South Carolina, Charleston. Allan Stuart is become a citizen of this state...24 May 1788.

Page 33: Charleston. George McCauley, Gentn., late a subject of the King of Great Britain, is become a citizen... 12 Oct 1784.

South Carolina, Charleston. David McCredie, Gentn., late a subject of the King of Great Britain, is become a citizen... 14 Nov 1785.

South Carolina, Charleston. Thomas Brown, Gentn., late a subject of the King of Great Britain, is become a citizen...7 April 1788.

South Carolina, Charleston. William Scarborough is become a citizen...25 June 1784.

Page 34: South Carolina, Charleston. David Haig is become a citizen of this state...24 May 1788.

South Carolina, Charleston. William McWhann, late a subject of Great Britain, is become a citizen...14 May 1784.

South Carolina, Charleston. Willm. Shields is become a citizen of this state...26 May 1788.

South Carolina, Charleston. Alexander Cammeron is become a citizen of this state...27 May 1788.

Page 35: South Carolina, Charleston. Alexander Abernethie is become a citizen...27 May 1788.

South Carolina, Charleston. John Langstaff, late a Subject of Great Britain, is become a Citizen....24 May 1788.

It appears on the Journals of the Privy Council that Christopher Knight was admitted a Citizen of this State 26 March 1783.

It appears on the Journal of the Privy Council that John Casper Folker was admitted a Citizen of this State, 26 March 1783.

Charleston, South Carolina. 21st April 1784. Humphry Courtney is a Citizen of this State, he having taken the oath of allegiance, and resided here upwards of twelve months.

Pp. 35-36: State of South Carolina) Personally appeared Francis
Charleston District) Mitchell...on the 22d day of April 1784, he took the oath of allegiance and received a Certificate which is unfortunately lost.

Page 36: South Carolina) Lewis Jerome Newhouse, Gentn., late a
Charleston) Citizen of Erlach in the Canton of Berne, Switzerland, is become a Citizen...23 Dec 1785.

James Barron is a Citizen of this state he having subscribed one year therein and taken the oath of allegiance...7th May 1788.

South Carolina) Edward Lownds, Gentn., late a Subject of the
Charleston) King of Great Britain is become a Citizen...6 Dec 1784.

Page 37: South Carolina) David Alexander, late a subject of
Charleston) his Britannick Majesty is become a citizen of this state...13 June 1788.

South Carolina) James Peirson is become a citizen...3 Dec 1785.
Charleston)

Patrick Hayes is a Citizen of this state, he having taken the oath of allegiance, 20th April 1784.

South Carolina) Jan Melich, late a Subject of the United Nether-
Charleston) lands, is become a citizen...8 July 1788.

Page 38: South Carolina) William Huxham, late a Subject of
Charleston) Great Britain, is become a Citizen... 11 May 1784.

Page 39: William McCleod, late a Subject of Great Britain, is become a Citizen of this state...3 Aug 1784.

South Carolina) William Rugge, Gentn., late a Subject of the
Charleston) King of Great Britain, is become a citizen of this state...3 May 1787.

South Carolina) Edward Wright, Gent., late a Subject of the
Charleston) King of Great Britain, is become a Citizen of this state...21 July 1785.

Sylvester Commerford is a Citizen of this state, he having taken the Oath of Allegiance...19 Sept 1788.

Page 40: South Carolina) James Millar, late a Subject of Ireland,
Charleston) is become a Citizen...19 June 1784.

South Carolina) Mr. Robert Stewart, late a Subject of the King
Charleston) of Great Britain, is become a citizen...25 Sept 1788.

South Carolina, Charleston. Thomas Stafford is become a citizen ...2 Oct 1788.

Page 41: South Carolina, Charleston. Will Bell, late a Subject of the King of Great Britain, is become a citizen... 9 July 1787.

South Carolina) James Down is become a citizen...27 Oct 1788.
Charleston)

South Carolina) Mr. Charles Godfrey Corre, late a citizen of the
Charleston) city of Dantzicke, became a citizen of this state...3 Nov 1788.

John Berney is a citizen of this state...19 Dec 1788.

Page 42: South Carolina) Rowland Cookson is become a citizen...
Charleston) 26 Jan 1789.

South Carolina, Charleston. John Champneys, late a Subject of the King of Great Britain, is become a Citizen of this state... 25 March 1789.

South Carolina) The Reverend Mr. James Wilson, late a Subject
Charleston) of the King of Great Britain, is become a citizen of this state...15 April 1789.

South Carolina) Paul Smith is become a citizen of this state...
Charleston) 10 Feb 1789.

Charleston) On the 23d day of May 1789, Richard Gilbert Wall
South Carolina) personally appeared and took the oath of allegiance ....

Page 43: South Carolina) Mr. James Baker, late a Subject of the
Charleston) King of Great Britain, is become a citizen of this state...25 May 1789.

Charleston, State of South Carolina. John Francis Chior, Gentleman, late of the United Provinces of Holland, is become a citizen ...23 April 1789.

State of South Carolina, Charleston. William Forester is become a citizen of this state...12 Dec 1785.

South Carolina, Charleston. Robert Quan is become a citizen... 9 Sept 1785.

Page 44: State of South Carolina, City of Charleston. Mr. Anthony Desverneys, late a subject of the King of France,is become a citizen...15 Sept 1789.

South Carolina. Mr. William Price hath taken and subscribed the oath of allegiance...2 Nov 1789.

South Carolina. Keiran Fitzpatrick, mariner, hath taken the oath of allegiance, 21 Nov 1789. Captn. Fitzpatrick also declares that in the course of the late war with Great Britain he sailed in the service of America and thinks himself from that circumstance to be a citizen of America....

State of South Carolina. Mr. Alexander Campbell hath taken the oath of allegiance...12 Nov 1789.

South Carolina) William Allenby and James White after having
Lexington County) taken the Oaths in Open Court...were admitted citizens. 23 Dec 1790.

Page 45: State of South Carolina. At a Meeting and Sitting of the Judges in Columbia...3 Dec 1796...Andrew Boddan came into court and made application to become a Citizen of the United States....

South Carolina) David Evans is become a Citizen...18 Feb 1785.
Charleston)

Page 46: State of South Carolina) Before one of the Judges of the
Richland District) Court of Common Pleas, personally appeared James Hamilton, who took and subscribed the oath of allegiance...he is a native of the Island of Great Britain, of the age of 53 years, and formerly resident of the City of London; his family consisted of the following persons, to wit, his wife Harriott Hamilton, age 38 years; his daughter Elizabeth, age 17 years; his son Samuel, age 15 years; his daughter Harriott, age 10 years; his daughter Caroline, age 8 years; and his son John Warner, age 4 years, all natives of the Island of Great Britain and formerly residents of the City of London. 29th April 1803.

Pp. 46-47: South Carolina) In the Common Pleas.
Kershaw District) Guardian of Negro Ben vs Mathew Coleman. Ravishment of Ward. We find for the plaintiff his freedom and $112.

Pp. 47-48: Before me Joseph Brevard, named in the following certificate, on the day mentioned...on 5 Sept 1803, John Cox, now of the Town of Columbia, in the State aforesaid, Bricklayer and plaisterer, appeared personally and being desirous of becoming a Denizen of the said state, took the oath of allegiance....he was born 28 Feb 1777 in Portmouth, in Hampshire, in that part of the Island of Great Britain, called England, and that he resided in Portsmouth aforesaid all his life (excepting only the time during which he was serving his apprenticeship)... he arrived with his Family in Charleston, 16 Feb 1801, that his Family now consists of his wife Frances late Frances Longley who was born 27 June 1778 in Dewsberry in Yorkshire, in England, aforesaid, and always resided in England untill she came with him as aforesaid to Charleston, and of a daughter and only child named Martha Ann who was born in Columbia aforesaid 6 Aug in the present year...the said John Cox has hereby become a Denizen ....

Page 49: State of South Carolina. John Cameron, now a resident in the District of Sumter in said state, and desiring the right and privilege of a Denizen...did declare on oath that he was born in the Parish of Dingwoll(?) in the County of Ross in Scotland, but resided last in Aberdeen, that he arrived in this state 16 Jan 1802, and hath since been an inhabitant of the same...he is an unmarried man...3rd March 1804.

Pp. 49-51: State of South Carolina. Before me Saml. Wilds, one of the Judges of the Court of Common Pleas of the State of South Carolina, on 26 April 1805, Benjamin Lawrence now of the Town of Columbia, being desirous of becoming a Denizen of said state...born in November 1757 in the County of Gloucester in that part of Great Britain called England, and that he resided there all of his life until he set out for these states, that he arrived with his family in Charleston, 4 Sept 1801, and that his family now consists of his wife Hanah late Hanah Miller of the same county of Gloucester in the Kingdom of England and now about 57 years old, and also one daughter Elizabeth Lee about 19 years old and one son called Benjamin about 14 years old, all of whom were born in Gloucester in England....

Pp. 51-52: State of South Carolina. Appeared Joseph Marie Lequinac Kerblay...made oath that he is 50 years of age and a native of Larzeau in France and lately residing in that State of Georgia, that his family consists of a Wife named Jeanne Marie Odette de Loin(?), aged 42 years, a native of Toulouse in France also of another Lady named Cecile Vaudeperre formerly the wife of Simon Harriot but since Legally divorced from him aged 48 years, a native of Braxelles in French Flanders & Lately residing in the said state of Georgia...5 Nov 1805.

Page 52: Appeared Robert Yates...made oath that he is 26 years of age, a native of the Parish of Handsworth & County of Stafford in England, and lately residing in the Borough of Janeworth...he hath a wife named Elizabeth about 30 years of age and a native of this state....30 Nov 1805.

Pp. 53-54: State of South Carolina. Appeared 27 Aug 1806, Esaias Moses, now of Columbia, being desirous of becoming a Denizen of the said state...born in Hanover in the German empire and that said Hanover was his former place of residence until he came to this state, and also that he has no family....

Pp. 54-55: Personally appeared James Young, 5 Dec 1806, now of Columbia, desirous of becoming a Denizen of sd. state...born in the vicinity of Edinburgh and that the said vicinity and the city of Glasgow were his former places of residence until he came to this state, and also that he has no family....

Page 55: State of South Carolina, Lancaster District. On 8 April 1807, at Lancaster Court house came before me William McKenna, who declared on oath that he is a native of that part of Europe called Ireland, that he was born in Donegal County, and resided formerly in the same place...desirous of becoming a denizen....

Page 56: State of South Carolina....William Shaw of the City of Charleston, attorney at Law, hath applied to be a citizen, 7 Aug 1784....

Page 57: State of South Carolina. I, William Parker, a native of London, in the Dominions of the King of Great Britain, for some years past a resident within the United States of America and for upwards of 12 months past a resident within the said state of South Carolina, being desirous of becoming a Denizen, & to be enabled to hold real property, do swear allegiance...21 Jan 1808. William Parker

William Parker, a native of the City of London, who hath resided in the city of Charleston, the Town of Columbia, & Town of Camden, and for several months previously in the City of New York, following the craft or trade of a cabinet maker...hath taken the oath to become a denizen....24 Jan 1808.

Page 58: State of South Carolina. I, Josiah Campbell, late of the County of Antrim, in Ireland, part of the Dominion of the King of Great Britain, for several years past a resident of the state of South Carolina, being desirous of becoming a Denizen...21 Jan 1808.

Josiah Campbell, aged 26 years, who has resided at Camden, from the year 1804, and prior to that period for a year and upwards in Charleston & elsewhere within the said state....

Pp. 59-60: I, Alexander Young, a native of Fifeshire, in Scotland, having resided for several years past in the United States of America, partly in the City of Baltimore, in that state of Maryland, & Partly in the Town of Camden, in the State of So. Carolina, at which last mentioned place, I reside at present, & where it is my intention to settle, being desirous of becoming a denizen....22 Jan 1808.

Page 60: South Carolina) On 13 April 1808 at Lancaster Court
Lancaster District) House personally appeared Michael Ryan...a native of Ireland in Europe, and resided last in the county of Tipperary...wishes to become a denizen.

Pp. 60-61: United States of America. State of South Carolina)
Charleston District)
At a Court of Common Pleas held in the City of Charleston, 3 June 1809, William McKenna, late of Ireland, made application to be made a citizen of the United States....

Pp. 61-62: State of South Carolina. Samuel Burns now residing in Chester District made application to become a denizen...he was born in the County of Antrim in the Kingdom of Ireland, and is now forty nine years of age, has a family consisting of a wife named Agnes about 45 years of age, a son named Archibald, 18 years of age, a son named Stuart, 16 years of age, a daughter named Jennet, 14 years of age, a daughter named Eliza 12 years of age, a son named Joseph ten years of age, a daughter named Agnes eight years of age, a daughter named Sarah four years of age, and a son named Samuel two years of age, and a daughter named Mary Ann, an infant, ten days old...7 Nov 1811.

Page 62: John Wylie now residing in Chester District made application to be admitted a denizen...born in the County of Antrim in the Kingdom of Ireland and is now 34 years of age, that he has a family consisting of a wife named Easther, about 37 years of age, a son named James 4 years of age, a son named Edward 2 years and four months of age, and a son named John, nine months of age...7 Nov 1811.

Page 63: South Carolina) Samuel Tom made oath that he is a
Laurens District) native of the County of Antrim in Ireland, Kingdom of Great Britain, that he is about 25 years of age, he has a wife Letitia who is also a native of the county of Antrim, also about 25 years of age, he has two children by his wife aforesaid to wit, Margarett about 3 years old and Mary Jane upwards of one year old, both born in the County of Antrim in Ireland...arrived in Charleston on 8 June last and immediately removed to Laurens District where he has resided ever since...15 April 1812.

Page 64: State of South Carolina) On 9 Nov 1813, at a Court of
Lancaster District) Common Pleas holden at Lancaster Court house, appeared Thomas P. Lewis, a native of in the Kingdom of Great Britain and Ireland, praying to be admit-

ted a citizen....

Pp. 64-65: State of South Carolina) On 15 Nov 1813, at the Court Kershaw District) of Common Pleas, holden at Kershaw Court House, appeared John Gilkeyson, a native of the Kingdom of Ireland. by his petition prayed to be admitted a Citizen of the U. S....

Pp. 65-66: State of South Carolina) On 11 Nov 1813, at the Court Lancaster District) of Common Pleas holden at Lancaster Court house...appeared Peter Downy, a native of the Kingdom of Great Britain and Ireland, by his petition prayed to be admitted a citizen....

Pp. 66-67: On 1 Oct 1813, Isaac Golden, of the Town of Charleston, merchant, appeared and being desirous of becoming a Denizen. .he was born on or about the year 1786 in Lensehua in Poland, that he left his native country in or about the year 1804 for the King of Great Britain, and that he removed from there to the United States of America about three years ago...he has neither wife nor children....

Pp. 67-70: The Petition of Lucas Creyon of the Town of Columbia, sheweth that he was born in or about the year 1788 in the County of Sligo and Kingdom of Ireland, that he left his native country and removed to the U. S. A., about the year 1803, and that since 1804 has been a resident of South Carolina. hath neither wife nor children...desirous of becoming a denizen...1 May 1815.

Page 71: State of South Carolina. I, Joseph Brevard, one of the Judges of the Court of General Sessions and Common Pleas ...that Doctor John Paton, a native of Scotland, in the Kingdom of Great Britain, who is now resident in the Town of Camden in the District of Kershaw, desires to become a denizen....

Pp. 71-72: South Carolina) At a circuit court held at Union Union District) Court House, 25 March 1815, Thomas Hancock, late of England and subject of the King of Great Britain, made application to become a citizen....

Page 72: State of South Carolina. Appeared Oct 1815, Peter Lalene DeLane of the District of Richland, being desirous of becoming a denizen...Peter Lelane DeLane of Bicay in the Kingdom of France...born in or about the year 1773, he left his native country and removed to the U. S. A. in the year 1809, and since the year 1809 has been a resident of South Carolina excepting nine months...6 Oct 1815.

Page 73: South Carolina) Locklin McIntosh, a native of Fairfield District) Scotland, who in the year 1800 imigrated to Nova Scotia, in the year 1804, removed to the State of New York, and from thence in the year 1807 to this state, wishes to become a denizen....

State of South Carolina) Christopher Flynn born in the city of Sumter District) Dublin in Ireland and subject of the King of Great Britain has this day taken the oath of allegiance ...13th March 1817.

Page 74: South Carolina, Columbia. George Herron, late a native of Ireland in the County of Down, a subject of the King of Great Brittain, is become a denizen....7 March 1817.

State of South Carolina) In the Court of Common Pleas holden
Fairfield District.) at Fairfield Court House, April Term 1817. Robert Cathcart, a native of Ireland and formerly resident therein, but now become resident in this state did take the oath of allegiance and is become a Denizen...21 Dec 1799.

Pp. 74-75: State of South Carolina) At a Court of Common Pleas
Fairfield District) holden at Fairfield Court House, 16 April 1817, James Bones, late of Ireland in the United Kingdoms of Great Britain and Ireland, now become a resident of this state, made application to become a Denizen.

Page 75: State of South Carolina. Appeared William Crowson Adams, native of Great Britain, and formerly a residence of the city of London, but now a resident in the Town of Camden...admitted a Denizen....19 Nov 1817.

Page 76: State of South Carolina. Appeared James Edmund a native of the Kingdom of Glasgow in Scotland, but now a resident of the Town of Camden...admitted a Denizen. 20 Nov 1817.

State of South Carolina. Appeared Michael Murray McCulloch, a native of Ireland, and formerly a resident of the city of Dublin, but now a resident of the town of Camden...admitted a Denizen. 19 Nov 1817.

Page 77: State of South Carolina) Petition of Thomas Heron, a
Abbeville District) native of Ruthwell County, Sartlung(?), where he formerly resided, but now a resident of So Carolina, Abbeville District about five years...wishes to become a denizen...21 March 1818.

Page 78: State of South Carolina) Petition of Dugald McKellar
Abbeville District) a native of Argyle County, Scotland, where he formerly resided but now a resident of So Carolina,Abbeville District about two years...21 March 1818.

Page 79: State of South Carolina. On 22 March 1818, appeared William Hacket of York District, desirous of becoming a denizen...his place of nativity and former residence was in the Town of Drumahagler in the Parish of Ballymoney, County of Antrim, Ireland, he has no family....

Page 80: South Carolina) Alexander Kirkpatrick, a native of
Laurens District) the County of Derey in Ireland, aged 33 years, did appear and took the oath...granting the privileges of Denizenship....16 April 1818.

Pp. 80-82: State of South Carolina. Petition of Francis William Donlevy of the Town of Columbia...was born in or about the year 1789 in the County of Sligo, Kingdom of Ireland, that he left his native country & removed to the U. S. A. in 1816 & since that period he has been a resident of the State of South Carolina...9 Oct 1818...he has neither wife nor children.

Page 82: State of South Carolina. James Kilpatrick and Thomas Kilpatrick did appear and took the oath of allegiance... the said James and Thomas are natives of Ireland, but at this time residents of Laurens District. 16th April 1819.

Walter B. Rutherford who was born in the Town Jacborough, Rorbinghshire, in Scotland, and resided there until the winter of 1815 was made a denizen of this state...16 April 1819.

Page 83:
State of South Carolina. Peter Lawrence Jumelle, native of the Island of St. Domingo, and a citizen of the parish government, for many years past a resident within the State of South Carolina ...desirous of becoming a denizen...22 April 1820. Peter Lawrence Jumelle, aged about 50 years who has raised (sic) within Camden, 17 years....22 April 1820.

Page 84: Chester District, Fall Term 1820. Petition of Robert Nelson sheweth that the petitioner being now about 39 years of age, emigrated from the Kingdom of Ireland, 28 June 1812, and landed at Charleston, in Sept. in the same year with his wife Isabella now about 39 years of age, Ireland having been the constant place of their residence until said emigration... wish to be admitted as Denizens....2 Nov 1820.

his
Robert + Nelson
mark

her
Issabella + Nelson
mark

Page 85: Chester Dist., Fall Term 1820. Petition of Wm Hamey sheweth that he is now about 18 years of age, emigrated from Ireland, 7 Dec 1818 and landed in Charleston in January 1819, Ireland having been the constant place of residence until said emigration.... 3 April 1820.
Certified by Henry Bradley, John Watts Esqr., Jno Kennedy.

Page 86: Chester District, Fall Term 1820. Petition of James Holden...being now about 27 years of age, emigrated from the Kingdom of Ireland on 29 Sept 1817 and Landed at Norfolk, Virginia, 25th November same year, Ireland having been the constant place of my residence until said emigration, and I have resided within the Bounds & under the Jurisdiction of the State of Virginia & South Carolina...prays to be admitted a Denizen...
certified by Jno McRee, Henry Bradley...3 Nov 1820.

Page 87: South Carolina, Laurens District. Frances Tourell, born in the City of Marseilles in France, but now a resident of the District and state aforesaid, took the oath...giving the right of Denizenship. 17 April 1821.

State of South Carolina, Laurens District. Samuel Austen, born in the County of Antrim, Ireland, but now a residence in the District and state aforesaid...took the oath...giving the right of Denizenship...17 April 1821.

Pp. 87-88: State of South Carolina. Petition of Jeremiah Winter a native of the County of Surry, in the Kingdom of Great Britain, who arrived in the U. S. A. about 1 Dec 1815 sheweth that he is desirous of becoming a Citizen...29 Oct 1816.

Pendleton District. Jeremiah Winter, a native of the County of Surry in the Kingdom of Great Britain, a Brick Mason, painter and Glazier, about 45 years of age...26 Oct 1821.

Page 89: Thomas J. Flinn took oath of allegiance...18 Oct 1821. Darlington District. Thomas J. Flinn born in the County of Dublin, Kingdom of Ireland, from which he removed to this state where he has since resided...18 Oct 1821.

Pp. 90-91: South Carolina) Petition of John Davis sheweth that Richland District) he is a native of England, has been in this country upwards of five years, desirous of becoming a denizen...born in Somersetshire in England, has resided in

Charleston about two months and since then has resided in Columbia about two years...3 May 1822.

Pp. 91-92: South Carolina) Petition of William Gray, a native
Richland District) of England, desirous of becoming
a Denizen of South Carolina...3 May 1822.
William Gray was born at Dorken in Surry in England, has resided since he removed from England in Columbia about three years besides a year at Boston and one in Augusta.

Pp. 92-93: South Carolina) Petition of Frederick Seybt...
Richland District) a native of Bayreath, Franconia,
and has hitherto been a subject of Frederick William the Sovereign of Prussia, aged 53. The petitioner has a wife and four children to wit Channette Perette, 18 years of age and born in Paris, Sophia Antoinette, 14 years old born in Paris, Augustine 12 years old and George Lewis Frederick ten years and six months old also of Paris, and said wife by name is Anne Renee Sierse born in Paris , arrived at Alexandria in the District of Columbia, 19 July 1818, and after staying there six months, he removed to this place where he has resided ever since with his wife and children...desirous of becoming a denizen...wife Anne Renee Tierse is 47 years old....10 May 1822.

Page 93: South Carolina) John Kennedy appeared and took the
Laurens District) oath of allegiance...entitled to the
priviledges of Denizenship...17 April 1822.

South Carolina) Archibald Craig appeared and took the usual
Laurens District) oaths...and family to wit his wife and Jane
aged 3 years and one month, James aged 1 year and 11 months...
15 April 1822.

Page 94: South Carolina) Robertson Hamilton, a native of the
Laurens District) County of Tyrone, Ireland, and latter-
ly a resident of the district aforesaid, took the oath of allegiance...22 Nov 1822.

South Carolina) William Baxton, a native of the County Antrim
Laurens District) Ireland, and latterly a resident of the district
aforesaid, took the oath of allegiance...22 Nov 1822.

South Carolina) Samuel Hamilton, a native of the County of
Laurens District) Monaghan, Ireland, and latterly a resident of
the district aforesaid, took the oath of allegiance....21 Nov 1822.

Page 95: State of South Carolina) John Webster a native of the
Pendleton District) Kingdom of Denmark, has been
a resident in the U. S. A. since 7 Aug 1813, petitioned that the oaths may be administered for the privilege of denizenship ...1 Nov 1822.

South Carolina. Petition of Michael Connor, a native of the Kingdom of Ireland, has been for some time and now is a resident of this state...desirous of becoming a denizen...
Chester District, oath administered 26 Aug 1822.

Page 96: South Carolina. Petition of Michael Collins, that he
is a native of Ireland, but has been for some time and
now is a resident of this state..desirous of becoming a denizen ...Chester District. Oath administered, 26 Aug 1822.

Pp. 96-97: State of South Carolina) Petition of Christopher H. Lexington District) Wiggins, a native of the Dukedom of Oldenburgh in the Empire of Germany of the age of 34 years, declared three years ago his intention to become a citizen of the U. S. A....has resided in the U. S. 11 or 12 years last past and within the State of South Carolina for the whole of that time...9 April 1823.

Page 97: State of South Carolina. On 9 July 1823 appeared William Fearis of York District...being desirous of becoming a denizen...his place of nativity and former residence was in the town and Parish of Glynn, County of Antrim in Ireland ....

Page 98: South Carolina. Sarah Ann Colchett did take the oath of allegiance with a view of becoming a Denizen... at Columbia, 30 Oct 1823.

South Carolina) Eliza M. McCord did appear and take the oath Richland District) of allegiance with a view of becoming a denizen. 30 Oct 1823.

South Carolina, Chester District. On 1 Nov 1823 appeared Willson Raney of York District, being desirous of becoming a Denizen... his place of nativity and former residence was in the Town of Balliwindland in the Parish of Balleymeng, County of Antrim, Ireland....

Page 99: South Carolina) November Term 1823. Jane Kirkpatrick Fairfield District) a native of Ireland, did this day on her own behalf and on behalf of her minor children Thomas Kirkpatrick,aged 18 years, Alexr Kirkpatrick aged 15 years, and Robert Kirkpatrick aged 13 years, all natives of Ireland...took oath of allegiance to become denizens...19 Nov 1823.

State of South Carolina. Hugh Wilson aged 38 years, of the County of Air of North Britain, took the oath of allegiance...becoming denizen. 30 Nov 1823.

South Carolina. Robert Bell aged about 38 years, a native of the County of Londonderry, Ireland, Kingdom of Great Britain, did take the oath of allegiance...to become a denizen. 19 Nov 1823.

Page 100: South Carolina. Robert Munro aged about 30 years, a native of Rophan, Scotland, took the oath of allegiance to become a Denizen...19 Nov 1823.

South Carolina. William Milligan, aged about 60 years, a native of the County of Antrim, Ireland, took the oath of allegiance... to become a denizen. 19 Nov 1823.

South Carolina. Thomas Fortescue, an alien born in the Kingdom of Ireland, took the oath to become a denizen...17 Nov 1823.

Page 101: South Carolina. John Cameron, aged about 21 years, a native of the County of Dengal, Ireland, took the oath to become a denizen...19 Nov 1823.

Personally appeared Christian Ernest Otto Breithaupt, who has been a resident of S. C. for two years previous to this date, he adjures all allegiance to the Sovereigns of Bavaria and Saxony, and also to the Emperor of Germany, intention to become a citizen...9 March 1824.

Patrick Elymott, aged about 30 years, a native of the County of Waxford, Ireland, took the oath of allegiance to become a Denizen. 16 April 1824.

Page 102: South Carolina. William Rauson, aged 36 years, a native of the County of Monaghan, Ireland, took the oath of allegiance to become a denizen. 16 April 1824.

South Carolina) James Rud, formerly of the Kingdom of Great Greenville District) Britain, and now about 27 years of age, took the oath of allegiance to become a denizen. Recorded 24 April 1824.

South Carolina) At a Court of General Sessions on the first Lancaster District) Monday after the fourth Monday in March in 1824, James Reed, a native of the County Donegal, Ireland, took that oath of allegiance to become a denizen...31st March 1824.

Page 103: South Carolina) John Ross, a native of Monaghan Laurens District) County, Ireland, took the oath to become a denizen. 16 April 1824.

South Carolina) John Rauson, a native of Ireland, and latterly Laurens District) a resident of the district aforesaid, took the oath of allegiance to become a denizen...13 April 1824.

Pp. 103-104: State of South Carolina. Archibald McCoy applies to be admitted as a denizen...native of Ireland, aged 44 years, and formerly a resident in the County of Antrim in Ireland...21 Oct 1824.

Page 104: South Carolina) Peter Gallager, a native of and Laurens District) formerly a resident of Ireland, but now a resident of the district aforesaid, took the oath of allegiance to become a denizen. 16 Nov 1824.

South Carolina. Andrew Kenedy, aged 31 years, a native of the County of Antrim, Ireland, took the oath of allegiance, 18 Nov 1824.

Page 105: South Carolina James Lemons, native of the County Down in the Kingdom of Ireland, has resided in the District of Fairfield for than one year. Certified 15 Nov 1824 by Caleb Clarke, Robert Cathcart.

State of South Carolina) Petition of Jerry OLeary...petitioner York District) was born in Ireland, in the County of Cork, and did arrive in Norfolk in the State of Virginia year 1821, hath resided in the U. S. ever since, and within the Jurisdiction of this state for the two last years past & is now about 25 years of age...intention to become a citizen. 23 Oct 1824.

Page 106: State of South Carolina) William Gildchrist, aged about Laurens District) 23 years, a native of Scotland, took the oath to become a Denizen. 19 April 1825.

South Carolina. John Campbell, aged about 35 years, a native of County Entrim (sic), took the oath to become a Denizen...20 April 1825.

Page 107: South Carolina) Petition of John Sweeny sheweth that Chester District) he is an alient, a native of Ireland, he emigrated to this Country in the year 1820, he had resided within the State of South Carolina principally during that time... born in the Parish of Loughmore, County of Tipperara, Ireland....

Certified 1 April 1825 by Charles Boyd, L. Strait, John Evans, Henry Bradley, James McClure, Wm. McClure.

Page 108: South Carolina) James Craig, aged about 42 years, Laurens District) a native of the County of Entrim (sic), Ireland, took the oath to become a Denizen...19 April 1825.

State of South Carolina. Samuel S. McGowan is over the age of 21 years, a native of the County Down, Ireland, took the oath of allegiance to become a denizen. 20 Nov 1825.

Pp. 108-109: Phillip Cummerford, aged about 26 years, a native of the County of Armagh, Ireland, took the oath of allegiance to become a denizen. 19 Nov 1825.

Page 109: State of South Carolina. Neil Morrison is above the age of twenty one years, native of Argyle County, Scotland, took the oath to become a denizen. 20 Nov 1825.

State of South Carolina. Samuel McCraken, is over the age of 21 years, a native of the County of Down, Ireland...took the oath to become a denizen.20 Nov 1825.

Pp. 109-110: Petition of Alexander Dullass sheweth that he is of the age of 29 years, he was born in Argyleshire, in Scotland, that he arrived at Wilmington, in the State of North Carolina, 10 Nov 1820, and came from thence to this state immediately where he has ever since resided... Alexr Dallas
Certified by John Craig, Strainger Perkins...8 Nov 1825.
South Carolina) Alexander Dallass make statement of
Chesterfield District) intention to become a citizen.

Page 111: Jacob Spoon, aged about 46 years, a native of the city of Copilius in Austria, and a subject of the King of Austria, took oath to become a Denizen...15 Nov 1825.

William Davidson, aged about 21 years, a native of the County of Derry, Ireland, took the oath of allegiance to become a Denizen. 15 Nov 1825.

State of South Carolina) Thomas Pringle, of the age of 50 years, Sumter District) a native of County of Monaghan in the Kingdom of Ireland, took the oath of allegiance to become a denizen...Sumterville, 17 March 1826.

Pp. 112-113: State of South Carolina) Petition of Lewis Levy, Lexington District) a native of England, is now about 22 years of age, and is desirous of becoming a citizen ...7 Nov 1825.
Certified by J. OHanlon, Wm. Jones, George Sawyer, Amos Banks.

Pp. 113-114: State of South Carolina) On the 4th Monday in Laurens District) September 1826,Matthew White, who was born in the County of Wakesford (sic), Ireland, took oath to become a denizen....

Page 114: State of South Carolina) At a Court of Sessions and Lexington District) Common Pleas...Robert Jones, did at Spring Term 1827, take the oath of allegiance...a native of Wales.

Page 115: Exparte Alexander McInnis. Petition for Citizenship. April term 1827, Orangeburgh District.

South Carolina) Petition of Solomon Simpson, a native of Chester District) the Kingdom of Ireland, desirous of becoming a denizen...22 Oct 1827. His place of residence was in the Parish of Donaghady, County Tryone, Ireland, aged about 29 years.
Certified by John Cherry, John McCreary, John Kennedy.

Page 116: State of South Carolina) On 18 April 1827, William Kershaw District) Kennedy, a native of Dunbartonshire, Scotland, prayed to be admitted a citizen....

State of South Carolina) James Divver, a native of & formerly Newberry District) residing in the County of Donegal, Ireland, took the oath to become a denizen...19 March 1828.

Page 117: South Carolina) Petition of William Scott, that he Chester District) is a native of the Kingdom of Ireland, and is desirous of becoming a denizen...
Certified 27 Oct 1827 by Robert Robinson, Charles Boyd, John Cherry.
William Scott, aged about 30 years, a native of County Antrim.

Pp. 117-118: South Carolina) Petition of David Lyle sheweth Chester District) that he is a native of the Kingdom of Ireland...25 Oct 1827.
Certified that they have known David Lyle for upwards of five years... Allen Jones Green, Robert Robinson, Geo Gill.
David Lyle resided the greatest part of his time in the Parish of Raloo, County Antrim Ireland, and believes his age to be 33....

Page 118: South Carolina) Antoine Gubal, a native of & Newberry District) formerly residing in the Town of Moulens in the department allier in the Kingdom of France... prays to be made a denizen...20 March 1828.

Page 119: State of South Carolina) Christian Henry Schmidt, a Newberry District) native of and formerly residing near the Town of Stutgard, Kingdom of Wirtemburg in Germany...praying to be admitted as a Denizen...22 Oct 1828.

State of South Carolina) Petition of David Wilson sheweth that Newberry District) he is a native of Sterlingshire, in the County of Sterling, in Scotland, and has resided within the limits of the U. S. A. for the period of four years, is desirous of becoming a denizen...25 April 1829.

Pp. 120-121: South Carolina) Patrick OFarrell is a native of Newberry District) the County of Longford, Ireland, that he has been within the limits of the U. S. A. for about nine years last past, and in this district for the last eight years...25 April 1829.

Pp. 121-122: South Carolina) Petition of John Baird sheweth Chester District) that he is a native of the Kingdom of Ireland, and has resided upwards of 7 years within the limits of this state, and has a family of three children and that he himself is aged 55 years, his son Cornelius Baird is age 18 years, and John Baird Jr. is aged 13 years, and William Baird is aged 10 years who were also born in the County of Londonderry...31 Oct 1829. Certified to have been acquainted with

John Baird upwards of six years. John McKee, John Kennedy.

Pp. 122-123: South Carolina) Petition of William Reynolds is Kershaw District) a free white person, and a native of Ireland, for more than one year last past a resident of the state of South Carolina, and wishes to become a denizen...1 April 1830.

Pp. 123-124: South Carolina) Petition of John Nauman...that Lexington District) he is a native of Saxony in the Kingdom of Great Britain, now a resident of South Carolina, Lexington District, his occupation is that of a vine dresser, the names, ages and places of nativity of his family are as following. John Nauman, of the age of 45; Hanah of the age of 42; Christiana, sixteen; Hanah, twelve; Recka, ten; Charles, seven; Carolina, six; Prata, three years of age, all natives of Saxony aforesaid...prays to be given the oath of allegiance... 28 Sept 1830.

Page 124: State of South Carolina. Appeared Mary Brown, a native of Scotland, where she formerly resided...a resident now of the Town of Columbia, wishes to become a denizen...14 Oct 1830.

South Carolina) At October Term 1830, Thomas Walsh, who Richland District) represents himself to be a native of the County of Queens, in Ireland, of the age of 26 years, has resided in the state of S. C. for about two years past, except about 15 months during which time he was absent on a visit to Ireland... 14 Oct 1830.

Page 125: James Kelly, a native of Galway, Ireland, made oath of intention to become a citizen... Richland District, 14 Oct 1830.

Michael Powers, a native of Waterford, Ireland, came and stated his intention to become a citizen.... Richland District, 14 Oct 1830.

Thomas Hennesey, a native of Kings County, Ireland, made oath that it is his intention to become a citizen...14 Oct 1830. Richland District.

Page 126: South Carolina. Samuel R. Todd, aged 21 years, a native of Monahon County, Ireland, took that oath to become a denizen...22 Nov 1828.

South Carolina. John Hamilton, aged about 22 years, a native of the county of Monaghon, Ireland, made oath to become a denizen ...21 April 1827.

Pp. 126-127: William Gray, a native of England, Surry County, made oath that it is his intention to become a citizen...Richland District, Nov. 5, 1825.

Page 127: South Carolina) John Forsyth made oath that it is Richland District) his intention to become a citizen ...3 April 1826. Certified in Lexington District also.

Page 128: South Carolina. In the Common Pleas, Lexington District. Petition of William Assman sheweth that he gave the requisite notice at the Fall Term in the District of Lexington in the year 1827 of his becoming a citizen, having resided in that state from that time to the present...8 March 1831.

Page 129: South Carolina) Petition of Elizabeth Welsh... Richland District) has been for some years past a resident of this state, that she is a native of Ireland, and is anxious to become a denizen...Columbia, 4 Oct 1831. She is a native of Kilkenny, Ireland.

her
Elizabeth X Walsh
mark

Page 130: South Carolina) At a common law Court held at Newberry District) Newberry, 30 April 1831, Antoine Gilbal late of the Kingdom of France,made application to become a citizen....

Page 131: State of South Carolina) At a Court of Common Pleas Abbeville District) held for the District of Abbeville, on the third Monday in March 1839...Maximilian Zuboff being desirous of becoming a citizen...name Maximilian Zuboff Iatronymick Fadovoorts, born in the City of Yourburgh, Province of Lithuania, under the dominion of the Emperor of Prussia about 7 Feb 1813, son and heir of Fador Martinavits Prince Zubuff... embarked for New York, August 1833, spent several years in the city of New York, then came from New York to Charlete (sic) South Carolina in May 1838, engaged since November 1838 in the Study of Law at Abbeville Court House, and expect to make settlement in this state...18 March 1839.

Page 133: Petition of John Dickey a native of Ireland, and emigrated to this state in the year 1834 and settled in Chester District...born in the County of Antrim, Ireland...__ April 1839.

END OF VOLUME.

Portions of the preceding volume are missing, specifically parts of pages 15 and 16. The document exists in a second copy, from Miscellaneous Records (Columbia series) Volume Q, from which the following are taken.

Page 19: Charleston. Bartholomew Carroll is become a citizen... 23 May 1785

Page 21: Joshua Hargraves, late a subject of Great Britain, is become a citizen, 22 July 1784.

James Bulgin is become a citizen...5 Dec 1785.

G. A. Petition No Date #177

Joseph Hazard formerly of the City of London but now of the City of Charleston, petition for citizenship [1791-1797]

G. A. Petition 1782 #1

Michael John Harris, a native of Britain, came to Charles Town in October 1780 in the line of a Merchant, with a considerable cargo of goods...19 Feb 1782

G. A. Petition 1783 #154

George Tunno of Charles town merchant...resided in this State for several years previous to the year 1777, at which time he went to the West Indies on a plan of Business...19 Feb 1783

G. A. Petition 1783 #397

John Thompson of Charlestown, merchant, a British subject who remained in this State under the protection of an agreement between Gov. Mathews and the British merchants...1783

G. A. Petition 1783 #396

Petition of Doctor Thomas Blair...who arrived in Charlestown Septr. 1782 from the West Indies...1783

Audited Account #6913

Thomas Sheafe, a native of Boston, left that place about 6 years ago being then a minor, with a view of settling the affairs of a Brother who had died in the West Indies, wishes to become a citizen.
Affidavit of Hext McCall. 27 Feb 1783.

G. A. Petition 1783 #2

Petition of Daniel Watson Turner, of Charles-Town, merchant... on many occasions has shewn himself friendly particularly in assisting and relieving distressed American prisoners.
Jan. 24, 1783

G. A. Petition 1783 #27

The Memmorial of the underwritten subscribers sheweth That your Memmorialists arrived in this State some time after the Reduction of the Capital by the British...are Prisoners on Parole waiting the determination of your Honorable house, tho' it is their sincere wish to become citizens.
Jan. 22, 1783

Henry Moses
Samuel Levy
Montague Simons
Hyam Solomons
Levy Solomon
Mordcay Lyon

G. A. Petition 1783 #28

John Vicars a native of Britain and came with Lut. Coll. Balfour as House Stuard...1783

G. A. Petition 1783 #66 and #119

John Collett Esquire late a Captain of the Prince of Wales's American Regiments...arrived in this state since the Capitulation of Charles Town...intention of becoming a citizen.

G. A. Petition 1783 #85

Robert Farquhar, merchant, prays he may be admitted a citizen Charles Town, 24th Jany 1783.

G. A. Petition 1783 #90

John Clark a resident in Charlestown, since the 12th day of May 1780...arrived from New York in the Mercantile Line, 7th August year aforesaid.
Charlestown 29th Janry 1783.

G. A. Petition 1783 #91

William Binnie...was formerly an inhabitant of this state, and left the same in 1778...settled in Saint Augustine...wishes again to become a subject of this state. 29 Jan 1783

G. A. Petition 1783 #92

William Blacklock arrived in this state in 1774...after the campaign against General Prevost in the summer of 1779, made a voyage to the Island of St. Eustatius...returned to Charles Town 20 Jan 1783

G. A. Petition 1783 #93

David Cameron...arrived in this state some time after the reduction of the capital by the British....
January 20, 1783.

G. A. Petition 1783 #94

James Gregorie of Charlestown, merchant...came to Charlestown from Britain in June 1780, where he has been ever since; always intended to become a citizen of the U. S. Jany 27, 1783

G. A. Petition 1783 #96

Christopher Knight...petition to become a citizen. 29 Jan 1783

G. A. Petition 1783 #98

Ralph Macnair...embarked his Family and Effects at New York, with full purpose to become a citizen of this State...arrived in this city in the latter end of October (1780?)...
Charlestown, 25th Jan 1783.

G. A. Petition 1783 #99

Andrew Miller...lived in the state of North Carolina at the time independence was declared...had his wife and four children then in that state, but his three eldest sons were then in Britain, where they had been for several years before... in 1776 went to Bermuda, from there to Antigua; in January, 1781, his sons arrived at the Island of Bermuda where he then was with his wife and five other children. In February 1781, he left that Island with his whole family and arrived in this town on a Brigantine of which he had purchased one half...now with wife, four sons and three

daughters; his fifth son has already taken the oath of allegiance to the State of North Carolina, and his sixth son who is under age has been cruising in a privateer belonging to that state for several months past.
Charlestown, January 24th, 1783.

G. A. Petition 1783 #100

John Walker arrived in this state some months past with a valuable cargo intending to reside in Charles Town...
Chs Town, Jany 23d 1783

G. A. Petition #105 and #111

Francis Speilmann a native of Strasburgh in the Alsace, a resident in Charlestown since the 12th of May 1780.
Charlestown 29th Janry 1783

G. A. Petition 1783 #116

John Kneeshaw, merchant...after the surrender of Charlestown arrived from Yorkshire in England with a cargo of goods.
30th Janry 1783

G. A. Petition 1783 #118

Ralph Dawes arriv'd in Charles Town, subsequent to its reduction by the British--being then a subject of that nation...since his arrival intermarried with a native of this state.
Jan 26th 1783

G. A. Petition 1783 #107

Richard Wilder Carr...was an inhabitant of Pensacola in West Florida, and upon that place being taken by the Spanniards, set off with his family in a flag of truce amongst others and arrived here in January 1782.
31st January 1783.

G. A. Petition 1783 #57

Francis Clarke, came to this state some time ago a British subject in the year 1781.
31 Jan 1783

G. A. Petition 1783 #123

Petition of John Casper Tucker, late an officer in the Second Battalion of New Jersey Volunteers, arrived in this state since the capitulation of Charles Town
1 Feb 1783

G. A. Petition 1783 #127

Petition of Peter Donworth late an officer, arrived in this state since the Capitulation of Charles Town.
31 Jan 1783

G. A. Petition 1783 #137

Petition of George Ross...came to this state the beginning of Septr. 1782. 10 Feb 1783

G. A. Petition 1783 #136 and #209

Petition of John Willson, late of Augusta in Georgia...was sent down a Prisoner to this Place in September 1780 by Col. Thomas Brown... 6 Feb 1783 Charlestown

G. A. Petition 1783 #139

Petition of William Cox...came to this state since the year 1780 a British subject.... 11 Feb 1783

G. A. Petition 1783 #140

Petition of Joseph Noland...an old commander from Great Britain to the West Indies...residing in this state for near two years. Charlestown 10th Feb 1783

G. A. Petition 1783 #181

Wm Freeman...is one of the merchants residing here...prays to be admitted a citizen.
Charlestown, Febry 1st 1783

G. A. Petition 1783 #191

Colin McLachlan has by long habitude and familiarity contracted a superior regard for America...prays to be admitted a subject of the United States. Charlestown 3 Feby 1783

G. A. Petition 1783 #196

Petition of Francis Ley...he is one of the merchants residing here...requests to admit him to remain here a Citizen.
5 Feb 1783

G. A. Petition 1783 #192

John Geyer...from a residence of about two Years in this State, greatest part of which time having lived entirely in the Country with his family. Charlestown Jany 30th 1783

G. A. Petition 1783 #193

John Manson...is a native of and was bred in Great Britain & never was in American until 1780...mercantel business...wishes to become a citizen. 1783

G. A. Petition 1783 #198

Abraham Newton arrived in this State with the British Army and that he never held any post under that government except by being a clerk in the Superintendants office...permit him to be a citizen. 5 Feb 1783

G. A. Petition 1783 #211

Arthur de Bardeleben...formerly held the Commission of Lieutenant of Infantry in the service of the Prince of Hesse Cassel and was among the number of those troops ordered by his Sovereign to do Duty in America...desires to become a Citizen...purchased a plantation in Charlestown Neck from Robert Williams...8 Feb 1783

G. A. Petition 1783 #217

William Parker...desires to become a citizen. 8 Feb 1783

G. A. Petition 1783 #202

George Selby is a Native of England and never was out of that Kingdom till his Voyage to this place in the latter end of 1781 and arrived here 10th day of December...
Charles Town 7 Feb 1783
No 30 on the Bay

G. A. Petition 1783 #206

John Thompson of Charlestown, merchant...is a British subject...
8 Feb 1783

G. A. Petition 1783 #205

These Memorialists arrived in this State some time after the reduction of this Capital....
Charles Town
February 3d 1783

Andrew Smith
Soln. Woolf
Henry Harris
Moses Simons
Jas. Martin

G. A. Petition 1783 #200

Saml. Blakely...resided in the State of Georgia six years and in the month of November 1780, removed to Charlestown, where he has been a storekeeper.
Feb 6, 1783

G. A. Petition 1783 #212

Samuel Graham...was born and bred up in Ireland to the black smith's trade, has resided in American about 18 years...he lived with and worked for a Mr. Rutherford near Wilmington, in North Carolina...Febry 6, 1783

G. A. Petition 1783 #221

Laurence Campbell...remained in Charlestown after the evacuation thereof by the British Troops...Charlestown, Feby 10th 1783

G. A. Petition 1783 #225

Thomas Gibb...formerly held the Commissions of Surgeon and Paymaster to one of the Regiments in the Service of the King of Great Britain...took refuge with the American lines...prays to be a citizen. 15 Feb 1783

G. A. Petition 1783 #226

Charles Goodwin late of the City of London but now resident in Charles-Town...established himself in Charles Town in the latter end of 1780. 10th Feby 1783

G. A. Petition 1783 #227

Willm. Gordon...being a Mechanick came a Passenger in a British Vessell from England in 1782...requests to be admitted as a Citizen. 15 Feb 1783

G. A. Petition 1783 #236

Alexander McIver of Charles Town, merchant...arrived in this Country in October 1780.
11th Feby 1783

G. A. Petition 1783 #243

Robt Squibb, seedsman, gardner & Professor of Agriculture... left England in 1780 to settled in Carolina...15 Feb 1783.

G. A. Petition 1783 #238

Peter Merselis, lately a resident of West Florida, planter... came to this state Novr. last... Charles Town Febry. 12, 1783.

G. A. Petition 1783 #232

Geo: Kiloh...lately came to this State...Chas Town 15 Febry 1783

G. A. Petition 1783 #233

Henry Legge arrived in this Province some short time after the evacuation by the British.... Charleston Febry 15, 1783

G. A. Petition 1783 #234

George Macaulay of Charlestown, merchant, came to this State with his Family about seven months ago...15 Feb 1783

G. A. Petition 1783 #244

Thomas Pashley, taylor...lately came to this State...15 Feb 1783

G. A. Petition 1783 #249

Barnard Richardson...was an inhabitant of Pensacola in West Florida and upon the fall of that place to the Spaniards removed to this State...15 Feb 1783

G. A. Petition 1783 #267

John Hepburn (Hypburn)...arrived in South Carolina in 1780... wishes to become a citizen of this Republick...22 Feb 1783

G. A. Petition 1783 #260

James Arkle...a printer, arrived in South Carolina in 1781...22 Feb 1783

G. A. Petition 1783 #272

James La Motte...came to this continent from England, solely with the views of Trade, resided in Charlestown upwards of two years...22 Feb 1783

G. A. Petition 1783 #280

James Phillips...settled in this Town when it was in possession of British Troops.... Charlestown Febry 16th, 1783

G. A. Petition 1783 #289

Willm Watson...your petitioner is a native of Great Britain and came to this Town in 1780...has lived the greater part of his

Time in the employ of Mr. Maurice Simons...Chas Town 19th Feby 1783

G. A. Petition 1783 #292

Gibbes Atkins...one of the British merchants who remained in Charlestown...21st Febry 1783.

G. A. Petition 1783 #294

Thomas Foster and Seth Foster...having resided sometime in this country...desirous of becoming citizens... Charles Town Febry 14th 1783.

G. A. Petition 1783 #295

Paul Hill...is a mechanick and came to this Town in 1781. 24 Feb 1783

G. A. Petition 1783 #166

Alexr Campbell...he being young when he arrived here with the British...bound himself apprentice to Mr. James Steedman, carpenter, of this town, and his time being out wishes to become a citizen. Febry 22d 1783.

G. A. Petition 1783 #163

James Cunningham...came into this country in August 1781 at the Evacuation of this Town...22 Feb 1783.

G. A. Petition 1783 #302

William Marshall, now of Charles Town...for upwards of sixteen years last past hath been a resident in West-Florida, that upon the capture of that place by the Spaniards in 1781...came in March 1782 with his family....24 Feb 1783

G. A. Petition 1783 #307

Peter Saul Ryan...a native of Ireland, arrived in 1781. Charlestown, 18th Febry 1783.

G. A. Petition 1783 #306

William Robinson, late of London, merchant...
Charles Town 18th Febry 1783

G. A. Petition 1783 #305

Thos. Richardson..an inhabitant of Pensacola in West Florida, upon the fall of that place to the Spaniards, removed to this State...24 Feb 1783

G. A. Petition 1783 #312

Thomas Withers, mariner, became an adventurer to this country in September 1780, since which he hath resided in Charlestown. Charlestown, February 16, 1783.

G. A. Petition 1783 #313

Elihu Hall Bay, late of West Florida...born in the State of Pennsylvania and educated in the city of New York, from whence he removed in the latter end of 1772 to Pensacola, then to Charles Town, 22 Feb 1783.

G. A. Petition 1783 #314

John Bay, late of Pensacola in West Florida...born in Pennsylvania, educated in New York, removed to Pensacola, remained there until February last, and came from thence.... Charles Town, 22nd Feby 1783.

G. A. Petition 1783 #315

Ebenezer John Collett,a native of England, came to Charles Town in December 1780, in the line of a merchant. Charles Town 24 Febry 1783

G. A. Petition 1783 #316

Joseph Purcell...was an inhabitant of Pensacola in West Florida removed to this State with his family...Charlestown, George Street No. 3 February 2d 1783

G. A. Petition 1783 #318

Samuel Watson and Nicol Primerose...are natives of Great Britain that they came to Charles Town in 1780, in the line of merchants... Charles Town 27th Febry 1783

G. A. Petition 1783 #219

Doctor Thomas Blair...arrived in Charles Town Septr. 1782 from the West Indies...1 March1783

G. A. Petition 1783 #320

Alexr Bethune...a British merchant...wishes to become a citizen. Charlestown 1st March 1783

G. A. Petition 1783 #308

Alexr Shirras...one of the merchants. Febry 19th 1783 No 30 Bay

G. A. Petition 1783 #321

Joseph Taylor...remained in Charlestown after the evacuation... Charlestown Febry 26th 1783

G. A. Petition 1783 #322

James Warington...a native of England, arrived in October 1781. Charlestown 3rd March 1783

G. A. Petition 1783 #323

Waller Keith...remained in Charlestown on its evacuation... came to Charlestown 2 Sept 1783. 5 March 1783

G. A. Petition 1783 #326

Daniel O'Hara...having resided some time in this country... Charlestown March 1783

G. A. Petition 1784 #28

George Duncan came to settle in this country in 1764, followed his trade as a wine cooper until June 1778 when he left this state. Charleston 10th Febry 1784

G. A. Petition 1783 #147

The Memorial of the Undersigned British Merchants residing in Charleston...parties to an agreement enter'd into between his Excellency Governour Mathews and themselves, bearing date October 1782 were permitted to remain six months under the Government and Protection of this State for the Purpose of disposing of their Goods and collecting their debts.

That the Time with which your Memorialists are indulged is inadequate to the Intention thereof... That as from the Lenity of the Government under which they are now protected, several may be desirous of becoming Citizens of the United States, these of your Memorialists who, by their Commercial Engagements, are prevented from making immediate application for that purpose, hope they will not be precluded from this Advantage provided they sollicit the same within the period of Neutrality granted.

Henry Shoolbred
Thos Stewart
E. Jn. Collett
Jonathan Lawson
Nicol Primerose
Jona. Simpson Jr.
Saml. Watson
Henry Shoolbred for the Estate of Wm Smith decd
Jona. & Wm Simpson for the estate of Anthony Lechmere deceas'd
Wm Simpson
William Thompson
James Wallace
William Lindsay
Daniel Silsby
James Stevens
Dugald Forbes
Benjamin Moodie
John Maitland
Thos Miller
David Lamb
William Brown
Will Tunno

David Millar
James Somervell
Wm Cam
Colin Campbell
Minton Collins
Patk. Hayes
Saml Fluitt
James Rule & Co.
David O'Hara
Jas. Bradford
John Macnair
Frederick Webber
Thos Barron
John Bryden
John MacIver
Geo: Troup
William Lennox
Fred Kisselman
John Ferrie
Alexd. Gordon
Thomas Withers
Willm. Simmons
Jas Peirson
James Miller
John Bethune
Robert Struthers
James Warington

Edward Crook

G. A. Petition 1785 #9

(original in French and German with translation)
Francois Philippe de Fabert...arrived a considerable time since from the Emperial (sic) City Vienna in Europe...wishes to become a citizen...his family consists of his wife, a son five years old and his brother.... 1785.

G. A. Petition 1786 #6

Alexander Baron, physician...about the beginning of last year preferred a Petition for Citizenship...7 Feb 1786.

G. A. Petition 1787 #43

Thomas Miller, clerk, a native of England, but now Rector of the Parish of St. Andrew...left England in April last and arrived here in the month of June following...having already taken the oath of allegiance and purposing with his family to pass the remainder of his days in South Carolina...William, Thomas and Giles his three sons.... Charleston, 20 Feb 1787.

 see p 77

G. A. Petition 1787 #64

Hugh Alexander Nixson served in the late war for the space of three years and upwards in the Navy of this state, and has resided therein for four years...wishes the rights of a citizen.
1 March 1787

G. A. Petition 1788 #6

Petition of Rev. Thomas Frost of Charleston...a native of England, having resided in this state three years...
October 22, 1788

G. A. Petition 1788 #7 and #68

James Down of Charleston...a native of England..came into this state 5 Oct 1787, and is desirous of settling at Charleston
25 Oct 1788

G. A. Petition 1788 #12

James Atkins of Camden...left Britain in 1786 and has ever since resided in Camden...14 Jan 1788

G. A. Petition 1788 #28

John Simpson, mercht., of Laurence (sic for Laurens) County... having come from Ireland.
January 2d 1788

G. A. Petition 1788 #76

Thomas Mills, clerk, a native of England, but now Rector of the Parish of St. Andrew...left England April 1786....24th Oct 1788

G. A. Petition 1789 #6 and #13

Richard Wrainch of Charleston, a native of England, having resided in this state for near five years...14 Jan 1789

G. A. Petition 1789 #14 and #101

Patrick Byrne of Charleston, a native of Ireland, having resided in this state near five years...14 Jan 1789

G. A. Petition 1789 #33 and #37

Petition of George Harding, a native of Ireland, having resided in this state near six years...30 Jan 1789

G. A. Petition 1789 #21 and #100

Edward Butler is desirous of becoming a citizen of this state
27 Jan 1789

G. A. Petition 1789 #39

Petition of Andrew McCulley of George Town, a native of Ireland, having resided in this state three years...30 Jan 1789

G. A. Petition 1789 #40 and #43

Petition of Andrew Smith of Laurance (sic for Laurens) County having come from Ireland about 18 months ago...4 Feb 1789

G. A. Petition 1789 #49

Paul Smith is desirous of naturalization...12 Feb 1789

G. A. Petition 1789 #52 and #75

John Fitzpatrick of Charleston, a native of Ireland, having resided in this state near five years...14 Feb 1789

G. A. Petition 1789 #53

James Burges...better than one year ago left Scotland his Native Country and arrived in this city with a design to become a citizen... Charleston, 10 Feb 1789

G. A. Petition 1789 #60 and #73

John Hartley Harris of Charleston...a native of England having resided in this state upwards of three years...Feb 18, 1789

G. A. Petition 1790 #5

Petition of Jan Molich of Charleston, mercht, a native of the United Netherlands, having resided in this state four years... on 8 July 1788 took the oath of allegiance...
Charleston, Dec. 28, 1789 Jan Mölich

G. A. Petition 1790 #12

Petition of Paul Coste, Minister of the Calvinistic Church of French Protestants in the city of Charleston...has been a resident 12 months.... Theodore Trezevant, Stephen Thomas, Bazill Lanneau and Lewis Poyas, Elders of sd. church. 7 Jan 1790

G. A. Petition 1802 #33

Petition of Barnerd Dierson of the city of Charleston, Grocer... born in the electorate of Hannover in Germany, and came into this state 14 years ago, resided uninterruptedly in Charleston, and was there married to his present wife, a native of South Carolina, and with whom he has issue now alive...took oath in due form before the Inferior City-Court at Charleston, the clerk whereof gave him a certificate of citizenship 24 Nov 1802

I do certify that on 15th May 1796, Mr. Barnerd Dierson, and Elizabetn Krebs, daughter of the late John Krebs, were joined together in matrimony and have now three children viz.
Margaret Catharine born 16 March 1797
Elisabeth born 15 Aug 1798
John William born 8 Dec 1799
24 Nov 1802. John Christian Faber, Minister of the German church.

Committee Report 1785 #9

Dr. Alexander Baron was never a citizen of this state...recommend that his petition be granted.

Committee Report 1783 #21

In the Senate 9 March 1783

The Committee to whom was referred the Petitions of several British Merchants residing in Charles Town, who have entered into agreement with the late Governor Mathews to depart this State in six months as also the Petitions of several persons British subjects found in said Town when General Greene took possession of it, and were paroled; and who have severally petitioned to be permitted to become subjects of this state. Report That your committee having taken every means of information they could devise to form a true judgement of the characters & dispositions of the several petitioners; recommend as their opinion that the following British subjects, Merchants and others be granted the prayer of their Petition, that they be received as Citizens of this state, and that they take the Oaths of Abjuration and Allegiance vizt.

(on Parole)

William Gordon
Francis Speilman
Abraham Newton
John Frederick Fulker
Samuel Blakeley
John Willson
Samuel Graham
Solomon Woolf
Henry Harris
Andrew Smith
James Martin
William Parker
Francis Clark
Archibald Smith
William Watson
Thomas Matthews
John London
William Marshall
George Tunno
Peter Saul Ryan
John Askew
John Elihu Bay
John Bay
Thomas Richardson
Daniel Watson Turner
John Clark
Charles Knight
Joel Poinsett
Ralph Dawes
Lieut. Debardelban
John Nicholson
Robert Squib
Bernard Richardson
Henry Legge
Peter Mercellis
Thomas Pashley
John Geyer
Thomas Gibb
Samuel Watson
Nicholes Primrose
Joseph Purcell
Ebenezer John Collet
Thomas Blair
George Kiloh
Paul Hill
Gibbs Atkins
Collin McLennan
William Brisbane
Walter Keith

That the Petitions of the following British Merchants be Granted

John Kneeshaw
William Freeman
George Selby
James Gregorie
Laurence Campbell
William Blacklock
Michael John Sharris(?)
James LaMotte
John Walker
Thomas & Seth Foster
Thomas Sheaffe
Thomas Withers
William Robertson
Alexander Bethune
James Warrington
Alexander Shirras
Joseph Taylor

That the Petitioners Andrew Miller, Ralp MacNair and Thomas Hooper be permitted to remain in this State until they apply to the Legislature of North Carolina (where they resided) at the next meeting of the General Assembly of that State and if accepted of as Citizens of the same, then they prayer of the Petitioners be granted, otherwise to depart this state on or before the 1st day of March 1784.

That the Petitioner William Scarborough be permitted to remain in this State, untill he applies to the Legislature of Masechusetts (sic) (From whence he came) and if admitted a Citizen there, then the prayer of the Petition be granted other wise to depart this State on or before 1st March 1784

That the Petitioners Andrew Turnbull and James Penman be permitted to remain in this State, untill the first day of March 1784 under the same restrictions as the British Merchants under compact with Govr. Matthews.

That the Petitions of the following Persons be rejected

John Collet
Peter Dunworth
John Francis Ley
John Thomson
John Hepburn
Samuel Taylor
George McCauley
James Herriott
William Simpson
James Phillips
James Arkle
Charles Goodwin

Committee Report 1789 #44

The Petitions of Richard Wrainch, Patrick Byrne, Edward Butler, George Harding, James Lambert Ransier, John Luckie, Andrew McCulley, Andrew Smith, Paul Smith, James Burgess and John Fitzpatrick and John Hartley Harris...recommend that they be granted. 18 Feb 1789

Committee Report 1789 #25

Petitions of Ed'd Butler, Paul Smith, Jas Burges, George Harding, John Fitzpatrick, And'w Smith, Rich'd Wrainch, Patrick Byrne, John Hartley Harris and James Down...recommend that they be granted. 28 Feb 1789

Committee Report 1790 #28

Petition of Jan Molich, the reverend Paul Coste...in the opinion of the committee, the Legislature is not competent to pass a Law for naturalization....8 Jan 1790

Committee Report 1800 #128ov

This committee report was a result of an election which was under question held in Charleston. Apparently each voter was questioned and asked to prove his citizenship or to give a statement thereof. Those persons who had been naturalized are listed with the pertinent information. Also as an exhibit in this report is found a list of aliens admitted citizens in the courts of sessions for Charleston District and the Federal Courts for South Carolina District.

Benjamin Booth...was admitted four or five years ago as a citizen of this state in the City Court.

Richard Brennan...is a citizen of the U. S. admitted in this state about 3 years ago.

Andrew Ballon...was admitted a citizen of the US about 8 years ago in the City Court

<u>Committee Report 1800 #128ov</u> (contd.)

Alexander Crawford was admitted a citizen of this State in the year 1783.

Collin Campbell...admitted a citizen of this state 18 August 1784 and produced a certificate from Judge Burke.

Thomas Cave...admitted a citizen in the Court of Common Pleas in the year 1798.

John Braer(?) became a citizen in this state in 1796 or 1797 in the Federal Court.

Moise Abrahams became a citizen in the Federal Court 7 May 1799.

Alex: Henry answers he became a citizen 2 March 1796...Federal Court.

Sam: Hyams answers he is a citizen admitted 18 June 1799...Court of Common Pleas.

M'Millan Campbell was admitted a citizen 17 June 1799 in the Court of Common Pleas.

Thos Coveney took oath of allegiance in New York, December 1783.

Thos Malcolm admitted in the Court of Common Pleas 1799.

John Dixon...produced a certificate from the Court of Common Pleas 13 June 1799.

Hume Greenhill became a citizen in the City Court 1794.

Wm Purvis...produced a certificate from the Court of Common Pleas, 29 May 1799.

George Viand...born in Germany, came here in 1780, took the oath of allegiance the second year after his arrival.

Caleb Robson...produced a certificate from the Federal Court, 1 June 1799.

Charles Crockray...a citizen, Court of Common Pleas, 1798.

Alex: England...became a citizen of the US, Court of Common Pleas, 1799.

John Sollee...admitted a citizen '93 or '94, certificate from the Secretary's office, dated 28 July 1798.

George Ruth...became a citizen in the City Court about 10 years ago.

James Hyndman...became a citizen of the US, Court of Common pleas, 1799.

J. G. Wurdeman, became a citizen in the Federal Court, 17 June 1799.

Charles McKenna...became a citizen in Dumfries in Virginia, in 1799, in the Federal Court.

Moses C. Levy, became a citizen of the US, 17 Feb 1795, from the City Court, but was admitted by Judge Grimke ten years before....

Committee Report 1800 #128ov (contd.)

Duncan Love...became a citizen in Philadelphia before the Mayor about 8 years ago.

Peter Hippers became a citizen of the US, 6 March 1795, City Court.

Samuel Nobles was admitted a citizen about 6 years ago in Federal Court.

Henry Moses arrived in Philadelphia in 1776 and became a citizen there in 1779, arrived in Charleston and became a citizen in 1783.

Thos Gordon...became a citizen of the U. S. in 1794 in City Court.

Daniel Cruckshanks...became a citizen in the City Court in '91 or '92.

Wm Liddy (or Lebby)...took oath of allegiance in 1784 before Judge Burke.

John Roche...produced a certificate from the court of Common Pleas 18 June '99.

Lewis Peigne...produced a certificate from Federal Court, 17 Sept 1792.

Wm Cruckshanks...born in Scotland, came to Charleston in 1793, then about 18 years of age.

Mordecai Lyon...came to Charleston in 1782, took oath of allegiance.

Humphry Marks...came to Charleston, Nov. 1783.

Malcolm McKay (spelt McCoy)...a native of Scotland, arrived in U. S., 1793.

Samuel Wyllie...admitted a citizen of the U. S. in the year 1794 in Richmond (Virginia).

Andrew Gordon...became a citizen of the U. S. in Philadelphia in October 1785.

Wm Gordon...became a citizen, 18 June 1798, in the Court of Common Pleas.

John M'Clure became a citizen of the U. S., Feb 1795.

James Gibson became a citizen in Philadelphia, August 1793.

Robert Walker became a citizen of the U. S., 13th June 1799, and produced a certificate from the Court of Common Pleas.

James Pearson...became a citizen in the year 1798.

John Otto, a citizen of the U. S., produced a certificate 12 August 1782, became so in Pennsylvania.

Robert Foster...became a citizen of the U. S., in the City Court, 1796.

George W. Annelly...admitted a citizen in Federal Court, 1796.

Edward McCann...became a citizen in the State of New York.

Committee Report 1800 #128ov (contd.)

Edward Poulton...born in Bermuda, came to Charleston, August 1785, married a wife of Charleston.

Richard R. Stowe...admitted a citizen in Charleston, Court of Common Please, 18 June 1799.

Alexander Stewart...became a citizen in the Court of Common Pleas, 18 Feb 1795.

Peter Wyatt...admitted in the Court of Common Please, about 2 years ago.

James Broadfoot admitted a citizen 30 January 1799, in the Court of Common Pleas.

"Aliens admitted Citizens in the Courts of Sessions for Charleston District, and the Federal Courts for South Carolina District"

Names of Persons	When Admitted
Adcock, John	October 15th 1792
Adancourt, Francis	August 12th 1796
Alexander, George	November 7th 1796
Albony, John B.	September 20th 1797
Anneley, George W.	" " "
Allan, John	November 29th 1797
Allan, William	January 16th 1798
Anthony, Joseph	May 22d 1798
Alexander, Abraham	September 4th 1798
Abrahams, Moses	May 8th 1799
Aveilhe, Jean B.	June 17th 1799
Bell, Alexander	May 13th 1790
Brodie, Alexander	May 25th 1792
Berry, Francis Hubert	September 17th 1792
Bradford, Thomas	May 27th 1794
Brailsford, Samuel	June 6th 1794
Blair, James	July 7th 1794
Boate, Thomas	September 29th 1795
Burch, Jeremiah	January 18th 1796
Brownlow, John	May 17th 1796
Bowen, William Jones	September 20th 1796
Booker, Anthony	September 26th 1796
Buckley, Philip	September 28th 1796
Branagan, John	October 8th 1796
Bordez, Des Roy	January 16th 1797
Bailey, David	January 17th 1797
Bailey, Thomas	January 17th 1797
Bethell, David	February 11th 1797
Blair, John	November 29th 1797
Bladen, Thomas D.	February 2d 1798
Brown, Samuel S.	March 9th 1798
Ballantine, David	March 21st 1798
Bigam, William	March 30th 1798
Broadfoot, William	April 2d 1798
Budde, Marke	September 19th 1798
Burk, Walter	February 25th 1799
Back, John M.	February 25th 1799
Carroll, James Parsons	June 12th 1792
Crowley, Michael	September 17th 1792
Conyers, John	March 15th 1795
Cameron, Samuel	September 10th 1795
Coste, John Paul	September 17th 1795
Campbell, John	January 19th 1796

Committee Report 1800 #128 ov (contd.)

Names of Persons	When Admitted
Charet, Prudent B.	July 6th 1796
Coleman, George	August 17th 1796
Corlett, Thomas	January 17th 1797
Cooper, Peter	March 25th 1797
Crawley, Elisha	July 6th 1797
Caruth, Peter	November 30th 1797
Cooling, Thomas	March 26th 1798
Cocquereau, Charles	April 2d 1798
Craig, William	April 2d 1798
Courtin, Francis	June 17th 1799
Carew, William	June 17th 1799
Dansie, Abraham	January 21st 1794
Dalton, Peter	January 19th 1796
Downes, Jeremiah	March 24th 1796
Dawson, Thomas	July 6th 1796
Duffy, Henry	September 20th 1796
Duffy, Barnard	September 20th 1796
Dowthwaite, Abraham	September 23d 1796
Dowthwaite, Robert	September 23d 1796
Dennison, James	December 12th 1796
Dupuy, Claude	December 14th 1796
Dickinson, John F.	March 20th 1797
Doran, William	August 10th 1797
Duffus, John	November 18th 1797
Dubois, Charles L.	April 2d 1798
Drevais, Adam	April 2d 1798
Dunn, John	May 29th 1799
Duffy, Patrick	June 17th 1799
Deishman, Charles F.	" " "
DeGrasse, Alexander F. A.	" " "
Dunn, John	June 17th 1799
Duncan, George	" " "
East, Richard S.	April 29th 1795
Eyhrick, John M.	September 25th 1795
Eakins, David	January 23d 1796
Ewing, Alexander	October 28th 1797
Forrest, Michael	September 23d 1791
Fraser, Alexander	January 24th 1792
Farquhar, Robert	September 1st 1795
Forster, John Robert	January 23d 1796
Findlarer(?), William	November 18th 1796
Fleury, Jean Baptiste	May 11th 1797
Faxley, Hance	March 4th 1799
Fullerton, James	June 14th 1799
Ferguson, Whitney J.	June 14th 1799
Geslain, Jacques B.	May 31st 1793
Greenhoff, Jacob	May 20th 1796
Grove, Samuel	July 20th 1796
Gernon, William	May 16th 1797
Glaister, Robert	November 14th 1797
Graham, John	November 29th 1797
Grochan, John	December 11th 1797
Goldie, Walter	December 11th 1797
Grehan, Edward	January 15th 1798
Greaser, Lewis A.	January 25th 1798
Gibson, William	January 25th 1798
Gregorie, James Junr.	" " "
Hoban, James	September 23d 1791
Hammet, William	May 29th 1793
Hart, Daniel	May 26th 1794
Hendrickson, Betze	September 17th 1794

Committee Report 1800 #128ov (contd.)

Names of Persons	When Admitted
Hands, John	September 29th 1795
Harlow, Thomas	October 1st 1795
Haslett, John	January 22d 1796
Henry, Alexander	March 2d 1796
Hutton, James	April 20th 1796
Harrison, William P.	September 1st 1796
Hunter, William	September 20th 1796
Horn, Gustavus	September 23d 1796
Hunter, James	October t6h 1796
Howard, Benjamin	October 25th 1796
Haasman, Jacob	May 16th 1797
Hamilton, James	July 24th 1797
Hyndman, Robert A.	September 25th 1797
Hass, Francis	December 11th 1797
Hoffman, Michael	December 11th 1797
Hanley, James	May 1798
Harrison, Samuel	May 8th 1798
Hunter, John	May 31st 1798
Hattier, Henry	July 27th 1798
Hill, Alexander	June 13th 1799
Hrabousky, John S.	" " "
Henriques, Elijah	August 20th 1800
Johnston, Robert	February 22d 1791
Johnson, Edward	October 7th 1795
Johnson, Thomas	October 20th 1795
Jaillet, Pierre	March 24th 1796
Johnston, Edward	March 25th 1797
Johnston, James	July 14th 1797
Innes, Daniel	August 10th 1797
Jeffords, Richard	March 21st 1798
Jones, Joshua	May 5th 1798
Johnston, Hugh	June 1st 1798
Joyce, Thomas	June 17th 1799
Josephs, Joseph	" " "
Kennedy, Andrew	March 27th 1794
Keptenius, Gustavus	August 31st 1796
King, James	January 16th 1797
Kennedy, Samuel	December 11th 1797
Kelly, Daniel	June 19th 1798
Levi, Moses	June 20th 1795
Laing, Peter	March 15th 1795
Lee, William	March 30th 1795
Laughton, William	January 18th 1796
Lewis, John	April 12th 1796
Levy, Nathan	September 23d 1796
Lamonte, James	October 6th 1796
Lane, Robert	December 11th 1797
Lamb, John	" " "
Love, John	March 20th 1798
Lecat, Francis	August 15th 1798
Lanchester, Henry	" " "
LeSeigneur, Vincent	June 17th 1797
McDonald, William	May 26th 1792
McKenzie, Andrew (Grocer)	
Murphy, James	September 15th 1794
McCormick, William	March 26th 1795
Marshall, William	July 7th 1795
McIntosh, John	October 30th 1795
McCaul, William	April 1st 1796
McDowell, Alexander	April 1st 1796
Manson, John	April 20th 1796

Committee Report 1800 #128ov (contd.)

Names of Persons	When Admitted
Maclean, John	April 20th 1796
Miller, James	June 17th 1796
Maurice, George	September 3d 1796
McBlair, William	September 20th 1796
McCormick, William	" " "
McEvoy, James	September 22d 1796
Martin, Patrick	October 4th 1796
Michau, John	" " "
Moore, Richard	" " "
Maxwell, John	October 6th 1796
McDonnald, Christopher	October 8th 1796
Merrieult, John Francis	October 25h 1796
Munroe, James	February t7h 1797
Morley, Mathew	March 20th 1797
Miller, Francis	April 13th 1797
McWilliams, Archibald	July 3d 1797
McCaw, Peter	November 14th 1797
Moran, Nicholas	November 29th 1797
Molcomson, Samuel	January 16th 1798
Myers, Michael	January 19th 1798
Moureau, Lewis Francis	February 2d 1798
McFarlane, Alexander	February 8th 1798
Martin, Frederick	April 2d 1798
Mulligan, Barnard	May 10th 1798
Mair, Thomas	May 27th 1798
McKay, Mungo C.	May 31st 1798
Monson, James	June 1st 1798
McCay, Joseph R.	July 26th 1798
McMillan, Alexander	" " "
Mullen, Daniel	June 13th 1799
Mooney, Patrick	" " "
Mulligan, John	" " "
McAffe, John	" " "
Macadam, James	June 17th 1799
Nightingale, Henry	September 21st 1792
Nobbs, Samuel	March 29th 1796
Neill, William	January 16th 1797
Napier, Thomas	July 17th 1800
O'Hara, William	February 7th 1797
Olivers, Thomas	August 11th 1797
Prince, Charles	
Peigne, Louis	September 17th 1792
Patterson, Hugh	September 17th 1793
Pourie, Bazil	January 23d 1794
Phillips, Benjamin	September 15th 1794
Pogson, Milward	December 14th 1795
Phepoe, Richard	April 20th 1796
Petit, Peter	November 7th 1796
Philips, John	March 20th 1797
Pearce, Charles	April 22d 1797
Parsons, Thomas	November 14th 1797
Peters, Henry	March 11th 1798
Powers, George	May 29th 1799
Pelletant, John A.	June 17th 1799
Quay, Alexander	September 20th 1796
Richards, William	March 12th 1791
Read, Robert	March 21st 1796
Rust, Peter	May 19th 1796
Rabb, John	" " "
Roberts, John	April 13th 1797
Ross, James	July 1st 1797

Committee Report 1800 #128ov (contd.)

Names of Persons	When Admitted
Reardon, Dennis	April 2d 1798
Reilly, Charles	April 3d 1798
Reid, James	" " "
Reynoulds, David	December 11th 1798
Roland, Henry	February 20th 1799
Rodick, James	May 4th 1799
Robson, Caleb	June 1st 1799
Reilly, Thomas	June 14th 1799
Scott, William	July 1st 1793
Stephens, Samuel	August 21st 1793
Sweetman, M. C.	June 6th 1794
Shroudy, William	July 17th 1794
Steedman, Charles	September 18th 1794
Skrimsher, William	September 25th 1794
Sanchez, Bernardine	November 1st 1794
Spinks, William	March 17th 1795
Shroudy, William	July 7th 1795
Smith, William	January 18th 1796
Sangster, John	February 8th 1796
Scott, Thomas	April 20th 1796
Schepeler, George	April 29th 1796
Salgado, Joseph R.	September 14th 1796
Sweeny, Bryan	September 22d 1796
Sergeant, John P.	September 29th 1796
Slater, Thomas	March 25th 1797
Sangster, William	October 27th 1797
Smith, Francis	" " "
Swart, John	December 11th 1797
Smith, James	January 21st 1799
Spies, John J.	" " "
Sudermann, John	" " "
Steinmetz, Jacob E. A.	June 13th 1799
Smith, William	" " "
Schofield, Edmond	" " "
Stevenson, James	" " "
Schirmer, John E.	June 14th 1799
Smylie, Andrew	July 7th 1800
Taylor, Alexander	February 5th 1793
Tate, James	September 5th 1795
Tate, John	February 9tn 1796
Toutain, Peter N.	December 2d 1796
Tombarel, John F.	December 14th 1796
Taylor, Alexander	February 22d 1797
Tromp, James	October 27th 1797
Thom, Robert	August 14th 1798
Truchelet, Joseph	" " "
Thomey, William	" " "
Taylor, John	March 18th 1799
Thompson, James	July 7th 1800
Vesey, Abraham	September 11th 1795
Villeneuve, John B.	May 16th 1797
Watson, Joseph	September 19th 1794
Williams, Cornelius	January 18th 1796
Wilson, William	January 19th 1796
Williams, William	February 1st 1796
Wilson, John	March 21st 1796
White, James	August 2d 1796
Walker, Thomas	September 20th 1796
Walsh, Edmond	September 28th 1796
Wilson, William	January 21st 1797
Wilkins, James	March 26th 1797

Committee Report 1800 #128ov (contd.)

Names of Persons	When Admitted
Wade, William	March 26th 1797
Waller, Bayfield	January 19th 1798
Winker, John H.	May 10th 1798
Wipon, Joseph	" " "
Westbury, John	January 2d 1799
Wurdeman, John G.	June 17th 1799

From Statutes at Large of South Carolina, by Cooper & McCord.

Volume V, pp. 15-16, No. 1357: Whereas, Richard Champion, a native of England, hath, by his petition to the Legislature, humbly prayed that he and his descendants might be partakers of the rights, privileges and immunities which the said natural-born citizens of the State of South Carolina do enjoy.... And whereas, Hugh Alexander Nixon, a native of Ireland, hath served in the navy of this State for upwards of three years, in the late was against Great Britain, and hath ever since resided in the said State.... In the Senate House, 27 March 1787.

Volume V, page 92, No. 1432: Whereas, the Reverend Thomas Frost, of Charleston, and the Reverend Thomas Mills, of Saint Andrew's parish, in the State aforesaid, have, by their respective petitions to the Legislature, humbly prayed that they and their descendants respectively may be partakers of all the rights, privileges.... In the Senate House, 4 February 1788.

I, 304-5: S. C., Lexington District, John Snyder petitioned on behalf of himself and his wife Catherine and his children Henry, Catherine, and Rebecca...his family are subjects of the emperor of Austria. He was born in the village of Bermingham, Hesse Cassel, he left 1 September 1833, and arrived in Charleston, 24 December 1833, and was 40 years of age last Christmas; wife Catharine, 39, son Henry 15, Catherine 11, and Rebecca, 18 months... 1 October 1835

I, 305: S. C., Lexington District, 3 October 1835. Christopher Maibus, born in the Village of Grueszin, Hesse Cassel, arrived in Charleston 24 December 1833, has two children, son Rinehart, 15, and Eustus, 12.

I, 306: S. C., Lexington District, Henry Degenhart, appeared 30 September 1835, born in the village of Erbenhaussen, Dannstadt, left there 1 July 1830, arrived in New York the last of August 1830, and came to Charleston, December 1831. He was 24, on 7 July last.

O, 19: S. C., Abbeville District, James Martin, about 22 years of age, born County Antrim, Ireland, arrived in Charleston, 13 December 1841, and 16 December arrived at Hamburgh, and removed to Abbeville District...is now made a denizen...20 March 1844.

O, 60: S. C., Abbeville District, William Henderson, about 23 years of age, born County Antrim, Ireland, arrived in Charleston, 23 November 1840, removed to Columbia, and then to Abbeville District, about 18 December the same year...is now made a denizen...20 March 1844.

O, 167: S. C., Abbeville District, Nancy Keown, widow, about 43 years of age, born County Monehan, Castle Blany, Ireland, emigrated with her husband Thomas Keown, in August 1825, sailed from Belfast, landed in Charleston, February 1827...her husband died 19 June this year, a naturalized citizen...12 July 1844.

P, 26: S. C., Williamsburgh District: Edward J. Porter , a native of Ireland, took oath of allegiance, 7 July 1845.

A-3, 438: Gabriel William Heintzen became a citizen...17 March 1786.

A-3, 444: James Parsons Carroll made a citizen, 12 June 1792.

B-3, 87: Michael Forrest became a citizen, 23 September 1791.

B-3, 278: William McDonald was made a citizen, 28 May 1792.

B-3, 388: Caleb Smith became a citizen, 7 November 1789.

B-3, 388: William Inglesby became a citizen, 10 March 1785.

B-3, 69: Charles Prince was made a citizen, 20 September 1791.

C-3, 81-2: William Smith, late a subject of the King of Great Britain, became a citizen, 4 August 1788.

C-3, 83: James Ellison took the oath of allegiance to this state 15 September 1788, and had taken oaths of allegiance to Georgia, July 1783.

C-3, 238: 9 March 1793, John Frederick Kern, gentleman, became a citizen.

C-3, 462: 16 September 1793, William Scott, late of the Kingdom of Ireland, became a citizen.

C-3, 517: 20 August 1793, William Muir of Charleston, merchant, was made a citizen.

C-3, 518: 29 May 1790, Thomas Hunter, now of Charleston, mariner, a native of Great Britain, was made a citizen.

C-3, 530: 6 June 1794, James Blair was made a citizen.

C-3, 560: October term, 1794, Andrew Kennedy,was made a citizen.

C-3, 540: William Skrymsher, 26 September 1794, was made a citizen.

D-3, 342: William Taylor, of Black Swamp, Beaufort District, was made a citizen, November term 1793.

D-3, 413-414: January term, 1794, on 7 February 1794, John Sewart of Charleston, was made a citizen.

D-3, 456: 26 May 1794, Daniel Hart was made a citizen.

D-3, 476: 6 June 1794, Samuel Brailsford, was made a citizen.

D-3, 497: Michael Copenger Sweetman, 6 June 1794, was made a citizen.

D-3, 511: Benjamin Phillips, 16 September 1794, was made a citizen.

D-3, 512: Jacob Harmon Lange made a citizen, 8 January 1793, in the Court of Wardens.

D-3, 512: Bazil Pourie, 24 January 1794, was made a citizen.

D-3, 512: 6 February 1794, Joseph Hargreaves of Charleston was made a citizen.

D-3, 514: 16 September 1794, James Murphy was made a citizen.

D-3, 517-8: September term 1790, Robert KirkPatrick was made a citizen.

D-3, 522: January term 1793, 1 January 1793, James Gairdner was made a citizen.

D-3, 524: Nathaniel Bliss Neale, 4 November 1794, was made a citizen in the Court of Wardens.

D-3, 576: 15 March 1795, Peter Laing, late of Great Britain, was made a citizen.

E-3, 60: Court of Wardens, 25 June 1793. Mr. Archibald Duncan took the oath of a citizen.

E-3, 359: 16 September 1794, S. C., at a court in Charleston, 16 September 1794, Betze Hendrickson, made application to become a citizen.

E-3, 404-5: Bernardino Sanches took oath in U. S. Court, 31 October 1794.

E-3, 440: George Alexander Wylie made application to become a citizen, 13 February 1795.

E-3, 441: 17 February 1795, Charles Henry Mey made application to become a citizen.

E-3, 443: 30 January 1794, William Lenox of the city of Charleston, made application to become a citizen.

E-3, 482-3: January 6th 1795, John Caig made application to become a citizen.

E-3, 483: Court of Wardens, January 18th 1793, Albert Danhnken, took the oath of a citizen.

E-3, 488: Court of Wardens, 5 February 1793, Hyam Levy took the oath to become a citizen.

E-3, 494: Jean Francis de Lorme, a native of France, has been admitted a citizen, 24 June 1793.

E-3, 499: South Carolina) Elias Smerden, late a subject of the
Charleston) King of Great Britain, is become a
citizen, 13 July 1789.

E-3, 510: 5 June 1795, William Carson took the oath of a citizen.

E-3, 560: South Carolina District, At a Court of Admiralty, 7 July 1795, Capt. William Shrowdy made oath....

E-3, 564: S. C., Charlestown District, on 13 July 1795, John Garrett, late of Ireland, prayed to become a citizen...

E-3, 613: S. C., City of Charleston. Court of Wardens, 11 Nov 1794, William Lauthausen took the oath of allegiance.

F-3, 2-3: S. C., in the common pleas, 16 February 1795, William Foster made application to become a citizen.

F-3, 3: S. C., In the Common Pleas, 16 February 1795, William Boyd made application to become a citizen.

F-3, 3-4: S. C., in the Common Pleas, 16 February 1795, John Gillespie, made application to become a citizen.

F-3, 4-5: S. C., in the Common Pleas, 16 February 1795, James Henderson, made application to become a citizen.

F-3, 24-25: S. C., in the Common Pleas, 21 February 1794, William Kevon made application to become a citizen.

F-3, 32: 16 February 1795, John McClure made application to become a citizen.

F-3, 32: 18 March 1795, William Spinks, late of the Kingdom of Great Britain, made application to become a citizen.

F-3, 38: At a Federal Court...29 March 1795, William McCormick, late of the Kingdom of Great Britain, made application to become a citizen.

F-3, 42: Court of Wardens, 6 June 1794, Thomas Meilloy, took the oath of allegiance.

F-3, 42: 12 March 1795, Oliver Carter, son of George Carter, phisician, made application to become a citizen.

F-3, 59-60: Certificate from New York, 13 January 1795, that Robert Benson is a citizen.

F-3, 60: Court of Wardens, 5 July 1793, Toney Fairman took the oath of a citizen.

F-3, 79-80: At a Federal Court, 28 April 1795, Richard Sears East, late of the Kingdom of Great Britain,made application to become a citizen.

F-3, 121-122: 2 June 1795, Herman Justur Floto, late of the Dukedom of Brunswick, gentleman, prayed to become a citizen.

F-3, 121: 3 February 1795, Joseph Simond made application to become a citizen.

F-3, 128-9: 21 June 1795, Cornelius O'Driscoll, late of Ireland, prayed to become a citizen.

F-3. 129-130: 22 June 1795, John Perinchief, late of the Island of Bermuda, prayed to be a citizen.

F-3, 130: 13 February 1795, Robert Mitchell made application to become a citizen.

F-3, 133: At a Federal Court, 7 July 1795, William Marshall made application to become a citizen.

F-3, 137-138: 11 July 1795, Jacques Staack, late of the city of Hamburgh, one of the Hanse Towns, made application to become a citizen.

F-3, 130-131: 13 February 1795, Edwin Gairdner made application to become a citizen.

F-3, 228: 13 October 1795, Henry Corner, late of Ireland, applied for citizenship.

F-3, 296: Certificate from Baltimore County, Maryland, 24 July 1793, that Frederick Roux was naturalized.

F-3, 297: 7 February 1795, George Henderson made application to become a citizen.

F-3, 308: Court of Wardens, 28 March 1794, Alexander Shaw took oath.

F-3, 357: 13 February 1795, Charles Carrere made application to become a citizen.

F-3, 377: 29 February 1796, Jean Matthieu Cousin de Longchamps made application to become a citizen.

F-3, 358: at Federal Court, 9 February 1796, John Tait, late of North Britain, made application to become a citizen.

F-3, 411-2: at Federal Court, 17 June 1796, James Miller, late of Eyreshire in North Britain, made application to become a citizen.

F-3, 412-3: 27 June 1796, Robert Murray made application to become a citizen.

F-3, 443-444: at Federal Court, 5 July 1796, Prudent Brice Charet, late of Nantz in Brittany, made application to become a citizen.

F-3, 458: Court of Wardens, 9 October 1792, Daniel McCawley took the oath of citizenship.

G-3, 46-7: At Federal Court, 1 September 1795, Abraham Vesey, late of the Island of Bermudas, took the oath of citizenship.

G-3, 128-9: on 4 Feb 1796, at a Court of Common Pleas in Charleston, Henry Lusher, late of the Island of Bermuda made application to become a citizen.

G-3, 129-30: on 5 Feb 1796, in Court of Common Pleas of Charleston, John Fraser, late of Scotland, made application to become a citizen.

G-3, 130-1: 11 Feb 1796, at a Court of Common Pleas at Charleston, appeared William Kewans, late of Scotland, made application to become a citizen.

G-3, 197: January term 1795, Common Pleas. On 6 Feb 1795, appeared Francis Depeau, and made application to become a citizen .

G-3, 197: January term 1796, Common Pleas. 13 Feb 1796, Nicholas Fitzsimmons made application to become a citizen.

G-3, 331-2: At a Federal District Court, 31 August 1796, Gustavus Keptinius, late of Lapland in Sweden, appeared and took the oath of a citizen.

G-3, 332: Court of Wardens, 20 December 1793, Zephaniah Kingsley took oath of allegiance.

G-3, 335: At a Court of General Sessions, 23 September 1796, Gustavus Horn, late of Sweden, took the oath of a citizen.

G-3, 337: In Common Pleas, January term 1795, on 13 February 1795, Lewis Chupien made application to become a citizen.

G-3, 342: on 21 October 1796, at Common Pleas for Charlestown District, Angus Bethune made application to become a citizen.

G-3, 405-6: At a Federal District Court, 20 March 1797, appeared Matthew Morley, late of Bristol in Old England and applied for citizenship.

G-3, 406-7: On 28 March 1797, appeared Alexander McDowall and made application to become a citizen.

G-3, 436-7: 3 May 1797, At a Court of Common Pleas in Charleston, George Mason appeared and applied for citizenship.

H-3, 11: 16 Feb 1796, at a Court of Common Pleas appeared Rene Laporte, late of the Republic of France, prayed for citizenship.

H-3, 40-41: January term, in Common Pleas. On 13 February 1795, Constant BoisGerard made application for citizenship.

H-3, 54-55: On 24 May 1796, at a Court of Common Pleas in Charleston, Alexander McClure, late of Scotland, applied for citizenship.

H-3, 56: 10 June 1796, at a Court of Common Pleas in Charleston, Ewing Ritchie applied for citizenship.

H-3, 62-63: At a Federal Court, 20 April 1796, Thomas Scott, late of Ireland,applied for citizenship.

H-3, 63: at a Court of Wardens, October 10, 1794, Joseph Heylegar took the oath of allegiance.

H-3, 143: At a Court of Equity for Charleston,Georgetown & Beaufort, 15 September 1796, James Moles, late of Scotland, applied for citizenship.

H-3, 152: At a Federal Court, 5 October 1796, Benjamin Howard, late of Somersetshire in England, made application for citizenship.

H-3, 152-153: At a Federal Court, 25 October 1796, John Francis Merrieult, late of Natchez in West Florida, made application for citizenship.

H-3, 202-203: Charlestown District, 24 January 1797, at a Court of Common Pleas, John Andrew Graeser applied for citizenship.

H-3, 215: At a Federal Court, 22 February 1797, Alexander Taylor, late of North Britain, applied for citizenship.

H-3, 217: January term 1795. In the Common Pleas, 16 February 1795, William Monies, gentleman, made application for citizenship.

H-3, 232: At a Federal Court, 11 May 1797, John Baptiste Fleury, late of Rouen in France, made application for citizenship.

H-3, 337: At a Federal Court, 20 July 1796, Samuel Grove, late of Great Britain, made application for citizenship.

H-3, 352: At a Federal Court, 17 September 1792, Jean Paul Coste made application for citizenship.

H-3, 425-6: At a Federal Court, 11 December 1797, John Grochan, 28 years old, late of Bourdeaux, department of Gironde, French Republic, made application for citizenship.

H-3, 426-7: At a Federal Court, 11 December 1797, Walter Goldie, about 6' 3", late of the County of Nithdale, age 20 years, applied for citizenship.

H-3, 427-8: At a Federal Court, 11 December 1797, Robert Lane, 5' 8", late of Lymsham, Somerset, England, aged 31 years, made application for citizenship.

H-3, 457: At a Federal Court, 5 January 1798, Edward Graham, late of Dublin, Ireland, made application for citizenship.

I-3, 95-96: At a Federal Court, 7 February 1797, James Munroe, late of North Britain, Fifeshire, made application for citizenship.

I-3, 99: Charlestown District, 14 February 1797, at a Court of Dommon Pleas, John Thornhill, applied for citizenship.

I-3, 189: At a Court of General Sessions, 17 September 1794, Charles Steedman made application for citizenship.

I-3, 214: At a Federal Corut, 13 April 1797, Francis Miller, late of Great Britain, made application for citizenship.

I-3, 279-80: at a Court of Wardens, Christian Philip Knippling, took the oath of allegiance, 17 February 1795.

I-3, 279: At a Court of Common Pleas, 27 May 1797, Nicholas Darrell, prayed to be a citizen.

I-3, 430: At a Federal Court, 21 March 1796, Robert Read, late of Ireland, made application for citizenship.

I-3, 431: At a Federal Court, 3 April 1798, Charles Reilly, of the County of Cavan, Ireland, made application for citizenship.

K-3, 46-47: on 13 March 1797, at a Court of Common Pleas, John Thompson, applied for citizenship.

K-3, 65: At a Federal Court, ______ 1796, Peter Nicholas Toutain, late of Rouen in French Normandy, made application for citizenship.

K-3, 70-71: At a Federal Court, 10 August 1797, William Doran, late of Wexford, Ireland, made application for citizenship.

K-3, 76-77: January Term 1795. In Common Pleas, 13 February 1795, John Conrad Landolt made application for citizenship.

K-3, 87-88: At a Federal Court, 20 September 1797, John B. Albony, late of Martinique, made application for citizenship.

K-3, 113: At a Federal Court, 5 September 1797, Robert Augustus Hyndman, late of Ireland, made application for citizenship.

K-3, 113-4: At a Federal Court, 5 September 1795, James Tate, late of Great Britain, made application for citizenship.

K-3, 205: S. C., Georgetown District: on 20 March 1794, at a Court of Common Pleas in Georgetown, Roger Heriot applied for citizenship.

K-3, 215: Court of Wardens. April 1, 1794, Mr. Jacques Lambert Ransier, took the oath of allegiance.

K-3, 252-3: At a Court of General Sessions, 17 May 1797, Casper Christian Schutt was admitted a citizen.

K-3, 369: At a Court of Quarterly Sessions held at the Court House for the County of Princess Anne, 2 June 1794, George Burns, a native of Scotland, took the oath of Fidelity to the Commonwealth of Virginia....

L-3, 3-4: At a Federal Court, 2 January 1798, William Gibson, 5' 10", late of Moffat, County of Dumfries, North Britain, made application for citizenship.

L-3, 5: S. C., Charlestown District, on 22 January 1798, in the Common Pleas, John Whalley prayed for citizenship.

L-3, 7: At a Federal Court, 8 February 1798, Alexander McFarlane, late of Nova Scotia, made application for citizenship.

L-3, 19: S. C., Charlestown District, 2 March 1798, at a Court of Common Pleas, John Boissiere applied for citizenship.

L-3, 76: Court of Wardens, Mr. Benjamin Booth Jr. took the oath of allegiance, 17 February 1795.

L-3, 148: Charlestown District, At a Court of Common Pleas, 31 May 1798, John David Thomas prayed to be a citizen.

L-3, 140: 13 June 1798, in the Court of Common Pleas, appeared Richard Brenan prayed to be a citizen.

L-3, 169: Office of Common Pleas, January term 1795. 13 February 1795, John Sollee made application for citizenship.

L-3, 169-70: Charlestown District, on 28 July 1798, in the Court of Common Pleas, Joseph Ravara, lately of Genoa, prayed to be a citizen.

L-3, 260-1: 1 October 1798, at a Court of Common Pleas, Andrew Domonic Sabourin appeared and prayed to be admitted a citizen.

L-3, 321: At a Federal Court, 11 December 1798, appeared Mr. Peter Fisher, merchant, late of Glasgow in North Britain, and made application to become a citizen.

L-3, 355-6: 30 January 1799, at a court of Common Pleas, James Broadfott appeared and made application for citizenship.

L-3, 361-2: on 21 July 1798, at a Court of Common Pleas, appeared John Baptist Grand, and prayed that the court admit him a citizen.

M-3, 1: At a Court of Common Pleas, 16 February 1795, John Turnbull prayed to be admitted a citizen.

M-3, 64: 18 May 1796, John Rabb, late of the Kingdom of Ireland, took the oath of allegiance.

M-3, 103: At a Federal Court, 28 March 1798, William Broadfoot, 5' 8" high, late of the Shire of Galloway, in North Britain, about 19 years old, made application to become a citizen.

M-3, 120-1: 29 May 1799, at a Court of Common Pleas, William Purvis prayed to be admitted a citizen.

M-3, 125: S. C., Charlestown District, 13 June 1799, at a Court of Common Pleas, John Duffus prayed to be admitted a citizen.

M-3, 126: Court of Wardens, May 3d 1793. Frederick Khone took the oath of allegiance.

M-3, 140: Charlestown District, 13 June 1799, at a Court of Common Pleas, John Fowler, late of Scotland, prayed to be admitted a citizen.

M-3, 144: At a Federal District Court, 13 June 1799, Frederick Deishman, late of Bassum, Lower Hessia, made application for citizenship.

M-3, 168: January Term 1795, in the Common Pleas, 13 February 1795, Francis Canut, gentleman, made application for citizenship.

M-3, 180: Charlestown District, 12 June 1799, at a Court of Common Pleas, Hugh Cameron, prayed to be admitted a citizen.

M-3, 186: Charlestown District, 15 June 1799, Thomas Stephens, a native of Ireland, auctioneer, prayed to be admitted a citizen.

M-3, 273: At a Federal District Court, 17 June 1799, Francis Courtin, late of Paris, merchant, made application to become a citizen.

O-3, 205: William Smith, a native of the town of Kilmarnock, shire of Ayr, Kingdom of Great Britain, called Scotland, now of the City of Charleston, merchant...took the oath of a denizen.

O-3, 289: 10 June 1799, at a Court of Common Pleas, appeared Charles Kiddell, and petitioned to become a citizen.

O-3, 289-90: In the Court of Common Pleas, January term 1795; 16 February 1795, Laurence Faures the elder, made application to become a citizen.

O-3, 290: In the Court of Common Pleas, January term 1795, 18 February 1795, Walter Forsyth made application to become a citizen.

O-3, 317: At a Federal District Court, 19 March 1798, James Gregorie the younger, late of Glasgow in North Britain, made application to become a citizen.

O-3, 336: Charlestown District, 18 June 1799, at a Court of Common Pleas, Thomas Malcom, late of Ireland, Merchants Clerk, petitioned to become a citizen.

O-3, 428: In the Court of Common Pleas, January term 1795; 16 February 1795, Joseph Lewis made application to become a citizen.

O-3, 441: 21 December 1799, William Collier, born in Gloucestershire, Kingdom of Great Britain, 17 December 1772, arrived in Charleston, 28 May 1784....

O-3, 501: 10 June 1801, appeared Justus Angel, a native of the Island of Santa Cruz, lately a resident of Bermuda, took the oath of allegiance.

O-3, 628: Court of Wardens, 11 April 1794. Mr. Archibald McLachlan took the oath of allegiance.

O-3, 713-4: 19 January 1803, Richard Graves, desirous of becoming a denizen, born 16 June 1757 at Gravesend, County of Derry, Ireland, and for several years past resided at Hamburg Fort, County of Devon, Great Britain, arrived at Charleston, 13 day of this month, he has a wife, late Caroline Louisa Colleton, of this state, and six children, one son and five daughters Samuel Colleton Graves, aged 14; Sophia Louisa Colleton Graves, aged 13; Carolina Victoria Colleton Graves, aged 12; Louisa Catharina Colleton Graves, aged 9; Septima Sexta Colleton Graves, aged 5, and Olivia Septima Colleton Graves aged 2; family are still in England....

Q-3, 99: January term 1795, in the Court of Common Pleas, 16 February 1795, Patrick Mair applied for citizenship.

Q-3, 99-100: January term 1795, in the Court of Common Pleas, 20 February 1795, John Frederick Henning made application for citizenship.

Q-3, 141-142: Charleston District, 17 June 1799, at a Court of Common Pleas, James Sweeny, a native of Ireland, merchant, prayed to be admitted a citizen.

Q-3, 213-14: 12 December 1800, at a Court of Common Pleas, Louis Niroth, a native of the Dutchy of Litherania and late a reisdent in the city of Kiden, in the Dutchy aforesaid, applied to be a denizen.

Q-3, 270: 29 December 1799, John Douglas, a native of Scotland, and lately a resident in Edinburgh, took the oath of allegiance.

Q-3, 361: At a Federal Court, 17 June 1798, HenryRose, 5' 9" high, late of Leipzig in Saxony, Germany, merchant, 35 years old, made application to become a citizen.

Q-3, 370-1: At a Federal Court, 17 June 1799, Jean Baptiste Aveilhe, Engineer, native of Merarde, Dept. Du Gene in Gascogne, made application for citizenship.

Q-3, 373: At a Federal Court, 14 December 1796, Claude Dupuy, late of the Province of Languedock, made application for citizenship.

Q-3, 374: At a Federal Court, 17 June 1798, Frederick Curtins, merchant 5' 9" high, late of Brunswick in Germany, maimed in the middle finger of his left hand, made application to become a citizen.

Q-3, 374-5: Court of Wardens, 12 September 1794, Charles Watts, of Charleston, took the oath of allegiance.

R-3, 78-9: State of Georgia, County of Chatham. Francois Choman is a citizen of the USA...13 July 1797.

R-3, 80-81: Commonwealth of Massachusetts. Among the records of our Supreme Judicial Court holden at Tannton for the County of Bristol, on Tuesday preceding the last Tuesday in October 1795, John Francis Monosiet late of the Island of Hispaniola in the West Indies, has resided here more than two years....

R-3, 328: 2 February 1798, at a Court of Common Pleas, William Milligan petitioned for citizenship.

R-3, 653: At a Federal Court, 28 September 1803, Thomas Gunnry Bushford, merchant, late of Belfast, Ireland, 27 years old, made application for citizenship.

R-3, 649-51: At a Federal Court, 4 August 1803, Thomas Marshall, aged 52 years, late of St. Clements in the city of London, brought up a Comedian, applied for citizenship.

R-3, 708: At a Federal Court, 23 January 1804, Hugh Crombie, about 23 years of age, late of Belfast, Ireland, merchant, applied for citizenship.

R-3, 727: At a Federal Court, 23 February 1804, Joseph Claret, aged 38 years, late of Narbonne, in Languedoc, France, merchant, made application for citizenship.

R-3, 728-9: At a Federal Court, 23 February 1805, John Williamson, aged 26, late of London, merchant, made application for citizenship.

R-3, 737-8: At a Federal Court, 24 July 1804, Henry Duvivier Peire, aged 27 years, late of St. Mare, Island of St. Domingo, applied for citizenship.

S-3, 245: At a Federal Court, 7 September 1803, Henry Harrison, aged 28, late of Cheshire in England, made application for citizenship.

S-3, 248-9: At a Federal Court, John Thomas grocer, aged 30 years late of Wales, made application for citizenship , 8 September 1803.

S-3, 249: At a Federal Court, 20 September 1802, Simon Felix Gallagher, minister of the Roman Catholic Church, late of the city of Dublin, Ireland, aged 40 years, made application for citizenship.

S-3, 303: At a Federal Court, 28 October 1803, Peter Manoel, 29 years of age, late of LaSalle in Languedoc, made application for citizenship.

S-3, 303-4: At a Federal Court, 28 October 1803, Auguste St. Martin, aged 25, late of St. Domingo, made application for citizenship.

S-3, 306: At a Federal Court, 13 November 1803, John Fyholl, merchant, aged 34 years, late of Fleshinge in Holland, made application for citizenship.

S-3, 322: At a Federāl Court, 12 December 1803, Charles Verguin, about 35 years of age, late of Toulon, France, merchant, made application for citizenship.

S-3, 344-5: At a Federal Court, 19 March 1803, John Nicholas Leboucher, late of Rouen, France, made application for citizenship.

S-3, 420: At a City Court in Charleston,7 May 1804, George Jean Bernard, of the City of New Orleans, made application for citizenship.

U-3, 16: At a Federal District Court, 19 March 1804, appeared Bertrand Depeau, aged 24, late of Bayonne in France, merchant, and made application to become a citizen.

U-3, 17-18: At a Federal District Court, 21 March 1804, Stephen Lefevre, aged about 71, late of Beaurdis, France, merchant, made application to become a citizen.

U-3, 31: At a Federal District Court, 19 April 1804, appeared Josiah Richards, aged 42 years, late of Wales, Kingdom of Great Britain, mariner, and made application to be made a citizen.

U-3, 47-48: 14 May 1804, at a Court of Common Pleas at Charleston, appeared George Lushar, a native of the Island of Bermuda, and prayed to be admitted as a citizen.

U-3, 48: 14 May 1804, at a Court of Common Pleas at Charleston, James Kennedy Douglas, a native of North Britain, prayed to be admitted a citizen.

U-3, 51-52: At a Federal District Court, 27 May 1798, Thomas Mair, near six feet high, late of Shetland, North Britain, made application to become a citizen.

U-3, 130-131: At a Federal District Court, 23 January 1796, John Campbell, born in North Britain, made application to become a citizen.

U-3, 135-6: Louisiana, New Orleans: on 18 June 1804, before me Francis Munhall, N. P., appeared Jean Baptiste Noel Marie de La Hogue, of said city, merchant, and says he was a citizenship of this place previous to 30 April 1803, and has resided in the province of Louisiana for more than 18 months.

U-3, 183: At a Federal District Court, 30 August 1804, "Francois dite Duboc" aged 34 years, late of Havre de Grace, Normandy, baker, made application to become a citizen.

U-3, 210: Certificate of Citizenship for Alexander Christie, late a subject of Great Britain, 1 August 1788.

U-3, 220-1: At a Federal District Court, 11 October 1804, Juhan Pedre Humeau, aged 33, late of New Orleans, merchant, made application to become a citizen.

U-3, 224-5: At a Federal District Court, 16 October 1804, Richard Hancock, aged 29 years, late of London, mariner, made application to become a citizen.

U-3, 229: At a Federal District Court, 10 December 1804, James Douglas, aged 32 years, late of Galloway, in Scotland, mariner, made application to become a citizen.

U-3, 230: At a Federal District Court, 27 August 1804, John Ambrose Dacqueny, aged 26 years, late of Honfleur in Normandy, France, a printer, made application to become a citizen.

U-3, 238-9: At a Court of Common Pleas, 31 January 1805, Robert Jackson, now of Charleston, merchant, applied for denizen...born 6 August 1780 in London, county of Middlesex, Great Britain, he resided in London about 19 years, removed to Charleston, January 1799....

U-3, 240: At a Court of Common Pleas, 4 February 1805, Morris Goldsmith of Charleston, desirous of becoming a denizen... born 23 April 1784 in London, and resided there till October 1799, and arrived in Charleston a few months after....

U-3, 243: At a Federal District Court, 12 October 1804, Marc Domec, aged 50 years, late of Cape Francois, Island of St. Domingo, merchant, made application to become a citizen.

U-3, 249-50: Certificate from the State of New York, that John Jousset applied for citizenship, 31 July 1798.

U-3, 297: At a Federal District Court, 22 April 1805, Henry Kunst, aged 27 years, late of Hanover, Germany, brought up to the mercantile business, made application to become a citizen.

U-3, 297-8: At a Federal District Court, 26 February 1805, John Witt, aged 27 years, a native of Holstein, in Denmark, made application to become a citizen.

U-3, 343: S. C., Greenville District: At March Term 1804, John Choland LaPlace, a native of St. Domingo, and an inhabitant of Greenville District, made application to become a citizen.

U-3, 364: At a Federal District Court, 23 November 1805, Hamilton Wilson, aged 25 years, late of the County of Down, Ireland, brought up to the mercantile line, made application to become a citizen.

U-3, 388: At a Federal District Court, 20 January 1806, Charles Della Torre, 28 years of age, late of Rowena in Italy, Mathematical Instrument Maker, made application to become a citizen.

U-3, 388-9: At a Federal District Court, 2 January 1806, John Baserga, formerly of Milan in Italy, merchant, petitioned to become a citizen.

U-3, 400: At a Federal District Court, 14 April 1806, John Pickenpack, aged 34 years of age, late of Hanover, grocer, made application to become a citizen.

U-3, 404-5: U. S., Orleans District, on 24 February 1806, Rene Gerard, deposes that he was an inhabitant of Louisiana previous to 30 April 1803....

U-3, 404: Maryland. At a court held for the Western Shore, at Annapolis, 2nd Tuesday in May 1794, Charles Asselin Dessables, was naturalized.

U-3, 431-2: At a Federal District Court, 25 July 1805, Laurence Frost, aged 34, late of Norway in the Kingdom of Denmark, mariner, made application to become a citizen.

U-3, 468-9: At a Federal District Court, 26 June 1805, Lewis Salomon, aged 40, late of Nantes in France, merchant made application to become a citizen.

U-3, 521: S. C., Georgetown District, on 5 April 1799, at a Court of Common Pleas, Robert Nesbitt appeared and prayed to be a citizen.

V-3, 6-7: At an Inferior City Court held in Charleston, 2 January 1804, Rene Delarue of the Republic of France, made application to become a citizen.

V-3, 7: At a Federal District Court, 14 November 1797, Robert Glaister, late of Cumberland in England, made application to become a citizen.

V-3, 8: At a Federal District Court, 23 January 1804, John Garnier, about 36 years of age, late of Rochfort, Republic of France, merchant, made application to become a citizen.

V-3, 26-27: S. C., Charleston District: On 7 February 1804, at a Court of Common Pleas, John Ker, a native of Cork in Ireland, prayed for citizenship.

V-3, 30: 9 May 1803, At a Court of Common Pleas for the District of Charleston, William Smith, a native of Scotland, merchant, prayed to be a citizen.

V-3, 31: At a Federal District Court, 10 February 1804, Peter Sartoris, aged 24 years, late of Geneva in Switzerland, made application to become a citizen.

V-3, 38-9: At the Inferior City Court in the city of Charleston, 7 March 1804, Jean Pebarte of St. Domingo, made application for become a citizen.

V-3, 45: At a Federal District Court, 19 March 1804, Peter Bournos, aged 23, late of St. Domingo, merchant, made application to become a citizen.

V-3, 46: At a Federal District Court, 19 March 1804, John James Le Bourg, aged 55, late of Quillebuff, Normandy, France, mariner, made application to become a citizen.

V-3, 46-7: At a Federal District Court, 19 March 1804, Peter Roger Girette, aged 40 years, late of Havre de Grace, mariner, made application to become a citizen.

V-3, 47-8: At a Federal District Court, 20 March 1804, David Wallace, aged 36, of Middlesex County, Great Britain, mariner, made application to become a citizen.

V-3, 48: At a Federal District Court, 21 March 1804, Peter John Duboc, aged 45, late of Normandy, France, made application to be made a citizen.

V-3, 49: At a Federal District Court, 21 March 1804, James Vegan, aged 39, late of Normandy, France, merchant, made application to become a citizen.

V-3, 49-50: At a Federal District Court, 5 September 1803, John Peter Chazal, a seaman and mariner, late of Cape Francois, St. Domingo, made application to become a citizen.

V-3, 65: At a Federal District Court, 16 April 1804, Joseph Durbec, aged 40, late of the Republic of France, brought up in the mercantile line, made application to become a citizen.

V-3, 65-6: At a Federal District Court, 16 April 1804, Paul Griot, aged 34, late of France, mariner, made application to become a citizen.

V-3, 68: On 12 January 1804, at a Court of Common Pleas in Charleston, Francois Faure, a native of France, prayed to be a citizen.

V-3, 73: At an Inferior City Court, 6 March 1804, held in Charleston, James Quin of Ireland, made application to become a citizen.

V-3, 96: At a Federal District Court, 11 June 1804, Jacob Nathan, aged 38 years, late of Nancy, Province of Louaine, France, merchant, made application to become a citizen.

V-3, 97: At a Federal District Court, 11 June 1804, Christopher Duboc, aged 35 years, late of Blaye, France, merchant, made application to become a citizen.

V-3, 109: on 21 May 1804, at a Court of Common Pleas in Charleston, Nicholas David Roquet, a native of the city of La Rochelle in France, prayed to be admitted as a citizen.

V-3, 121: At a Federal District Court, 23 February 1804, Thomas Wrench Naylor, late of Middlewich, Cheshire, England, made application to become a citizen.

V-3, 121: At a Federal District Court, 24 July 1804, Jonathan Lucas Senior, aged 51 years, late of Northumberland, England, a Millwright, made application to become a citizen.

V-3, 157: At a Federal District Court, 19 January 1796, William Wilson, aged 29 years, late of the County of Antrim, Ireland, mariner, made application to become a citizen.

V-3, 232-3: At a Federal District Court, 17 March 1805, Isabella Perrie, aged about 40, late of the Parish of Wick, County of Caithness, North Britain, midwife, made application to become a citizen.

V-3, 235: On 10 January 1804, at a Court of Common Pleas, Alexander Sinclair, a native of Perthshire in Scotland, prayed to be admitted as a citizen.

V-3, 242-3: On 2 June 1798, at a Court of Common Pleas, Charles Francis Norroy prayed to be a citizen.

V-3, 255-6: On 20 May 1805, at a Court of Common Pleas, Peter Bernard Boutan, a native of Roquelaure in France, aged 35, prayed to be admitted a citizen.

V-3, 257-8: North Carolina, Newbern District, Superior Court, January term 1805. Read the petition of Alexander Allen to become a citizen, 23 January 1805.

V-3, 258-9: On 7 June 1805, at a Court of Common Pleas, Hugh Hutchinson, a native of Ireland, mariner, aged 39, prayed to be admitted a citizen.

V-3, 259: On 11 June 1805, at a Court of Common Pleas, Mitchell Colin, a native of Scotland, prayed to be admitted as a citizen.

V-3, 283: On 6 June 1805, Eugene Reardon, now of Charleston, gentleman, desirous of becoming a denizen...born in the Town of Millstrut, County of Cork, Ireland, arrived in Charleston October 1803....

V-3, 401: S. C., York County. At an Intermediate Court, 8 May 1798, Jonathan Beatty took the oath to qualify as a citizen.

V-3, 416: At a Federal District Court, 11 December 1804, Jean Cabos, aged 47 years, late of Rochfort in France, Jeweller, made application to be made a citizen.

V-3, 427-8: At a Federal District Court, 20 January 1806, John Ker, aged 27, a native of Invernesshire, North Britain, petitioned to become a citizen.

V-3, 430: At a Federal District Court, 13 January 1806, Patrick McOwen, about 25 years of age, late of Loughkeen, County of Tipperary, Ireland, merchant, made application to become a citizen.

V-3, 477: At a Federal District Court, 27 August 1806, Loder Needham Rees, Doctor of Medicine, late of Oxfordshire, Great Britain, aged 24, made application to become a citizen.

V-3, 477: At a Federal District Court, 19 March 1806, Francis Bremar the younger, aged 22, late of London, made application to become a citizen.

V-3, 498: At a Federal District Court, 29 September 1806, Richard Stone Blayney, aged 29 years, late of Nauturich, Cheshire, England, merchant, made application to become a citizen.

V-3, 502: At a Federal District Court, 14 October 1806, Neil McNeill, aged 25, late of Sterlingshire, Great Britain, merchant, made application to become a citizen.

V-3, 502: At a Federal District Court, 14 October 1806, Peter Fayolle, aged 38 years, late of Rions, dept. of Geronde, France, a Dancing Master, made application to become a citizen.

V-3, 512-3: At an Inferior City Court at Charleston, 3 November 1806, Charles C. Tamores, of Berlin, made application to become a citizen.

V-3, 524: S. C., Marion District. At a Court of Common Pleas, 4 November 1806, Andrew Paul, a native of Scotland, aged 42, prayed to be admitted as a citizen.

V-3, 525: George Reid, Notary Public, in Charleston, certifies that Timothy McCormick, born in Ireland, 5'8" high, dark hair, grey eyes, and pitted with the small pox, is a citizen, 13 March 1798.

H-3, 31: At a Federal District Court, 1 April 1796, William McCaul, late of North Britain, made application to become a citizen.

H-3, 153: At a Federal District Court, 7 November 1796, Peter Petit, late of Picardy in France, made application to become a citizen.

K-3, 232: At a Federal District Court, 11 August 1797, Thomas Oliver, late of Cardinganshire in England, made application to become a citizen.

U-3, 237: At a Special Circuit Court, 12 January 1805, at Charleston, appeared Alexander Champy, aged 22, late of Point Petre, Island of Gaudoloupe (sic), brought up a Physician, and made application to become a citizen.

U-3, 298: At a Federal District Court, 23 April 1805, Thomas Christian, late of Douglas, Isle of Man, brought up to the mercantile business, made application to become a citizen.

U-3, 326: On 28 May 1805, at a Court of Common Pleas, Stephen Charzotte, a native of France, aged 27, made application to become a citizen.

U-3, 327: At a Federal District Court, 27 March 1805, John André, aged 34, late of Havre de Grace, France, brought up to the mercantile business, made application to become a citizen.

W-3, 93: At a Court of Common Pleas, January term, 1795, 16 February 1795, Hector Depestre made application to become a citizen.

W-3, 102: At a Federal District Court, 27 March 1805, Abraham Rodrigues, aged 30 years, late of Bordeaux, France, brought up in the mercantile business, made application to become a citizen.

W-3, 197: On 22 May 1805, at a Court of Common Pleas, David McKelvey, a native of Ireland, aged 25 years, prayed to be admitted as a citizen.

W-3, 474: At the Inferior City Court of Charleston, 10 May 1803, John Corrie, a native of Scotland, made application to become a citizen.

W-3, 481-2: Maryland. By return of the General Court, for the western shore at Annapolis, 2nd Tuesday in May 1796, on December 1794, John L'Engles Senior, took the oath to become a citizen.

W-3, 520: At a Federal District Court, 6 July 1805, John Brooks, aged 23, late of Yarmouth in England, made application to become a citizen.

W-3, 536-7: At a Federal District Court, 22 July 1805, Martyn Alken, aged 43 years, late of London, brought up to the mercantile business, made application to become a citizen.

W-3, 563-4: On 7 June 1805, at a Court of Common Pleas in Charleston, James Peyton, a native of Ireland, mariner, aged 21, prayed to be admitted as a citizen.

W-3, 572: Joseph Marie Lequinio Kirblay applied to be a denizen... 50 years of age, a native of Sarzean, France, lately residing in the state of Georgia, has a wife Jeanne Marie Odette de Lewis, aged 42 years, a native of Toulouse, France, and another lady, Cecile Vandeperre formerly wife of Simon Hamot, but since legally divorced, aged 48 years, a native of Bruxelles in French Flanders, 5 November 1805.

W-3, 576: At a Federal District Court, 2 January 1806, George Charles Mazger, about 44 years of age, late of Frankfort, Germany, merchant, made application to become a citizen.

W-3, 576-7: at a Federal District Court, 14 January 1806, John M. Laviette, merchant, late of Grand Canary Island, about 32 years old, made application to become a citizen.

W-3, 577-8: At a Federal District Court, 14 January 1806, Peter Charles Beckennel, a seaman and mariner, late of Lorient in France, about 33 years old, made application to become a citizen.

W-3, 595: On 14 February 1806, at a court of Common Pleas, Peter Bouisseven, a native of Tholouse, France, aged 41 years, mariner, made application to become a citizen.

W-3, 600-1: Charleston District, on 8 February 1806, Marin Detargny, a native of Lawzann, in Pays de Vaux, Switzerland, aged 33, prayed to be admitted as a citizen.

W-3, 601-2: At a Federal District Court, 2 January 1806, Bertrand Lange, aged 35, late of Bayonne in France, merchant, made application to become a citizen.

W-3, 625: City of NewYork. Charles Pinsan, of the city of New York, merchant, appeared in the Mayors Court, 15 November 1804, a subject of France, made application to become a citizen.

W-3, 682: State of Maryland, at a General Court for the Western Shore at Annapolis, 14 May 1799, Christopher Lusher, a native of Great Britain, made application to become a citizen.

W-3, 704: At a Federal District Court, 29 August 1806, John Quay, aged 40, a mariner, late of the Isle of Mann, Great Britain, made application to become a citizen.

Y-3, 3-4: At a Federal District Court, 27 August 1806, William Corlett, aged 23 years, mariner, late of the Island of Jamaica, made application to become a citizen.

Y-3, 11-12: At a Federal District Court, 10 November 1806, Francis Roux, aged 20 years, late of Jeremie, Island of St. Domingo, brought up in the mercantile business, made application to become a citizen.

Y-3, 28: At a Federal District Court, 16 April 1804, Peter Laurans, aged 43, late of France, merchant, made application to become a citizen.

Y-3, 30: At a Federal District Court, 29 November 1806, Jonathan Heulan, a Physician, 23 years old, late of the City of St. Domingo, made application to become a citizen.

Y-3, 125: At a Federal District Court,24 September 1802, Bernard Mulligan, about 28 years old, late of Westmeath, Ireland, made application to become a citizen.

Y-3, 160-1: Court of Wardens, October 17, 1794. Whiteford Smith, a native of the Orkney Islands prayed to be admitted as a citizen.

Y-3, 161: On 12 May 1807, Edward Griffith, a native of the Island of St. Thomas, West Indies, lately arrived in South Carolina, wishes to become a denizen.

Y-3, 293: At a Federal District Court, 9 November 1807, Andrew Hannah, late of Gallowayshire in North Britain, merchant made application to become a citizen.

Y-3, 374-5: Alexander Black Waugh, now of Charleston, 7 January 1808, wishes to become a denizen...born in the City of London, arrived in Charleston, November 1806....

Y-3, 465: William Shaw, of Charleston, applied to Thomas Heyward Esqr., a Judge of the Court of Common Pleas, 7 August 1784, and took the oath of allegiance.

Y-3, 610: At a Federal District Court, 26 October 1808, John James Heulan, aged 37 years, late of Dondon, Cape Francois, Island of St. Domingo, teacher, of Music, made application to become a citizen.

Z-3, 2: At a Federal District Court, 16 April 1804, Peter Frederick Lafrentz, aged 28, late of the City of Hamburgh, merchant, made application to become a citizen.

Z-3, 6: At a Federal District Court, 18 March 1807, JohnMorrison, aged about 21 years, merchant, late of Fifeshire in North Britain, made application to become a citizen.

Z-3, 11-12: On 20 March 1807, Joseph William Garratt, wishes to become a denizen...born in Great Britain.

Z-3, 12: on 20 March 1807, William Musgrave, wishes to become a denizen...born in Great Britain.

Z-3, 13-14: On 20 March 1807, Charles Hodgkin, wishes to become a denizen...born in Great Britain.

Z-3, 21-22: At a Federal District Court, 28 March 1807, Thomas DeLisle, aged about 30, late of the Island of Guernsey, merchant, made application to become a citizen.

Z-3, 40: At a Federal District Court, 24 January 1804, Benjamin Leefe, aged 25, made application to become a citizen.

Z-3, 41-42: At a Federal District Court, 27 March 1805, James Huston, late of Harrymount, County of Down, Ireland, brought up a Taylor, made application to become a citizen.

Z-3, 45: At a Federal District Court,23 April 1807, John Vidal, aged 39, a Grocer, late of Montpellier, in France, made application to become a citizen.

Z-3, 49-50: At a Federal District Court, 24 May 1804, William Russell, aged 34 years, late of Aryshire, Scotland, merchant, made application to become a citizen.

Z-3, 49: U. S., Orleans District: on 17 April 1805, Antoine Boggiano, appeared in New Orleans, and stated that he was an inhabitant of this province before 30 April 1803.

Z-3, 50: At a Federal District Court, 4 May 1807, Charles Martin, aged about 28 years, late of Mitau, in the empire of Russia, merchant, made application to become a citizen.

Z-3, 51-52: At a Federal District Court, 27 April 1807, Francis Mabille, aged about 41, late of Valenciennes in France, merchant, made application to become a citizen.

Z-3, 62: On 15 May 1807, at a Court of Common Pleas in Charleston, Charles Harbert Menzy, a native of Douzier in the Province of Champaigne in France, aged 25, made application to become a citizen.

Z-3, 66: At a Federal District Court, 18 May 1807, Joseph Howell, aged about 27, late of Chester in England, merchant, made application to become a citizen.

Z-3, 69-70: At a Federal District Court, 20 May 1807, Nicholas Aspinall, aged about 24 years, late of London, merchant, made application to become a citizen.

Z-3, 79: At a Federal District Court, 30 may 1807, James Ball, aged about 35 years, late of London, merchant, made application to become a citizen.

Z-3, 80: On 2 June 1807, at a Court of Common Pleas in Charleston, Joseph Harper, a native of Norwich, County of Norfolk, Great Britain, aged 50 years, prayed to be a citizen.

Z-3, 81: At a Federal District Court, 27 May 1807, John James Joseph Miniere, aged about 39, late of Cape Francois, planter, made application to become a citizen.

Z-3, 81-2: At a Court of Common Pleas in Charleston, 7 February 1806, Benjamin Colman, a native of Jermany (sic), aged 32, a shop keeper, made application to become a citizen.

Z-3, 90-91: On 29 May 1807, at a Court of Common Pleas in Charleston, Peitro Primauesi, a native of Cassato, in Italy, aged about 36 years, prayed to be a citizen.

Z-3, 91: On 25 May 1807, at a Court of Common Pleas in Charleston, Anthony Marinone, a native of Sangedelle, State of Milan, Italy, aged 33, prayed to be a citizen.

Z-3, 92: On 2 June 1807, At a Court of Common Pleas in Charleston, Josephe Marzoratti, a native of the Town of Breignano in Italy, aged 37 years, prayed to be a citizen.

Z-3, 93-94: On 3 June 1806, at a Court of Common Pleas, in Charleston, George Sherwood, a native of Bristol, Island of Great Britain, mariner,aged 32 years, prayed to be a citizen.

Z-3, 118: At a Federal District Court, 30 August 1807, Archibald Armstrong, aged about 33 years, late of Dublin, Ireland, merchant, made application to become a citizen.

Z-3, 119: On 19 August 1807, Samuel Calborne, wishes to become a denizen..born in Great Britain.

Z-3, 132: Georgia District, May Term 1803; at Savannah, Jacques Dessenti L Homaca, a citizen of France, petitioned to become a citizen.

Z-3, 143: At a Federal District Court, 26 November 1807, Christopher Stanke, aged about 46 years, late of Hanover, Germany, mariner, made application to become a citizen.

Z-3, 150-151: At a Court of Common Pleas, 7 January 1808, John Hunt, desirous of becoming a denizen...born in Dumfernlein inScotland, arrived in Charleston, November 1803.

Z-3, 219-220: At a Federal District Court, 9 April 1808, Loui Coste, aged 44 years, merchant, late of Montpellier in France, made application to become a citizen.

Z-3, 313-314: At the Inferior City Court on 5 September 1808, Christian Pagels of Hanover in Germany, made application to become a citizen.

Z-3, 314: At the Inferior City Court, in Charleston, 5 September 1808, JohnRivers of Stetlin, Prussia, made application to become a citizen.

Z-3, 315: At the Inferior City Court in Charleston, 6 September 1808, John Christopher Jahns of Hanover, Germany, made application to become a citizen.

Z-3, 315: On 2 February 1808, at a Court of Common Pleas in Charleston, Hans Jochin Dresler, a native of Bramsledt, Denmark, aged 38, made application to become a citizen.

Z-3, 316: On 2 February 1808, At a Court of Common Pleas in Charleston, Henry Drewes, a native of Nammen in Prussia, aged 38 years, prayed to be a citizen.

Z-3, 317: At the Inferior City Court, in Charleston, 7 September 1808, Peter Elizabeth Benjn. Raynal, of the Province of Champagny, in Old France, made application to become a citizen.

G-3, 459: At a Federal District Court, 3 July 1797, Archibald McWilliams, late of Air in North Britain, made application to become a citizen.

B-4, 211: At a Federal District Court, 11 January 1810, Louis Peter Rabie, aged about 21 years, late of Cape Francois, but now of Charleston, made application to become a citizen.

B-4, 237-8: At a Court of Common Pleas in Charleston, 15 January 1810, Dennis Louis Cottineau de Kerloguen, late of Nantz in Britainy, aged 27 years, made application to become a citizen.

B-4, 254: At a Federal District Court, 24 June 1805, Samuel McCartney, aged about 25 years, late of Kirkcudbright, County of Galloway, North Britain, merchant, made application to become a citizen.

B-4, 254-5: At a Federal Circuit Court, 10 May 1798, John Henry Wienges, 5' 3" high, late of Bremen, made application to become a citizen.

B-4, 255: At a Federal District Court, 15 August 1805, William Cruckshanks, aged about 30 years, late of Murry Shire, North Britain, made application to become a citizen.

B-3, 260: Court of Wardens, Read petition of Patrick Duncan, to be admitted a citizen, 26 September 1794.

B-4, 260-1: At a Federal District Court, 2 January 1806, Alexander Kirk, aged about 24 years, late of Airth, Sterlingshire, Scotland, merchant, made application to become a citizen.

B-4, 263-4: At a Court of Common Pleas in Charleston, 25 January 1810, Louis Peyson, late of Paris, France, aged 33, jeweller, made application to become a citizen.

B-4, 264: At a Federal District Court, 29 January 1806, Henry Bryce, aged 23, late of Edinburgh, Scotland, merchant, made application to become a citizen.

B-4, 264: At a Federal District Court, 17 June 1799, James Macadam, merchant, late of the Parish of Drynum, by Glasgow in Scotland, made application to become a citizen.

B-4, 266: At a Federal District Court, 18 May 1807, Alexander Morton, aged about 28 years, late of Leith, in North Britain, merchant, made application to become a citizen.

B-4, 268: Thomas Salmond, Clerk of the Court of Common Pleas of the District of Kershaw, certify that Alexander Mathison was admitted a citizen at the Court of Common Pleas at Kershaw Court House, 5 Nov 1804.

B-4, 275-6: At a Federal District Court, 14 December 1807, Samuel Patterson, aged about 22 years, late of Coleraine in Ireland, merchant, made application to become a citizen.

B-4, 356: At a Federal District Court, 15 March 1810, Peter Esnard, aged 49 years, late of the Province of Daugounois, France, made application to become a citizen.

B-4, 367-8: At a Federal District Court, 31 October 1810, Mrs. Ann Blair Ker, aged about 21 years, late of Edinburgh in North Britain, made application to become a citizen.

C-4, 16-17: At a Court of Common Pleas in Charleston, 13 February 1809, John Reigne, late of Castillon, Province of Gugenne, in France, aged 45, merchant, made application to become a citizen.

C-4, 23-4: At a Federal District Court, 2 April 1798, Charles Coquereau, about 5' high, late of Rochelle, in the French Republic, made application to become a citizen.

C-4, 32: At the Inferior City Court, 6 July 1809, Daniel Donoghoe, of Ireland, 35 years old, made application to become a citizen.

C-4, 43-44: At an Inferior City Court,10 November 1808, George A. Schroebal, a native of Wirtemberg, Germany, made application to become a citizen.

C-4, 77-78: At the Inferior City Court at Charleston, 6 July 1809, Andrew Kippenberg, formerly of Goslar in Germany, aged 30, took oath....

C-4, 102-3: At the Inferior City Court, 1 January 1810, Peter Ulrick Bergsten, of Gottenberg in Sweden, aged 27, made application to become a citizen.

C-4, 104: At the Inferior City Court, at Charleston, 2 January 1810, Mathias Mehlen of Holstein in Germany, aged 36 years, made application to become a citizen.

C-4, 116: Michael King of Fifeshire, Scotland, took the oath of a citizen, 6 February 1810.

C-4, 230: At a Court of Common Pleas Thomas Cooper Vanderhorst, a native of England, but residing in Charleston, 25 January 1810, made application to become a citizen.

C-4, 365-6: At the Inferior City Court, 7 May 1810, Mary Huntington of Queens County, Ireland, aged 48 years, made application to become a citizen.

C-4, 338: At a Court of Common Pleas, 13 February 1809, Stephen Dubarry, late of Danzelas, Province of Begorre, France, aged 56 years, Shopkeeper, made application to become a citizen.

C-4, 568-9: At a Federal District Court, 4 September 1802, Isaac Lewis,late of London, merchant, made application to become a citizen.

C-4, 569-70: At the Inferior City Court, 5 July 1811, Peter McPherson, a native of Greenock, Scotland, aged 32 years, a tallow chandler, made application to become a citizen.

C-4, 603: At a Court of Common Pleas, Christopher Happoldt, 23 September 1811, of Charleston, butcher, desirous of becoming a denizen...born in Braunspah in Germany, arrived in Charleston, __ October 1809.

C-4, 608-9: City of New York. Certificate 13 February 1808 that Anthony Charlson, renounced fidelity to the King of Prussia, and took oath of a citizen.

C-4, 701: On 22 February 1812, William Twaits, a native of London, wishes to become a denizen....

C-4, 746-7: At a Federal District Court, 24 May 1811, Henry H. Moore, aged 32, Schoolmaster, late of the County of Kerry, Ireland, made application to become a citizen.

C-4, 752: At the Inferior City Court, 4 November 1811, John Christian Frederick Miller, a native of Strout, Duchy of Brunswick, aged 31, grocer, made application to become a citizen.

C-4, 762: At the Inferior City Court, 5 May 1812, James Descleaux, a native of Sept in Languedoc, France, aged 47, made application to become a citizen.

C-4, 777-8: At a Court of Common Pleas, 1 June 1812, Alexander Placide, late of Bordeaux in France, aged 55, made application to become a citizen.

C-4, 786-7: At the Inferior City Court, 5 March 1810, James Morrison, a native of Scotland, made application to become a citizen.

C-4, 793-4: At the Inferior City Court, 6 July 1812, Johann Lewis Linser, a native of Neider Veassel on the Rhine, Kingdom of Prussia, made application to become a citizen.

E-4, 20-1: At a Court of Common Pleas, 8 March 1811, Hugh Maguire, now of Charleston, merchant taylor, desirous of becoming a denizen...born in the town of Fentona in County Tyrone, Ireland, arrived in Charleston, 29 March 1808....

E-4, 24-5: At a Federal District Court, 13 November 1807, John Magrath, aged about 27 years, merchant, late of Waterford, Ireland, made application to become a citizen.

E-4, 25: At a Federal District Court, 18 March 1811, Martin William Hand, a mariner, aged about 30 years, late of Stelten in Prussia, made application to become a citizen.

E-4, 31: At a Federal District Court, 19 March 1806, James Wilson, aged 24 years, late of Dublin in Ireland, physician, made application to become a citizen.

E-4, 40-1: At a Court of Common Pleas, 3 April 1811, John Pyne, now of Charleston, desirous of becoming a denizen... born County Cork, Ireland, and for several years previous to his arrival in America, resided in the town of Nenagh, County of Tipperary...arived in Charleston, 28 February 1808.

E-4, 62-3: At a Federal District Court, 27 March 1811, Madame Bointe Plane, Veuve Deonna, late of Chamberi, Capital of Savoy in France, aged about 60 years, made application to become a citizen.

E-4, 63: On 3 February 1804, At a Court of Common Pleas, Jonathan Lucas Junior, a native of the village of Egermont, County of Cumberland, aged 29 years, prayed to be a citizen.

E-4, 79: At a Court of Common Pleas, January term 1795, 16 Feb. 1795, Alexander Nisbit, made application to become a citizen.

E-4, 160: At a Court of Common Pleas, 7 June 1811, Jeremiah Murray, late of Farnane, County of Waterford, Ireland, aged 28 years, made application to become a citizen.

E-4, 236: At a Court of Common Pleas, 24 January 1812, John Maillet, late of Copenhagen, Denmark, made application to become a citizen.

E-4, 240: At a Court of Common Pleas, 21 January 1812, Robert Magwood, took oath of allegiance.

E-4, 284: At the Inferior City Court, 4 March 1812, Mathias Probzt, a native of Bremen, aged 41 years, a mariner, made application to become a citizen.

E-4, 472-3: At a Federal District Court, 21 September 1812, Alexander Black Waugh, aged 27 years, a merchant, late of London (who has been admitted a denizen) made application to become a citizen.

E-4, 508-9: At a Federal District Court, 19 November 1812, Placide LeChartier, mariner, aged 26 years, late of Morlaix in France, made application to become a citizen.

E-4, 510: At a Federal District Court, 19 November 1812, Pierre Charriol, mariner, aged 42 years, late of Lisbourne, France, made application to become a citizen.

E-4, 578: Court of Wardens, 10 October 1794, James McDowall, took oath of allegiance.

E-4, 584: At a Federal District Court, 5 March 1813, Johan Myers, mariner, aged 35 years, late of Westphalia in Germany, made application to become a citizen.

E-4, 585: City of New York. Robert Wallace, 3 October 1811, took oath...from Great Britain.

E-4, 585: At a Federal District Court, 5 June 1812, George Hall, aged about 32 years, merchant, late of Roxburghshire, North Britain, made application to become a citizen.

G-4, 133-4: At a Federal District Court, 14 June 1799, Jacob Eberhard August Steinmetz, late of Etree in East Friesland, made application to become a citizen.

G-4, 187-8: At a Federal District Court, 16 August 1805, Paul E. Lorent, merchant, aged 24, late of Hamburg, made application to become a citizen.

G-4, 197: At a Federal District Court, 31 August 1813, Thomas Cousins, aged 26, merchant, late of London,made application to become a citizen.

G-4, 246: At the Inferior City court of Charleston, 3 November 1813, William Scott, a native of County Armagh, Ireland, aged about 37 years, mill wright, made application to become a citizen.

G-4, 265: At a Federal Special Circuit Court, 11 December 1813, Robert Aitchison, merchant, aged 29, late of Roxburghshire, North Britain, made application to become a citizen.

G-4, 555: At a Federal District Court, 17 April 1815, Jean Baptist Pellessier, aged 24, late of Cape Nicholas Niole, St. Domingo, made application to become a citizen.

H-4, 57-8: At a Federal District Court, 7 May 1814, John Wilson, engineer and surveyor, aged about 24 years, late of Lanarkshire, North Britain, made application to become a citizen.

H-4, 68: At a Court of Common Pleas, 28 May 1814, Louis Sollier, late of Porssy, France, aged 42, merchant, made application to become a citizen.

H-4, 182: At a Federal District Court, 8 May 1815, Francis Girard, aged about 32 years, late of Bordeaux, in France, merchant, made application.

H-4, 185-6: At a Federal District Court, 10 May 1815, Francis Tirvert, merchant, late of Ypreville, Normandy, France, made application to become a citizen.

H-4, 210: At a Federal District Court, 12 April 1815, Antoin Pretens, aged 40, late of Marseilles, France, made application to become a citizen.

H-4, 223: At a Federal Circuit Court, 13 June 1815, Claudius Bicais, aged 52, cabinet maker, late of Provence in France, made application to become a citizen.

H-4, 226-7: At a Federal District Court, 12 July 1815, Laurence Marie Rabot, late of Denan, in Brittany, France, formerly a resident in Louisiana when ceded to the United States, made application to become a citizen.

H-4, 384: S. C., Georgetown District. Richard Hynes, a native of the County of Dublin, Ireland, about 40 years of age, took the oath of a denizen...20 October 1815.

H-4, 420-1: At a Court of Common Pleas, 22 December 1815, Joseph George Holman, now of Charleston, desirous of becoming a denizen...born London, lived in England and Ireland, arrived in April last in this state.

N-4, 3-4: At a Court of Common Pleas, Peter Duval, made oath that he was born in the Province of Chartret, Normandy, 25 April 1770, resided in France and St. Domingo...wishes to become a denizen...7 February 1817.

N-4, 44-45: Petition of James Hevey, a native of Langford County, Ireland, a resident of South Carolina, aged 36, desirous of becoming a denizen...30 January 1817.

N-4, 45: John Corcoran, a native of the County of Longford, Ireland, aged 28, desirous of becoming a denizen...30 January 1817.

N-4, 47: On 6 March 1817, Felix Lewis L'Herminier, a native of Paris, and formerly a resident of Guadaloupe, West Indies, desirous of becoming a denizen.

N-4, 79: Petition of James Ferrall, a native of the County of Longford, Ireland, aged 38, desirous of becoming a denizen...30 January 1817.

N-4, 148: 21 April 1817, Lewis Glenet, a native of France, took oath of a denizen.

N-4, 257: Petition of Frederick Schwach, a native of Saxony, Germany, arrived in the United States 11 years ago, is 29 years old, desirous of becoming a denizen...28 May 1817.

N-4, 262: James Sutcliffe took oath...he is a native of London, about 30 years of age, wife Sophia a native of Canterbury, aged 26 years, and a daughter Ruth, a native of Gravesend, County Of Kenry, about 3 years of age...28 May 1817.

N-4, 418-9: At a Federal District Court, 22 October 1805, Peter Barreyre, aged about 36, late of Bordeaux, France, baker, made application to become a citizen.

N-4, 424: Petition of Charles Henry Dencken, has resided in the U. S. for 2 years, in South Carolina...desirous of becoming a denizen...a native of the Dutchy of Mecklenburgh... 16 March 1818

O-4, 7:At a Court of Common Pleas, Arnold John Baptiste Fourgeaud, took oath, he is a native of Charoux, Commune of St. Aquitin, Department of La Dordogne, France, aged about 31 years, arrived in United States, 19 February 1808...desirous of becoming a denizen...22 May 1817.

O-4, 50: Jean Dufort appeared in the Court of Common Pleas... born in Casset, Dept. of Lallier, France, 27 July 1778, arrived in Charleston, 15 March 1804, has married here and had a child Marie Urane Dufort...desirous of denizenship...1 July 1817.

O-4, 256: At a Court of Common Pleas, 24 January 1818, John Rudolph Herbers, a native of Germany, took oath to be a denizen....

O-4, 276-7: Petition of Just Viel, a native of France, aged about 25 years, arrived in this city, November 1815, has resolved on being a citizen...10 February 1818

O-4, 278-9: Peter Buchanan, a native of Perthshire in Scotland, took oath to become a denizen. 10 February 1818.

O-4, 371: State of New York: Francis LaRoussiliere, a subject of the Emperor of the French, applied to become a citizen... 10 September 1817

O-4, 377: At a Court of Common Pleas, George Jacob Lorent, born in the city of Hamburgh, Germany, and formerly residing in Gottenburgh in Sweden, took oath of a denizen...9 May 1818.

R-4, 40: At a Federal District Court, 9 January 1816, John Aberegg, watchmaker, late of Canton of Bern, Switzerland, made application to become a citizen.

R-4, 342-3: Charles Marshall, a native of Lincolnshire, Great Britain, aged 33 years, wishes to become a denizen... 16 October 1819.

R-4, 447: At a Court of Common Pleas, 28 February 1805, Pierre Jacques Baunay, a native of Havre de Grace, France, aged 27 years, prayed to be admitted a citizen.

R-4, 510: At a Federal Circuit Court, 13 September 1808, Raymond Clissey, aged 46 years, coach and harness maker, late of Badeaux, France, made application to become a citizen.

R-4, 522: S. C., Laurens District: John Pearson took the oath of a denizen...21 April 1820.

R-4, 544: At a Court of Common Pleas, John A. Groves, a native of England, aged 39, resided in this state for 17 years, took oath of a denizen...17 May 1820.

R-4, 544-5: At a Federal District Court, 16 May 1820, Conrad Wienges, late of Bremen, Germany, made application to become a citizen.

R-4, 545: At a Federal District Court, 16 May 1820, Jacob Wienges, late of Bremen, Germany, made application to become a citizen.

R-4, 593: City of New York. Charles Frederick Volckman, 4 April 1807, remounced allegiance to the King of Prussia, and took the oath of a citizen.

T-4, 64-5: 14 December 1819, Petition of Michael O'Donovan, a native of Grenand, County of Limerick, Ireland, has resided since 24 May 1803 in this state, desirous of becoming a denizen....

T-4, 295: Petition of John Maxton, a native of Perthshire, Parish of Crieff, Scotland, __ August 1820, took the oath of a denizen.

T-4, 295-6: At a Court of Common Pleas, petition of John Saml. Peake, a subject of the United Kingdom, desirous of becoming a denizen.

T-4, 339: Petition of Frederick Blum, a native of Germany, aged about 32 years, arrived in Charleston __ December 1811, desirous of becoming a denizen...7 November 1820.

T-4, 460: N. C., County of Montgomery, Court of Pleas & Quarter Sessions, 1st Monday in April 1814, Thomas Higham, a native of England, made application to become a citizen.

T-4, 535-6: At a Federal District Court, 10 May 1815, Peter Augustine Deguer, late of Nantz, Brittany, made application to become a citizen.

U-4, 1: Petition of Thomas Still, a native of Armagh, Ireland, aged about 30 years, has resided in this state five years, desirous of denizenship...12 April 1820.

U-4, 143: At a Court of Common Pleas, John Lockhart, a subject of the Emperor of Austria, a native of Germany, hath resided in this state since 1805, aged 45 years, wishes to be a denizen...12 December 1820.

U-4, 176-7: At a Federal District Court, 26 January 1821, Henry Mohr, late of Grünendeich, Hanover, made application to become a citizen.

U-4, 182: Petition of Robert Harret, a native of Ireland, arrived in Charleston, 1817, wishes to be a denizen, 26 January 1821.

U-4, 275-6: 13 June 1821, Robert Dubois, a native of Havre de Grace, France, took oath of a denizen.

U-4, 477-8: At a Court of Common Pleas, Thomas How, born and formerly resided in the town of Berwick upon Tweed, in Great Britain, aged about 21 years, desirous of becoming a denizen...11 October 1822.

W-4, 260: At a Court of Common Pleas, 31 May 1822, Patrick Mead, born in the County of Limerick, Ireland, but brought up in the County of Cork, arrived in Charleston 15 April 1822, desirous of becoming a denizen.

W-4, 326: On 20 January 1823, The Right Rev. Doctor John England, a native of Ireland, took the oath of a denizen.

W-4, 331-2: At a Court of Common Pleas, Francis Henderson, took the oath of a denizen...born in Great Britain.

W-4, 334: Petition of Christian David Happoldt, a native of Wirtemberg, Germany, has resided in Charleston since 8 November 1816, desirous of becoming a denizen.

W-4, 340: S. C., Abbeville District, Petition of James R. Ware, a native of London, admitted a denizen...19 March 1823.

W-4, 356: S. C., Marion District, John McClenaghan, born in the town of Belfast, Ireland, aged about 30, took oath of allegiance, 30 October 1823.

W-4, 405: Petition of John Hall, born in Roslin, County of Edinburgh, Scotland, 19 August 1785, is over 38 years of age, has a wife Susannah Hall, aged 33, born in Edinburgh, and has five children: Janet, aged 12, born in London; John age 11; Jemima, aged 8; Margaret, aged 5, born at Brighton; and Jane, one year old, born in Versailles in France...23 April 1824.

W-4, 467-8: At a Federal District Court, 5 August 1825, Pascal Etienna Meinadier, late of Montpellier, France, made application to become a citizen.

Y-4, 155: Petition of John Scannel Jr., born Clonakilly, Ireland, late of Liverpool, but now of Charleston, desirous of becoming a denizen...25 October 1822.

Y-4, 166: 12 November 1822, Thomas J. Summers, a native of London, sail maker, aged 36, and has a wife...desirous of becoming a denizen.

Y-4, 258: At a Federal District Court, 14 April 1823, John F. Hageman, late of Bremen, Germany, made application to become a citizen.

Y-4, 276-7: Petition of Joseph Urban, a native of France, arrived in Charleston, 1819, now is 27 years old, desirous of becoming a denizen.

Y-4, 287: At a Federal District Court, 24 March 1813, John Andrew Battker, shop keeper, aged 31 years, late of Wittenberg, Mecklenburg, made application to become a citizen.

Y-4, 317: On 5 August 1823, James McKenzie, a native of Roxburghshire, Scotland, and lately resident in Grenock, but now of Charleston, plaisterer, aged 29, has a wife aged about 20, whose place of nativity is Charleston...took oath of a denizen.

Z-4, 4: Petition of William Davenport, born in Guernsey, brought up to the business of the Sea, and is now about 37 years of age, born 14 September 1786, arrived in this State, March 1816, wishes to become a citizen, 23 January 1823.

Z-4, 51: Petition of Thomas Price, a native of Wales, aged about 44 years, arrived in Charleston, March 1810, from London, it is his intention to become a citizen, 15 February 1823.

Z-4, 51: Petition of Alice Cassidy, a native of Ireland, where she formerly resided, for many years a resident of South Carolina, wishes to become a denizen...28 February 1823.

Z-4, 80: City of New York. Charles A. Bollen who hath resided here five years, at a court held 16 August 1804, took oath to be a citizen.

Z-4, 276-7: At a Court of Common Pleas, Frederick Schaffner, now of Charleston, made application to become a citizen, __ December 1823.

Z-4, 347-8: At a Court of Common Pleas, Justus Hartman, 26 March 1824, now of Charleston, grocer, desirous of becoming a denizen.

Z-4, 383: At a Court of Common Pleas, 17 May 1824, Catharine Lazarus, a native of London, now a resident of Charleston, store keeper, aged about 38 years, desirous of becoming a denizen....

Anderson-Pendleton

The following are abstracts of records from LDS microfilm R. K. 292 "Old Naturalization Papers of Pendleton District 1806-1825." Some are after 1825, even though they are on the same reel. Some, but not all, of the originals survive. These originals are in the South Carolina Archives.

S. C., Pendleton District: Petition of James Erskine, a native of the County of Antrim in Ireland, arrived at Charleston in 1789. The following attested to his character and stated that they had known him since 1800: Danl Bryson, John Scot J. P, E. Browne, John Warnock, David Sloan, Wm. Center(?).

S. C., Anderson District: Thomas Gwynn (Gwinn), born in County Doublin (sic) in Ireland, is about 24 years of age, arrived at Philadelphia, about 14 months since, a laborer by proesssion... 3 March 1829.

Petition of Robert Waugh, a native of the County of Antrim in Ireland, arrived in Charleston, December 1786.
The following attested to his character and stated that they had known him since 1794: J. B. Earle, James Wood, Wm. Hunter, J. Miller Sen., Wm. Hamilton. 31 October 1807

S. C., Pendleton District: October term 1809. Petition of James Ruzk, a native of County Antrim in Ireland. The following attested to his character and stated that they had known him since 1805: Thomas Farrar, Obadiah Trimmier, David Sloan, James McKinney, Wm. Thompson, David Sloan Junr., Andrew Brown, J. B. Earle.

October Term 1818. Petition of James McGiffert, a native of County of Down in Ireland, arrived in the U. S., December 1817...28 Oct 1818.

S. C., Pendleton District. Petition of Daniel Drummond, a native of the county of Antrim in Ireland, has been a resident in the U. S. A. 15 years, and the whole time in this state...October 26, 1813. The following attested to his character and stated that they had known him for 5 years: John T. Lewis, Patrick Norris, John McFall, James Todd, Nerman Moore, John Bryce J. P., E. Herring, Nathan McAlester, Andrew McAlester.

S. C., Pendleton District. Joseph Moore, born County Down in Ireland, above the age of 35 years, emigrated to America and arrived at Charleston, 13 November 1819, is a Millwright...20 August 1821.

Petition of Richard Johnston, aged 34 years, a native of ______, County Down, Ireland, arrived in the U. S., November 1819. Took oath 30 March 1821.

Petition of Henry Dickey, a native of Antrim County, Ireland, arrived in the U. S. A., January 1805, now follows farming, is now 28 years of age...1820 October 25th.

S. C., Pendleton District. Petition of Robert Todd, known as Irish Robert, a native of County Antrim in Ireland, has resided in the U. S. since 23 April 1802, and has been a resident 10 years and upwards in this state, aged about 29...26 October 1813.
The following attested to his character and stated that they have known him since the year 1802: Nathan McAlester, John Bryce, Capt. James Thomson.

COUNTY RECORDS

Anderson-Pendleton

Petition of John C. Dench, a native of the county of Cambridge, Kingdom of Great Britain, arrived in U. S. the last day of November 1807, notice of intent...25 March 1817. The following attested to his character and stated that they had known him 15 years: F. W. Symmes, George Lewis, David Cherry, Saml Cherry, A. Lawhon, J. C. Kilpatrick, Th. Harbin, Thos Louton, Aaron Broyles, E. B. Benson, R. Anderson, John S. Lewis.

Petition of Adam Richards, a native of the County of Antrim, Ireland, arrived in the city of Charleston, 31 May 1803...27 Oct 1814. The following attested to his character and stated that they had known him since 1806: Thomas Richards, Jas. C. Griffin, John Harris, George Reese.

Petition of William McKee, waggon maker, a native of County Antrim, Ireland, has resided in the U. S., since 5 December 1788... __ October 1806. The following attested to his character: Danl Bryson, Jno Moffett, E. Browne, Jas. Thomson, Patrick Norris.

S. C., Pendleton District. Petition of John George, a native of the County of Antrim, Ireland, arrived in Charleston, January 1791...1 November 1806. The following attested to his character: Geo. Bowie, Pat. Norris, Thomas Farrar, David Sloan, Robert Anderson.

Petition of William Duncan, born in Islean(sic) or Ireland in 1762, left Ireland in 1789 and he has resid (sic) in the State of South Carolin ever since Christmas Eve of the year last mentioned, he has resided in the district of Pendleton, 16 years, desirous of becoming naturalized...23 February 1814. The following attested to his character: Samuel Black, Jas Major J. P., John Warnock, Elisha Bennett, Daniel Major, James Blag, Thomas Cristian, Samuel Mafield, T. W. Burford, Lowden Low, John McDowell, Wm Smith, Artchible H. Burton, Daniel Drummond, Ibzan Rice, Jas Mattison Capt., Armsted Carter, Lewis Davis, Wm Williamson, Robert McClenden, Robert Brackenridge, Newman Moore, Aaron Tood, Jehu Orr.

S. C., Pendleton District: Petition of Alexander Shaw, a native of County Antrim, Ireland, arrived in Charleston, January 1795... The following attested to his character and stated that they had known him since 1803: John Taylor, James Wood, Saml Cherry, Elam Sharpe. 25 March 1807.

Certified from a Federal Circuit Court, 27 July 1805, William Richards, late of the County of Antrim in Ireland.

Petition of Robert McLees, a native of the County of _____, Ireland, arrived in Charleston, January 1787...25 March 1807. The following attested to his character: Robert Anderson, Jas Thomson, P. Keys.

Petition of John Brewster Burke, born in Nottinghamshire, Great Britain, he is 26 years old, emigrated to the U. S. A., arrived in the city of New York, 18 October 1820, is a schoolmaster, 29 March 1825. Statement of intent.

S. C., Pendleton District. Petition of Alexander Calhoun, a native of County Tyrone, Kingdom of Ireland, has been a resident in this district ___teen years, October 27, 1813. The following attested to his character and stated that the had known him for nine years: Newman Moore, David Sloan, Samuel Cherry, Benj. Dickson, Jno. McFall, John McMillian.

Anderson-Pendleton

S. C., Pendleton District. Petition of Barnett McCully, a native of County Antrim, Ireland, arrived in the U. S., November 1818... 23 October 1827. The following attested to his character: Major Lewis, James Bell, Joseph Mooney, Hugh Gaston, Richd. Johnson, Jno. Sharpe, Thomas Clark, ___ Moorhead Senr., John McFall.

Petition of George J. Gray, born Bath(?), Somersetshire, England, he is 27 years old, arrived in the city of Boston, October 1818, he is a physician...25 October 1826.

COUNTY RECORDS

Charleston

Name	Date	Description
Amiel, John W.	2 Oct 1838	Made a Citizen
Abrahams, Moses	11 Oct 1830	Made a Citizen
Alley, Thomas H.	28 Jan 1834	Made a Citizen
Abnegg, Gotlief	12 Oct 1830	Notice of Intention
Artope, George B.	22 May 1800	Notice of Intention
Allan, William W.	11 Oct 1832	Made a Citizen
Alley, Luder	3 Oct 1837	Notice of Intention
	26 Sep 1837	Denizen
Allen, James	13 Oct 1828	Made a Citizen
Armand, Peter	6 Oct 1832	Made a Citizen
Alley, John B. P.	10 Oct 1836	Citizen
Almers, Luder F.	30 Jan 1841	Notice
Agrell, Charles	30 Jan 1841	Notice
Ahrens, Christopher	26 May 1841	Citizen
Almers, Luder Frederick	30 Jan 1841	Notice
Albrecht, Neclaus	26 Feb 1844	Notice
Allan, Alexander	13 Jul 1844	Notice
Arndt, H. L.	27 Jun 1844	Notice
Anderson, Wm.	11 Aug 1845	Notice of Intention
Adicks, John	1 Jun 1847	Citizenship
Apeler, Jno. Fred.	5 Oct 1846	Notice of Intention
Albrecht, Nicholas	11 May 1846	Citizenship
Albrecht, John	27 Mar 1848	Notice of Intention
Aharan, Patrick	11 Oct 1847	Notice of Intention
Anderson, James	15 Dec 1848	Notice of Intention
Anderson, Carl G.	5 Nov 1849	Citizenship
Alfs, Christopher	14 Oct 1850	Notice of Intention
Boothroyd, Jabez	17 Jun 1799	Citizen
Brown, George	4 Oct 1830	Citizen
Breen, Michael	12 Oct 1830	Citizen
Blaumon, J.	12 Oct 1830	Citizen
Bourren, Joseph	11 Oct 1830	Citizen
Blanchard, John	8 Oct 1830	Citizen
Beco, A.	9 Oct 1830	Citizen
Bosse, Vincent	12 Oct 1830	Citizen
Blair, David	12 Oct 1795	Citizen
Biggs, Henry J.	9 Oct 1826	Citizen
Boyd, John A.	5 Oct 1830	Citizen
Barber, Frederick C.	7 Oct 1830	Citizen
Blake, Daniel	23 Jan 1833	Citizen
Burn, A.	8 Oct 1831	Citizen
Bilton, George	12 Oct 1830	Citizen
Betner, Peter C.	12 Oct 1830	Citizen
Bunkman, A.	9 Oct 1832	Notice of Intention
Bendalier, Jean	12 Oct 1830	Notice of Intention
Barton,Aaron	3 Oct 1831	Notice of Intention
Bissinger, Konrad	7 Oct 1831	Notice of Intention
Burger, Nicholas	8 Oct 1832	Notice of Intention
Blacks, Robert	31 May 1823	Notice of Intention
Brunton ,Archibald	25 Jan 1836	Notice of Intention
Brocklebank, William	5 Oct 1832	Notice of Intention
Burke, William	27 Jan 1838	Notice of Intention
Brady, Patrick	6 Oct 1837	Notice of Intention
Bevan, Daniel	3 Jun 1837	Notice of Intention
	13 Jun 1837	Denizen
Brady, Edward	11 Oct 1831	Notice of Intention
	13 Oct 1834	Denizen
Benger, John	14 Oct 1834	Citizen
Brown, Peter	11 Oct 1834	Citizen
Brown, Thomas	12 Oct 1796	Citizen

Charleston

Name	Date	Description
Barre, John	10 Oct 1832	Citizen
Blake, Daniel Jr.	31 Jan 1831	Citizen
Battiste, John	11 Oct 1834	Citizen
Brodie, Alexander	26 Mar 1790	Citizen
Burke, Martin	11 Oct 1828	Citizen
Blanchard, Edward	6 Oct 1832	Citizen
Brown, Francis	6 Oct 1832	Citizen
Bousquet, Peter	8 Oct 1832	Citizen
Brown, John	14 Oct 1834	Citizen
Betzen, Samuel F.	10 Oct 1831	Citizen
Bingley, William	9 Oct 1820	Citizen
Blanchard, William	12 Oct 1830	Citizen
Berry, John	11 Oct 1830	Citizen
Brady, John	6 Oct 1837	Citizen
Blanchard, Stanislaus	10 Oct 1836	Citizen
Bolger, H. H.	11 Oct 1836	Citizen
Bolger, Christopher	2 Jan 1840	Notice
Bretliff, Wm.	11 Jun 1841	Citizen
Bohler, Luder E.	7 Jan 1840	Citizen
Brady, Patrick	1 Feb 1840	Citizen
Bazille, Joseph	20 May 1841	Notice
Benson, John	20 Jan 1841	Notice
Besser, Charles	29 Jan 1841	Notice
Benjamin, Solomon A.	22 Jan 1841	Notice
Binda, Jos. A.	10 Jun 1841	Citizen
Bischoff, Albert	28 May 1841	Citizen
Boylin, Philip	26 May 1841	Citizen
Burtliffe, Wm.	11 Jun 1841	Citizen
Becher, Fred. Aug.	13 Jan 1842	Notice of Intention
Bockelhoff, P. C.	18 May 1842	Notice of Intention
Bennett, James	20 Feb 1843	Notice of Intention
Blake, John	8 Nov 1842	Notice of Intention
Borner, Frederick	18 Mar 1843	Notice of Intention
Burk, Edmund	10 Apr 1843	Notice of Intention
Boyce, Jerome	10 Apr 1843	Notice of Intention
Bredenberg, C. F.	22 Mar 1843	Citizenship
Butler, John	6 Oct 1843	Notice of Intention
Bluett, John Joshua	2 Nov 1843	Citizenship
Benson, John	15 Nov 1843	Notice of Intention
Becher, F. A.	19 Mar 1844	Citizen
Behre, Christian	2 Jul 1844	Notice
Brady, Patrick	4 Apr 1844	Notice of Intention
Bruns, Hermann C.	23 May 1844	Notice of Intention
Bulwinkle, Jacob	18 Jun 1844	Notice of Intention
Butler, And.	10 Nov 1843	Citizenship
Bailey, Wm.	23 Nov 1844	Notice of Intention
Bennett, James	29 Mar 1845	Citizenship
Blake, Jno.	11 Apr 1845	Citizenship
Borner, Frederick	26 Mar 1845	Citizenship
Breidert, Henry	7 Nov 1844	Notice of Intention
Brett, Nicholas	16 Apr 1845	Notice of Intention
Burke, John	5 Dec 1844	Notice of Intention
Burns, Edward	4 Dec 1844	Notice of Intention
Barry, Richard	25 Aug 1845	Notice of Intention
Bockelhoff, P. C.	6 Nov 1844	Citizenship
Bolage, Harman	1 Nov 1845	Notice of Intention
Boyce, J. J.	17 Nov 1845	Citizenship
Buckhiet, Philip	13 Nov 1845	Notice
Butler, Jno.	10 Nov 1845	Citizenship
Brady, Patrick	14 Oct 1834	Notice
Barragan, Wm.	12 Oct 1846	Notice

Charleston

Name	Date	Description
Booker, Francis Edwd.	26 Jun 1843	Notice
Brandt, Jno. Wm.	11 Mar 1846	Notice
Brolley, A. P.	7 May 1847	Citizenship
Buhre, J. F.	16 Dec 1846	Notice
Burke, John	26 Apr 1847	Notice
Bressel, Jno. F.	1 Sep 1846	Notice
Bolage, Herman	8 Nov 1847	Citizenship
Blase, C. F.	30 Jan 1841	Citizenship
Brady, Patrick	13 Jun 1846	Citizenship
Bembrook, Wm.	29 Mar 1848	Notice
Bonaud, Auguste	10 Jan 1848	Notice
Brenan, P. S.	20 Jul 1847	Notice
Brophfy, Jno.	2 Aug 1847	Notice
Bruggeman, F. W.	7 Feb 1848	Notice
Buckley, Daniel	16 Jun 1847	Notice
Buhre, Dederick	7 Sep 1847	Notice
Burk, John	17 Aug 1847	Notice of Intention
Burleigh, Wm.	31 Dec 1847	Notice of Intention
Beauerschmieth, Henry	11 Sep 1848	Notice of Intention
Bennett, Theophilus	2 Aug 1848	Notice of Intention
Boesch, Jno. James	28 Aug 1848	Notice of Intention
Bosnahan, Daniel	22 Apr 1848	Notice of Intention
Brunner,Christian	30 Aug 1848	Notice of Intention
Buhrman, Henry	12 May 1848	Citizenship
Bohl, Jno.	8 Dec 1848	Notice of Intention
Boning, Dederick	7 Nov 1848	Citizenship
Bourke, Ormsby	17 Feb 1849	Notice of Intention
Brugger, Jos. Lorentz	9 Feb 1849	Notice of Intention
Bucking, Jno. H.	4 Nov 1848	Citizenship
Bullwinkle, D.	5 Jan 1849	Notice of Intention
Brunges, Wm.	23 Oct 1849	Notice of Intention
Bourke, Jno.	18 Oct 1848	Notice of Intention
Bussell, Jno. F.	11 Nov 1848	Citizenship
Brophy, Jno.	21 Feb 1849	Notice of Intention
Behrens, J. H.	25 Mar 1849	Notice of Intention
Barnes, James	24 May 1849	Citizenship
Block, Henry A.	19 Jul 1849	Notice of Intention
Brophy, John	28 Jun 1849	Notice of Intention
Brinkenborg, Jno. H.	9 Apr 1849	Notice of Intention
Burk, Edmund	18 May 1849	Citizenship
Baas, Joachim	9 Jan 1850	Notice of Intention
Backes, Francis	31 Oct 1849	Notice of Intention
Balleer, Wm.	31 Oct 1849	Notice of Intention
Baurmeister, Geo. C.	5 Mar 1850	Notice of Intention
Bidault, Alex.	26 Jun 1850	Notice of Intention
Brenna, Patrick	3 Jun 1850	Citizenship
Brennan, Luke	15 Feb 1850	Notice of Intention
Briggmann, Wm.	10 Nov 1849	Citizenship
Broge, J. H. F.	19 Apr 1850	Notice of Intention
Byron, James	13 Feb 1850	Notice of Intention
Barrett, Thomas	14 Oct 1850	Notice of Intention
Baer, Marie Elisa	28 Jul 1850	Notice of Intention
Behrens, Jno. D.	14 Nov 1850	Citizenship
Bischoff, Jacob	10 Oct 1850	Notice of Intention
Bornemann, F. W.	7 Oct 1850	Notice of Intention
Brandt, H. F.	28 Oct 1850	Notice of Intention
Brassel, Jno.	30 Nov 1850	Notice of Intention
Brockmann, Charles	29 Oct 1850	Notice of Intention
Brunyes, Wm.	9 Nov 1850	Citizenship
Bunch, Philip	5 Jul 1850	Notice of Intention
Burke, Jno.	9 Nov 1850	Notice of Intention

Charleston

Name	Date	Description
Corbett, Patrick	11 Oct 1836	Citizen
Cooper, Peyton	6 Feb 1832	Denizen
Cantey, Owen	12 Oct 1830	Citizen
Carpenter, Peter	12 Oct 1830	Citizen
Crowley, Timothy	9 Oct 1830	Citizen
Colina, J. L.	11 Oct 1830	Citizen
Cassidy, John	12 Oct 1830	Citizen
Clarken, Richard	13 Oct 1834	Notice of Intention
	19 May 1838	Citizen
Clarken, John	13 Oct 1834	Notice of Intention
	27 Jan 1837	Citizen
Clifford, Loftus C.	21 Jan 1835	Notice of Intention
Clarke, Charles	7 Oct 1830	Citizen
Cormier, Francis	8 Oct 1830	Citizen
Caw, Peter	4 Oct 1830	Citizen
Colson, Charles	6 Oct 1830	Citizen
Currin, William	11 Oct 1830	Citizen
Crean, Henry	11 Oct 1830	Citizen
Cotton, Thomas	9 Oct 1830	Citizen
Clark, Charles	20 Oct 1832	Notice of Intention
Campbell, James	14 Oct 1834	Citizen
Campbell, James	8 Jun 1833	Notice of Intention
Crosier, William	6 Oct 1832	Notice of Intention
Cross, Jacob	12 Oct 1830	Citizen
Cull, James	30 Jan 1832	Notice of Intention
Cachon, Arcene	14 Jul 1825	Notice of Intention
Callen, Thomas	21 May 1830	Citizen
Carricks, Gilbert	16 Jun 1823	Notice of Intention
Cambridge, Saint John	8 Oct 1831	Citizen
Channer, Christopher J.	11 Oct 1831	Citizen
Cay, Raymond	8 Oct 1831	Citizen
Cahill, Thomas	22 Oct 1834	Notice of Intention
Casey, John	26 Jan 1838	Notice of Intention
Casey, Rose	26 Jan 1838	Notice of Intention
Cantwell, John	16 May 1838	Notice of Intention
Clement, Finlater	2 Jun 1812	Citizen
Cantwell, Patrick	10 Oct 1826	Citizen
Caldwell, John Jr.	14 Oct 1828	Citizen
Conter, Pierre	3 Feb 1812	Citizen
Caminade, Henry	12 Oct 1830	Citizen
Cleland, John C.	14 Oct 1828	Citizen
Cordes, Jacob	10 Jan 1837	Citizen
Cassidy, Alice	15 Oct 1831	Citizen
Cruickshanks, Robert	10 Oct 1831	Citizen
Crop, Jacob	13 Oct 1834	Citizen
Castilio, Michael	5 Oct 1832	Citizen
Campbell, Stevenson	(no date or description)	
Clark, Charles S.	11 Oct 1834	Citizen
Curran, Patrick	20 May 1839	Notice of Intention
Cooper, John	23 Jan 1839	Notice of Intention
Charlou, Francis	7 Jan 1841	Notice of Intention
Clarke, Thomas J.	Jan 1840	Notice of Intention
Castrillon, Diego A.	12 May 1841	Notice of Intention
Charlon, Francis	7 Jan 1841	Notice of Intention
Cooper, John	26 Jan 1841	Citizen
Carlstran, Mangs	18 Oct 1842	Notice of Intention
Crawley, Richard	18 Oct 1842	Notice of Intention
Coffey, Patrick J.	25 Jan 1843	Notice of Intention
Casey, John & Rose his wife	20 Apr 1843	Citizenship
Cronin, Michael W.	5 Aug 1843	Notice of Intention
Collins, Patrick	31 Aug 1843	Notice of Intention

Charleston

Name	Date	Description
Cattenhorns, Dederick	5 Oct 1843	Notice of Intention
Caffin, Nicholas H.	18 May 1825	Citizen Com P Journal 18 May 1825
Cannon, John	5 Jul 1844	Notice
Cassidy, Francis	15 Mar 1844	Notice
Charlon, F.	12 Mar 1844	Citizenship
Coche, Joseph	6 Feb 1844	Notice of Intention
Croughan, Stephen	1 Jan 1841	Notice of Intention
Costallo, Thomas	4 Nov 1842	Notice of Intention
Camack, John	28 Apr 1845	Notice of Intention
Carrell, Barney	15 Nov 1844	Citizenhip
Coffee, Thomas	21 Oct 1844	Notice of Intention
Crawley R.	13 Mar 1845	Citizenship
Culbert, James	29 Mar 1845	Notice of Intention
Cumming, Thos J.	(no date)	Notice of Intention
Castaillon, Diego A.	29 Oct 1844	Citizenhip
Clauss, John Henry	25 Nov 1845	Notice of Intention
Crowley, Daniel	22 Jul 1845	Notice of Intention
Curtis, Thomas	31 Oct 1845	Notice of Intention
Curtis, Thomas	31 Oct 1845	Denizenship
Cagny, Jno. J.	17 Oct 1846	Notice
Camach, John	27 May 1847	Citizenship
Campbell, Hugh	29 Mar 1843	Notice
Cameron, Hugh P.	19 Oct 1846	Notice
Claassen, Siebrand	4 Feb 1847	Notice
Collins, Edward	4 Dec 1846	Notice
Collins, Patrick	6 May 1846	Citizenship
Corcoran, Patrick	27 Jul 1847	Notice
Culbert, John	21 May 1846	Notice
Cunnien, Michael	8 Mar 1847	Notice
Campsey, Jno.	1 Apr 1848	Notice
Cary, Cornelius	27 Sep 1847	Notice
Conway, John	22 Nov 1847	Notice
Corcoran, Pat	28 Oct 1847	Notice
Cotter, John	22 Oct 1847	Notice
Crohan, Peter	8 Nov 1847	Notice
Culbert, John	29 May 1848	Cirizenship
Cain, Edward	1 Mar 1849	Notice of Intention
Clarke, Thomas	7 Nov 1848	Notice of Intention
Coglen, P.	13 Nov 1848	Notice of Intention
Connolly, Pat.	25 Mar 1849	Notice of Intention
Cordes, Geo. H.	18 Oct 1848	Notice of Intention
Currier, J. H.	25 Mar 1849	Notice of Intention
Campbell, Owen	27 Jul 1849	Notice of Intention
Carroll, James	2 Jan 1849	Notice of Intention
Caulier, George	21 Apr 1849	Notice of Intention
Cohen, Edward D.	12 Apr 1849	Notice of Intention
Collins, William	1 May 1849	Notice of Intention
Canning, Charles	24 Sep 1849	Notice of Intention
Carty, Thos.	27 Sep 1849	Notice of Intention
Croughan, Jos.	27 Sep 1849	Notice of Intention
Cahill, Thos.	29 Nov 1850	Notice of Intention
Carey, Jas.	27 Aug 1850	Notice of Intention
Carey, Thos.	28 Aug 1850	Notice of Intention
Carmody, Jno.	27 Nov 1850	Notice of Intention
Carty, Jno.	11 Oct 1850	Notice of Intention
Clarke, Wm.	11 Oct 1850	Notice of Intention
Collins, Patrick	31 Aug 1850	Notice of Intention
Corcoran, Patrick	13 Nov 1850	Citizenship
Cosgrove, Jas.	12 Nov 1850	Notice of Intention

Charleston

Name	Date	Description
Dalzel, Joseph	12 Oct 1830	Citizen
Daniels, William	16 Jun 1834	Notice of Intention
Dascher, Claus	10 Jun 1834	Citizen
Desgraves, Peter	7 Oct 1826	Citizen
Dwyer, Patrick	15 Oct 1831	Notice of Intention
Doyle, John	27 Jan 1838	Notice of Intention
Droppenstadt, Diederick	5 Oct 1839(?)	Notice of Intention
Dunn, George	5 Jun 1837	Notice of Intention
Draine, William	9 Oct 1832	Notice of Intention
	10 Oct 1834	Citizen
Dunn, Richard H. W.	4 Oct 1832	Notice of Intention
Dwyer, Thomas	15 Oct 1832	Notice of Intention
Davidson, Thomas	4 Feb 1832	Notice of Intention
	9 Oct 1834	Citizen
Dinges, Christian	7 Oct 1831	Notice of Intention
Dowd, Thomas	3 Oct 1831	Notice of Intention
Doud, John	15 Oct 1831	Notice of Intention
	7 Oct 1834	Citizen
Duffy, James	10 Oct 1826	Citizen
Deery, James	7 Oct 1834	Notice of Intention
	9 Oct 1836	Citizen
Dunn, William	9 Oct 1834	Citizen
Dieckman, John H.	28 Jan 1834	Citizen
Duffy, Thomas	12 Oct 1830	Citizen
Davenport, William	26 Jan 1826	Citizen
Due, Francis A.	12 Oct 1830	Citizen
Duval, J. B.	12 Oct 1830	Citizen
Dalton, Martin	5 Oct 1832	Citizen
Dollelende, Peter	6 Oct 1832	Citizen
Douglas, Anthony	6 Oct 1832	Citizen
Delmold, C. E.	2 Jun 1832	Citizen
Dircks, Henry	11 May 1838	Citizen
Doucin, Morelle	11 Oct 1831	Citizen
Dligraph, C.	10 Oct 1831	Citizen
Doyle, Edward	20 May 1839	Notice of Intention
Doyle, Edward	17 Jan 1840	Notice of Intention
Dierssen, William	26 May 1841	Citizen
Doherty, John	Jan 1841	Notice
Doogan, Patrick	26 Jan 1841	Notice
Doscher, Hinrich	30 Jan 1841	Citizen
Doyle, Patrick	30 Jan 1841	Notice
Doyle, Edward	12 Jun 1841	Citizen
De Haan, Saml. L.	20 Mar 1843	Citizenship
Dempsey, Edward F.	13 May 1842	Citizenship
Donovan, Patrick	18 Oct 1842	Notice of Intention
Doscher, Dederick	30 Mar 1843	Citizenship
Delahunt, James	7 Apr 1843	Notice of Intention
Doyle, Edward	3 Nov 1843	Citizenship
Diehl, Henry W.	4 Jun 1844	Notice
Dounohn, Andrew	16 Apr 1844	Notice
Dwyer, Dennis	28 Feb 1844	Notice
Dailey, Thomas	12 Apr 1845	Notice
Daly, Henry	6 Sep 1844	Notice
Darcy, Timothy	28 Nov 1844	Notice
Doscher, B. H.	25 Feb 1845	Notice
Dougherty, John	30 Sep 1844	Notice
Dryer, Geo.	5 Nov 1844	Notice
Duls, Henry	29 Oct 1844	Citizenship
Dolan, John	8 Jul 1845	Notice
Dowling, John	27 Jul 1845	Notice
Dunlap, Rob. C.	29 May 1843	Notice

Charleston

Name	Date	Description
Davidson, James	3 Jun 1847	Notice
Delahnut, Jas.	13 Jun 1846	Citizenship
Donahoe, Thos	9 Sep 1846	Notice
Dunn, John	31 Mar 1845	Notice
Dunn, John	20 May 1847	Citizenship
Daily, Francis	5 Apr 1848	Notice
Day, Jno.	1 Nov 1847	Notice
Dey, Andrew	4 Sep 1847	Notice
Diefenbach, Johan C.	29 Sep 1847	Notice
Dillon, Thos.	20 Oct 1847	Notice
Dolahanty, Jno.	24 Aug 1847	Notice
Doscher, Luder	30 Nov 1847	Notice
Dugan, Patrick	1 Jan 1848	Notice
Denis, Jno. A.	21 Aug 1848	Notice
Donald, Jno.	22 Sep 1848	Notice of Intention
Dosher, Jno. H.	9 Sep 1848	Notice of Intention
Dunn, Brian	16 Jun 1848	Notice of Intention
Donerhue, Patrick	27 Nov 1848	Notice of Intention
Dorbaum, Jno. C.	8 Jan 1849	Notice of Intention
Dorin, Thos	2 Nov 1848	Notice of Intention
Drayer, Otto W.	6 Oct 1848	Notice of Intention
Duffy, Patrick	3 Nov 1848	Notice of Intention
Dunn, John	11 Nov 1848	Citizenship
Dunning, Hugh	29 Sep 1848	Notice of Intention
Darcy, Michael	27 Jul 1849	Notice of Intention
Doyle, Jno.	27 Jul 1849	Notice of Intention
Doogan, Patrick	23 May 1850	Citizenship
Darcy, Timothy K.	13 Jun 1850	Citizenship
Donohoa, Dennis	15 Oct 1850	Notice of Intention
Doherty, Luke	17 Dec 1850	Notice of Intention
Doscher, Luhr	22 Nov 1850	Citizenship
Diefenbach, Johann C.	2 Nov 1850	Citizenship
England, John Right Rev.	20 Jan 1823	Denizen
Evans, Charles	4 Oct 1838	Notice of Intention
Elliot, Robert	3 Jul 1793	Citizen
Esterslat, Peter	8 Oct 1830	Citizen
Enston, William	6 Oct 1834	Citizen
Eyland, James	12 Feb 1824	Citizen
English, William	8 Oct 1834	Citizen
Eickell, John	10 Feb 1812	Citizen
Evenius, Friederick or Fritz	27 Jan 1841	Citizen
Eikerenketter, Augustus	5 Apr 1843	Citizenship
Edwards, Joseph	8 Jul 1844	Notice
Ehrichs, Henry	19 Jul 1844	Denizenship
Ehrichs, Henry	16 Jul 1844	Notice of Intention
Englart, William	11 Nov 1844	Notice of Intention
Epping, J. P. M.	28 Nov 1844	Notice of Intention
Ehrichs, Henry	7 May 1847	Citizenship
Early, Luke	12 Jul 1848	Notice of Intention
Ellard, William	16 Jun 1848	Notice of Intention
Edmonds, Thos.	1 Mar 1849	Notice of Intention
Englebert, Geo.	26 Mar 1849	Notice of Intention
Enslon, Hannah Mrs.	7 May 1849	Citizenship
Faber, Jno. C.	29 May 1790	No action marked
Fielding, John	5 Feb 1831	Notice of Intention
	25 Jan 1836	Citizen
Finn, Daniel	25 Jan 1823	Notice of Intention
Farrell, James	15 Oct 1836	Notice of Intention

Charleston

Name	Date	Description
Fay, Patrick	8 Oct 1831	Notice of Intention
	10 Oct 1834	Citizen
Flinn, Daniel	11 Feb 1824	Notice of Intention
Francis, Edward	19 Jan 1833	Notice of Intention
Forbes, George	6 Jun 1822	Citizen
Ferguson, Hugh W.	10 Oct 1820	Citizen
Fogaurs, John A.	7 Oct 1834	Citizen
Feagan, Simon	6 Feb 1822	Citizen
Fink, Jens Peter	10 Oct 1835	Citizen
Fleming, William S.	17 Jun 1824	Citizen
Fox, Richard W.	6 Oct 1832	Citizen
Fox, James	11 Oct 1828	Citizen
Fullarton, Alexander	9 Oct 1832	Citizen
Fox, William	11 Oct 1828	Citizen
Feria(?) , James	11 Oct 1837	Citizen
Fay, James	12 Oct 1830	Citizen
Fleming, Patrick	12 Oct 1830	Citizen
Ferguson, William	7 Oct 1830	Citizen
Forsyth, Arthur	9 Oct 1830	Citizen
Francis, Michael	12 Oct 1830	Citizen
Francisco, Emanuel	12 Oct 1830	Citizen
Farrell, F.	25 Jan 1835	Notice of Intention
Frieze, Frederick	12 May 1840	Notice of Intention
Duerst, Daniel Herman	3 Jun 1841	Citizen
Ficken, Jno. F.	29 Jan 1841	Citizen
Faber, George	14 Jan 1842	Notice of Intention
Frates, Joseph	11 May 1842	Notice of Intention
Farmer, Richard	18 Oct 1842	Notice of Intention
Fiken, William	12 Apr 1843	Notice of Intention
Frieze, Frederick	20 Mar 1843	Citizenship
Freitag, Christian	20 Mar 1843	Notice of Intention
Fitzpatrick, James	12 Jul 1843	Notice of Intention
Ferrell, Daniel	8 May 1844	Notice of Intention
Fink, Peter Jens	20 Dec 1843	Notice of Intention
Fitzgibbon, Patrick	20 Mar 1843	Citizenship
Fanning, John	15 Mar 1845	Notice of Intention
Ferrall, Jno. J.	21 Nov 1844	Notice of Intention
Fink, Bog H.	16 Oct 1844	Notice of Intention
Francis, George	13 Mar 1845	Notice of Intention
France, James	22 Oct 1845	Notice of Intention
Fisher, Samuel	13 Dec 1845	Notice of Intention
Frey, Geo. J.	31 Oct 1846	Notice of Intention
Frintrup, Wm.	12 Jan 1846	Notice of Intention
Fay, Wm.	23 Aug 1847	Notice of Intention
Flynn, Patrick	17 Jul 1847	Notice of Intention
Fisher, Samuel	10 Jun 1848	Citizenship
Finck, Jacob Fred.	26 Sep 1848	Notice of Intention
Fehrenback, Sigmund	26 Mar 1849	Notice of Intention
Fitzsimons, Bernard	22 May 1849	Notice of Intention
Flynn, John	18 Jul 1849	Notice of Intention
Frier, De Jno.	13 Jun 1849	Citizenship
Frey, Geo. Joseph	9 Jun 1849	Citizenship
Figeroux, Benj.	22 Jan 1850	Notice of Intention
Fischer, Jno. Henrich	15 Oct 1849	Notice of Intention
Foei, Charles	6 Sep 1849	Notice of Intention
Funke, H. H.	19 Apr 1850	Notice of Intention
Fellers, Patrick Fallos	12 Nov 1850	Notice of Intention
Ferrell, Thos.	14 Nov 1850	Notice of Intention
Fenner, Henry	28 Oct 1850	Notice of Intention
Flood, James	23 Oct 1850	Notice of Intention
Francis, Antnony	13 Jan 1850	Notice of Intention

Charleston

Name	Date	Description
Freer, Martin	26 Jul 1850	Notice of Intention
Gerdts, Henry	3 Oct 1837	Notice of Intention
	26 Sep 1837	Denizen
Garcia, J. R.	4 Oct 1836	Notice of Intention
Giraud, Anne	20 Jan 1812	Citizen
Gallagher, J. W.	7 Oct 1834	Citizen
Gairdner, James	1 Jan 1793	Citizen
Gidiere, Margaret	23 Jan 1813	Citizen
Guieu, Philip	17 Jan 1805	Citizen
Gibson, Charles R.	11 Oct 1836	Citizen
Gunderman, Anton	20 Oct 1836	Citizen
Guillenran, Peter	10 Oct 1836	Citizen
Gilfillin, Alexander	5 Oct 1836	Citizen
Greig, Alexander	13 Oct 1834	Citizen
	12 Oct 1830	Notice of Intention
Greenhill, John	14 Oct 1834	Citizen
Gordon, George	11 Oct 1834	Citizen
Guinand, Henry	8 Oct 1832	Citizen
Gay, Louis	6 Oct 1832	Citizen
Geise, Charles	11 Oct 1830	Citizen
Gillespie, Thomas	12 Oct 1830	Citizen
Gonfierville, Theodore	14 Oct 1834	Citizen
Gamboa, John	5 Oct 1831	Citizen
Gonzales, John	11 Oct 1831	Citizen
Gallagher, John	6 Oct 1832	Citizen
Greer, John M.	29 May 1834	Citizen
Good, Francis	13 May 1812	Citizen
Gunderson, William	12 Oct 1830	Citizen
German, John	21 Jan 1811	Citizen
Gannon, John	15 Jun 1839	Citizen
Garrett, George	8 May 1839	Notice of Intention
Graman, Henry	29 Jan 1841	Notice of Intention
Gerdts, Henry	26 May 1841	Citizen
Grebbs, Henry	5 Jun 1841	Citizen
Gissel, R.	8 Jun 1841	Citizen
Gissell, H.	8 Jun 1841	Citizen
Garrott, George	7 Jun 1841	Citizen
Gallagher, John	8 Jan 1841	Notice of Intention
Garrett, George	7 Jun 1841	Citizen
Gaynor, Nicholas	13 Jan 1841	Notice
Gerdts, Carsten	30 Jan 1841	Citizen
Gerdts, Henry	26 May 1841	Citizen
Gissel, Hanke	7 Jun 1841	Citizen
Gissel, Reimert	7 Jun 1841	Citizen
Gramman, Henry	29 Feb 1841	Notice
Grant, Edward	21 Jan 1841	Notice
Grebb, Henry	6 Jun 1841	Citizen
Gray, Andrew	28 Jan 1840	Denizenship
Gallagher, John	8 Apr 1843	Citizenship
Glucklick, Ignaz	9 Jan 1843	Notice of Intention
Gibbon, Patrick Fitz	20 Mar 1843	Citizenship
Grammann, Henry	5 Apr 1843	Citizenship
Gray, Andrew	12 Apr 1843	Denizenship
Guenther, Charles	28 Mar 1843	Citizenship
Gallagher, Edward	11 Apr 1843	Notice of Intention
Gambati, Alexander	3 Oct 1843	Notice of Intention
Geraty, Christopher	15 Nov 1843	Notice of Intention
Gambati, Alexander	26 Mar 1844	Denizenship
German, Geo. A.	13 Mar 1844	Notice
Geverd, Garbonne	23 Aug 1844	Notice

Charleston

Name	Date	Description
Garden, Benj.	6 Oct 1845	Notice
Garner, James	4 Nov 1845	Notice
Gibson, Charles	30 Sep 1845	Notice
Gottschalk, Jno. A.	14 Oct 1845	Notice
Graver, Jno. H.	29 Jul 1845	Notice
Gelabert, Jno.	7 Jun 1847	Citizenship
Gerdes, C. H.	14 Oct 1846	Notice
Gerk, Francis H.	8 Mar 1847	Notice
Greenwald, Jno. J.	28 May 1847	Citizenship
Goldman, Meyer	3 & 13 Nov 1846	Citizenship
Goodwin, Geo. M.	28 Jan 1846	Notice
Gerety, Bernard	13 Oct 1847	Notice
Gorman, Jno.	18 Feb 1848	Notice
Goury, Jno.	17 Jul 1847	Notice
Grace, Patrick	4 Aug 1847	Notice of Intention
Green, Patrick	13 Sep 1847	Notice of Intention
Green, Hugh	25 Sep 1847	Notice of Intention
Gibson, Charles	23 May 1848	Citizenship
Gerken, Peter	9 Sep 1848	Notice of Intention
Gourlay, W. K.	2 Jun 1848	Notice of Intention
Gerdes, Charles H.	30 Oct 1848	Citizenship
Gieven, Wm.	16 Jan 1849	Notice of Intention
Girvan, Jno.	20 Oct 1848	Notice of Intention
Gruendel, Aug.	8 Jan 1848	Notice of Intention
Goodwin, Geo. M.	18 May 1849	Notice of Intention & Citizenship
Gallagher, Nathaniel	28 Jun 1850	Notice of Intention
Garden, Benj.	9 May 1850	Citizenship
Gerdis, Eimmer	3 Nov 1849	Notice of Intention
Gilmore, Thos.	11 Oct 1849	Notice of Intention
Gardiner, Edward	18 Feb 1850	Notice of Intention
Goold, Patrick	16 Oct 1850	Notice of Intention
Gormon, James	7 Oct 1850	Notice of Intention
Hackell, Patrick	25 Jan 1836	Notice of Intention
Hosse, Johan Gotlieb	27 Jan 1838	Notice of Intention
Hosse, Juliana Augusta	27 Jan 1838	Notice of Intention
Hartje, Henry	6 Oct 1837	Notice of Intention
Hughes, Thomas	27 May 1837	Notice of Intention
Hyde, Joseph	10 Jun 1837	Notice of Intention
Hogan, Daniel	4 Oct 1832	Notice of Intention
Hanasy, Thomas	13 Oct 1832	Notice of Intention
Hewy, M.	8 Oct 1831	Notice of Intention
Hyams, Isaac	8 Jun 1812	Citizen
Highet, Campbell D.	11 Oct 1834	Citizen
Hamill, Thomas	13 Oct 1828	Citizen
Hadler, John	30 Mar 1827	Citizen
Hill, William	13 Oct 1834	Citizen
Happoldt, Charles L.	14 Oct 1828	Citizen
Happoldt, John M.	14 Oct 1828	Citizen
Headden, Joseph	9 Oct 1830	Citizen
Holmes, Charles	6 Jun 1811	Citizen
Hughes, Charles	9 Oct 1832	Citizen
Hawey, Edward	16 Jun 1832	Citizen
	29 May 1830	Notice of Intention
Henry, Edward	11 Oct 1828	Citizen
Halden, John	12 Oct 1830	Citizen
Henry, Robert	20 Feb 1794	Citizen
Haslett, John	22 Jan 1796	Citizen
Hounsley, Charles W.	11 Oct 1831	Citizen
Hernandez, Peter	20 Oct 1831	Citizen

Charleston

Name	Date	Description
Hendrick, Joseph	8 Oct 1831	Citizen
Hilson, John	7 Jun 1830	Citizen
Hill, Caspar	5 Oct 1832	Citizen
Hodgson, William	12 Oct 1832	Citizen
Hosterholtz, John	22 Oct 1836	Citizen
Husman, H.	11 Oct 1836	Citizen
Herschgartner, Martin	22 Oct 1836	Citizen
Heilman, Albert	5 Oct 1832	Citizen
Herbey, John R.	24 Jan 1818	Denizen
Healy, John	10 May 1839	Notice of Intention
Heissenhuttle, Gisset	29 Jan 1841	
Hagan, Patrick	26 May 1841	Citizen
Haartje, Henry	8 May 1840	Citizen
Habernicht, John D.	28 Jan 1841	Citizen
Hogan, Patrick	12 May 1841	Citizen
Hamel, George	8 Jan 1841	Citizen
Harris, George	29 Jan 1841	Notice
Heisenbuttle, Gefert	29 Jan 1841	Notice
Healy, John	3 Jun 1841	Citizen
Henderson, John	19 May 1841	Notice
Henchen, Martin	3 Jun 1841	Citizen
Hencken, Wm. Henry	3 Jun 1841	Citizen
Hogan, Richard	21 Jan 1841	Notice
Holst, Charles F.	28 Jan 1841	Notice
Howell, J. K.	9 Jun 1841	Citizen
Hervey, George	24 Jan 1842	Notice of Intention
Harbers , Ann Gesche	28 Jan 1842	Notice of Intention
Harbers , Jno. A.	28 Jan 1842	Notice of Intention
Hamilton, Jane	17 Jan 1843	Notice of Intention
Hanratty, Patrick	19 Oct 1842	Notice of Intention
Harbers, Geo. Henry	4 Apr 1843	Notice of Intention
Hassard, Jno.	20 Apr 1843	Notice of Intention
Heimsath, John	17 Apr 1843	Citizenship
Hogan, Michael	8 Apr 1843	Notice of Intention
Hogan, Richard	20 Mar 1843	Citizenship
Holst, Charles F.	13 Mar 1843	Citizenship
Heide, Louis E.	5 Oct 1843	Notice of Intention
Harbers, K. F.	8 Nov 1843	Citizenship
Harenburg, Jno. F.	30 Aug 1843	Notice of Intention
Hahn, Herman Henry	5 Feb 1844	Notice of Intention
Harbers, Hannah	13 Mar 1844	Notice of Intention
Harbers, Ann G.	18 Mar 1844	Citizenship
Heine, Wierich	4 Jun 1844	Notice of Intention
Harbers, Jno. A.	29 Mar 1845	Citizenship
Harttz, Jno. C.	18 Apr 1845	Notice of Intention
Heischel, Charles L.	8 Apr 1845	Notice of Intention
Heissenbuttle, Gefert	12 Apr 1845	Citizenship
Hora, Michael	3 Jan 1845	Notice of Intention
Hanratty, Patrick	8 Nov 1845	Citizenship
Hogan, John	22 Nov 1845	Citizenship
Holland, Wm.	31 May 1843	Notice
Harenburg, Jno. F.	7 Nov 1845	Citizenship
Hagemeyer, K. C.	27 Jan 1846	Notice
Harding, Mathew	19 Oct 1846	Notice
Heckman, A.	14 Jun 1847	Notice
Hellen, Jacob H.	5 Oct 1846	Notice
Hogen, Jno.	17 Mar 1847	Notice
Heyer, Jno. H.	5 Aug 1847	Notice
Hill, Edward	21 May 1847	Notice
Hadeler, Adolph	12 Sep 1848	Notice
Hartigan, Thos	21 Sep 1848	Notice

Charleston

Name	Date	Description
Hamill, Owen	19 Aug 1848	Notice
Hervey, Geo.	10 Jun 1848	Citizenship
Herwig, Wm.	23 May 1848	Notice of Intention
Hausman, Carl	19 Oct 1848	Notice of Intention
Herling, Charles	8 Jan 1848	Notice of Intention
Hilken, Jno. H.	27 Dec 1848	Notice of Intention
Hoben, John	23 Oct 1848	Notice of Intention
Hartman, George	30 Mar 1849	Notice of Intention
Hastedt, Harman	30 Mar 1849	Notice of Intention
Hickmann, Adolph	16 Jun 1849	Citizenship
Hill, Edward	24 May 1849	Citizenship
Hynas, John	23 Jul 1849	Notice of Intention
Hammarskold, C. W.	29 Jun 1850	Notice of Intention
Harbers, Died. H.	7 May 1850	Citizenship
Hasett, Jno.	15 Oct 1849	Notice of Intention
Heins, D.	24 May 1850	Citizenship
Hogan, Peter	20 Apr 1850	Notice of Intention
Hogan, Martin	24 Sep 1848	Notice of Intention
Hubert, Otto Charles	24 May 1850	Notice of Intention
Hynes, Henry	1 Jan 1850	Notice of Intention
Harrison, Wm.	30 Aug 1850	Notice of Intention
Hayes, Thos	12 Nov 1850	Notice of Intention
Healy, Patrick	19 Oct 1850	Notice of Intention
Herbert,Thomas	6 Oct 1850	Notice of Intention
Hennesey, Charles	12 Dec 1850	Notice of Intention
Hett, Andrew	23 Nov 1850	Notice of Intention
Hogan, Dennis	30 Aug 1850	Notice of Intention
Hollarin, Patrick	6 Jan 1850	Notice of Intention
Holley, Jno.	6 Oct 1850	Notice of Intention
Hude, Arad	27 Sep 1850	Notice of Intention
Jahan, Mary	6 Feb 1836	Notice of Intention
Ingoldsby, Felix	14 Oct 1822	Notice of Intention
	4 Oct 1826	Citizen
Johnson, William	27 Jan 1832	Notice of Intention
Janson, P.	11 Oct 1836	Citizen
Justus, Herman	2 Jun 1795	Citizen
Jackson, Henry	20 May 1796	Citizen
Jamieson, John	23 Oct 1830	Citizen
Jones, Thomas	11 Oct 1831	Citizen
Irvine, George	9 Oct 1830	Citizen
Jamradt, M. F.	12 Oct 1830	Citizen
Jordan, Thomas	15 Jun 1839	Notice of Intention
James, Jordan	23 Jan 1841	Notice of Intention
Judge, Mary Ann	28 May 1841	Notice of Intention
James, William	30 Jan 1840	Citizen
Jordan, James	23 Jan 1841	Notice
Judge, Mary Ann	28 May 1841	Notice
Judge, James	26 May 1841	Citizen
Judes or Indes, Charles	6 Oct 1843	Notice of Intention
Jagler, Christiana	29 Mar 1844	Notice of Intention
Johnson, Thomas	14 Jun 1844	Notice of Intention
Jordan, James	8 Nov 1844	Citizenship
Jush, C. F. A.	20 Feb 1845	Notice of Intention
Jessen, Hains	27 Apr 1845	Notice of Intention
Jessen, Henry	5 May 1847	Citizenship
Justi, Carl F.	20 May 1847	Citizenship
Justi, J. A. W.	14 Oct 1847	Notice
Jones, Thomas	3 Feb 1849	Notice
Jinson, Martin	6 Jun 1849	Notice
Johnson, Wm	19 Nov 1849	Citizenship

Charleston

Name	Date	Description
Justi, J. A. W.	27 Oct 1849	Citizenship
Killroy, Patrick	16 May 1838	Notice of Intention
Kevinstein, August	4 Oct 1837	Notice of Intention
	5 Oct 1837	Denizen
Kester, Jacob	5 Oct 1837	Notice of Intention
Koch, John C.	7 Jun 1837	Notice of Intention
Kickham, William	12 Oct 1830	Notice of Intention
Kalb, John	10 Oct 1832	Notice of Intention
Kalb, Jacob	21 Jan 1832	Notice of Intention
Kuhl, Henry	12 Oct 1832	Notice of Intention
	13 Oct 1834	Citizen
Kane, Christopher	16 June 1834	Citizen
Kottman, John F. F.	5 Oct 1832	Citizen
Kelly, John A.	4 Oct 1832	Citizen
Krain, Adolphus	8 Oct 1832	Citizen
Kidd, Charles	13 Oct 1828	Citizen
Kirkpatrick, Andrew	14 Oct 1828	Citizen
Konefick, Daniel	11 Oct 1828	Citizen
Kelly, Edmund B.	7 Oct 1831	Citizen
Kalb, George	27 Jan 1832	Citizen
Ker, Henry	8 Aug 1798	Citizen
Kennedy, W.	5 Oct 1830	Citizen
Kenny, James	8 Oct 1830	Citizen
Kennedy, Stewart	16 Jun 1832	Citizen
Kenaghan, Thomas	6 Oct 1835	Citizen
Keenan, Edward	8 Oct 1830	Citizen
Koch, John C.	7 Jun 1839	Citizen
Kennedy, Dennis	1 Feb 1840	Notice
Kennedy, Henry	17 May 1841	Citizen
Kester, Chris	26 May 1841	Citizen
Kremer, Philip	8 Jun 1841	Citizen
Kelly, Thos Hughes	20 Jan 1840	Notice of Intention
Kennedy, Dennis	1 Feb 1840	Notice of Intention
Koster, Jacob	10 Jan 1840	Citizen
Kilroy, Michael	20 Jan 1840	Notice of Intention
Kilroy, Patrick	1 June 1840	Citizen
Keebey, Thos. M.	18 Jan 1841	Notice
Kemme, D. K.	27 Jan 1841	Notice
Kennedy, Henry	17 May 1841	Citizen
Kester, John Christopher	26 May 1841	Notice
Kremer, Philip	8 Jun 1841	Citizen
Kuhlmann, Herman	30 Jan 1841	Notice
King, Matthew	26 May 1842	Notice of Intention
Keeleg, Thomas M.	15 Mar 1843	Citizen
Keetz, Frederick H.	17 Jan 1843	Notice of Intention
Kennedy, Dennis	11 June 1842	Citizenship
Kilroy, Michael	7 Apr 1843	Citizenship
King, Jno	18 Oct 1842	Notice of Intention
Kruger, Christian	22 Apr 1843	Citizenship
Kolnitz, Henry Von	7 Sep 1843	Notice of Intention
Kirby, John	15 Nov 1843	Citizenship
Knebel, Frederick	26 Apr 1844	Notice of Intention
Kelly, James	23 Jan 1845	Notice of Intention
King, Mathew	29 Nov 1844	Citizenship
Klein, Jno. C.	4 Nov 1844	Notice of Intention
Koster, Jno. C.	13 Nov 1844	Citizenship
Kappelman, Marcus H.	19 Jun 1846	Notice
Kennedy, James	2 Jun 1847	Notice
Kessal, John	11 Jun 1847	Citizenship
King, Jeremiah	14 May 1846	Citizenship

Charleston

Name	Date	Description
Klien, Jno. C.	11 May 1847	Citizenship
Klein, Claus	20 May 1847	Citizenship
Kohlman, Fried.	17 Sep 1846	Notice
Konig, Jno. H.	28 Oct 1846	Citizenship
Kunhenne, F. W. H.	5 Feb 1846	Notice
Kelly, Daniel	6 Dec 1847	Notice
Kenealy, Cornelius	1 Dec 1847	Notice
Kennedy, Jno. G.	12 Nov 1847	Notice
Keoley, James	4 Aug 1847	Notice
Kenerty, Jno.	4 Sep 1847	Notice
Kite, Jacob	13 Mar 1848	Notice
Klein, Jas. J.	11 Nov 1847	Citizenship
Kleimbeck, Jno. D.	7 Feb 1848	Notice
Korber, Geo. Henry	17 Nov 1847	Citizenship
Kurth, Christian	28 Feb 1848	Notice of Intention
Kerstein, Herman	27 Sep 1848	Notice of Intention
King, Jno.	14 Jul 1848	Notice of Intention
Keegan, Edwd.	15 Feb 1849	Notice of Intention
Kelly, Peter	10 Nov 1848	Notice of Intention
Kelly, Patrick	30 Jan 1849	Notice of Intention
Kelly, Hugh	29 Sep 1848	Notice of Intention
Keran, Mathew	17 Feb 1849	Notice of Intention
Kuck, Henry	6 Dec 1848	Notice of Intention
Kunhenne, F. W. H.	1 Nov 1848	Citizenship
Keenan, John	27 Jul 1849	Notice of Intention
Kennedy, Michl. D.	16 Apr 1849	Notice of Intention
King, Archibald	16 Apr 1849	Notice of Intention
Kennedy, John	5 Oct 1849	Notice of Intention
Kenny, Jas.	13 Nov 1849	Citizenship
Kleimbeck, Jno. D.	27 May 1850	Citizenship
Knoche, Anton	7 Feb 1850	Notice of Intention
Kelly, Michael	19 Sep 1850	Notice of Intention
Kennelly, Jno.	5 Oct 1850	Notice of Intention
Kennedy, Jas.	15 Oct 1850	Notice of Intention
Kilroy, Edward	30 Dec 1850	Notice of Intention
Kirker, Jas.	18 Sep 1850	Notice of Intentnion
Laurens, Peter	8 Oct 1832	Notice of Intention
Lordar, Patrick	6 Oct 1823	Notice of Intention
Landon, James C.	10 Oct 1833	Notice of Intention
Legrex, John P.	8 Oct 1831	Citizen
Livingston, Henry	15 Jun 1810	Citizen
Ladeveze, R.	6 Feb 1813	Citizen
Le Camset, F.	13 Feb 1795	Citizen
Lear, John	6 Jun 1812	Citizen
Lyle, William	7 Oct 1833	Citizen
Lowe, Robert	14 Oct 1828	Citizen
Lopez, Joseph	7 Oct 1834	Citizen
Lachecotte, Julius	25 Jan 1832	Citizen
Lowther, Thomas	10 Oct 1828	Citizen
Lankenan, John H.	11 Oct 1830	Citizen
Lewis, William	11 Oct 1831	Citizen
Leslie, James	May 1794	Citizen
Lindsey, Samuel	11 Oct 1830	Citizen
Lodwick, Nicholas	11 Oct 1830	Citizen
Lowe, Charles	9 Oct 1830	Citizen
Leyman, C. K.	7 Jun 1841	Citizen
Linning, Phillip	1 Jun 1841	Notice
Leeburk, Deidrick	26 May 1841	
Landreth, D. M.	6 Jun 1840	Citizen
Lampe, Frederick	28 Jan 1841	Notice

Charleston

Name	Date	Description
Lewis, Jacob	Jan 1841	Notice
Linning, Philip	1 Jun 1841	Notice
Ludders, Frederick	30 Jan 1841	Citizen
Lange, Jno. H.	18 Mar 1843	Notice of Intention
Lutterman, Herman	22 Nov 1843	Notice of Intention
Lyons, Charles	14 Jul 1843	Notice of Intention
Lubs, P. S.	30 Aug 1843	Notice of Intention
Langan, Michael	17 Nov 1843	Notice of Intention
Lawles, John	7 Jun 1844	Notice of Intention
Linde, Luder G.	15 May 1844	Notice of Intention
Lonergan, James	25 Apr 1844	Notice of Intention
Lyons, James	18 May 1844	Notice of Intention
Lange, Jno. H.	29 Mar 1845	Citizenship
Laux, Martin	17 Mar 1845	Notice of Intention
Ling, Samuel	5 Nov 1844	Citizenship
Luttermann, H.	22 Mar 1845	Citizenship
Leopold, Fred.	25 Jul 2845	Notice
Lindfors, C. J.	1 Nov 1844	Notice
Lribs, P. S.	4 Nov 1845	Citizenship
Lucken, Henry	25 Jul 1845	Notice
Lissak, J. J.	27 Jan 1847	Notice
Lucas, Jonathan	12 Jun 1847	Citizenship
Luhren, C.	4 Jun 1847	Citizenship
Lunn, Charles A.	10 Aug 1846	Notice
Lynass, Michael	19 Jul 1847	Notice
Lyons, Michael	2 Feb 1848	Notice
Lathers, Richd.	17 May 1848	Citizenship
Luers, Frederick	31 Jul 1848	Notice of Intention
Leary, Daniel	27 Nov 1848	Notice of Intention
Leonard, Richard	22 Mar 1849	Notice of Intention
Lissack, J. J.	11 May 1849	Citizenship
Leitch, James	7 Jun 1849	Notice of Intention
Leman, Morris	13 Aug 1849	Notice of Intention
Loughry, James	15 Jun 1849	Notice of Intention
Laffan, Jas.	5 Oct 1849	Notice of Intention
Lyons, Darby	30 Mar 1850	Notice of Intention
Lanagan, Pat.	11 Oct 1850	Notice of Intention
Larsen, Jno. C.	6 Jan 1850	Notice of Intention
Lawler, Thos.	2 Jan 1850	Notice of Intention
Levy, Marse	9 Nov 1850	Citizenship
Lins, Henry	6 Nov 1850	Citizenship
Longbourues, Richd.	5 Oct 1850	Notice of Intention
Myer, Luder	26 May 1837	Notice of Intention
Mathuren, E. M. Miss	18 May 1837	Notice of Intention
Magee, John	27 May 1823	Notice of Intention
Mulloy, William	19 Jan 1832	Notice of Intention
McDermott, Edward	4 Oct 1831	Notice of Intention
McLaren, James	8 Jun 1833	Notice of Intention
McGolrich, Edward	7 Feb 1833	Notice of Intention
Memminger, G. C.	11 Feb 1824	Notice of Intention
McLeish, James	14 Oct 1836	Notice of Intention
	18 May 1839	Citizen
Murphy, Thomas	25 Jan 1836	Notice of Intention
Myer, John	13 Jun 1812	Notice of Intention
	9 Oct 1832	Citizen
Marshall, John T.	18 Oct 1834	Notice of Intention
Myer,Johan	5 Oct 1837	Notice of Intention
McFeeter, Andrew	9 Oct 1830	Citizen
Maynard, John	11 Oct 1830	Citizen
Massalow, J. F.	18 May 1837	Citizen

Charleston

Name	Date	Description
McDermot, Timothy	11 Oct 1830	Citizen
McKinley, John	13 Jun 1812	Citizen
Martinez, Joseph	5 Oct 1831	Citizen
Matthiessen, John Mathias	3 Oct 1831	Citizen
McKenzie, George	10 Oct 1831	Citizen
Mairs, Levi	10 Oct 1831	Citizen
Martineau, John M.	10 Oct 1831	Citizen
McDonald, William	26 May 1792	Citizen
McKenzie, Archibald	11 Oct 1831	Citizen
Mullins, Charles P.	10 Feb 1821	Notice of Intention
	7 Oct 1834	Citizen
McBurney, John R.	12 Oct 1830	Citizen
Michell, John	12 Oct 1830	Citizen
McDonald, B. B.	10 May 1836	Citizen
Mitchell, William	8 Oct 1836	Citizen
Meynardie, C.	9 Oct 1830	Citizen
McDuffie, N.	9 Oct 1830	Citizen
McCullough, James P.	12 Oct 1830	Citizen
Miller, Francis F.	23 Oct 1830	Citizen
McClelland, Jackson	10 Oct 1836	Citizen
Marlow, James	11 Oct 1836	Citizen
Magee, J. J.	12 May 1838	Citizen
Myres, John	5 Oct 1832	Citizen
Miller, Robert	4 Oct 1832	Citizen
Morton, F. L.	3 Oct 1832	Citizen
Miller, Charles	11 Oct 1834	Citizen
Montgomery, Andrew	9 Oct 1832	Citizen
Miller, James C.	11 Oct 1824	Citizen
Myer, Gerd A.	9 May 1838	Citizen
Morrison, John	15 Jun 1799	Citizen
Moutt, William	19 May 1832	Citizen
McLean, Peter	19 Oct 1834	Citizen
Murray, John M.	13 Oct 1828	Citizen
McKeegan, John	20 Oct 1828	Citizen
Moss, Joseph	28 Jun 1833	Citizen
Magwood, Robert	21 Jan 1812	Citizen
McCauley, William	22 Oct 1830	Citizen
McGowan, Archibald	6 Oct 1830	Citizen
Moise, Cherry	16 Jun 1810	Citizen
Murray, Jeremiah	7 Jun 1811	Citizen
Moore, Hugh	4 Jun 1830	Citizen
Miller, John Christian	3 Jun 1839	Citizen
Mertens, Frederick	1 Feb 1839	Citizen
Maghre, Jno. G.	8 Jan 1841	Notice
Mehrtens, H. Wehlmen	19 Jan 1841	Notice
Maher, Thomas	28 Jan 1841	Notice
Meyer, M. K.	20 May 1841	Citizen
Middendorff, Henry	5 Jun 1841	Citizen
Moffett, George	26 May 1841	Citizen
McNatty, S.	5 Jun 1841	Citizen
McDonald, John	25 Jan 1840	Notice of Intention
McEnny, Barney	23 Jan 1840	Citizen
McHugh, Patrick	25 Jan 1840	Notice of Intention
McKeogh, John	10 Jan 1840	Notice of Intention
McNamara, Laurence	22 Jan 1840	Notice of Intention
Meredith, Richard	19 Jan 1840	Notice of Intention
Metzler, William	30 Jan 1840	Notice of Intention
Miller, Jno. Haig.	21 Jan 1840	Notice of Intention
McAuliff, Richard	24 May 1841	Citizen
McDonough, P.	Jan 1841	Notice
McKenzie, John	19 May 1841	Notice

Charleston

Name	Date	Description
McNally, Samuel	5 Jun 1841	Citizen
Maher, Thomas	28 Jan 1841	Notice
Mehrtens, H. Wilhelm	28 Jan 1841	Notice
Mehrtens, H. W.	29 May 1841	Citizen
Meyer, B. H.	28 Jan 1841	Notice
Meyer, M. K.	20 May 1841	Citizen
Middendorf, Herman Henry	5 Jun 1841	Notice
Moffett, George	26 May 1841	Notice
McLaren, James	20 Jan 1839	Citizen
McAndrew, Patrick	7 Jan 1842	Citizen
Mancinelli, Louis	20 Jan 1842	Notice
McKeogh, John	16 Mar 1843	Citizenship
McLean, William	22 Apr 1843	Notice of Intention
Maher, Thomas	17 Mar 1843	Citizenship
Mahler, Henry	1 Apr 1843	Citizenship
Menzanmaier, Charles F.	24 May 1843	Notice of Intention
Meredith, Richard	16 Mar 1843	Citizenship
Meyer, Jno.	7 Apr 1843	Notice of Intention
Meyer, Andreas	24 Nov 1842	Notice of Intention
Moroso, Anthony	19 Oct 1842	Notice of Intention
Muhlenbrink, H.	20 Mar 1843	Citizenship
Murray, James	6 Mar 1843	Notice of Intention
Marjenhoff, Eibe Henning	30 Aug 1843	Notice of Intention
Moore, Thomas	27 Sep 1843	Notice of Intention
Meyer, Henry	6 Oct 1843	Notice of Intention
McClure, John B.	12 Apr 1844	Citizenship
McEnernay, Michael	15 Jun 1844	Notice of Intention
McLeish, Archibald	27 Jun 1844	Notice of Intention
McNamara, Lawrence	22 Mar 1844	Citizenship
Magrath, Michael	6 Jul 1844	Notice of Intention
Meyer, Cord	1 Apr 1844	Notice of Intention
Miller, Frederick	9 Jul 1844	Notice of Intention
Molony, John	2 Jul 1844	Notice of Intention
Murray, Edward	1 Jun 1844	Notice of Intention
McInherpeny, Michael	18 Jan 1845	Notice of Intention
Meyer, John	10 Mar 1845	Citizenship
Meyer, C. J.	20 Feb 1845	Notice of Intention
Mokler, John	19 Feb 1845	Notice of Intention
Munzanman, C. F.	17 Mar 1845	Citizenship
McCarey, Jas.	19 Jul 1845	Notice
McEvoy, Wm.	23 Oct 1845	Notice
McKenna, James C.	16 Jul 1845	Notice
Mc Lean, Wm.	22 Nov 1845	Citizenship
Meyer, Christ.	20 Feb 1845	Notice
Monohan, Thos	16 Sep 1845	Notice
McGary, Francis P.	23 Apr 1846	Notice
Magrath, Roger	23 Sep 1846	Notice
Maguire, Thomas	14 Dec 1846	Notice
Maher, Wm.	22 Jan 1846	Notice
Marjenhoff, Eibe H.	11 May 1846	Citizenship
Meyer, Jno	29 Apr 1846	Notice
Mokler, Jno	8 Jun 1847	Citizenship
Murchen, Ahrend	27 Jun 1846	Notice
McCormick, Jas.	23 Sep 1847	Notice
McCormick, Peter	14 Aug 1847	Notice
McCormick, Jno.	14 Aug 1847	Notice
McGaines, Jas.	12 Jun 1847	Citizenship
McKeough, Timothy	14 Aug 1847	Notice
McLeish, Wm.	2 Aug 1847	Notice
Maha or Moka, Jno.	1 Sep 1847	Notice
Maloney, Thos	30 Jul 1847	Notice

Charleston

Name	Date	Description
Manahan, Timothy	11 Oct 1847	Notice
Mansfield, Terrance	17 Jul 1847	Notice
Martin, Isaac	31 Mar 1848	Notice
Mayer, Henry	20 Mar 1848	Notice
Meyer, C. G.	26 Jan 1848	Notice
Morris, P.	27 Oct 1847	Notice
Muirhead, Rob.	19 Nov 1847	Notice
Murphy, Jas.	5 Jan 1848	Notice of Intention
Murray, Jos.	21 Feb 1848	Notice of Intention
McAndrew, James	17 Aug 1848	Notice of Intention
Masher, Jas.	17 Jun 1848	Notice of Intention
Meahe, Wilhelm	12 Aug 1848	Notice of Intention
Meyer, Jno.	8 Jun 1848	Citizenship
Meitzler, Jno.	2 May 1848	Notice of Intention
Mollard, Jno.	24 Jul 1848	Notice of Intention
Mulvaney, Michael	17 Jul 1848	Notice of Intention
McDonald, Owen	12 Jan 1849	Notice of Intention
McGrath, Michael	25 Mar 1849	Notice of Intention
Macdonald, Alex. T.	10 May 1848	Notice of Intention
Mehrtens, C. F.	10 Nov 1848	Notice of Intention
Meyer, Oswald	8 Jan 1849	Notice of Intention
Meyer, Cord.	23 Jun 1847	Citizenship
Miller, Jno. L.	26 Feb 1849	Notice of Intention
McCabe, James	1 Aug 1849	Notice of Intention
McNamara, Jos.	27 Mar 1849	Notice of Intention
Maguire, Thomas	31 May 1849	Citizenship
Metzler, Emiel	3 Jul 1849	Notice of Intention
Meyer, Jno. C.	9 Jun 1849	Citizenship
McCormick, Peter	13 Nov 1849	Citizenship
McDowell, Rob L.	29 Jun 1850	Notice of Intention
McGarrty, Michael	17 Sep 1849	Notice of Intention
McKenna, Jas. C.	23 Nov 1849	Citizenship
McKenna, F.	24 Aug 1849	Notice of Intention
McManus, Michael	14 Nov 1849	Notice of Intention
Martin, Isaac	1 Jun 1850	Citizenship
Maynard, W. J.	3 Jun 1850	Notice of Intention
Mehrtens, Henry	7 Sep 1849	Notice of Intention
Misdorf, Jacob	2 Nov 1849	Citizenship
Morrison, Kenneth	13 Nov 1849	Notice of Intention
Muirhead, Rob.	19 Nov 1849	Citizenship
Murphy, Laurence	21 Mar 1850	Notice of Intention
Murray, Michl J. & his son J. H. Murray	15 Nov 1849	Notice of Intention
McDonnell, Patrick	27 Sep 1830(?)	Notice of Intention
McSweeny, Daniel	24 Dec 1850	Notice of Intention
Maguire, Wm.	12 Aug 1850	Notice of Intention
Meyer, Jno	28 Aug 1850	Notice of Intention
Meyer, Claus	8 Nov 1850	Citizenship
Meyer, C. H.	10 Oct 1850	Notice of Intention
Meyer, Jno.	3 Jun 1850	Citizenship
Morrison, Thos.	14 Oct 1850	Notice of Intention
Murphy, Jno:	21 Dec 1850	Notice of Intention
McBride, Owen	8 Oct 1850	Notice of Intention
Novertney, Ignes	16 Jun 1823	Notice of Intention
Neville, John	5 Feb 1831	Notice of Intention
Newton, William		
Niel, Adrian Jaques	5 Feb 1812	Citizen
Nelson, Richard	4 Oct 1831	Citizen
Naylor, William	3 Oct 1832	Citizen
Naylor, William	12 Feb 1824	Citizen

Charleston

Name	Date	Description
Newman, John	9 Oct 1830	Citizen
Ninitz, Wm	29 Jan 1841	Citizen
Nihaus, Jno. Wm. Frederic	6 Jan 1840	Notice of Intention
Nantz, Wm.	29 Jan 1841	Notice
Nash, Wm.	14 Jun 1844	Notice of Intention
Nunan, George	5 Sep 1844	Notice of Intention
Nevin, Patrick	30 Aug 1845	Notice of Intention
Naumann or Neumann, P.	3 Mar 1846	Notice of Intention
Nunan, Geo.	5 Jun 1846	Citizenship
Nimitz, Charles H.	29 Sep 1847	Notice of Intention
Noelkin, Christian	28 Aug 1848	Notice of Intention
Natale, Peter	2 Mar 1849	Notice of Intention
Nunan, Jno.	24 Oct 1848	Notice of Intention
Neeson, T. P. L.	30 Dec 1848	Notice of Intention
Naumann, Philip	17 Nov 1849	Citizen
Neuts, Andries	3 Dec 1849	Notice of Intention
Nicholson, Jno.	6 May 1850	Notice of Intention
Nowlan, Michael	4 May 1850	Notice of Intention
Nugent, Michael	9 Dec 1850	Notice of Intention
Oliver, Joseph	6 Oct 1832	Notice
O'Sullivan, Denny	16 May 1838	Notice
O'Neill, Thomas	8 Jan 1838	Notice
Oberhaussen, Johannes	6 Jun 1836	Notice
	19 Jan 1839	Citizenship
O'Reilly, Eugene	4 Feb 1822	Notice
O'Brien, Thomas	6 Oct 1832	Notice
	9 Oct 1834	Citizenship
O'Brien, William	5 Feb 1834	Notice
Owen, John Leslie	10 Jun 1832	Citizen
Oslaide, Thomas C.	7 Oct 1832	Citizen
O'Hanlon, Charles	7 Oct 1832	Citizen
Ormond, James	7 Oct 1832	Citizen
Ogilvie, Mathew	3 Oct 1832	Citizen
O'Farrell, James	7 Oct 1836	Citizen
O'Keefe, Arthur	11 Oct 1828	Citizen
Owen, Thomas	11 Oct 1830	Citizen
O'Brien, Peter	8 Jan 1841	Notice
OMara, John	1 Feb 1840	Notice
O'Neill, Edmund	12 Oct 1830	Citizen
Oetgen, Henry	17 May 1841	Citizen
Oldenberg, Henrick	28 Jan 1841	Citizen
Omara, John	11 Jun 1842	Citizen
O'Brien, Peter	6 Apr 1843	Citizen
Oelrich, F. W.	16 Apr 1844	Citizen
O'Neill, Bernard	6 Sep 1848	Notice
Osterholtz, Jno. D.	20 Mar 1844	Citizen
O'Brien, Jeremiah	1 Nov 1844	Citizen
Ostendorff, A. C. A.	1 Jun 1846	Citizen
Osbahrt, Wm.	8 Nov 1848	Citizen
O'Brien, John	14 Jun 1849	Notice
O'Callaghan, Patrick	12 Apr 1849	Notice
O'Connor, W. B.	5 May 1849	Notice
Oetgen, John C.	29 May 1849	Citizen
Otgen, Jno. C.	14 Jun 1849	Citizen
O'Connel, Jas.	20 Nov 1849	Notice
O'Connor, Jas.	6 May 1850	Notice
O'Neill, Patrick	13 Feb 1850	Notice
O'Brien, John	10 Oct 1850	Notice
O'Neil, Wm	20 Nov 1850	Notice
O'Neil, Patrick	20 Nov 1850	Notice

Charleston

Name	Date	Description
O'Neil, Thos	20 Nov 1850	Notice
O'Rourke, Bernard	12 Nov 1850	Notice
O'Brien, Peter	8 Jan 1841	Notice
Osterholtz, Jno. Deiderik	28 Jan 1842	Notice
O'Sullivan, James	30 May 1842	Notice
O'Connell, Jeremiah	25 Jan 1843	Notice
O'Callaghan, Dennis	5 Dec 1844	Notice
O'Neill, Richard	19 Nov 1844	Notice
O'Neill, John	16 Dec 1844	Notice
Oppert, Vincent	31 Oct 1844	Notice
Oetjen, Jno. C.	28 Apr 1847	Notice
Oland, C.	6 Aug 1846	Notice
O'Brien, And	28 Mar 1848	Notice
O'Connell, Patrick	20 Sep 1847	Notice
O'Connor, Jno.	28 Sep 1847	Notice
Oldenburg, Henry	3 Nov 1847	Notice
O'Neill, Wm.	8 Mar 1848	Notice
Otten, Peter	6 Mar 1848	Notice
O'Callaghan, D.	9 Jun 1848	Notice
Pranninger, Leonard	22 Feb 1812	Notice
Passmeyer, A. B.	14 Oct 1836	Notice
Peixotto, Solomon	14 Oct 1834	Notice
Panknin, Charles	11 May 1837	Notice
Preston, John	11 Oct 1831	Notice
Patterson, James	3 Oct 1825	Citizen
Pritchard, Edmund C.	4 Oct 1836	Citizen
Pritchard, William Jr.	21 Oct 1796	Citizen
Pemberton, George	14 Oct 1834	Citizen
Podestor, Louis	14 Oct 1834	Citizen
Placide, Alexander	1 Jun 1812	Citizen
Powell, Thomas	8 Oct 1832	Citizen
Pedimant, John	8 Oct 1830	Citizen
Pearce, John	3 Oct 1838	Citizen
Phelan, Richard	12 Oct 1830	Citizen
Parker, Henry	11 Oct 1823	Citizen
Pansin, Charles	6 Oct 1831	Citizen
Penot, John	8 Oct 1831	Citizen
Payne, W. J.	8 Oct 1831	Citizen
Poland, Oliver	9 Oct 1830	Citizen
Preston, James	7 Feb 1831	Citizen
Petit, William	12 Oct 1830	Citizen
Potorino, Stephen	11 Oct 1830	Citizen
Purdy, James	21 May 1807	Citizen
Pagnanski, G.	17 Jan 1841	Notice
Panknin, Charles	27 May 1840	Citizen
Perram, William	May 1841	Citizen
Prior, William	30 Jan 1841	Notice
Peterson, Christian	28 May 1842	Citizen
Pass, Alexander	5 Apr 1843	Citizen
Passailaigue, Eulalie	29 Mar 1843	Citizen
Prior, William	13 Mar 1843	Citizen
Puder, Geo. C.	23 Oct 1843	Citizen
Payne, Thomas	9 Nov 1843	Citizen
Park, Robert	23 Jan 1845	Notice
Pindar, Louis	9 Dec 1845	Notice
Prior, B. R.	18 Jun 1846	Notice
Patterson, Jno.	2 Aug 1848	Notice
Power, Morris	24 Jul 1847	Notice
Paturzo, Ferdinando	7 Oct 1848	Notice
Park, Mary	24 Oct 1849	Citizen

Charleston

Name	Date	Description
Phillips, Tho.	10 Jun 1850	Citizen
Pontz, Law	1 Mar 1850	Notice
Prince, Geo.	13 Jun 1850	Notice
Prior, B. R.	7 May 1850	Citizen
Petter, Jno.	11 Sep 1850	Notice
Punch, T. J.	5 Jul 1850	Notice
Quin, John	7 Oct 1830	Citizen
Quinlan, John	12 Oct 1830	Citizen
Quigly, Edward	27 Jan 1838	Notice
Quirk, Wm.	28 Mar 1832	Notice
Quirk, Wm.	11 Apr 1845	Citizen
Quale, Jno. N.	3 Sep 1846	Notice
Quinn, Arthur	20 Jul 1847	Notice
Quigley, Charles	29 Aug 1849	Notice
Quinn, Daniel	27 Jun 1849	Notice
Rose, William P.	20 May 1836	Notice
Richtey, John Jr.	21 Apr 1829	Notice
	5 Sep 1831	Citizen
Rowe, James	31 Jan 1826	Notice
Ryan, Oliver	5 Oct 1837	Notice
Rigelo, John	12 Oct 1830	Notice
	7 Oct 1834	Citizen
Reges, Joseph	5 Oct 1831	Notice
Reid, John T.	13 Oct 1836	Notice
Recardo, Joseph	6 Oct 1834	Citizen
Richards, John	10 Oct 1834	Citizen
Ryley, Joseph	5 Oct 1832	Citizen
Ryan, James	11 Oct 1830	Citizen
Rooney, Paul	11 Oct 1828	Citizen
Ryan, Francis	14 Oct 1834	Citizen
Rousseau, Jules	14 Oct 1834	Citizen
Rickerty, Laureny	9 Oct 1830	Citizen
Rainey, James	8 Oct 1832	Citizen
Rock, John	6 Oct 1832	Citizen
Ryan, John	11 Oct 1828	Citizen
Roumillat, Eugene	12 May 1830	Citizen
Routereau, Charles	11 Oct 1830	Citizen
Riviere, J. P.	11 Oct 1831	Citizen
Ryan, Thomas	4 Jun 1823	Notice
Rene, Bossiere	12 Oct 1830	Citizen
Roberts, Nathaniel	12 Oct 1838	Citizen
Roe, James	8 Oct 1830	Citizen
Rosenbohm, John H.	7 Oct 1830	Citizen
Revell, George	12 Feb 1806	Citizen
Rams, Thomas	9 Oct 1830	Citizen
Ridley, James	11 Oct 1830	Citizen
Rabb, Jacob	12 Oct 1830	Citizen
Reguier, A. J. B.	12 Oct 1830	Citizen
Reilly, John P.	11 Oct 1830	Citizen
Reilly, Charles	11 Oct 1836	Citizen
Rogge, Conrad	10 Oct 1836	Citizen
Ryan, Patrick	10 Oct 1826	Citizen
Rose, Richard	28 May 1839	Citizen
Reynolds, Michael	29 Jan 1841	Notice
Riddock, Arthur	30 Jan 1841	Notice
Rosentreter, G. F.	1 Jun 1841	Notice
Reynolds, Michael	29 Jan 1841	Notice
Rieekweg, William	27 Jan 1841	Citizen
Rosenburg, Morris	Jan 1841	Notice

Charleston

Name	Date	Description
Rosentreter, Geo. F.	1 Jun 1841	Notice
Riddock, Arthur	30 Jan 1841	Notice
Rowland, Peter	30 Nov 1842	Notice
Rowland, Michael	30 Nov 1842	Notice
Riecke, Carshen	12 Apr 1843	Notice
Rogers, John	19 Jun 1844	Notice
Rosis, T. M. V.	3 Jun 1844	Notice
Ryan, Michael	26 Feb 1844	Notice
Rassau, Jno. H.	16 Aug 1844	Notice
Roberts, Francis	8 Nov 1844	Citizen
Robinson, Jos. A.	4 Nov 1844	Notice
Rosis, Joseph	12 Sep 1844	Notice
Reed, Jno. T.	17 Oct 1846	Notice
Rians, Peter	13 Jan 1847	Notice
Riecke, Henry W.	13 Oct 1846	Notice
Rogers, Samuel	15 Jun 1847	Notice
Runcken, Henry	1 Mar 1847	Notice
Ryan, Jno. L.	11 Mar 1845	Citizen
Rey, Geo.	1 Mar 1848	Notice
Riley, Alex.	18 Nov 1847	Notice
Ryan, Patrick	18 Dec 1847	Notice
Rasilly, Rhos.	7 Mar 1848	Notice
Reid, Jno. P.	10 Nov 1848	Citizen
Rimrod, Lewis	17 Dec 1848	Notice
Roark, Felix	6 Nov 1848	Notice
Read, Charles	27 Jun 1849	Notice
Ryan, Paul	16 Jun 1849	Citizen
Ryan, Elizabeth	16 Jun 1849	Citizen
Ryan, Wm.	21 May 1849	Notice
Reilly, Wm.	11 Jun 1850	Notice
Rohfling, Heinrich	6 Nov 1850	Notice
Ryan, O'Callaghan P.	21 Dec 1850	Notice
Shroder, Charles	8 Oct 1832	Notice
Scharff, Frederick	6 Oct 1837	Notice
Shanley, Daniel	8 Oct 1832	Citizen
Shea, Brown	12 Oct 1830	Notice
	7 Oct 1834	Citizen
Smith, Patrick	12 Oct 1830	Notice
	6 Oct 1834	Citizen
Stockfleet, John	12 Oct 1832	Notice
	13 Oct 1834	Citizen
Sweeny, Michael	6 Oct 1832	Notice
Steicke, John	11 Oct 1831	Notice
Stevens, Charles	11 Oct 1836	Notice
Short, James	11 Oct 1836	Notice
Smith, James	14 Oct 1836	Citizen
Schutte, John Henry	12 May 1829	Notice
Simoni, Francis	21 Jan 1812	Citizen
Sweegan, M.	12 Oct 1830	Citizen
Salvo, Conrado	25 Jan 1826	Citizen
Sollier, Louis	28 May 1814	Citizen
Salomois, Sarah	16 Jun 1834	Citizen
Siless, Peter	13 Oct 1834	Citizen
Stark, Charles	9 Oct 1826	Citizen
Smith, Samuel	6 Oct 1831	Citizen
Sampson, Emanuel	14 Oct 1834	Citizen
Sheridan, Jno. J.	14 Oct 1828	Citizen
Sweeney, Edward Revd.	20 Oct 1828	Citizen
Saburn, Thomas	22 Jan 1812	Citizen
Satterthwaite, Tho. W.		Citizen

Charleston	Date	Description
Smith, James	5 Oct 1836	Citizen
Schroder, Christian	11 Oct 1836	Citizen
Shanks, Charles	11 Oct 1830	Citizen
Simpson, James	7 Oct 1830	Citizen
Smith, Mary M.	12 May 1835	Citizen
Stubble, William Daniel	5 Oct 1832	Citizen
Stuardi, John B.	9 Oct 1830	Citizen
Smyth, Francis	8 Oct 1830	Citizen
Storm, James Gordan	7 May 1839	Citizen
Stelling, John	17 May 1839	Citizen
Strain, Louis	15 Jun 1839	Citizen
Seebeck, Dederik	14 May 1839	Notice
Sherman, Clarke	14 May 1839	Notice
Silcox, Jeremiah	18 May 1839	Citizen
Scharleck, Alexander	29 May 1839	Citizen
Scharlock, George	23 May 1839	Citizen
Singstock, Herman	29 Jan 1841	Citizen
Scroder, J. D. W.	15 Jan 1841	Notice
Schnewyer, Henry	28 Jan 1841	Notice
Schwing, Charles	14 Jan 1841	Citizen & Notice
Schroder, John	28 May 1841	Notice
Scharff, Frederick	9 Jan 1840	Citizen
Schroder, Jno. William	31 Jan 1840	Notice
Sullivan, Timothy J. Revd.	20 Jan 1840	Notice
Seibeck, Dederick	26 May 1841	Citizen
Scherfersee, August	4 Jun 1841	Notice
Schmidt, Conrad	30 Jan 1841	Citizen
Schmidt, Ernst	29 Jan 1841	Citizen
Schnapel, William	29 Jan 1841	Citizen
Schneger, Henry	28 Jan 1841	Notice
Schnilker, Arend	23 Jan 1841	Citizen
Schroder, Jno. D. William	15 Jan 1841	Notice
Schroder, John	28 May 1841	Notice
Schuchmann, Lewis	30 Jan 1841	Citizen
Scharing, Charles	14 Jan 1841	Notice
Seaman, Arp	28 Jan 1841	Citizen
Seba, Bruns	30 Jan 1841	Citizen
Sengstock, Herman	29 Jan 1841	Citizen
Soin, Charles	8 Jan 1841	Notice
Sturcken, Herman	30 Jan 1841	Citizen
Sullivan, Revd. T. J.	24 Jan 1842	Citizen
Sripdorff, Jno. Gustavus	13 Jan 1842	Notice
Simpson, Abram	21 Jan 1842	Notice
Schmetzer, Geo. Charles	11 Apr 1843	Citizen
Schroeder, Jno. D. W.	14 Mar 1843	Citizen
Schroder, Jno. Wm.	20 Mar 1843	Citizen
Schwing, Charles	16 Mar 1843	Citizen
Shanahan, Thomas	25 Jan 1843	Notice
Soin, Charles	17 Mar 1843	Citizen
Streffatter, John	21 Mar 1843	Citizen
Streffatter, Andrew	21 Mar 1843	Citizen
Streffatter, Martin	22 Mar 1843	Citizen
Stein, Francis	17 Mar 1843	Notice
Stelling, Henry	31 Mar 1843	Citizen
Schnetter, John	6 Oct 1843	Notice
Sullivan, Phillip	14 Nov 1843	Citizen
Sancken, John	29 Nov 1843	Notice
Sinclair, Daniel	15 Nov 1843	Citizen
Schafer, Joseph	11 Mar 1844	Notice
Schroder, Christopher	6 Apr 1844	Citizen
Sherman, Thomas	1 Jun 1844	Notice
Schwing, Charles	4 Jun 1844	Denizenship
Sahlman, Carsten	22 Jul 1844	Notice

Charleston

Name	Date	Description
Segar, Solomon	12 Sep 1844	Notice
Schermer, Simon	28 Dec 1844	Notice
Schlepegrell, C.	5 Oct 1844	Notice
Schulken, Martin	12 Aug 1844	Notice
Sheridan, John	11 Nov 1844	Notice
Stein, Francis	19 Mar 1845	Citizen
Stender, H.	23 Aug 1844	Declaration of Intention
Sussdorff, Jno. G.	8 Nov 1844	Citizen
Schacte, Wm.	25 Jul 1845	Notice
Seevers, Henry	2 Sep 1845	Notice
Stein, Francis	19 Mar 1845	Citizen
Stelling, Diederick	25 Oct 1845	Notice
Stockfleth, Henry	17 Nov 1845	Citizen
Sahlman, Carsten	20 May 1847	Notice
Sandberg, Charles	2 Mar 1847	Notice
Scharlock, A.	11 May 1847	Citizen
Schoneman, H. G.	6 Feb 1846	Notice
Seeba, Christopher F.	20 Dec 1845	Notice
Shanahan, Thomas	13 Jun 1846	Citizen
Shea, Robert	3 Jun 1846	Notice
Sheridan, John	7 May 1847	Citizen
Siemenson, Theo.	11 Sep 1846	Notice
Streckfuss, Jno. F.	2 Jun 1847	Notice
Sahlman, Harman	3 Aug 1847	Notice
Sally, Wm.	14 Aug 1847	Notice
Schael, Jno. M.	12 May 1847	Notice
Schotter, N.	29 Nov 1847	Notice
Schreiner, Mary H.	2 Nov 1847	Notice
Seckendorff, Isaac	19 Nov 1847	Notice
Shanahin, Daniel	21 Oct 1847	Notice
Singleton, Jos.	4 Oct 1847	Notice
Spilmann, Jno.	25 Sep 1847	Notice
Stetling, Diederick	5 Nov 1847	Citizen
Sutton, Michael	19 Nov 1847	Notice
Schoneman, Harman G.	8 Jun 1848	Citizen
Schreck, H.	14 Apr 1848	Notice
Seeba, Christopher F.	20 May 1848	Citizen
Stoman, Jno.	8 Apr 1848	Notice
Sweany, Thoma	8 Jul 1848	Notice
Schulken, Fred.	18 Oct 1848	Notice
Schwartz, F. W.	13 Nov 1848	Notice
Seely, J. W.	2 Mar 1849	Notice
Seymour, T. Tucker	28 Nov 1848	Notice
Siebern, C. G.	8 Jan 1849	Notice
Steinmeyer, J. D.	28 Sep 1848	Notice
Stetling, Dederick	4 Nov 1847	Citizen
Sutherland, Wm.	7 Dec 1848	Notice
Sachtleben, Aug.	7 Oct 1848	Notice
Schnickenberger, G. A.	22 May 1849	Notice
Shanahan, Timothy	24 Jul 1849	Notice
Smith, Michael	23 Aug 1849	Notice
Streckfuss, Jno. F.	9 Jun 1849	Citizen
Schreiner, Mary H.	5 Nov 1849	Citizen
Schroder, Fred.	29 Apr 1850	Notice
Sheridan, Jas.	13 Oct 1849	Notice
Siepel , Geo. Jno.	19 Apr 1850	Notice
Stewart, Jno.	7 Mar 1850	Notice
Stellor, Peter	29 Jan 1850	Notice
Sullivan, Jno.	31 Aug 1849	Notice
Schaller, Charles	17 Oct 1850	Notice

Charleston

Name	Date	Description
Schroder, Carl F.	29 Oct 1850	Notice
Speiske, Jno. F.	29 Oct 1850	Notice
Stenhouse, Thos.	17 Oct 1850	Notice
Thompson, Robert	16 Jun 1823	Notice
Trescot, Joseph	22 Feb 1812	Notice
Timmonay, Peter	11 Oct 1830	Citizen
Turnbull, Joseph	9 Oct 1830	Citizen
Taveau, Augustus	31 Jan 1835	Citizen
Thrane, G. W.	31 Jul 1831	Citizen
Tobin, Richard	8 Oct 1836	Citizen
Taylor, James	20 Jun 1825	Citizen
Tavet, Julius	12 Oct 1830	Citizen
Thompson, James	13 Oct 1828	Citizen
Troude, Victor	11 Oct 1831	Citizen
Toersen, Henry	5 Oct 1832	Citizen
Trittan, George H.	5 Oct 1832	Citizen
Thomas, John N.	14 Oct 1828	Citizen
Thrane, G. W.	6 Jul 1830	Citizen
Tinken, Diedrick	16 May 1834	Citizen
Tevelin, Pat:	27 Jan 1841	Notice
Tietyen, Jno.C.	28 Jan 1841	Citizen
Tietyen, John H.	29 Jan 1841	Citizen
Tobin, William	5 May 1847	Citizen
Thomas, Michael	18 Oct 1842	Citizen
Thomas, Henry	18 Oct 1842	Citizen
Tarrants, Joseph	28 Jul 1843	Notice
Teppe, Wm.	4 Jan 1844	Notice
Torrant, John	18 May 1844	Notice
Tighe, Owen	8 May 1844	Notice
Tiedeman, O.	29 Mar 1845	Citizen
Thomas, Michael	13 Mar 1845	Citizen
Thomas, Henry	13 Mar 1845	Citizen
Torck, J. D.	11 Nov 1844	Notice
Touky, Maurice	4 May 1842	Notice
Temmerman, A. H.	11 Mar 1846	Notice
Thees, Henry	5 Jun 1847	Citizen
Thompson, Ninian	31 May 1847	Citizen
Todd, James	29 Sep 1846	Notice
Tolle, John	11 Mar 1846	Notice
Thomsaden, Edward	1 Apr 1848	Notice
Trou, A. W.	31 Jan 1848	Notice
Thompson, Thomas	5 Jul 1848	Notice
Tolle, Jno.	1 May 1848	Citizen
Torck, Jno. D.	11 Jun 1847	Citizen
Teppe, Wm.	18 May 1849	Citizen
Thode, H. P.	7 Oct 1850	Notice
Thompson, Hary	1 Oct 1850	Notice
Timmerman, Harman	25 May 1850	Citizen
Tracy, Wm.	16 Dec 1850	Notice
Underwood, Thomas	15 May 1838	Notice
Vidal, James F.	31 Jan 1831	Notice
	16 May 1834	Citizen
Vidal, Louis	9 Jun 1832	Notice
Vissor, John	10 Oct 1826	Citizen
Valance, Isaac	10 Oct 1831	Citizen
Vogel, Martin	8 Oct 1831	Citizen
Valentine, Samuel	17 Jan 1831	Citizen
Upmann, Diederick	20 May 1841	Citizen
Van Sprecken, Frederick	28 Jan 1841	Citizen

Charleston

Name	Date	Description
Van Glahn, Henry	20 Apr 1843	Citizen
Von Kolnitz, Henry	7 Sep 1843	Notice
Van Eitzen, Diederick	16 Aug 1844	Notice
Vogelsang, Meno Mrs.	10 Aug 1844	Notice
Von Glahn, John	20 Nov 1844	Citizen
Vonhollen, Henry W.	29 Nov 1844	Notice
Von Glahn, Henry	12 Nov 1845	Citizen
Van Eitzen, P.	20 May 1847	Citizen
Von Behn, Jacob	10 Jul 1848	Notice
Vanderlieth, E. H.	24 Aug 1849	Notice
Vogelsang, Mina	14 Nov 1849	Citizen
Volger, G. H. B.	29 Apr 1850	Notice
Wiley, Samuel	26 Jun 1823	Notice of Intention
	25 Jan 1826	Citizen
Wanless, A.	11 Oct 1831	Notice of Intention
Waller, William	15 Jun 1811	Citizen
Winchley, John	6 Feb 1812	Citizen
White, Timothy	13 Feb 1830	Citizen
Werner, Christopher	7 Oct 1835	Citizen
Weiman, Joseph	8 Oct 1830	Citizen
Wilken, Jurgen	5 Oct 1832	Citizen
White, James	13 Feb 1830	Citizen
Whitty, Edward	12 Oct 1830	Citizen
Wiley, W. J.	7 Oct 1836	Citizen
Wagner, Peter C.	10 Oct 1836	Citizen
White, Thomas	11 Oct 1836	Citizen
Woolf, Ralph	11 Oct 1836	Citizen
Wood, Edward	14 Jun 1826	Citizen
Weller, William	28 May 1814	Citizen
William, David	12 Oct 1830	Citizen
White, Charles L.	13 Feb 1830	Citizen
Wittpen, Frederick	7 Jan 1839	Citizen
Wagener, John A.	14 May 1839	Citizen
Woolfe, John F.	30 Jan 1841	Citizen
Walker, Henry Pinckney	Jan 1841	Denizenship & under special act
Watson, James	8 Jan 1841	Notice
Westerlon, C. F.	17 May 1841	Notice
Ward, Bernard	18 Oct 1841	Notice
Wildhagen, Charles	16 Dec 1842	Notice
Wilson, John	17 Oct 1842	Notice
Welch, William	27 Sep 1843	Notice
Wall, John	6 Oct 1843	Notice
Winkelhaus, Paul	18 Nov 1843	Citizen
Wartman, Henry	19 Jul 1844	Notice
Wellcocks, Thomas	23 May 1844	Notice
Walker, R. T.	10 Aug 1844	Notice
Ward, Barnard	13 Mar 1845	Citizen
Wickenberg, Fabian R.	4 Sep 1844	Notice
Wienholtz, Jno. T.	20 Mar 1845	Citizen
Wahrmann, Jno. H.	21 Nov 1844	Notice
Williams, Henry	13 Nov 1845	Notice
Waterman, Christian	12 May 1846	Citizen
Watson, Jno.R.	20 Apr 1847	Notice
Weber, Wendel	8 Feb 1847	Notice
Wienholtz, Frederick	20 May 1847	Citizen
Wilson, John	20 May 1846	Citizen
Wise, Alfred	31 May 1847	Denizen
Wise, Alfred	31 May 1847	Citizen
Wuhrmann, Jno. H.	20 May 1847	Citizen

Charleston

Name	Date	Description
Winckelmann, Aug. F.	14 Feb 1848	Notice
Woodall, Wm.	30 Mar 1848	Notice
Warnken, H. G.	18 Sep 1848	Notice
Wiemer, Gerhard	30 Sep 1848	Notice
Warnaka, Wm.	6 Sep 1848	Notice
Weiser, St. O.	26 Feb 1848	Notice
Weinfeldt, Oyzias	28 Feb 1849	Notice
Wohlcken, Lewis	3 Nov 1848	Notice
Watson, Jno.R.	9 May 1849	Citizen
Wendelken, Carsten	28 Aug 1849	Notice
Wendelken, Martin C.	18 Aug 1849	Notice
Wendelken, Martin	22 May 1849	Notice
Winberg, Jno. W.	9 May 1849	Notice
Wallace, Samuel	10 Aug 1849	Notice
Wolf, Jacob	9 Jun 1849	Notice
Walseman, Wm.	6 Nov 1850	Notice
Welsh, Jno.	9 Oct 1850	Notice
Whitting, Wm. Jos.	14 Nov 1850	Notice
Widau, Henry	7 Oct 1850	Notice
Wiemer, Gerhard	28 Oct 1850	Citizen
Yrela, Anastano	6 Oct 1834	Citizen
Young, Archibald	11 Oct 1831	Citizen
Zachariah, Jonathan	10 Jan 1843	Notice
Zehe, Henry	13 May 1846	Notice
Zehe, Henry	17 Nov 1849	Citizen

COUNTY RECORDS

The following are abstracts of all extant citizenship petitions and notices of intent for Charleston County/District through the year 1850. The originals are in the South Carolina Archives in Columbia.

Petition of Rev. John Christopher Faber, minister of the German Lutheran Church at Charleston...a native of the Dukedom of Wirtemberg in Germany, arrived in this City of Charleston, 14 July 1787...Charleston, May 29th 1790.
The Vestry and Wardens of the German St. John's Church testify that Rev. John Christopher Faber has conducted himself to our entire satisfaction: George Hahnbaum, Jacob Williman, Daniel Strobel, Abram. Markley, George Youn sen., Peter Dever, Jacob Sass, Jacob Martin, John C. Martin, John Burckmyer.

Notice of Intent of Henry Herman Funke, aged 30, carpenter, born in Oldenberg, arrived in Charleston 1847...19 April 1850.

Petition of Alexander Fullerton, aged 26, mariner, born in Scotland, arrived in Philadelphia, 1823, then a minor under 18 years, has made Charleston his home for five years...9 Oct 1832.

Notice of Intent of Anthony Francis aged 25, mariner, born West Indies, arrived at Fall River in Massachusetts, and came to Charleston in 1845, renounces allegiance to the Queen of Portugal ...15 March 1845.

Petition of John Fanning, aged 23, labourer, born Dublin County, Ireland, arrived at New York in December 1840, and came to South Carolina...15 March 1845.

Notice of Intent of Edward Francis, aged 44, manufactorer of Tobacco, born in France, arrived in Baltimore, September 1817, was attached to the American naval vessel "Franklin 74" for three years...20 Oct 1834.

Notice of Intent of James France aged 42, laborer, born in Lancashire, England, arrived in 1835 in New York, came to Charleston ...11 Octo 1845.

Notice of Intent of George Francis, aged 42, labourer, born Waterford County, Ireland, arrived in the U. S. in New York, September 1844, and came to Charleston in December of the same year...12 March 1845.

Petition of Michael Francis, aged about 38, mariner, born in Madarea, arrived in Charleston, 1 January 1811...renounces allegiance to the King of Portugal...12 October 1830.

Petition of Emanuel Francisco, born in Lisbon, embarked at the Port of Bordeau, arrived in Charleston, has been as resident of the U. S. for 18 years...he was about 18 years old when he arrived ...12 Oct 1830.

Notice of Intent of Joseph Frates,aged 48 years, fruit merchant, born in the Island of Mederia, arrived in New York, December 1832, and in Charleston August 1837...11 May 1842.

Notice of Intent of George Joseph Frey, aged about 36, repairer of musical instruments, b. Ruppertysberg, Canton Newstadt an der Haard, Rhein Pfalz, Kingdom of Bavaria...__ Oct 1846.

Notice of Intent of Christn. Freitag, aged 28, a storekeeper, born Ratzeburg, Dukedom of Holstein, 15 April 1815, arrived in Charleston December 1839...20 March 1843

COUNTY RECORDS

Charleston

Notice of Intent of Frederick Freize, aged 29 years, farmer, born in the Village of Diepholtz, Hanover in Germany, arrived in Baltimore 1832, came to Charleston, November 1836...12 May 1840. Petition for Citizenship dated 20 March 1843.

Notice of Intent of Martin Freer,aged 25, laborer, born in Ireland, arrived in New York, May 1845, came to Charleston August 1848... 26 July 1850.

Petition of John DeFries, 25, a Boarding House Keeper, born Holland, came to New York, 1839, and to Charleston in 1845...13 June 1849.

Notice of Intent of William Frintup, aged 39, painter, born in the Kingdom of Prussia, Germany, arrived at Baltimore, August 1843, and came to Charleston in the same year...12 Jan 1846.

Petition of Charles Stewart, late of the City of Bristol in Great Britain, has resided in Charleston four years past...2 November 1797.

Notice of Intent of Peter Rowland, aged 21, clerk, born in the Parish of Glennhest, County of Mayo, Ireland, arrived in New York, 1842...30 Nov 1842.

Petition of John Rushton, linnen draper, late of Great Britain, has resided in Charleston six years past...20 Sept 1796.

Petition of Francis Nelson, Shipwright, a native of Copenhagen, Denmark, hath resided in this state upwards of eight years... 15 Sept 1796.

Petition of Charles Morgan, Shipwright, a native of the Kingdom of Great Britain, has resided in this State upewards of seven years...15 Sept 1796.

Petition of Jules Rousseau, aged 23 years, tavern keeper, born in the town of Gonigny, France, arrived in New York, February 1827, then aged 16...13 October 1834.

Petition of Charles Rotureau, born in France, arrived in America in 1793, resident of Charleston 37 years...11 October 1830.

Petition of Gerhard Wiemer, aged 37, clerk, born in Oldenberg, arrived in Charleston, November 1842...28 October 1850.

Declaration of Intent from Kings County, New York; John Ganner, 4 November 1835.
Petition in Charleston District. John Ganner, aged 26, labourer, born Ireland, arrived in New York in April 1833, resided in Charleston two years. Filed 15 June 1839.

Petition of Joseph Gamboa, aged 23, mariner or rigger, born on the Island of Marguerite, dominion of the Republic of Colombia, arrived in Charleston, 19 October 1824...5 October 1836.

Petition for Denizenship of Alexander Gambotti, born Rovigo, Empire of Austria, aged 42 years, resided in U. S. since 1833...15 March 1846. Notice of Intent Alexander Gamboti, aged 42, artist of music...3 October 1843.

Charleston

Petition of Patrick Galaher, 30 years of age, born in the north of Ireland, arrived in Boston at age 17...11 Oct 1830

Petition of John Gallagher, aged 33, porter, born County Donegall, Ireland, arrived in the U. S., 1 June 1836, and resided in this state five years...gave notice of intent June 1841...8 April 1843.

Petition of John W. Gallagher, born Ireland, arrived in New York 1828, resided in this state five years...7 Oct 1834.

Notice of Intent of John Gallagher, aged 30 years, porter or packer of glass ware (see above)...8 Jan 1841.

Petition of John Gallagher, born Ireland, County of Donegall, arrived in New York, 12 May 1828, lived in this state three years....

Notice of Intent of Edward Gallagher, aged 25, clerk, born County of Leitrin, Ireland, arrived in the U. S., 1837...11 April 1843.

Notice of Intent of Benj. Garden, aged 40, apothecary, born Elburg in Prussia, arrived in the U. S. at New York, 6 Sept 1836, and in Charleston since 1840...6 Oct 1845.

Notice of Intent of George Garrett, aged 31, Boot maker, born Mickleover, Ireland, arrived in Charleston, 17 Jan 1831...6 May 1839.

Notice of Intent of Nathaniel Gallagher, aged 24, laborer, born Ireland, arrived in New York in 1844, came to Charleston, Sept. 1848...28 June 1850.

Petition of James Gairdner, having resided in this state for two years and upwards...1 January 1793.

Petition of William Gunderson, aged 22, born Kingdom of Norway, arrived at Baltimore 1823...12 Oct 1830.

Notice of Intent of Gererd Garbonne, aged 28, grocer, born Hanover, arrived in New York 1836, and in Charleston, 1837...23 Aug 1844.

Notice of Intent from the City of New York. James Gardner, 17 Oct 1840, late of the Kingdom of Great Britain and Ireland. Petition in Charleston District, James Garner, aged 25, clerk, born Queens County, Ireland, arrived in New York, 1838, came to Charleston October 1839...4 Nov 1845.

Petition of Lewis Gay, aged 52, Goldsmith, born France, arrived Charleston, 1800...6 Oct 1832.

Petition of George Garrett, aged 33, boot-maker, born Micklover in England, 10 May 1807, arrived in Charleston, 1830, gave notice of intent 7 May 1839...7 June 1841.

Notice of Intent of Nicholas Gaynor, aged 26, mercer and tailor, born Ireland, arrived in New York, 13 June 1836, and Charelston, 1 April 1838. Filed 13 January 1841.

Petition of Benjamin Garden, aged 45, apothecary, born Elsburg in Prussia...8 May 1850.

Charleston

Petition of James Robert Garcia, Professor of Music, aged 42 years, born Dunkirk, in French Flanders, migrated from Havre de Grace, arrived in Charleston, May 1832...4 Oct 1836.

Petition of Eimmer Gerdis, aged 27, store keeper, born Hanover arrived in Charleston, in the year 1840...1 Nov 1849.

Notice of Intent of Henry Gerdts, grocer...3 Oct 1837. Petition of Henry Gerdts, aged 29, grocer, born Laacke, Kingdom of Hanover, arrived in Charleston, November 1832. Filed 26 May 1841.

Notice of Intent of C. H. Gerdes, aged about 30, grocer, born Hanover, arrived in the U. S. at New York in 1838, moved to New Orleans, 1840, and in 1841 to Charleston...14 Oct 1846.

Petition of Carsten Gerdts, aged 24, grocer, born Altluneberg, Hanover, 22 August 1816, arrived in Charleston 18 June 1834...30 Jan 1841.

Notice of Intent of Christopher Geraty, aged 23, grocer, born County Westmeath, Ireland, arrived in the U. S., at New York, May 1839, and at Charleston in October of the same year. 15 Nov 1843.

Notice of Intent of Bernard Gerety, aged 25, laborer, born Ireland, arrived in New York in May 1846, came to Charleston, January 1847. 13 Oct 1847.

Notice of Intent of Francis H. Gerb, aged 38, laborer, born Heidelberk, Baden, arrived at Baltimore, 1837...8 March 1847.

Notice of Intent of Peter Gerken, clerk, aged 26, born in the town of Dorom, Hanover, arrived in Charleston, September 1846... 9 Sept 1848.

Notice of Intent of George A. German, aged 37, store-keeper, born German, Clousen, Bavaria, arrived in the U. S. 14 July 1831...12 March 1844.

Petition for Denizenship of Henry Gerdts, a native of Laacke, Neuhaus District, Hanover, born 11 February 1812, arrived in New York 30 October 1832, and a few weeks after came to Charleston ...now aged 25 years, 7 months and 15 days...23 Feb 1837.

Petition of John Gellabart, aged 21, Iron founder, born Island of Minerca, arrived at Baltimore, 1842, a minor of 16 years, and removed to Charleston...7 June 1847.

Notice of Intent of C. H. Gerdes, aged 30 grocer, native of the Kingdom of Hanover, arrived in New York, 1838, then went to New Orleans, and in 1841 to Charleston...14 October 1846. Petition for citizenship dated 30 October 1848.

Petition of Charles Giese...born in Prussia, and has been a resident of the U. S. for 7 years...11 Oct 1830.

Petition of Thomas Gillispie...born in Sterlingshire in Scotland, emigrated to the U. S. in 1817, in January...took oath in 1818 in the city of New York...12 Oct 1830.

Petition of Alexander Gilfillin...a native of Ireland, 25 years old, came to Charleston 1826 and has resided here ever since... at the time of his arrival, he was under 18 years...5 Oct 1836.

Charleston

John Girvan, born Ireland, arrived at New York, 15 May 1848 from thence came to Charleston...notice of intent...20 Oct 1848.

Petition of Anne Giraud McKernan...has resided in the U. S. 14 years, between 18 June 1798 and 14 April 1802 and during the greatest part of the same period in Charleston...a native of Nantz in France, aged 36 years...filed 20 January 1812.

Petition of Hanke Gissel, aged 23, grocer, born Wolsdorf, Hannover, 2 September 1817, arrived in New York, June 1835 and in Charleston 1836...7 June 1841.

Petition of Reinelt Gissel, aged 22, grocer, born Wolsdorf, Hannover, 2 April 1819, and arrived in New York 3 August 1837...7 June 1841.

Notice of Intent of Charles Gibson, aged 33, a laborer, born Liverpool, Great Britain, arrived in the U. S. at NewYork 12 May 1832 and was a seaman...now resides in Charleston...30 Sept 1845.

Notice of Intent of Thomas Gilmore, aged 22, laborer, born Ireland, arrived in Boston, August 1849, and from thence came to Charleston..11 Oct 1849.

Petition of Charles P. Gibson, aged 24, born Belfast, Ireland in 1812, arrived in the U. S. at Charleston, then a minor...11 Oct 1836.

Petition of Margaret Gidiere, a native of Cape Nicholas Mole, Island of St. Domingo...she has resided in the jurisdiction of the U. S. 1798 and 14 April 1802...Jan. 23, 1813.

Notice of Intent of William Gieven, aged 23, merchant, born in Ireland, arrived at Charleston, 19 Dec 1845...26 Jan 1849. Wm. Given.

Petition of Charles Gibson, aged 35, laborer, born England, arrived in the U. S. 12 May 1832, hailed from the U. S. as a seaman till 1835, gave notice of intent 30 Sept 1845...23 May 1848.

Notice of Intent of Ignaz Glücklick, aged 35, merchant, born Hungary in Austria, arrived in the U. S. 30 May 1840 at New York ...9 Jan 1843.

Petition of John Gonzales, aged 53, shoe maker, born Kadis, arrived at Charleston, 1811...11 Oct 1831.

Petition of Francis Good...resided withint the limits of the U. S. 18 June 1798 and 14 April 1802...native of Germany, aged about 51 years, shop keeper...13 May 1812.

Petition of George Munro Goodwin, aged 26, Dry goods store keeper, born Bury suffolk in England, arrived in the U. S. at New York, April 1842, and at Charleston, February 1844...18 Jan 1846.

Petition of Patrick FitzGibbon, aged 29, merchant, born Gallanamonah, Ireland, arrived in the U. S. at New York in 1830, then a minor... 20 March 1843.

Notice of Intent of George Gordon, aged 28, Baker, born Edinburgh, Scotland, arrived in Philadelphia, November 1828, resident of Charleston for five years...10 Oct 1834.

Charleston

Notice of Intent of Patrick Goold, aged 24, laborer, born Ireland, arrived in New York, April 1849, and in Charleston in May 1849... 16 Oct 1850.

Petition of John Gorman, a resident upwards of 10 years, born England, and is 32 years of age...19 January 1811. Certificate of his residence from Horry District.

Notice of Intent of J. A. Gottschalk, aged 37, Chandler, born Amt(?), Hagen, Kingdom of Hannover, 6 Jan 1808, arrived in the U. S. at Charleston, 6 Nov 1838...14 Oct 1845.

Notice of Intent of John Gorman, laborer, aged 29, born Ireland, arrived at New York, 6 July 1843, and then to Charleston...18 Feb 1848.

Notice of Intent of William Kennaway Gourlay, aged 26, mariner, born Exeter, County of Devon, England, 1822...arried New York, October 1839...2 June 1848.

Notice of Intent of James Gorman, aged 19, laborer, born Ireland, arrived in Charleston, January 1850...7 October 1850.

Notice of Intent of John Goury, aged 35, laborer, born County of Limerick, arrived New York, 1834, to Charleston in 1836...17 July 1847.

Petition of Theodore Goutueville, aged 29, a Dyer, born Dieffe, Kingdom of France, arrived in New York 1827, aged 17 years...14 October 1834.

Petition of Meyer Goldman, aged 29, merchant, born Cracow, Poland, arrived in U. S. at New York, July 1841, to Charleston in 1843, gave notice of intent, 25 Oct 1844 in New York...4 Nov 1846.

Notice of Intent of Patrick Grace, aged 32, laborer, born in the County of Tipperary, Ireland, arrived at New York 1833, to Boston, then to Charleston in 1838...4 Aug 1847.

Notice of Intent of Patrick Green, aged 30, Tailor, born Ireland, arrived in Charleston, 1842...13 Sept 1847.

Petition of John J. Greenwald, aged 25, a conductor on the Rail Road, born Heidstadt, Hesse Cassell, arrived in the U. S. at Norfolk, Va., in 1839, and was of the age of 18...28 May 1847.

Petition of John Greenhill, aged 33, born in England in 1801, arrived in the U. S. at Savannah, 1819, gave notice in Darlington District, S. C....John Greenhill, 14 Oct 1834.

Petition of John M. Greer, aged 26, bookseller, born in the Town of Belfast, Ireland, arrived in Charleston December 1826...gave notice of intent Feb. 1832...28 May 1834.

Petition of Alexander Gregg, born Scotland, arrived in the U. S. 1820, and gave notice of intent in 1830...13 Oct 1834.

Notice of Intent of Henry Gramann, aged about 40, merchant, born Nanstedt, Kingdom of Hanover, 27 March 1800, arrived in the U. S. at Charleston, 14 April 1833...filed 29 Feb 1841.

Charleston

Court of Common Pleas. John Henry Graver, aged about 27 years, clerk, arrived at Charleston, December 1839, a subject of Ernest Augustus, King of Hanover...29 July 1845.

Notice of Intent of Edward Grant, aged 32, born in Ireland, arrived in the U. S. at Boston, 1832, and at Charleston, Nov 1838 ...filed 21 Jan 1841.

Petition of Andrew Gray, born at St. Cuthberts, Scotland, florist and gardener, aged 39 years, arrived in May 1834, and in S. C. in 1835...__ Jan 1840.

Petition of Henry Grebb, aged 27, laborer, born Darmstedt, Upper Hessia, 28 April 1814, arrived in the U. S. at Baltimore, 1832, enlisted as a private in the Army of the U. S., August 1834... filed June 6, 1841.

Notice of Intent of Augustus Gruendel, aged 27, Lock-smith, born Prussia, arrived in New York, June 1847, and to Charleston in July 1847...8 Jan 1848.

Petition of Henry Graman, aged 43, Tailor, born Nanstedt, Kingdom of Hanover, arrivdd at Charleston, 14 March 1833, gave notice of intent 29 January 1841...20 March 1843.

Petition of John Gannon, aged about 26, laborer, born Ireland, arrived at New York, April 1833, resident in Charleston two years...Oath from New York City Municipal Court, 4 Nov 1835.

Petition of Joseph Gamboa, aged 23, born Island of Marguerite, Republic of Colombia, arrived Charleston, 19 Oct 1824...5 Oct 1831.

Notice of Intent of John Gallagher, aged 30, born County of Donegal, Ireland in 1810, arrived in New York, 29 May 1836, left for Charleston, October 1838...8 Jan 1841.

Petition of John Gallagher, born Ireland, County of Donegal, arrived at NewYork, 12 May 1828...6 Oct 1832.

Notice of Intent of George Garrett, aged 31, boot maker, born Mickleover, Kingdom of Great Britain and Ireland, arrived at Charleston, 27 January 1831...6 May 1839.

Notice of Intent of Nathaniel Gallagher, laborer, aged 29, born Ireland, arrived at New York, 1844, and at Charleston, September 1848...28 June 1850.

Notice of Intent of Hugh Green, aged 33, Taylor, born Ireland, arrived at New York September 1847, came to Charleston in the same month...25 September 1847.

State of Louisiana. Nov. 23, 2840. Appeared Charles Guenther, a native of Berlin (Prussia) aged 32, arrived at Charleston, S. C., in 1835, and since 4 November 1840 has been a resident in the state of Louisiana...New Orleans, 23 Nov 1840.
Petition for Citizenship at Charleston...says he is an accountant... 14 March 1843.

Petition of Philip Guieu, aged 21, born Port au Prince, St. Domingo, arrived at Norfolk, Virginia, September 1796, with Orman & Burke, merchants, then returned to his parents at St. Domingo, arrived at Carolina 5 September 1803...17 Jan 1805.

Charleston

Petition of Peter Guillemin, aged 31 years, farmer, born in the City of Macon, France, in 1805, arrived in New York in 1811, then a minor under the age of 6...stated his intent in Charleston in 1825...10 Oct 1836.

Petition of Henry Guinard, aged 41, silversmith and watch maker, born in Prussia, arrived at Boston in 1806, then about 15, resident in this state for the last four years...8 Oct 1832.

Petition of Anthony Gunderman, born Hanover, is of the age of 21 years, arrived in the U. S. at Baltimore in 1830, then aged 15, resided there till 1834 and came to Charleston...Anton Gundermann. 10 Oct 1836.

Petition of Joseph Frey, aged 39 years, born Ruppertsberg, Canton Neustadt an der Haard, Rhein Pfalz, Kingdom of Bavaria, arrived in the U. S. at Charleston 28 Jan 1842, declaration of intent, 31 Oct 1846...a repairer of musical instruments, signed George Joseph Frey.

Petition of William Fox, born Ireland, arrived in America eight years ago, then a minor, now upwards of 25 years...11 October 1828.

Petition of Richard W. Fox, aged 39, mariner, born England, arrived in New York in 1807, then a minor, resident of Charleston for 10 years...6 Oct 1832.

Notice of Intent of Charles Foei, born Sweden, arrived in Charleston in September 1847...6 Sept 1849.

Notice of Intent of Daniel Farrell, aged 37, a mason, born Ireland, County of Tipperary, arrived in the U. S. at New York, 27 May 1840, and at Charleston in October of the same year...8 May 1844.

Notice of Intent of Richard Farmer, aged 30, laborer, born Ireland, arrived in the U. S. at Charleston, 12 Jan 1840...filed 18 Oct 1842

Petition of Hugh W. Ferguson, born in the parish of Rogart, County of Southerland in North Britain, and emigrated to the U. S., Nov. 1820...gavei notice in Federal Court 1820...10 Oct 1826.

Notice of Intent of John J. Ferrall, aged 23, clerk, born Longford, Ireland, arrived in the U. S. in New York, autumn of 1840, and remained one month and came to Charleston...21 Nov 1844.

Petition of Jacinth Ferera, aged about 24, carpenter, born on the Island of Madera 1813, arrived in the U. S. at Charleston in 1824...2 Oct 1837.

Petition of William Ferguson, born in Scotland in 1807, arrived in America in 1821, then a minor, resided 8 years in South Carolina...7 Oct 1830.

Petition of John N. Fegarus, aged 53, stiller(?), born East Florida in 1781, and was a citizen when Florida was ceded to the U. S., arrived in Charleston, 25 years ago...7 Oct 1834.

Notice of Intent of Thomas Ferrall, aged 25, carpenter, born Ireland, arrived in the U. S. at New York in 1846, and came to Charleston October 1847...14 Nov 1850.

Charleston

Petition of Daniel Herman Feaurst, arrived in the U. S. at New York February 1833, resided in S. C. upwards of five years... registered his notice of intent in March 1833 in New York...3 June 1841.

Petition of Peter Jens Fink, born Holstein in Denmark, arrived at New Port, September 1830, on 2 October 1834 gave notice of intent...10 Oct 1836.

Notice of Intent of Sigmund Fehrenback, a potter, born in Baden, arrived in the U. S. at Charleston...26 March 1849.

Petition of Simon Feagan, a native of Ireland, born County of Longford, aged 29 years, arrived in the U. S. at New York 2 Sept 1815, and to Columbia, __ Oct 1816, then to Charleston...gave notice of intent 29 July 1818...filed 6 Feb 1822.

Notice of Intent of Patrick Faltos, aged 23, laborer, born Ireland, arrived New York Sept. 1848, and to Charleston July 1850... 12 Nov 1850.

Petition of Rev. John Fielding, a native of Ireland, arrived Nov 1829... dated 29 Jan 1836. Notice of Intent states born in Ireland, County of Kilkenny, arrived in S. C. 6 Nov 1829, aged 23...5 Feb 1831.

Petition of James Fitzpatrick, common laborer, a native of the County of Kildare, Province of Leinster, residing in Charleston... age 37...12 July 1843.

Notice of Intent of Jacob Frederick Finck, carpenter, born Hanover, arrived at Charleston, 15 Dec 1841...26 Sept 1848.

Notice of Intent of Samuel Fisher, aged 56, merchant, born Walworth, County of Surry, England...arrived at New York in 1830, came to Charleston 1836...13 Dec 1845.

Notice of Intent of Bernard Fitzsimmons, aged 32, saddler, born Ireland, arrived at Boston, about 1834, to Charleston 1837...22 May 1849.

Petition of Daniel Finn, aged about 19, born in the City of Dublin, left Ireland in Sept 1819, and arrived at Charleston December 1819...25 Jan 1823.

Notice of Intent of Peter Jens Fink (or Finck), aged 24, born Denmark, Island of Silt, 28 April 1829, arrived in Charleston 19 Dec 1843...20 Dec 1843.

Petition of John Heinrich Fischer, aged 25, years, tailor, born Derum, Kingdom of Hanover, arrived at Charleston 2 Dec 1846... notice of intent. 15 Oct 1849.

Petition of John F. Ficken, aged 31, grocer, born Utleda, Kingdom of Hanover, 12 Aug 1810, arrived in the U. S. 5 April 1828 at New York...29 Jan 1841.

Notice of Intent of William Fiken, born Bremen, arrived in the U. S. in 1835...12 April 1843.

Notice of Intent of Henry Fenner, aged 26, a moulder, arrived in the U. S. at New York Feb 1847, came to Charleston Feb 1849... 28 Oct 1850.

COUNTY RECORDS

Charleston

Notice of Intent of Benjamin Figerour, aged 42, merchant, born Guadaloupe in the West Indies, arrived in the U. S. in 1839... 22 Jan 1850

Notice of Intent of Patrick Flynn, aged 23, laborer, born Ireland, arrived at New York in April 1850 and came to Charleston in May of the same year...27 Sept 1850.

Petition of Patrick Fleming, arrived in the U. S. previous to 28 June 1812, born Ireland, lived in this state 12 years...12 Oct 1830.

Petition of William S. Fleming, a native of Ireland, born in the County of Managhan, 30 years of age,arrived at New York 17 April 1810...notice of intent...filed 23 Jan 1822.

Notice of Intent of James Flood, aged 24, laborer, born Ireland, arrived in Charleston, 1849...23 Oct 1850.

Notice of Intent of John Flynn, age 26, sailor, born Ireland, arrived at Boston, August 1846, came to Charleston Dec. 1848... 18 July 1849.

Petition of Notice of Intent of Daniel Flin, a native of the City of Dublin, Kingdom of Ireland, arrived in U. S. December 1819...11 Feb 1824.

Notice of Intent of Patrick Flynn, aged 25, born County of Limerick, Ireland, arrived at Whitehall, New York, 1841, came to Charleston 1845...12 July 1847.

Certificate from Richland District, S. C., for the citizenship of Richard Flannagan, aged 21 years, born Ireland..resident in the Town of Columbia...28 Feb 1849.

Petition of George Forbes of the Kingdom of Great Britain, arrived in the U. S.,October 1817..6 June 1822.

Petition of Arthur Forsyth, born in Ireland, emigrated to the U. S. many years since...9 Oct 1830.

Petition of James Fox, a native of Tyrone, Ireland...11 Oct 1828.

Notice of Intent of George Faber, aged 36, merchant, born Giessen in the Grand Dukedom of Darmstadt, arrived in the U. S. at New York 18 Oct 1841, went to New Orleans, then to Charleston...14 Jan 1842.

Notice of Intent of James Farrell, aged 26, born County Meath, Ireland, arrived May 1831 at Charleston...15 Oct 1836.

Petition of Rev. Francis Ferrall, a native of Ireland, arrived in North Carolina, 15 August 1832, thence to Charleston...29 Jan 1836.

Notice of Intent of William Fay, aged 35, shoemaker, born in the city of Dublin, Ireland, arrived in New York in 1837, then to Charleston in the same year...23 Aug 1847.

Petition of James Fay, born County of Cavan, Ireland, and now about 34 years of age, arrived in New York, August 1816, declared his intent at Newtown in Sussex County... _____ 1830.

Charleston

Notice of Intent of Patrick Fay, aged 40, storekeeper, born in the County of Cavan, Ireland, arrived in the U. S., October 1823, resident of Charleston sine 1826...7 Oct 1831.

Petition of Robert Elliot, having resided in the U. S. upwards of seven years...3 July 1793.

Petition of Eugene Roumillat, born on the Island of St. Domingo, emigrated to the U. S. when ten years of age, resided in the U. S. 19 years, twelve years in S. C....12 Oct 1830.

Petition of John Eckells, a native of Fallerleben in Prussia, aged 32, resident in the U. S. between 18 June 1798 and 14 April 1802...10 Feb 1812.

Petition of Augustus Eikerenketter, aged 24 years, grocer, born Warburg, Prussia, 1819, arrived at New York in 1836, and came to Charleston in the same year...4 April 1843.

Petition for Denizenship of Henry Ehricks, born Hambergen, Hanover, 14 June 1812, went to London in 1829...19 July 1844. Notice of Intent states age 32, storekeeper, born Hanover, arrived in U. S. 1836 at Charleston...16 July 1844. Certificate dated 16 July 1844. Petition for citizenship dated 5 May 1847.

Petition of the Right Reverend Dr. John England, a native of Ireland, aged 36 years, arrived in Charleston December 1820...20 Jan 1823.

Petition of Charles Evans, turner, born County of Maith, Ireland, arrived in the U. S., at New York 1818, and at Charleston 1819... 4 Oct 1838.

Petition of Fritz (Friedrich) Evenius, aged 22, born Albringhausen, Hannover, 18 March 1819, arrived in the U. S. at Baltimore, and to Charleston in April....23 Jan 1841.

Petition of Peter Esterhat, a native of Sweden, born in Kalsen, arrived in Charleston, a minor under 20, Dec 1816...8 Oct 1830.

Notice of Intent of Boy Hendrick Fink, aged 21, clerk, born Halsten, Denmark, arrived at Charleston, 14 March 1844...16 Oct 1844.

Petition of Patrick Fay, aged 43, storekeeper, born County of Cavan, Ireland, arrived in the U. S., October 1823...10 Oct 1834.

Notice of Intent of Thomas Edmunds, aged 30, born Ireland, arrived at New York about 1832, and thence to Charleston...1 March 1849.

Notice of Intent of Joseph Edwards, aged 40, manufacturer, born Cheshire, England, arrived in the U. S. at New York, March 1829, resided there nine years, afterwards lived in the Wisconsin Territory, then to Charleston...8 July 1844.

Notice of Intent of Luke Early, aged 28, born Ireland, arrived in New York in 1846, came to Charleston same year...12 July 1848.

Notice of Intent of William Ellard, aged 22, laborer, born Ireland, arrived at New York, in 1845, to Charleston in 1847...15 June 1848.

Charleston

Petition of William English, aged 21, born Ireland, arrived in the U. S. in 1821, then a minor under 21 years...8 Oct 1834.

Notice of Intent of George Engelbert, aged 38, sail maker, born Bavaria, arrived at Charleston, 1833...26 March 1849.

Notice of Intent of William Enston, aged 26, born in the City of Canterbury, Great Britain, in 1808, came to Philadelphia in 1822...6 Oct 1834.

Notice of Intent of William Englert, aged 28, shoemaker, born Hoffstaden, Baden, arrived in New York, May 1838, resident of Charleston four years...11 Nov 1844.

Notice of Intent of James Eyland, a native of Walsall, England, arrived in the U. S., September 1818...12 Feb 1824.

Notice of Intent of John Peter M. Epping, aged 27, druggist, born Oldenburg, arrived in the U. S., Charleston 1836...28 Nov 1844.

Petition of Hannah Enston, wife of William Enston, merchant and dealer in furniture, aged 39, born Melton, Mowbray, Leicestershire, England, arrived in Philadelphia, 20 July 1824, then an infant, came to Charleston 28 August 1834...23 April 1849.

Chester

A unique situation exists with the naturalization/citizenship records of Chester County/District. These records were recorded in separate volumes, title Naturalized Citizens, Volume A 1802-1832 and Volume B 1832-1868. These volumes are still in the Office of the Clerk of Court in Chester, but LDS microfilm is available of these volumes. The entries within these volumes are not in strict chronological order. However, the abstracts below are in a page by page sequence. No entries have been included in these abstracts after the year 1850; therefore, some pages in the latter part of Volume B are omitted. Many of the original loose petitions are also extant and might be helpful if an actual signature of the applicant or petitioner is desired. These originals are also in the Office of the Clerk of Court in Chester, and also LDS microfilm of these is available.

Page 1: Thursday 18th November 1802. Joseph Johnston & George Kennedy, Samuel Omelveny & John Kennedy Senior & John Kennedy Junior, and James Kennedy, all natives of Ireland, came into court and made application to be admitted citizens....

Page 2: The Petition of Joseph Johnston...is a native of Ireland from whence he emigrated in the year 1796...landed in the city of Charleston in the same year....18 November 1802.

Page 3: The Petition of Geo. Kennedy...is a native of Ireland whence he emigrated in the year 1796...landed in the city of Charleston in the same year...and now acting as Post Master at Chester C. H. commissioned thereto in the year 1798 & also as Notary Public for Chester District & has also heretofore acted as deputy Clk of this County under Saml. Lacy....Nov. 18th 1802

Page 4: Petition of Samuel Omelveny, a native of Ireland, from whence he emigrated in the month of October 1793...landed in the city of Charleston in the month of December of the same year... November 1802.

Page 5: The Petition of John Kennedy..is a native of Ireland from whence he emigrated in the month of October 1787...landed in the city of Charleston in the month of December in the same year... November 18th 1802.

Page 6: The Petition of James Kennedy...is a native of Ireland, from whence he emigrated in the month of October in the year 1787...landed in the City of Charleston in the month of December in the same year....Novemr. 18th 1802.

Page 7: The Petition of John Johnston...a native of Ireland, whence he emigrated in the month of June 1787...landed in the City of Charleston in September in the same year...15th Novemr. 1802.

Page 8: The Petition of John Kennedy...is a native of Ireland, from which he emigrated in the year 1792 and landed in the City of Charleston....Nov. 18th 1802.

Page 9: The Petition of Alexander Inglish, John McCully, Thomas Galyspie and James Martin...emigrants from Ireland from whence they all and each of them emigrated at least eleven years ago... landed in the City of Charleston at different periods...Alexander English occupying the trace of clothes and dyer, John McCully occupying the tract of Blacksmith and Thomas Galyspie occupying the occupation of a farmer or planter and James Martin farmer... 19th April 1803.

Chester VOLUME A

Page 12: Petition of Edward Blackstocks and Andrew Crawford... emigrated from Ireland to wit Edward Blackstock in the month of September 1792 and landed inthe City of Charleston in the latter end of said year...17th April 1804.

Page 15: Tuesday 16th April 1805. Petition of James Allen...an emigrant from Ireland from whence he emigrated at least seventeen years ago...trade of a farmer. April 15th 1805.

Page 18: Friday 8th November 1805. Petition of John Cherrey... a native of Ireland from whence he emigrated in or about the year 1785...landed in the City of CKarleston in August in the same year....8th November 1805.

Page 21: The Petition of James Morrow...a native of Ireland whence he emigrated in the year 1788...landed in the City of Charleston in December in the same year....31st March 1806.

Page 23: Wednesday 2d April 1806. Petition of James Woodburn... was born in Ireland and emigrated from Ireland in the year 1789 ...April 2d day 1806.

Page 25: Petition of Charles Boyd Senr...born in the Kingdom of Ireland...has resided at least five years within the limits of the US and two years within the state of SC...2 Apl 1806.

Page 26: Petition of James Lowry. born in the Kingdom of Ireland ...has resided at least five years within the US and at least one year in South Carolina...April 2nd 1806.

Page 28: Petition of Hugh Reid...born in the Kingdom of Ireland ...has resided at least five years within the limits of the US and one year at least within this state...April 2d 1806.

Page 29: Petition of Jas. McConnell...born inthe Kingdom of Ireland ...resided at least five years withint the US and one year within this state...2 April 1806.

Page 31: Petition of Robert Gibson, born in Ireland...emigrated from Ireland in 1788....April 2d 1806.

Page 33: Petition of Matthew McClintock...born in Ireland... has resided at least five years within the US and two years within this state...2 Apl 1806.

Page 34: Petition of Alexander Boyd...born in the Kingdom of Ireland...has resided at least five years within the US and one year in this state...2d April 1806.

Page 36: Petition of Joseph Boyd...born in the Kingdom of Ireland ...hath resided at least five years within the US and two years within this state...2 Apl 1806.

Page 37: Petition of Robert Hamilton, born in the Kingdom of Ireland...has resided at least five years within the US and one year in this state...3d April 1806.

Page 39: Petition of Alexander Johnston..born in the Kingdom of Ireland, that he has previous to this time resided at least nineteen years within the US and in this state...April 3d 1806.

Chester

VOLUME A

Page 40: Petition of James McCaulley...born in the Kingdom of Ireland...has resided at least five years within the US and two years in this state...3 April 1806.

Page 41: Petition of Charles Miller, carpenter, born in the Kingdom of Ireland...has resided in the Us five years and at least two years in this state...April 2d 1806.

Page 43: Petition of James McClintock, born in the Kingdom of Ireland...has resided at least eighteen years in the US and in this state...April 3d 1806.

Page 44: Petition of Thos Adams, born in the Kingdom of Ireland ...has resided at least five years in the US and one year in this state. 3 Apl 1806.

Page 46: Petition of James Meek, born in Ireland, emigrated from Ireland in the year 1788...November 3d day 1806.

Page 47: Petition of Robert Meek, born in Ireland, emigrated from Ireland in the year 1788...Novbr. 3d day 1806.

Page 49: Petition of John Simpson, born in Ireland, has resided at least five years in the US and one year in this state...Nov. 3d 1806.

Page 50: Petition of Patrick Finney, born in Ireland, emigrated from Ireland in the year 1786...Novbr. 3d 1806.

Page 52: Petition of Hugh Simpson, born in Ireland, emigrated from Ireland in the year 1787...Nov. 4 1806.

Page 54: Petition of John Cunningham, emigrated from Ireland in the year 1792...Novr. 5th 1806.

Page 55: Petition of Robert Sanderson, James Brandon, James Cowzey, Robert Ingram, John Murphy, and Jonas McCullough... born in Ireland, and that they emigrated from Ireland viz sd. Robert Sanderson in the year 1790, James Brandon in the year 1789, James Cowsey (Cowsert) in the year 1790, the sd. Robert Ingram in the year 1792 and the sd. John Murphy in the year 1787. Novr. 3d 1806.

Page 57: Petition of James Armstrong, born in the Kingdom of Ireland...has resided at least five years within the US and one year in this state...Novr. 3d 1806

Page 58: Petition of William Egnew, born in the Kingdom of Ireland, he emigrated from Europe in the year 1790...Novr. 6th 1806.

Page 60: Petition of William McKee, born in the Kingdom of Ireland, has resided at least five years within the US and at least one year within this state...Novr. 3 1806.

Page 61: Petition of John Colwell, born in the Kingdom of Ireland, emigated from Ireland in the year 1786...resided at least five years within the US and one year in this state...Novr 7th 1806.

Page 63: Petition of John Barr, born in Ireland, emigrated from Ireland in the year 1792.......1st April 1807.

Chester

VOLUME A

Page 65: Petition of William Adair, born in the Kingdom of Ireland...has resided at least five years within the US and one year within this state...Novr 2d 1807.

Page 66: Petition of Jonathan Beatty, born in Ireland, emigrated from Ireland in the year 1796....November 4th 1807.

Page 68: Petition of Thomas Johnston, born in Ireland, emigrated from Ireland inthe year 1788....

Page 69: Petition of Hugh Park, born in the Kingdom of Ireland, resided at least five years within the US and one year within this state...November 2d 1807.

Page 70: Petition of Andrew McKee, born in the Kingdom of Ireland, ...has resided at least five years in the US and one year in this state...November 2d 1807.

Page 72: Petition of John Barr, born in the Kingdom of Ireland, has resided at least five years within the US and one year in this state...Novr. 4th 1807.

Page 73: Petition of Terrence Foy, born in the Kingdom of Ireland, has resided at least five years in the US and one year in this state...April 4th 1808.

Page 75: Petition of John McCown and Hugh McCown, born in the Kingdom of Ireland, from whence they emigrated...have resided at least five years within the US and one year in this state... April 6th 1808.

Page 77: Petition of Samuel Wright, born inIreland, emigrated from Ireland in the year 1787...6th Apl 1808.

Page 78: Petition of Patrick Spence, born in Ireland, emigrated from Ireland in the year 1794...7 Apl 1808.

Page 80: Petition of John McElmoil, born in Ireland, emigrated from Ireland in the year 1796...7th Apl 1808.

Page 82: Petition of Charles Boyle, born in Ireland, emigrated from Ireland in the year 1796...7 Apl 1808.

Page 84: Petition of Samuel Wright, a native of Ireland, residing in the US between 18 June 1798 and 14 April 1802...1 November 1808.

Page 85: Petition of George Clark, a native of Ireland, residing in the US between 18 June 1798 and 14 April 1802....2d November 1808.

Page 86: Petition of James Elliot, a native of Ireland, residing in the US between 18 June 1798 and 14 April 1802...2 November 1808.

Page 87: Petition of William Love, a native of Ireland, residing in the US between 18 June 1798 and 14 April 1802...2d November 1808.

Page 88: Petition of Elias Love, a native of Ireland, residing in the US between 18 June 1798 and 14 April 1802...2d November 1808.

Chester

VOLUME A

Page 89: Petition of Richard Wylie, a native of Ireland, residing within the US between 18 June 1798 and 14 April 1802...2 November 1808.

Page 90: Petition of John Glynn, a native of Ireland, was residing in the US between 18 June 1798 and 14 April 1802...October 3, 1808.

Page 92: Petition of Samuel Wylie, a native of Ireland, residing in the US between 18 June 1798 and 14 April 1802...3d November 1808.

Page 93: Petition of James Robeson, a native of Ireland, residing in the US between 18 June 1798 and 14 April 1802...3d November 1808.

Page 94: Petition of Alexander Parkeson, a native of Ireland, residing in the US between 18 June 1798 and 14 April 1802... 3d November 1808.

Page 96: Petition of Maurice OCallaghan, a native of Ireland, residing within the US between 18 June 1798 and 14 April 1802... 4th November 1808.

Page 97: Petition of Robert Milling, born in Ireland, residing in the US between 18 June 1798 and 14 April 1802...4th April 1809.

Page 99: Petition of James Andrew, a native of Ireland, residing in the US between 18 June 1798 and 14 April 1802...4th April 1809.

Page 101: Petition of Doctr. Simeon Bevens, a native of Britain, residing in the US between 18 June 1798 and 14 April 1802... 4 Apl 1809.

Page 102: Petition of William Walker, a native of Ireland, residing in the US between 18 June 1798 and 14 April 1802... 31st October 1809.

Page 104: Petition of Andrew McCully, a native of Ireland, residing in the US between 18 June 1798 and 14 April 1802...2d November 1809.

Page 105: Petition of John McClintock, a native of Ireland, residing in the US between 18 June 1798 and 14 April 1802... 2d November 1809.

Page 106: Petition of Peter Wilson, a native of Ireland, residing in the US between 18 June 1798 and 14 April 1802...2d November 1809.

Page 108: Petition of Henry Bradley, a native of Ireland, residing in the US between 18 June 1798 and 14 April 1802...3d November 1809.

Page 109: Petition of John McKee, a native of Ireland, residing in the US between 18 June 1798 and 14 April 1802...3d November 1809.

Page 110: Petition of William Miller, a native of Ireland, residing in the US between 18 June 1798 and 14 April 1802... 3d November 1809.

Chester VOLUME A

Page 111: Petition of John Anderson, a native of Ireland, residing in the US between 18 June 1798 and 14 April 1802... 3rd November 1809.

Page 113: Petition of Thomas Walker, a native of Ireland, residing in the US between 18 June 1798 and 14 April 1802...4th April 1810.

Page 114: Petition of John Walker, a native of Ireland, residing in the US between 18 June 1798 and 14 April 1802...4th April 1810.

Page 115: Petition of Samuel McKeown, a native of Ireland, residing in the US between 18 June 1798 and 14 April 1802... 4th April 1810.

Page 117: Petition of Moses McKeown, a native of Ireland, residing in the US between 2nd August 1785 and 14 April 1802...4th April 1810.

Page 118: Petition of John Stockdale, a native of Ireland, residing in the US since 3 December 1788...4th April 1810.

Page 119: Petition of David Graham, a native of Ireland, residing in the US since December 1794...29th October 1810.

Page 120: Petition of Saml Gordon, a native of Ireland, residing in the US since 1 October 1792...29th October 1810.

Page 122: Petition of Samuel McCluney, a native of Ireland, residing in the US since December 1794...30 October 1810.

Page 123: Petition of James Lilly, a native of Ireland,residing in the US since October 1798...30 October 1810.

Page 124: Petition of Archibald Wilson, a native of Ireland, residing in the US between 25 December 1794 and 30 October 1802...30 October 1810.

Page 125: Petition of Francis Egnew, a native of Ireland, residing in the US since September 1789...1 Nov 1810.

Page 127: Petition of John Bingham, a native of Ireland, residing in the US since 20th September 1800...1 November 1810.

Page 128: Petition of Wm. McKean, a native of Ireland, residing in the US between 15 December 1794 and 30 October 1802...Novr 1st 1810.

Page 129: Petition of Mathew Elder, a native of Ireland, residing in the US since October 1798...1 Novr 1810.

Page 131: Petition of James Black, a native of Ireland, residing in the US before 1795... 2d November 1810.

Page 132: Petition of Archibald Stewart, a native of Ireland, residing in the US before 1795...2d November 1810.

No pages 134-137 in this volume.

Page 138: Petition of Wm. Croset, a native of Ireland, residing in the US since 17 July 1792...2 April 1811.

Chester

VOLUME A

Page 139: Petition of Wm Lyles, a native of Ireland, residing in the US since 17 July 1792...3 April 1811.

Page 140: Petition of Wm Fee, a native of Ireland, residing in the US since January 1793....31st March 1812.

Page 141: Petition of Robert Fee, a native of Ireland, residing in the US since January 1793...31st March 1812.

Page 142: Petition of Hugh Kennedy, a native of Ireland, residing in the US since August 1787...31 March 1812.

Page 144: Petition of Wm. Tate, a native of Ireland, residing in the US since 1786...31st March 1812.

Page 145: Petition of Moses Lemon, a native of Ireland, residing in the US since December 1791...2nd November 1813.

Page 146: Petition of Stephen Kennan, a native of Ireland, has resided in the US for five years and in this state for at least one year...2d November 1813.

Page 148: Petition of James Wilson, a native of Ireland, residing in the US since January 1790...2 Novr. 1813.

Page 149: Petition of Alexander Jameson, a native of Ireland, residing in the US since January 1794... 2 November 1813.

Page 150: Petition of Thomas Jameson, a native of Ireland, residing in the US since January 1794...2 November 1813.

Page 152: Petition of William Skelly (Scelly), a native of Ireland, residing in the US since May in 1801...2 November 1813.

Page 153: Petition of Thomas Kennedy, a native of Ireland, residing in the US since August 1787...3d November 1813.

Page 154: Petition of William Omelveny, a native of Ireland, residing in the US since 18 January 1798...2 November 1813.

Page 155: Petition of Charles Robinson, a native of Ireland, residing in the US since December ______....Novr 3 1813.

Page 157: Petition of James Robinson, a native of Ireland, has resided in the US since 1 March 1792....3 November 1813.

Page 158: Petition of John Wylie, a native of Ireland, residing in the US since April 1807....__ Novr 1813.

Page 159: Petition of Thomas McKean, a native of Ireland, has resided in the US five years and in this state for at least one year...3rd November 1813.

Page 161: Petition of James McKinstry, a native of Ireland, resided in the US since December 1789....3rd November 1813.

Page 162: Petition of Joseph Wham, a native of Ireland, residing in the US since May 1807....3rd November 1813.

Page 163: Petition of Samuel Burns, a native of Ireland, residing in the US since 1806....3rd November 1813.

Chester

VOLUME A

Page 165: Petition of James S. Stockdale, a native of Ireland, residing in the US since Feby 1793...3rd Novr 1813.

Page 166: Petition of Joseph McCosh, a native of Ireland, has resided in the US since September 1807...4 Novr 1813.

Page 167: Petition of Andrew Quay, a native of Ireland, has resided in the US since May 1805...5th November 1813.

Page 169: The Petition of John Junkin, a native of Ireland, residing in the US since April 1807...4 November 1813.

Page 170: Petition of John Johnston, a native of Ireland, residing in the US since August 1785... 5 November 1813.

Page 171: Petition of Jane Beard, an alien in the dominions of the King of Great Britain, residing in the US between 14 December 1805 and 27 October 1813...5 Novr 1813.

Page 173: Petition of William Graham, a native of Ireland, has resided in the US since September 1788...29 October 1814.

Page 174: Petition of David Kirk, a native of Ireland, residing in the US since December 1793...2 Novr 1814.

Page 176: Petition of William McKee, a native of Ireland, residing in the US since May 1794 and one year in this district ...1 Novr 1814.

Page 177: Petition of John Junkin, born in Ireland, emigrated in April 1807...Novr 6th 1811.

Page 178: Memorial of John Wylie, born in Ireland, landed in this state April 1807...7 Novr 1811.

Page 178: Petition of Samuel Mahor, a native of Ireland, residing in this state since April 1801...3rd Novr 1814.

Page 180: Petition of William Dunn, a native of Ireland, has resided in the US since December 1801...7 Apl 1814.

Page 181: Petition of William Ferres, a native of Ireland, has resided in the US since December 1803...7 Apl 1814.

Page 182: Petition of William Simpson, a native of Ireland, has resided in the US since March 1790...7 April 1814.

Page 184: Petition of John Gleghorn, a native of Ireland, has resided in the US since August 1790...7 Apl 1814.

Page 185: Petition of James McCalla, a native of Ireland, has resided inthe US since 1794...7 Apl 1814. (Signed James McCullough)

Page 187: Petition of Geo. McCullough, a native of Ireland, residing in the US since first of May 1806...7 Apl 1814.

Page 188: Petition of John McCullough, a native of Ireland, has resided in the US since 1794...7 Apl 1814.

Page 189: Petition of John Adair, a native of Ireland, has resided in the US since 1789...7 Apl 1814.

Chester

VOLUME A

Page 191: Petition of David McCann, a native of Ireland, has resided in the US since 1798...7 Apl 1814.

Page 192: Petition of William Smith, a native of Ireland, has resided in the US since 1795...7th April 1814.

Page 193: Petition of Charles Erwin, a native of Ireland, has resided in the US since June 1803...7th April 1814.

Page 195: Petition of Robert Ross, a native of Ireland, he has been residing in the US since October 1788..31 October 1815

Page 196: Petition of James Gillespy, a native of Ireland, has been residing in the US since August 1790...1st November 1815.

Page 197: Petition of James Garner, a native of Ireland, has been residing in the US since June 1801...7th Novr 1817.

Page 199: Petition of John Adams, a native of Ireland, has resided in the US since August 1789...April 4th 1818.

Page 200: Petition of James Oliver, a native of Ireland, has been residing in the US since February 1811...4th April 1821.

Page 201: Petition of George Wilson, a native of Ireland, has resided in the US upwards of thirty years last past...4th April 1820.

Page 203: Petition of David Junkin, a native of Ireland, has resided in the US since December 1811...26th March 1822.

Page 205: Petition of William Campbell, a native of Ireland, about 38 years of age, sandy hair, stout made, about five feet nine or ten inches high, intention to become a citizen...7th November 1818.

Page 206: Petition of William Campbell, an alien of Ireland, whence he and his wife Mary Campbell emigrated in the month of January 1818, on 7 November 1818 gave notice...25 March 1823.

Page 208: Petition of John Rodman (Rodment), a native of Ireland, emigrated to the US in December 1790...25th March 1823

Page 209: Petition of Samuel McNinch, a native of Ireland, from whence he, his wife, and eight children, emigrated in the month of January 1818, on 7 November 1818, he gave notice...27th March 1823.

Page 211: Petition of William Poag, a native of Ireland, has resided in the US since 1787...15 July 1823.

Page 212: Petition of John Poag, a native of Ireland, has resided in the US since 1787...15 July 1823.

Page 213: Petition of Samuel Irwin, an alien of Ireland, from whence he emigrated together with his wife Elizabeth Irwin, William Irwin, Samuel Irwin, and John Irwin, and arrived in the city of Charleston in January 1819...on 4 April 1821, gave notice...25th March 1824.

Page 216: Petition of Alexander Anderson, an alien of Scotland, from whence he emigrated with his wife Elizabeth Anderson and arrived in Charleston, 1 December 1817...30th March 1825.

Chester VOLUME A

Page 217: Petition of James Holliday, an alien of Ireland, from whence he emigrated in August 1818, arrived in Charleston, on 15 November 1818 gave notice....29th October 1829.

Page 219: Petition of Robert McNinch, an alien of Ireland, emigrated from Ireland and arrived in the City of Charleston in January 1829...on 25th March 1823...28th March 1826.

Page 221: Petition of Robert Nelson, an alien of Ireland, emigrated from Ireland and arrived in Charleston, September 1812...gave notice 28 August 1822...__ March 1826.

Page 223: Petition of Peary Cahil, an alien of Ireland, emigrated from Ireland and arrived in Charleston November 1820...gave notice 3 April 1821...28th March 1826.

Page 225:Petition of James Ross, an alien a native of Scotland, emigrated from Scotland and arrived in Philadelphia, on 22 May 1819, arrived inCharleston 24 May 1820...on 25 March 1823 he gave notice...29th March 1826.

Page 227: Petition of Joseph Baird, an alien of Ireland, emigrated from Ireland and arrived in Charleston January 1820, gave notice 1 April 1826...1st April 1829.

Page 228: Petition of John Sweny, an alien of Ireland, emigrated from Ireland and arrived in Charleston, November 1820, gave noitce 28 March 1822...24th October 1826.

Page 230: Petition of Thomas Bell, a native of Ireland, from whence he emigrated in March 1823...arrived in Charleston, 26 Novr 1817, and on 28 March 1823 gave notice of intention...1st April 1826.

Page 232: Petition of Morris Fitzgarrald, an alien of Ireland, emigrated from Ireland and arrived in the City of Bosont, June 1815, has resided in the US in the states of Massachusetts, Connecticut, New York, South Carolina, and Georgia, five years of which time he has resided in South Carolina, on 1 November 1823 gave notice...24 April 1828.

Page 233: Petition of Charles McCulloch, an alien of Scotland, emigrated from Scotland and arrived in the city of New York in October 1818, resided about two years in Virginia, and the remainder of the time in South Carolina, gave notice 10 November 1823....28th October 1828.

Page 235: Petition of William Simpson, an alien of Ireland, emigrated from Ireland and arrived in the city of Baltimore, August 1819, on 25th October 1826, gave notice...1st November 1828.

Page 237: Petition of William McCandless, an alien of Ireland, arrived in the City of Charleston, November 1821...gave notice 28th October 1826...4th April 1829.

Page 238: Petition of Soloman Simpson, an alien of Ireland, arrived in the city of Charleston, in 1821, gave notice on 22 October 1827...29 March 1830.

Page 240: Petition of John Miller, an alien a native of Ireland, emigrated from Ireland with his family about 35 years ago, at which time your petitioner was an infent ten or twelve months

VOLUME A

old, has resided in SC ever since...4th April 1831.

Page 242: Petition of William Rowland, an alien of Ireland, arrived in the City of Charleston, February 1823...gave notice 27th March 1828...6 April 1832.

VOLUME B

Page 1: Petition of William Rainey (Reany), an alien of Ireland, emigrated from Ireland and arrived in South Carolina in October 1806...6th November 1811, gave notice....22d October 1822.

Page 3: Petition of Samuel Snoddy, an alien a native of Ireland, arrived in Charleston in 1818...gave noitce on 28th March 1825... 6th October 1832.

Page 4: Petition of John Adams, an alien of Ireland, emigrated from Belfast and arrived in the city of Charleston in the Winter of 1821, on 25 October 1824 gave notice...22d October 1832.

Page 6: Petition of John McCisick (McIssick), an alien of Ireland, emigrated from Ireland and arrived in the City of Charleston, November 1821...on 2 April 1825 gave notice...22d October 1832.

Page 8: Petition of Thomas McGuire, an alien of Ireland, emigrated from Ireland by the way of Quebeck and arrived in the US at New York in May 1819...gave notice 28th October 1824...22d October 1832.

Page 9: Petition of Robert Bradshaw, an alien of Ireland, emigrated from Ireland and arrived in Charleston about 1791...22 October 1832.

Page 10: Petition of John Bradshaw, an alien of Ireland emigrated from Ireland and arrived in Charleston about 1791... 22 October 1832. Certificate delivered, 6th February 1843.

Page 12: Petition of Thomas McDowell, an alien of Ireland, arrived in Charleston in 1811...22d October 1832.

Page 13: 1st November 1828. Report of Samuel Kirkpatrick, an alien from Ireland, arrived in the City of Charleston November 1822...Samuel Kirkpatrick, born Inves: County Antrim, Ireland, aged 50 years. Petition of Samuel Kirkpatrick, dated 22 October 1832.

Page 16: Report of George Mcl. McNeill, an alien of Ireland, who arrived in the city of Charleston, 20 December 1822, at Court held 21 April 1828. born Ireland, aged 22 years. Petition dated 23 October 1832.

Page 18: Report of Hugh McGinnis, an alien from Ireland, who arrived in the city of Philadelphia, June 1818, at Court held 1st November 1827...born County Armagh, aged 38 years. Petition dated 23 October 1832.

Page 20: Petition of Adam Elliott, an alien of Ireland, emigrated from Ireland, and arrived in Charleston, 10 March 1822...gave notice 28th March 1825...23d October 1832.

Chester VOLUME B

Page 21: Petition of Robert Lathan, an alien of Ireland, emigrated from Belfast and landed in Charleston, 11 November 1819...gave notice 2nd April 1825...23rd October 1832.

Page 23: Petition of George Keenan, an alien, born in Ireland, emigrated from Ireland and arrived inCharleston, January 1817... gave notice fourth Monday in March 1828...24th October 1832.

Page 24: Petition of James Beaty, an alien of Ireland, arrived in Charleston, December 1823...gave notice 28th October 1824... 23rd October 1832.

Page 25: Petition of Charles Morrison, an alien of Ireland, emigrated from Ireland and arrived in Charleston, 1787...23rd October 1832.

Page 27: Petition of Samuel Keenan, an alien born in Ireland, emigrated from Ireland and arrived in Charleston, January 1825... gave notice 27th March 1828...10th October 1832.

Page 28: Report of Robert Gowley, an alien who arrived in the city of Charleston, November 1820...made 23 October 1832...aged 32, born Scotland, emigrated from Greenoch...24th October 1832.

Page 30: Petition of Thomas Bradshaw, an alien of Ireland, emigrated from Ireland and arrived in Charleston about 1791...24 October 1832.

Page 31: Petition of Robert McDowell, an alien a native of Ireland, has resided in the US since 1811...24th October 1832.

Page 33:Petition of John McDowell, a native of Ireland, has resided in the US since 1811...24th October 1832.

Page 34: Petition of John Montgomery, an alien of Ireland, emigrated from Ireland and arrived in Charleston about 1791... 25th October 1832.

Page 35: Petition of James B. Magill...an alien of Ireland, emigrated from Ireland to Charleston in the year 1823...on 15 July 1823 gave notice...__ October 1832.

Page 36: Petition of John J. Anderson, an alien of Ireland, emigrated from Ireland and arrived in Charleston August 1818... on 28th October 1826 gave notice...6th October 1832.

Page 37: Report of Hugh McDowal, an alien from Ireland who arrived at Charleston November 1821, made for himself and family...21 April 1828....born Raloo, County Antrim,Ireland; Hugh McDowell aged 43, Elizabeth McDowell aged 44, my son Thomas aged 16, Mary aged 14, and Ann aged 11.

Page 38: Report of John Kearney, a native of Ireland, arrived in Charleston, 1 December 1823...born Monygran Parish, of Killray,County Londonderry, Ireland, 2 April 1830.

Page 39: Report of John McKelvey, an alien from Ireland, who arrived in Charleston, 18 March 1820, made for himself and family, 25 October 1832...John McKelvey aged 61, born Clough Co., Ireland; Sarah McKelvey, born County Antrim, Ireland, aged 50; James Barr, aged 19....25th October 1832.

Chester

VOLUME B

Page 39: Petition of John M. Strain, an alien a native of Ireland, emigrated from Ireland in the year 1817 and arrived in Charleston, on the 25th Decembr same year...gave notice 2 April 1825... 6th April 1833.

Page 41: Report of James Barnet, an alien from England, who embarked from that place in 1821 and arrived in the City of New York and then removed to Philadelphia and continued there two years and then removed to South Carolina in 1823...born County Lancaster, aged 31...4th April 1833.

Page 42: Report of David Lyle, an alien from Ireland, who arrived in the city of Charleston November 1817...26th October 1829; born in County Antrim, Ireland, and now 35 years of age....26th October 1829. Petition dated 4th April 1833.

Page 44: Petition of William Cherry, an alien of Ireland, emigrated from Ireland and arrived in Charleston about 1785... November 1st 1833.

Page 45: Petition of Robert Y. Russell, born beyond the limits of the US that he has been residing within the limits of the US since his infancy, and before 18 June 1812...30th October 1833. (Later referred to as the Rev. Robert Y. Russell).

Page 47: Report of John McCaughey, an alien from Ireland who arrived in Charleston April 1825, made from himself 30th October 1830...born County Londonderry; petition dated 1 November 1833.

Page 49: Petition of William Cook, an alien of Ireland, emigrated from Ireland 11 December 1819...on 25th March 1824, gave notice ...2nd April 1834.

Page 50: Petition of William English, an alien of Ireland, emigrated from Ireland and arrived in Charleston, latter end of December 1823...gave noitce 28th October 1824...23rd September 1834.

Page 52: Report of Wm. S. Stuart, an alien from Ireland, who arrived in the City of Charleston, February 1825, made for himself, 24th October 1831...born Glyn, County Antrim, aged 22, petition dated 28th October 1834.

Page 54: Report of Samuel Paisley, an alien from Ireland, who arrived in New York in June 1819, made for himself on 25 October 1830...born Parish of Aughilurchor, County Fermaugh (sic), 26th Octr 1830. Petition dated 27th October 1835.

Page 56: Report of Samuel Sterling, an alien who arrived in Charleston, November 1819, report made 23 October 1832...aged 32, born County Antrim, Ireland, emigrated from Belfast... petition dated 27th October 1835.

Page 58: Report of David Welch, a native of Cork in Ireland, aged 32, report dated 28 October 1830. Petition dated 27th October 1835.

Page 60: Petition of Peter Johnston, an alien of Scotland, emigrated from Scotland and arrived in Savannah, Georgia, November 1819...at Novemter Term 1832, gave notice in the District of Fairfield...18th October 1836.

Chester

VOLUME B

Page 61: Report of Wm. Sanderson, an alien from Ireland, who arrived in Charleston, February 1825, report made for himself 24 October 1831...born Glyn,County Antrim, Ireland, aged 24 ...26 Octr 1831. Petition dated 21 October 1836.

Page 63: Report of Hugh McCreary, an alien who arrived in the US 2 March 1822, made report...born County Antrim, Ireland, age 33...24th October 1832. Petition dated 21st October 1836.

Page 65: Report of William Ford, an alien from Ireland, who arrived in Charleston, December 1822, made report 21 October 1836...born County Antrim, aged 36.

Page 66: Report of John Beggs, an alien from Ireland, who arrived in Charleston, November 1820...made report 7 April 1832: born County Antrim, aged 60. Petition dated 20th October 1836....

Page 68: Report of Hugh McDowell, an alien from Ireland for himself and family viz Elizabeth McDowell, Thomas McDowell, Mary McDowell and Anne McDowell...21 April 1828.

Page 70: Report of William McKissack and David Walsh, natives of Ireland; Report of William McKissick an alien who arrived in Charleston, January 1826, made...October 1830.

Page 71: Report of George McCormick, an alien from Ireland, who arrived in Charleston, December 1822...25 September 1834... born County of Antrim, Ireland, aged 34. Petition dated 27th October 1837.

Page 75: 24th October 1832: Robert Gourley, Samuel Stirling, Hugh McCreary, John McCormick, and Daniel Tafts, natives of Ireland, made oath that it was their intention to become naturalized citizens.

Report of John McCormick, born County of Antrim, aged 18...24 October 1832. Petition dated 6th April 1837.

Page 78: John Kerney, Leut Cahill, and Stephen Keenan, natives of Ireland, made application to beo admitted citizens....

Petition of John Kairney, an alien of Ireland, whence he emigrated in December 1823, gave notice 2 April 1830...6th April 1838.

Page 80: William Adams, a native of Ireland, made application to be admitted a citizen...Petition of William Adams, an alien of Ireland, arrived in Charelston about 1788....28th October 1839.

Page 82: Archibald English, a native of Ireland, made application to be admitted a citizen...emigrated in the month of December 1823...gave notice 28th October 1824, his father Samuel English did give notice...2d April 1839.

Page 84: Steven Keenan, John Robinson, and John Biggards, natives from Ireland, made report of themselves...1st November 1833.

Report of Stephen Keenan, an alien from Ireland, who arrived in Charleston, 1st November 1819...born County of Londonderry, aged 27 years, emigrated from County of Antrim, Belfast...1st November 1833. Petition dated 5th April 1838.

<u>Chester</u> VOLUME B

Page 87: David Watters, a native of Ireland, made application to be made a citizen...Petition of David Waters, an alien of Ireland, emigrated from Newry and arrived in Philadelphia, in June 6th day 1812....26th October 1840.

Page 89: Report of John Biggart, an alien from _____ who arrived in the US on 10 December 1824, report: born County Antrim, Ireland, aged 25 years, place of intended settlement, York District, SC...1st November 1833. Petition dated 29th March 1841.

Page 93: Petition of James Watson, a native of Ireland, emigrated from Ireland, arrived in CHarleston in 1832...gave notice at Chester Court House...30th March 1841.

Page 95: James Barr, Samuel English, and William Ford, natives of Ireland, made application to be admitted citizens...

Petition of William Ford, a native of Ireland, emigrated from Ireland and arrived in Charleston, December 1822...made notice on 21st October 1836...1st April 1841.

Page 97: Petition of James Barr, a native of Ireland, emigrated from Ireland, arrived in Charleston, 18th March 1820...gave noitce 25 October 1832...John McKelvey with whom he emigrated and in whose family he resided report him as an alien....__ April 1841.

Page 99: Petition of Samuel English, an alien of Ireland, emigrated in the month of November 18__...gave notice 24 October 1824...1 April 1841.

Page 101: William Ross, an alien from Ireland, made report of himself...arrived in the city of New York in April 1828...made report 28 October 1837...born Antrim County, Ireland, aged 33... Petition dated 2 April 1841.

Page 104: John Craig, a native of Ireland, made application... Petition of John Craig, an alien of Ireland, emigrated from Ireland and arrived in Charleston, December 1822...gave notice 3 March 1823...27 October 1841.

Page 106: Report of Daniel Tafts, an alien, who arrived in the US 22 July 1825, made report 25 October 1832...aged 27, emigrated from County Antrim, Ireland...24th October 1832.

Page 107: Report of John Robinson, an alien who arrived in the US on 22 April 1822, made report...aged 37, born County Down, Ireland, emigrated from County Antrim, place of intented residence, York District.

Page 108: Report of Mr. Lant Cahill, an alien from Ireland, who arrived inthe US in the city of Savannah, Ga., 15 June 1830, and came to Chester District, SC...report made 5 April 1834... born Tipperary, aged 39 years. Petition dated 6 April 1838.

Page 110: Report of Robert Wallace, an alien from Ireland who arrived in Charleston, 4 March 1822...born County Antrim, filed 23 September 1834.

Page 111: Report of William Wallace, an alien from Ireland, who arrived in the US at Charleston, 4 March 1822...aged 34 years, born County Antrim...23d September 1834.

Chester VOLUME B

Page 112: Report of Michael Cragle, an alien from Strasburg, in Germany, who arrived in the City of Charleston, January 1831 ...report 3 April 1837...born Strasburg, aged 25...

Page 112: Report of John Dickey, an alien from Ireland, who arrived in the US in Charleston, 9 January 1834...report 7 April 1833. born County Antrim, Ireland, aged 29.... Petition dated 9th April 1844.

Page 114: Report of John McGowen, an alien from Ireland, who arrived in Charleston in April 1824...born County Antrim, Randlestown, aged 32 years, place of intended residence York District.

Page 115: Report of Samuel McCormack, an alien who arrived in the US 23 December 1823...report made 3 April 1839...born County Antrim, Ireland, aged 50....Petition dated 5th April 1848.

Page 117: Report of James McMillen, an alien from Ireland, who arrived in the US in Charleston, February 1826...report 29 March 1841...Jas McMillen aged 45, wife Mary aged 43, Mary aged 22, Ann, aged 17, and William aged 15. Born County Down, Ireland. Petition dated 8th April 1844.

Page 119: Report of Thomas Orr, an alien from Ireland, who arrived in the US in Charleston, December 1824...report 29 March 1841...born County Antrim, Ireland, aged 35 years... Petition dated 9th April 1844.

Page 121: Report of John Marlin (Merlin) and family as aliens... arrived in the City of New York, December 1831...report made 30 March 1841. John Merlin, aged 46, Hugh Merlin, aged 20, John Merlin aged 19, James Merlin aged 14, Ralph Merlin, aged 13, Hamelton Merlin aged 12, David Merlin aged 10, Henry Merlin aged 9, Robert and William Merlin aged 4. All born County Derry, except Robert and William born in Chester District, S. C; family emigrated from County Antrim. Petition dated 9th April 1844.

Page 123: Report of John Charles, an alien from Ireland, who arrived in the US in the city of Charleston, January 1831... report 29th March 1841...born County Antrim, Ireland, aged 27 years...31st March 1841. Petition dated 9th April 1844.

Page 126: Report of Edward Sloan and family as aliens...who arrived in Charleston, 22 December 1834, report made 1 April 1841 ...Edward Sloan aged 51, Margaret Sloan his wife, aged 51, Susannah Sloan, aged 18, Margaret Sloan aged 15, Nancy Sloan aged 13, Edward Sloan aged 11, Eliza Sloan, aged 9, and Sally Sloan aged 4, all born County Antrim, Ireland... Petition dated 1 November 1844.

Page 128: Report of Daniel Carroll, an alien from Ireland, who arrived in the City of New York in June 1836...report made 2 2 April 1844...born Ireland, County Tiperrary, aged 20 Petition dated 11 April 1844.

Page 131: Report of Andrew Moore,an alien from Ireland, who arrived in the US at Charleston, January 1833...report 28th October 1839. born County of Antrim, Ireland, aged 28 years... Petition dated 13th November 1845

Chester   VOLUME B

Page 133: Petition of John McAdams, an alien of Ireland, arrived in Charleston,March 1843....9th April 1844.

Page 135: Report of Thomas Charles, an alien from Ireland, who arrived in Charleston, January 1832...report 4 April 1842... born County of Antrim, aged 62.

Page 136: Report of Thomas McAfferty, an alien from Ireland, who arrived in the US at Charleston, January 1838...report 4 April 1832..born County Antrim, aged 28½... Petition dated 9th April 1845.

Page 138: Report of Michael Keenan, an alien from Ireland, who arrived in Charleston, 1 January 1825...report 1844...born County of Londonderry...13 April 1844.

Page 139: Report of Jeremiah Hagerty, an alien from Ireland, who arrived in East Port, State of Main, in June 1836...report made October 1844...born County of Cork, Ireland...12th November 1844.

Page 140: Report of Charles Bell, an alien from Ireland, who arrived in Charleston, November 1838...made 12 April 1844... born Ireland, County Antrim,aged 28.

Page 141: Petition of James Beatty English, a native of Ireland, emigrated in December 1823...gave notice 28th October 1824...13 November 1844.

Page 143: Report of Thomas Charles Junior, an alien from Ireland, who arrived in the US at Charleston, 8 January 1831...report made November 1844...born County of Antrim, aged 29...

Page 144: Report of William Reid, an alien from Ireland, who arrived in the US at Charleston, 27 November 1840...report October 1844...born County of Antrim, Ireland, aged 30...

Page 145: Report of Samuel Adams, an alien from Ireland, who arrived in the US at Charleston, 15 November 1821...report October 1844...born County of Antrim, Ireland.

Page 146: Report of John Brice, an alien from Ireland, who arrived in Charleston, December 1840...report 16 November 1844. born County Antrim, Ireland, aged 49...

Page 147: Report of Francis Nelson, an alien from Ireland, who arrived in Charleston, December 1840...report 16 November 1844 ...born County Antrim, aged 24...

Page 148: Report of John C. Curry, an alien from Ireland who arrived in Charleston, 1 January 1837...report March 1846... born County of Antrim in Ireland, aged 32... Petition dated 3rd April 1849.

Page 150: Report of Sarah Keenan, an alien who arrived at Charleston, 15 January 1838, and made application...report November 1847...born County of Antrim Ireland, aged 26.

Page 152: Petition of Samuel Woodburn, an alien of Ireland, who arrived in Charleston about the middle of December 1819... at that time about 18 years of age, he has since resided in Fairfield District, on 15 November 1826 reported himself and gave notice in Fairfield District...4th April 1848.

COUNTY RECORDS

Chester VOLUME B

Page 154: Report of Robert Sloan, an alien from Ireland, who arrived inthe US at Charleston, March 1834...report April 1848. born County Antrim Ireland, aged 30 years... Petition dated 2d April 1851.

Page 157: Report of John Woodburn, an alien from Ireland, who arrived in the US about 1 December 1835...report 4 November 1844...no place of birth or age given in report. Petition dated 15th November 1848.

Page 160: Report of John Bennett, an alien from Ireland, who arrived in New York, 12 June 1836...report March 1849...born County of Cavan in Ireland, aged 25 years...place of intended residence, Union District, SC...

Page 161: Report of John McCullough, an alien from Ireland, who arrived at Charleston, 13 May 1846...report 4 November 1850... John McCullough, aged 47, wife Elizabeth aged 46, Mary aged 20, William aged 18, John aged 16, Grace aged 14, Robert aged 11, James aged 8, Charles aged 5, and Sara Jane aged 3.

Page 162: Report of Henry McCord, an alien from Ireland, who arived in the US in Charleston, 3 February 1835...report April 1848...born County of Antrim Ireland, aged 34....

Page 164: Report of William Thompson, an alien from in Great Britain, who arrived in Charleston, 7 March 1842; report April 1848...born County of Antrim....

Page 168: Report of Alexander McNeill, an alien from Ireland, who arrived in Charleston, 3 December 1842...report March 1845... born County of Antrim, aged 29 years

Page 173: Report of George Keenan, an alien from Ireland, who arrived in Charleston, 14 December 1824...report made April 1849...born County of Londonderry...Filed 2nd April 1849.

Darlington

The following petitions have been supplied by Mr. Horace Fraser Rudisill, Darlington County Historical Commission. With the exception of that petition of James Bell (which comes from private papers), all are from the unpaginated Sessions Journal 1806-1826 in the Darlington Courthouse.

Petition of James Bell...a native of the County of Antrim, Kingdom of Ireland, born 8 May 1814, removed to South Carolina about 20 September 1838, three years ago stated his intention...16 April 1844. Certified by W. R. Wingate, J. A. Dargan.

Petition of Andrew Gilmour, 25 March 1825.

Thomas Little, petition, reported himself as an alien, 1813, born in the Dominion of George III...October term 1818.

Petition of Mathew Lyles, 19 March 1812.

Francis Walsh, a native of Ireland, left in the fall of 1809, arrived in Charleston the December following, has been enroll'd with the clerk of court for admission as a citizen for upwards of two years...18 March 1813. signed by Lam. Benton, Moses Sanders, Jno. E. McIver, Josiah J. Evans, Geo. Bruce, Wm. Zimmerman, James Ervin.

Thomas Moore, a native of the county of Antrem(*sic*), Kingdom of Ireland, states his intention...(no date)

Dr. Thomas J. Flinn, aged 23 years, born in Dublin, Kingdom of Ireland, removed to this state in the year 1816, gives notice of intention...19 Oct 1821.

Fairfield

The following are abstracts of the original loose citizenship papers from Fairfield County/District now at the South Carolina Archives.

Nov. term 1813. Petition of John Wiley, a native of Ireland, emigrated to the US in 1787, resided in the US between 18 June 1798 and 14 April 1801...19 November 1813.

Nov. term 1813. Petition of James Wiley, a native of Ireland, emigrated to the US in 1787, resided in the US between 18 June 1798 and 14 April 1801...19 November 1813.

Petition of James Barkley, born in Ireland...17 April 1806.

Petition of Alexander Kincaid, born in Ireland...16 April 1806.

Petition of Hugh Barkley, born in Ireland, resided at least five years in the US...17 April 1806.

Petition of Samuel Johnston, born Ireland...17 April 1806.

Petition of Stuart Grafton, born Ireland...16 April 1806.

Petition of John McGuire, born Ireland...16 April 1806.

Petition of John McVea, born Ireland...15 April 1807.

Petition of Andrew Boyd, born Ireland...15 April 1807.

Petition of Robert Bones, born Ireland...13 April 1807.

Certificate of Naturalization of Andrew Crawford, 15 April 1807. resided in the US previous to 14 April 1802.

Petition of James Stewart, born Ireland...14 April 1807.

Petition of James Barber, born Ireland...13 April 1807.

Petition of James Richie, born Ireland...16 April 1807.

Petition of David Johnston, born Ireland...15 April 1807.

Petition of William Johnston, born Ireland...16 April 1807.

Petition of David Weir, born Ireland...13 April 1807.

Petition of James Weir, born Ireland...15 April 1807.

Petition of James Douglass, born Ireland...13 April 1807.

Petition of George Reed, born Ireland...13 April 1807.

Petition of William Adger, born Ireland...13 April 1807.

Petition of William McCulloch, born Ireland...14 April 1807.

Petition of Thomas McCullough, born Ireland...14 April 1807.

Petition of John Barkley, born Ireland...13 April 1807.

Petition of William Merrian, born Ireland...13 April 1807.

Fairfield

Petition of Daniel McCullough, born Ireland...14 April 1807.

Petition of James Beaty, born Ireland...14 April 1807.

Petition of Thomas McCauley, born Ireland...13 April 1807.

Petition of James Barkley, born Ireland...14 April 1807.

Petition of Christian F. Breithaupt, born Germany, a subject of the King of Saxony...16 November 1807.

Petition of Samuel Montgomery, born Ireland...21 April 1808.

Petition of Samuel Banks, born Scotland...19 April 1808.

Petition of Hugh Barkley Junior, born Ireland...19 April 1808.

Petition of Alexander Douglass, born Ireland...29 April 1808.

Petition of John Allen, born Ireland...19 April 1808.

Petition of Moses Camak, born Ireland...18 April 1808.

Petition of Breighton Buchanan, a native of Ireland...19 November 1808.

Petition of John Russell, a native of Ireland...19 November 1808.

Petition of James Hodge, born in Ireland...18 November 1808.

Petition of Samuel McGill, a native of Ireland...18 November 1808.

Petition of Thomas McKinstrey, born Ireland...14 November 1808.

Petition of Samuel McKinstrey, born Ireland...14 November 1808.

Petition of Henry McBride, born Ireland...21 April 1809.

Petition of James Kennedy, born Ireland, aged 55 years...18 April 1809.

Petition of James Gardner, born Ireland, aged 46 years...20 April 1808.

Petition of James Camak, born Ireland...21 April 1809.

Certificate of Naturalization of Robert Boyd, dated 18 April 1809.

Petition of David Hume, born Ireland, aged 45 years...21 April 1809.

Certificate of Naturalization of Alexander Harvey...18 April 1809.

Petition of Robert Gamble, born Ireland, aged 40 years...21 April 1809.

Petition of William Smith, born Ireland, 22 April 1809.

Petition of William Hamilton, born Ireland, aged 48 years...18 April 1809.

Petition of Alexander Wilson, born Ireland, aged 33 years...19 April 1809.

Fairfield

Petition of David Wilson, born Ireland, aged 51 years...19 April 1809.

Petition of Alexander Harvey, born Ireland, aged 50 years...18 April 1809.

Petition of James Harvey, born Ireland, aged 45 years..18 April 1809.

Petition of John Barber, born Ireland, aged 38 years...18 April 1809.

Petition of James Linn, born Ireland, aged 55...18 April 1809.

Petition of William Kiernaghan, born Ireland, aged 45...19 April 1809.

Petition of Christopher Plunkett, born Ireland...19 April 1809.

Petition of David Patton, born Ireland, aged 33...20 April 1809.

Petition of Hugh Penny, born Ireland, aged 46...19 April 1809.

Petition of John Kirkpatrick, born Ireland, aged 30....19 April 1809.

Petition of James Perry, born Ireland...18 April 1809.

Petition of James Rogers, born Ireland, aged 37...18 April 1809.

Petition of Samuel Bones, born Ireland...14 April1802.

Petition of Robt. Boyd, born Ireland...17 April 1809.

Petition of James McGill, born Ireland, aged 35...19 April 1809.

Petition of Robert Thompson, born Ireland, aged 24...19 April 1809.

Petition of Gan Thompson, born Ireland, aged 51...19 April 1809.

Petition of James Brice, born Ireland, aged 35...19 April 1809.

Petition of James Caldwell, born Ireland, aged 69...16 April 1809.

Petition of Gan Curry, born Ireland, aged 55...18 April 1809.

Petition of Robert Caldwell, born Ireland...19 April 1809.

Petition of Patrick Gladney, born Ireland, aged 45...19 April 1809.

Petition of Michael Moore, born Ireland, aged 55...22 April 1809.

Petition of John Brice, born Ireland...16 November 1809.

Petition of Samuel Caldwell, born Ireland...14 November 1809.

Petition of James Murdock, born Ireland...14 November 1809.

Petition of David Wilson, born County of Antrim, Ireland, aged 35...18 April 1810.

Petition of Alexander Thompson, born County of Antrim, Ireland, aged about 32 years...18 April 1810.

Fairfield

Petition of Joseph Caldwell, born County of Antrim, Ireland, aged 34...18 April 1810.

Petition of Alexander Stewart, born Ireland...18 April 1810.

Petition of James Thompson, born Ireland...14 April 1810.

Petition of John Neal, born Ireland...19 April 1810.

Petition of Samuel Bondes, born County of Antrim, Ireland...18 April 1810.

Petition of Robert Bryson, a native of Ireland, resident in the US between 1791 and 1811...19 November 1811.

Petition of James Nason, born Ireland...19 November 1811.

Petition of James Thompson, a native of Ireland, resident in the US between 179 and 1811...19 November 1811.

Petition of William Holmes, a native of Ireland, resident in the US between 1789 and 1811...19 November 1811.

Petition of William Telford, born Ireland...20 November 1811.

Petition of Robert Stett, a native of Ireland, resident in the US between 1791 and 1811...22 November 1811.

Petition of James Barkley Junr., born Ireland, resident in the US 22 years... 20 November 1811.

Petition of Robert Lathan (Leathen), born Ireland, landed at Charleston, 5 December 1788...14 April 1812.

Petition of Frances Elliott, born Ireland, emigrated to the US in 1791...18 November 1813.

Petition of Gardner Miller, born Ireland, emigrated previous to 18 June 1798...18 November 1813.

Petition of William Brafton, born Ireland, emigrated to the US in 1790...16 November 1813.

Petition of William McCreight Junr., born Ireland, emigrated to the US in 1792...16 November 1813.

Petition of John McMaster, born Ireland, emigrated to the US in 1790...16 November 1813.

Petition of James Blair, born Ireland, emigrated in 1790...18 November 1813.

Petition of James McCrorey, born Ireland, emigrated in 1793... 15 November 1813.

Petition of William Blair, born Ireland, emigrated to the US in 1790...17 November 1813.

Petition of Thomas Craig, born Ireland, emigrated to the US in 1789...19 November 1813.

Petition of John Parkerson, born Ireland, emigrated to the US in 1789...15 November 1813.

Fairfield

Petition of William McCrorey, born Ireland, emigrated to the US in 1785...17 November 1813.

Petition of Thomas Blair, born Ireland, emigrated to the US in 1793...15 November 1813.

Petition of William McClure, born Ireland, emigrated to the US in 1790...15 November 1813.

Petition of Roderick McDonald, a native of Scotland, emigrated to the US in 1789...16 November 1813.

Petition of David Drennan, born Ireland, emigrated to the US in 1797...16 November 1813.

Petition of John Neal, born Ireland, emigrated to the US in 1789...15 November 1813.

Petition of Joseph Neel, born Ireland, emigrated to the US in 1789...16 November 1813.

Petition of Robert Andrews, a native of Ireland, emigrated to the US in 1794...17 November 1813.

Petition of John Andrew, a native of Ireland, emigrated to the US in 1794...18 November 1813.

Petition of Robert Neelands, born Ireland...15 November 1813.

Petition of George Miller, a native of Ireland, emigrated to the US in 1795...23 April 1814.

Petition of Peter Hamilton, a native of Ireland, resident in the US since December 1791...23 April 1814.

Petition of Hugh Rodman (Rodmont), a native of Ireland, emigrated to the US in 1783...23 April 1814.

Petition of Hugh Kerr, a native of Ireland...23 April 1814.

Petition of Mathew Hutchison, a native of Ireland, emigrated to the US in 1809...19 April 1814.

Petition of Samuel Corke, a native of Ireland, emigrated to the US in 1792...23 April 1814.

Petition of James Swan Senr, a native of Ireland, emigrated to the US in 1788...23 April 1814.

Petition of William Cupit, a native of Ireland, emigrated to the US in 1787...23 April 1814.

Petition of Archibald McHenry, a native of Ireland, on 17 April 1809 declared his intention...23 April 1814.

Petition of Daniel Cupit, a native of Ireland, emigrated to the US in 1789...16 November 1814.

Petition of Samuel Clark, a native of Ireland, emigrated to the US in 1789...16 November 1814.

Petition of James Hindman, a native of Ireland, emigrated to the US in 1787...15 November 1814.

Fairfield

Petition of Robert Hindman, a native of Ireland, emigrated to the US in 1787...15 November 1814.

Petition of Thomas McCulley, a native of Ireland, emigrated to the US in 1789...15 November 1814.

Petition of Robert Marshall, a native of Ireland, emigrated to the US in 1786...17 April 1815.

Petition of John Dickson, a native of Ireland, emigrated more than nine years ago...19 April 1815.

Petition of Joseph Gladney Senr., emigrated from Ireland, August 1810...18 April 1815.

Petition of Richard Nason, a native of Ireland, emigrated to the US in 1801...18 April 1815.

Petition of Lachlan McIntosh, a native of Scotland, emigrated in 1800 and settled in Nova Scotia, in 1804 removed to the state of New York and in 1807 to SC...20 April 1816.

Petition of Robert Cathcart, a native of Ireland...22 November 1817.

Petition of William Perry, a native of Ireland, came to this country in 1801...22 November 1817.

Petition of John McCollum, a native of Ireland, emigrated to the US in 1801...22 November 1817.

Petition of William Wier, a native of Ireland, emigrated more than 19 years ago...18 November 1817.

Petition of David Wier, a native of Ireland, emigrated more than 19 years ago...18 November 1817.

Petition of Samuel Gault, a native of Ireland, came to this country 19 years ago...14 April 1819.

Petition of James Harper, a native of Ireland, emigrated to this country eight years ago...15 April 1819.

Petition of Michael Mahon, born County of Tipperary, Ireland, aged 33...16 April 1819.

Petition of James McGrady, born Parish of Glenavy, County of Antrim, Ireland...aged 16...12 July 1819.

Thomas Rogers, born County of Londonderry, Ireland, aged 21... 17 April 1819.

Robert Beaty, born County of Antrim, Parish of Killead, Ireland, aged 26...1 December 1818.

Petition of James Akin, born County of Antrim, Parish of Killard, aged 27...13 August 1819.

William Carlisle, a native of Ireland, declaration of intention... 20 April 1820.

Alexander Smith, a native of the County of Antrim, Ireland, came to Charleston 1 November 1819, then 23 years of age...18 April 1825.

Fairfield

Robert Mathews, a native of Ireland, declaration of intention... 29 April 1820. Report states that he was born County of Antrim, Parish of Ahoghill, aged 25.

James Crawford, born County Antrim, Ireland, aged 33...15 September 1820.

William Linn, a native of Ireland, emigrated 14 years ago... November term 1820.

Petition of John Gladney, a native of Ireland, emigrated 10 years ago...14 November 1820.

James Marshall, a native of Ireland, emigrated more than 30 years ago...14 November 1820.

Robert Pogue (Poge), a native of Ireland, emigrated 27 years ago...November term 1820.

James Linn, a nativeof Ireland, emigrated 14 years ago...November term 1820.

Petition of James Bones, a native of Ireland...13 November 1820.

Petition of James Harper, a native of Ireland, emigrated 10 years ago...November term 1820.

Petition of Patrick Gray, a native of Ireland, emigrated in 1814 ...18 November 1820.

Petition of Alexander Gladney, a native of Ireland, emigrated 10 years ago...14 November 1820.

Mathew Smith, a native of Ireland, emigrated to this country eight years ago...__ November 1820.

Petition of David Milling, a native of IReland, emigrated nine years ago...15 November 1820.

Report of Samuel Loughridge, born County Antrim, Ireland, aged about 60 years, resident in this state since 1790...19 April 1821.

William Aiken, a native of Ireland, declaration of intention... 19 April 1821. Report states that he was born in County Antrim, Ireland, and he is aged 23.

David McBurney, declaration of intention...15 November 1821.

John McNance, declaration of intention...15 November 1821.

Thomas McGrady, born County Antrim, Parish of Glenavy, aged 30 years...9 October 1821.

James McGrady, declaration of intention...16 November 1821.

Archibald Strain, born County Down, Ireland, aged 53...17 April 1822.

Michael Odonoho, born County of Kirk, Ireland, aged 26 years... 15 April 1822.

James Cathcart, born County Antrim, Ireland, aged about 27 years... 9 April 1822.

COUNTY RECORDS

Fairfield

Alexander Reid, born County Antrim, Ireland, aged about 35...7 April 1822.

James Wright, born County Tyrone, Ireland, aged about 28...__ April 1822.

Moor Smith, born County Antrim, Ireland, aged about 23...19 April 1822.

William McCombs, born County of Antrim, aged about 23...landed at Charleston 12 November 1820...16 October 1822.

John Carlile, born Ireland, aged 22..a native of County Antrim... 21 November 1822.

James Carlile, born County of Antrim, Ireland, aged 57...landed at Charleston 4 December 1821, has himself and family: wife Mary Carlile and children Alexander a son aged 19, Mary a daughter aged 16, Thomas McKeen Carlile, a son aged 13 and Henry, a son aged 13. 21 November 1822

James Carlile, born County of Antrim Ireland, aged 26...21 November 1821

William Mundell, born County of Antrim, Ireland, aged 41...landed at Charleston 2 December 1819, has wife Elizabeth and children Esther Mundell a daughter aged 14, Samuel Mundell a son aged 11, and Mary Mundell a daughter aged 9. 19 November 1822

Robert Gordon, a native of Ireland, declaration of intention...20 November 1822

John McGrady, arrived in the US 1 January 1821...aged 26, born County of Antrim, Parish of Glenavy , Ireland, 14 November 1822.

James Lemmon, born County of Antrim, Ireland, aged 25...19 November 1822.

James Welsh, born County of Antrim, Ireland, aged 21...arived in Charleston 1 November 1819...21 November 1822.

James Elder, born County Antrim, Ireland, aged 21...21 November 1818.

Thomas Lauderdale, born County of Down, Ireland, aged 27...__ November 1822.

William McGowan, born Randalstown, Ireland, aged 22...22 November 1822.

William Lauderdale, arrived at Charleston, 1 November 1817...born County Down, Ireland, aged 50, has wife Jane Lauderdale, and children: David a son aged 15, Mary Ann a daughter aged 19, and William a son aged 13. 20 November 1822

Robert Gordon, born County of Antrim, aged 23...20 November 1822.

John B. Philips, a native of Ireland, declaration of intention... 16 April 1823.

Michael McKinley, a native of Ireland, declaration of intention... 19 November 1823.

Fairfield

Alexander McDowell, born Antrim County, Ireland, aged 55...17 April 1824.

William Gibson, born County Armagh, Ireland, aged 32 years...landed at Charleston 15 January 1818...20 April 1821.

John R. Buchanan, a native of the Parish of Conner, County of Antrim, Ireland, emigrated from Belfast to Charleston 23 or 24 December 1818, then inthe 22nd year of his age....

Andrew McFadden, born Antrim County, Ireland, aged 36...__ November 1824.

John Antonie, a native of Portugal, declaration of intention... 8 November 1824.

Petition of John D. Crawford, a native of Ireland...20 April 1825.

Petition of Andrew Bartholomew, a native of County Antrim, Ireland ...18 April 1825. Report states that he was born County Antrim, Tullygarb(?), aged 21...17 November 1820.

Petition of James Cathcart Jr., a native of Ireland, on 9 April 1822 , declared his intention...21 April 1825.

Petition of Mathew Brown, desirous to become a citizen...10 November 1825.

Joseph Smith, a native of Ireland, declaration of intention... 12 April 1823.

Robert Quigley, a native of Ireland, made declaration of intention...9 November 1825.

Petition of Richard Cathcart, emigrated from Ireland in 1816, and landed in Charleston, was a minor and arrived with his father and family...17 April 1826.

Report of Charles Laughlan, born County Antrim, Ireland, aged 26 ...20 November 1822.

Petition of Joseph Smith, a native of County Antrim, Ireland, emigrated from Belfast to Charleston, 28 October 1820, then being 64 years of age...on ___November 1822, made declaration of intention...12 April 1826.

Report of William L. McCombs, November term 1826...born Drummand, County Antrim, Ireland.

Report of James Rogers, November term 1826...born County Monaghan, emigrated from Belfast.

Report of William Harper, 15 November 1826...aged 27, born Craigs, County Antrim, Ireland.

Report of John Markes, born Straid(?), County Antrim, Ireland, aged 27...15 November 1826.

Report of William McGookin, November tern 1826...born County Derry, Ireland, emigrated from Belfast.

Fairfield

Petition of James Harper, born Ireland, aged about 27, resident in the US since 9 November 1819, declared his intention November 1826...12 November 1828.

Report of John Matchet, aged 48, wife Susan aged 46, children: Alice 13, Richard 12, Eliza 10 and Thomas 7, born Parish of Glenavy, County Antrim, Ireland...15 November 1826.

Report of Thomas Chisam, born County Antrim, aged 30...November term 1826.

Report of James Chisam, born County Antrim, aged 19 years... November term 1826.

Report of Alexander McGrady, a minor at the time of his arrival (aged 20), born County Antrim, Ireland...15 November 1826.

Report of Robert Harper, __ Nov 1829, born County of Antrim, Ireland, aged 46...emigrated in 1822.

Report of Samuel McCombs, born County Antrim, aged 23...15 November 1826.

Report of Bryant McCaula, born County Antrim, Ireland, aged 30 years...November term 1826.

Report of Patrick Gilhooly, __ November 1826, born County of Leitrim, Ireland, aged 29....

Report of Robert Bell, November term 1826...borun County Monaghan, Ireland, aged about 40...

Petition of William Mundel (Mundle), a native of Ireland 15 November 1826.

Report of Joseph Davisson and family...Joseph Davisson aged 56, wife Margaret aged 48; children: James 20, Moses 17, Anne 15, Margaret 11, Joseph 13 and Jane 9, born County Antrim, Parish of Glenavy, Ireland...15 November 1826.

Petition of William McCombs, a native of County Antrim, Ireland... 15 November 1826.

Report of Richard Welch...15 November 1826; aged 32, born County Cork, Ireland.

Report of John Woodburn, 18 November 1820...born Craigs, County Antrim, Ireland...aged 30.

Petition of Wm Aiken, a native of the County of Antrim, emigrated from Belfast to Charleston, December 1819...then 22 years of age...11 December 1826.

Report of Ephraim Wilson, 7 November 1826..aged 38, born County Antrim, Ireland....

Report of Daniel Creamer, November term 1826...born County Cork, Ireland.

Report of Patrick Cunningham, born County Monaghan, Ireland, aged about 30 years...9 November 1826.

Petition of John McGrady, a native of Ireland...15 November 1826.

Fáirfield

Report of George Peters, November term 1826...born County of Symusel, Italy, aged 22, emigrated from Marsells (sic), France.

Report of Isaac Walker, __November 1824..born County of Monaghan, Ireland, aged 28.

Report of Archibald McGinnes, __ April 1826; born County of Antrim, Ireland, aged 27.

Report of John McCrea, 10 April 1827...born County of Antrim, Ireland, aged 26.

Report of Edward Philips, __ April 1827; born County of Antrim, Ireland, aged 23.

Report of Robert McMaster, __ April 1827, born County of Antrim, Ireland, aged 30.

Report of James Miller, November term 1827...born County Entrim(sic), Ireland, aged 37.

Report of Patrick Brennan, Ncvemter term 1827...born Queens County, Ireland, aged 29...emigrated from Waterford County, Ireland.

Petition of James Welsh, a native of County Antrim, Ireland, emigrated 1 November 1819, then aged 29...10 April 1828.

November term 1828: Petition of James Patton, a native of County Down, Ireland.

Petition of William Harper, born Ireland...resident in SC since 9 November 1819...gave notice of intention November 1826...12 November 1828.

Report of Armand Godfroy, April term 1829; born Baueux, Dept. of Calvados, France, aged 32, emigrated from Normandy.

Report of John Laney (Lanna), aged 28, born County Antrim, Ireland...emigrated from Belfast...November term 1826.

Report of John Murdock, born County Kildare, Ireland, aged 28; November term 1829. Petition dated 10 November 1829.

Petition of John Mark, a native of County Antrim, emigrated to Charleston December 1824, then about 24 years of age, has resided in Fairfield and Chester districts...13 April 1830.

Petition of Thomas Chisam, a native of County Antrim, Ireland, emigrated from Belfast to Charleston, 17 November 1819, then 25 years of age, made declaration of intention 15 November 1826... 6 November 1830.

Petition of James Chisam, a native of County Antrim, Ireland, emigrated from Belfast to Charleston 17 November 1819, then 11 years of age, made declaration 15 November 1826...6 November 1830.

Petition of David Walker, a native of Ireland, County Antrim, resident in SC upwards of 5 years...18 April 1837.

Report of Thomas B. Macartney...born Belfast, Ireland, aged 23, 1 October 1830.

Fairfield

Petition of Stewart Mitchel, a native of Ireland, resident in the District of Fairfield upwards of 5 years...12 April 1831.

Petition of William Brown, a native of Ireland, resident in the District of Fairfield upwards of 5 years, on 14 November 1827 declared his intention...1 November 1830.

Petition of John Boyd, a native of Ireland, resident in Fairfield District upwards of 5 years...Fall term 1830.

Petition of Hugh Bruce, a native of Ireland, resident in the District of Fairfield upwards of 5 years...8 November 1830.

Report of Henry Aime Joseph Leroy, 11 November 1830, born Lille, France, aged 30.

Petition of Robert Boyd, a native of Ireland...6 November 1830.

Report of Wilson Dalrymple, 14 April 1827...born County of Antrim, Ireland, aged 26.

Report of Francis Divine, 15 October 1831...born County Tyrone, Parish Donaugheady, aged about 36....

Petition of James Patton, a native of County Down, Ireland...14 April 1832.

Petition of Andrew Loole, a native of the County of Antrim, Ireland, 11 April 1832.

Petition of Patrick Brennan, a native of Queens County, Ireland, 12 April 1832.

Petition of William McCarol, a native of County Antrim, Ireland, resident in the US 5 years...16 April 1832.

Petition of Wm McDowell, a native of County Antrim, Ireland... 16 April 1832.

Report of Margaret Boyd...April term 1828...born County Derry, Ireland, aged 45.

Report of Peter Johnston, aged 38, born Duns Parish, Scotland, Barkshire County, intended residence is Chester District..__ November 1832.

Report of Mathew Petticure, aged 22, born County Armagh, Ireland, 3 November 1832.

Petition of Robert Gordon, a native of County Antrim, Ireland... 3 November 1832.

Petition of John Harper, born County Antrim, Ireland...November term 1832.

William Colgan, declaration of intention, 17 November 1824.... "sent a copy to Chesterfield C. H. Sept. 25th 1833."

Declaration of Intention of Kyle Quigley, a native of Ireland... 11 November 1834.

Petition of William Robinson, a native of County Antrim, Ireland... 7 April 1835.

Fairfield

Petition of William Gore, a native of County Antrim, Ireland... 7 November 1838.

Petition of William McDonald, a native of County Fermannah (sic), Ireland...7 November 1838.

Petition of Michael Gearty, a native of County Roscommon, Ireland...7 November 1838.

Petition of William Woolrich, a native of Newport, Shropshire, England, declared his intention 3 years ago...18 April 1840. A copy of declaration from Marine Court of New York, dated 24 December 1836 included.

Petition of Robert Miller, a native of Ireland...17 July 1840.

Report of William Wilson, aged 34, born County Antrim, Ireland... 9 November 1841.

Petition of George M. Leventrell, a native of County Underhauken (sic), Bavaria, about 28 years of age, a resident of the Town of Winnsboro, Fairfield District, arrived in the US September 1839...18 November 1843.

Petition of Joseph Cummings, a native of Ireland...22 February 1844.

Petition of John McKinney, a native of Ireland...19 February 1844.

Petition of Charles McCormick, a native of Ireland...29 March 1848.

Petition of Saling Wolf, a native of Newmark, West Prussia, aged about 26, arrived in the US, July 1839...24 February 1844.

Report of Thomas Kirkpatrick, November 1833...born County Antrim, Ireland, aged 28....

Petition of John Johnston, a native of County Antrim, Kingdom of Great Britain, 28 October 1846.

Petition of James Hutcheson, a native of County Antrim, Kingdom of Great Britain, aged about 46, arrived in this district 18 December 1839...22 November 1844.

Petition of James McElhenny, born County of Denigall (sic), Ireland, aged about 24, arrived in this state May 1841...23 November 1844.

Petition of James M. Crawford, a native of County Down, Ireland, aged about 23...22 November 1844.

Report of William Patterson, born County Antrim, Ireland, aged 23...18 November 1844.

Petition of John U. Zurcher (Zucher), a native of Switzerland... 23 November 1844.

Petition of William Simpson, a native of County Antrim, Ireland, aged about 30, arrived here in 1840...22 November 1844.

Fairfield

Petition of Francis Gourdin, a native of County Antrim, Ireland, arrived in Charleston, 21 December 1839...20 November 1844.

Petition of John Nobbs, a native of County Norfolk, Great Britain, aged about 25...23 November 1844.

Petition of James Stevenson, a native of County Antrim, Ireland, in the 61st year of his age...arrived in America fifty-three years ago...22 November 1844.

Petition of William Claxton, born County of Quinn (sic), Ireland, aged about 27, arrived in New York, April 1841...22 July 1845.

Petition of Eliza Bell, a native of County Antrim Ireland...23 July 1845.

Report of Martha Glover, born Ireland...23 July 1845.

Declaratino of Intention of Jane Corke, a native of Ireland...23 July 1845.

Petition of James McGuiger, a native of County Antrim, Ireland, arrived in SC, November 1840...22 November 1844.

Report of Sarah Keenan, born County Antrim, Ireland, aged 26, residence inChester District...3 November 1847.

Petition of William Claxton, declared his intention 22 July 1845....

Petition of John Hare, aged about 30, farmer, born County of Monahan, Castle Blany, Ireland, arrived in Philadelphia, 17 April 1849....26 October 1849.

Petition of Robert Stevenson, farmer, born County Armagh, Ireland, arrived in New York, 1 December 1848...23 October 1849.

Petition of Henry Reynoldson Curtis, aged 22, profession of medicine, born City of London, England, arrived in the US at Bangor, Maine, in 1834, and in SC in May 1842, resided two years in Alabama...24 October 1849.

Petition of Richard Cabeen, a native of Ireland, born County Antrim, Ireland...26 March 1850.

Petition of Chestnut Morrison, born County Antrim, Ireland...26 March 1850.

Petition of Robert McIlroy, aged 30, tailor, born County Antrim, Ireland, arrived in the US 19 December 1842...28 March 1850.

Petition of Joseph K. Crawford, aged 26 years, carriage marker, born County Down, Ireland, arrived in New York, 1 August 1843... 1 November 1850.

Petition of Charles Crawford, aged 25, tavern keeper, born County Down, Ireland, arrived in New York, 30 April 1839...1 November 1850.

Greenville

Following are the entries from the index to miscellaneous papers of the Court of Common Pleas for Greenville District pertaining to naturalization and abstracts of the few extant records.

Name	Date of Notice	Date Admitted	Label	File
Adams, John	6 Apr 1846	12 Apr 1848	1	24
Bull, Wm.	9 Nov 1847		1	37
Clarke, Alex	10 Apr 1849	13 Apr 1853	1	121
Gibson, Mrs. E.		25 Jul 1845		
Gullen, James	12 Apr 1848	15 Apr 1850	1	16
Johnson, Sam	16 Oct 1844		1	6
Keating, S.	15 Oct 1846		1	29
McCawley, John	10 Nov 1847	15 Apr 1850	1	38
Paulmann, L.		11 Nov 1844	1	7
Saxton, L.	16 Nov 1844		1	8
Scott, Alex.	31 Aug 1844		1	5

Label 1 File 1 (this entry does not appear in the index)

William Rabe...intention to become a citizen; born in Breslau, Kingdom of Prussia, 15 April 1818, now 21 years of age... left Rotterdam in Holland 15 Sept 1837 and arrived in Baltimore 1 November ensuing...10 Oct 1839. Tooak oath 28 Oct 1839.

Label 1 File 5

Petition of Alexander Scott...born in Dundee, Scotland, July 1821; sailed from Liverpool, England, for the U. S., 1841 and landed in the City of New York, October following; has resided in S. C. two years. (no date)

Label 1 File 6

Petition of Samuel Johnson aged 42 years...born in Frankfort, Germany, August 1804, sailed fromFrankfort, October 1815, arrived in Albany, New York, fall 1835...is desirous of becoming a citizen...__ April 1847.

Label 1 File 37

William Bull was born in the county of Kenty, Parish of Stone, Kingdom of Great Britain, 13 May 1816...sailed from London, 29 April 1839 and landed in New York 30 May, and left from Greenville District, SC...21 Oct 1847.

Kershaw

The following are from the Miscellaneous Index to the Records of the Court of Common Pleas for Kershaw District. This original index is now in the South Carolina Archives. The papers themselves are not known to be extant.

Name	Date of Notice	Date of Admission
Charlesworth, Jos.	Spring term 1841	
Douglas, Robt	Spring term 1841	
Durk(?), Joseph	October term 1841	
Douglas, Robert	23 October 1844	
Goodlad, John B.	October term 1838	October term 1841
Geirs, John Jos.	October term 1844	October term 1844
Gardner, William	April term 1832	18 March 1845
Gardiner, Andrew Young	29 October 1849	
Gardiner, James M.	29 October 1849	
Gatman, Jacob	30 October 1849	
Hubert, Francis	Spring term 1841	
Hopkinson, George	30 October 1849	
Johnston, William B.	October term 1838	October term 1841
Kennedy, Anthony M.	October term 1838	October term 1841
Kennedy, Robert	13 November 1847	Spring term 1850
Koopman, M.	30 October 1849	
Laboures, Felix	March term 1845	
Matheson, Farquhar		October term 1839
Macrae, Colin	Spring term 1844	April term 1847
Moffat, K. S.	2 April 1849	2 April 1849
O'Connell, W. L.	Spring term 1841	
Oaks, F. J.	2 April 1849	2 April 1849
Riddle, James	Spring term 1842	
Reynolds, John	Spring term 1842	
Robinson, Andrew	March term 1845	
Reynolds, Marcus		Spring term 1844
Smith, Jno. R.	October term 1841	
Smith, John R.	21 March 1845	
Stevenson, Wm.	13 November 1847	
Wilson, Robert	20 March 1845	
Wilson, Thomas	March term 1845	
Wilson, James	11 November 1847	5 April 1851
Wilson, William John	9 April 1849	
Worthington, ___	5 April 1850	
Young, Andrew	Spring term 1841	

Lancaster

The following entries are from the Miscellaneous Index at the Lancaster County Courthouse, which commenced in 1839. It may or may not include earlier entries. The original petitions and papers have not yet been found, but may be extant. No dates appear in the index. Only those entries for Petitions for Naturalization have been included (the index also includes Prison Bounds & Insolvent Debtors).

Name	Number
Adams, James	37
Beaty, John	8
Blackstocks, William	23
Bradley, John W.	28
Craig, John	24
Cooper, Samuel	25
Campbell, Michael	29
Costow, John	38
Douglass, Samuel	5
Douglass, Robert	6
Downey, Peter	20
Dobbin, Robert	30
Davidson, Henry	41
Graham, John	7
Gettys, John	18
Gare, Thomas M.	34
Gardner, Henry	39
Gardner, John	40
Garside, Hugh	46
Grim, Alexander	48
Hagan, John	9
Hunter, Joseph	17
Hayman, George	45
Johnston, John	15
Johnston, Peter	27
Kerr, Robert	4
Kenney, Patrick	14
Ketchins, Thomas	32
Lewis, Thomas P.	22
Marshall, John	1
McDowall, Robert	2
McAteer, James	3
McAteer, Francis	16
McElmoyl, John	26
McDowall, William	31
Maley, James	32
McMullan, William	33
McCary, John	34
McKenna, Patrick	35
Mayblume, N.	42
Porter, John	19
Quigley, Daniel J.	47
Roberson, Thomas	10
Robison(?), Thos. H.	36
Scott, John	9
Scott, James	10
Steel, Francis	12
Steel, James	21
Summervill, William	43
Spence, Saml	44
Simpson, Bartholomew	49
Wilson, Robert	11

Lancaster

The following entries are from the Lancaster County/ District Common Pleas Journals (WPA copy at South Carolina Archives # A489).

p. 76, April 8, 1807. James Douglass, Samuel Douglass, James Scott and James Anderson...are natives of Ireland; James Douglass and Samuel Douglass have resided in this state for 20 years last past; James Scott for 15 years, and James Anderson for 13 years.

pp. 112-113, April 11, 1809. John Steel and Francis McAteer, natives of Ireland, pray to be citizens.

p. 114, April 11, 1809. Patrick Kenny, a native of Ireland, prays to be a citizen.

p. 224, November 10, 1814. Petition for naturalization of Robert Robertson.

Laurens

With the exception of the petition of Dennis McNamara, the following naturalization petitions are from the Georgia Genealogical Magazine (No. 37, No. 42, and No. 43), used with the kind permission of the editor, Rev. Silas Emmett Lucas, Jr. The original petitions from which those abstracts were made cannot now be located.

Petition of Dennis McNamara...a native of the County of Tipperary in Ireland, that he arrived in Charleston on 7 March 1811 and has resided in this state ever since....18 Nov 1813. (from Laurens County Citizenship Petitions Roll 52, label 2, original at South Carolina Archives)

Label 1

Roll #1: James Kyle, a native of Ireland, petitiond for naturalization on April 15, 1806 and stated that he had resided in the U. S. about twelve years and in South Carolina for eight years. Certifying as to his character were George Bowie, Thos Lewers, Benj. Tankersley, Sam'l Law, Jr., Jno Simpson, M. Hunter.

Roll #2: Alexander Stuart petitioned for naturalization April 16, 1806, stating that he was a native of County Antrim, Ireland, and that he has resided in the U. S. ten years and upwards and in this state for this space of time. Certifying as to his character were Wm. Caldwell, Jno. Simpson, Wm. Dunlap, George Bowie, Wm. Nibbs, J. W. McKebbin.

Roll #3: John Black petitioned to be admitted a citizen of the U. S., 18 Nov 1806, stating that he was a native of Scotland, and that he had resided in this state seven years. Certifying concerning his character were Robt. Creswell, John Simpon, Chas. Griffin, Jno. Garlington, Jno. Watts, Jas. Caldwell, Abner Pyles.

Roll #4: Samuel Todd and Robert Alexander Todd petitioned the court for citizenship on 17 April 1807, stating that they were subjects of Great Britain, but had resided in the U. S. and in this state since the year 1800. Character testimonials by B. H. Saxon and Silvanus Walker, Jr.

Roll #5: Charles Little petitioned the court for citizenship on 16 April 1807, stating that he was a native of Ireland and had resided in this state for 13 years. Citizens certifying as to his character were Robt. Hutcheson, Jno. Simpson, Jas. Simpson, A. Rodgers Jr., Wm. Hutchinson, W. Burnside, Wm. Dunlap, David Speers.

Roll #6: William Cowan, a native of Ireland, stated that he had resided in the U. S. and in this state for 10 years and wishes to become a citizen. Certifying were R. Creswell, Wm. Hutchinson, Thos. Parks, Thos. Wright, Starling Tucker, Robt. Hutcheson, Charles Allen, W. Burnside. Petition filed 14 April 1807.

Roll #7: David Whiteford, a native of County Antrim, Ireland, petitioned the court for citizenship and stated that he had resided in S. C. upwards of 17 years. Certifying as to character were W. Burnside, Matthew Hunter, Jno. Wiseman, Jas. Young, Wm. McCredy, Jno. Watts, Rich'd Watts. Filed 14 April 1807.

Roll #8: The petition of James McCarey stated that he was a native of Ireland and that he sailed from Ireland 14 April 1792 and arrived in Charleston 26 July 1792; also that he had resided in the U. S. and this state for 15 years. Petition filed 17 April 1807. Character witnesses: Jno. Simpson, Starling Tucker, Thos. Lewers,

Laurens

Jno. Ritchey, Joshua Hitch, Robt. Hutcheson, Sam'l Todd.

Roll #9: The petition of Alexander Henry showed that he was a native of Ireland and that he had resided in the U. S. and this state for 15 years. Character witnesses: Benj. Lewis, W. Burnside, Wm. Craig, J. Puckett, Robt. Hutcheson, James Park, Abner Rodgers, Jno. Davis, Jno. Simpson, Z. Bailey, Charles Allen. Filed 15 April 1807.

Roll #10: The petition of Joseph Lyons stated that he was a subject of the King of Great Britain, and that he had resided in the U. S. and particularly in this state since the year 1781. Character witnesses: Dan'l Wright, Andrew B. Moore, Jno. Meador, Wm. Bowen, Thos. Parks, Jonathan Downs. Petition filed 13 April 1807.

Roll #11: James Hunter, a native of Ireland, filed petition for naturalization 17 April 1807 in which he stated that he embarked from there 15 or 16 years before and that he arrived at the harbor in Charleston some short time thereafter; also that he had resided in this state 14 years. Testifying that they have known Hunter for 10-12 years were Jas. H. Lawing, Chas. Smith, Thos. Wright, George Ross, W. Fowler, Wm. Barksdale, Thos. Porter, Robt. Hutcheson, W. F. Downs, J. Rodgers Jr.

Roll #12: The petition of Matthew Hunter showed that he was a native of Ireland and had resided in this state 14 years. Character witnesses: Wm. Dunlap, Jno. Garlington, Jno. Simpson, Elihu Creswell. Filed 17 April 1807.

Roll #13: The petition of David Greer showed that he was a native of Ireland and had resided in the U. S. and this state for 10 years. Character witnesses: Jno. Simpson, Wm. Dunlap, Jno. Black, James Nickels. Filed 20 April 1808.

Roll #14: Petition of David Little showed that he was a native of Ireland and that he had resided in this state 14 years. Character witnesses: Chas. Allen, Robt. Long, Robt. Hutcheson, Jno. Boyd. Filed 18 April 1808.

Roll #15: Andrew Todd, a native of Ireland, stated in his petition that he had resided in the U. S. since Jan. 1794 and in this state. Character witnesses: M. Hunter, Thos. Lewers, Sam'l Todd, Jno. Cook. Filed 19 April 1808.

Roll #16: William McGowan, a native of Ireland petitioned for naturalization and stated that he had resided in the U. S. since May 1801 and for seven years past in this state. Testifying as to character were Josiah Evans, Samuel Lemon, Meshac Ovaby, Jno. Beasley. Filed 18 April 1808.

Roll #17: Maxwell McCormack, a native of Ireland petitioned the court for naturalization and stated that he had resided in the U. S. since October 1790 and for 18 years in this state. Testifying as to character were Chas. Simmons, Thos. Porter, Thos Lewers, Sam'l Todd, B. Nabers, Chas. Allen, P. Brannon, M. Hunter. Filed 19 April 1808.

Roll #18: David Glen made petition for naturalization and stated that he was a native of Ireland and that he had resided in the U. S. and this state for 20 years. Testifying as to character were Wm. Cowan, Starling Tucker, David Speers, Jno. Simpson, Robt. Hutcheson. Filed 19 April 1808.

Laurens

Roll #19: James Laughridge, a native of Ireland, petitioned for citizenship and stated that he had resided in the U. S. since July 1801 and for 3 years past he resided in this state. Certifying as to character were Thos. Porter, Thos. Wright, Jonathan Downs, John Simpson. Filed 19 April 1808.

Roll #20: John Crawford, a native of Ireland, petitioned for naturalization and stated that he had resided in the U. S. and this state for 18 years. Testifying were Jno. Simpson, Wm. Dunlap, Jas. Nickels, Jno. Black. Filed 20 April 1808.

Roll #21: James Boyd Jr. petitioned for naturalization, stating that he had resided in the U. S. and this state for 6 years. Certifying as to character were Wm. Kingsborough, Jno. Simpson, Jas. Nickels, Robert Hutcheson, John Black, Wm. Dunlap. Filed 20 April 1808.

Roll #22: John Todd, a native of Ireland, petitioned for naturalization and stated that he had resided in the U. S. and this state since December 1790. Testifying: Thos Lewers, David Glen, Wm. Cowan, David Conor, Sam'l Todd. Filed 21 April 1808.

Roll #23: William Black, a native of Scotland, petitioned for naturalization and stated that he arrived in Charleston about 1 November 1803 and has since resided in Laurens District. Citizens and freeholders testifying as to character were R. Word, Jno. Clark, Wm. Dendy, W. Burnside, Jno. Simpson, David Anderson, Robt. Creswell, Jno. Garlington. Filed 16 Nov 1808.

Roll #24: William Holiday petitioned for naturalization and stated that he was a native of Ireland and that he had resided in this state 18 years. Testifying as to character were Robt. Hutcheson, W. Burnside, Saml Cunningham, Thos Lewers, Jos. Downs, David Anderson. Filed 16 Nov 1808.

Roll #25: James Boyd, a native of Ireland, petitioned for naturalization and stated that he had resided in the U.S. between 1795 and 1796 and for the last 13 years in this state. Testifying as to character were Jno Simpson, Robt. Hutcheson, Jas. Holley, W. Burnside, R. Campbell, Jonathan Downs, Jas. Abercrombie. Filed 15 Nov 1808.

Roll #26: Samuel Wier, a native of Ireland, petitioned for naturalization and stated that he had resided in the U. S. between 25 Dec 1792-1793 and for the last 10 years had resided constantly in this state. Testifying were Chas. Allen, David Speers, Jno. Simpson, Captors Hugens, Robt. Hutcheson, W. Burnside. Filed 15 Nov 1808.

Roll #27: William Fulton, a native of Ireland, petitioned for naturalization, stating that he had resided in the U. S. between 4 Sept 1787-1788 and for the last 20 years in this state. Testifying were B. H. Saxon and Chas. Allen. Filed 16 Nov 1808.

Roll #28: Walter Stewart, a native of Ireland, petitioned for naturalization and made oath of allegiance to the U. S.; also that had had resided in this state 20 years. Filed Nov. 1808. Among those testifying were James Fleming, Robert Brown,J. A. Elmore, Jas. Mills.

Laurens

Roll #29: Thomas Fulton asked for naturalization and made oath; he stated that he was a native of Ireland and had resided in the U. S. since the 15 June 1795 and for the last 17 years in this state. Testifying as to character were Joseph Downs, Thos. Lewers, Chas. Allen. 16 Nov 1808.

Roll #30: Robert Fleming petitioned and made oath, stating that he was a native of Ireland and had resided in this state 11 years. Testifying were Robt. Word, A. Lawrence, Thos. Parks, John Wil-laism. Filed 16 Nov 1808.

Roll #31: Robert Gilliland, a native of Ireland, petitioned and made oath; also stated that he had resided in this state 22 years. Testifying were Andrew Rodgers Sr., Benj. Byrd, Robt. Word, Jno. Puckett. Filed 17 April 1809.

Roll #32: John Luke, a native of Ireland, petitioned for naturalization and made oath; also stated that he had resided in this state 15 years. Among those testifying were George McNary, James Holley, George Ross. Filed 18 April 1809.

Roll #33: Alexander Luke, a native of Ireland, petitioned for naturalization and made oath; also stated that he had resided in this state 15 years. Testifying were Alexander Fillson, Alexander Henry, James Park. Filed 14 April 1809.

Roll #34: John Wilkerson, a native of Scotland, petitioned and made oath; also stated that he had resided in this state 24 years. Testifying were H. T. Martin, J. Underwood, Wm. Dendy. Filed 14 Nov 1809.

Roll #35: Alexander Wilkinson, a native of Scotland, petitioned nade made oath; also stated that he had resided in this state 25 years. File 17 April 1810.

Roll #36: John Stewart, a native of Ireland, petitioned and made oath; also stated that he had resided in this state 21 years. Testifying were George Adair, W. H. Alexander, John Cochran, Samuel Taylor. Filed 17 April 1810.

Roll #37: Petition and oath of Samuel Stewart, a native of Ireland, stated that he had resided in this state 21 years. File 17 April 1810. Testifying were Jno McLaughlin, J. A. Elmore and others.

Roll #38: Wm. Boyd Jr., a native of Ireland, petitioned and made oath; also stated that he had resided in this state 6 years. Filed 12 Nov 1810.

Roll #39: Samuel Boyd, a native of Ireland, petitioned and made oath; stated that he had resided in this state 6 years. Filed 12 Nov 1810.

Roll #40: Robert Sinkler, a native of Ireland, petitioned and made oath; also stated that he had resided in this state 6 years. File 12 Nov 1810.

Roll #41: Patrick Todd, a native of Ireland, petitioned and made oath; also stated that he had resided in this state 7 years. Testifying were James Strain and Jonathan Johnson. Filed 13 Nov 1810.

Laurens

Roll #42: Francis Stewart petitioned for naturalization and made oath; also stated that he was a native of Ireland and had resided in this state 15 years. Testifying were Jas. Fairbairn, George Jones, and Isaac Underwood. Filed 13 Nov 1810.

Roll #43: John Boyd, a native of Ireland, petitioned and made oath; stated that he had resided in this state 5 years. File 2 Nov 1810.

Roll #44: William Boyd Sr., a native of Ireland, petitioned and made oath stated that he had resided in this state 6 years. Filed 12 Nov 1810.

Roll #45: Jon McGowan, a native of Ireland, petitioned and made oath stating that he had resided in the U. S. since Dec. 1791 and in this state. Filed 15 April 1811.

Roll #46: William Black, a native of Scotland, petitioned and made oath; stating that he arrived in the City of Charleston in the Spring of 1803 and immediately removed to Laurens District. At the november term of court in 1808 he gave notice of his intention to become a citizen. Among those testifying was William Nibbs. Filed 19 Nov 1811.

Roll #47: William McCullough, a native of Ireland, petitioned for citizenship and stated that he had resided in S. C. since 1796. File 19 Nov 1811.

Roll #48: Samuel Thomb, a native of County Antrim, Ireland, petitioned, giving notice of his intention to become a citizen. He stated that he arrived in Charelston in June 1811 and immediately removed to Laurens District where he has resided ever since. Filed 14 April 181.

Roll #49: John Patterson, a native of Ireland, petitioned and made oath; stating that he had resided in the U. S. since 1793 and in this state for same time. File 16 April 1812.

Roll #50: Joseph McCullough gave notice of becoming a citizen, native of Ireland. Lived in U. S. and S. C. since Feb. 1808. Filed 16 April 1812.

Label 2

Roll #51: File 21 Sept 1812. John Johnson, born in the Kingdom of Prussia and about 32 years of age; arrived in the U. S. at the Port of New Orleans, in 1807; is a preacher or the Gospel, had no family.

Roll #53: John Drennon, a native of Ireland, filed petition for naturalization and took oath 16 Nov 1812; stated that he had resided in the U. S. and in the state of S. C. since Feb. 1787. Among those testifying as to his character were N. Durkee, Jas. Longridge and Willis Farr.

Roll #54: Robert Sloan, a native of County Antrim, Ireland, filed his petition and took oath in open court 10 Nov 1813. He stated that he arrived in Charleston 7 Jan 1800. In May he left there and resided in Newberry where he spent seven years; then he came to Laurens District where he since resided. John Sloan made a sworn statement that this was true.

Laurens

Roll #55: Jame Gage, a native of Ireland, took oath 19 April 1814; he was of Union District.

Roll #56: Henry Fearnes, a native of Warwickshire, England, petitioned for naturalization and took oath 16 Sept 1814; arrived in Charleston 25 Jan 1811.

Roll #57: John McWilliams, a native of Ireland, petitioned for naturalization and stated that he had resided in the state of South Carolina since Nov. 1805.

Roll #58: David Graham, a native of County Antrim, Ireland, petitioned the court 16 Nov 1815. He arrived in Dec. 1788 and had ever since resided in S. C.

Roll #59: Alexander Austin Sr., James Austin Sr., James Austin Jr., J. Alexander Austin Jr., petition for naturalization, filed 14 Nov 1815; natives of County Antrim, Ireland; arrived in Charleston 13 Nov 1804 and immediately removed to Laurens District where they ever since resided.

Roll #60: Petition and oath of George Cruickshanks filed 14 April 1819; a native of the north of Scotland, aged 23, born in the province of Rhynie, Aberdeenshire; left Scotland 1 June 1817; landed in Quebec, lower Canada the end of July; left lower Canada 18 Jan 1818; had been in Laurens District 12 months or 20 April 1819; aged 23 years in May 1819.

Roll #61: Petition of Francis Glenn filed 14 April 1819; native of Ireland, resided in S. C., since Feb. 1788.

Roll #62: Thomas McCarley, a native of Ireland, filed petition for naturalization 16 April 1819. Landed in the U. S. August 1800 in the state of Delaware; removed to S. C. in 1802 and resided there ever since. Among those testifying as to his character were C. Saon and Thomas F. Jones.

Roll #63: William Hamilton filed his intention to become a citizen 16 Nov 1810; he was upwards of 50 years of age; migrated from the County of Trine(sic) in Ireland; arrived in U. S. Dec 1803 and settled in S. C., Laurens District.

Roll #64: James Garner, a native of Ireland, arrived at Georgetown, S. C., July 1796 and has ever since resided in this state. Sworn in court 19 Nov 1819.

Roll #65: Reverence Alexander Kirkpatrick, a native of County Antrim, Ireland, appeared in open court 18 Nov 1817; arrived in Charleston 16 Nov 1816 and immediately removed to Laurens District where he has ever since resided.

Roll #66: Andrew Todd, a native of the County of Monaghan, Ireland, filed notice of intention to become a citizen and took oath 19 Nov 1817; arrived at Charleston 16 Nov 1816; immediately removed to Laurens District where he has resided ever since.

Roll #67: John Pearson, a native of England, aged about 32 years, made petition and took oath 20 April 1820.

Roll #68: John Henderson, a native of Ireland, made petition and took oath 15 Nov 1820. Resided in U. S. since June 1818; Character testimonials made by Jason Meadors, James Tolland, and Elisha Adair.

Laurens

Roll #69: John McWilliams, a native of Ireland, petitioned and took oath 15 Nov 1820. Resided in Laurens District for 15 years.

Roll #70: Robert Ross, a native of Ireland, resided in U. S. since December last. Filed and took oath 16 Nov 1820.

Roll #71: Alexander Austin Jr., a native of Ireland, filed petition and took oath 15 Nov 1820. Arrived in Charleston November 1805 and came to this district where he had ever since resided.

Roll #72: Thomas Quinn, a native of the County of Sligo in Ireland and Parish of St. John's arrived at port of Charleston in 1817 from which place he removed to Chester District and from thence to the district of Laurens where he intended finally settling himself, aged 28 years. Filed notice of becoming a citizen 16 Dec 1820.

Roll #73: Samuel Austin petitioned for denizenship and gave notice of his intention to become a citizen 18 April 1821; a native of County Antrim, Ireland, aged 60 years.

Roll #74: Francis Tourell, a native of the City of Versailles in France, 51 years of age, born under the allegiance of Louis 18th, filed 18 April 1821, petition for denizenship and also notice of intention to become a citizen.

Roll #75: Alexander Austin Sr. petitioned for naturalization and took oath 18 April 1821; a native of County Antrim, Ireland. Arrived in Charleston about 17 years ago; immediately removed to this district where he has ever since resided. Filed notice 14 Nov 1815 of his intention and obtained from the Clerk of Court of Laurens District a certificate of same. Took oath 18 April 1821.

Roll #76: Archibald Craig petitioned for denizenship 15 April 1822; a native of Scotland; arrived in Charleston 15 June 1821, had family of children, viz: (1) Jane aged 3 years and 1 month (2) James, 1 year and 11 months, born inScotland; oath taken 15 April 1822.

Roll #77: John Kennedy, a native of Ireland, petitioned to become a denizen of the state of S. C., 17 April 1822; had resided in U. S. since 10 Nov 1819; oath taken 17 April 1822.

Roll #78: Andrew Todd, a native of Ireland, filed petition for naturalization 20 Nov 1822; certificate drawn; resided in U. S. and S. C. since Nov 1816, certificate dated 19 Nov 1817; sworn 21 Nov 1822. Testifying as to character: Wm. Ranson,Ambrose Hudgens Jr., Henry C. Young.

Roll #79: Robertson Hamilton, born in County Tyrone, Ireland; aged 26; petitioned to become a denizen and gave notice for naturalization. Filed 19 Nov 1822.

Roll #80: Samuel Hamilton, a native of County Monaghan, Ireland, filed petition and took oath 20 Nov 1822, arrived in Charleston about 26 Nov 1816 and ever since resided in this state.

Roll #81: William Baxter, a native of County Antrim, Ireland, aged 26, petitioned and took oath 18 Nov 1822.

Roll #82: Alexander Kirkpatrick, a native of Ireland, filed application 19 Nov 1822; took oath 12 Nov 1822; emigrated to the U. S. 1816 and had lived in the state and district nearly 6 years.

Laurens

Roll #83: Robert Bell, a native of the County of Londonderry, Ireland, aged 28 years; had been a resident of this district about four years and intended to continue a resident of this state; oath taken 19 Nov 1823, filed same date.

Roll #84: Hugh Wilson, a native of County of Air (Eire) in North Critina, born in 1778, about 45 years old; arrived in S. C. in October 1822 and intended settling in Laurens District; had wife Jannet about 42 years of age; three children viz: (1) William about 20 years of age (2) John about 11; (3) Hugh about 3 years; the whole of whom were born in the County of Air, except wife Jannet who was born in the County of East Lothan in North Britain; arrived in S. C. at the same time with the petitioner in district of Laurens and had resided in same state about a year. Oath 20 Nov 1823. Filed 15 Nov 1827.

Roll #85: Anthony McFaul (McFall), a native of County Antrim, Ireland, aged about 26 years, arrived in U. S. month of Nov. 1811 and had ever since resided in this state. Certificate of denizenship of this state dated 20 Nov 1824. Oath taken 21 Nov 1823.

Roll #86: John Cannon, a native of County Dengal (sic, for Donegal?), Ireland, aged 21, had been a resident of Laurens District about 6 months. Oath taken 19 Nov 1823.

Roll #87: Andrew Matthews, a native of the City of Londonderry, Ireland, arrived in the City of Baltimore, Md., Sept 1818 and had since resided in the U. S. in Nov. 1819, he removed to Columbia in this state and on 1 April 1820, he filed his petition in the Court of Common Pleas for Richland District. Reunuciation in Columbia 1 April 1820. Oath taken in Laurens 13 Nov 1823.

Roll #88: Robert Monroe, 30 years of age, born in County of Rophair, Scotland; had been a resident of this state about 5 years; took oath 19 Nov 1823; filed his petition for denizenship and naturalization the same day.

Roll #89: William Milligan, a native of County Antrim, Ireland, aged 60 years; had been a resident of this state nearly 20 years; oath taken 19 Nov 1823; filed same day.

Roll #90: John Ranson, a native of County of Monaghan, Ireland; resided in the state of S. C. since 1 Dec 1818; sworn in open court 14 April 1824; filed petition same day.

Roll #91: Patrick Synnott, a native of Waxford, Ireland, aged 30, had been a resident of this state since 1821 and of this district since 1822; oath and reunuciation of allegiance 14 April 1824; filed petition same day.

Roll #92: William Ranson, a native of County Monaghan, Ireland, aged 36, a resident of this district since 1812; oath and renunciation made 14 April 1824.

Roll #93: John Ross, a native of County Monaghan, Ireland; had resided in U. S. and S. C. since 20 April 1823; oath and renunciation 15 April 1824.

Roll #94: Thomas Kirkpatrick, a native of Londonderry, Ireland, aged 28; sailed from Belfast and arrived in S. C. in 1818 where had had lived since that time and still intends to reside. Oath 19 Nov 1824.

Laurens

Roll #95: Andrew Kennedy and family; Andrew Kennedy, a native of County Antrim, Ireland, aged 41; wife Mrs. Ann Kennedy, aged 40, born in same county. Three children (1) Cunningham Moore Kennedy, born Antrim, aged 17 (2) Isabella, aged 14, born in County of Meath, Ireland (3) John aged 13, born County of Meath; arrived in Charleston from Belfast in October 1823 and had resided in this district about 12 months. Kennedy took oath 18 Nov 1824.

Roll #96: Peter Galaher, a native of County Leitrim, Ireland, aged about 35 years; left Ireland June 1822 and arrived in Charleston 11 Sept. following; filed petition 16 Nov 1824.

Roll #97: William Gilchrist, a native of Scotland, aged 23 years old, arrived in Charleton 5 June 1821; filed petition 19 April 1825.

Roll #98: John Campbell, a native of County Antrim, Ireland, aged 35 years; embarked from Port Rush in North Ireland; had been a resident of this district since 1820. Filed 20 April 1825.

Roll #99: James Craig, a native of County Antrim, Ireland, aged about 42 years; wife, Mrs. Katharine Craig, aged about 43, who was born in the U. S. Arrived in Charleston from Belfast about the middle of April 1821; had resided in this district 18 months and planned to continue here. Filed 19 April 1825.

Roll #100: William Davidson, a native of County Derry, Ireland, aged 21, arrived at Port of Charleston via New York from Belfast Sept 1823; had resided in this district. Filed petition 15 Nov 1825.

Lexington

The following entries are from the index on LDS microfilm titled "Old Index to Citizenship Petitions,' which is actually the Miscellaneous Index from the Court of Common Pleas of Lexington District/County. The papers are not known to be extant.

Name	Date of Notice	Date of Application
Bachman, Henry L.	26 Oct 1847	30 Oct 1850
Doughens, Patrick	11 Apr 1840	
Eagans, James	15 Apr 1843	23 Oct 1849
Frederick, Frederick	1 Nov 1850	
Frank, Christian	15 Apr 1843	30 Apr 1846
Horens, James	11 Apr 1840	
Miller, John Lebright	13 Nov 1844	26 Oct 1847
Schenk, Michael	14 Apr 1842	
Younginer, John		10 Apr 1844

Marlboro

The following are abstracts of the original loose petitions from Marlboro(ugh) District, now in the South Carolina Archives.

Allen Macfarlan...declaration of intention...3 June 1839. Certified copy of report from Chesterfield District, SC.

Petition of James McKellar, a native of Scotland (no date)

Petition of William Cooper, born Tarbert, County of Argyleshire, Scotland, 28 years of age, came from Greenock, and arrived in Charleston, December 1821...9 March 1830.

Petition of Angus Colquhoon, planter, a native of Scotland, resident in the U. S. since 1790, and in South Carolina upwards of 18 months...5 Nov 1806.

Petition of Hugh McColl of the District of Darlington, planter, and native of Scotland...resident in the U. S. upwards of 16 years...5 Nov 1806.

Petition of John McLeran, a native of Scotland, resident of the U. S. 16 years, and 5 years in this state...4 Nov 1806.

Petition of Lachlin McLaurin Junr., a resident in the U. S. before 29 February 1795, resident in the District of Marlborough ten years...19 March 1805.

Petition of Daniel McLucas, resident in the district of Marlborough before 29 February 1795...19 March 1805.

Petition of Hugh McLaurin, resident in South Carolina before 19 February 1795, in Marlborough three years...filed 19 March 1805.

Report of Joseph Halliburton, born in the County of Cumberland, England, aged 28 years, arrived in Charleston, June 1818...4 November 1819. Petition dated 7 April 1825.

Petition of Duncan McNabb, born on the Island of Ilay, Scotland, about 31 or 32 years of age, came from Greenock, and arrived in Charleston...11 March 1830.

Petition of Angus McIntyre, born in the County of Morvin, Argyleshire, Scotland, 36 years of age, arrived in Charleston, October 1822...1 January 1827.

Petition of Peter McNab at fall term 1827, made oath...4 October 1831.

Murdock McLennan reports...born in Sterlingshire, Scotland, 1798, sailed from Greenock, 25 April 1818, on board the ship *Roger Stewart*, landed in Charleston, 14 June 1818...3 August 1820.

William Mudd, born Yorkshire in England, 22 years of age, sailed from Liverpool, arrived in Charleston, 1842...18 Nov 1845.

Petition of Daniel McLaurin, Hugh McLaurin, and Lachlin McLaurin, planters...residents of the U. S. since 15 Nov 1790, residents in this state upwards of eight years...4 November 1806.

Eugene Keenan, notice of intention...born County Clare, Ireland, 1786...4 April 1820.

Marlboro

John Battles, desirous of becoming a citizen, born in Stralsund, Prussia, about 35 years of age, arrived at Charleston...17 April 1830.

Thomas Robinson,desirous to become a citizen, born Brampton, County of Cumberland, England, 28 years of age, came from Liverpool, arrived at Savannah, Ga., May 1823...8 March 1830.

Petition of Donald McDearmud, resident in the U. S. 20 years, in this district upwards of 10 years...6 April 1809.

Petition of Hugh McLeran, planter, native of Scotland, resident in the U. S. near 15 years, and upwards of 13 years in this state ...4 November 1806.

Petition of John McColl, of the District of Darlington, planter, native of Scotland, resident in the U. S. upwards of 16 years, and in S. C. upwards of 10 years...5 November 1806.

Petition of John McLucas, planter, native of Scotland, a resident of the U. S. upwards of 15 years, and this state upwards of 18 months...4 November 1806.

Petition of John Douglas,planter, native of Scotland, resident in the U. S. for 18 years, and in this state 16 years...4 November 1806.

Petition of Patrick Mahoney, carpenter, a native of Ireland, resident in the U. S. upwards of 20 years...in this district upwards of 8 years...6 April 1808.

Petition of Neill McLaurin (McCleran), planter, native of Scotland, resident of the U. S. since 15 November 1791, resident in this state one year...4 November 1806.

Petition of Philip Miller, aged 47 years, tavern keeper, born Frankfort on the main, Germany, arrived in the U. S. at Baltimore, 1830, resided one year in Philadelphia and New York, two years in Charleston, fifteen years at Bennettsville...on __ April 1837 made declaration of intention...13 October 1849.

Donald Matheson, desirous of becoming a citizen, born Rossshire, Scotland, 26 years of age, sailed from Port Glasgow, arrived in Charleston, November 1825...17 April 1837.

Hugh McDonald, desirous of becoming a citizen, born in the county of Invernessshire, Scotland, 27 years of age, came from Greenock, arrived in New York, December 1826...13 March 1833.

Michael Joyce, aged 28, born in the city of Cork in Ireland, arrived in the U. S. at New York, September 1841, resident two years in New York and since 1843 in this state...gave notice 13 October 1848....Fall term 1850.

Alexander Livingston, desirous of becoming a citizen, born Argyleshire, Scotland, aged 35, sailed from Liverpool, arrived at New York, and thence landed at Charleston by 1835, and since resided in S. C....11 October 1848. Petition dated 14 October 1850.

The following petition exists only in typescript in the WPA copy of Marlboro County Minutes of Court 1807-1826: Petition of Peter Stewart Ney...notice of intention; born Sterling Shire, Scotland, AD 1787...__ March 1820.

Newberry

The following abstracts were made from the original loose papers (petitions, notices, etc.) now at the South Carolina Archives.

Petition of Peter Braselman, a native of Germany, and has resided in this state for twenty years past...1 September 1808.

Petition of Arthur P. Brolley, a native of Londonderry County, Ireland, has resided in the US since 6 July 1834...19 April 1845.

Petition of Alexander Chalmbers, a native of Ireland, has resided in this state for seven years past...30 October 1808.

Petition of David Chalmbers, a native of Ireland, has resided in this state for seven years past...30 October 1808.

Petition of James Chalmbers, a native of Ireland, has resided in this state for seven years past...30 October 1808.

Petition of William Chalmbers, a native of Ireland, has resided in this state for seven years past...30 October 1808.

Petition of James Clarey, a native of Ireland, has resided in this state for seven years past...30 October 1808.

Petition of John Clary, a native of Ireland, has resided in this state for seven years past...1 November 1808.

Petition of James Copeland, a native of Ireland, has resided in this state for twenty two years...27 March 1811.

Petition of Joseph Craft, a native of the Duchy of Baden in Bermany, on 23 October 1837 stated his intention, has resided in this state more than five years...2 April 1841.

Petition of William Culken (Kulkin), a native of Sligo, Ireland, resided in the US since February 1839...wish to become a denizen ...29 October 1842. Petition for citizenship, 21 October 1846.

Petition of James Divver, a native of Ireland, has resided in this state more than five years...27 April 1831. Declaration, 19 March 1828, states that he was a native of Donegal County, Ireland.

Petition of Robert Drennon, a native of Ireland, has resided in this state twenty three years...23 October 1810.

Petition of Caesar Duval, aged 74 years, entered the service of the US during the Revolution...born Picardy in France, 25 August 1758, sailed from Brest in the Spring of 1780 and landed at Newport, Rhode Island in July...(long account of service)...23 April 1833.

Petition of Lezar Duval, a native of Boulogne in France, has resided in this state since 1796...27 March 1811.

Petition of Robert Eckels, a native of Ireland, has resided in this state nineteen years...1 November 1808.

Petition of Mathew Evans, a native of County Tipperary, Ireland, has resided in this state for six years...31 October 1808.

Newberry

Petition of Alexander Fillson, now of Laurens District, a native of Ireland, has resided in this state for seven years...5 April 1808.

Petition of James Fleck, a native of County Antrim, Ireland, on 16 April 1844, declared his intention...18 October 1847.

Petition of John Garmany, a native of Ireland and the county of Monaghan, has resided in this state for twenty years...31 October 1808.

Petition of Antoine Gilbal, a native of Montier, department of Allier, France...declared his intention upwards of three years ago (20 March 1828)...30 April 1831.

Petition of John F. Gottshau, aged 34 years, brick mason, born in the Dukedom of the Grand Duke of Oldenburg, Germany, arrived at New York, 20 July 1838, and in SC 3 May 1839...declaration of intention...19 November 1850.

Petition of David Griffith, a native of Nova Scotia, arrived in the US upwards of 24 years ago, resident in the US between 1798 and 16 October 1804...(no date).

Petition of John Herman, a native of Ireland, has resided in this state for seven years past...30 October 1808.

Petition of Edward Hill, a native of Ireland, has resided in this state for seven years past...30 October 1808.

Petition of Robert Hill, a native of Ireland, has resided in this state for seven years past...1 November 1808.

Petition of Michael Hook, a native of the county of Fruburg, Kingdom of Baden, has resided in the US between five and six years...2 November 1839.

Petition of Hugh Hopper, a native of Ireland, has resided in this state for seven years past...31 October 1808.

Petition of George Hunter, a native of Ireland, was residing in the US between 18 June 1798 and 14 April 1802...(no date)

Petition of James Hunter, a native of Ireland, was residing in the US between 18 June 1798 and 14 April 1802...(no date)

Petition of Joseph Hunter, a native of Ireland, was residing in this US between 18 June 1798 and 14 April 1802...(no date)

Petition of Nathan Hunter, a native of Ireland, was residing in the US between 18 June 1798 and 14 April 1802...(no date)

Petition of Nathan Hunter Jr., a native of Ireland, was residing in the US between 18 June 1798 and 14 April 1802...(no date)

Petition of William Hunter, a native of Ireland, was residing in the US between 18 June 1798 and 14 April 1802...(no date)

Petition of Samuel Johnson, a native of Ireland, was residing in the US between 18 June 1798 and 14 April 1802...(no date)

Petition of Samuel Johnson, born in the County of Antrim, Ireland, May 1757, left Ireland, November 1801, and arrived in Charleston

Newberry

2 May 1802...3 November 1807.

Petition of John Jones, a native of England, has resided in this state for seven years, and was residing in the US between 1798 and 14 April 1802...(no date)

Petition of Simon Keary, a native of Ireland, has resided in this state for 23 years...1 November 1808.

Samuel Kendal, a native of Lancanshire (sic), Kingdom of Great Britain, where he resided until five years past when he arrived in Charleston..is about 30 years of age, and previous to his removal from England, had a child Mary about 11 years of age, and whom he brought with him; since his arrival, he married Sarah a native of the state and district aforesaid (Newberry) and by whom he has had two children: Isabella about two years old and Elizabeth, about six months of age...28 March 1811.

Petition of Sebastian Kraft, a native of the Grand Duchy of Baden, on 22 March 1849, declared his intention...22 March 1849.

Petition of James Law, a native of Ireland, resided in this state for fifteen years...1 November 1808.

Petition of Samuel Law, a native of Ireland, resided in this state for sixteen years...23 October 1810.

Petition of William Law, a native of Ireland, resided in this state fifteen years...1 November 1808.

Ann McCalla, born Donaghadel, County of Down, Ireland, aged 46 years, emigrated to SC, 30 November 1817 from Belfast...__ October 1824.

Robert McCalla, born Newtownards, County of Down, aged 26 years, emigrated to SC 30 November 1817, from Belfast...__ October 1824.

Petition of Samuel McCalla, a native of Ireland, has resided in this state for seven years...31 October 1808.

On 21 October 1825, James McCann appeared, born Muckamore, County Antrim, Ireland, 1783, aged now 42, emigrated from Belfast. Petition dated 27 April 1833.

Petition of Robert McKee, a native of Ireland, resided in this state for seven years. (no date)

Petition of George McKitrick, a native of Ireland, resided in this state for seven years...1 November 1808.

Petition of Robert McKitrick, a native of Ireland, resided in this state for seven years...1 November 1808.

Petition of Joseph McKown, a native of Ireland, was residing in the US between 18 June 1798 and 14 April 1802...(no date)

Petition of John McLane (McClane), a native of Ireland, resided in the US upwards of 14 years...October term 1815.

Petition of Patrick McNary (McNeary), a native of Ireland, was residing in the US between 18 June 1798 and 14 April 1802... (no date)

Newberry

Patition of James McNeel, a native of Ireland, has resided in this state upwards of 23 years...was residing in the US between 1798 and 10 January 1802 (no date)....

Petition of James McQuerns, a native of Ireland, was residing in the US between 18 June 1798 and 14 April 1801...Filed 15 March 1812.

Petition of Samuel McQuerns, a native of Ireland, resided in this state for 23 years...23 October 1810.

Petition of Samuel McQuerns Junr.,a native of Ireland, was residing in the US between 18 June 1798 and 14 April 1802... Filed 25 March 1812.

Petition of John Madan, a native of Ireland, resided in this state for seven years past...3 November 1808.

Petition of John Marpurt, a native of one of the principalities of Germany, namely that of the Prince of Hanau, born 24 July 1756, left that principality in 1784, landed at Philadelphia and came to SC in 1787, wishes to become a citizen; he has seven children: Joshua, aged 20; Polly, aged 17; John, aged 13; Philip,aged 10; Daniel, aged 7; Billy, aged 5; and Michael, aged 3; 3 November 1807.

Petition of George Marshall, a native of Ireland, resident of this state for seven years...31 October 1808.

Petition of James Marshall, a native of Ireland, resident of this state for seven years...31 October 1808.

Petition of Joseph Marshall, a native of Ireland, resident of this state for seven years...1 November 1808.

Petition of Alexander Martin, a native of Ireland, County of Antrim, born September 1780, left Ireland in June 1789 and landed in Charleston, he afterwards proceeded up the country with his father Patrick Martin to Newberry County, now District...he has two children James aged 2 and John aged 1...3 November 1807.

Petition of John Martin, a native of County Antrim, Ireland, born October 1781, left Ireland June 1789 and landed in Charleston, proceeded up the country with his father Patrick Martin... 3 November 1807.

Petition of Patrick Martin, a native of County Antrim, Ireland, born December 1759, left Ireland, June 1789, proceeded up the country, resided in this state upwards of 18 years; he has 7 children: Alexander, aged 27; John, 26; George, 16; Agnes, 14; Jennet, 12; Patrick, 10; and William, 6...3 November 1807.

Petition of Moretz Mayblum, a native of Unter Franklin, Bavaria, on 28 July 1843 declared intention..22 March 1848.

Petition of Meredith William Moon, a native of Scotland, born 24 June 1770, left Scotland and went to England, then to Ireland, then to America, landed in Charleston, 28 January 1794...after his arrival in this district he intermarried with Mrs. Sarah Robertson now about 40; he has seven children: Peter Moon, aged about 11; and Sarah of the same age; Maria, aged 9; Meredith William Moon, aged 7; Delton Lark Moon, aged 5; Dennis Fletcher Moon, aged 3, and Elizabeth Ann Moon an infant...2 November 1807.

Newberry

Petition of Robert Moore, a native of Ireland, resided in the US between 1798 and 14 April 1802...(no date)

Petition of James Morehead, a native of Ireland, resident in this state 22 years past...1 November 1808.

Petition of William Muckle, a native of Great Britain, resided in the US between 18 June 1798 and 14 April 1802...(no date)

Petition of Jerry Murphy, a native of County Cork, Ireland, resided in the US since 15 June 1845...filed 19 October 1847

Petition of Lewis Nehr, a native of Lauta Maria(?), France, has been in the US four years and 8 months...15 July 1844.

Petition of David Nelson, a native of Sterlingshire, Scotland, resided in the US for 4 years...15 April 1829.

Petition of John Nelson, a native of Ireland, has resided in this state 18 years...27 March 1811.

Petition of Robert Nelson, a native of Ireland, has resided in the US 20 years, and was residing in the US between 18 June 1798 and 14 April 1802...28 March 1814.

Petition of John Nestley (Johann Nestle), a native of the Kingdom of Wertermburgh (sic), Germany, has resided in the US six years and six months...16 April 1844.

Petition of William O'Connor, a native of the town of Carrickon-chair(?), County of Waterford, Ireland, resident in the US since 29 April 1829 and in SC from 25 October 1833...26 November 1834.

Petition of Thomas O'Donnell, a native of the County of Tipperary in Ireland, has resided in the US since June 1836...filed 18 October 1848.

Petition of James Patterson, a native of Ireland, has resided in this state for 16 years...30 October 1808.

Petition of Robert Powell, a native of the County of Limerick, Province of Munster, Ireland, born 12 November 1758, left Ireland on 12 August 1787, and landed in Charleston 10 October, and went immediately to Newberry County; he now has three children: Catherine, aged 23; Elizabeth, aged 9;and Mary Ann, aged 6

Petition of Thomas Raney (Reainey), a native of Ireland, was resident in the US between 18 June 1798 and 14 April 1802... (no date)

Petition of James Red, a native of Ireland, resided in the US between 18 June 1798 and 14 April 1802...(no date)

Petition of Robt. Red, a native of Ireland, resided in the US between 18 June 1787 and the present day being 25 October 1813....

Petition of David Reid, native of Ireland, resided in this state 10 years...1 November 1808

Petition of Charles Russell, a native of IReland, resident in this state for 7 years...3 November 1808

Newberry

Petition of Christian Henry Schmidt, a native of Wurtemburg, born near the town of Stutgard, resided in the US from 18 July 181 and in SC since 1820...wishes to become a denizen...22 October 1828.

Petition of William Seymour, a native of Ireland, resident in this state for 7 years...30 October 1808

Petition of Cornelius Shea, a native of County Kerry, Ireland, resided inthe US 3 years...21 November 1835

Petition of Lewis J. Simmons, a nativeof London, United Kingdom, resided in the US since 25 October 1842...22 November 1844.

Report of Adam Smith, born County Derry, Ireland, aged 24 years, ...filed 7 October 1826.

Petition of Leslie Smyth, a native of the town of Aberdeen, Scotland, on 3 April 1840 gave notice of intention...22 April 1843.

Petition of Charles Snow, a native of Sweden, came to Boston, 22 February 1801, and remained about 5 years; and 29 January 1806 came to Charleston...Filed 26 March 1812.

Petition of Samuel Spence, a native of Ireland, born 10 June 1775, left Ireland in January 1800 and landed in Charleston 29 April the same year...4 April 1808.

Petition of Robert Sprowl, a native of Ireland, resident in this state for 7 years...31 October 1808.

Petition of William Taylor, born Ireland, County of Armagh... aged 25 years...28 October 1822

Petition of John Tinsley, a native of Ireland, resident in this state 20 years...27 March 1811.

Petition of John Toland, a native of IReland, resident in this state seven years past...31 October 1808.

Petition of Frederick Joseph Wallern, a native of the Austrian Dominions of Germany, resident in this state upwards of 20 years...22 October 1810.

Petition of Samuel Warnock, aged 33, watch maker, born County Down, Ireland, arrived in the US at New York 2 May 1848...26 October 1850.

Petition of William Watt, a native of Ireland, resident in this state for 19 years...4 April 1809.

Petition of John Christian Waukle, a native of Germany, resided in the US between 18 June 1798 and 14 April 1802...5 October 1811.

Petition of Benjamin Williamson, a native of Ireland, resident in the US between 18 June 1798 and 14 April 1802...(no date)

Petition of James Williamson, a native of Ireland, resident in this state for 10 years...1 November 1808

Petition of John Williamson, a native of County Antrim, Ireland, resident in this state for 9 years...31 March 1807.

Newberry

Petition of James Wright, a native of Ireland, resident in this state 10 years...3 November 1808.

Petition of James Wood, a native of Great Britain, resident in the US between 18 June 1798and 14 April 1802...29 October 1811.

Pickens

Pickens District was formed in 1826 from Pendleton District. For records prior to that year, see County Records, Anderson-Pendleton. The following are the only citizenship/naturalization records through the year 1850 which have been found. These appeared in The Georgia Genealogical Magazine, No. 57 (Summer 1975) and are included by kind permission of the editor.

Petition of Samuel B. Dawson, aged 28, a native of Maidstone, Kent, England, arrived at Charleston, about the 2 February 1846, nor residing in Pickens District, SC, declared his intention to become a citizen...4 April 1848.

I, Daniel Horlbeck, Clerk of Court for Charleston District, do certify that Martin C. Wendelken, aged 30 years, a grocer, appeared and declared that he arrived in Charleston, Dec. 1839, where he has ever since resided, renounced all allegiance to Earnest Augustus, King of Hanover...18 August 1849.

Pickens District: Petition of Martin C. Wendelken, aged 32, grocer, a native of Hanover, Germany....November 1851.

Petition of Joseph Dawson, aged 51 years, sheweth that he is a native of Lyme Regis, Dorsetshire, England, that he arrived at Charleston about 2 February 1846, and that he is a resident of Pickens District, declared his intention to become a citizen... 4 April 1848.

COUNTY RECORDS

Union

The following are abstracts of the petitions and notices from Union District (County) from LDS microfilm, #U. R.4646.

No. 1 Thomas H. Armstrong, a native of Ireland, took oath of allegiance, 8 October 1836; emigrated to US in 1820, and resided in this state since 1828.

No. 2 Thomas Beauchamp, a native of Ireland, took oath of allegiance, 25 March 1820.

No. 3 Petition of William Bryce, a native of Scotland, desirous of becoming a citizen...October term 1808.

No. 4 March 24th 1828. William Cowan, born in County Antrim, Ireland, is about 50 years of age, and has resided about eight years in SC; he has a wife and eight children: Elizabeth, his wife, aged about 50; five children under 21--William, John, Elizabeth Mary and Jennet; three children above 21: James, Jane, and Margaret...11 March 1828.

No. 5 Petition of Lacke Crosby, born in Ireland, has resided in this state for three years...October term 1823; a native of the County of Tyrone, left Ireland and arrived in SC, 9 September 1819, and is an instructor in an academy, declaration of intention.

No. 6 Petition of James Clark, a native of Scotland, has resided in the US since 18 June 1798 and 14 April 1802...intention to become a citizen.

No. 7 Petition of Alexander Campbell, a native of the county of Armagh in Ireland, aged about 26, migrated to SC and landed at Charleston, 26 October 1824...declaration of intention...7 October 1826.

No. 8 Report of James Ewing, an alien born in Ireland, to clerk of court, 27 September 1813; aged 25, has no family but himself, resides at Thomas C. Taylors at Pinckneyville, Union District, a farmer...declaration of intention.

No. 9 In the Court of General Sessions and Common Pleas, 6 Oct 1831. Robert Gunney, born County Down, Ireland, more than three years past declared his intention...declaration dated 10 March 1828.

No. 10 Petition of John Gage Junr., an alien, a native of Ireland, has been resided in the US fromabout 15 September 1803. (no date)

No. 11 Petition of Edward Gillmore, a native of Ireland, desirous of becoming a citizen...4 October 1826.

No. 12 James Gage, a native of Ireland, took oath 8 October 1836.

No. 13 Petition of Alexander Hay, a native of Scotland, resided in the US, before 18 June 1798 and 14 April 1802...desirous of becoming a citizen...12 March 1810.

No. 14 Petition of William Hemmingway, a native of Yorkshire in England, intends to become a citizen...has resided in the US since October 1793...24 October 1811.

No. 15 25 March 1815, Thomas Hancock took oath of allegiance; born in England, has resided in the US since 1793...24 March 1815.

<u>Union</u>

No. 16 Petition of William Hood, an alien born in Ireland, emigrated from Scotland, arrived in Charleston, SC, January 1819, gave notice at Chester C. H., 31 March 1827...6 October 1832.

No. 17 Certified Report of John Hood from Chester District... an alien from Ireland, arrived at Charleston, January 1819... 25 October 1825. John Hood, born in County Antrim, Ireland, aged 24 years, emigrated from Belfast; petition dated 6 October 1832.

No. 18 Petition of James Hamilton, a native of Ireland, arrived in Charleston,January 1822, gave notice 28 October 1826 at Chester C. H....5 October 1832.

No. 19 Petition of Alexander Hay, a native of Scotland, born County of Nairn, Parish of Auldeas, came to US June 1828; he is about 31 years of age...25 July 1838.

No.20 Petition of James Hay, a native of Auldean Parish, Scotland, for some years past a resident of Union District...24 March 1838.

No. 21 Petition of Adam Kilpatrick, a native of Ireland, has resided in the US since 20 June 1790 and 16 October 1812...17 October 1812.

No. 22 John Knowles, took oath of allegiance, 17 October 1821.

No. 23 Notice of Intention of Anne Laverty, 20 October 1821; born in Ireland is now 46 years old on 13 April last, and lived in Ireland in the County of Armah (<u>sic</u>), landed in the town of Boston, 6 August 1800, and resided in Massachusettes for nine years....

No. 24 Petition of Daniel McMahan, a native of Ireland, resided in the US before 18 June 1798 and 14 April 1802...23 October 1808.

No. 25 (missing on microfilm)

No. 26 (not a petition for citizenship)

No. 27 Petition of John McElwain, a native of Ireland, resident in the US before 23 December 1822 till the present time...Fall term 1830. 14 October 1830. Notice of Intention states that he is a native of County Down...7 October 1826.

No. 28 Petition of John Nogher, born in Ireland, and resident in the US since 1790...17 October 1810.

No. 29 Petition of James Orr, born in Scotland...oath of allegiance. 14 October 1823.

No. 30 Petition of Barney Onealle, a native of Ireland, prays for rights of denizenship. 4 October 1862.

No. 31 Petition of John Rogers, a native of Ireland, resident within the limits of the US before 18 June 1798 and 14 April 1802...22 March 1810.

No. 32 Petition of Mary Riley, a native of Ireland, resident of SC since February 1794...13 March 1822.

Union

No. 33 Petition of William Smith, a native of Ireland, has resided in thie state two years...21 October 1820.

No. 34 Petition of James Service, a native of Ireland, gave notice on 2 April 1825 at Chester C. H....6 October 1832. Copy from Chester District: James Service, a native of Ireland, born in Parish of Balliston, County Antrim, now about 28 years of age...28 October 1826.

No. 35 Petition of William Toomey, intention to become a denizen...12 October 1822.

No. 36 Petition of Thomas C. Taylor, a native of Ireland, resident in the US before 18 June 1798 and 14 April 1802....

No. 37 Petition of Peter P. Taylor, a native of England, and born in the County of Lankeshire (sic), has resided in the US for three years...25 March 1820.

No. 38 Citizenship of John Knowles, October term 1826.

No. 39 Certificate of William Orr's citizenship, 5 March 1815.

Also in No. 39 At Circuit Court, 25 October 1815, Thomas Hancock, late of England, made application to become a citizen... (no date)

No. 40 Petition of John McDowell, born in Ireland, resident in the US since 1796...18 October 1810.

No. 41 Certificate of Wm Hemmingway, 21 October 1814, late of England.

No. 42 Petition of Patrick Flynn, a native of Cavin, in Ireland, emigrated to US in 1831, and has been a resident for five years, on 18 March 1838, declared his intention...5 October 1840.

No. 43 Petition of Robert Fairbridge, a native of Northumberland in England, emigrated to US in 1818, on 11 November 1826, declared his intention...October 1840. Declaration of intention from Fairfield District, November Term 1826.

No. 44-A Petition of James Laverty, born in Ireland, resident in SC since 1810...6 August 1818.

No. 44 Petition of Alexander Brodie Senr, a native of Ireland, County, Tyrone, arrived in New York in 1806 or January 1807, then in his 17th year, having neither parent nor guardian in the US; arrived at Columbia, SC in 1808...26 September 1840. (Headed Richland District; stricken and Union District written in.)

No. 45 Petition of Thomas Levy, a native of the United Kingdom of Great Britain and Ireland, whence he emigrated in 1833; on 24 October 1835 declared his intention; October 1840. Declaration of intention from New York, certified copy with application.

No. 46 Petition of Duncan McKinlay, a native of Argyleshire, Scotland, arrived in Charleston, December 1819 or 1820, and has continued to reside in NC and SC; gave notice of intention 24 March 1838 at Columbia...26 September 1840.

Union

No. 47 Petition of John O'Connor, a native of the United Kingdom of Great Britain and Ireland, emigrated to the US, and arrived at New York 18 January 1835; gave notice of intention before the Marine Court of New York 30 January 1837...7 October 1840.

No. 48 Petition of Augustus G. Nagel, emigrated from Anhalt in Saxony for the US in 1806; arrived at Savannah, Ga., and took up residence in Edgefield until 1824 when he removed to Columbia... October 1840.

No. 49 Petition of Charles Swan, a native of the United Kingdom of Great Britain and Ireland, arrived at Philadelphia 1821, has resided in SC since 1825; on 1 November 1827 declared his intention...8 October 1840. Declaration at Richland District, SC, states that he is a native of Antrim County, Ireland, 1 November 1827.

No 50 Petition of Andrew Wilson, a native of Ireland, arrived at Philadelphia 20 Mary 1833; on 5 October 1836 he declared his intention...8 October 1840. Andrew Wilson, a native of Donegal, Ireland, gave notice of intention in Richland District, 5 October 1836.

No. 51 11 October 1841; Petition of Thomas Slattery, a native of Ireland, born in Dungarvin, County of Waterford, came to US in March 1838, and landed at Savannah, Ga., has been in SC since 1 May 1839 and in Union District since 5 December 1840.

No. 52 Petition of John Clowney, on behalf of himself, his wife Nancy and four minor children: John, William James, Samuel and Robert Clowney, all natives of Ireland, born County Down, Parish of Dromore, came to US, July 1840; he is 54; his wife Nancy is 46; John about 9, William James about 7, Samuel about 5 and Robert about 3...11 October 1842.

No. 53 Petition of James Cunningham, and also on behalf of his wife Mary and child Elizabeth, natives of Ireland, born County Down, Parish of Dromore, arrived in the month of July 1840; he is about 25, wife Mary is 26 and Elizabeth is one year old... 11 October 1842.

No. 54 Petition of Joseph Clowney, a native of County Down, Parish of Dromore, arrived in the US July 1840 is about 24 years of age...11 October 1842.

No. 55 Petition of James Lynch and wife Jane, born County Londonderry, Parish of Killowen, and Town of Colerain; came to US in September 1841; he is 34 and wife Jane is about 36...11 October 1842.

No. 56 Petition of Julius Schwinn, a native of Prussia, arrived at New York in 1836, and resided six years in SC...14 October 1844.

No. 57 Petition of Patrick Dougen, a native of Ireland, arrived at New York, July 1834; resided five years in SC; on ____ 1840 declared his intention at Lexington C. H...15 October 1844.

No. 58 Petition of Moses Clowney, a native of Ireland, born County Down, Parish of Dromore, arrived in US, July 1840, is about 23 years of age...15 October 1842. Petition for Citizenship 21 March 1848.

<u>Union</u>

No. 59 Petition of Ernest Gorden Park, a native of Aberdeen, Scotland, emigrated to the US 22 September 1842...resident of Union District since 10 November 1842...21 March 1845. Oath 9 October 1849; by profession a carpenter.

No. 60 Petition of John G. Hay, house carpenter, arrived in US, October 1842, and in this state 10 November of the same year ...21 October 1850. Petition dated 21 March 1845.

No. 61 (not on film)

No. 62 Petition of James Stewart, aged about 21 years, a native of Ireland, County Dunegal (*sic*) from which he emigrated 15 May 1837, and landed at Philadelphia...15 March 1847.

York

The following petitions have been gleaned from the General Sessions Journal for York District, 1800-1820, on S. C. Archives microfilm (C1668).

Pp. 124-125: Petition of John Blair...born in Ireland, resident at least five years in the US and one year in this state... October 28th 1806.

Pp. 125-126: Petition of James Ditty, born in Ireland, resident at least five years in the US and one year in this state... October 28th 1806.

Pp. 136-137: John Street on 28th October 1807 took the oath of allegiance to become a citizen.

P. 142: William English on 29 March 1808 took the oath of allegiance to become a citizen.

Pp. 153-154: Petition of George Smith, a native of Ireland, resident in the US between February 1788 and this date, October 26th (1808).

Pp. 154-155: Petition of William Beatty, a native of Ireland, resident in the US between 18 June 1798 and 14 April 1802... (October term 1808)

Page 155: Petition of Patrick Higgins, a native of Ireland, resident in the US between 18 June 1798 and 14 April 1802... (October term 1808)

Page 156: Petition of Thomas Duncan, a native of Ireland, resident in the US between 18 June 1798 and 14 April 1802... (October term 1808)

Pp. 156-157: Petition of Robert Wallace, a native of Ireland, resident in the US between 1 January 1792 and October 26, 1808, this date.

Pp. 157-158: Petition of John Flynn, a native of Ireland, resident in the US between 18 June 1798 and 14 April 1802...(October term 1808)

Page 158: Petition of Andrew Smith, a native of Ireland, resident in the US between 18 June 1798 and 14 April 1802...(October term 1808)

Page 159: Petition of John Miller, a native of Ireland, resident in the US between 18 June 1798 and 14 April 1802...(October term 1808)

Pp. 159-160: Petition of William Coker, a native of England, resident in the US between 18 June 1798 and 14 April 1802...27 October 1808.

Page 160: Petition of Mathew Boyers, a native of Ireland, resident in the US between 18 June 1798 and 14 April 1802...(October term 1808)

Page 161: Petition of John Lynn Henderson, a native of Ireland, resident in the US between 18 June 1798 and 14 April 1802... October 26, 1808.

York

Page 170: Petition of James Lindsay, a native of Ireland, resident in the US between 18 June 1798 and 14 April 1802...29th March 1809.

Page 177: Petition of Michael Gaffney, a native of Ireland, resident in the US between 18 June 1798 and 14 April 1802... October 23rd 1809.

Page 178: Petition of John McClure, a native of Ireland, resident in the US between 18 June 1798 and 14 April 1802...(October term 1809)

Page 179: Petition of William Kennedy, a native of Ireland, resident in the US between 18 June 1798 and 14 April 1802... (October term 1809)

Pp. 179-180: Petition of James Wallace, a native of Ireland, resident in the US between 18 June 1798 and 14 April 1802... (October term 1809)

Page 180: Petition of William Caldwell, a native of Ireland, resident in the US between 18 June 1798 and 14 April 1802... (October term 1809)

Page 181: Petition of James Scott, a native of Ireland,resident in the US between 18 June 1798 and 14 April 1802...(October term 1809)

Page 194: Petition of Hugh McWhorter, a native of Ireland, resident in the US between 18 June 1798 and 14 April 1802... (October term 1810)

Pp. 194-195: John Smith, a native of Ireland, resident in the US between 18 June 1798 and 14 April 1802...28th October 1810

Pp. 195-196: Petition of Thomas Whiteside, a native of Ireland, resident in the US between 18 June 1798 and 14 April 1802... 23d October 1810.

Page 216: October 27, 1812. Joseph Oneal signified his intention to become a citizen and took oath....

Pp. 238-239: Petition of William Hacket, a native of Ireland, resident in the US between 18 June 17798 and 14 April 1802... 29 October 1813.

Page 239: Petition of Samuel Neeley, a native of Ireland, resident in the US between 18 June 1798 and 14 April 1802..(October term 1813.)

Page 240: Petition of Matthew Harper, a native of Ireland, resident in the US between 18 June 1798 and 14 April 1802...(October term 1813)

Pp. 240-241: Petition of Robert Smith, a native of Ireland, resident in the US between 18 June 1798 and 14 April 1802...(October term 1813)

Page 241: Petition of Henry Smith, a native of Ireland, resident in the US between 18 June 1798 and 14 April 1802...(October term 1813)

York

Pp. 241-242: Petition of Hugh Finch, a native of Ireland, resident in the US between 18 June 1798 and 14 April 1802... (October term 1813)

Pp. 242-243: Petition of Joseph Smith, a native of Ireland, resident in the US between 18 June 1798 and 14 April 1802...27 October 1813.

Page 243: Petition of William Love, a native of Ireland, resident in the US between 18 June 1798 and 14 April 1802...October 29th 1813.

Pp. 243-244: Petition of Francis Nisbet, a native of Ireland, resident in the US between 18 June 1798 and 14 April 1802... (October term 1813)

Pp. 244-245: Petition of Robert McCulloch, a native of Ireland, resident in the US between 18 June 1798 and 14 April 1802... 30 October 1813.

Page 245: Petition of Hugh Simpson, a native of Ireland, resident in the US between 18 June 1798 and 14 April 1802...(October term 1813)

Pp. 245-246: Petition of James Dickson, a native of Ireland, resident in the US between 18 June 1798 and 14 April 1802... (October term 1813)

Pp. 246-247: Petition of Samuel W. Faries, a native of Ireland, resident in the US between 18 June 1798 and 14 April 1802... October 26, 1813.

Page 247: Petition of John Ewing, a native of Ireland, resident in the US between 18 June 1798 and 14 April 1802...28 October 1813.

Pp. 247-248: Petition of James Wallace, a native of Ireland, resident in the US between 18 June 1798 and 14 April 1802... (October term 1813)

Page 248: Petition of John Miller, a native of Ireland, resident in the US between 18 June 1798 and 14 April 1802...29 October 1813.

Page 249: Petition of Thomas Simpson, a native of Ireland, resident in the US between 18 June 1798 and 14 April 1802...28 October 1813.

Pp. 249-250: Petition of James Arnold, a native of Ireland, resident in the US between 18 June 1798 and 14 April 1802...28 October 1813.

Page 250: Petition of Joseph Hopkins, a native of Ireland, resident in the US between 18 June 1798 and 14 April 1802...(October term 1813)

Page 251: Petition of Joseph Pearson, a native of Ireland, resident in the US between 18 June 1798 and 14 April 1802...28 October 1813.

Petition of Henry Harrison, a native of Ireland, resident in the US between 18 June 1798 and 14 April 1802...(October term 1813).

York

Page 252: Petition of Joseph Miller Junior, a native of Ireland, resident in the US between 18 June 1798 and 14 April 1802... (October term 1813)

Pp. 252-253: Petition of Daniel Graham, a native of Ireland, resident in the US between 18 June 1798 and 14 April 1802... 28 October 1813.

Page 253: Petition of Andrew Love, a native of Ireland, resident in the US between 18 June 1798 and 14 April 1802...(October term 1813)

Page 254: Petition of Daniel Kerr, a native of Ireland, resident in the US between 18 June 1798 and 14 April 1802...29 October 1813.

Page 255: Petition of William Dickson, a native of Ireland, resident in the US between 18 June 1798 and 14 April 1802... 25 October 1813.

Pp. 255-256: Petition of Samuel Waller, a native of Ireland, resident in the US between 18 June 1798 and 14 April 1802... 28 October 1813.

Page 256: Petition of Charles Bradley, a native of Ireland, resident in the US between 18 June 1798 and 14 April 1802... 25 October 1813.

Page 257: Petition of Michael Bradley, a native of Ireland, resident in the US between 18 June 1798 and 14 April 1802... (October term 1813)

Pp. 257-258: Petition of James Quin, a native of Ireland, resident in the US between 18 June 1798 and 14 April 1802...28 October 1813.

Page 258: Petition of James Neeland, a native of Ireland, resident in the US between 18 June 1798 and 14 April 1802...(October term 1813)

Pp. 258-259: Petition of James Davison, a native of Ireland, resident in the US between 18 June 1798 and 14 April 1802... (October term 1813)

Page 259: Petition of Robert Love, a native of Ireland, resident in the US between 18 June 1798 and 14 April 1802...29 October 1813.

Page 260: Petition of William Ardery, a native of Ireland, resident in the US between 18 June 1798 and 14 April 1802... 28 October 1813.

Pp. 260-261: Petition of Andrew McWhorter, a native of Ireland, resident in the US between 18 June 1798 and 14 April 1802... 28 October 1813.

Pp. 261-262: Petition of Sarah McCarter, a native of Ireland, resident in the US between 18 June 1798 and 14 April 1802... (October term 1813.)

Page 262: Petition of Margaret McElderry, a native of Ireland, resident in the US between 18 June 1798 and 14 April 1802... 28 October 1813.

York

Page 263: Petition of David Barr, a native of Ireland, resident in the US between 18 June 1798 and 14 April 1802...28 October 1813.

Pp. 263-264: Petition of William Love, a native of Ireland, resident in the US between 18 June 1798 and 14 April 1802... 28 October 1813.

Page 264: Petition of Thomas McWhorter, a native of Ireland, resident in the US between 18 June 1798 and 14 April 1802... 28 October 1813.

Page 265: Petition of John McWhorter, a native of Ireland, resident in the US between 18 June 1798 and 14 April 1802...28 October 1813.

Pp. 265-266: Petition of Elizabeth Wallace, a native of Ireland, resident in the US between 18 June 1798 and 14 April 1802... 29 October 1813.

Page 266: Petition of John Barr, a native of Ireland, resident in the US between 18 June 1798 and 14 April 1802...28 October 1813.

Page 267: Petition of Andrew Davison, a native of Ireland, resident in the US between 18 June 1798 and 14 April 1802...28 October 1813.

Pp. 267-268: Petition of William Ewing, a native of Ireland, resident in the US between 18 June 1798 and 14 April 1802...28 October 1813.

Page 380: Petition of Samuel Blair, a native of Ireland, resident in the US since 8 June 1812...27 March 1819.

INDEX

PROBLEMS OF PEACE
NINTH SERIES

PACIFISM IS NOT ENOUGH

LECTURES DELIVERED AT THE GENEVA INSTITUTE OF INTERNATIONAL RELATIONS
AUGUST 1934

by

WILLIAM E. RAPPARD
A. E. ZIMMERN
ETIENNE DENNERY
G. P. GOOCH
CLEMENT ATTLEE, M.P.
SIR NORMAN ANGELL
ALVAREZ DEL VAYO
E. J. PHELAN
J. B. CONDLIFFE
ROBERT MacIVER
LELAND REX ROBINSON

Essay Index Reprint Series

BOOKS FOR LIBRARIES PRESS
FREEPORT, NEW YORK

First Published 1935
Reprinted 1970

STANDARD BOOK NUMBER:
8369-1609-3

LIBRARY OF CONGRESS CATALOG CARD NUMBER:
70-111832

PRINTED IN THE UNITED STATES OF AMERICA

INTRODUCTION

THIS volume contains a number of the lectures delivered at the meeting of the Geneva Institute of International Relations held in Geneva in August 1934.

It follows closely the lines of its predecessors, but on this occasion it is less of a commentary on a variety of current international topics than an exposition from different angles of one central problem, the problem of securing and maintaining peace.

Professor Gooch shows how the essential elements of that problem as it faces the statesmen of to-day are to be found in the rise of nationalism: Professors Rappard and Zimmern discuss the rôle and responsibilities of the great and the small nations in the present collective system; the French view, an essential element in any realist consideration of the problem, is set out by Professor Dennery, and the socialist attempt to see the problem logically and completely is brilliantly described by the Rt. Hon. C. R. Attlee, M.P.; Sir Norman Angell analyses the fundamental issues involved with his usual convincing lucidity; Señor Alvarez del Vayo treats with unique authority of the Chaco dispute, and Mr. Phelan discusses the relations between Peace and Social Justice.

The volume concludes with three papers on economic subjects: The Trends of Recovery by Dr. J. B. Condliffe, National Economic Planning and International Organisation by Professor MacIver, and the International Implications of the Financial Aspect of the "New Deal" by Dr. L. R. Robinson.

This list of subjects and authors should suffice to promise

that the volume will not be inferior in interest to any of its predecessors.

It only remains to add that the opinions expressed therein commit only their respective authors and not the Institute or its members.

NOTE

Particulars of the short annual session to be held from 18 to 24 August, 1935, may be obtained from:

The Honorary Secretary, The Geneva Institute of International Relations, 15 Grosvenor Crescent, London, S.W.1.

The Assistant Secretary, The Geneva Institute of International Relations, The Disarmament Building, quai Wilson, Geneva.

The League of Nations Association of the United States, 6 East 39th Street, New York City.

The main subject for consideration this year will be: "*The attempt to establish an international public order.*"

CONTENTS

CHAPTER I

THE GROWTH OF NATIONALISM

by

DR. G. P. GOOCH
Ex-President of the Historical Association

i. *What is a Nation?*

NATIONALISM is the self-consciousness of a nation, the affirmation of its personality. But what is a nation? It is the result of a combination of material and spiritual factors. The material factor is the possession of a home, a defined and recognized territory in which it lives. For want of such a geographical home the Jews are rightly described as a race, not a nation. The spiritual factor is the will of the members of a community to live together. This desire is strengthened by community of blood and language and by common experiences, and that nation is the toughest where such unifying influences are most numerous. But the spiritual element often triumphs over manifold diversities, as in the case of Belgium, Switzerland, and the United States. 'What constitutes a nation', declared Renan in his celebrated lecture *Qu'est ce qu'une nation?* 'is not speaking the same tongue or belonging to the same ethnic group, but having accomplished great things in common in the past and the wish to accomplish them in the future.' Still better is the definition of Professor Zimmern. 'Nationality, like religion, is subjective; psychological; a condition of mind; a spiritual possession; a way of feeling, thinking, and living.' Nationalism thus denotes the resolve of a group of human beings to share their fortunes and to exercise exclusive control over their own actions. All attempts to penetrate its secrets by the light of mechanical interpretations break down before the test of experience. Where such a conscious determination to live together exists there should be a State, and there will be no abiding peace till there is a State. Where there is a soul there should be a body in which it may dwell.

ii. *The Political Organization of Society before the Nation.*

Now that we realize what is meant by a nation we discover how modern a phenomenon it is, and how recently the doctrine of nationalism has come into the world. The civilizations of the Ancient East gave us our first recorded lessons in science and the arts, but they thought in terms of Empire, not of nationality. To the Greeks we owe a conception of political society which substituted the doctrine of partnership for the bleak relationship of the ruler and the ruled. But there is no trace of the nation in Plato's *Republic* or the *Politics* of Aristotle, and the matchless Periclean oration was a hymn of praise to the city-state. Just because the Greeks lived in little separate communities, instead of combining into a formidable unity, they went down like ninepins before the impact of Philip of Macedon. In Roman civilization, again, we find the ideal of a world-wide system, resting on common principles of law and controlled by an irresistible executive entrenched on the Seven Hills. And finally the Middle Ages, stretching from the fall of the Roman Empire to the Renaissance, from Augustine to Macchiavelli, were saturated with universalism. Nations were coming into existence, but national sovereignty in the modern sense was unknown. For in ecclesiastical affairs the Roman Catholic Church was supreme, and the noble conception of a *Respublica Christiana*, a Christian Community, coloured the thought of the Western world. There stood the Holy Roman Empire, with God the invisible King, and His appointed representatives on earth, the Emperor and the Pope. It was an age of divided allegiance, not of concentrated power.

iii. *From Joan of Arc to Hobbes.*

The nation-state came in with the Renaissance and the Reformation. The pioneer of self-conscious nationalism was Joan of Arc, who fought under the inspiring watchword of France for the French. The rejection of Papal authority by Northern Europe strengthened the power of the temporal ruler, and enthroned the notion of a government supreme within and without. England and France finally emerged from the feudal era, the union of Aragon and Castile created the Spanish monarchy, and Ivan the Terrible began to knock Russia into shape. The State grew steadily in strength as the competing authority of the great nobility and the Church wilted away. At the end of the sixteenth century a new nation was born when the Dutch in heroic conflict threw off the alien yoke of Spain, and the Protestant world looked on with admiration.

The march of events was accompanied by significant changes in the realm of ideas. In the Middle Ages political science was a branch of Christian theology, the principles of which were regarded as valid over the whole field of human experience. It was the historic task of Macchiavelli to sever politics from ethics, to secularize thought, to proclaim the empirical method, to judge conduct by its results. The message of *The Prince* is not the *Respublica Christiana*, in which States and citizens were bound together by a thousand ties visible and invisible, but *La Raison d'État*, the overriding interest of the State as conceived and applied by its ruler. The doctrine of the unfettered sovereignty of the State, implicit in the writings of Macchiavelli, was worked out by Bodin in the crisis of the French religious wars, and received its classic embodiment in the following century at the hands of Hobbes at the height of our constitutional struggles. The doctrine of partnership in a wider unity based on the recognition of common principles had disappeared. Modern Europe had emerged, a tangle of Sovereign States, without a thought of obligation or allegiance to any Power outside or above themselves. Europe had become a geographical expression, for the era of atomistic nationalism had dawned.

iv. *Nationalism Becomes an Accepted Doctrine.*

The latter half of the eighteenth century witnessed a sensational advance in the theory and practice of nationalism. The birth of the United States of America was an event so stupendous that the Old World watched the swaying struggle with bated breath. Here was a community of civilized white men testifying by years of struggle and sacrifice to their desire to share their destiny and control their fortunes. Only less profound an impression than that caused by the birth of one nation was produced by the death of another. In the middle of the century Poland was one of the largest States in Europe. A generation later she had vanished from the map. The third and final Partition, carried through at the moment that her unworkable Constitution had made way for a reasonable system, struck even a realistic and rather cynical age as a crime of the first magnitude. Nations, like individuals, it was coming to be felt, had a right to live, possessing as they did not only bodies but souls. 'They have swallowed you,' cried Rousseau; 'take care they do not digest you.'

The French Revolution is a landmark both in the evolution of democracy and in the history of nationalism. In 1789 the French people snatched the rudder from the nerveless hands of a dynasty which had forgotten how to rule, challenging thereby not only a monarchical tradition of centuries but the autocratic practice of the Continent. A collision with its neighbours was virtually inevitable, and when the Duke of Brunswick's manifesto threatened Paris with pain and penalties the soul of revolutionary France caught fire. Raw levies hurled back the Prussian and Austrian invaders, and Creasy included the cannonade of Valmy among his fifteen decisive battles of the world. On the evening after the skirmish Goethe, who accompanied his master Karl August, Duke of Weimar, on the campaign, was asked what he thought. 'Those of you who are here to-day', he replied, 'will be able to boast that you were present at the birth of a new era.' Whether or no he improvized the oracular phrase on that rainy evening in 1792 or at a later period is irrelevant. For Valmy was in fact the beginning of the age of self-conscious and flamboyant nationalism which was to dominate the nineteenth century and to extend its peremptory sway across the world.

Napoleon was the child of the French Revolution, and he fully understood its clamorous demand for equality before the law. But he never grasped the power of the sentiment of nationhood, and his ignorance was his undoing. Torpid Spain roused herself when French armies flooded the peninsula, and with the aid of Wellington flung them back across the Pyrenees. Russia set fire to Moscow, and the

Grand Army was buried beneath the snow on her icy plains. Seven years of French rule in Germany kindled the fires of the Wars of Liberation, which were fed by the lectures of Fichte and the songs of Körner and Arndt. The most enduring legacy of Napoleon to Europe was the quickened sense of national self-consciousness generated by the rigours of a despotic military empire. An emotion had flowered into a doctrine.

v. *The Nineteenth Century.*

After a generation of ceaseless war it was natural that the victors of Leipzig and Waterloo should strive for a period of peace abroad and tranquillity at home. In fighting Napoleon, Metternich felt that he was fighting the French Revolution, and though the emperor had gone the struggle continued. The sovereignty of the people and the gospel of nationality he regarded as high explosives which had set the world aflame, and which needed to be kept under lock and key if another conflagration was to be escaped. The statesmen of the Holy Alliance and the Quadruple Alliance called a momentary halt to their victorious advance, but they could do no more; for the forces which they set out to control were stronger than courts and armies. Greece cast off the numbing yoke of the Turks, Catholic Belgium escaped from the unwelcome embrace of the Protestant Dutch, and South America blossomed into a bouquet of independent republics. In addition to the emergence of these new nations the leaven was at work elsewhere. O'Connell in Ireland, Palacky in Bohemia, Szechenyi and Kossuth in Hungary, Mazzini in Italy proclaimed the gospel of national rights. Every people, declared the great Italian prophet, had a special part assigned to it in the scheme of things in accordance with its peculiar circumstances and gifts. Italy for the Italians, by all means! But above Italy and the nations towered God and Humanity.

The nineteenth century was the era of democracy, nationality, and applied science; but the most dramatic event in the life of Europe was the birth of two large nations. Italy and Germany were placed on the map by a combination of diplomacy and arms, and entered the privileged circle of the Great Powers. Shortly afterwards Turkish rule was cast off in Roumania and Bulgaria, Serbia and Montenegro. That all or most modern wars have arisen from economic causes is a fable; for economic motives played no part in the titanic conflict of 1792, the Crimean struggle, the campaigns engineered by Cavour and Bismarck, the Balkan uprisings and Russia's intervention in the seventies. Men fought and died for differences of political system, for the balance of power, for the expulsion of alien influences or alien rule. Religious wars in Europe ended with the Treaty of Westphalia in 1648, but as the theological temperature fell the political temperature rose. Nations became acutely conscious of their personality, and the face of Europe was transformed by the change of mood.

The wars of nationality seemed to have ended with the birth of the Balkan States, but the leaven continued to work and to spread. In Ireland Parnell raised aloft the banner which O'Connell had dropped a generation before. In South Africa the plucky struggle of the Dutch Republics against the might of the British Empire evoked the sympathy of the world. Norway threw off the Swedish yoke after a century of unwilling partnership. Finland's efforts to retain the autonomy granted by Alexander I on her transfer from Sweden to Russia were applauded by the Western nations, as the unavailing struggles of the Poles had been applauded in 1830 and 1863. The realm of the Hapsburgs began to crack as its racial minorities came of age. A new spirit arose in Asia, where Russian encroachments called Persian nationalism into life, where the seed sown by English culture ripened in the Indian Congress, where the Japanese victory over Russia sent a thrill through the dark-skinned races, and where the overthrow of the Manchu dynasty transferred control of the largest nation in the world to men who had drunk deep at the wells of Western thought. Campbell-Bannerman's declaration, intended to justify the grant of representative institutions to the Boers, that good government was no substitute for self-government, expressed the growing mood of the age and echoed round the world. Imperialism was at its height; but its sway was challenged with ever-increasing insistence by the claim of nations to live their own lives.

vi. *The Great War Redraws the Map of Europe.*

The World War is connected with the development of nationalism in various ways. Firstly, the sufferings of Belgium and Serbia focussed attention on the fortunes and aspirations of little peoples. Secondly, the proclamation by a thousand tongues that the Allies were fighting for the principle of self-determination awoke or encouraged dreams of independence in many lands. And finally the collapse of four powerful empires paved the way for the creation of new States and the consolidation of racial units. The withdrawal of Russia from the fray improved the chances of a liberal settlement, and President Wilson voiced with ever-increasing authority the principle that peoples should be consulted in regard to their fate and not handed about from conqueror to conqueror as if they were flocks of sheep.

The new map of Europe, like the old, contains many millions of discontented citizens, and the problem of minorities, despite the minority clauses in the treaties, remains acute. So mixed are the racial elements in several parts of Europe that a committee of archangels could not have allotted every one to the State of his choice. But there can be no doubt that the treaties which ended the World War created a Continent in which the doctrine of national self-determination was applied over a wider area than ever before. The defeat of Germany restored the Rhine provinces to France, and North Schleswig to the Danes. But it was in Central and Eastern Europe that the most dramatic changes occurred and long-vanished nations rose from their tombs. When war broke out in 1914 the Poles could look forward to a possible unification, but not to the still more coveted goal of independence; for whichever side won was certain to include a more or less reunited people in its own sphere of influence. By what may well have seemed to patriotic Poles a miracle at the end of the struggle, they could look round on the three Powers who had torn their country to pieces in the eighteenth century and see their proud empires lying prostrate in the dust. Next to the creation of the League of Nations, the reappearance of Poland as a united and Sovereign State after more than a century of partition and subjugation may be regarded as the greatest constructive result of the war. The situation would have been still more satisfactory had it proved possible to revive the Polish-Lithuanian partnership of earlier days.

Only less important than the restoration of Poland was the resurrection of Bohemia. The World War was inaugurated in Vienna, and just because the Hapsburg Empire was a mosaic, not a nation-state, it was bound to break up into its component parts in the event of defeat. German Austria and a greatly reduced Hungary emerged as independent republics, South Tyrol went to Italy, the Jugoslav provinces to Serbia, Galicia to Poland, Transylvania to Roumania, and the richest province of them all regained her place among Sovereign States which she lost on the death of her last king at the Battle of Mohacz in 1526. Before the war the great majority of Czechs would have been content with the revival of the Bohemian Kingdom within the Hapsburg Empire, Bohemia possessing the same rights as Hungary. But a party led by Professor Masaryk gradually reached the conviction that the Hapsburgs were unteachable and that Bohemia must regain her independence if she could. Such a consummation was only possible as the result of a world-wide catastrophe in which the Central Empires should suffer a crushing defeat. The fortunes of war favoured the Czechs as they favoured the Poles; and Czecho-slovakia, with Masaryk as her first President, has perhaps a fairer prospect of success than any of the new States of Central and Eastern Europe.

The collapse of Russia brought into being not only an independent Poland, but a litter of tiny States on the Baltic. The world rejoiced when Finland escaped from the yoke of a country not only alien in blood, language, religion, and tradition, but definitely inferior in the scale of civilization. While the claims of Finland had long been known, it was not till the Great War that we all became aware of the national aspirations of the Baltic Provinces. Esthonia, Livonia, and Courland have for centuries been the pawns and victims of their larger neighbours, and their history is the record of their successive domination by Teutonic knights, Swedes, and Russians. A Russian victory would have riveted the yoke of St. Petersburg, and a German triumph would have made them the serfs of Berlin. Here again the unexpected downfall of both empires opened the way to independent life. So long as Bolshevist Russia pursues its present course of avoiding external adventures, the frail little republics of Finland, Esthonia, and Latvia are safe enough. While several States have thus been born or reborn, one only disappeared as the result of the World War; for the little Kingdom of Montenegro was swallowed up in the consanguineous realm of the Jugoslavs.

vii. *The Strength and the Insufficiency of Nationalism.*

The story of the growth of nationalism, needless to say, does not come to an end with the creation of a League of Nations. It was psychologically inevitable that new States, enlarged States, and diminished States should all, from their respective angles, develop an acute and in some cases almost morbid self-consciousness. Moreover, the prolonged horrors of the struggle had emphasized the fact that modern war is a conflict of resources even more than of men. The relentless pressure of our naval blockade on the fighting strength of our foes was carefully noted in every chancellery of the belligerent and neutral world, and the doctrine of economic nationalism enshrines the lesson taught by grim memories of starvation and collapse. No community in the world possesses all the raw materials requisite for the waging of war, and many States are dependent on external sources for a considerable part of their food supply. But so long as war is an alarming possibility statesmen will naturally aim at the maximum of self-sufficiency in the economic field.

Looking round the world to-day most observers would conclude that nationalism is stronger than ever. Japan snaps her fingers at solemn treaty obligations as she takes advantage of the weakness of China to pursue her aims in Manchuria. India strides forward from provincial dyarchy to a partial control of the central government. Persia has cast off the tutelage of Russia and England under the leadership of a rough soldier who has climbed into the seat of the Shah. Mustapha Kemal surveys a new and virile Turkey from the rocky heights of Angora—not an empire, but a nation-state. Though British garrisons remain in Egypt, the country is ruled no longer from Downing Street but from the palace of the King. Mussolini and Hitler preach the gospel of national and racial pride in raucous tones. Even the Bolshevists, whose thoughts run on economic rather than political lines, are now beginning to beat the patriotic drum, for the spectre of a second Japanese war hovers before their eyes.

Two dominant impressions force themselves upon us as we look back over the road we have travelled. The first is the massive strength of nationalism both in theory and practice. Here is a new and mighty force that has entered the world, and it is clear that it has come to stay. The gospel that a people with a distinct national culture and self-consciousness should be allowed to live its own life in its own home is the expression of a profound and legitimate instinct. Its explosive force has torn unjust treaties to shreds and shattered despotic empires. Its prophets and its martyrs are enshrined in the hearts of grateful and contented peoples.

A second impression is equally inescapable: the insufficiency of nationalism is as obvious as its strength. It has fostered savage racial passion and repulsive national arrogance. The cult of *sacro egoismo* has almost obliterated the sense that civilization is a collective achievement and a common responsibility. It has not only caused innumerable wars, but has justified them in the name of sovereignty. It has given us order within our respective boundaries at the cost of chronic anarchy outside. Our thought in the sphere of international relations has stood still while the world is shrinking before our eyes. The miracles of science have made us all close neighbours, and the provincialism of the last four centuries is out of date.

The supreme task of the twentieth century is to adjust our ideas and institutions to the new and overwhelming realities of an interdependent world. We can never organize the life of mankind as a whole on the basis of self-sufficing sovereign units. We shall retain all that is precious and vital in nationalism, but it must be transcended and enlarged. We shall march forward, not only because to do so is the only alternative to ceaseless war, but because without the close co-operation of national units the ordinary peace-time business of the human race can no longer be efficiently carried on. The world state of which Mr. Wells dreams is beyond our range, and perhaps beyond our powers. But a co-operative commonwealth is well within our reach. The clearest thinkers of our time have come to realize that in the new international machinery which we are painfully learning to work is to be found not only the strongest bulwark against the recurrence of war, but the only security that the peoples will retain their rightly treasured national life.

CHAPTER II

SMALL STATES IN THE LEAGUE OF NATIONS

by
WILLIAM E. RAPPARD
Professor at the University of Geneva
Director of the Graduate Institute of International Studies, Geneva

i. *Great Powers and Small States before the World War.*

ANYONE at all conversant with the political literature of the day will readily understand what is meant by Small States, when mentioned in relation with the League of Nations. But he who idly believed that words had no other significance than that given by the dictionary might well be surprised. China, with a population about ten times as great as that of France or of Italy, is a Small State. Brazil, with an area ten times as large as those of France and Italy combined, was, until discontented with her status as such, a Small State member of the League. Spain, Poland, India, Australia, Canada, are counted as 'small members' of the League, as are Sweden, Holland, Luxembourg, Albania, Belgium, Hungary, Denmark, Switzerland, Liberia, and Panama.

It is obvious, therefore, that smallness depends neither on population nor area. Nor does the status of a Small State stand in any relation to its place in history, to its neutrality or belligerency in the World War, to its geographical situation, to its form of government, to its possession of colonies, to its degree of civilization, to its *per capita* wealth, nor to its aggressive or pacific policies. In fact, the so-called Small States within the League of Nations have nothing in common which distinguishes them from others, except that they enjoy no permanent representation on the Council. And they are deprived of this privilege because they are not co-called Great Powers. And they are not so-called Great Powers because they are not considered as such. And they are not considered as such because in the history of the nineteenth and of the early twentieth centuries they have not been militarily dominant or at least prominent. Small States are, as my friend Max Huber called them already before the war, 'Nichtgrosstaaten'.[1] And they are 'Nichtgrosstaaten' because their relative weakness is reassuring for their more powerful neighbours.

Such are the plain facts of the case. They may shock those who are innocent of the cynicism of history. But they are familiar, even if they do not necessarily seem justified, to all students of the past.

In the introductory chapter of his magnificently ambitious and most promising illuminating recent work entitled *A Study of History*, my friend Professor Toynbee suggested another definition of a Great Power. He writes:

> 'The spirit of Nationality is a sour ferment of the new wine of Democracy in the old bottles of Tribalism. The ideal of our modern Western Democracy has been to apply in practical politics the Christian intuition of the fraternity of all Mankind; but the practical politics which this new democratic ideal found in operation in the Western World were not Œcumenical and humanitarian but were tribal and militant. The modern Western

---

[1] Cf. Max Huber, *Die Gleichheit der Staaten*, in Reichtswissenschaftliche Beiträge, Josef Kohler's Festgabe, Stuttgart, 1909, passim.

democratic ideal is thus an attempt to reconcile two spirits and to resolve two forces which are in almost diametrical opposition; the spirit of Nationality is the psychic product of this political *tour de force*; and the spirit of Nationality may be defined (negatively but not inaccurately) as a spirit which makes people feel and act and think about a part of any given society as though it were the whole of that society. This strange compromise between Democracy and Tribalism has been far more potent in the practical politics of our modern Western World than Democracy itself. Industrialism and Nationalism, rather than Industrialism and Democracy, are the two forces which have exercised dominion *de facto* over our Western Society in our age; and, during the century that ended about A.D. 1875, the Industrial Revolution and the contemporary emergence of Nationalism in the Western World were working together to build up "Great Powers", each of which claimed to be a universe in itself.

'Of course this claim was false. The simple fact that there were more Great Powers than one proved that no single one of them was co-extensive with the sum total of that society which embraced them all. Every Great Power, however, did succeed in exerting a continual effect upon the general life of Society, so that in some sense it could regard itself as a pivot round which the whole of Society revolved; and every Great Power also aspired to be a substitute for Society in the sense of being self-contained and self-sufficient, not only in politics and economics but even in spiritual culture. The state of mind thus engendered among the people of communities which constituted Great Powers spread to communities of lesser calibre. In that age in the history of our Western Society all national States, from the greatest down to the least, put forward the same claim to be enduring entities, each sufficient unto itself and independent of the rest of the World.'[1]

---

[1] Arnold J. Toynbee, *A Study of History*, vol. i, London, 1934, pp. 9, 10.

Thus a Great Power would be one 'which claimed to be a universe in itself'. That, I think, is an accurate as it surely is an ingenious definition. But it defines the Great Power by its psychological effect on its citizens rather than by the external circumstances which surround its birth. A Great Power is one which having imposed its recognition as such on its neighbours by actual or potential force—that is why it is called a 'Power', a 'Puissance', a 'Macht'—then proceeds to impose its recognition as a universe on its people by the grandeur of its prestige.

The modern world has always known an hierarchy of States, even if it has very generally, if not quite universally, proclaimed the equality of States as a fundamental principle of international law. In the introduction of his book on *The United States as a World Power*, my lamented colleague Professor Coolidge, of Harvard University, recalled the evolution of Great Powers in Europe, with the precision and concision of the true historian. He wrote:

'. . . by the close of the fifteenth century, certain States had assumed a position which entitled them to the modern designation of "great European Powers". The Holy Roman Empire, still first in dignity; France, after she had recovered from the Hundred Years' War and had broken the might of her great feudal nobles; England, in the firm hand of Henry VII; the newly formed Kingdom of Spain, which had finally ended Moorish rule in the peninsula—all these held a position unlike that of their neighbours. The difference between them and such Powers as Denmark, the Swiss Confederation, and Venice was one of rank as well as of strength. Politically they were on another plane: they were not merely the leaders, they were the spokesmen, the directors, of the whole community.

'As time went on, changes took place in their membership. In the course of the sixteenth century, when the Empire became so dislocated that it was hardly a Power at all, its place was taken by Austria, a strangely conglomerate formation, which protected the eastern frontier of Christendom against the Turks. Spain was for a while a real World Power, overshadowing all the others, dominant in Europe, supreme in America, and dreaded even in remote Japan. The seventeenth century witnessed the decline of Spain, the primacy of France, and the temporary rise of Sweden and the Netherlands; but the greatness of these last rested on too small a material foundation to support it after the countries themselves had outlived their heroic period. The eighteenth century saw them subside into relative insignificance, and in their stead two newcomers step to the forefront of European affairs. The huge semi-Asiatic empire of Russia was now, by the genius of Peter the Great, transformed into the outward semblance of a European State; and the little military Kingdom of Prussia, the representative of Northern Germany, won for itself a position which its resources hardly warranted, but which, thanks to the extraordinary ability of its rulers and the sense of discipline of its people, it succeeded in maintaining.

'After the violent episode of the French Revolution and the Napoleonic wars, the European continent settled down to what seemed to be a stable organization with five Great Powers—Russia, England, Austria, Prussia, and France, for the skill of Talleyrand at Vienna prevented France from being even temporarily excluded after her disasters.'[1]

This famous Pentarchy had grown out of the concert of the anti-Napoleonic coalition whose four members had already at Châtillon, on 5 February, 1814, boldly spoken 'in the name of Europe'.[2]

At the end of the interminable and ever-renewed wars

[1] A. C. Coolidge, *The United States as a World Power*, rev. ed., New York, 1918, pp. 2, 3.

[2] Charles Dupuis, *Le Principe d'égalité et le concert européen*, Paris, 1909, p. 122.

into which revolutionary and imperial France had plunged Europe for almost a generation, the general need was for peace, order, and security. On 17 August, 1817, Metternich, addressing Emperor Francis, wrote:

> 'One of the first notions, I should say even the basis of contemporaneous policy is and should be tranquillity; now the fundamental idea of tranquillity is security of possession. If the principal Powers of Europe adopt this principle the Small States which can hardly stand alone (qui peuvent à peine se tenir debout) must adopt it also, whether they like it or not (de gré ou de force).'[1]

In order to maintain peace and order among themselves as well as against the Small States, which even 'if they could hardly stand alone' might always become turbulent, the Pentarchy, at Aix-la-Chapelle on 15 November, 1818, laid down their principles and the rules governing their future meetings. They decided that they would usually meet alone, to discuss measures for the maintenance of 'general peace'. But that in case they had to deal with 'affairs especially connected with the interests of other European States, they would meet only when formally invited to do so by such States, with the express reservation that they would always have the right to take part in such conferences'.[2]

When we compare the membership of the European Directorate thus set up with the seven Great Powers of to-day, we note that only two States, Great Britain and France, have completely maintained their political identity. We note further that the U.S.S.R. has taken the place of Russia, and Germany that of Prussia. Austria, the main

[1] Dupuis, op. cit., p. 153.

[2] Dupuis, op. cit., p. 163.

victim, as she was also the immediate author of the World War, has disappeared. Italy crept into the concert of Europe, guided by the genius of her master statesman and true founder, even before she acquired national unity. When, in February 1855, Cavour had succeeded in bringing first France and Great Britain and then his own Parliament to allow his country to participate in the Crimean War, he exclaimed: 'The glory which our soldiers will not fail to reap on the banks of the Orient will do more for the future of Italy than all the declamations of the world have done.'[1] And so it proved to be. Admitted on equal terms with the Great Powers to the Congress of Paris in 1856, in spite of Austria's opposition and the reluctance of all others, except Napoleon III and Great Britain, the Kingdom of Sardinia thus prematurely began its brilliant diplomatic career.[2] Since her foundation in 1861 Italy has regularly taken her place as the sixth Great Power of Europe until the World War.

Although never formally recognized as such, since the days of Metternich, the six European Great Powers came as a matter of course to consider themselves the true masters of the Continent. Thus, during the second Balkan war, the British Foreign Secretary, to avoid a European catastrophe, proposed what in his memoirs he called a 'Conference of the Powers'. It went without saying and without any discussion that the membership of such a conference was limited to the representatives of Great Britain, France, Italy, Germany, Austria, and Russia.[3] The same were naturally

[1] Paul Matter, *Cavour et l'unité italienne*, vol. ii, 1848–56, Paris, 1925, p. 317.

[2] Matter, op. cit., pp. 327 et seq.

[3] Grey of Fallodon, *Twenty-five Years*, 1892–1916, vol. i, London, 1925, p. 264.

invited to the abortive Conference of the Powers summoned by Grey in July 1914.[1]

The United States, always officially hostile to world entanglements, became a World Power by reason of her growing wealth and influence, almost in spite of herself. The Spanish-American War of 1898 is usually looked upon as the turning-point in her history in this respect.[2]

As for Japan, her military victories over China in 1894, and over Russia ten years later, would have entitled her to the rank of a Great Power, even if her policy during the World War had not made of her the preponderant force in the Far East.

ii. *Small States and the Covenant.*

When after the World War the victors decided to set up a league of nations, all concerned realized that the co-operation of the five principal Allied and Associated Powers was essential to its success. In order to secure their co-operation, most authors agreed that a position of special influence and responsibility should be reserved for them in the structure of the new organization.

The first British and American plans, to be sure, did not specifically provide for a small council, but they were based on the assumption of the preponderance of the Great Powers.[3]

In his *Practical Suggestions*, published in December 1918, General Smuts foresaw the establishment of a Council which was to do 'the real work of the League'. As for its membership, he proposed:

[1] Grey, op. cit., p. 314. [2] Coolidge, op. cit., p. 121.

[3] D. H. Miller, *The Drafting of the Covenant*, 2 vols., New York, 1928; vol. i, pp. 10, 40; vol. ii, pp. 3 et seq., 7 et seq., and 12 et seq.

'In the first place, the Great Powers will have to be permanent members of it. Thus the British Empire, France, Italy, the United States of America, and Japan will be permanent members, to whom Germany will be added as soon as she has a stable democratic Government. To these permanent members I would suggest that four additional members be added in rotation from two panels, one panel comprising the important intermediate Powers below the rank of Great Powers, such as Spain, Hungary, Turkey, Central Russia, Poland, Greater Serbia, etc., and the other panel comprising all the minor States who are members of the league. Each panel will provide two members, who will be selected from it in rotation according to rules to be laid down in the first instance by the permanent members, who will also fix the two original panels. The council will therefore have nine or ten members according as Germany is or is not a stable democratic Great Power in future.'[1]

Lord Robert Cecil's first plan provided for an 'annual meeting of Representatives of British Empire, United States, France, Italy, Japan, and any other States recognized by them as Great Powers'.[2]

The French plan called for a 'Permanent Delegation' of fifteen members, to be elected by the International Council representing all the members of the Société des Nations.[3]

In the Italian plan provision was made for a council of nine members, of whom five were to represent the five victorious Great Powers, and four were to be elected by the Conference of all the other members.[4]

Before the first meeting of the Commission which drafted the Covenant there were several exchanges of views

1 Miller, op. cit., vol. ii, p. 41.
2 Miller, op. cit., vol. ii, p. 61.
3 Miller, op. cit., vol. i, p. 11; vol. ii, p. 46.
4 Miller, op. cit., vol. ii, p. 248.

on the composition of the Council between the members of the American and the British delegations. The British, that is Lord Robert Cecil and Mr. C. Hurst (as they then were), would have restricted membership to the Great Powers. President Wilson, however, favoured some such plan as that proposed by General Smuts.[1]

The draft finally put before the League Commission on behalf of the American and British delegations had been written by Mr. Hurst, and was worded as follows:

> 'The representatives of the States, members of the League directly affected by matters within the sphere of action of the League, will meet as an Executive Council from time to time as occasion may require.
>
> 'The United States of America, Great Britain, France, Italy, and Japan shall be deemed to be directly affected by all matters within the sphere of action of the League. Invitations will be sent to any Power whose interests are directly affected, and no decision taken at any meeting will be binding on a State which was not invited to be represented at the meeting.'[2]

This plan, it may be noted, was in essence the same as that which the Great Powers had adopted for the Directorate of Europe at Aix-la-Chapelle a century before. It was calculated to answer the same purpose, and it was destined to arouse the same opposition.

As a matter of fact, it was reluctantly abandoned by its authors when they were faced by the unanimous protests of the representatives of the Small Powers, backed by those of France and Italy.[3]

[1] Miller, op. cit., vol. i, pp. 36, 57, 72; vol. ii, pp. 61, 67, 98, 108, 132, 142, 146.

[2] Miller, op. cit., vol. ii, p. 232.

[3] Miller, op. cit., vol. i, pp. 134, 137 et seq., 146 et seq.; vol. ii, pp. 257 et seq.

The text as finally adopted reads as follows:

'1. The Council shall consist of Representatives of the Principal Allied and Associated Powers, together with Representatives of four other Members of the League. These four Members of the League shall be selected by the Assembly from time to time in its discretion. Until the appointment of the Representatives of the four Members of the League first selected by the Assembly, Representatives of Belgium, Brazil, Spain, and Greece shall be Members of the Council.

'2. With the approval of the majority of the Assembly, the Council may name additional Members of the League, whose Representatives shall always be Members of the Council; the Council with like approval may increase the number of Members of the League to be selected by the Assembly for representation on the Council.

'3. The Council shall meet from time to time as occasion may require, and at least once a year, at the Seat of the League, or at such other place as may be decided upon.

'4. The Council may deal at its meetings with any matter within the sphere of action of the League or affecting the peace of the world.

'5. Any Member of the League not represented on the Council shall be invited to send a Representative to sit as a Member at any meeting of the Council during the consideration of matters specially affecting the interests of that Member of the League.

'6. At meetings of the Council, each Member of the League represented on the Council shall have one vote, and may have not more than one Representative.'[1]

---

[1] On 29 July, 1926, the following additional paragraph came into force as an amendment to the Covenant:

'2 bis. The Assembly shall fix by a two-thirds majority the rules dealing with the election of the non-permanent Members of the Council, and particularly such regulations as relate to their term of office and the conditions of re-eligibility.'

We do not propose to analyse all the discussions which led to this change. It is interesting, however, and directly relevant to our main purpose, to examine some of the arguments put forward in support of the various solutions urged. The problem, as generally conceived, was to reconcile the principle of the equality of States with the necessity of setting up a body sufficiently strong to carry decisive weight with the world community, while small enough to be capable of executive action.

The principle of equality itself was openly challenged by no one, and indeed expressly proclaimed by most of the authors of the Covenant.

The most critical was undoubtedly Lord Robert Cecil. Even he did not publicly repudiate the principle, however. But his ardent desire to make a success of the League and his conviction that success depended exclusively on the co-operation of the Great Powers led him to brush aside, as an undesirable obstacle to that end, the plea of the Small States for representation on the Council. On 16 January, 1919, discussing privately with Mr. D. H. Miller the various drafts that were being considered, he declared 'that the Great Powers must run the League, and that it was just as well to recognize it flatly as not'.[1]

His impatience with the Small States and with what he held to be their excessive demands was shown not only in the debates on the League Commission, but also in his private papers. Thus in his 'Notes on a Permanent Court', communicated to Mr. Miller a few days later, he recalled how in his opinion the Small States had 'wrecked the plan for a Permanent Court' at The Hague in 1907. He added that 'their ground of opposition was a plea of equality of

[1] Miller, op. cit., vol. i, p. 53.

rights which not only is theoretically preposterous but which is entirely incompatible with the conception of a League of Nations'.[1]

President Wilson's attitude was appreciably different. He was no less anxious for the success of the League, but he was too fundamentally attached to the principle of equality entirely to disregard the claims of the Small States. Throughout the war he had preached the gospel of right as opposed to might, and demanded equal consideration for strong and weak alike. Thus, for instance, in his address to the Senate on 22 January, 1917, he had explicitly declared: 'The equality of nations upon which peace must be founded if it is to last must be an equality of rights.'

If he had been tempted to forget this generous doctrine, his Secretary of State would have reminded him of it. On 21 December, 1918, Lansing had drafted some 'Suggestions as to an International Council', in which 'a Supervisory Committee' of five elected members was to perform functions analogous to those entrusted to the Council of the League. Lansing's plan was, as he states, 'based on international democracy and denies international aristocracy'. He had placed it before President Wilson 'in order to prevent, if possible, the United States from becoming sponsor for an undemocratic principle'.[2]

Lansing's doctrine was that of the traditional legalist. Thus he wrote:

> 'Equality in the exercise of sovereign rights in times of peace, an equality which is imposed by the very nature of sovereignty, seemed to me fundamental to a world organization. . . . Any

---

[1] Miller, op. cit., vol. i, p. 64.

[2] Robert Lansing, *The Peace Negotiations*, London, 1921, pp. 52 et seq.

departure from that principle would be a serious error fraught with danger to the general peace of the world and to the recognized law of nations, since it could mean nothing less than the primacy of the Great Powers and the acknowledgment that because they possessed the physical might they had a right to control the affairs of the world in times of peace as well as in times of war.'[1]

This theoretical legalism was hardly calculated to impress President Wilson. While holding firmly to the formula of equality, he was quite prepared to countenance and indeed to recommend practical measures hardly compatible with a strict interpretation of it. The general principle he stated with all the more force and eloquence, as he did not intend to apply it literally. Thus, on 11 April, 1919, at the last meeting of the League Commission, President Wilson opposed a proposal of Japan, whose delegates would have wished to insert in the Preamble of the Covenant 'the endorsement of the principle of equality of nations and just treatment of their nationals'. In the course of his attack on this proposal, President Wilson declared:

'This League is obviously based on the principle of equality of nations. Nobody can read anything connected with its institution or read any of the articles in the Covenant itself, without realizing that it is an attempt—the first serious and systematic attempt made in the world—to put nations on a footing of equality with each other in their international relations. It is recognized everywhere that this is an attempt, a most hopeful attempt, to secure for those nations which could not successfully protect themselves if attacked by the stronger nations of the world, the support of strong nations of the world in their defence. It is a combination of moral and physical strength of nations for

[1] Robert Lansing, *The Peace Negotiations*, p. 53.

> the benefit of the smallest as well as the greatest. That is not only a recognition of the equality of nations, it is a vindication of the equality of nations.'[1]

But this 'recognition' and 'vindication' of equality had not prevented President Wilson from supporting at first Cecil's original proposal for a Council made up of Great Powers only. He had done so by showing

> 'that the chief physical burdens of the League will fall on the Great Powers whether these burdens are military or economic. He said that the adoption of the League will depend upon whether it can be done without making the Powers too uneasy. It is desirable to make the plan acceptable that the Great Powers should be in the Executive Council. Then it should be considered what other elements, if any, there should be to it. The general idea is that the Executive Council will consist of those other Powers whose interests are affected. The scheme is to have the Executive Council consist of the interested parties. The Great Powers are always interested.'[2]

The French delegates were no less insistent on equality of rights as a principle, but somewhat less prepared to sacrifice the principle to expediency in the composition of the Council of the League. In their official draft, we recall, the French drew no distinction between various classes of States, but relied on election to secure permanency of tenure for the Great Powers in the 'Permanent Delegation' of fifteen members which they provided for. It is therefore not surprising that their delegates should have supported the Small States in their revolt against the original British proposal. They were perhaps the more inclined to do so as the Anglo-American hegemony, exercised by Wilson and

[1] Miller, op. cit., vol. i, p. 463. [2] Miller, op. cit., vol. i, p. 146.

Cecil in the League Commission, increased their understanding of and their sympathy with the feelings of their minor colleagues. Thus, on 4 February, Léon Bourgeois combated the British exclusivism by expressing the fear 'that if too much power is given to the Great Powers they will act rather for peace than for peace founded on justice',[1] an uncommonly acute political observation.

At a subsequent meeting, his colleague, Dean Larnaude, of the Paris Law School, went further both in the verbal denunciation of Great Power claims and in their actual justification. He

> 'wanted it clearly understood that no implications were carried by the use of the terms "Great Powers" and "Small Powers". It was only a convenient form of expression for dealing with a certain difference in fact. Indeed, he thought that the use of the general terms "great" and "small" was inadvisable, and that it was proper that the five Powers (whom they were classing as great) should be specifically named. For the League is the outcome of this war. Of course the five Powers are not the only ones who have made vast contributions of lives and principle. Belgium, the first bulwark against German invasion, has gained because of this a great place in history. But the matter is not one to be discussed in the abstract or on the basis of sentiment; but a thing of cold fact; and the fact is that the war was won by Great Britain, France, Japan, Italy, and the United States. It is essential that the League be formed around these effective Powers so that at its birth it shall carry with it the influence and prestige of the nations that conquered Germany.'[2]

The delegates most active in the defence of the rights of the Small States in the League Commission were Messrs.

[1] Miller, op. cit., vol. i, pp. 148, 152.
[2] Miller, op. cit., vol. i, pp. 159, 160.

Hymans of Belgium, Vesnitch of the Serb-Croat-Slovene State, Pessoa of Brazil, Wellington Koo of China, and Reis of Portugal. While unanimously basing their case on the principle of equality, as well as on the necessity of securing the effective co-operation of the nations they represented, they all realized and admitted that in the composition of the Council account should be taken of the various degrees of international importance of members of the League.

Thus they opposed the original British plan of no representation of Small States as entirely unacceptable, and the first concession of two delegates as insufficient. The former, Mr. Pessoa declared, would make of the Council, 'not an organ of the "League of Nations", but an organ of "Five Nations", a kind of tribunal to which everybody would be subject'.[1] The latter, Mr. Hymans repudiated hotly, declaring to Lord Robert Cecil: 'What you propose is nothing else than the Holy Alliance.'[2]

The solution finally adopted—five permanent Great Powers and four elected Small States—was clearly a compromise. It was a compromise not only between the Great Powers—of whom Lord Robert Cecil said that their support was 'the chief need in making the League a success'[3]—and the Small States—of whom Mr. Wellington Koo said that while 'it was probably true' that the interests of any one of them were less than those of any so-called Great Power, 'it was certainly true that no one Great Power had interests greater than the aggregate interests of the so-called secondary powers',[4] it was also a compromise between law and politics, between juristic theory and tradition and political expediency. Thus even Mr. Pessoa, of Brazil, recognized 'that it was

[1] Miller, op. cit., vol. ii, p. 257.
[2] Miller, op. cit., vol. i, p. 162.
[3] Miller, op. cit., vol. i, p. 161.
[4] Miller, op. cit., vol. i, p. 152.

clear that the question could not be settled entirely by the rigorous principles of law. The injunctions of political reason must also be considered'.[1]

The latter compromise was much more significant than the former. The political inequality between Great Powers and Small States had always existed, but the formal and general recognition of legal inequality between them was a truly revolutionary innovation. Whether it will prove to have been a constructive or a destructive innovation remains to be seen. That it has aroused jealousies and irritation, that it has temporarily or permanently deprived the League of the co-operation of Argentina, Brazil, and Spain, that it occasioned a major crisis in 1926 over Germany's admission, and may create a similar crisis in the near future over the admission of the U.S.S.R., is certain. That it was inevitable was claimed in 1919, but not really demonstrated.

Of course, an international organization like the League must have, besides a general assembly, a smaller body for executive action. And of course the Great Powers must always be represented on the latter. But why that representation should not depend upon periodical election by the whole international community rather than be based on an express constitutional provision is by no means clear.

The provisions of Article 4, whose origin we have just considered, are the only clauses of the Covenant which set up a permanent legal inequality in the League between Great Powers and Small States. But through their operation other effective and indeed inevitable inequalities have arisen. Thus, as the composition of the Permanent Court of International Justice is based upon concurrent but separate

[1] Miller, op. cit., vol. ii, pp. 301, 470.

elections by the Council and by the Assembly, the Great Powers have always seen judges of their nationality elected to the Court. The fact that a judge of the United States has always been elected also, although the American Government was represented neither on the Council nor on the Assembly, is an interesting indication of the international community as to the advisability of securing the co-operation of the Great Powers.

Furthermore, as practically all the committees and commissions of the League are appointed by the Council and as they are very often, if not quite universally, composed of nationals of States represented thereon, one may speak of the repercussion of the inequality established under the Covenant in respect of the membership of the Council on that of most of the consultative bodies of the League.

Finally, a similar repercussion may be noted in the case of the Secretariat. The privileged position of nationals of the Great Powers on the civil service of the League is also due to, and may even be justified by, the only other inequality sanctioned by the Covenant as at first drafted. We refer to the unequal national contributions by which the League is financed. We recall that, according to Article 6, § 5 of the original Covenant, 'the expenses of the Secretariat should be borne by the members of the League in accordance with the apportionment of the expenses of the International Bureau of the Universal Postal Union'. According to this apportionment, the Great Powers which, with six other States, were all in the first category, were to pay twenty-five times more towards the expenses of the Secretariat than the Small States who paid least. This system was soon found to be unfair. It was unfair not because of its excessive, but on the contrary because of its insufficient, inequality. It was accordingly altered through the operation of an amendment to the Covenant which came into force in 1924. It reads: 'The expenses of the League shall be borne by the Members of the League in the proportion decided by the Assembly.'

To-day the ratio of contributions between the States permanently represented on the Council and other States is as follows:

United Kingdom	105	India	56
France	79	China	46
Germany	79	Spain	40
Italy	60	Canada	35
Japan	60	Poland	32

Albania (for example) 1.[1]

It will be noted that in this realistic realm of finance we are very far from the legal theory of equality. Not only are there very great differences between burdens incumbent upon the Great Powers and the Small States, but in neither category is there anything even approaching equality. These figures show more clearly than any abstract demonstration not only the unreality of the fiction of international equality but also the artificial character of the bipartite division of countries into Great Powers and Small States.

It was the sense of this unreality that had led General Smuts to suggest, as we have seen, the establishment of an intermediate category of countries. This suggestion, taken up by President Wilson, was abandoned at the second meeting of the League Commission, on 4 February, 1919, after it had been criticized by the Portuguese delegate.[2] It was to be revived, however, in 1926. It will be recalled

[1] League of Nations, *Official Journal*, 14th Year, No. 10, 2nd part, Geneva, 1933, p. 1258.

[2] Miller, op. cit., vol. i, p. 147.

that, as a result of the difficulties surrounding the entry of Germany into the League as a permanent member of the Council, that body was then remodelled. The number of permanent members, which had fallen to four through the absence of the United States, was again raised to five through the admission of Germany. The number of non-permanent members, which had been raised from four to six in 1922, was then increased to nine. But these nine were divided into two categories, calculated roughly to correspond to States in the intermediate and in the minor classes. Thus, to-day, we have in the structure of the Council three categories: the Great Powers, the Small States and, between them, Poland and Spain, who by a two-thirds majority of the Assembly, have been declared to be immediately re-eligible to the Council.

This structure is obviously not destined to last. Even if Poland should wisely desist from her suspected ambition of being placed in the Great Power class on the admission of the U.S.S.R., Argentina, China, Mexico, Turkey and probably others may aspire to promotion from the ranks of the Small States at least to the intermediate class. This position, which already seems threatening and which may at any moment become critical, is the inevitable outcome of the establishment of the principle of legal inequality between States in the structure of the League.

iii. *Small States within the League.*

Having examined the origin and the nature of this inequality, let us now consider how the Small States have reacted to it. Their reaction, as could be expected, has varied with their own importance, and more particularly with their own sense of their own importance.

While all have been what one may call inferiority-conscious, some have openly revolted against the legal inequality, but, with more or less critical reserve, the others have accepted it as the price to be paid for the advantages which it was hoped the organization of the international community would bring to all, and particularly to its weaker members. That price, even if unnecessarily high, would be deemed excessive only if those advantages were to prove illusory.

To the category of revolting States belong the Argentine Republic, Brazil, Spain, and Poland. When representatives of these States, as they frequently do, insist on the beauties of equality and deplore the legal inequalities prevailing in the League,[1] one cannot escape the impression that it is less from their faith in a general principle than from an accidental national disappointment. Thus the Argentine Republic, in 1920, proposed an amendment to the Covenant to suppress the distinction between Great Powers and Small States and to render all seats on the Council elective. When the examination of this and of her other proposed amendments was adjourned, her delegation left Geneva. It reappeared there only in 1933, to accept election to the Council.[2] Thus Brazil and Spain, protesting their love of equality, gave notice of their intention to withdraw from the League in 1926, when faced with the alternative of either consenting

[1] de Gimeno (Spain), ii, 208; Skirmunt (Poland), iv, 45. Our references are to the Records of the Assembly published as Special Supplements of the *Official Journal* of the League. The Roman figures refer to the number of the Assembly, the Arabic to the page of the corresponding volume of the Records. Thus de Gimeno (Spain, ii, 208, means declaration by de Gimeno, delegate of Spain, made at the Second Assembly, page 208 of the corresponding Records.

[2] Cf. Assembly Records, i, 91, 277; xiv, 36, 58.

to Germany's alone becoming a new permanent member of the Council or of their not being re-elected thereto. Brazil persisted in her intention, while Spain abandoned it when offered the possibility of being re-elected as an indefinitely re-eligible member. The latter possibility, offered to Poland also, certainly contributed to prevent her from imitating her two irascible would-be Great Power colleagues.[1]

The other Small States, with the possible exception of China, Turkey, Mexico, and perhaps some others, have more or less definitely accepted the present arrangement. They are resigned not only to the structure of the Council as it is and to the breach of the principle of legal equality which it entails, but also to their non-inclusion within the ranks of the privileged Great Powers. This resignation, however, is dependent upon the fulfilment of certain conditions which are constantly being recalled in the course of the debates of the Assembly. The privilege enjoyed by the Great Powers on the Council must not be abused and unduly extended to the Secretariat,[2] to the League Commissions,[3] and especially to the Court.[4] The Council must accept the full and free discussion of its decisions by

[1] League of Nations, *Official Journal*, Special Supplement, No. 42, Records of the Special Session of the Assembly, March 1926, Geneva 1926, p. 25. Cf. also *Official Journal*, 7th Year, No. 7, pp. 881, 887, 1004; No. 10, p. 1528; 9th Year, No. 4, pp. 432, 584, 585; No. 5, p. 603.

[2] Sastri (India), ii, 215; Beelaerts van Blokland (Holland), viii, 39; Hambro (Norway), viii, 57 et seq.; Caballero (Paraguay), viii, 100; Blythe (Ireland), ix, 77; Vasconcellos (Portugal), x, 83; Blythe (Ireland), xi, 96.

[3] Frangulis (Greece), ii, 277; Arfa (Persia), vii, 42; Franco (Dominican Republic), vii, 42; Hambro (Norway), vii, 49; Khan Foroughi (Persia), viii, 37; Stauning (Denmark), x, 41.

[4] Diaz Rodriguez (Venezuela), i, 167 et seq.; Antuna (Uruguay), x, 38.

the Assembly.[1] Above all, the Great Powers must pursue policies of peaceful international co-operation and impartiality, and they must assume responsibilities of leadership corresponding to and commensurate with their privileged position.[2]

This general attitude of the Small States is due to their attachment to the League of Nations and to their willingness to sacrifice a measure of theoretical equality to the cause of international organization. This cause is dear to them for three main reasons of very different importance.

In the first place, being Small States, that is militarily weak States, they have everything to gain from the establishment of law and order in the world. Anarchy, international as well as municipal, may sometimes be temporarily profitable for the mighty. Because of their superior force the strong may, in a state of anarchy, not only successfully defend their own rights, but sometimes also with impunity invade the rights of others. For the weak, on the other hand, law is not only justice for all, but particularly also security for themselves. It is therefore neither surprising nor especially creditable that the Small States should be willing to contribute to the establishment of world order, even at the expense of

[1] Hagerup (Norway), i, 92; Branting (Sweden), ii, 61; Nansen (Norway), iv, 61; Mowinkel (Norway), ix, 43; Frasheri (Albania), ix, 62; Hymans (Belgium), xi, 60.

[2] Rowell (Canada), i, 170 et seq.; Arfaed-Dovleh (Persia), iv, 37; Allen (New Zealand), iv, 48 et seq.; Caballero (Paraguay), vi, 37; Arfa (Persia), vi, 56; Cielens (Latvia), viii, 44; Löfgren (Sweden), viii, 46; Moltesen (Denmark), viii, 52; Apponyi (Hungary), x, 86 et seq.; Paradas (Dominican Republic), x, 92; Apponyi (Hungary), xi, 87 et seq.; Ala (Persia), xi, 117; Mitter (India), xii, 49; Guthrie (Canada), xii, 52; Hymans (Belgium), xii, 88; Salnais (Latvia), xiv, 53; O'Kelly (Ireland), xiv, 55.

their national sovereignty and of the principle of international equality. When, before the war, Professor Max Huber defended the doctrine of legal equality against all encroachments, it was expressly because he did not then believe in the possibility of such a world order. But, as he wrote, 'it is obvious that an association of States endowed with the authority to command and to coerce must possess a form of organization corresponding to the relative force of its members. In joining such an association, the weaker members of the community will be compensated for the loss of equality by increased security in the enjoyment of their own rights.'[1]

So it is felt to be to-day in Geneva, and so it has often been expressed in the Assembly. This view was expounded in the following terms by Mr. Sandler, the Swedish Foreign Minister, on 29 September, 1933, while he was discussing the problem of disarmament and the equal obligations incumbent upon all States members of the League under Article 8 of the Covenant:

> 'While upholding the above fundamental principle, the Swedish Government desires to point out that there is no question of the absolute legal equality of former times. What we want for the future is controlled equality. We know from experience what the old kind of equality means; it was nothing but the right of everybody to do whatever he liked and we know to what disastrous consequences it led. Pre-war equality is the fratricidal fraternity of the war period and the impoverished liberty of the post-war period. To return to an equality of that kind would be to restart the vicious circle of earlier times. That circle must be broken by a convention.'[2]

---

[1] Huber, op. cit., p. 116.

[2] xiv, 43.

Secondly, the Small States realized that through the organization of the League they have gained in effective influence on world affairs much more than they have lost in theoretical equality. This sentiment was clearly expressed at the Thirteenth Assembly on 28 September, 1932, by Mr. Motta, of Switzerland, when he said:

> 'No Government in the world it seems to me could contemplate with equanimity the collapse of this institution [the League of Nations], this our great hope. For the Small Powers it would mean renouncing all possibility of bringing their influence—their beneficial influence—to bear on international matters. For the Great Powers it would mean the inevitable return to the old system of big alliances.'[1]

Twelve years before Mr. Hymans, of Belgium, in closing the First Assembly on 18 December, 1920, had already declared:

> 'One of the features of this Assembly has been the recognition of the equality of States. It is a feature to which we must draw attention more particularly because we are emerging from a period still very recent when a strange and artificial distinction was drawn between the States which were called States with limited interests and those which were called States with general interests. The interests of humanity and the interests of the world are universal interests. The Small States, whatever the size of their territory and whatever their population, have the same interest as large States in the safety of humanity. *Nihil humani a me alienum puto.*'[2]

This curious and apparently paradoxical statement can be understood only when it is remembered that its author had bitterly suffered from the humiliation of national insignifi-

[1] xiii, 39. [2] i, 761.

APPENDIX A

Date	Place	Conference	Chairman	Nationality
1920				
April 13	London	Typhus	Astor	British
Sept. 24	Brussels	Financial	Ador	Swiss
Oct. 25	Paris	Passports	Loudon	Dutch
1921				
March 10	Barcelona	Communications	Hanotaux	French
June 30	Geneva	Traffic in Women	Lévie	French
Aug. 22	Geneva	Russian Refugees	Jovanovitch	Jugoslav
Nov. 23	Geneva	Upper Silesia	Calonder	Swiss
1922				
Feb. 4	Geneva	Upper Silesia	Calonder	Swiss
March 20	Warsaw	Typhus	Chodzo	Polish
Nov. 15	Geneva	Communications	Conti	Italian
1923				
Aug. 31	Geneva	Obscene Publications	Deschamps	French
Oct. 15	Geneva	Customs Formalities	Buxton	British
1924				
May 15	Rome	Migration	de Michelis	Italian
Nov. 3	Geneva	Opium	van Wettum	Dutch
Nov. 17	Geneva	Opium	Zahle	Danish

1925				
May 4	Geneva	Arms Traffic	Carton de Wiart	Belgian
Nov. 20	Paris	Inland Navigation	Mathieu	French
1926				
May 12	Geneva	Passports	Pusta	Esthonian
May 26	Geneva	Economic	Theunis	Belgian
Sept. 23	Geneva	Permanent Court	van Eysinga	Dutch
1927				
May 4	Geneva	Economic	Theunis	Belgian
July 27	Geneva	Assistance	Kuelz	German
Aug. 23	Geneva	Communications	de Aguero y Bethancourt	Cuban
Aug. 23	Geneva	Press	Burnham	British
Oct. 17	Geneva	Trade Restrictions	Colijn	Dutch
1928				
March 14	Geneva	Hides and Bones	Serruys	French
June 29	Geneva	Hides and Bones	Serruys	French
July 3	Geneva	Trade Restrictions	Colijn	Dutch
Nov. 26	Geneva	Economic Statistics	Rappard	Swiss
1929				
April 9	Geneva	Counterfeit Money	Pospisil	Czech
Aug. 29	Geneva	Hides and Bones	Serruys	French
Sept. 4	Geneva	Permanent Court	van Eysinga	Dutch
Nov. 5	Paris	Foreigners	Devèze	Belgian
Dec. 5	Paris	Trade Restrictions	Colijn	Dutch

APPENDIX A—*continued*

Date	Place	Conference	Chairman	Nationality
1930				
Feb. 17	Geneva	Economic Action	Moltke	Danish
March 13	The Hague	Codification	Heemskerk	Dutch
May 13	Geneva	Bills of Exchange	Limburg	Dutch
Oct. 6	Lisbon	Buoyage	Vasconcellos	Portuguese
Nov. 17	Geneva	Economic Action	Colijn	Dutch
Nov. 17	Geneva	River Navigation	de Ruelle	Belgian
1931				
Feb. 23	Geneva	Bills of Exchange	Limburg	Dutch
March 4	Geneva	Counterfeit Money	Delaquis	Swiss
March 16	Geneva	Economic Action	Colijn	Dutch
March 30	Geneva	Road Traffic	Eckhardt	German
May 27	Geneva	Opium	de Brouckère	Belgian
June 29	Geneva	Rural Hygiene	Pittaluga	Spanish
Oct. 12	Geneva	Communications	Vasconcellos	Portuguese
1932				
Feb. 2	Geneva	Disarmament	Henderson	British
Sept. 5	Stresa	Economic	Bonnet	French
1933				
June 12	London	Economic	MacDonald	British

cance at the Paris Peace Conference. There Belgium, in spite of her glorious war record and in spite of her status of theoretical equality with the Great Powers, had continuously been bullied and slighted by the Big Five, whereas at Geneva, in spite of her theoretical inequality, she had played a truly leading part in the debates over which her eminent Foreign Minister had brilliantly presided.

This suggests the third compensating circumstance which has led the Small States in the League to accept their position of theoretical inferiority, but of effectively enhanced prestige and influence. While deprived of permanent seats on the Council, they have played an exceptionally important part in supplying international conferences and commissions with presidents and chairmen. Thus the fourteen ordinary Assemblies have had thirteen presidents, all drawn from Small States, that is in turn from Belgium, Holland, Chile, Cuba, Switzerland, Canada, Jugoslavia, Uruguay, Denmark, Salvador, Roumania (twice), Greece, and South Africa.

Similarly, of eighteen International Labour Conferences, nine have been presided over by citizens of Small States. Furthermore, of fifty other international conferences held under the auspices of the League in the course of the last fifteen years, which we have been able to consider from this point of view, thirty-three have had chairmen from Small States. This statement is based upon the list of conferences in Appendix A, which, although not necessarily complete, the term international conferences being susceptible of various interpretations, may prove of some general interest.

Finally, as arbitrators, mediators, and conciliators in countless tribunals, committees and sub-committees of the Council and of the Assembly, representatives of Small States have, thanks to the League, been called upon to play a part in world affairs, which was quite unexampled before and would be quite inconceivable without a permanent international organization. The influence they have thus exercised, equally flattering to their personal pride and to the national honour of their respective countries, has undoubtedly been an important although imponderable factor in reconciling the Small States to the loss of their theoretical equality.

All these circumstances have, however, tended to stress rather than to erase the distinction between Great Powers and Small States in the League. A close examination of the debates of the successive Assemblies reveals an interesting change in the attitude of the latter towards the former. While, at the beginning of the League's existence, the delegates from the Small States were inclined to assert the principle of equality and deny the validity of any legal distinction, they have tended of late to recognize and indeed to emphasize this distinction. They have done so mainly, it would seem, to throw the responsibility for the League's failures on the Great Powers and to call upon them for more constructive leadership.

We have already noted how Mr. Hymans, on closing the First Assembly, had declared the recognition of the equality of States to have been one of its main features. Eleven years later the same Belgian statesman, speaking of the impending Disarmament Conference, declared, on 12 September, 1931: 'The part the Small States have to play in the field of disarmament is naturally limited. Their policy will naturally depend on that of the Great States.'[1]

At the same Assembly, four days earlier, Sir Brojendra Mitter, delegate of India, had already voiced a similar

[1] xii, 88.

sentiment, saying: 'We rely on the Great Powers to instal trust in the place of suspicion and to establish their moral pre-eminence as they have already established their material pre-eminence.'[1]

At the Assembly of 1933, after the weakness of the League's action displayed in the Sino-Japanese conflict, the failure of the World Economic Conference and the sterile debates of the Disarmament Conference had created an atmosphere of acute discouragement, the general tendency of the Small States was to blame the Great Powers for their lack of leadership and for the ensuing disappointments. Thus, on opening the Fourteenth Assembly as President of the Council, on 25 September, 1933, Mr. Mowinkel, of Norway, speaking more particularly of the failure of the Economic Conference, declared:

> 'The reason is that it has not been possible to establish in advance a basis of co-operation between those States which through their importance and their power exercise a decisive influence in the world. When even those States—or perhaps particularly those States—come to big conferences with views that are difficult to reconcile, it may be said in advance that it will not be possible—even if all the others are agreed—to arrive at fruitful results.'[2]

Similar feelings were re-echoed throughout the debates of the last Assembly. Thus, on 30 September, Mr. Salnais, Foreign Minister of Latvia, declared that it was 'indispensable to establish a basis of co-operation between the States which, through their importance and force, exercised a decisive influence in the world'.[3]

Immediately after Mr. Salnais, Mr. Sean T. O'Kelly,

[1] xii, 49. [2] xiv, 29. [3] xiv, 53.

Vice-President of the Executive Council of the Irish Free State, attributing the failure of the League not to any defect in its machinery, but to the fact that it had not been used to the full, stated: 'The responsibility for that failure must lie with the Great Powers who, owing to their importance and their resources, exercise a decisive influence in the world.'[1]

Finally, let us quote the closing words of the presidential address of Mr. te Water, of South Africa, delivered on 11 October, 1933, at the end of the last Assembly: '. . . let the leaders of the Great Powers change their policies, from the policy of fear and of resentment, to one of generosity. . . . Will not the great nations go forward in this new spirit, so that the peoples of the earth may have peace?'[2]

Thus, under the stress of disappointment, we see emerging on the lips of representatives of the Small States not only a recognition of the distinction between them and the Great Powers but almost a new definition of the latter.

iv. *Small State Policies?*

We have sought briefly to outline the attitude of the Small States in the League *vis-à-vis* the structure of the League itself, and to define their own position within that structure. Is it possible to go further? Is it possible to discern any particular policies common to all the Small States which might be said to distinguish them as a group from the Great Powers? Except as regards a general conception of the League itself, which we will touch upon in conclusion, we do not believe it.

We have already noted at the beginning of this study the

[1] xiv, 55.

[2] xiv, 96.

complete lack of homogeneity of the Small States. How could Poland and Uruguay, Hungary and Czechoslovakia, Switzerland and Australia, Sweden and Ethiopia be expected to see eye to eye on any matter of political or economic import? It will be sufficient to mention some of the major problems which have arisen since the war to illustrate this point.

On reparations, in particular, and on a punitive as opposed to an impartial settlement of peace in general, the policies of the Small States of Poland or Czechoslovakia much more closely approximated those of the Great Power, France, than those of Sweden or South Africa.

The idea of a closer European union was launched by a Great Power, France, enthusiastically endorsed by several Small States of Europe, such as Greece, Czechoslovakia, and Austria, as well as by Cuba in America, was viewed with critical reserve by Great Britain as well as by Switzerland and most non-European Small States.

The Briand–Kellogg Pact, to be sure, was accepted by practically all the Small States of the world. But so it was also by all the Great Powers. It is therefore not even necessary to examine the very appreciable national differences which mark the spirit of the unanimous acceptance of that uncertain formulation of a nebulous doctrine to realize that here was no specifically Small-State policy.

The Four-Power Pact, put forward by a Great Power, Italy, was favourably received by Great Britain and Germany, accepted with many reservations by France, violently resented by Poland, considered with ill-disguised hostility by Czechoslovakia, but not without favour and hope by most of the former neutral Small States of Europe.

The general policy of political blocks, of which the

members of the Little Entente, all Small States, are the chief protagonists, is almost as unpopular in several other Small States of Europe, and quite as unpopular in Hungary as it is in Italy, a Great Power.

Even in the matter of disarmament, which would seem to be of special importance to all Small States, there is no common policy by which one could distinguish them as a group from the equally heterogeneous group of the Great Powers. To be sure, Norway and Hungary, for instance, are more insistent, although for different reasons, on the urgency of an immediate substantial reduction of armaments than France, but so are Great Britain and Germany, but not so Poland and Jugoslavia.

The same lack of uniformity of outlook may be observed in the field of economic policies. The present gold block comprises two or three Great Powers and three or four Small States. Protectionism, ever more exclusive and aggressive, has come to be practised by all, great and small alike, even though theoretically repudiated by almost all, great and small alike. When we think of Holland, Belgium, and the Scandinavian States, we may be tempted to look upon freer trade as an ideal peculiar to Small States in the contemporary world. But what of the extreme economic nationalism of such other Small States as Ireland, Hungary, or Australia?

Nothing more decisively proves the fragility of the concepts of Small States and Great Powers than the lack of any doctrine or creed uniting either of the two groups and opposing it to the other. In only one sphere of world politics can one find anything approaching unity among all those States 'whose importance and resources do not allow them to exercise a decisive influence on human affairs', as the new formula runs. The sphere in question is that of the activities and functions of the League of Nations.

We believe it to be generally true that all Small States agree in looking upon the League mainly as an instrument for the promotion of peace through justice. It is not unnatural, although it may give rise to cynical comment: the nations whose only material bond is a common lack of might are spiritually linked together by a common love of right.

This legal and ethical conception of the League, which Léon Bourgeois had already foreseen in Paris in 1919 when he expressed the fear lest the Council, exclusively composed of Great Powers, would tend to seek peace rather than peace founded on justice, has led the Small States to insist on certain specific political postulates.

Realizing that justice, in international affairs as elsewhere, was conditioned and promoted by impartiality, and that the less the League resembled a partial alliance and the more it approached a world association the better the chances for impartiality, the Small States have been the most consistent champions of the principle of universality.

Mr. Motta was surely expressing the feeling of the overwhelming majority of the Small States when, as President of the Swiss Confederation, on opening the first meeting of the First Assembly, on 15 November, 1920, he declared: 'The more universal the League of Nations becomes the more its authority and impartiality will be guaranteed.'[1]

Realizing that the Permanent Court of International Justice was more apt faithfully to serve the ideals of right

[1] i, 28. Cf. also Pueyrredon (Argentine Republic), i, 91; Zahle (Denmark), iv, 63; de Torriente (Cuba), iv, 157; Ramaswami Ayyar (India), viii, 35; Morales (Panama), viii, 102.

than the political Council, they have consistently advocated the strengthening of the judicial arm of the League and the extension of its jurisdiction. Having failed, in 1920, to render its jurisdiction compulsory, they hailed the introduction of the optional clause, which had already been proposed at The Hague in 1907 by Professor Max Huber, of Switzerland, and for the first years of the existence of the Court they persistently urged the Great Powers to follow their example in adhering to this clause.[1]

Realizing that justice was more apt to triumph in the public debates of the Assembly than at the secret negotiations around the Council table, the Small States have been the most ardent advocates of open diplomacy and of a strict interpretation of the Covenant in the League, as well as the constant defenders of the rights and influence of the Assembly. The firm and bold attitude of several of their representatives in such circumstances as the Corfu conflict in 1923, the crisis over the admission of Germany in 1926, and especially the recent Sino-Japanese conflict[2] shows that the stand of the Small States in these matters is not the expression merely of an academic preference for honesty, but of the deep-rooted belief that it is effectively the best and indeed the only safe world policy.[3]

[1] Diaz Rodriguez (Venezuela), i, 167; Motta (Switzerland), iv, 58; Nansen (Norway), v, 37, 38; Ador (Switzerland), v, 84; Apponyi (Hungary), v, 94; Fernandes (Brazil), vi, 84; Lange (Norway), viii, 76; Antuna (Uruguay), x, 38; Venizelos (Greece), x, 65; Motta (Switzerland), x, 82; Apponyi (Hungary), x, 86 et seq.

[2] Cf. Sean Lester, 'The Far East Dispute from the Point of View of Small States', *Problems of Peace*, 8th Series, London, 1933, pp. 120 et seq.

[3] Hagerup (Norway), i, 92; Motta (Switzerland), i, 160; Branting (Sweden), ii, 61; Radeff (Bulgaria), iii, 43; Nansen (Norway), iv, 61; Arfa (Persia), vii, 42; Foster (Canada), vii, 45.

Finally, realizing the importance of an independent and impartial civil service, the Small States have often emphasized the necessity of recruiting the members of the Secretariat from the greatest number of countries and of freeing them from the bonds of national allegiance.[1]

In stressing the legal characteristics and duties of the League rather than its political functions and in tending to give justice precedence over expediency, the Small States are insisting on what is most novel in the Geneva institution. Secret negotiations and diplomatic bargainings there have always been, ever since representatives of various States have assembled to adjust their respective interests or to jeopardize those of their neighbours. What is new and truly revolutionary in the conception of the League as defined in the Covenant is the attempt to bring the conduct of nations in their mutual relations into conformity with certain specific standards of morality. By their advocacy of this conception the Small States may therefore rightly look upon themselves as the most faithful champions of the League itself. This, we repeat, is less due to their superior virtue than to their inferior power. If Small States are on the whole internationally less sinful than Great Powers, it is not because they are more saintly, but because they are less apt to be successful sinners. By serving the League they are not only defending justice, they are also most effectively promoting their national interests. Compared with the Great Powers, they are gaining more, while risking less, by subordinating their own ambitions to the cause of law and order in the world. One of their spokesmen, Mr. Moltesen, of Denmark, could therefore without indulging in cant declare at the close of a remarkable speech delivered

[1] Sastri (India), ii, 215; Blythe (Ireland), xii, 78.

at the Eighth Assembly on 7 September, 1927: 'The League has now found allies . . . in all the smaller States, which, let us hope, may serve—to quote the simile of an English statesman—as the consecrated vessels in which the Divinity dispenses the sacred wine.'[1]

These are fine words. Fine words, however, will not suffice to insure the success of the League of Nations, nor to maintain the peace of the world, which is its chief task.

The love of peace is not so universal to-day that war could be prevented by the effective co-operation of less than all the pacific nations. In this co-operation the heaviest duty undoubtedly falls upon the Great Powers. But the Small States also have their part to play.

Their spokesmen, being less responsible, usually enjoy more freedom of speech than their major colleagues on contentious and delicate matters which oppose national and international interests. Being freer to speak their own mind, they can more simply and more faithfully express the general sentiment of the world community as it exists in large and small States alike. Thereby they are in a position to secure for the League a measure of popular confidence and support that is often denied the more diplomatic oratory and the mystifying reticence of the leaders of the Great Powers. This is an opportunity which representatives of Small States should not underestimate and never miss. The example of Branting and Nansen suffices to illustrate its reality and its possibilities.

As we have seen, the general tendency of the Small States is at present to insist on the impotence of their good-will and to call upon the Great Powers for bold and constructive leadership. If the Small States continue, through

[1] viii, 53.

their spokesmen, thus to say 'we would if we could', and the Great Powers, through their attitude, tacitly to reply 'we might but we won't', it is obvious that the League will not succeed in maintaining the peace of the world. That goal can be attained only if Great Powers and Small States agree in adopting and in applying to their foreign policy the stern maxim attributed to William the Silent: '*Point n'est besoin d'espérer pour entreprendre ni de réussir pour persévérer.*'

CHAPTER III

THE GREAT POWERS IN THE LEAGUE OF NATIONS

by

ALFRED ZIMMERN

Montague Burton Professor of International Relations, Oxford.

i. *Relations Between the Great Powers and the Essential League Problem.*

TO discuss the Great Powers in the League is really to discuss the League itself. Without the smaller States the League would be an oligarchy—perhaps a tyranny; but it would still exist and function; it would still be a League. But without the Great Powers the League would be nothing more than a debating society. This is not to cast discredit on the Smaller States, whose standards in international politics, thanks to their relatively sheltered life, are in some, though not in most, cases higher than those of any of the Great Powers—it is simply to face the facts of the international scene as we find them.

Thus the Great Powers constitute the specific League problem. If they could agree amongst themselves, the League would function harmoniously. In so far as they do agree amongst themselves on any particular problem, the League is able to deal with it satisfactorily. It is not the Small States, numerous and heterogeneous as they are, unscrupulous and unruly as many of them are, which have obstructed the work of the League during the last fifteen years. Small States never persist in making trouble when the Great Powers are united and determined to bring them to reason. It is when the Great Powers are at loggerheads that the League functions badly, or is even temporarily put out of action.

What has just been said is, no doubt, familiar to every student of international affairs. It is being confirmed and illustrated day by day. But there are two conclusions arising out of it which are not so universally recognized.

One is that nothing is to be gained by trying to amend the unanimity rule. It is tempting to argue that a body of nearly sixty members cannot be expected to be unanimous and that, therefore, some method for arriving at a decision without unanimity ought to be introduced. But, in point of fact, the unanimity rule has hardly ever, if at all, proved a real obstacle at Geneva. The Smaller States are always ready to give way in the last resort. They are never desirous of pushing things to extremes and impairing the life of the League, where they fare better than they would under any practicable alternative system. As for the Great Powers, when there is a serious disagreement between them, it is idle to imagine that it can be overcome by a majority vote. The result would most probably be to drive the Power in the minority out of the League. It is not by mechanical devices of this sort that wide differences of opinion and divergences of interest can be overcome.

The second practical conclusion is that, when the Great Powers are in disagreement on a particular subject, it is of no use to expect it to be solved by 'referring it to the League'. Some such problems are best discussed at Geneva: others are best discussed between the capitals concerned by the ordinary means of diplomacy; both methods have their advantages, and there is no peculiar merit in either. The procedure best adapted for any particular case must be decided according to its nature. But, whatever method is adopted, it will be the same Governments and the same public opinion between which agreement has to be secured. This is not always understood by those who have acquired the habit of crying 'Leave it to Geneva'—as though the League was in a position to *impose* a settlement over the head of the Power concerned.

This is only another way of saying that the League is not a world-government, but simply an agency of co-operation between States which remain independent and masters of their own affairs. A Foreign Minister who treated the League as a world-government would very soon find himself in difficulties with his Cabinet, his Parliament, and his public opinion—just as the Resident Minister of a British Dominion in London would soon discover whose servant he was if, under the influence of the atmosphere, he allowed himself to think that he owed any obedience to His Majesty's Government in Great Britain!

Co-operation is of the essence of the League. Statesmen and peoples who have not learnt the art—the admittedly difficult art—of co-operation are not helpful members of the League. That is not to say that they should not be allowed to serve their apprenticeship.

ii. *The Great Powers in the Covenant.*

Students of the Covenant who know it only as a paper document sometimes claim that it is unfair in conferring special privileges on the Great Powers. Complaint is made that the Great Powers occupy permanent seats on the Council, whilst the other Powers are only entitled to temporary seats, to which they are elected by the Assembly.

Proposals have even been put forward in some quarters for putting all the Council seats on the same electoral footing.

Those who argue in this way do not realize how the present system came into existence, or what was in the minds of those who were responsible for it. They seem to have a picture in their minds of the world of international politics reduced to a state of nature in which the only realities were some sixty entities called Sovereign States; and they behold these Sovereign States, in the exercise of their 'rights', drawing up a covenant of association in which special privileges are granted to some of their number. This, it is argued, is 'undemocratic', and should be corrected as soon as possible!

But, of course, this is not at all what really happened. It is metaphysics, not history or politics, or (for the matter of that) law either. What actually took place was that the *League was built round the Great Powers.* It could not have been built in any other way—or it would have been, not a product of historical forces, but, as has already been said, simply a debating society. It could never have become a going concern. Even as it was, the absence of one of the Great Powers—the greatest of all—very nearly prevented it from becoming a going concern, and has greatly diminished its authority and usefulness. We know exactly what was in the minds of the British statesmen who were concerned with the drafting and subsequent sponsoring of the Covenant; for their views were set forth in an official Commentary presented to Parliament and published in June 1919—and still obtainable at the cost of twopence.[1] Here the Council is described as 'the central organ of the League' and as 'a political instrument

[1] Cmd. 151, Miscellaneous, No. 3, 1919.

endowed with greater authority than any the world has hitherto seen'. On what is this authority based? On a metaphysical delegation of powers from the sixty sovereigns in a state of nature? Of course not. It is based on the facts of the world of international politics as they were at that moment. 'If it [the Council] is to exercise real authority,' says the Commentary, 'it must be [a body] which represents *the actual distribution of the organized political power of the world.*' And it goes on to say that though 'in form its decisions are only recommendations', 'when those who recommend include *the political chiefs of all the Great Powers* and of four other Powers selected by the States of the world in assembly, their unanimous recommendations are likely to be irresistible'.

Nor is this simply a British view. One of the greatest Continental authorities, Professor Max Huber, of Zurich, later President of the Permanent Court of International Justice, analysing the Covenant in a lecture[1] delivered in December 1919, describes the League as the product of a process of *codifying practical politics*—'co-ordinating' would perhaps be a term more familiar to the British mind, since the word 'code' suggests a legal rather than a political system. The Covenant, Professor Huber explains, was not drawn up by a process of bargaining or contract, like an ordinary treaty, nor by a process of constitution-making such as is to be found in the paper projects for a League of States put forward by Sully, Penn, Cruie, the Abbé St. Pierre, and others. It is something different in method from either of these; it is a 'systematic co-ordination of all those elements in the politics of the last hundred years which are either of direct service to the cause of peace'

[1] Reproduced in the *Zeitschript tär Völkernicht*, vol. xii, Nos. 1–2.

(e.g. The Hague machinery and administrative agencies like the Universal Postal Union), or have originally belonged to the system of Power Politics, and can now be made use of in the cause of general peace.'

The Covenant, then, was not a brand-new constitution for the world, but a co-ordination, an adjustment, an attempted harmonization of the political forces actually existing in the world at the time. Amongst these forces those represented by the Great Powers were undoubtedly the strongest. It was inevitable, therefore, that a League conceived on these lines should be built round the Great Powers.

Let us pause to examine what this implies.

It implies, firstly, that the League was not built round a law-court. There is a school of writers who think, or write as if they think, that all that the world needs in order to enjoy undisturbed peace is that the sixty odd States should sign and ratify an agreement to settle all their differences by peaceful means before tribunals suited to the various classes of disputes. Such writers are always casting reproaches at the Great Powers because they are unwilling to do this or because when, in response to the appeals of the Smaller Powers and their own 'advanced' politics, they do consent to do so, they are careful to make reservations which retain for them considerable freedom of action as well as a time-limit for their signature. But when the Smaller States clamour for these signatures they are not doing so in the name of the Covenant, but of a more academic, if more symmetrical, conception of international relations. The Covenant provides facilities for the peaceful settlement of disputes, but it does not provide for compulsory litigation. And the reason is that the Covenant was drawn up, in the main, by representatives of Great Powers who knew that their peoples were not yet ready to submit themselves to the rulings of what is called international law.

Why were they not ready to do so? Partly for not wholly respectable reasons; but partly also for a reason that is not only respectable but extremely cogent—namely, that law-courts cannot function satisfactorily (except perhaps for issues of small moment) in a world in which order is not yet assured. A framework of order is needed before the authority of the law can be recognized and enforced. Laws are rules to facilitate men's living together. They are drawn up on the assumption that men desire to do so and have organized themselves to give effect to this desire. But in a world which is still unruly, in which there is little or no consciousness of membership of a common 'society', law cannot take root. Thus it is mere realism on the part of the Great Powers to treat law-courts, at this stage of international development, as being of secondary importance; or perhaps it would be better to say, as signposts pointing to the future rather than as important working institutions for to-day. That is why there is no mention in the Covenant of The Hague and the treaties drawn up there before the war. The framers of the Covenant were politically minded, not legally minded. They acted on the maxim: 'First things first.'

In the second place, the Covenant was not built round an economic system, but round a political system, a system of *States*.

Its framers might have said—according to many present-day writers they ought to have said—'our principal task is to abolish war. Since the causes of war are to be found in the existing economic system, it follows that we cannot abolish war without changing that system; we propose therefore to set on foot a new economic system, immune from the defects of its predecessor.'

The framers of the Covenant did not do this. It would indeed have been difficult to accomplish, though much less difficult under the conditions that existed in the winter of 1918–19 than it would be to-day. But they did not even try to do so, or consider that they ought to try. And the reason is very simple. They did not think that the chief causes of war lay in the economic system. On the contrary, they thought that they lay in the political system, in the relations between *States* or independent political bodies, not in the relations between buyers and sellers, or between employers and employed. And, in particular, they believed that they lay in the relations between the more important States or Great Powers—in other words, in what is called *Power-Politics*.

This view on their part has received striking confirmation in recent months. For some time after the war the territory we call Russia was governed by men who did not consider that they were in charge of the destinies of a State, or independent political body, but of a local branch of the world-wide organization of a particular social *class*, and they conceived of this organization as not being simply political but also economic. As time went on this theory became more and more untenable under the impact of fact. To-day Russia is once more in the full sense a State—and indeed a Great Power. She has her own particular economic organization—but so have other States. But for the purpose of preventing the outbreak of war and eliminating war from present-day civilization, she is co-operating with other States whose economic systems differ greatly from her own.

Evidently her rulers consider that the most urgent task for the time being is to grapple with the *political* causes of war rather than to concentrate on the building up of a new economic system.

This is not to say that the existing economic system is working satisfactorily. It is not. It is only to say that, of the two problems, the problem of Power-Politics and the problem of what may be called Greed-Economics, the former is at the present stage of human history the more urgent. To put it in another way: there are two evil spirits whose influence is conspicuous in our midst. There is Moloch, whose lust is for Power, and Mammon, whose lust is for Profit. But the more dangerous of the two is Moloch. Mammon may have corroded our civilization, but Moloch can destroy it in a single stroke, as Samson brought down the Temple.

iii. *Force and Law as Elements in the League System.*

Is the League, then, it may be asked, a system of partnership between the Great Powers—a sort of syndicate of the strong reducing the little to nothingness?

No; the League is much more than that. To understand how its various elements are related and interpenetrate it is necessary to go back briefly over the history of the Great Power system.

The disorder or 'anarchy', as some writers call it, which the framers of the Covenant hoped to redress by harmonizing the relations of the Great Powers dates from the break-up of the mediaeval world. When the verity of Christendom disappeared the system of Sovereign States arose in its place. The essence of this system was that the monarch or prince or sovereign was bound by no overriding law. He was a law unto himself. He was the embodiment of the supreme power. He *was* the State . . .

L'état c'est moi.

This purely self-regarding system, with the anti-social attitude resulting from it, lasted throughout the seventeenth and eighteenth centuries. It was broken in upon sharply by the French Revolution, which gave the monarchs a rude lesson as to the need for co-operation. It was in 1791 that they first discovered that they had a common interest—in checking the rise of Republican France. After the final defeat of Napoleon, the child of the French Revolution, they came together once more and, following upon the abandonment of a more ambitious scheme, fell back upon what we should to-day describe as a *Consultative Pact*; it was known at the time as the Concert of Europe.

The Concert of Europe, as its name implies, dealt only with the affairs of Europe and the Near East—a region which was for most of its members not simply the centre of the world but the whole world. It was a system of rights without corresponding duties. The Great Powers had a *right* to be consulted on any matter affecting the peace of Europe, and any one of them had a *right* to demand that a Conference be summoned to deal with it. But the members of the Concert were not allies: they were not bound to go to one another's help in war-time, or to protect one another's frontiers.[1]

This system of consultation and occasional conferences

[1] The best short statement of the functions and limitations of the Concert is to be found in the late Sir James Headlam Morley's *Studies in Diplomatic History*, pp. 116–18.

functioned intermittently, at times with greater at times with less success, until 1913, when the British Foreign Secretary presided over a Balkan Conference in London. In retrospect it seems to many little less than anarchy; but it is to its credit that no major war broke out in Europe between 1815 and 1914. From 1871 onwards, however, Bismarck, then the predominant statesman on the Continent, linked it up with a system of alliances, and, after his disappearance, these in their turn, from 1891 onwards, led to counter-measures. Through the threat to her sea-power Britain was drawn reluctantly into one of the two opposing camps. It was out of this system of opposing alliances rather than out of sheer anarchy that the Great War took its rise.

During almost the whole of this period down to the Spanish-American War (1898) and the Anglo-Japanese Alliance (1902) Great Britain occupied the predominant position in the overseas world owing to her unchallenged naval supremacy. This very summary sketch will have been sufficient to indicate the place which the British framers of the Covenant intended the League to fill. It was to 'co-ordinate' the elements of pre-war international politics through the establishment of an *improved consultative system.* How was it to be improved?

Firstly, its membership was to be extended to all the Great Powers, and its scope from Europe to the whole world. Thus the consulting Powers would be Great Britain, France, Germany, Italy, Russia, the United States, and Japan.

Secondly, it would be provided with a permanent organization or secretariat, and would hold regular meetings.

Thirdly, room would be found in the new organization

for the Smaller States, though they would occupy no large place in the 'central body' or Council.

Fourthly, the Powers would be bound by a Charter or Covenant which would involve duties and obligations as well as rights.

It will be seen that the third and fourth features introduce elements entirely foreign to the pre-war system. The weak are to sit side by side with the strong, and both are to be bound by common obligations or rules. These obligations are indeed not numerous; they cannot even by a stretch of language be described as a code. But, if not numerous, they are extremely important; they mark the introduction of the *spirit of law* into what had hitherto been the domain of independent and self-regarding force.

Thus the Covenant can be described as a union between Force and Law, or, better still perhaps, as involving a recognition by the Great Powers, representing predominant force, of the *need for law* and of their responsibility for promoting conditions of order in which law could develop and with authority. If a terminology had been adopted corresponding to the design the *Great Powers* should henceforward have become known as the *Great Responsibles.*

Here again it is worth while pausing to drive home certain implications.

The scheme of the Covenant assumes that there is *a place for Force in politics.*

There is a widespread opinion or, to be more exact, a widespread sentiment in the English-speaking countries to the effect that force should be banished from the domain of international politics. It is admitted that force is provided for in the Covenant, but this is regarded as an unfortunate blemish, and the Articles concerned are accepted with a mental reservation. In this way thousands of persons, whose clear-headedness and intellectual integrity is not on a level with their undoubted goodwill, have contrived to consider themselves as 'supporters of the League', and have even held a prominent place in the counsels of some of the organizations which exist to promote its cause.

Some of these persons are opposed to the use of force under any circumstances. Others, remembering the local police-court, admit the need for force in domestic affairs, but consider that it is not needed, or ought not to be needed, or should not be admitted to be needed, in international affairs. Why law should be expected to function without force to back it up in the international domain, where much less support is as yet available than in home matters from the free co-operation of citizens, is not very clear; but, of course, the impulse which had led to this illogical distinction between the two realms of force is horror of war. Force in the international realm is associated in the mind with war, whilst force in the domestic realm is associated with the homely policeman.

The Covenant, of course, knows nothing of any such distinction. The distinction which it draws is an entirely different one. It does not approve of the policeman and condemn the soldier and sailor. It distinguishes between the *right and wrong use of force.* To regard all force as inherently wicked is, on this view, to drift into materialism. It is to attach a peculiar vice to a warship or a gun or a rifle, or even a stick. It is to ignore the fact that a warship may be used to free slaves on the high seas, as a stick may be used to prevent an assault on a child. In other words, the evil which is connected with force lies in the *motive* of those who use it or command its use. In international politics this evil lies in the motives of States and their rulers —that is, in Power-Politics as opposed to Responsibility-Politics.

The object aimed at in the Covenant, therefore, is not to eliminate force but to moralize it; to secure that States whilst remaining, as they cannot help remaining, vehicles of Power, should become more and more agencies for well-being, using their power to promote the moral life of the community.

This is not the place in which to pursue this argument in its religious bearings. Suffice it to say that the view embodied in the Covenant is not only based on appreciation of political realities, but also on the general consensus of Christian doctrine. The opposing views, of which so much is heard to-day from many whose contact with Christian teaching is of the slightest, is that of a small other-worldly minority. It is in essence monastic. In its modern form it may be described as quasi-monastic, for most of its devotees remain in the 'world', enjoying full social intercourse, benefiting by the ordered freedom and the amenities which the State provides, but considering at the same time that they have a right to contract out of certain civic obligations of their own choosing. In so far as this view is held as an article of religious faith there is nothing that can be said to its adherents except that they should interrogate their conscience once again to make sure whether a less capricious reply may not be forthcoming. But it is clear that if such an opinion became at all general, it would lead to the disintegration of political life and of the civic values associated with it. Not by such means as these will the advanced communities increase their influence or ensure peace and the stability of civilization. The problem of rendering unto Caesar the things that are Caesar's cannot so lightly be dismissed. The task before all men and women of good will is to realize the nature of Caesar's problems and to co-operate in *moralizing his motives* and activities; in other words, the League is not simply an organization for co-ordinating and adjusting the policies of the Powers, rubbing off their rough edges, so to speak; its aim is to make statesmen and people more conscious of the *common values* which States exist to promote. To put it in a single phrase drawn from the Greeks, the League exists *to promote the good life for mankind.*

iv. *Democracy and the League.*

President Wilson, the great sponsor of the League at its inception, connected its world-wide aim with the predominance of democracy as a form of government. Democracy and internationalism were for him two interdependent themes. He desired world peace in order to make 'the world safe for democracy'; and he desired the spread of democracy, amongst other reasons, because he thought that a democratic regime was more likely to be peaceful.

What was the ground for this view?

Ir was based on the conclusion for which there is good warrant in history, that Caesar can only be kept virtuous—at least in the long run—when he has to render an account of his actions to the main body of citizens; in other words, that the best way to ensure that Governments shall use their power to promote human welfare is to provide that the people shall be in a position to control them.

Thus it was that President Wilson's hopes for the League were bound up with his expectation that democracy would be the predominant political system in the post-war world.

Has this expectation been disappointed?

The political map of the world is indeed very different from what it was in 1919 and 1920. At that time all the Great Powers except Japan were democracies in name, and new constitutions on the democratic model were being introduced throughout Central and Eastern Europe. In Russia, the workers and peasants (that is by far the most numerous section of the population) were ostensibly in control of the State, whilst Japan was becoming steadily more responsive to Western ideas.

To-day the situation has changed. Of the leading Powers only three, Great Britain, the United States, and France remain democratic, whilst Germany, Italy, Japan, and Russia, together with important States such as Poland and Yugoslavia, have adopted varying forms of Governments all equally opposed to the democratic system. This raises the issue: Has the set-back to democracy made the League system unworkable?

Two separate questions are involved here.

The first is whether we are entering upon a new era in the practice of Government in which democracy will be more and more superseded.

The second is whether or not the democratic States are still predominant in the world as they were in 1919–20.

To take the first question first. It is quite true that the world has entered upon a new era in the practice of government. Governments have to meet demands to-day with which political organization as it was understood in pre-war days is quite unable to cope. In this sense there is a crisis. But it is not a crisis in democracy or in Parliamentarism, it is a *crisis in Government.*

Public affairs in the post-war world demand swift

decisions and a strong organization of the State. These demands have been met in some countries by the adoption of what is quaintly called 'the leadership principle' (as though the history of democracy was devoid of great leaders), and by vesting supreme power in a single executive head or 'dictator'.

Can the democratic system meet these demands of the new age without sacrificing its principle of popular control? For anyone who will look round the world to see what is actually happening instead of allowing himself to be deafened and bemused by official propaganda the answer is clear. Democracy not only can meet these demands, but is doing so—and indeed far more efficiently than the heterogeneous array of inexperienced States, ranging from Central Europe to Central and Eastern Asia, which have found the democratic system too difficult to manage and have therefore fallen back upon cruder methods.

What are the facts?

Of the States which were solidly democratic before 1914—where democracy was rooted in the life of the people, and not, as for instance in most Latin-American States, simply set down in a document—*not one has changed its regime.* In the economic storm that has swept over Europe since 1927 many young trees have been uprooted; but the old masters of the forest are all unscathed.

These pre-war democracies include three Great Powers—Great Britain, the United States, France, and a group of smaller European States: Belgium, Holland, Switzerland, Sweden, Denmark, and Norway. To these may be added a group of post-war democracies which have weathered the storm: in Europe, Czechoslovakia, Finland, Iceland, and the Irish Free State, whilst overseas Canada,

South Africa, Australia, and New Zealand have acquired full powers for their existing systems of responsible government. In all these cases the main demands upon government have been realized and met in various ways. It has been found possible to strengthen the executive without destroying its responsibility to Parliament. In Great Britain, Australia, New Zealand, South Africa, and Holland the adjustment has taken the form of a temporary coalition of parties. A solution on these lines is at present under discussion in France, where the stabilization of the franc was carried through by a temporary arrangement of this kind. In Switzerland and Czechoslovakia custom has ensured wide authority for the Executive. Thus all in all there is no reason whatever to conclude that the democratic system is being, or is likely to be, superseded.

Moreover, the democratic States, though numerically a minority, as they always have been, constitute *the most powerful group of States* in the world of to-day. Together they have an overwhelming preponderance of sea-power, and by far the largest share of the world's natural resources, particularly the resources needed for effective armament. Thus, by the standards of Power-Politics, the world has become far more safe for democracy than it was in 1914. That this is not generally realized is largely due to the ignorance which prevails in democratic countries as to the changes which have taken place in the art of war since 1914, and this in its turn springs partly from the tendency already mentioned to regard force and all that is connected with it as sinful, and therefore unworthy of close study or attention. When the democratic peoples on both sides of the Atlantic at last awaken to the *political responsibility* involved in the control of the so-called Key-minerals, as well as in their sea-power, not only democracy but the Rule of Law will be far more assured in the world than it is to-day.[1]

A final question remains to be answered. Is it not unjust, it may be asked, that the democratic peoples should have so large a share of the world's goods, and therefore under modern conditions of the World's Power?

To this there are two answers.

The first is that Justice in the sense of the equal division of this world's goods is an ideal beyond the attainment of statesmanship. All that statesmanship can do for the poor or the helpless or the less gifted within each State, as for the less happily situated peoples in the existing condition of the world, is to lay down minimum standards and to frame policies which will result not in equality but in a greater approximation to equality. But such measures can only be carried through under conditions of assured peace and within a framework of order. In a world in which war remains a constant factor, injustice is bound to be rampant also; for one injustice corrected by force will only be succeeded by another injustice on the opposite side. The establishment of the Rule of Law is therefore not simply in the interest of the Haves. It is still more in the interest of the Have-nots. The most important group of Have-nots in the world at the present time is of course not that of the European peoples defeated in the last war, but

[1] On this subject, see *World Minerals and World Politics*, by C. K. Leith, New York, 1931, and two articles by Sir Thomas Holland, his Presidential Address to the British Association in 1929, reprinted by the Carnegie Endowment (International Conciliation Pamphlets, No. 266, price 5 cents), and in the *Journal of the Royal Society of Arts*, 14 February, 1930. Details are also to be found in the *Armaments Year-book*, published by the League of Nations.

that of the non-white peoples who have been exposed to the results of their weakness for the last four centuries.

The second answer is that the predominance of the democratic peoples in the world of to-day is neither wholly unjust nor wholly accidental. It is due, at least in very large part, to the fact that there is an inner connection between Freedom and Power. Power in the modern world is not brute force: neither is it mass obedience subject to 'leadership'. It is *organized intelligence*; that is to say, a product of the minds and wills of human beings. But to employ either the mind or the will effectively *freedom* is required—freedom not as a political right but as a quality in the soul—the modern world with its science, its inventions, its vast and elaborate organization has come into existence through the working of free minds and wills. It is therefore no accident, but according to the nature of things that the free peoples should have become the *powerful* peoples.

Will they realize the responsibilities that this power involves? Will they co-operate to discharge them more swiftly and more effectively? Will this co-operation serve as an inspiration and a rallying-point for the less mature, less freedom-loving, and less socially minded peoples? The future of the League of Nations is bound up with the answers to these questions.

CHAPTER IV

FRENCH FOREIGN POLICY

by

ETIENNE DENNERY

Professor at the Institut des Hautes Etudes Internationales, Paris.

i. *General Tendencies and Particular Anxieties.*

I THINK that the majority of French people would be greatly astonished if they were told that the external policy of France is stable and continuous. One of the essential characteristics of the Frenchman is always to criticize the politics of his Government, even when he is most devoted to it and votes regularly for it. The Frenchman thinks particularly of the instability of his Government, and logically feels that a regularly established external policy cannot be made by chiefs, whose political life seems to him ephemeral. The usual reproach of foreign opinion is, on the contrary, that French foreign policy is immutable. Such was the expression of Signor Mussolini when he formerly criticized the cloyed, satisfied, and conservative nations. Such also is the expression of the Germans when they so often oppose the dynamic conceptions of their people to the static conceptions of ours.

These two ideas are not necessarily contradictory, but neither corresponds exactly to reality. In France the Ministries are thrown down more often than the leaves fall from the trees. But it should first be noticed that the men who lead foreign politics change less than is generally thought. For example, there is no important country in the world where a man has since 1914 occupied for a longer period the position of Minister of Foreign Affairs than has Aristide Briand in France. And the policies of the Ministers who replaced him before or after his death (with perhaps only one exception which confirms the rule, in 1923) have not been very different from his own. Yet I do not think either that it is possible to say that French politics are conservative. If our Ministers continue to be directed by the same principles, these principles are far from being accomplished.

The continuity of aim in French policy is determined by the persistent reality of facts and the very principles of the French mind. The facts, or rather the one fact that predominates all others is the question of environment. My statement is not meant to be in any way official, and I therefore prefer to be frank rather than prudent. The average Frenchman of to-day has no feeling of hatred towards Germany. Up to these latter years he has followed hopefully all the attempts to bring together France and Germany, and each time at the moment of the French elections the question of foreign politics has been of greater importance than that of home politics. The French people have voted for the parties that they thought most favourable to good relations with Germany. But the French mistrust their neighbour in the East. They suspect that the 60 millions of inhabitants in Germany are moved by a desire for revenge and expansion, and that if they do not actually desire war they at least have a passionate taste for everything military.

I do not want to flatter the Frenchman more than he deserves. Socially speaking, there is no doubt that he is not very internationalist. His traditional reputation of not knowing geography is, undoubtedly, well earned.

Foreigners travelling in France often complain, and not without reason, that it is difficult to penetrate into French circles, and that they frequently meet with a certain reserve. From an economic point of view the Frenchman, as a native of the European country which is the most self-supporting, is not very internationalist either. But intellectually he is an internationalist, and very profoundly so, as a consequence of his being a rationalist. All foreigners are astonished at the formulae, often abstract, but general, in which French statesmen try to hide their direction of foreign politics, formulae which could be applied to the mass of men and nations, to the individual such as came out of the French Revolution.

The Frenchman interests himself in the world, but he finds that a precise and terrible reality must occupy him at his very door. He realizes that there are on the globe to-day events infinitely more profound and more important than those traditional Franco-Germanic relations: Asiatic expansion, consequences of the new economic situation as regards international relations, and many other questions. But he always returns to the question of Germany.

It is the conflict between general tendencies and particular anxieties which dominates French policy and gives it a permanent nature.

ii. *Franco-German Relations.*

Does a Franco-German problem actually exist? I think if one puts aside questions of a psychological order it is easily seen that there is, literally speaking, no direct Franco-German problem at all.

First, from an economic point of view, there are fewer reasons for conflict between France and Germany than there would be between other large countries which have been for very many years on very friendly political terms. Whilst the economic systems of the two countries are not entirely complementary, they do nevertheless make economic co-operation possible. Germany needs agricultural products, whilst France is an important exporter. Germany has a surplus of coal and needs iron, France has an excess of iron ore and needs coal. France exports, above all, luxury goods; Germany manufactured necessities, specialized goods, or tools for industrial equipment. In spite of political or psychological difficulties the flow of commerce between the two countries is important for each. In 1930 German products amounted to 13 per cent of French imports. French products to nearly 10 per cent of Germany's imports.

Since 1927, in their commercial and custom agreements, France and Germany have without doubt often shown more consideration to one another than they have exercised in their negotiations with other countries. Between 1927 and 1932 France granted more than once to Germany customs concessions which were only granted much later to neighbouring countries. In 1934 the German currency restrictions and the new French quotas made the commercial relations between the two countries more difficult, but did nothing better for their commercial relations with other countries. From the point of view of production there are no two countries where the agreements between industrialists have been more numerous than between France and Germany since 1926.

The economic situation, then, is no reason for tension, but rather an inducement to collaboration between the two countries. So much so that since the summer of 1932 and the Lausanne Conference the French Government has practically agreed (although conditionally) to renounce almost entirely her debt for Reparations.

Even from a territorial point of view the frontier between France and Germany does not in reality give rise to any immediate problems. There is no official discussion about Alsace and Lorraine. There remains only the question of the Saar, but from the French point of view, and more especially from the Government's point of view, the question of the Saar is not a Franco-German question, but rather a question for the League of Nations. It is a question that must be settled automatically by the League of Nations, according to the provisions foreseen by the Treaties.

The question of the mines must be gone into after the assignment of the territory. The mines, of which the production is to-day equivalent to about a quarter of the French production of coal, have been ceded to France absolutely by the Peace Treaty, as a compensation for the destruction by the Germans of her mines in the North of France. But there again the procedure was provided for by the Treaty. France's rights to the mines situated in that territory were to be bought in a block by Germany at a price payable in gold. The Treaty provided that this price should be determined by three experts voting by majority: one to be named by Germany, one by France, and one by the League of Nations.

The policy of the French Government has been to ensure the liberty, secrecy, and the sincerity of the vote. M. Barthou worked actively for this end. It was decided that for the period prior to the plebiscite a superior Court of plebiscite would be formed, composed exclusively of native citizens of disinterested countries and of eight private Courts.

It was decided that the regular and county police force could be reinforced and completed with the aid of neutral elements. The Plebiscite Court is to be maintained in the Saar for a year after the definitive regime comes into power, to be used as a Court of Appeal for any inhabitants who wish to complain of retaliation or of any discrimination shown by the new authorities. France and Germany, moreover, bound themselves by a solemn declaration to abstain from all reprisals or any discriminatory measures. In short, both of them solemnly agreed to abstain from all direct or indirect pressure that could affect the liberty or sincerity of the vote. In a recent speech Herr Hitler declared that the only territorial question directly separating France and Germany was the question of the Saar.

The question of the Franco-German relations can in reality be set forth in two ways: on one side the question of psychology, and on the other the question of the German and European relations.

Psychologically, there is no doubt that the tension might come from traditional rancour and reciprocal sentiments of insecurity. But to-day on the French side the tension arises mainly, as I have already said, from feelings of distrust. The Frenchman fully realizes the present state of ferment in Germany. Nobody can hide from him the display of uniforms and the noisy manifestations, directed more often than not against a foreign country, which are not always a direct call for war but which might create an explosion at any moment. He knows that the organization of the German associations was based on the Army, and that even the workmen are subject to military organization. He hears people talking of all this literature which, from the school books up to those of the Chancellor himself, is impregnated with hatred towards France. He knows that the principles of the men actually ruling Germany are, to-day at least, those of biological and racial superiority. And does not all this amount to the official affirmation of the superiority of force over rights universally accepted in the Western countries?

The Frenchman realizes the dangers of this potential psychology of war when once the equality of material armaments is accomplished. In any case, he is persuaded that if the question of the western frontier of Germany is not actually raised officially, it will be raised the day that German expansion is accomplished in the south and east, towards Austria, Czechoslovakia, Poland, or Russia.

These preoccupations of the French people, I think, are understood by many people outside France, or even Europe, but in France they are *very strongly* felt. That is why France more than ever puts in the forefront of her policy the organization of her security, and why her attitude regarding the question of disarmament may seem to some people not sufficiently conciliating.

iii. *Disarmament.*

To say that the policy of France has been an impediment to disarmament is inexact. France has, since 1920, reduced in a very appreciable way her effective army. She had reduced by two-thirds the length of her military service. Recently, again in a year, from June 1932 to June 1933, she reduced by two and a half millions her credits for National defence. Some accuse the French Governments of having made Paragraph I of Article 8 of the Covenant too cheap. This Article says: 'The members of the League recognize that the maintenance of peace requires the reduction of national armaments to the lowest point consistent with national safety and the enforcement by common action of international obligations.' A minimum of armaments compatible with her national security is the aim which has been upheld with great continuity by all successive French Governments. Barthou's action on this point was consistent with that of Paul Boncour, Herriot, and Tardieu.

To say that there have been no differences with regard to the minimum of armaments compatible with security would be inexact. But the differences have never been as great as one might think.

M. Paul Boncour in October 1933 agreed to the realization of equality in a system of security—a principle already admitted in December 1932. But he insisted on the fact that the rights of equality were only to be realized after a trial period of four years. The political atmosphere of Europe had to be purified before any substantial reduction of armaments could even be considered; and, above all, the system of control of all armaments had to be one that would be carried out loyally, reciprocally, promptly, automatically, and periodically. The idea of control was again specified by M. Paul Boncour in his Note of 1 January, 1934, handed to Berlin by the French Ambassador. According to this Note it was impossible not to take into some account the para-military organizations, who often receive what is in effect a military education, the outlines being often supplied by the Reichwehr. Their equipment can be compared to that of the militia. They are grouped in companies, squadrons, and regiments, as the Reichwehr which is made up of motor sections, of cavalry units, and engineers. The Note protested against the realization of equality of rights through an immediate increase of German armaments and army force, concomitant with a decrease of French armaments. It only agreed to provide, in the final stage towards the realization of equality, progressive licence to Germany for authorized defence material.

Most of these propositions, the automatic control of armaments, the importance of counting to some extent the para-military formations, are to be found in M. Barthou's Note, handed to London on 17 March, 1934, in reply to the British propositions. But in the latter Note the protest against authorized rearmament of Germany was more energetic.

Moreover, M. Barthou subordinated disarmament to security still more clearly than had M. Paul Boncour. He rejected the British memorandum proposing a consultation between the Powers in case of the violation of one of the Conventions for disarmament, as he esteemed that guarantee to be insufficient. Lastly, in a short Note handed to London a month later, he denounced with vigour the heavy increase (an increase of 352 millions of marks) in the Reich budget.

I am attempting to explain, not to judge, French policy, and it seems to me that the stiffer attitude taken up by M. Barthou is above all explained by the evolution of French opinion.

French public opinion was very vividly impressed by the events of October 1933, by the sudden departure of Germany from the Disarmament Conference, and especially from the League of Nations. At that time, seeing the emotion which really took hold of the man in the street in France, one was able to judge what the League of Nations really meant to the middle-class Frenchman.

Now a large part of French opinion has again been

surprised to see that, following this outburst, the Governments of countries, Members of the League of Nations, continue their negotiations as in the past, with a more conciliatory spirit than before. The French and English Notes of January 1934 showed on many points (notably on the duration or even the existence of the trial period) an attitude more favourable to Germany than the declarations of October 1933. The man in the street in France, as in most countries, is generally a pacifist but not always a diplomat. He did not understand the attitude of his chiefs. The Parisian agitations of 6 February, 1934, were due almost solely to home political reasons. But I am not so sure that, at the bottom of it all, those feelings of uneasiness about foreign relations did not play their part.

Finally, M. Barthou, at the sessions of the General Disarmament Commission held at the end of May and at the beginning of June 1934, reiterated the idea that any limitation, any reduction of armaments, necessarily calls for a reinforcement of security. On 11 June he secured the approval of the General Disarmament Commission for the creation of a Security Committee and of a Control Committee. The Security problem again is assigned a prominent place, not only by France but by the General Disarmament Commission.

iv. *Security*.

I would like to recall very briefly the stages of the search for security made by France since the war, for M. Barthou's policy showed on this point such continuity with that of his predecessors that it is impossible to understand it if we detach it from past history.

The Peace treaties have not given to France the organized

security which it has been seeking ever since the war. France, however, thought it *had* acquired security when to the Treaty of Versailles was annexed an Assistance Treaty between the United States, England, and France. But the United States refused to ratify the Treaty. England, seeing the refusal of the Americans, no longer agreed to participate. Since then England has hesitated between participation in and abstention from the various schemes for security proposed by France.

There remained on the morrow of Peace Treaties, as the only system of security, the Covenant of the League of Nations. But the Covenant does not condemn all wars, and, moreover, the articles dealing with collective action and sanctions are subject to various interpretations by the signatories. At first, in 1920, it seemed as though they would never be carried out.

When the first arrangements agreed upon at Versailles for mutual assistance between England, France, and the United States fell through, France sought a more general plan. And this, of course, led eventually to the 1924 Protocol. France is faithful to the principle of mutual assistance, which really saved it during the war. The object of the Protocol was that of universal organization for security, according to fixed and automatic regulations. The definition of the aggressor was to be automatic; the application of sanctions by the signatories compulsory. This plan was admirably suited to French ideas. It was said of it that it would tend to transform the world into a French garden, with regular geometric perspectives!

But after some hesitation the Protocol was not adopted owing to the opposition from England. The French Government did not abandon the project of a Mutual

Assistance Pact, but as the general plan was not admitted it sought mutual assistance in a more modest frame, in a regional frame. A Treaty may gain in precision what it loses in generality, and Locarno (the phrase is, I believe, Aristide Briand's) is a fragment from the broken mirror that was the 1924 Protocol.

Locarno is the first real guarantee. It is England and Italy who guarantee the inviolability of the frontiers between Germany and Belgium, and between Germany and France, as well as the observance of the provisions of the Treaty concerning the demilitarized zone of the Rhine. One can say that Locarno has been the principal contribution brought by any document to European security. It is so still to-day.

It is certain that for France the value of Locarno still depends to-day to a large extent on her relations with the two guarantors—that is to say, with England and Italy. Security is not only a question of Treaties, but depends in the highest degree on relations with other countries; their sentiments towards one another give to the lines of the Treaty their real value.

The realization of a close French-English collaboration has, I think, been one of the aims proclaimed by all successive French Governments. The approval of this desire for a close understanding has been found so regularly in all the ministerial declarations of all Governments that its expression does not astonish anyone in France any more, and becomes something like a usual formula. There is no doubt the French Government did not always find itself of the same opinion as the British Government—notably on the relative importance of security and disarmament. But this desire for collaboration is actually stronger in France than it has ever been. The sentiment of fidelity as regards political liberty, liberty of conscience, and of thought in a Europe where these become more and more rare, creates a new bond. Of course many French people know to-day (it has so often been repeated to them) the reason why English people are hesitating to unite their fate with that of Europe. There are the interests and duties of the Empire; the fear of seeing themselves in a conflict; a shade of insular contempt also, it must be admitted, with regard to this European continent which manages its affairs so badly; a mutual incomprehension of methods that I can in no way illustrate to you better than by referring you to an extract from an article by Professor Zimmern in the *Contemporary Review* of June 1934. Professor Zimmern opposes the English and French conception of the League of Nations.

> 'For them [the French] the League, or any collective system, signifies a concentration of power against an aggressor State, whereas to us it represents something resembling our own decentralized Commonwealth, a group of States co-operating together, because they are animated by mutual good-will. Thus our motive in forming the League was to consolidate a condition of good-will which we assumed to exist amongst its members. But the motive of the French and most other European peoples (the Northern nations excepted) was to establish conditions of safety out of which good-will should ultimately emerge.'

But the Frenchman also thinks that geographically England is very near to Europe, that the fact of her being an island means little in view of the progress of aviation, and especially military aviation; that Great Britain will be in case of a general European conflict inevitably brought into it, and that if England were to take in advance a definite attitude the risks of being drawn into a clash would be infinitely less than the chances of avoiding it altogether.

As to the other guarantor, Italy, her relations with France have considerably improved since 1932. There is no doubt there remain still between the two countries more than one question that has not been finally solved: the status of the Italians in Tunis, the question of Colonial compensations to Italy (France having promised during the war certain colonial advantages, and Italy finding those offered to her insufficient), the difference of policies in the Balkans, France's friendship with Yugoslavia, and, lastly, the question of naval parity. But most of the dissensions over these subjects will be easily resolved the day that the moral understanding between the two peoples is complete. The French Press on the Left has given up for many years past its ironic tone regarding the Duce that so irritated the Italians. The Italian Press devotes itself more rarely to violent attacks against France, so frequent only two years ago. To-day the same opposition to the Ainschluss helps to bring together the two countries. The Pact of Four, even modified at France's initiative and brought back to the League of Nations, has never been so popular in France. It was with a conciliatory aim towards Italy that M. Daladier's Government agreed to sign it. The tension between France and Italy has become a collaboration with eclipses. But uncertainty is better than opposition. And the Franco-Italian relations have improved to such an extent that the French people sincerely hope for a continuation of this evolution.

Such are the relations between France and the two

countries who guarantee the Pact of Locarno. Locarno I regard as a most important contribution towards the organization of European Security. But Locarno has still many gaps.

The intervention of the guarantors is not as yet as automatic as the French Government would have liked it to have been; it is still too subject to the interpretation of parties. Besides, the French Government has never hidden its preference for a Mutual Assistance Pact, truly reciprocal; the reciprocity of services that can be rendered is a sure guarantee of the solidarity of treaties.

But, above all, Locarno only directly concerns Germany's frontiers with Belgium and France. Locarno does not assure any Security in Central and Eastern Europe. In this region the possibilities of a conflict originating are to-day great. A Treaty of Arbitration between Germany and Poland was signed as an annexe to the Treaty of Locarno, as was also a treaty between Germany and Czechoslovakia, but they are simply *Arbitration* Treaties. The only *Assistance* Treaties which have been signed besides the Pact of Locarno itself, are the Treaties between Poland and France, and between Czechoslovakia and France, which, moreover, reproduce partly the conventions signed between France and these two countries just after the war.

v. *Eastern and Central Europe.*

The French Government has always desired the organization of Security for Eastern and Central Europe. Here the problem is still more delicate than in Western Europe as the question of the revision of frontiers had, of course, been raised by a certain number of countries.

The French Governments have always upheld energetically the idea of a European territorial *status quo*. Without doubt there were mistakes over some details when the frontiers were determined at the Peace Conference. This can be as readily understood in France as in other countries. But the French believe that it is Utopian to think that a revision of frontiers can be carried out pacifically in Europe to-day, especially in Eastern and Central Europe, where all the Governments have affirmed that they are ready to defend with arms their territorial integrity.

Although faithful to the idea of the territorial *status quo*, I do not think it is possible to say, even concerning this question, that French policy is conservative. Hostile to the question of the revision of frontiers, it looks, however, towards another aim, towards minimising in Europe the whole idea of frontiers. If the frontiers are not to be modified, arrangements should be made to diminish the impediments they bring to the relations between various countries. Such was the meaning of the European Union proposals of Aristide Briand. When, owing to the disturbed state of mind in Europe, the idea of European Union had to be at least temporarily abandoned, the French Government again took up on a regional basis the idea which it had not succeeded in carrying through in a more general way; the proposal for a Danubian Economic Union made by M. Tardieu in 1931 extends M. Briand's idea. When, in 1933, the 'Little Entente' took a legal and economic character, the French Government was very pleased to see that the three nations belonging to it expressed the desire to see the other Danubian countries take part some day in this organization. The same year in Rome, in March and in May, so-called triangular agreements were concluded between Italy, Austria, and Hungary. Besides the guarantees of territorial independence and integrity that these nations granted to each other, they accorded reciprocally a series of Customs preferences. The States forming part of the 'Little Entente' upheld by France had already made known that they were disposed to a general accord on the principles announced by Italy, on condition that the 'Little Entente' would not abdicate, legally speaking, that France and eventually Germany would associate in the same way as Italy, and that on this occasion no question be asked regarding the revision of frontiers. Similarly, with regard to the Balkans, the signing of the Balkan Pact followed by closer relations between Yugoslavia and Bulgaria was received with undisguised satisfaction in Paris.

M. Barthou's visits to the capitals in Eastern Europe, Warsaw, Prague, Bucarest, and Belgrade were no departure from principles accepted by his predecessors. These journeys allowed France to test the ties of friendship with those peoples whose independence she has always upheld. The conversations were also related to the question of relations with Russia. France desires that Russia should in the future collaborate in this organization of Security in Eastern Europe.

Franco-Russian relations have so rapidly improved since 1932 that France and Russia's points of view concerning the organization of European Security are now very much the same. In 1931 it was still to Germany that the Soviets looked for their European help. They declared themselves openly against the Treaty of Versailles. The Bessarabian question turned them against Roumania, recollections of a trying war after the signing of the Peace Treaties made them hostile to Poland, and behind Poland and Roumania they felt there was France. But since 1931 more imminent dangers have made them forget old subjects of rancour. In the Far East there has been the expansion of Japan and Japanese threats against the Russian maritime provinces. In the West, Russia has witnessed the rise of Hitlerism and the Nazi conquest of power. There are also the German plans for colonization towards the East, the expression of which is found in the 'Chancellor's Memoirs', as well as in 'Hugenberg's Memorandum' in London. Russia knows that she needs guarantees on her Western frontier, as well as on that of the East. She is the more attached to Peace as her economic crisis and the elaboration of her second quinquennial plan both demand for her external tranquillity.

In this desire for Security, for a guarantee of her frontiers, it was quite natural that she should turn to France. In November 1932, therefore, a non-aggression Pact was signed between Russia and France; a Pact which is not isolated but which forms a part of a group of Pacts with which Russia during the last two or three years has been trying to surround herself. With the Slav countries of Central and Eastern Europe these Pacts have been rapidly concluded; the non-aggression Pact with Poland was concluded before even that with France.

On the question of European Security, the Russian and French Press are not at present very far apart. 'When we talk of a progressive bettering of our relations with other countries, we must evoke above all France,' Litvinoff said in January 1934. 'After the signature of the non-aggresssion Pact our relations with France have made rapid progress, owing to the absence of political opposition, and particularly our common desire to collaborate actively for the maintenance of peace in general.' With France, Poland, and the 'Little Entente' Russia has become anti-revisionist. 'The stipulations of Versailles are not perfect,' Stalin said recently. 'But an attempt to modify them would bring about a massacre, the first victims being workmen and peasants.' This idea corresponds to that of French opinion regarding revision. Again, recently at Geneva at a General Commission for Disarmament, the point of view regarding the question of Security upheld by M. Litvinoff was very near the views expressed in M. Barthou's speech.

This analogy of present views on the question of peace organization has brought the French Government to hope for Russia's collaboration in a Pact assuring security in Eastern Europe. France is actually trying hard to bring about the realization of this Eastern Pact.

This project has already been baptized by the name of 'Locarno of the East', but this does not quite correspond with the real situation. In Locarno, England and Italy guarantee their help without reciprocity to other countries: to France and Belgium in case of aggression from Germany; to Germany in case of aggression from France and Belgium. The Eastern Pact would, on the contrary, be strictly reciprocal between all its members. There would be no guarantor not benefiting from its assistance in case of conflict with one of its signatories. It would be, in a word, a Pact of Mutual Assistance, established, it would seem, on the model of Treaties envisaged in 1928 by the Assembly at Geneva.

England and Italy have already made it known that they approve of the creation of such a Pact, but the British Government made it very clear that England would not belong to it. The signatories of such a Pact could be

France, Belgium, Germany, Poland, Czechoslovakia, Russia and perhaps the Baltic States.

You must note that of all the signatories of such a Pact, France would be the one to benefit least from new and direct guarantees of security, as she already has with certain of these signatories Treaties which provide for Mutual Assistance in case of aggression. Germany, on the other hand, would receive guarantees which would be new.

Naturally, on certain points this Pact would have to be in harmony with the Pact of Locarno. If France, for instance, in order to uphold Russia (attacked by Germany and Poland) or Poland (attacked by Germany) had to intervene on the Rhine, she would have to obtain the authority of the guarantors of the Treaty of Locarno.

You have already been able to judge of the reception accorded to the proposals for an Eastern Pact. Two countries to-day seem to hesitate to become parties thereto —Germany and Poland.

To the system of Pacts of Mutual Assistance the German Press seems to oppose the system of bilateral Pacts, which it claims to prefer. The French Government shows that it does not ignore the advantages of bilateral Pacts, as it has already signed many. But France has always placed above these Pacts without sanctions, Pacts providing first of all the union of forces against an aggressor.

As to Poland, it has been said that coming after the signature of the German-Polish declaration renouncing recourse to force, this attitude shows clearly the abandonment of Poland's traditional attitude towards France. One must not exaggerate. There have been, and still are, misunderstandings between France and Poland. The Polish Government has reproached the French Government during the last few years for not keeping her sufficiently informed of her political projects. The signing of the Four-Power Pact by France undoubtedly did annoy Poland. Poland was afraid of not being treated on an equal footing, and, consequently, wanted to prove her independence. But, on the occasion of M. Barthou's visit, Marshal Pilsudski declared that the understanding between France and Poland remained the basis of Polish policy. I do not think that the desire to prove her independence of France and her reluctance to do anything which might displease Germany can explain Poland's hesitations with regard to the project of the Eastern Pact. There is no doubt that the Polish Government would prefer first of all the conclusion of a treaty which would confirm her territorial status, and definitely guarantee existing frontiers, as did the Pact of Locarno. Above all, Poland is afraid that the Eastern Pact would make of its soil in case of a conflict a passage for foreign armies, even if it happened to be allied armies. She has suffered already too much from this state of affairs in her past history.

It is difficult to say yet in what measure the project of the French Pact will be realized. Concerning France, it may seem at first sight that with such a Pact the risks of the engagement to which she would subscribe would be much greater than the advantages of the direct guarantees she would receive. Any conflict in the near future is much more likely to be in Eastern Europe than on the Western frontier of Germany. Some French newspapers have already pointed this out. But, in reality, the prospect of more durable peace in Eastern Europe seems to the French Government to be in itself an important guarantee.

French opinion is fully aware that in any case, with or

without a Pact, there is very little chance that a conflict that would overthrow Eastern Europe would not at the same time destroy Western Europe. It believes also that the promise to unite against the aggressor, while reducing the chances of a conflict, is an act of prudence, much more than an act of temerity.

These negotiations are only one more illustration of the fundamental conception which lies at the basis of all French efforts to organize Security. It has often been said that French policy in this direction is based on a pessimistic idea of humanity, since it seeks to enforce wisdom by the fear of sanctions rather than to rely upon reciprocal good will between the peoples. But the organization of Security itself supposes that those who consent to take part possess good will and a spirit of solidarity.

It has also been said that this Pact policy is highly abstract. It has gone through the same attacks and the same criticisms as the League of Nations. However, in the everyday reality this form of political action does seem to us in France to present very great advantages. It applies to terribly concrete and precise national clashes, but it denationalizes them to some extent. Willingly or unwillingly the French Governments have all worked for ten years to denationalize the Franco-German problem, seeking its solution in the most general form in the organization of Security and Mutual Assistance.

The principles which directed the actual policies of recent French Governments remain constant. But Europe is upset and anxious. French public opinion demands that its leaders bring to the organization of peace much firmness in planning and much energy in acting.

CHAPTER V

THE SOCIALIST VIEW OF PEACE

by

THE RT. HON. C. R. ATTLEE, M.P.

i. *Capitalism, Nationalism, and War.*

I WOULD preface my remarks by saying that Peace to the Socialist is not a mere negation, an absence of War. It is a positive condition of human society wherein there is a realization of the essential unity of mankind and of the common interests of the great majority of the world's population. Those interests which make for peace are in our view so much greater than the causes that make for war, and the bonds uniting us one to the other are so much stronger than the forces which tend to divide us that it is imperative that we should make them effective by every means in our power. We feel that we must go beyond the negation of 'No more War', and even beyond just Disarmament. Only by building up a world society can we ensure peace. An uneasy equilibrium of balanced forces in an armed world is only a truce.

Hobbes in his *Leviathan* expressed this truth very well when speaking of individuals. He said:

> 'Hereby it is manifest that during the time men live without a common Power to keep them all in awe, they are in that condition which is called War. . . . For War consisteth not in Battle only or the act of fighting but in a tract of time wherein the Will to contend by battle is sufficiently known: and therefore the notion of Time is to be considered in the nature of War as it is in the nature of weather. For as the Nature of Foul Weather

> lieth not in a shower or two of rain but in an inclination thereto of many days together so the nature of war consisteth not in the actual fighting but in the known disposition thereto during all the time there is no assurance to the contrary. All other time is Peace.'

Thus in our view during all the period of the balance of power in Europe there was no real Peace, but only an intermittent state of Warfare.

Let me now consider briefly the world position to-day. From a superficial view the post-war period seems to be marked mainly by a violent recrudescence of Nationalism. It is arguable that the doctrine of self-determination of nations preached as an ideal by President Wilson and others, but certainly adopted by the Allies in the Great War as a convenient weapon against the Central Powers, has let loose forces far beyond the expectation of the leaders in the war. The Balkanization of Europe, the arousing of Japan, China, India, and the East, and the exaggerated racial claims put forward by Nazis and Fascists may all be traced to this origin. But in our view, if we wish to explain the post-war period we must consider not merely political causes of unrest but economic conditions which provide the soil wherein political movements grow. Political Nationalism and Economic Nationalism go hand in hand. The two features of the world situation which would strike a hypothetical visitor from another planet would be these:

The first, Nations renouncing War as an instrument of Policy, repeatedly entering into solemn engagements of non-aggression and mutual assistance, and discussing disarmament, while at the same time busily arming to the teeth. The second, Governments on the one hand making elaborate plans for the relief of unemployment and for the mitigation of the worst rigours of poverty, while at the same time subsidizing the destruction of wealth in the form of food and raw materials. I think that these are the two paradoxes which would first strike the stranger. Later, of course, he would note the comparatively minor absurdities of all the nations endeavouring to sell commodities without buying anything in exchange, and of loyal members of the disarmament conference selling munitions of war to two of their fellow-members engaged in hostilities.

We Socialists connect these phenomena of starvation in the midst of plenty and preparation for War in a world pledged to Peace. We hold that there is something very wrong in a world that behaves thus. We believe that we understand the reason for it, and the remedies which we propose spring from our analysis of the position. Socialist writers have proved right in their predictions as to what would happen as the system of production for profit developed, and that gives us confidence in our analysis of the situation. It is not my purpose here to give you an account of Socialist theory, nor of what errors of over-simplification of a complex problem have been made in the past. Readers of Mr. G. D. H. Cole's *What Marx Really Meant* will have found there a very frank discussion. But it is, I think, undeniable that in many respects the Socialist analysis has been proved correct by the facts.

Briefly our analysis is that production for profit inevitably leads to a struggle for markets. It is of the essence of capitalism as we know it that it fails to distribute purchasing power among the masses of the workers in the country where it operates. The capitalist has to find a market for his production outside his own country. He exports goods as loans for the development of countries less industrially advanced than his own. The continuance of his system of production depends on finding ever fresh markets as the old ones become saturated, and sooner or later this brings him into rivalry with capitalists of other nations. In the struggle for markets and concessions the rival groups of interests enlist the support of their respective Governments, which is exerted by diplomacy and threats of war. Ultimately war breaks out.

It is a matter of history that there was a tremendous outburst of imperialism and a desperate struggle for markets throughout the second half of the last century, and that this struggle produced wars and war situations. The underlying cause of the Great War was commercial rivalries and the desire for markets and colonies. The war aims on both sides and the peace terms of the victors also very plainly revealed the predominant influence of economic and financial interests.

Those causes still operate. M. Theunis, one of the most eminent financiers and business men of Belgium, who certainly cannot be suspected of any Socialist leanings, was President of the League Economic Conference of 1927. Speaking in that capacity he said: 'Economic conflicts and the divergence of economic interests are perhaps the most serious and the most permanent of all the dangers which are likely to threaten the peace of the world. No machinery for the settlement of international disputes can be relied upon to maintain peace if the economic policies of the world so develop as to create not only deep divergencies but a sense of intolerable injury and injustice.'

Since that speech was delivered economic nationalism has increased the rivalries and injustices to which M. Theunis referred.

The situation has become particularly acute in the Far East. The Lytton Report makes it quite clear that the driving-force behind the Japanese invasion of Manchuria was the desire of Japanese big business to obtain a monopoly market and source of raw materials, particularly war materials. Of late it has become clear that the Japanese occupation of Manchuria in its turn is merely the first step to the subjugation of China, in order to put an end to the Open-Door policy and drive the Western Powers out of Eastern Asia. The very Powers that remained indifferent to the violation of the Covenant and the Nine-Power Treaty in Manchuria, because they had no 'interests' at stake, are showing considerable alarm at the Japanese threat to their trade and investment interests in China. That anxiety is being translated into a new race in armaments and a growing war atmosphere throughout the Far East.

In this connection may I draw your attention to the following statement by my friend Sir Arthur Salter in the *Manchester Guardian* of 23 June. In a discussion of the international economic importance of China, he writes:

> 'As we survey in retrospect the rapid rise and decline of our competitive capitalist system we cannot fail to be struck with the fact that its earlier period of prosperity was largely due to the constant opening of new markets. Without such new outlets the system becomes congested. The outlets are closing. Scarcely anywhere is there the possibility of a new one which is comparable to that of the increased purchasing power of four hundred millions whose needs, except the barest, are now unsatisfied.'

The same issue of the *Manchester Guardian* in an editorial comments on Sir Arthur's statement as follows:

> 'It must be obvious that the future of the capitalist system, as

it still exists, is closely bound up with the future of China. That system has depended and depends for its prosperity upon the constant opening of new markets. If it appears to be decaying, that is largely for the reason that of late new markets have not opened nearly fast enough to swallow the tremendous output of competing and developing industrial States.'

Those statements are interesting because they come from acute, independent, and liberal-minded believers in the present economic system, and are at the same time a perfect, if unconscious, illustration of the Socialist case.

When one reads statements such as these by thoughtful and experienced men, one realizes how far we have travelled from the rather naïve mid-Victorian optimism of Cobden, the theory of a world of individual capitalists peacefully competing in a world which had not only an Almighty God to keep it in order but a self-acting mechanism which converted individual self-interest into public welfare. The dream of international Free Trade in a world of bourgeois Liberalism had its counterpart in a policy of *laissez-faire* at home. Both eminently suited the interests of capitalist nations and capitalists, but necessarily failed to enlist the support of the exploited.

I do not wish to suggest that all wars are entirely due to economic causes, still less to contend that men are only moved by economic impulses. There have been wars of religion and wars of nationalism, but in all modern wars there is the economic motive. It is a tribute to human nature that it has been found necessary to represent the causes of war as lying in the region of the ideal, and not the material. Patriotism, Religion, Freedom, and Justice must be inscribed on the banners and on the War Memorials.

Modern States are controlled by capitalists, except in

Russia. But they are enlightened capitalists in so far as they realize the need for idealism in the world. Great Britain as the earliest of the great capitalist Powers led the way in this. Our capitalists were generally able to persuade the majority of the nation that when we went to war we did it from the most altruistic motives, and that acquisitions of territory were in the earlier period to bring the blessings of Christianity to the heathen, and in a more sceptical age to introduce Law and Order in place of barbarous anarchy.

It is suggested by some that what is needed is a patriotic reformation that would civilize patriotism. If, say they, we could get away from the extremes of nationalism we might have a peaceful capitalist cosmopolitan world. But we must realize that the Power-Politics of the nineteenth and twentieth centuries grew up alongside of capitalism. It is the capitalists who have used nationalism for their own purposes, and who are its strongest supporters. We cannot afford to deal with the theoretical possibilities of capitalist economics. We must face the hard fact that nationalism and capitalism stepped onto the stage of history hand in hand, and have kept company ever since. In their youth both were generous and liberating movements. The rise of the middle class was accompanied by the shaking off of any number of feudal, aristocratic, and dynastic fetters on human development, and resulted in a tremendous release and growth of the power of production and a rise in the standards of human welfare. At least in England, where the advantage was obvious, capitalism believed in free trade and world peace, although it did not include in the latter a series of Colonial wars. Cobden and Bright thought that commerce was going to draw the nations together and eliminate war, just as Mazzini dreamed that nationalism would not only throw off the yoke of the rotting reactionary régimes throughout Europe but lead to a union of free nations. But as foreign trade gave place to foreign investment, capitalism became increasingly monopolistic in outlook. A man may learn to tolerate business rivals, and may even dimly grasp that trade breeds trade, and is not to be thought of in terms of war to the knife. But when a company has built a railway or opened a mine there is not room for anyone else to do the same, and in placing contracts and securing 'law and order' to work these investments the tendency is to deal with the whole matter on a nationalist and monopoly basis.

Nationalism, too, changed its character with advancing years. The late Israel Zangwill once said that 'imperialism supervenes on nationalism like a moustache on the lip of puberty'. We have all seen that happen.

In short, capitalism as it exists, not as it theoretically might be, lives by nationalism, and in its turn keeps nationalism alive. The champions of private enterprise are also the upholders of national sovereignty. Patriotism has become the last refuge of the profiteer. We have seen this on a vast scale in Italy and in Germany, where the connection between big business and the violent nationalist movements that seized power is notorious. In Japan the same process has been at work. Even in Great Britain we have a Conservative Government which upholds the interests of big business, and at the same time has embarked on an arms race and is reverting to international anarchy. It calls itself 'National', and declares that party politics are dead, which is its mild and gentlemanly way of asserting the Fascist claim to a monopoly of government and treating political opponents as outside the pale of the nation.

I am not suggesting that there are any wicked people called capitalists who are deliberately planning war, or even consciously desire war. The evil lies much deeper than that. The drive to war is the result of the working out of blind forces, of a multitude of petty interests each concerned with its own private good, and all jostling each other and following the line of least resistance. The late Bonar Law once defined war as the failure of human wisdom. The war system is simply international anarchy, which itself is merely one aspect of the anarchy of capitalism. The whole trouble about the capitalist system is that it is not a system at all, but the absence of all system. The drift toward war is the absence of a drive toward peace. Let me illustrate again what I mean by quoting from a man who is not a Socialist, and who has had a perhaps unique experience of gaining insight into the actual working of the economic system of to-day. I refer to Sir Arthur Salter, who, as he keeps insisting himself, is not a professional economist, but who has gained his knowledge of economics first as a British Civil Servant, then during the war, then on the Reparations Commission as an inter-Allied Civil Servant, and finally, as Director of the Economic and Financial Section of the League Secretariat as an international Civil Servant. Writing in his book *Recovery*, Sir Arthur says:

> 'To imagine that at the centre of the intricate web of man's economic activities stand a few constructive and controlling intelligences is to entertain a romantic illusion. There are no such Olympians. The intricate system of finance has been built and is operated by thousands of men, of keen but limited vision, each working within the limits of his own special sphere. For the most part the system has constructed itself from the separate work of specialists who built into the environment they found

about them. Those who have made and worked this system have normally not understood it as a whole; those who have come nearest to understanding it, the academic economists, have not made it and do not direct it. The economic and financial structure under which we have grown up was indeed, at the moment of its greatest perfection, more like one of the marvellously intricate structures built by the instincts of beavers or ants than the deliberately designed and rational works of man.'

In the course of a series of three lectures at Cambridge University last year, Sir Arthur gave an illustration drawn from real life of the way in which capitalist economics work in practice:

'The present tariffs are scarcely ever the expression of what in any reasonable sense can be called either national or any kind of policy. It is rarely possible to discover in the mind of any Government a general conception of economic policy for their country of which their detailed tariffs are the logical development. Ideas of improving the balance of trade, or of securing self-sufficiency, or of making the foreigner pay, float about, but they operate, not to determine the character and proportions of the actual tariff system, but merely as arguments and forces to secure the acceptance of tariffs. The tariffs themselves are selected, and their height determined, in most cases as the net result of organized competitive pressures. For some years at Geneva, during the tariff negotiations there, I tried to discover what were the real springs of action, what were really the dominant anxieties and preoccupations in the minds of Ministers of Commerce and their chief officials when they were defending existing tariffs or proposing changes. In nearly every case, when it was possible to penetrate behind the words to the thoughts of the persons concerned, it was not a conception, whether wise or unwise, of general economic national policy, but a calculation of prospective political forces that was determining action. Tariffs as we have them now in the world have not been planned but improvised, and improvised under organized pressure.'

I should certainly be prepared to confirm this analysis after having seen the MacDonald Government at work at Westminster during the last three years. As an example, just before the House rose the Government introduced two subsidies, one to help the home producer of meat, the other to assist the shipping industry, which carries the rival imported supplies.

In other words, tariffs are what we in England call a ramp, and what in the States they call a racket. The same thing applies to armaments. You know that the Covenant pledges the members of the League to put an end to the evils of private manufacture of arms. Those of you who have read the Report of the League Chaco Commission, or any of the various books or pamphlets on the subject, will have some idea of the way in which the hunt for profits works out in the field of armaments. This is a clear case of the way the theory works out in practice, that if every man pursues his private profit the result will be the public good. May I in this connection draw your attention to a little book called *The Economics of Re-Armament*, by Paul Einzig. The author expressly states that he is not a Socialist, but believes in something that we may called 'Planned Capitalism', although from the Socialist point of view that phrase is a contradiction in terms. Mr. Einzig tells us that—

'It is beyond question that, as far as Germany is concerned, the economic improvement since the advent of the National-Socialist régime was largely the result of feverish rearmament. The spectacular reduction in German unemployment during

1933 was due in a high degree to the increase in the Government's armament expenditure. . . . Economic recovery in Japan was also connected with increased armament expenditure and with the rise in prices caused thereby. Apart from these two examples, however, few, if any, of the capitalist countries actually increased their armaments in 1933. Several of them have every intention of doing so. President Roosevelt's programme of public expenditure for providing employment includes the construction of a number of new battleships which, in the ordinary course of events, would not have been constructed, or at any rate not in the immediate future. There is also every likelihood of an increase in air defence expenditure in Great Britain. Should the disarmament negotiations definitely fail, France will most certainly increase her military expenditure and other countries will follow her lead. All this is bound to provide a certain amount of employment, and it is therefore conceivable that what was true in 1933 only in the isolated cases of Japan and Germany may become true in 1934 concerning a larger number of countries . . .

'Notwithstanding this, it is an exaggeration to attribute the trade revival in 1933 exclusively to rearmament.'

Need I remind you that since this was written the Vinson Bill has been passed in the United States for an enormous naval building programme to be put in hand immediately, with ambitious air plans in the background, and that Great Britain has entered with a will into the race in armaments, with particular attention to the air?

Einzig goes on to comment on the facts he has brought out. He says:

'Until comparatively recently it was considered the supreme task of mankind, in the sphere of economics, to produce more so as to be able to improve the standard of living of consumers. Any raw material and labour spent on armament was considered a dead loss because it reduced the volume of goods available for consumption. At present, however, thanks to scientific inventions and the application of more efficient methods of production, the problem is no longer the same. It is no longer production that has to make desperate efforts to keep up with consumption; it is consumption that is lagging far behind productive capacity, and even behind actual production. In such circumstances disarmament means the reduction of the world's capacity and willingness to consume, while rearmament means an increase of that capacity. . . . The question is whether there are no better ways of stimulating the demand for goods than through rearmament. Evidently there are many; in fact, it is difficult to imagine worse ways of stimulating demand. . . . There are innumerable tasks before every Government which are at present left unfulfilled merely on account of timidity as regards raising the requisite funds. To carry out the schemes which at present are considered to be beyond the bounds of practical politics would produce a demand infinitely more beneficial to trade than rearmament. Unfortunately, the money which is made available, by fair means or by foul, for armament expenditure is not forthcoming for such productive purposes. . . .

'In our absurd economic system war . . . is capable of bringing an economic depression to an end. . . . The economic arguments against rearmament and in favour of disarmament lack convincing force so long as production and distribution remain in their present haphazard state. Pacifism would find more fertile soil under a system of planned economy, when the consumers would have to bear the full burden of preparation for war, and when increased armament expenditure does not increase but reduce prosperity. The way towards true pacifism lies, therefore, through economic planning.'

What does all this mean? It means that when you get whole communities dominated by the doctrine that 'business is business', which is the modern way of saying 'All's fair in love and war', war in the end is the result. It is not that anyone wants war. But nations put defence above peace, and by defence they mean readiness to use armed force to protect their own view of their rights and interests. You all know the phrase 'Protection of British'—or, as the case may be, American, or Japanese—'lives and property', and you know in practice it means what has become known as 'the gunboat policy', or, as I believe is more familiar in the States, the 'policy of landing marines'. This is all right so long as the State that does the protecting enjoys an overwhelming military superiority over what I may call the 'protectee'—although with the spread of nationalism and such new ideas as the boycott, the system does not work very well even then. But the danger is that the 'protectee' may be able to bring some rival protectors into the field, or that two States of approximately equal strength may differ as to the way to protect their competing interests—such interests being almost invariably private economic and financial interests.

For the arms racket and the tariffs racket and the scramble for markets racket are all part of the general capitalist racket which proceeds under the noble motto 'Business is Business'. Capitalism, as it recovers from the shock of the World War and begins to emerge from its latest and worst slump, is feverishly concentrating on war preparation as the best way to make profits, and to produce the kind of political atmosphere in which it can survive and feel at home. Big business, when faced with the certainty of more or less rapid extinction through the advance of Socialism in a world that is democratic and where peace is secure, prefers to take its chance of survival through Fascism and the risk of war.

I hope that I have said enough to show what we Socialists

mean when we say that war is the result of the anarchy of capitalism. That anarchy is both economic and international. Socialists believe that the only way to strike at the roots of war is to attack simultaneously the twin and connected evils of capitalism and nationalism. For we are just as hostile to international anarchy as to economic anarchy—in fact, the two things in our eyes are but different aspects of the same root evil. It may be admitted that theoretically it would be possible to preserve Peace in a world of capitalist States, and to have war between rival sovereign Socialist national States. But in actual fact Socialism and Internationalism are inseparable. 'Workers of the World Unite' was the first Socialist slogan, and internationalism has always been part of the Socialists' living faith. It must be admitted that Socialists failed to stop war in 1914. But at least Socialists in all belligerent countries during and since the war have stood for a saner international outlook than any other political parties. On the peace settlement, reparations, the evacuation of the Rhineland, disarmament, international security, on all the problems that have vexed the world since the war Socialist parties have managed to keep together and to work out common solutions which time has proved to be sound. I think that the two British Labour Governments, weak as they were, and the various Socialist or semi-Socialist Governments on the Continent have shown that we know how to translate our international faith into practical action for organizing peace.

I should myself be prepared to admit that Socialists both before and after the war devoted too little attention to working out the implications in the international field of their Socialist creed. I think that they have too often been content to follow Liberal instead of Socialist solutions. But that has been largely due to their political weakness.

ii. *Weaknesses of the League System.*

I have tried to show you what is the Socialist view of the forces at work in the world to-day. I have explained why I believe that on the one hand Capitalism and Imperialism, and on the other hand Socialism and Internationalism, are inseparable. I now come to how Socialism proposes to tackle the job of putting the world right.

When we address ourselves to this task, we find ourselves faced by two big facts:

(*a*) In the first place the capitalism that is limping out of the last and worst slump is a changed capitalism. The statistics published by the League Economic Intelligence Service show that whereas production is picking up, international trade remains at little more than a third of what it was in 1929. That is because States are developing their home markets, which means regulating economic life by Government intervention of various kinds, such as tariffs, quotas, subsidies, currency manipulation, etc. Competitive private enterprise has so completely broken down that the world has been forced into a series of crude, haphazard, and improvised experiments in national planning and 'directed economy'.

As Sir Arthur Salter puts it in his book *Recovery*:

> 'The clue to the maze of intricate problems through which we have to find our way is to be found in the fact that we are now in a stage intermediate between these two systems—the self-regulating, automatic system in which supply adjusted itself to demand under the stimulus of competitive gain, with the guidance of changing prices, and the system under which future

needs are estimated, production is directed and controlled, and distribution is organized. . . . We have, in our present intermediate position between these two systems, lost many of the advantages of both and failed to obtain the full benefits of either. Without securing the advantages of deliberate planning, we have enough official control and private privilege and monopoly to impede the automatic adjustments, and to restrict the benefits of competition to the consumer. From this worst of both worlds we must certainly escape.'

Let us be clear what we mean by planning. Planning has become a blessed word used by all and sundry. Many Conservatives talk of planning, but that does not mean that they agree with us. I would put the difference between us in this way.

The Conservative would place society on the lines of the old English village. There would be a large mansion for the squire, a smaller one for the parson, a good-sized house for the retired colonel who protects the village from foxes and hares, and a row of small cottages for the workers.

In our new world everyone has an adequate dwelling, but the only big buildings are those devoted to the common needs of the community, such as schools, libraries, and public baths.

In short, our planning is for an equalitarian world. Socialists do not believe that the attempts to blend private profit-making with public control can be other than a temporary compromise. We consider that the world has definitely passed away from the individualist conception of business, and is inevitably tending towards a planned economy. This planned economy may be either on Socialist or Fascist lines. The latter carries within it the seeds of conflict and dissolution. The totalitarian State is really the political expression of big business. The State as the controller of the economic life of a nation takes the place of the old capitalist anarchy. The process is comparable to the supersession of a number of small businesses by a combine. The State becomes, as it were, a kind of holding corporation directing the general policy of a number of businesses of different kinds. The Trust did not bring industrial peace except where it became international. The mid-Victorian competition of individual businesses against the individual businesses of other nations is replaced by the competition of organized national trusts, just as in the sphere of war the frontier bickerings of border lords was replaced by war carried on by organized national armies. The result was not peace but intensified warfare.

As we see it, the totalitarian Fascist State, wherein all the activities of a nation are organized for competition, must necessarily be militarist. The resulting war will be worse than 1914.

It is therefore essential that the national planning in which we believe should be supplemented by world planning. But planning for what? Planning in the interests of the peoples of the world, not of the rulers, political or economic.

We Socialists recognize that there are to-day capitalist and proletarian countries. Debtor and creditor nations. Exploiters and exploited. We must recognize that we cannot build up a new world on the assumption that there are classes among the nations, some of which are entitled to a higher standard of life than others. We have to apply our democratic faith in equality beyond the bounds of our own country. Peace must be based on justice. There are many who we think fail to realize the impossibility of stabilizing a fundamentally unjust state of affairs. This was the error which has brought the world into its present condition, i.e. the attempt to build a new world on a basis of injustice.

(*b*) The second big fact is the League of Nations. The work of Socialist thinkers, e.g. G. Lowes Dickinson, H. N. Brailsford, Leonard Woolf, had a good deal to do with the conception of the League; the insistent demand of the Socialist parties helped to bring the League into existence; and Socialists have been the strongest supporters of the League ever since. But from the outset part of the Socialist movement has been critical of the League, and in the last three years that critical attitude had spread. We feel that the Covenant is too deferential to sovereignty, and that the League has suffered increasingly from that fundamental vice. Its organization is too particularist, too much hampered by unanimity. Governments and nothing but Governments are in a position to take decisions, or even to make their voices authoritatively heard (I make a partial exception for the International Labour Organization). The League was built on the assumptions that economic questions would continue to be primarily a matter of private concern, that the existing social order would not be seriously challenged, and that capitalist democracy would continue to be the prevailing system of government. The framers of the Covenant did not foresee the strains and stresses, the violent nationalisms and titanic social conflicts of this age of transition.

But at the same time we realize that the only alternative to the League to-day, however weak and imperfect the League may be, is a relapse into international anarchy. The League has developed into something different from what its founders intended, and if it is to survive it will no doubt continue to change. The Covenant was so framed as to allow plenty of room for adaptation and growth.

I can best illustrate the attitude of most Socialists to the League to-day by two analogies: the first is with the way the Republicans in the thirteen States that had broken loose from England regarded the Articles of Confederation in the seven years between 1776 and 1783. As you know, the framing of the Constitution of the United States was put through by people who had grown dissatisfied with the weakness and inadequacies of the loose and ramshackle Confederation. But supposing even that loose Confederation had been threatened by disruption—as in fact the Federal Union was subsequently threatened by the Civil War. Then even those who felt most keenly how unsatisfactory were the Articles of Confederation would have joined with the supporters of the Confederation to defeat the attempt at disruption.

My second analogy is with the Socialist attitude toward parliamentary democracy. Socialists are rightly critical of the insufficiency of capitalist democracy. Their avowed aim is to convert political democracy into economic democracy through public ownership of the means of production. But Socialists realize the necessity of defending parliamentary democracy against any attack from Fascists, and in doing so would be ready and eager to join forces with all who believe in democracy. At the same time, we believe that the best way of defending parliamentary democracy is to show that it is capable of delivering the goods, and by that I mean that Parliament must be used and reformed by the Socialists for Socialist ends. When we say that we believe in constitutional democracy that does not mean that we give up our desire to establish a Socialist Commonwealth, but that we propose to use and adapt our existing democratic institutions for that purpose.

In international relations a political instrument is necessary for the carrying out of Socialist policies, just as much as in domestic matters. At home the political instrument is Parliament; abroad it is the League of Nations. The fact that the instrument is weak and imperfect must be balanced against the fact that it is the only instrument in existence, and that if it collapsed Socialism would be as powerless to organize peace as it is powerless to establish itself in countries where parliamentary democracy has been abolished by Fascism. In the latter case, Socialism has been obliged to become an underground revolutionary movement, and if the collective peace system were destroyed the Socialist resistance to war would have to assume a purely revolutionary form.

iii. *Armaments and the Collective Peace System.*

So much for the Socialist view of the problem of peace. I now come to the policy by which we propose to seek peace and ensue it.

Our task as we see it is to develop the League of Nations as a real expression of the fact of world unity. The League must not be something superadded to national Governments, but the Government of the World. It must not be a mere instrument for settling disputes, but a controlling force in world economics which will deal with the causes of war.

In our view, as I have shown you, economic questions are the chief cause of war in the modern world, and the only radical way of dealing with that cause is to substitute the interests of all for the mass of competing interests. We desire to see in every country a planned economy co-ordinated into a world plan. We recognize the right of each nation to decide the general lines of its economic life. If a nation decides that it wants to remain agricultural, or desires to develop industries of this or that nature, it has a perfect right to do so, but that right is conditioned by its duty not to injure other nations. We cannot admit the right of a nation controlling the supply of some necessity holding the rest of the world to ransom any more than we admit the right of a landlord to hold up the community in right of his private ownership. We can no more admit the right of one nation to insist on another taking its goods than we can admit the right of the private employer to force his workers to buy from a company store.

We hold that owing to scientific development the world is to-day an economic unity, and therefore that the exchange of goods and services must be organized on a world scale. To-day in most countries trading is controlled to a greater or less degree by the State. By instruments such as tariffs, quotas, subsidies, and agreements political power controls the lines of economic activity. Trade between nations is becoming a matter of treaty regulation. Unfortunately the Governments themselves are the expressions of the power of the capitalists, and all trade is considered in terms of individual profit. When the State is controlled by Socialists as trustees for the masses, bargainings between countries will be carried on on the basis of use, not profit, but these bargainings should, we think, be co-ordinated.

Few people would deny that one of the central difficulties of the world to-day is the absence of a sound system of exchange and currency. We do not think that it is beyond the wit of man to devise an international system of exchange and an international currency whereby the peoples of the world would be enabled to exchange their goods and services on a just basis.

You may think these ideas far-fetched, but I may remind you that the Constitution of the International Labour Organization begins by saying that 'the League of Nations has for its object the establishment of universal peace, and such peace can be established only if it is based on social justice.' We hold that only by getting rid of production for private profit and by substituting production for the use of the community can social justice be attained.

The constitution of the I.L.O. explains that 'conditions of labour exist involving such injustice, hardship, and privation to large numbers of people as to produce unrest so great that the peace and harmony of the world are imperilled'. Few would deny that the European unrest of to-day is due in the main to the conditions which have arisen out of the anarchy of capitalism in decline.

Economic policy we look upon as an attack on the causes of war, as erecting the sub-structure of peace. But the greatest public interest is of course centred in the direct peace measures. The most obvious and alarming symptom of the parlous state of the world to-day is the new race in armaments. The only effective way to stop that race and to put an end to the growing danger of war it represents is, in the Labour view—and it is a view on which the Labour Party will act the moment it has the opportunity—to submit to all nations at Geneva a bold, far-reaching plan both for all-round disarmament and for the international organization of security. The plan should provide for:

(*a*) the abolition of all the arms forbidden to the Central

Powers by the 1919 Treaties, with a system of regular supervision and guarantees of execution;

(*b*) the limitation of Armaments' Budgets;

(*c*) the abolition of national air forces, the internationalization of civil aviation, and the creation of an international air police force;

(*d*) the nationalization and drastic international control of the manufacture of and trade in arms;

(*e*) a treaty of non-aggression, clarified by a definition of aggression, and linked with the sanctions system of the League; and

(*f*) machinery and obligations for settling all disputes by pacific means.

It would carry me beyond the scope of this lecture, and certainly beyond your patience, if I attempted to deal in detail with these proposals. But I would pause to stress the vital importance of real disarmament and of the creation of an international police force.

I am entirely sceptical as to the efficacy of reduction in armaments by itself. The existence of national armaments in my view inevitably leads to competitive arming. I do not believe that limitations either qualitative or quantitative, or even budgetary, can be effective. I often compare the state of the world to-day with the condition of England at the time of the Wars of the Roses. Then you had numerous great lords with their private armies, making their temporary alliances, and constantly on the look-out for impending dangers from their neighbours. All, it is true, bore fealty to the king, but the king was often too weak to assert himself. I do not think limitations on the thickness of armour, the length of spears or the number of retainers would have been effective to stop private warfare. It was only definitely stopped when the king became possessed of the master weapon—artillery. The Tudor possession of artillery stopped private war for ever in our country.

The master weapon to-day is the Air Force. I want the League to have the Master Weapon, and thus to render obsolete all national armaments other than those required for internal policing. Further, it is agreed that an international air force must be supplemented by the control of civil aviation. I want the entire main air services to be internationalized, with strict control over private flying. With this must go the internationalization of aircraft construction.

I will not develop this further, except to say that I believe it is the most imperative step to avert war, and, further, that it would be a beginning to the internationalization of all through transport. Modern warfare depends on transport. The world is brought together by transport. Internationalize the means of communication between country and country, and we shall have made a start in building up the new order. We shall have removed from private interest and from national interest one enormous service of vital importance.

If this cannot be done for the whole world, I should like to see a start made by a group of countries that really mean peace.

I will not go into the policy for restoring peace and meeting the menace of war that the Labour Party proposes with regard to Europe and the Far East—those who are interested will find it set out in the two pamphlets *Labour's Foreign Policy* and *For Socialism and Peace*.

But I must now take up the question of ways and means: the League, as I have pointed out, will be the indispensable instrument of Labour's foreign policy. But we must face the fact that the unanimity rule and the existence of violently Nationalist States within the League raise difficulties. Here again, however, the wise elasticity of the Covenant shows the way out, for under Article 21 it is possible for groups of States to conclude regional agreements to promote any of the purposes of the League, and as this Article was interpreted by the Assembly they may even for this purpose use the machinery of the League to prepare and hold regional conferences for this purpose. One of the cardinal points in Labour's foreign policy is that we are prepared to go ahead on the basis of regional agreements with States that are prepared to go the whole way with us, including pooled defence, joint social and economic policies, and common duties of citizenship on the issue of peace. In practice, the States that would be prepared to embark on such a policy would, I think, turn out to be the democratic and Socialist countries in Europe. We should hope to have the Soviet Union within this group, and the United States on terms of friendly co-operation with it, preferably through some form of association with the League.

The Labour Party attaches great importance to Russia's membership of the League, and if membership unhappily does not yet prove possible in the case of the United States, at least to getting that country into the closest possible working relationship with the League on the basis of some form of non-agression and consultative pact, and an undertaking not to oppose League sanctions, such as has been offered by President Roosevelt in connection with the Disarmament Conference. We have on several occasions strongly expressed the view that the only hope of avoiding war in the Far East is to make it clear beforehand that the

Soviet Union, the British Empire, and the United States will adopt a concerted attitude against aggression and the violation of Treaties on the basis of the Nine-Power Treaty, the Paris Pact, and the Covenant, as they have been interpreted in the unanimous Report of the League Assembly.

We believe that the Dominions in the British Commonwealth would gladly join as partners in a foreign policy of this sort. The various Imperial Conferences, and in particular the unofficial Conference at Toronto in September 1933, have brought out strikingly the fact that the only basis for a concerted attitude in international relations within the British Empire is the collective peace system. Policies of Imperial isolation, Empire free trade, or what not, provoke friction rather than enthusiasm, and lead to insistence by Dominions on their economic independence and right to neutrality. The only international policy which is big enough to evoke their joint enthusiasm and loyalty is the policy of organizing the world for peace and against aggression.

Finally, I come to a group of measures which although they are merely a logical development of Labour's previous attitude in these matters, are nevertheless new, and in the strict and literal sense revolutionary. I refer, first of all, to the statement by the Labour Party that it has turned its back once for all on the Balance of Power, and adopted instead as its grand objective the establishment of a Co-operative World Commonwealth. The Balance of Power we regard as a negative, competitive idea, based on the dogma of sovereignty and the belief that States are hostile entities, and war is sooner or later inevitable. When States pursue the Balance of Power game, either through isolation or alliances, they are drawn into a race in armaments, for each wishes to be stronger than his neighbours in the desire to tip the balance in his favour. That kind of game, with the play of economic rivalries behind it, foments the blind fears and suspicions of primitive nationalism and ends in war.

The establishment bit by bit and step by step of a World Commonwealth is a forward-looking, constructive, co-operative idea. It rejects the pessimism of those who believe in the dying social order, and therefore cannot imagine that mankind will ever rise above the present level of political organization into States and Empires. It dares to dream of a time when the world shall be organized as one society, and where there shall be neither class nor national nor racial barriers.

One Great Power in the world already is committed to the view that the division of the world into Sovereign States is an anachronism which has drowned the earth in blood and is doomed to disappear. I refer to the Union of Socialist Soviet Republics. But the Communist idea of how to achieve the aim of world union has so far been so remote from reality that it has exerted little influence on Soviet policy. Let us hope that in this respect matters will change with the entry of the Soviet Union into the League.

The Labour Party is the first major political party in a Great Power to base its foreign policy on this new conception of world unity. We believe with Graham Wallas that 'the consciousness of a common purpose in mankind, or even the acknowledgment that such a purpose is possible, would alter the face of world politics at once'. We have proclaimed that common purpose, and we are not without hope that others in other countries will follow our example. We propose to approach the League and all current problems, whether of defence, or economics, or social or international relations, in such a way as to make our short-term measures fit into our long-range policy of organizing the World Commonwealth.

iv. *Loyalty to the World Commonwealth: the Proposed Peace Act.*

Finally, we propose to take steps at home that will translate this idea of a World Commonwealth into immediate political realities. I refer to the Labour proposal for a Peace Act of Parliament, and to our proclamation of a world peace loyalty.

Under the collective peace system Great Britain with other nations has assumed obligations to submit disputes to pacific procedure, to refrain from the use of force as an instrument of national policy, and to take part in collective action to put an end to breaches of the peace. The Covenant is the foundation of this system; it has been extended by the Optional Clause, the General Act of Arbitration, and the Paris Pact. There are still gaps in the system, but *on paper* it is already fairly complete. It is almost impossible now for a State to resort to violence without breaking treaty obligations that render it liable to sanctions. But this is not much use if an aggressor State may nevertheless count on the enthusiastic support of its own people, and feel fairly confident that the rest of the community will not lift a finger in execution of their own treaty obligations to stop aggression. Somehow or other this paper system must be made a reality.

There are two ways in which the Labour Party proposes to do this: In the first place, we wish to put on the Statute

Book in the shape of a Peace Act of Parliament our national interpretation of our international obligations. We wish to make it part of the law of the land that our Government shall submit its disputes with another State to pacific procedure, and shall in no case resort to force as an instrument of national policy; even if it feels compelled to use force in self-defence it shall immediately report the whole matter to the League and abide on the basis of reciprocity with the League's injunctions for restoring peace. That would, in our view, add nothing to the obligations of the British Government, but it would mean that if the latter behaved disloyally to the collective system and tried to take the law into its own hands and to use force for its own ends, it would be violating not only treaties but the Constitution, and get itself into the most serious kind of trouble at home. We want foreign nations and our own public opinion to know exactly what we mean by our obligations under the collective peace system, and we want them to know further that we intend to live up to those obligations in all circumstances. For this purpose the Peace Act is also to include an Enabling Act, giving the Government the power to take part in any collective economic and financial action directed to cutting off relations with a peace-breaker.

In the view of the Labour Party, our country's membership of the League and signature of the Paris Pact have made us already citizens of a world community pledged to peace. We look upon the Covenant and the Paris Pact as the rudimentary constitution of a nascent World Commonwealth. We say that because the common purposes to which the membership of this community are pledged are strictly limited, our world duties of citizenship are also limited. But we contend that we already owe allegiance to a world peace loyalty that overrides the claims of the Government in war. Or, to put it in another way, we consider that the rights of the State over its citizens in war are subordinated to the way in which the Government of that State performs its duty to the World Community on the issue of the preservation of peace.

We have formulated the following three duties of world citizenship by which we consider we are already bound:

(1) Arbitration-insistence—this means the duty to insist that our Government should settle all its disputes by pacific means and in no case resort to force as an instrument of national policy;

(2) Sanctions-assistance—this means the duty to stand unflinchingly by the Government in meeting any risks or consequences that may ensue from performing its duty to take part in world-wide action to refuse supplies to a peace-breaker;

(3) War-resistance—this means the duty of demanding that any claim to use force in self-defence must be submitted to the test of arbitration or to the judgment of the international community, and to back up this demand by refusing to serve or to support in any way, either by military service, or work of national importance, or the payment of taxes, a Government that would be condemned by the League as an aggressor, or that got involved in war as a result of refusing arbitration.

These are revolutionary doctrines, and they may seem strange and disturbing to some. But to Socialists they are a direct consequence of our principles and our faith. We yield to none in our love of country. But to us it seems obvious that love of country must be fused with loyalty to civilization which can survive only through peace being made secure by world unity. We do not deny the claims of patriotism, but to a Socialist true patriotism blends with his faith in the international solidarity of the workers, with the belief that all men are brothers. Throughout mankind we have in a real and tangible sense become members one of another, and are being driven by hard facts to live according to the principle of 'work of each for weal of all'.

CHAPTER VI

'PACIFISM IS NOT ENOUGH'

by

SIR NORMAN ANGELL

IF the knowledge which results from our study of international affairs is to find expression in policy; if, in fact, it is to have any bearing upon policy, upon what men do about this problem of world disorder, then there are two distinct questions we must keep before us. One is to find the facts, the objective truth; what constitutional devices for the establishment of a world order would be fair and workable if applied. That is one side of the problem. But if our work is to be practical it has another side, which is much more difficult. And that is to discover why men don't see the objective truth, are not guided by the facts, do not apply methods that are both fair and workable if only they were tried.

The two problems are separate and distinct. It is no good pointing out the way of salvation, if for some reason you have not taken into account men won't see that it is the way. It is no good drawing accurate charts for these dangerous seas if the men who are to navigate the ship cannot or will not look at charts at all. You may recall the remark of Henri IV, I think it was, to the author of a plan for peace. 'It is perfect,' the King said. 'Perfect. I see no single flaw in it save one, namely, that no earthly prince would ever agree to it.'

It is naturally this aspect of the task which most impresses a man who for thirty years as a journalist, writer, publicist, has almost daily in one form or another wrestled with the public mind on this subject. Parenthetically it is for me a rather appalling reflection that it is now forty years since I was a student in Geneva. But that—for me—disturbing fact does enable me to take stock of two generations of internationalist and peace effort, to compare the post-war approach with the pre-war, and to examine, with at least some experience to go upon, a question which some who are now starting out on the road I took thirty years since, cannot too often ask. The question is this: Why is it that our peace efforts meet at some points with such small measure of success? Does the fault lie with us at all, with our methods of exposition, our approach? Does experience seem to reveal any outstanding defects in the technique of the peace movement?

Looking back, I think I see certain undoubted mistakes, and I would like briefly to list them.

i. *Men Desire Peace and Defence.*

The first mistake perhaps is this: Too often organized effort towards peace seems to proceed on the assumption that we shall solve our problem by intensifying the will to peace, intensifying the hatred of war. But the general will to peace exists. Everybody, broadly speaking, wants peace; and everybody goes to war. Our problem is to find out why the intention is frustrated. It is not a problem of evil intention, but of discovering the error which causes good intention to miscarry. Wars are not made by wicked men knowing themselves to be wrong, but by good men passionately convinced on both sides that they are right. When I am told that it is selfishness which makes men go to war,

I think of the youngsters who have gone singing to their deaths, as to a feast. Do you think that men can die gladly from avarice? Hardly, unless they are quite unusually certain of their mansions in the skies.

This does not mean, of course, that evil motives do not enter into the policies which lead to war. Evil motives enter into the building of cathedrals—contractors' profits, or what not. But you don't explain the presence of great cathedrals by the fact that builders wanted to make profits. Nor, do I think, can we explain great wars by the fact that armaments-makers are seeking profits. About as truly might we say that Americans drank bootleg liquor because Al Capone wanted to make money. Al Capone made money because Americans wanted to drink bootleg liquor. We are sometimes told that fifty armament-makers caused the Great War. But why did tens of millions, hundreds of millions of ordinary folk obey fifty men?

When I have put that question, which is the real question, on a hundred occasions has come the answer: 'Because the people are forced to.' Forced by whom? By fifty obese gentlemen sitting in board-rooms? And again and again to that question I have had the reply 'Yes', plainly revealing that those who make the reply have not considered the meaning of the words they use.

Fifty people cannot 'force' fifty millions, for obviously the force is on the side of the millions. The only force the fifty can use to oppress the people is force supplied by the people themselves: armies recruited from the people, paid for by the taxes furnished by the people; armed with equipment made in factories staffed by the people. We talk of Dictators ruling by force. But force can only enter after a long process of persuasion, of getting at human wills.

Sir Oswald Mosley cannot 'force' the British people to make him Dictator; nor can his financial backers. Whether he is ever able to use force or not, whether the capitalists who may be associated with him ever get any power through using him, all depends upon whether the British people or large sections of it will or will not respond to certain ideas, certain suggestions which he makes to them. The first process (and the last) must be persuasion; putting certain ideas into the minds, first of his Blackshirts, then perhaps of a Party, then of sections of the army perhaps, or of the Cabinet, or the public.

Unless the capitalists are successful in inducing the public or large sections of it to respond to the suggestions they make, they (the capitalists) will be utterly impotent, and force can never come into operation at all. The thing which constitutes the force is not the existence of fifty or five hundred men desiring to make money. It is the response of great sections of the public—hundreds of thousands, millions—to false and dangerous ideas. It is that public tendency which is the important thing, and the thing we ought to examine. Unless the public, the public who are not capitalists at all, respond to the capitalist suggestions, force can never come into question. For force can only act as the instrument of human wills. Guns don't get themselves made, nor pointed, nor fired.

It is the common people, the mass of the voters, who make possible the passing of those budgets out of which armament firms derive their profits. They continue to do this because while they want peace they also want something else, defence, and insist upon the adoption of a form of defence which makes effective defence impossible and war inevitable.

I think I would make a second point in criticism of the

usual technique of peace societies, that it puts peace in one watertight compartment as it were and defence in another, instead of treating the two as one, and presenting the orderly organization of the world first and last as the only means of achieving a really secure national defence.

Let us examine the point.

All nations proclaim sincerely enough their desire for peace. But all nations proclaim, by the policies which they follow, that there is one thing they place before peace, namely defence. We do so equally with the others. We repeat easily, and again sincerely enough, the phrase about the greatest interest of the British Empire being peace, but we do not quite believe it. Without quite realizing it we make certain reservations. We mean that we want peace so long as we are not attacked. If that were not so, if we really did put peace above everything else, we should not maintain our Army and Navy. If we literally put peace above everything else, we should say: 'Invasion by foreign armies, rule by foreign Governments are bad things, but they are not as bad as war, and we shall suffer them rather than provoke a state of war by resistance.' Neither we nor any other great State takes that position. If peoples as a whole took that position, Governments could not, year after year, go on taxing and burdening the peoples as they do for war preparation. People do not like the burdens that so-called 'defensive measures' involve, they are sincere, the world over, when they speak of their hatred of war, but they will accept these sacrifices rather than surrender the armed defence of the nation and suffer invasion or the dictation of foreign nations, or the placing of their national rights at the mercy of stronger Powers.

This decision to stand by the armed defence of the nation

is common to all Great States—to ourselves, to America, to Russia, to Italy, to France, to Germany. It is a decision proclaimed not only by the words and professions of statesmen, but by their acts and the policies that they pursue. All nations, however intense their desire for peace, have determined to defend themselves by arms.

That decision, to abide by armed defence, is the fact from which, I suggest, our presentation of the Peace case should start.

ii. *Old and New Ideas of Defence.*

There are, of course, two ways of using arms for defence, the old each for himself method, or the collective method, that of the League Covenant, of common resistance to the war-maker.

Now there are many of us, of whom I am one, who believe that it is best to leave force out of it altogether. I personally am of the opinion that the risks of unilateral disarmament are infinitely less than those of going on with armament competition; that there is a great case for simple non-resistance. If you believe that case, argue it, state it. I happen on one part of its economic side to have been arguing it all my life. I have tried to show that wealth can no longer be seized by a conqueror to his advantage, that in that sense it has become intangible. By all means make the case for taking boldly the position that the Lesser States—Switzerland, Denmark, Norway, Sweden, Finland, Holland, perhaps the most civilized nations in the world—are compelled to take without by that fact being any more insecure than the Great States, the position, namely, that they are not in the armaments race at all.

But while you are making that case do not refuse to answer

a question which large sections of the public put to us of the Peace Movement. That public says in effect:

> 'We cannot accept your view of the adequacy of non-resistance as a means of defence. We are determined to defend our country by arms. What we want you as the organized peace movement to tell us is, which of the two ways of using arms for defence, the old competitive way of everybody being stronger than anybody else, or that of the Collective system of the League, is less likely to lead to war; which is, from your point of view, the less dangerous. Don't tell us that you don't believe in arms at all, for that would not be answering the question which we put. Which is the less dangerous way of using power for defence, the nationalist way or the internationalist way?'

Now I suggest that we cannot dodge or evade that question if we profess to be dealing with realities at all. I suggest that there is only one way in which those of us who do not believe in force can answer it, and that is to say that though we firmly believe pure pacifism and non-resistance the quickest and effective road to peace. Of the two ways of using arms or power, the internationalist, as opposed to the nationalist, way of using them is by far the less dangerous. Both are dangerous, and we don't want either, but if arms there are to be, let them be an international rather than a national instrument.

Do we surrender any single pacifist non-resister conviction in making that reply? I suggest that we surrender none, are guilty of no compromise, and that indeed it is the only honest answer to that particular question which we can possibly make.

We have failed in our attempts to bring home to the big public the basic fallacy at the root of the Nationalist method of defence, for that fallacy is as much in evidence in the

London Press to-day in 1934 as it was in the years immediately preceding 1914.

A British Cabinet Minister, in a speech to a gathering of Manchester merchants a year or so before the outbreak of the last war, said this:

> 'Gentlemen, there is just one way in which you can make your country secure and have peace, and that is to be so much stronger than your prospective enemy that he won't dare to attack you. This, I submit, is a self-evident proposition which should be the guiding light of our national policy.'

That is to say: Here are two nations or two alliances likely to quarrel. How shall they both be secure, and both keep the peace? Our Cabinet Minister replies that both will be defended, and each will keep the peace when each is stronger than the other.

Among much that is doubtful in this subject there are a few truths in relation to it that are not doubtful at all, are in the nature of mathematical truth, as unquestionable as that two and two make four.

Thus, if it be true that in order to be adequately defended a nation must be stronger than a possible rival, then that rival, guided by the same principle, must go without defence. It is mathematically certain that if all Great States putting national defence by preponderance of power over others before all other objects of national policy, act on the principle that a free people should rather die than be inferior in power to another, there must follow a movement of forces bound by their very nature to produce conflict, that is to say war. To say that in order for both of two parties to a dispute—nations or alliances—to keep the peace and have security each must be stronger than the other is not only absurd in the Euclidian sense but as demonstrably so as any proposition that Euclid propounds.

Yet men, whole nations, all great nations, act upon that absurdity, base high policy upon it. It defeats its object, defence, produces war, and must by its very nature defeat defence and produce war. Yet it is to-day as much alive, men put their faith in it as much as they did when I first knew the Peace Movement more than a quarter of a century ago. We have not shifted the public mind from a self-evident absurdity. In so far as the fault is ours at all, it is due, I think, in considerable part at least to the assumption that in the forces leading to war it is the will and intention which is at fault and not the understanding.

If you examine the Press agitation now going on in favour of increased air forces you will find daily certain other assumptions made about defence no whit less absurd than the one I have just examined—much quotation, for instance, of the scriptural line that the strong man armed keepeth his goods in peace, without, however, the second line, which was plainly the point of the whole parable, the line to the effect that when a stronger than he comes along what then becomes of the first's security? For, as used by our Press, the quotation is made to support the isolationist position of each arming himself. As one young man put it, householders knew perfectly well in the days of the highwaymen that they had to keep a blunderbuss under the bed. 'Our air force is our blunderbuss.' Now the simple and obvious truth is that when every householder did have a blunderbuss over his bedstead they were very much more insecure than to-day, when not one householder in a thousand has a firearm about the place. For so long as each householder had to depend upon his own force alone he was at the mercy of any gang that could overcome one household. When, with the scientific organization of the community for mutual defence, a competent police system came into being, so that the highwayman or his gang had to meet not one frightened paterfamilias with a shaky fowling-piece but all the forces of the nation, then indeed were the Dick Turpins done in. So long as the citizen relied on the blunderbuss he was insecure; when he turned to organization with his neighbours his insecurity came to an end. The scriptural lesson is daily turned by our Press exactly upside down.

But of course the illustration, the talk of householders defending themselves against burglars, distorts the whole defence problem in another way. If you ask the average sincere supporter of increased armaments what he means by defence he will stare at such a question, deeming that the nature of defence is self-evident. Defence means keeping the foreigner out of our national house, in precisely the same way that Mr. John Smith defends his silver spoons against Mr. William Sykes.

Well, let us see. You will agree that our wars of the past have been defensive wars. But you will also have to face this curious fact about them: for very nearly one thousand years every war that we have ever fought has been fought in someone else's country. I once tried to make a list of those countries that have never seen the British Army or the British Navy in any form, and when I was through the list was a short one: Greenland. Yet there is one country where, for very nearly a thousand years, our army has never fought a foreign foe, this country.

Does that mean that our numberless wars were aggressive wars because they were fought in other people's countries?

It does not. But it does mean that defence cannot be merely a defence of the nation's soil. Defence must include a defence of the nation's interests, rights. Defence of its interests in such matters as those relating to access to its undeveloped territory, the settlement of that new land, free and assured use of this or that strait, passage through that inter-oceanic canal, protection of citizens in disorderly countries, extra-territoriality in the Far East, capitulations in the Near East, rights on the High Seas, the list is endless. Defence must include the defence of such interests, such rights.

But if defence means, as it must, defence of our rights in a dispute with others, note where the demand for preponderance of power for defence leads you. One State says in effect to another:

> 'It is quite true that we ask for greater power than you, but we give you our most solemn assurance to Heaven that that power will be used purely for defence. That is to say, when we get into a dispute with you as to what your rights are and our rights are in a given matter, where it is a question of judging whether you are right or we are right, all we ask is that we shall be judge of the question and so much stronger than you that you will just have to accept our verdict without a demur.'

If a foreign nation should use that language to us, what would be our retort? We should reply, with perfect truth, that the demand was outrageous, the demand of one of the litigants to be the judge.

Then why do we ask foreigners to occupy a position which we refuse to occupy when he asks us?

Yet this situation is inseparable from the old method of using arms for defence. Under the old dispensation each

State is inevitably placed in the position of asking another to occupy a position of inferiority that the first refuses to occupy. It meant putting might, not behind right, but behind the denial of right, the denial, that is, to the other party, of that right of judgment we claim for ourselves.

Do we really suppose that upon such a system of the mutual denial of right, secure national defence can be based? And this is a further point we have perhaps failed to clarify, a further question which we should compel those who support the old method of armed defence to answer. Is it or is it not true that by the method of preponderance we do indeed put our might behind the denial of right, that we do indeed deny to others the right of judgment we claim for ourselves? I have been putting that question for thirty years and have never had an answer. Never. Now this is not just a logician's dialectical dilemma, it is the actual situation presented to us in the tragedies of international affairs again and again and again. It was the impasse which landed us in the catastrophe of 1914. As Germany's power grew, we said in fact that it would soon be so great that we should have no means of defending our national rights. A German victory over France and Russia would place us in a position of such manifest inferiority as to deprive us of all defence, would place us in a position in which we should have to accept the verdict of a foreign nation as to our rights in any dispute with her about them. We declared, with justice, that this was a situation which no free people should occupy. We therefore proposed to Germany that she should occupy it. And to prove to her that she could safely occupy a position of inferior power to us and trust to our sense of justice to do the right thing, when we had the predominant power we made the Treaty of Versailles. That Treaty is the outcome of British naval power, plus French military might. To-day one could perhaps get into one omnibus all those Englishmen who would be prepared to stand up and say that the Treaty of Versailles was a perfectly just Treaty. Yet we made it, we and our allies.

To-day, of course, Germany is pointing to the Treaty as the sort of thing that happens when you are inferior in power to others; as proof that unless a nation is stronger than its neighbours, it will suffer the kind of fate which Germany and Hungary suffered. The lesson, from the point of view of the German people, is so plain that they are taking immense risks to challenge the power of their enemies. They are nursing, by all the means which a Fascist and totalitarian State can employ, a sense of grievance and vengeance. We are advised to keep out of any Continental entanglement, to let France, if needs be, suffer the fate which, only sixteen years ago, we gave a million of our youths to prevent. If, as the result of this isolationism, Germany establishes her preponderance once more in Europe, she will make a new Treaty of Versailles. It won't be better than the one we made. It will be worse. For the Germans are no more competent to be judges in their own cause than the French or the English. Having obtained that hegemony which we waged the last war to prevent, Germany would certainly not hesitate to ask for the return of her colonies and 'reparation' of other kinds at our expense. *We* should then be the victims of a new Treaty of Versailles, which it would be our duty to revise by means of war. Assuming we were successful in our new war against injustice we should then make a Versailles Treaty No. 3. It would not be any improvement on No. 1, because we should have so much more to avenge. Then, of course, would be the turn of the other side—except that long before that European civilization would have vanished utterly.

But as bearing upon this problem of defence certain other aspects are still disregarded by the public we are supposed to educate.

What is it that we propose to defend?

Whatever else it includes it must include protection of property, of wealth, of trade, of money, of investments. Both in Britain and in America great emphasis has been thrown on the part which the navy is intended to play in protecting, in Britain's case, the overseas trade by which we live; in America's case that wealth which, but for the strong arm of American power, might offer too great a temptation to the foreigner. What is the technique by which you use military victory after a war to take the defeated enemy's trade? How does military victory give you economic advantage? When you have had your war and are completely victorious, how do you control the markets? We have had our war with Germany. We won that war. We are apt to forget it, but we did. We British were completely victorious over our greatest economic rival, and we were promised a certain transfer of trade. Where is it? Where is this trade that somehow the victory, promoted we are told by the capitalists, was to give us? How does military power come into this matter at all?

Before the war we were told that the protection of our wealth, the protection, for instance, of our monetary gold demanded a big navy; that, but for the navy, foreigners would come in and take our gold and bust up our financial system. I have been rather interested to observe these last few years that foreigners have been coming in and taking the gold from the Bank of England. What has the navy been doing about it? The navy seems to have been inactive. It is true that you also have lost wealth which the navy does not seem to protect. You have lent money to the foreigner, and foreigners have run off with it. Why don't you send your navy after it?

What has victory, what has military power to do with these things? In so far as capitalism enters into these conflicts, it is because the capitalist thinks not as a capitalist but as a nationalist. And it is rather suggestive that, if the capitalist system goes to pieces, as I think it may, much of the disintegration will have been due, not to the inherent defects of capitalism as such, at this stage at least, but to the chaos produced by nationalism. If the capitalist had thought more as a capitalist and less as a nationalist, we should probably not have had the war, and capitalism would not be in the desperate state that it is.

If we are to defend our wealth effectively we must note certain changes in the character of wealth which bear upon our problem.

During the course of the tenth century Anlaf came twice into Essex, and on each occasion he made a pretty good thing of it. His ships moved out of the estuaries deeply laden with corn and hides, with fine cloth from the monasteries, with plate and ornaments, sometimes with women and slaves.

Obedient to the injunction to remember that the underlying forces of history and the motives of men remain unchanged, I have tried to imagine the British, now that they have the upper hand, returning the compliment ten centuries later—our navy loading up a goodly part of our mercantile marine with the agricultural and industrial wealth of the Scandinavian peninsula, and pouring into Britain shipload upon shipload of butter, bacon, and milk products; of Swedish wood pulp, paper, furniture, iron, hardware, textiles; bringing into Britain the shops of the Baltic, and then . . .

Yes, and what then?

Dumping them upon the British market.

And then our troubles would begin.

One remembers what happened when some of our own producers discovered that foreign Governments were subsidizing the shipment to this country of certain products like sugar. We called international conferences for the purpose of preventing the entrance into this country of foreign goods which were obtained by some of our people at something below their cost of production. But what would happen if some modern British Anlaf obtained vast quantities of foreign goods for nothing more than the cost of seizing them and began dumping them on the market?

The British farmer and industrialist would immediately insist upon a tariff or a convention to prohibit this somewhat too simple manifestation of the 'struggle for bread'. We have plainly here a complication that Anlaf did not have to face. The fluctuations of the produce markets, agricultural prices, the political pull of the Manufacturers' Associations did not particularly embarrass him.

But these would not be the only complications which would follow upon a sort of Attila raid into the Baltic and wholesale confiscations by invading British hordes. The British coal trade with Scandinavia and the Baltic is an extremely important one; and on that trade depends also much of our shipping industry. It is the fact of taking out coal and getting a cargo both ways that has given to us so much of the carrying trade of the world; and if our modern sea-rovers began sacking Stockholm or Copenhagen or Christiania they would in fact be sacking the working-class homes of Newcastle or Barrow or Cardiff almost as disastrously, reducing to unemployment and starvation British miners, British factory men, British shipbuilders, British sailors.

I doubt whether, when Anlaf sacked Maldon or Colchester, the Scandinavian carrying trade was greatly affected, or the unemployment rate increased. But this is only the beginning of the complications with the modern Anlaf. British insurance companies have insured the very buildings that our British Vikings would be burning; the shares of our businesses now sacked are held by British investors; British banks have lent money to the now ruined merchants, or discounted their bills; or lent money to their merchants who had discounted the bills; and if the sacking across the North Sea were at all extensive, we should find British banks gravely embarrassed, and for safety's sake calling in loans extended to British men, raising the British bank-rate, increasing the cost and difficulty of financing British business and British enterprise, thus depriving British investors of their property and British workmen of their jobs.

I have not studied Viking history very carefully, but I doubt very much whether Scandinavian stock exchanges were greatly affected when Anlaf ravaged Essex.

Still, very learned people, writers of histories and books on statecraft, tell me that 'the same struggle—the struggle for bread', which more than a thousand years ago 'drove the Teutonic warriors across the Rhine', must still go in much the same way. Well, I suggest there will be complications.

We live in a world in which every nation is trying its

utmost, not to seize the food and resources of other nations, but to keep them out by insurmountable tariff walls, a fantastic world in which we go in terror, not of scarcity, but of plenty; where a considerable proportion of its population stands idle by idle machines, because it has not yet learned how to distribute the food it already produces. Brazil burns coffee, Canada burns wheat, but neither burns the coal of the British miner, who goes without both the coffee and wheat.

If we are to do the best with our world resources—if we are to do the best with our nation's—we must so organize the traffic on the commercial highways of the world that there are no traffic blocks, stoppage jams, none of the confusion, congestions, fights, wrangles, uncertainties as to what the other will do when he drives his powerful car, all of which are likely to bring the flow to a stop. If that takes place the particular product of each becomes valueless. Plainly, the need here is agreement as to what the traffic rules shall be—system, organization.

It is just as impossible for anarchy to work effectively in the international field as it would be for anarchy to work within the State, for us to live at peace within the frontiers of the nation without the institutions of Government, without law, without a Constitution, without Courts—just as impossible for peace to be maintained between nations travelling the highways of the world as it would be for accidents to be avoided on the modern motor-car road if each drove as he saw fit, and be damned to traffic rules.

If on our modern motor roads each made his own rule, so that an Englishman accustomed to driving all his life to the left, going to the Continent should say, 'What! abandon the habits of a lifetime at the dictation of mere foreigners and now drive to the right? I shall continue to drive to the left'—it would be inconvenient.

And if we repudiated rules in that way there would be accidents, and, of course, the accidents would always be the fault of the other fellow. We might say we did not want accidents, did not believe in accidents. But accidents would happen. They would happen, not because men were particularly evil, not because one was worse than the other, but because that whole basic method of travelling the roads together without any real rules was simply unworkable.

And that is a truth which becomes truer every day. The need for rules was not always so great. In the days of the oxcart it was possible to travel without any elaborate rules. If two teams met, one driving to the left and the other to the right, each driver, after the appropriate blasphemy, could disentangle his team and go on his way rejoicing. But if, on the modern motor-car road, with the new Ford travelling at seventy miles an hour, you do not really know whether the other fellow is going to drive on the right or left, well, the discussion afterwards will probably be academic.

We must make our public see that just as the old method defies arithmetic, so does it defy morals and ethics, that by the old method of isolated power if one is secure, the other is not, and that if one has what he calls justice, the other is deprived of it; that we are all the time asking the other to occupy a position which we refuse to occupy when he asks us.

Mankind has only found one way out of this: To take arms from the hands of the litigants and pass them over to the law. And the problem at this stage is not as between a world of force and no force, coercion and no coercion. I am in favour of a world without coercion, but you, the public as a whole, are not. There remains therefore one of two alternatives: force behind the law, or force behind the litigants. I regard both as evil, but of the two I accept the less, and suggest that it is better that power, if you must have power, should be in the hands of the judge, than that it should be in the hands of the rival litigants. The problem which confronts us in Geneva is just that—to make this transfer of power from litigants to law.

iii. *A Problem of Understanding.*

We all want peace, and we all follow policies that make war inevitable because we do not see the relation between the policy which we follow and the result in war. It is thus a problem of understanding, not of evil intent. War is not made by evil men believing themselves to be wrong. It is unfortunately made by good men, passionately convinced that they are right. And they are passionately convinced they are right because both parties alike are basing their whole method of international life upon the wrong fundamental assumption that each can be independent, sovereign, go its own way, whereas, of course, the independence and sovereignty of each in an organized society is a contradiction in terms.

You cannot have an organized society unless each is prepared to limit his independence at least sufficiently to make co-operation possible. So long as we do not realize that, emotion and good intention won't do. Again, it is a problem of understanding. We have to bring science now not merely into the field of physics but into the field of human relationships; to apply to the understanding of those relationships the same cold intellectual rectitude that we have devoted to the understanding of matter.

We do not seem able to do that. As soon as we attempt to apply science to society we seem to be led astray by old pugnacities, hostilities. We always seek to find *who* caused the war instead of trying to find out *what* caused it. We want a scapegoat. We want to indulge pugnacities, the passions of retaliation. We do not believe that intelligence is necessary. We still in this matter—and here again I agree in the condemnation of much pacifist effort—believe it is a matter of better intentions. It is very much more a matter of better understanding. And we tend to disparage the need for understanding, for intelligence.

We English particularly have always had that feeling that understanding does not much matter; that our difficulties can be solved by what we call character. We think if a man's heart is stout, it doesn't matter how thick his head is.

I once heard at Geneva, in reply to a Frenchman, one of our Ministers repudiate the idea that logic mattered in these things. 'Logic!' he said in reply to the Frenchman, '*We* are not guided by logic. We are guided by intuition, by empirical methods; by this and that. We muddle through.'

A Frenchman turned to me in irritation and said, 'Really, you know, I think you British believe your stupidity is a gift of God. Well, it may be, but it is a gift that ought not to be abused.'

We must not abuse it, and in framing this new order, in creating now the international society which is necessary, we must try to understand as well as to feel. We must look upon the 'brotherhood of man', not as a mere emotional aspiration, not as a mere windy phrase to be used as a peroration, but as something to be organized scientifically, a problem to be solved, and a problem which can only be solved by what I have called intellectual rectitude, a determination to face our own share in past failures. Let us give up the effort to find scapegoats, the habit of blaming either a guilty nation or a guilty class. Then only may we do for human society what we have done for matter, conquer it and manage it; reshape it to something that shall be more worthy of what I feel we can still hope shall prove to be 'man's unconquerable mind'.

CHAPTER VII

THE CHACO WAR

by

SENOR ALVAREZ DEL VAYO

Chairman of the League of Nations Commission of Enquiry into the Chaco Dispute

i. *Historical Antecedents.*

MY subject is one of the most senseless wars of history. I wish to discuss it not as President of the League's Commission of Enquiry, but as a man who has seen the disaster in the Chaco at first hand, and who feels impelled as a result of that impression to do everything within his power to see that war brought to an end. The collective opinion of the Commission may be found in the Report submitted to the Council at its meeting in May 1934.

It is necessary by way of introduction to say a few words about the historical antecedents of the Chaco dispute. There is not time to take you with me over the endless and exhausting road of controversy and argument which we were obliged to travel. A date will be enough. On the initiative of Bolivia, the first negotiations between that country and Paraguay for the demarcation of their common border took place in 1879. There followed fifty-five years of negotiations, interrupted for shorter or longer periods. The interruptions abound in bloody incidents. The war that is going on to-day was declared in the summer of 1932.

Three treaties—those of Decoud-Quijano, Aceval-Tamayo, and Benitez-Tchaso—were concluded in the latter part of the nineteenth century, but none of them succeeded in obtaining the necessary parliamentary approval. Instead of bringing the adversaries nearer, each of these attempts to settle the controversy on judicial grounds led to a wider difference of views. Upon their return home, following each of these attempts to reach an agreement, the negotiators met only reproach and suspicion, instead of acknowledgment of their efforts. They were suspected of having capitulated to the enemy, and their careers were destroyed by the part they played in the negotiations. As a consequence there came into being a type of reluctant and hard negotiator who confounds patriotism and obstinacy, and who feels better and surer of his own position in his own country if he comes back from the negotiations empty-handed and covered with the reputation of being an unyielding delegate than if he returns with a basis of agreement. From the point of view of national politics in Bolivia or Paraguay, it is dangerous for an individual to win the reputation of being too conciliatory a diplomat.

This consideration represents a psychological factor which plays an incalculable role in later negotiations. The negotiations are infinitely complicated, too, by the activities of lawyers and historians who have exhumed from their countries' archives, brilliantly but uselessly, the material on which to base the contentions that have led to the struggle in the controversial field of the Chaco.

The discussion that has raged over the legal titles on which each claimant bases its rights of possession in the Chaco has gone on endlessly. It is a discussion that concerns opposite conceptions of the real value of the depositions taken by the Spanish Crown, the exact application of the principle of *utis possidetis* (1810) in the legislation of the new continent. The epic of the Spanish conquest, as told by the chief historians of the two countries, together with more recent tales of modern American and European travellers, furnishes an inexhaustible amount of material to support the opposing points of view.

The number of the expounders, historians, geographers, and jurists who have been given birth to and find their livelihood in the Chaco dispute is legion. For both adversaries the world is being slowly reduced to the Chaco plane. In Asuncion and La Paz people talk or write about little else. The Chaco dispute is the inevitable subject of the editorial in every morning paper, and the subject of familiar conversation before going to bed. It is the 'good morning' and the 'good night' during the whole year.

Consequently the question has become so entangled that every mediator has been obliged to devote most of his efforts simply to discovering a ground on which normal discussions can be carried on, away from so much beclouded argument.

ii. *Recent Attempts at Settlement.*

The Buenos Aires Conferences that opened in September 1927, to be suspended three months later, were able, for instance, only to reach the conclusion that it was impossible to achieve either of the two aims of the negotiations, viz., the settlement of the substantive question,[1] or, at least, an agreement on a *modus vivendi.* The same fate awaited the Commission of Neutrals appointed in 1929 by the International Conference of American States. It is of unusual interest to read the valuable *Proceedings of the Commission of Inquiry and Conciliation—Bolivia and Paraguay* published in Washington both in English and in Spanish. It was

[1] By substantive question, 'cuestion de fondo', is meant the solution of the ownership of the Chaco.

my travelling book on the journey to South America, a book which might easily discourage anyone not possessed of both a determination to bring peace and a certain amount of good humour. It is the best proof of the capriciousness and untenability of the objection made that our Commission was 'too European', and therefore incapable of penetrating American psychology, an objection that was made when our proposals did not please.

The Commission of Neutrals which met in Washington was composed exclusively of Americans—citizens of the United States, Colombia, Cuba, Mexico, and Uruguay. During several years they worked with admirable devotion and patience. They enjoyed the deserved support of the neighbouring States and of the nineteen American republics specially congregated to proclaim, in the declaration of 3 August, 1932, that they 'will not recognize any territorial arrangement of this controversy which has not been obtained by peaceful means, nor the validity of the territorial acquisitions which may be obtained through occupation or conquest by force of arms'. The Commission of Neutrals also enjoyed the support of the Council of the League, which at that time considered it desirable, in order to avoid a duplication of jurisdictions, to confine its action to supporting the efforts of the Commission of Neutrals to secure peace.

After having tried to bring about an understanding, the Washington Commission disbanded in December 1932, when, as a consequence of the concrete proposals submitted by it to both parties for the cessation of hostilities, the Government of Paraguay withdrew its delegation and put an end to the negotiations.

Nor did the formula of Mendoza fare any better than

these previous efforts. This proposal was the result of the combined efforts of the Argentine and Chilean Foreign Ministers, who met in that Argentine town in February 1933 to make a new supreme attempt at arbitration on the eve of the declaration of war announced by Paraguay. Subsequently the League Council decided on 20 May, 1933, to send a Commission to the Chaco. The departure of our Commission was deferred, however, by the new desire of Bolivia and Paraguay to have the Commission's mandate entrusted to the four adjacent Powers—Argentina, Brazil, Chile, and Peru. We left for South America at the end of October 1933, after the adjacent States, which had exchanged views and been in constant consultation with each other during August and September, informed the Council that they could not accept the invitation made as a result of the suddenly announced suggestion of the parties to the Chaco controversy.

When we arrived the Bolivian and Paraguayan armies had been fighting in the Chaco for eighteen months. If from afar, through the reliable reports which we had, the war had seemed to us an absurd monstrosity, the impression became solidly established in our minds as we proceeded to both countries and realized for ourselves the ruination that eighteen months of fighting had brought.

It was not the reaction of persons who considered themselves charged with an historical peace-making mission, and therefore inclined to over-emphasize the necessity of repudiating war as a means of settling disputes between nations; it was, at least in my own case, more of an intellectual reaction than a moral one.

I found simply stupid a war that, even from the military point of view, offered no clear issue whatsoever.

iii. *Military Considerations.*

To the military experts of the Commission—to Generals Freydenburg (France), Robertson (Great Britain), and Lieutenant-Colonel Rivera Flandes (Mexico)—belongs the credit of having realized at once very clearly the senselessness of fighting in the Chaco. The report which they laid before us when they returned from their visit to the front in November 1933 could be published to-day without having lost in the meantime anything of interest or actuality.

The victorious Paraguayan offensive during the beginning of December 1933 was forecast at that time. I remember that when we went to La Paz, after we had completed our visit to Paraguay, the opinions of our experts about the inevitable advance of the Paraguayan Army were received with scepticism and a gently hidden irritation. But we had just arrived in La Paz when news came from the front to justify the calculations of our military experts. The Paraguayan Army forced back the Bolivians and took from them a great quantity of arms and war material, in addition to thousands of prisoners. That part of their predictions was fulfilled. But in our experts' report there was a second part which displeased the Paraguayans as much as the first part had displeased the Bolivians. Our experts maintained that in spite of the predicted successful attacks carried out by the Paraguayans the nature of the war was such that it could not be decided by arms. Here, too, their foresight has been confirmed by the events that have since taken place.

When we were in Buenos Aires at the end of January 1934 the Paraguayan view, shared by high Argentine officials, was that the Paraguayan Army would be in Ballivan, one of the most important centres of Bolivian resistance, not later than the middle of February. Our experts were kindly but ironically smiled upon when they spoke of three months at least. It is easy to imagine the prospect for both countries if one remembers that, when the Paraguayans thought the fall of Ballivan was a matter of weeks, the Bolivians maintained that even the fall of Ballivan would not end the war, and that, in case they lost their outpost, the Bolivian Army simply would retreat to Villa Montes, where it would entrench itself on the Bolivian border. The prospect ahead of both countries is continual years of fighting without any concrete result. Thus the situation is in accord with the expectation of our military experts, who said that, failing any development particularly favourable to Paraguay, it might be supposed that the equilibrium reached in October 1933, 200 kilometres to the west of the Paraguay River, would be reached anew at a greater distance from the river, and that the two armies would be drawn up again in fortified systems.

I would not risk entering into a technical consideration of why for many months the military situation has turned steadily in favour of the Paraguayan Army. But let me say something about certain social aspects of the situation which I think are often overlooked.

iv. *Social Factors.*

We are frequently told that the Bolivian soldier, born in and used to high altitudes, finds himself at a disadvantage when he must fight the Paraguayan soldier in the Chaco plain. That is true. The Paraguayans would be at a similar disadvantage if their chiefs, in an *élan de victoire*, attempted to take them to those centres of mineral production in the interior of Bolivia where the nerve centres of Bolivia's wealth lie. And these centres are the only places where a successful stroke of the Paraguayan Army could decide the war by a triumph of arms.

But I believe that the lesser endurance of the Bolivian soldier is not to be explained entirely by climatic causes. In this connection I am not speaking of the Bolivian officers, whose gallantry is unanimously praised even by their adversaries. I believe another factor plays a big role. I refer to the social condition of the Bolivian soldier.

Most of the men in the Bolivian Army are pariahs. In civilian life they are submitted to an economic regime of the worst kind of capitalism. They lack even a shadow of modern protective legislation which in other places disguises capitalistic exploitation. The Bolivian Indian makes up the bulk of the army. As a native of Bolivia, he may have a feeling for his land that derives from having been born in it, from seeing its landscape, from his family connections there, and from the routine of life which he follows. But he is devoid of any strong and active identification with his country as a State, and he has no love for a ruling class that regards him only as a payer of tribute, or as a being to send to the military front.

Thus one notes in Bolivia the lack of a good social policy designed to benefit the Indian population, a policy of the type, for instance, that has been carried out by the Mexicans since their revolution.

Because I had the honour of representing the first Spanish Republican Government in Mexico, the contrast between Mexico and Bolivia in this respect was particularly striking. While I was in Bolivia I recalled the trips I had taken through the Mexican states, sometimes as a simple traveller, at other times accompanied by high officials and members of the Cabinet. I remembered that the Mexican authorities had devoted great care to improving the situation of the Mexican Indians. I thought of the Indian assemblies I had seen in the states of Michoacan, Sonora, and Morelos, where a rural population, set free by the revolution and which before the revolution was no better off than the Bolivian population, was able after several years of educational work by the Government to compete with the rural population of any country in its ability at self-administration. These Mexican Indians, too, I recalled, had been taught a sense of social responsibility and a spirit of co-operation.

In the few years since the Mexican Government has established rural schools throughout the country it has spent millions and millions of pesos to educate the Indians, and the result is evident. I will never forget my visit to the state of Guewero with the Minister of Education. We went, sometimes on mules the whole day, through steep mountains, opening new schools in many districts. It was a great thing to see the enthusiasm of those Indian peasants and their gratitude to the Minister of Education because he had made a personal visit to open their school. The Indians themselves had erected the school buildings, sometimes bringing the stones from afar. They were built in such a fashion that in every village the school was the best building in the middle of the wonderful Mexican landscape.

One could not help thinking of all this in Bolivia and of how much more sensible it would be to devote to a similar programme the money now being expended for destruction and for war. How much more sensible it would be to exploit in peace the territory that they have! Whatever the extent of their land after the settlement of the Chaco dispute, it would still be immense in proportion to their population.

The social condition of the Bolivian Indian soldier may explain, in my opinion, the apathy of which the Bolivian officers complain when they speak frankly. The Bolivian Indians are asked to die for a State that has sadly neglected them.

On the other hand, the war is for both parties to the controversy the catastrophe which we described in our report to the Council. It is a singularly pitiless and horrible struggle in an exceedingly trying climate. There is inadequate attention for the sick and wounded. The lack of adequate medical attention is the result of the difficulty of developing, with limited resources, a medical service large enough in proportion to the size of the effectives that have been mobilized.

v. *Procedure of the Commission.*

The Commission did everything in its power to stop that catastrophe. I will try here to give a résumé, in general lines, of its work.

When the Commission sailed for South America the representatives of both parties to the controversy had accepted the report made to the Council on 20 May, 1933. Already, however, divergent views had made their appearance during the discussion of that report. It was Paraguay's view that cessation of hostilities should precede the negotiations for the establishment of an arbitration agreement. Bolivia maintained that the establishment of the arbitration agreement should precede the cessation of hostilities. This difference of opinion continued even after the final adoption of the Council's report, and it was from the beginning a serious obstacle that confronted the Commission throughout the negotiations.

We assumed that the Council expected that the disagreement regarding procedure would not prevent the re-establishment of peace if we succeeded in finding a happy solution of the substantive question. That was our hope, and therefore, in spite of the fact that our arrivals in Asuncion and in La Paz were coloured by concern over the divergence of viewpoint in regard to procedure, we faced our task without discouragement.

We counted on Paraguay's fear of risking a subsequent renewal of the war as a factor which would overcome Paraguay's main objection to entering into negotiations about the substantive question without a previous cessation of hostilities. This point was made very clear in the address delivered by President Ayala on the occasion of our reception in Asuncion.

'The kind of peace that is desirable', said President Ayala, 'is one that is not founded on the conception of victor and vanquished. In spite of everything, the peoples have need of one another, and they cannot give each other any useful help if there is a gulf of hatred between them. A just peace is a peace without victory and without defeat. It is a peace without rancour. That seems doubtful. International justice, we must confess, has still but little power. Unhappily the production of a judgment or a solemn pact does not suffice to confer a sense of protection.'

Paraguay's justified claim, then, was for protection against a renewal of the war if negotiations failed, or if the judgment reached by the arbitration group did not satisfy the opponent. From the very start we gave that point the attention it deserved, and in our draft treaty of peace handed to both countries the security clauses played a prominent part. The draft treaty contained the following military measures: demobilization of the two armies, their reduction under supervision to an equal strength until the decision fixing the frontier between the two countries should have been executed, and an undertaking under supervision not to acquire any armaments during the same period. These military provisions were written into the draft treaty for the purpose of giving adequate security to both countries, and especially to Paraguay. We gave to Paraguay also the right to police a large part of the Chaco in the important section where the civilian settlements, industrial and rural properties, tannin-producing establishments, and stock-breeding *estancias* were the result of Paraguay's efforts at colonization. These conditions of security were, in our minds, enough to give Paraguay satisfaction, and to protect that country from the danger of aggression. Perhaps these proposals did not provide 'absolute security', but I wonder if there is a country in the world to-day which possesses 'absolute security'. Surely, even at the risk of stating a paradox, it is correct to say that 'absolute security' is always a relative term.

At any rate, a desirable solution was not to be found in a peace that resulted from capitulation, or from humiliation of one of the adversaries. It was President Ayala, as we have seen, who was the first to proclaim that a desirable peace was a peace without victor and vanquished. That was also the firm conviction of the Commission, and our attitude was not altered by the December victory.

It was our desire to arrive at such a kind of peace settlement. The Commission was moved by that desire, and at the same time we tried, on the one hand, to give satisfaction to Paraguay on the question of security, and, on the other hand, to the equally justified claim of Bolivia that the Treaty of Peace should contain definite stipulations for the settlement of the substantive question. Any attempt, as the Bolivian delegation put it, to 'dodge' that question was doomed in advance to the same failure that had met previous attempts at settlement.

vi. *The Draft Treaty.*

At the end of March, and after numerous meetings during weeks and months of negotiations, the Commission firmly held to the conviction that the parties to the controversy would not of their own accord make concessions sufficient to bring about an agreement. Since the Commission felt by that time that it had found the exact point at which, given a real desire for peace on the part of the adversaries, diametrically opposite theses and aspirations could be brought together, we submitted the following draft treaty of peace to both delegations in Buenos Aires. It said:

'The Governments of Bolivia and Paraguay,

'Being desirous of bringing to an end the state of war existing between the two countries by the adoption of adequate measures to ensure the final cessation of hostilities, as well as the definitive determination of their frontiers, by means of legal arbitration and in conformity with the principle laid down in the declaration made by all the other American Republics on August 3rd, 1932,

'Have agreed on the following provisions:

'(1) Hostilities shall cease twenty-four hours after the entry into force of the present Treaty.

'(2) In the following twenty-four hours, both armies shall

begin to evacuate the positions occupied by them at the time of the cessation of hostilities and shall within forty-five days withdraw to the following positions:

(*a*) Bolivian Army: Villa Montes and Roboré;
(*b*) Paraguayan Army: the River Paraguay.

'(3) The demobilization of both armies shall begin at the same time as the withdrawal provided for in Article 2. All demobilized soldiers shall return to their homes within three months;

'(4) At the end of these three months, and so long as the final judgment of the Permanent Court of International Justice fixing the frontier between the two countries has not been fully implemented, neither army shall exceed 5,000 men.

'So long as the above clause limiting the strength of the two armies is in force, the two Governments undertake not to acquire arms or other war material.

'Nevertheless, if during that period one of the two Governments should deem that an increase of its army or armaments is necessary, the Council of the League of Nations will have the power to grant such an increase, at the request of the Government concerned.

'If one of the two Governments is of opinion that the provisions of the present article are not being carried out, the Council of the League of Nations will also deal with the question, at the request of that Government.

'For the execution of the provisions of this article, the decisions of the Council will be taken without the votes of the Parties being included.

'(5) Pending the execution of the final judgment of the Permanent Court of International Justice fixing the frontier between the two countries, the latter may keep such police forces as will be necessary for the maintenance of order, as follows:

'Bolivia will exercise police rights along the Upper Pilcomayo, in the regions lying to the east of the Chiriguanos Mountains and the Parapiti River, as well as in the regions lying to the south of the Chochi Mountains and Otuquis River.

'For such police operations as may be necessary in those regions, Bolivia, in order to avoid possible difficulties with the Paraguayan police, undertakes not to go beyond meridian 62° (Greenwich) to the east, and parallel 19° 30′ to the south.

'Paraguay will exercise police rights along the Lower Pilcomayo and in the regions lying to the west of the River Paraguay and the River Negro (or Otuquis).

'For such police operations as may be necessary in those regions, Paraguay, in order to avoid possible difficulties with the Bolivian police, undertakes not to go beyond meridian 61° 30′ (Greenwich) to the west, and parallel 20° to the north.

'Paraguay will, however, exercise police rights north of parallel 20° along the western bank of the Negro (or Otuquis) River, as far as Galpón. Police rights on the eastern bank of that river will be exercised by Bolivia. Paraguay will also exercise police rights, to the west of meridian 61° 30′ (Greenwich) along the northern bank of the Pilcomayo River up to meridian 61° 55′ (Greenwich).

'As to the narrow strips of territory which, according to the above provisions, the police of neither country is allowed to enter, the two Governments shall agree on such police action as may be necessary.

'If, notwithstanding the firm resolve of both Governments to observe scrupulously the above provisions, incidents occur between Bolivian and Paraguayan police, and if such incidents cannot be rapidly settled, the Permanent Court of International Justice shall have the power to indicate provisional measures according to Article 41 of its Statute.

'(6) After the coming into force of the present Treaty, the Permanent Court of International Justice, at the request of the Party which first brings the case before it, shall exercise jurisdiction over the dispute between the countries, Bolivia maintaining on the one hand that her frontier with Paraguay is the Paraguay River and that her rights extend down to the confluence of the Pilcomayo and Paraguay Rivers, Paraguay maintaining, on the other hand, that her rights to the west of the Paraguay River extend: to the north, up to the frontiers between the former Paraguay province and the former military government of Chiquitos; to the west, up to the frontiers between that same province and the entities or provinces of Upper Peru, and that the Court must establish which were those frontiers.

'Nevertheless, in a spirit of conciliation, and on the understanding that the concessions mentioned below will neither weaken in any way the legal contentions or titles which either Party may think fit to submit to the Permanent Court of International Justice, nor, if the present Treaty does not enter into force, be invoked as precedents possessing any legal or moral value;

'Bolivia, on the one hand, renounces the reservations she has made concerning the award to Paraguay by President Hayes of the territory between the Verde River and the main branch of the Pilcomayo River;

'Paraguay, on the other hand, renounces the reservations she has made concerning the determination of the frontier between Bolivia and Brazil by the Treaty of Petropolis and consequently declares that she claims as her frontiers: to the north, the Chochi Mountains, the Aguas Calientes, Otuquis and Negro Rivers; to the west, the Parapiti River and the Chiriguanos Mountains, and, to the south, the Pilcomayo River.

'(7) In the eight days following the entry into force of the present Treaty, the two countries shall take the measures which are necessary for the repatriation of the prisoners, in conformity with international rules. The two Governments agree to send a request to that effect to the International Committee of the Red Cross and to accept the arbitration of its delegates for any difficulties which may occur. The expenses of those delegates shall be borne by the two Governments.

'(8) The two Governments agree that, after the Permanent Court of International Justice has rendered its judgment, they will request the Pan-American Union to convene the Conference of neighbouring Powers, contemplated in the resolution adopted by the International Conference of American States on December 24th, 1933, the mandate of the said Conference of neighbouring Powers being "to study the co-ordination of all geographical and economic factors which might contribute to the development and prosperity of the sister nations".'

Then follow the articles about ratification by the respective national congresses and registration of the Treaty in the Secretariat of the League.

In presenting this draft treaty we were honestly convinced that if both parties really had any earnest will to make peace, the proposal presented an honourable and practical solution for their old quarrel. The substantive question, around which the controversy of half a century had turned, here was brought to the only possible plane on which it was possible to settle it. Attempts to arrive at a compromise by the division of the territory into different zones—one, for instance, to be adjudged to Bolivia, one to Paraguay, and the third to be regarded as in dispute—had always failed. Such attempts at settlement were bound to fail. It is obvious that if Paraguay considered herself entitled to the whole of the Chaco, there was no reason for her to cede part of it to Bolivia by direct agreement; it was also true that if Bolivia considered herself the lawful owner of the whole tract, there was no reason to expect that she would cede a part of it to Paraguay.

vii. *Arbitration.*

Arbitration, therefore, was the only way out of the long-standing deadlock. Arbitration was the method we recommended for the whole disputed territory, exception being made only of the Hayes zone, which was adjudicated to Paraguay in 1878 by President Hayes, and of the zone north of Bahia Negra, which gave Bolivia access to the Paraguay River as a consequence of the Treaty of Petropolis. We decided to stipulate the Permanent Court of International Justice—the World Court—as the arbitration body, because it had to its credit a body of jurisprudence built up since 1921, and because three Spanish-American nations belong to the Court—Cuba, Colombia, and El-Salvador. We considered that the membership of these three nations in the Court ought to serve as a guarantee to Bolivia and Paraguay that the Court was familiar with American legislation, and knew the problems peculiar to the South American Continent.

From the point of view of a durable peace, arbitration such as was suggested by the Commission was the best solution, and, in my opinion, the only one to be carried out. It was also the best solution from the point of view of the internal policy of the two adversaries. In fact, both Governments should have felt happy at finding a way out of future difficulties. As in every war, propaganda had been exalted in Bolivia and Paraguay during the Chaco conflict, and the people had been promised much more than even a great victory could have given. A direct arrangement, on the basis of compromise, would always have left a certain section of public opinion disappointed. In one country as in the other, someone inevitably would have made himself heard, and would have pretended that better direction and greater effort on the part of the Government would have benefited the country in a larger way. And in South America, where personal motives play such a considerable part in politics, to leave the way open at the conclusion of the war for bitter home controversy as to how the direct arrangement ought to have been negotiated is to expose the country to unrest and mutiny. Under arbitration, therefore, the chances were better that this domestic strife might be avoided, and that the energy of politics might be devoted after the achievement of peace to the restoration of what the war had destroyed, to the improvement of the living conditions of the populace, to popular education, to public health, and to a grand programme of social betterment that ought to have absorbed the attention of both Governments for many years.

viii. *Forces Behind the Scenes.*

Besides the parts of the Draft Treaty designed to introduce a real system of security and to settle the substantive question, the proposal embodied, in Article 8, a plan to convoke a post-war economic conference of the neighbouring States. Such a conference was recommended by the Montevideo Conference on motion of the Argentine. It was our conviction—at least it was my own absolute conviction—that beneath the dispute on the legitimacy of certain legal titles, economic interests played a most important part, and foreign economic interests more than home interests. It was a behind-the-scenes fight in which it was not difficult to see the hand of that typical sort of foreign capitalism which believes it has found in the less socially and economically developed countries of South America the ideal paradise for its policy of exploitation. If it had not been for the tannin interests on the one side, and for the oil interests on the other—not so much for what can be obtained in the Chaco at present, but for the future prospects of developing oil reserves throughout the territory—and if it had not been for the wealth of mining in general in this tract, I feel very much inclined to believe that the war in the Chaco would have been over a long time ago. If this were not so, a peaceful decision would have been enforced by now. But stronger than the desire for peace in South America have been these contending economic interests, including those already branded by the moral sense of the world with the name of 'merchants of death'. Tannin, oil, arms, and materials of every kind of destruction, dividends and profits—all these have played their part under the surface of a struggle that appears to be only a fight between contenders for the juridical rights. For this reason we were very much in favour of the convocation of an economic conference that would be able to make a resolute attack upon the series of essential economic problems that arise in the Chaco.

I must say that in spite of the uncompromising spirit shown by both delegations in the course of the negotiations there was still a good deal of hope in the Commission that the draft treaty could be accepted in its fundamental lines, even though it might be altered by slight counter-suggestions. For the second time after our arrival in South America we felt near to a satisfactory conclusion when the Draft Treaty was presented. The first had been on the occasion of the armistice proposed by the President of the Republic of Paraguay on 18 December, 1933, while we were in La Paz. The armistice was accepted by Bolivia partly under our pressure. Later Paraguay agreed, as a result of our urging by telephone to Asuncion, to extend the armistice to 6 January, 1934. We could not believe in those days, once an armistice had been agreed to and arms had been laid down, that the people would be blinded again by a call to war. That was an illusion shared by the whole Montevideo Conference, which was sitting at that time, and which was unanimous in its anxiety for a pacific settlement of the conflict, and in giving its official support to the Commission on our arrival in the Uruguayan capital. I would like to pay tribute here, while speaking of that attitude, to the noble interest shown in the work of the Commission by the United States Secretary of State, Mr. Cordell Hull, and to the encouragement which he gave us. It was Mr. Hull who introduced at the Conference the important resolution reminding Bolivia and Paraguay that they were bound by the Covenant of the League, expressing the unalterable opinion that the question of honour was not involved as to either nation, and that therefore both parties could cease fighting with entire credit to themselves, and declaring that fighting, consequently, could not possibly be justified.

Our hopes were deceived both times—when the armistice was agreed upon, and again when we submitted our Draft Treaty—by the suicidal obstinacy of those who seem to have no other national programme to offer to their countries than to continue the war until there are no more soldiers to be sent into the trenches. The conflict may last two years more, perhaps four.

ix. *The Chaco as a Source of War Infection.*

During our mission we often called to the attention of American public opinion the danger that at any time, and despite the precautions taken by the neighbouring States, the war might spread. The Chaco controversy is in fact a dispute that every day is poisoning the entire South American Continent more and more. Sometimes in our debates in the Commission, when we were alone, I used to employ the word 'calcanization'. And truly the Chaco is to the South American Continent, in a certain sense, what the Balkans were to Europe before the World War—a focus of complications. Perhaps there were some individuals who found us too propagandist when we talked about that danger, who may have thought us too interested in impressing and mobilizing the different Foreign Offices, but the recent diplomatic collision between Chile and Paraguay may perhaps have modified their opinions somewhat. There will be one, two, or three minor and overlooked incidents, until some day things will be hopelessly entangled.

The very nature of the conflict makes it deadly. As I said earlier, decades of discussion have turned the Chaco controversy into the most venomous dispute recorded in the history of international relations. It is not possible to face it with normal logic. One has to deal with a morbid susceptibility, inclined to see in any reaction of other people's common sense a sign of hostility as soon as that reaction contradicts a dearly held point of view.

In such an atmosphere it is evident that a real conception of neutrality cannot survive. Neutrality is for both belligerents something that is spoken of in the official communications—nothing else. At bottom both knew only allies or enemies. This is true in the case of countries as it is true in the case of negotiators.

The growing irritation may any day prove stronger than all official declarations of neutrality. Any frontier incident, any disagreeable tone in a reply to an attempt at mediation, any newspaper campaign may provoke in the public opinion of other countries not yet implicated in the war a reaction that cannot be controlled. One must not forget that public opinion in South America is already so tired of the Chaco dispute, and so tired of both belligerents, that anything may happen. As long as the Chaco War goes on, no neighbouring country can feel that its own peace is assured.

The warm reception given to the Commission's report proved to what an extent people are anxious to be told the truth. For me it was not a revelation. I am for the truth not only on the ground of international morality, but because I am firmly convinced that to speak the truth is the way to serve and to strengthen the League of Nations. Those whose supreme aim is to try to move always in an official sphere, and who disguise everything by the unsubstantial language of ambiguous resolutions that do not mean anything and do not say anything in order to avoid displeasing this or that delegate, do not realize how much human support is lost for the League through their tactics. They do not realize that there are in the world millions of people ready to back the League if they were given a real chance to do so. But to win the support of these millions the language of truth must be employed. It is the support of men in the street that a human institution like the League wants. It is on the men in the street and not on the producers of arms and munitions that a solid policy of peace can be built.

The Commission's statement that the arms and war material of every description used in the Chaco are not manufactured locally, but are supplied to the belligerents by American and European countries, led the Council to adopt the embargo resolution at its meeting in May 1934. The mere announcement of the embargo created everywhere a strong current of sympathy and confidence in Geneva. It was something precise; it went beyond mere words. The moral sense of the world was one in the desire that the embargo should be carried out without any deception, excuse, or pretext. More worthy of condemnation, indeed, than the war itself, and than the obstinacy of those who are misled into attempting to settle by arms what can be settled only by arbitration, would be the conduct of members of the League who, bound by the Covenant of the League, might make it easy by a passive attitude or through a desire to participate in the traffic in arms for two other members of the League to continue their warfare. I hope that the Assembly of the League will be inexorable on this point, if it comes up before the Assembly in September, as is expected. And I hope that the majority of the League members will favour a strong position in this respect. Underneath the deceptive appearances of peace, this world of 1934 is too menaced from different sides to regard with indifference a new attack on the prestige of the League. The prestige of the League requires that the Chaco War be brought to an end. The time is long past for the finish of that conflict.

CHAPTER VIII

SOCIAL JUSTICE AND WORLD PEACE

by

E. J. PHELAN

Assistant Director of the International Labour Office

WHAT, if any, is the connection between social justice and world peace?

That connection is affirmed, in very definite terms, in the Constitution of the International Labour Organization, the Preamble to which states that—

> 'Peace can be established only if it is based on social justice.'

What is the value of that affirmation? Is it just a grandiloquent phrase, or is it a basic principle of the highest importance? Is it a self-evident truth or a reasoned conviction, and if it may be regarded as a reasoned conviction what reasons can be advanced for holding it?

No doubt the question could be discussed in philosophical terms, but it will be simpler to tackle it as a severely practical issue. Social justice and Peace are not easily definable, nor even easily recognizable concepts. Social injustice and War are more concrete phenomena which we can more readily identify. So let us see if we can establish the proposition that social injustice makes war more probable.

i. *How Do Wars Break Out?*

If we were to make a list of how wars have in fact begun we should perhaps find it difficult to arrange it in the most suitable order, but it may be taken as fairly certain that we should have at one end of the scale violent and unprovoked aggression, and at the other end a drift towards war in a situation growing steadily more menacing.

But in either case there has been a long period of incubation which culminates either in the sudden violent explosion or in the situation in which the fuse is steadily burning towards the powder-barrel, and the feet that should stamp on it seem inexplicably paralysed.

During that period of incubation it is evident that our peace machinery has failed, or that there has been a refusal to use it. Are we to regard this failure or refusal as the triumph of a war movement over the peace movement?

There are, of course, forces in the world making for war. There are also forces, active or latent, making for peace. I think we can take it that the forces making for peace are the stronger. Without attempting to make any comparative analysis it would seem safe to make this assertion, for the general reason that the overwhelming majority of men and women in the world do not want war.

They may find themselves at war at one moment or another, they may be led to believe that war is inevitable like a storm, or necessary like a surgical operation, but they no more desire war than they desire bad weather or the surgeon's knife.

As Professor Delisle Burns put it, war 'is a survival irreconcilable with modern civilization', and men are coming more and more to believe that it, like typhoid, can and should be eliminated by appropriate measures of sanitation. Plagues, like typhoid, are no longer regarded by the majority as visitations of vengeance, or punishment which it is futile to combat. 'War', to quote Delisle Burns again, 'is becoming less respectable.'

Hence we may take it that the overwhelming majority of men and women are anti-war, and that if their will could be effective there would be no war.

But their will must be effective at the right time, and the right time is in fact all the time.

This collective will must be exercised to control all the contributory causes of war before their cumulative effect becomes too great. For at that moment the will against war would conflict violently with the momentum of the movement towards war, and war—though in this case civil war—might be the result. And civil war is a temptation to, and therefore a potential cause of international war.

Let us look at some of the other causes of war. Attempts have been made to analyse them by several writers, but it will suffice for our purpose to take a few more or less at random.

There are psychological causes like 'the Defence Complex'[1] which has its roots in unanalysed fears and uncritical suspicions, but which is nourished by the wrong teaching of history, by Press campaigns, by the propaganda of certain interests, and by professional appeals. There are industrial causes like the private manufacture of and traffic in arms; economic causes; racial and religious animosities; and above all bad foreign policies, either unwise and unwittingly dangerous or deliberately adopted to distract attention from home policies which are giving rise to criticism or discontent.

Any of these, or any combination of them, may develop to danger-point unless they are controlled directly within

[1] See Delisle Burns, *War*. See also *The Causes of War*, by Salter and others.

the nation, or unless they are dealt with successfully through the international peace machinery, and war may be the result. Since some of them may in given circumstances not be susceptible of control nationally, for example, a case of acute economic friction between two countries, we must add to our list of causes of war, defects in the peace machinery, or the inability to make it function. No one would pretend that, admirable as the existing peace machinery is, it is yet perfect or complete. But the imperfections in it are of little importance in comparison with the fact that in one vitally important sphere it is non-existent. Not all international disputes are of such a nature that they can be settled by the procedures of conciliation and arbitration, or by legal decisions from the Permanent Court, any more than all disputes within a nation can be settled by the corresponding national procedures.[1] There are causes where the needs of the community require a change in the law, and the provision for the international treatment of cases of this kind has so far remained a dead letter.

Governments and Statesmen have so far failed to make any real constructive effort in the direction of filling this lacuna, and until they succeed in doing so it would be folly to exaggerate the perfection of the machinery which we at present possess.

For our present purpose, however, it is enough to note that this lacuna in our peace machinery is, if not a cause of war, at all events a symptom that the will of the majority against war is not effective. The same, of course, is true of the insufficiency of national control or reaction to the other examples of factors making for war which we noted above. It is clear that if the will against war were effective

[1] See Brierly, in *Problems of Peace* (3rd Series).

there would be a deliberate active policy for dealing with all factors making for war within the nation, and a similar policy as regards the operation and extension of the international peace machinery.

ii. *Social Justice the Essential Condition of Responsible Democratic Government and Peace.*

We are led to ask, therefore, how the will of the mass of men operates. The answer is that it expresses itself through what is called public opinion.[1] And public opinion can influence the instruments of Government and determine their action in the fields we have been considering.

But in order to operate effectively in this way public opinion must be definite and coherent. It must also possess a knowledge of the way in which it can influence and control the governmental machine. Power and a programme are not in themselves sufficient, any more than the possession of an automobile and the intention to go to Edinburgh are enough unless the possessor of them has the technical knowledge necessary in order to drive a car. A great deal of technical knowledge is indispensable nowadays before any body of public opinion, however strong and however clear-minded, can hope to exercise any effective control of the governmental machine. The governmental machine, guided by astute politicians, may of course deviate temporarily in the direction that public opinion demands, or public opinion may be persuaded that (to resume our simile) the car is really going to take it to Edinburgh, though it happens to be heading rapidly along the road from London to Land's End. But that is not the same thing, it only

[1] For a discussion of public opinion, see *Problems of Peace*, 8th Series.

means that the owner of the car is at the mercy of the chauffeur.

The need for the education of citizens in the effective exercise of their rights and duties in the modern State has recently been recognized in England, where an association has been founded under imposing patronage to promote this very object.

Any such effort is undoubtedly of the highest value. But it only touches one-half of the problem, and the less important half. It solves, or would solve if it were successful, the problem of the teachers. But what of the pupils?

The pupils, if they are not only to benefit by such teaching but to be able to apply what is taught, must fulfil certain conditions. They must presumably live in conditions in which learning is possible. No schoolmaster could hope to make a success of pupils who were unhealthy in body or exhausted by nervous strain, or perpetually preoccupied with the material problems of existence.

If we are to have intelligent, active, and enlightened citizens we must first have healthy citizens. And, secondly, these citizens must have time: time to learn, time to read, time to criticize what they read, time to follow political issues, local, national and international, time to participate in the discussion of those issues, time to take a share of active leadership in one or other field—in other words, time to master and fulfil all the essential duties of a citizen of a modern State.

How are health and time to be provided?

The answer is of course obvious. By such measures as the abolition of slums and the provision of healthy houses, by the protection of women and children, by the provision of free and equal educational facilities for all, by the prohibition of employment at too early an age, by provision for sickness, old age, and unemployment, by the limitation of hours of work, by the guarantee of leisure each day, by provision for a weekly rest and paid holidays, by securing for all the possibility of a decent standard of life—in other words, by the abolition of all and any of those conditions of social injustice which at present differentiate the lot of the great mass of the people from that of a favoured and privileged minority.

So we can summarize our argument as follows: To have peace you must have Governments who will carry out the peoples' will to peace; to have such Governments you must have politically active and enlightened citizens, citizens with the time and the knowledge required to control the Governments responsible to them, and such citizens will be more numerous and better equipped for their task in the degree in which social justice triumphs over social injustice.

If the solemn affirmation in the Constitution of the International Labour Organization has a meaning, it is presumably this, and it would seem impossible to deny its validity.

It may, of course, be urged that it is equally true that in order to have social justice we must have peace. There is no doubt that this is so. It is hardly necessary to show that if the wealth and energy of a community are consumed in war the progress towards social justice will in all likelihood be arrested. Moreover, since the successful pursuit of social justice involves international collaboration, it is clear that that international effort cannot be pursued if such collaboration is impossible. Hence we can affirm that peace is a condition of the successful pursuit of social justice.

But are these two principles, first that peace is based upon social justice, second that social justice is based upon peace, of equal value? A little reflection will show that the latter is only a truism. To say that social justice is based upon peace is only to say that war destroys or impedes certain peace activities. Though social justice may be unattainable without peace, it does not follow that peace, in the sense of the absence of war, will of itself produce social justice. And if by peace we mean a positive living thing, the continuous effort of man to preserve, strengthen, and embellish his civilization, then to say that peace is a condition of social justice only amounts to saying that social justice will not be achieved if no effort is made to achieve it. To say, however, that the pursuit of social justice is a potent factor in the establishment of peace is to state a principle which is more than a truism. It suggests, on analysis, a whole policy which, if successfully applied, should result in a peaceful world, a policy which, be it noted, will 'establish' peace, not just maintain it in some kind of unstable equilibrium

The argument, of course, may be stated otherwise: since peace is admittedly a necessary condition of social justice, then our efforts must be primarily directed to the maintenance of peace in order that the effort towards social justice may be possible. This implies that we can establish a certain priority among our peace activities. Put in concrete terms, it means that our major effort should be put into the peace-maintaining machinery and that our efforts to secure social justice should take a secondary place.

If we look at the problem from this angle we may note first that it is a question of the relative importance of our effort, and not of priority in time. No one would suggest that all our peaceful activities, or what we may call peace-contributing activities, should stop until a peace machinery functions with absolute certainty. What we have to examine is whether we can best *establish* peace by giving our major attention to strengthening and rendering more effective the peace machinery, or whether an equal or even greater effort should not be made to secure social justice. It would seem to follow from our earlier analysis that this latter principle is the sounder. Our peace machinery is necessarily a machinery between Governments. No matter how perfect it may be, the only guarantee that it will be made to function is that the Governments shall be peace-seeking Governments. And if we attempt to examine how best peace-seeking Governments may become the rule of our civilization we are led back to the problem of the citizen and his conditions of life.

Thus there would seem to be ample justification for writing into the Peace Treaties the principle that 'peace can be established only if it is based on social justice,' and no reason for astonishment at not finding the converse proposition affirmed in the same solemn manner.

iii. *The Preamble to the Constitution of the International Labour Organization and Its Implications.*

Philosophical historians may perhaps be tempted to discuss at some future date how clearly the implications of the principle we have been discussing were seized by those who wrote it into the Preamble of the Constitution they were drafting.

It is an interesting fact that the Preamble was written, not before, but after the earlier drafts of the Constitution had been made, and subsequently the Preamble received little or no discussion.[1]

Assuming it to be fundamental, let us now examine to what conclusions it would have led if it had been taken as the starting-point of a logical effort to give it practical application.

In the first place, it implies international action. The obstacles in the way of social progress which arise from international competition are too well known to need discussion here, and the necessity for international action to overcome them may be taken as established. International action implies, of course, some form of international organization through which it can operate.

In the second place, it is clear that the membership of that organization should be universal, and that there should be no barrier to its becoming as universal as possible. The fact that social progress in one country is hampered by its absence elsewhere means that any organization to promote it must endeavour to include all States. Its endeavour to do so must not be hindered by other considerations, such as, for example, the political relations between the States which may be willing to co-operate in its efforts. This principle is important because there has been some legal controversy in the past as to whether a State which ceased to be a Member of the League of Nations could continue to be a Member of the International Labour Organization, and as to whether the International Labour Organization could include Members who were not Members of the League. Whatever the value of the legal objections advanced (there are legal arguments on the other side of perhaps equal or

[1] See *The Origins of the International Labour Organization*, edited by Professor Shotwell, Columbia University Press.

greater weight) they have been overridden by the facts, and it is interesting to note that a consideration of purely theoretical principle leads to the same conclusion. If it be true that social justice is the foundation of peace, there is clearly no illogicality in the foundations being more extensive than the political structure which it may be possible to build on them at any given time. Thus while Membership of the League should involve Membership of the International Labour Organization, it would be both unwise and illogical to insist on the converse proposition that Membership of the Labour Organization must involve Membership of the League.

The third conclusion to which we are led is that the Organization must function continuously. We have seen above that the proper time for the action of the will against war is all the time. An organization to pursue social justice is not just this reform or that, or even any theoretically complete programme of reform. It is not a measure or a series of measures to be taken, but a way of life which needs to be perpetually adapted to the conditions of a changing civilization.

In the fourth place, we reach a conclusion of fundamental importance. Social justice is not only a way of life; it is a way of living. That means that its achievement concerns the individual in the things which affect him most. It concerns his home, his health, his education, the detailed conditions in which he works, and his leisure. It is definitely connected with, and in fact has no meaning apart from those questions which of all others are the most domestic in the sense of that term as it is used in international law.

From the international lawyer's point of view domestic

questions lie at the extreme limit of the operation of the law which is his province. Even as regards the Covenant and the competence of the Court, these domestic questions are regarded as only exceptionally subject to international interference or even concern, except where, as in the case of minorities, specific provision has been made—and that, be it noted, has only proved possible when it could be made on the occasion of the creation of a new State, or when an existing State secured a great extension of territory hitherto under other rule.

But international action as regards social justice means continuous international concern and possible interference in a host of questions which hitherto have been regarded as solely an affair between a State and its subjects. Hence it involves a surrender of sovereignty deeper and wider than that involved in any other international action.

Moreover, many of these domestic questions are, so to speak, so domestic that they escape to some extent from the regulation of the different national Governments: they often concern matters with which Governments or Parliaments hesitate to deal without consultation, and indeed agreement, with the interests concerned. Industry in the highly developed modern State is practically self-governing: Governments hesitate to do more than give legislative sanction to matters on which employers and workers have agreed, since, where substantial agreement is lacking, legislation would in all probability remain a dead letter. Hence international action in questions of this kind cannot operate solely through Governments. If it is to be effective it must have direct contact with and operate in negotiation with non-governmental elements. Representatives of the organized interests of employers and workers must form part of its machinery just as much as representatives of Governments. Here, again, we must have a vital breach in the theory of sovereignty, since sovereignty can hardly be reconciled with international negotiations carried on through delegates who are not purely Government nominees, and who are responsible to elements within the nation and not to the constitutional national authority.

The practical application of this principle will of course lead us into further novelties. International negotiation if it is successful leads to agreement, and agreements are embodied in treaties. But we shall clearly need a new form of treaty if the negotiations include other than those who usually conclude treaties on behalf of Governments. We shall need a new treaty technique.

Our next conclusion must be that unparalleled as these inroads on national sovereignty may be, they cannot be limited in advance. We cannot say that international action shall concern, for example, only wage-earners or industrial workers. The problem is wider than that of those who are paid wages, and it is not confined to industry. Nor would it do to take the very wide definition of all those under a contract of labour, whether engaged in the manufacturing, transport, and agricultural industries, or in commerce. This definition will not do for the simple reason that it excludes those whose case is most urgent, those whose case is urgent because they are not engaged at all, but are unemployed. And it might also be held to exclude measures regarding those who are employed but who should not be, children who work at too early an age, and women who work at processes or occupations which are specially dangerous to the essential social function of motherhood. Moreover, there can be no theoretical reason for excluding other workers who would not be covered by the above definition, for example, intellectual workers and civil servants. It may, of course, be neither possible nor desirable to deal with certain of these classes of workers at a given moment. The point is that the nature and extent of the regulation required cannot be foreseen in advance, and hence no limited definition of competence is possible. The Organization must therefore be autonomous in the fullest sense of being able to define its own competence as occasion may require.

This is equally evident if we regard the problem of its competence from the point of view of the questions which it may have to regulate. In dealing with social insurance, or hours of labour, or wages, its competence clearly extends to what the economists call the problem of distribution. Thus the economic field cannot be considered as excluded from its competence. And it is easy to imagine political questions which are in essence questions of a social kind. Hence, by neither *rational*, *personal* nor *routine* material can the competence of the Organization be pre-determined, but it must be defined by the action which is found possible and desirable in whatever circumstances may arise. And in consequence it must be an organization of the first rank, that is to say, that no other international organization can be considered as superior to it and capable of limiting its powers.

It does not fall within the compass of this paper to take the constitution of the International Labour Organization and, by analysing its provisions, determine how far it fulfils these logical deductions from the affirmation contained in its preamble. Historical analysts may one day attempt to discover whether these theoretical *desiderata* were in fact consciously translated into the written Constitution of the Organization by its authors in Paris. But whether they were conscious of the vast implications of the principle which they inscribed in the Preamble or not, the fact remains that it is difficult to find anything in it which conflicts with the theoretical conclusions which we have reached. Moreover, where the Constitution is silent legal decisions by the Court have gone in the direction indicated above, and the actual practice of the Organization has created a kind of case law which has steadily tended to make it approach to the kind of organization which its fundamental purpose would seem to imply. The representation of non-governmental interests is of course a permanent feature of its structure, and has proved not only workable but an element adding enormously to the vitality and authority of its action. Its interference with 'domestic' questions has led to no outcry about the violation of sovereignty. Its membership has been steadily widening towards the universal, and it has taken within the ambit of its decisions not only Colonies but Mandated Territories. The direct penetration of the activities of the Organization into the economic field has not yet perhaps been great, but it has been significantly begun.

Thus whatever may be the philosophical implications of the dictum that 'peace can be established only if it is founded on social justice', it has in fact served to guide an institution which has succeeded in concentrating and rendering effective a world-wide effort towards the improvement of social conditions. If that institution continues in the same spirit, can there be any doubt that it will make a vital contribution to the cause of peace, and that while the League performs the essential political service of attempting to preserve an unstable international equilibrium, the dangerous quicksand upon which it is at present based may be steadily replaced by that solid foundation of social justice upon which alone Peace can be made secure.

CHAPTER IX

TRENDS OF RECOVERY

by

DR. J. B. CONDLIFFE

Member of the Economic Intelligence Service of the League of Nations Secretariat

i. *The Meaning of Recovery*

THE term 'recovery' has come to have a technical meaning when applied to the fluctuations of economic activity that make up the business cycle. The recovery phase of a cycle follows immediately after the phase of depression and precedes that of prosperity. Recovery therefore is equivalent to convalescence rather than health, and evidence of recovery is always to be noted before anything like full restoration of business activity has been achieved. Moreover, recovery, like convalescence from a complicated illness, is usually uneven. Some aspects of economic life and some areas of activity are slower to recover than others, and the patient is always liable to relapses.

With this preliminary qualification and definition one may proceed to state in general terms the evidence of recovery that may be observed up to the middle of 1934. Looking back over the statistical material now available, it seems clear that the lowest point of the depression was reached, in the world as a whole, in the middle of 1932. In some countries production was increasing, unemployment was diminishing, and disequilibria in the economic structure were being righted, before that date. On the other hand there were important economic and financial relapses, notably the banking crisis in the United States, after that date. But there is a notable convergence of the world indices; for example, those of world production and world unemployment, which indicates the summer of 1932 as the turning-point between the depression and recovery phases of the cycle. In so far as any one single event can be said to mark this turning-point, that event was the successful issue of the Lausanne Conference in July 1932, which effectively disposed of the Reparation problem which had complicated both the political and the economic relations of post-war Europe. Not only was this sore spot healed, but there was hope of rapid action concerning War Debts and concerning international co-operation. It is important to recall the fact that even the promise of such relief from international strain and strife immediately brought an uprush of returning confidence, sufficient to check depression and mark the turning-point to recovery. Delay and disappointments ensued, and setbacks were inevitable; but the lesson of Lausanne remains.

It will be noted that in the preceding paragraphs use was made of the terminology familiar to students of business cycles. The economic developments from 1925 to 1934 follow in fact the course of a major cycle, and, while there are, undoubtedly, very confusing and complicating elements in that cycle arising both from long-term population, production, and consumption trends, and from Government policies, the recovery so far achieved has followed in the main the characteristic cyclical pattern. That is to say, that a large part of the progress so far made has been due to the adjustments and initiative of countless numbers of individuals in their search for daily bread under difficult conditions. The resilience and adaptability which is a characteristic feature of the system of free enterprise has enabled production to be carried on and profits to be made, even in the troubled and disorderly circumstances of recent years.

One is tempted, indeed, to follow further at this point the medical metaphor with which this paper began. Accurate diagnosis of the complicated troubles from which the world has been suffering for many years is not yet finally established; but two points seem to be clear. First, the patient had several ailments, some of them organic, and some the results of a nasty fall (in prices). And, secondly, both of these sorts of ailment seem to have been aggravated by a prolonged spell of (credit) intoxication. As usual in such situations also, one must take account of the psychological distress, as well as the realization of physical disorders, that ensues when the patient sobers up. The author of the *Anatomy of Melancholy* described this situation perfectly when he wrote: 'The State was like a sick body which had lately taken Physick, being not well cleared of its Humours, and weakened so much by Purging, that nothing was left but Melancholy.' The remedies prescribed for such a combination of troubles have naturally been numerous and varied—some indeed may quite definitely be classed as quack remedies. But the chief prescriptions seem to fall into two or three main groups. There is, first, the stern remedy of a strict regime, supplemented by cold douches of deflation. More kindly has been the removal of the patient to a more temperate (currency) climate. Another favourite remedy has been to prescribe a tonic, though there is a danger of such tonics resolving themselves into habit-forming drugs. The sceptical observer, however, in the midst of such confusion of remedial counsel, is likely to conclude that much of the recovery so far achieved has been due to the tough constitution and natural recuperative powers of the patient, which have enabled him to survive both the illness and the remedies.

ii. *The Improvement in* 1933–4.

From about the middle of 1933, after the world recovered somewhat from the fresh shock of the American banking collapse in February and March, recovery was definitely accelerated. Let me cite some of the statistics which may be used to measure the extent of recovery in 1933–4.

The following brief table summarizes the world indices of production that are available. They are calculated on an annual basis, and therefore do not show either the turning-point in the middle of 1932 or the full extent of the recovery to the middle of 1934; but they indicate definite and substantial increases of production for the year 1933 as compared with the preceding year.

WORLD PRODUCTION OF CRUDE FOODSTUFFS,* RAW MATERIALS,* AND INDUSTRIAL PRODUCTION.†

(Base: Average 1925–9 = 100)

	1925	1929	1930	1931	1932	1933
Crude Foodstuffs .	98	103	104	102	104	103
Raw Materials:						
Agricultural . .	97	105	103	103	96	100
Non-Agricultural	90	114	101	86	73	82
Industrial Production	91	112	98	87	77	86

* League of Nations, *World Production and Prices*, 1925–33, Geneva 1934.

† 'Institut fur Konjunkturforschung', Berlin.

The largest increase, it will be noted, has been in industrial production and in the production of non-agricultural raw materials, the aspects of production which suffered most heavily in the depression. It should be said, however, that the indices of industrial production are compiled in different countries by different methods. In nearly all, raw materials loom large, and in some indirect measures such as employment and raw materials imported are used. These indices do not, therefore, represent manufacturing production. The world index given above is simply a weighted average of the national index-numbers of some important industrial countries. The gain in 1933 as compared with 1932 was 4 per cent in agricultural raw materials and almost 12 per cent in industrial production, while the production of foodstuffs remained almost stationary. The world index of unemployment calculated by the International Labour Office shows a decline of 6 per cent in 1933, compared with 1932.

If the monthly index-numbers of industrial production compiled by many countries are compared for the month of June in each of the last three years it is obvious that the pace of recovery has differed in the various countries, but in most the increase of production has been fairly substantial since June 1932. The index for June 1934 showed the greatest rise in Canada, Germany, the United States and Sweden, and a substantial rise in the United Kingdom. There was on the other hand a distinct fall in France (*see table on next page*). The unemployment index is available only up to April, but compared with April 1933 it fell by over 24 per cent.[1]

[1] *International Labour Review*, July 1934, p. 116.

THE INCREASE OF INDUSTRIAL PRODUCTION IN CERTAIN COUNTRIES FROM JUNE 1932 TO JUNE 1934*

(Base: 1928 = 100)

Country	Index Numbers—June			Percentage	Increase
	1932	1933	1934	1932–4	1933–4
France . .	73·2	87·4	78·0	6·6	—10·8
United States† .	53·2	82·9	77·5‡	45·6	— 8·3
Belgium . .	65·9	72·8	70·2	6·5	— 3·6
Netherlands .	58·6	68·7	70·0	19·4	1·9
Norway . .	—	111·6	114·8	—	3·1
Austria† . .	63·2	65·6	68·1§	7·8	3·8
Chile† . .	105·1	117·5	125·6	19·5	6·9
Poland† . .	54·4	57·8	62·1	14·2	7·4
Italy . . .	62·7	79·1	65·7	36·7	8·3
Finland‖¶ . .	101·5	117·5	130·0	28·1	10·6
Hungary† . .	51·9¶	81·2¶	90·9**	75·4	12·0
United Kingdom¶	89·4	91·7	104·0††	16·3	13·4
Japan§ . .	108·9	126·0	143·5	31·7	13·9
Czechoslovakia‡	67·6	63·0	74·0	9·5	17·5
Canada† . .	65·3	67·1	80·8	23·7	19·4
Germany† .	60·7	69·5	68·1	45·8	27·3
Roumania** .	—	88·8	116·8	—	31·4
Sweden† . .	76·9	81·7	107·7	40·1	31·8

* League of Nations, *World Economic Survey, Third Year*, 1933–4.
† Adjusted for seasonal variations. ‡ May. § April.
‖ 1926 = 100. ¶ 2nd quarter. ** 1st quarter. †† Provisional.

It will be obvious that there is a marked difference between the developments in the countries on and off the gold standard. In the former, especially in those where there has been the added stimulus of heavy Government expenditures, the increase has been greater, and in the latter, with the notable exception of Poland, where deflation came early and was very thorough, the increase has been small, or there has been an actual decrease. Inspection of the monthly indices shows that a tendency to decline set in during the latter half of 1933 when the dollar depreciated, and this was reinforced, e.g. in France, when further deflationary measures were introduced in the early months of 1934. Italy is a notable exception, but in that country the recent strain on the balance of payments indicates that the increase of production is somewhat out of harmony with the external situation.

iii. *The Recovery in 'Investment' Goods.*

If one turns to analyse the nature of this increase in production two main trends of development may be noted. In the first place the increased production, in those countries which show the greatest increase, has been mainly in 'investment' goods—that is, the production of such commodities as iron and steel, which are used in the production of other goods, and which demand an investment of capital for a long period. This is shown quite clearly in the table on the next page.

It will be seen that in the first four countries the increase of production has been greatest in investment goods, and that the production of investment goods proportionately to consumption goods produced has moved back towards the 1929 ratio. In the United Kingdom in the first quarter of 1934 the ratio was practically back to that of 1929. In the United States it remained very low.

In the three gold countries, however, the increase from

the quarter of lowest production has been mainly in consumption goods, and the ratios have moved downward from the 1929 levels. This is particularly marked in the case of France.

THE PRODUCTION OF INVESTMENT AND CONSUMPTION GOODS*

Country	Quarter of Lowest Production	Percentage Decline from 1925–9 Level to Minimum		Percentage Rise from Minimum to 1st Quarter, 1934		Percentage Ratio of Investment to Consumption Indices (1925–9)=100	
		Investment Goods	Consumption Goods	Investment Goods	Consumption Goods	Lowest Quarter	1st Quarter, 1934
Germany	III 1932	−60	−17	+63	+22	48	64
Sweden	III 1932	−27	− 7	+41	+26	78	88
United Kingdom	III 1932	−28	−15	+35	+16	85	99
United States	III 1932	−75	−24	+96	+17	33	55
France	II 1932	−30	−29	+ 9	+34	99	80
Netherlands	III 1932	−49	−24	+25	+45	67	58
Poland	I 1933	−51	−44	+20	+43	88	74

* League of Nations, *World Production and Prices*, 1925–33.

iv. *Production for the Home Market.*

The second trend that may be noticed is a distinct tendency for production to increase, in the great industrial countries, in the home market rather than the export market industries. This trend is clearly shown in a diagram published both in *World Production and Prices*, 1933–4, and the *World Economic Survey*, 1933–4, which is not available for reproduction here. The following table, however, illustrate both this trend in the industrial countries and the reverse trend in the raw material exporting countries.

PRODUCTION FOR EXPORT AND HOME MARKET INDUSTRIES IN SWEDEN AND FINLAND*

(Base: 1929 = 100)

	1930	1931	1932	1933	1934 (1st Quarter)
Sweden:					
Export . .	97	78	66	72	85
Home Market .	97	89	87	88	101
Finland:					
Export . .	93	86	92	104	117
Home Market .	95	82	83	97	99

* League of Nations, *World Production and Prices*, 1925–33.

Finland depends largely upon the export of raw materials—wood products—which, as will be shown later, have been relatively less restricted than other classes of commodities entering into international trade. The increased production shown in the export industries in this case is paralleled by similar increases in such countries as the British Dominions, South American, and tropical countries which produce mainly raw materials. Where the export of foodstuffs from those countries has not been restricted up to the present, as in the case of the British Dominions, recovery has been even more pronounced. The development shown for Sweden, on the other hand, is even more marked in the case of France, Germany, the United Kingdom, and the United States.

v. *Changes in World Trade.*

The importance of this development may be further illustrated by the statistics which measure changes in the quantum of goods entering into world trade. These are given below:

QUANTUM OF WORLD TRADE IN FOODSTUFFS, RAW MATERIALS, AND MANUFACTURES

(Base: 1929 = 100)

	1932	1933
Foodstuffs . . .	91	83·5
Raw Materials . .	80	86·5
Manufactures . . .	58	59

The value of world trade, measured in gold, was still falling in the middle of 1934, as it had been falling steadily since the outset of the depression in the latter part of 1929. Measured in terms of sterling, however, the decline appears to have been stayed in the latter part of 1933, and the quantum of trade increased slightly in that year, the further continuing fall in value being due to the downward tendency of gold prices.[1] The increase in quantum, however, is mainly due to the substantial increase in the quantum of raw materials traded, those raw materials going mainly into the production of goods for the home market in the great industrial countries. This is clearly shown by the figures given above. In 1933, as compared with 1932,

[1] League of Nations, *Review of World Trade*, 1933–4.

the quantum of trade in raw materials increased by over 8 per cent, that in manufactures by less than 2 per cent, while the quantum of trade in foodstuffs fell by rather more than 8 per cent.

vi. *Agricultural Protection in the Industrial Countries.*

This fall in the quantum of foodstuffs traded is, of course, due to the tightening of agricultural protection in the industrial countries, a policy which shows no signs of relaxation up to the present, and which may even be extended to a restriction of food imports from the British Dominions into the United Kingdom when the Ottawa agreements expire in 1935. The importance of agricultural protection in the industrial countries may be illustrated by the statistics of wheat production up to 1933. Parallel movements might be demonstrated in respect of other important food commodities, such, e.g., as rice in the Far East, meat and dairy produce. The restrictions imposed upon wheat imports came earliest, and the difficulties of cereal producers in the great exporting areas caused a marked shift from cereal to animal farming in those areas, so that, at a later stage of the depression, the production of meat and dairy produce increased rapidly and the demand grew up in the industrial countries for restrictions upon the import of those commodities also. The table opposite shows the development of wheat production in three main groups of countries—the four major exporters (the Argentine, Australia, Canada, and the United States), the Danubian exporters (Bulgaria, Hungary, Roumania, and Yugoslavia), and importing Europe (the other European countries).

THE PRODUCTION OF WHEAT 1928–9 TO 1933–4*

	1928–9	1930–1	1931–2	1932–3	1933–4
Four Major Exporters					
Area (Hectares) .	48·9	50·1	45·5	46·9	43·6
Yield (Metric tons)	54·5	46·9	44·4	43·3	33·0
Danubian Exporters					
Area (Hectares) .	7·9	8·1	8·5	7·6	8·0
Yield (Metric tons)	10·0	9·6	10·1	6·1	9·9
Importing Europe					
Area (Hectares) .	19·5	19·9	20·2	20·9	21·5
Yield (Metric tons)	26·6	24·9	26·5	32·9	34·2

* League of Nations, *World Production and Prices*, 1925–33.

Several features of this development are worth noticing; but first it should be remarked that the statistics cited above do not include the production of the U.S.S.R., or of a number of minor producing areas which must be reckoned with in the total of world production. With the large accumulated stocks that have hung over the market since 1928–9, and the low prices that have prevailed, competition from outside producers has not been important in recent years, but a substantial rise in the price of wheat might cause an increase of production once again in these areas. Since 1930–1 there has been no great export surplus from the U.S.S.R., recent harvests having been poor, while less emphasis is placed in the second Five-Year Plan upon the necessity of marketing an export surplus of grain in order to obtain raw materials and machinery for industrial development.

The most important figure in the table above is that which shows that for 1933–4 (not including the 1934 harvest in the northern hemisphere) the production of wheat in importing Europe was actually greater than in the four main exporting countries, though at the beginning of the depression it was less than half as great. While this figure is partially explained by harvest failures (in the United States particularly) and by acreage reduction, the steady increase of European production is very impressive.

It will be noted also that the yield per acre is greater in Europe than overseas. The obverse of this fact is that the cost of production by the intensive labour-consuming methods of Europe is much greater than that in the major exporting countries. Greater production at a higher cost, and diminished production at a lower cost, is an achievement which requires political rather than economic organization. We have lived to witness the curious spectacle of Governments in high-cost areas subsidizing the production of a basic commodity which Governments in low-cost areas are paying their farmers not to grow, or, having grown, to destroy.

vii. *The Outlook.*

So far as the trends of recovery could be measured in the summer of 1934, therefore, they might be summarized somewhat as follows. Industrial production, having fallen about 30–35 per cent during the depression, had regained about a quarter of the lost ground; unemployment having trebled, had decreased again to rather more than double its 1929 total; international trade having fallen in gold value to a third, and in sterling value to about half, of its pre-depression level had ceased to shrink in volume, but still remained about three-fourths in quantum of what it had been. Raw materials were moving more freely, but the quantum of manufactured goods traded was not increasing much, and new restrictions were being imposed upon the exchange of foodstuffs. The main recovery in production so far registered had taken the form of increased production for the home-markets of the great industrial countries.

All the indications pointed to the fact that the business cycle was doing its best to stage a quite normal type of recovery based upon a revival of the investment industries. The recovery, however, was unevenly distributed over the various countries, and some part of it in the countries whose currencies were depreciated could be attributed, in the carefully chosen phrase of the International Chamber of Commerce, to the 'tacit acquiescence' of those countries whose currencies had not depreciated. In other countries the rapidity of the recovery was quite obviously due to rather large doses of the stimulant of Government expenditure.

The middle of the year is always a period of hesitation, of halting between opinions. As usual in the northern summer there is a seasonal recession of economic activity. Recovery has slowed down, and doubts have inevitably arisen concerning its hoped-for resumption in the autumn. Statistical inquiry can yield no answer to the questions that naturally arise at such a time; but some of the questions may now perhaps be put. Will the recovery of those countries which have responded to large tonic doses of Government expenditure continue to develop if those doses are diminished, or must the stimulant be renewed in larger doses? Can the domestic markets continue to absorb even greater production, or is the recovery based upon domestic expansion nearing its limits? How long can the countries which have suffered in neutral markets from the depression of their competitors' currencies continue to bear the strain imposed upon them? Is there any indication that a wider field for recovery is likely to be opened up by a relaxation of the restrictions upon international trade? And, finally, is individual initiative sufficient, and are the adjustments so far made adequate to enable the business cycle to emerge from recovery to the prosperity phase of the cycle?

CHAPTER X

NATIONAL ECONOMIC PLANNING AND INTERNATIONAL ORGANIZATION

by

ROBERT MACIVER

Professor of Political Science, Columbia University

i. *The Logical Problem of Organization.*

IN the study of international organization it is of importance to distinguish the logical problems involved in the effective co-ordination and harmonization of interests from the subjective difficulties which are associated with them. By the subjective difficulties I mean the historical traditions, prejudices, fears, emotional impulses, temperamental differences, and mass misunderstandings which divide nation from nation. I include all the attitudes and aspirations, whether to be admired or to be deplored, whether to be reverenced or to be pitied, which make up what is often called, though with what I regard as a false implication of mystical entity, the 'soul of a people'. By the logical problems I mean the questions of social engineering analogous to those faced by the management of a plant, by the directorate of a merger, by all who on any scale seek to combine a group of established interests or units into a more comprehensive system for the greater specific advantage of all the interests concerned. Such problems would exist even if men were completely rational beings, and in so far as they are rational beings such are the problems—social, economic, and political—which they set themselves to solve. It is to a problem of this order that I seek to address myself here. Like all international problems, it is in a high degree complicated or obscured by subjective factors, but again, like all such problems, it deserves examination in its pure or rational quality. For logic and reason do fitfully guide the strange processes of social opinion, so that what we call its soul may even in a rational people be a mind. To help towards this most important approach every aspect of international problems should be set forth without compromise, and if on that account they call us theorists and visionaries, we have no reason, in the present kind of world, to be ashamed of the appellation. In effect we persistently tend to over-simplify the logical problems of international co-operation. We are so impressed with the subjective difficulties that we neglect the architectonic problem.

ii. *The Principle That Technological Advance Necessitates International Order.*

I take it for granted that a real international order is inevitable, that the world-role of Geneva has scarcely begun. I am convinced that this is true no matter what setbacks or disasters may intervene. Even were the present League to dissolve, the idea it imperfectly embodies is as eternal as the necessity which inspired it. In time men come to terms with necessity, though it is sometimes incredible how long they must suffer before they will learn. Every new discovery of science, every new engine of power, every new means of communication, every new application of chemistry, every new technique of mass production, every device that transforms money from a concrete good into a symbol of effective demand—in short, every further irrevocable step that man takes towards both the understanding and the control of his world, leads him deeper into the necessity of an international order. There was a time when an international order would have been merely an insurance against warfare and a safeguard of secondary commerce, now it has become a condition of civilization itself.

The general principle that an international system is the logical implication of technological advance is sometimes regarded as having an important exception. It is held that the trend towards national economic planning is a serious and perhaps even fatal impediment of international co-operation. National economic planning is taken to imply the concept of the self-directed and even the self-sufficient national State. In some quarters it is regarded as inevitable that the admitted advantages of international trade and of the international movement of capital must be sacrificed for the sake of the economic stability which the unified direction of the nation's economic affairs is intended to assure. And the sacrifice itself is minimized by reference to another supposed exception to our general principle—advancing technology reduces in certain respects the comparative advantage in productive efficiency which is the classical argument for international trade. If rainy Lancashire had an advantage in cotton-spinning at one technological stage, a new advance of technology enables the Southern United States or the arid plains of India to enter into effective competition. The differentials determined by geography are reduced as transportation becomes quicker and cheaper and as local sources of power, whether water-power, coal, or oil, are converted into the more transmissible energy of electricity. The differentials determined by traditional skill are levelled by fool-proof machinery or by industrial education, as Japan and other countries have shown. Many countries can, in short, be more nearly self-supporting at somewhat higher standards of living than formerly, from which fact the inference is drawn, falsely as I believe, that international trade is of continuously lessening importance for the prosperity of nations. We have in consequence to-day two schools of economic thought, a vigorous resurgent school of economic nationalism and an opposing, but too often merely defensive, school which links national prosperity with international trade, international movements of capital, international monetary and credit standards, international economic co-operation in all its potentialities. And the issue between them is joined most decisively in the largely unexplored terrain of the planned economy.

iii. *Misconceptions of Economic Planning.*

Regarding the nature of a planned economy there is much misconception. It is not a Socialist as contrasted with a Capitalist economy. A Socialist economy inevitably involves national planning, but a Capitalist economy may no less undertake it. It is not a Fascist as contrasted with a Democratic system. A Fascist system has a seemingly freer hand in putting a comprehensive plan into operation, but in fact it is subject thereby merely to a different set of limitations from those which arise out of the impermanence of democratic administrations. National economic planning does not, or should not, mean the internal regulation by the State of the various units of the economic system. If that were indeed what it meant, then it would be no new thing, but the returning ghost of an ancient order for which Colbert stood and against which Adam Smith fought. National economic planning is the emergent principle of a world as remote from the thought of Adam Smith as from that of Julius Caesar, a world of crises and depressions and recoveries, a world of complicated interdependence, a world of vast corporations, a world in which new industries rise and old ones fall, a world in which the departure of one country from the gold standard affects the price-level in every other, a world in which the failure of an Austrian bank sends a shiver through the United States, a world which owes gigantic debts on one side of the ledger and on the other owns gigantic investments, but in such a manner that the debts mount and the investments dwindle, or perhaps *vice versa*, through the invisible forces which govern the level of prices and the activity of business. This is the kind of world in which national economic planning persistently seeks to emerge. It is in the light of such a world that we must endeavour to understand and to assess it.

iv. *In Economic Planning the State Assumes but Does Not Usurp a Function.*

What, then, is the true difference between a planned economy and the mere political regulation of economic activity? In a word it is this. When a State exercises some economic control which is a *substitute* for the control otherwise exercised by private business, when it runs a railroad instead of having a corporation run it, when it fixes wages instead of letting employers fix them, or letting employers and employees decide them by bargaining and conflict, when it lays down rules for factories which supersede the kind of rules which the factory owners would have laid down, then we are in the presence of political regulation. The State is then exercising authority over things so as to supersede the various authorities to which they would otherwise be left. There were excellent reasons why the

State should have stepped in to supersede, to limit or to modify the controls exercised by private industry. But that is beside the point of my argument. For what constitutes economic planning is precisely the undertaking by the State of economic tasks which no one, no business man, no trust, no banking corporation, consciously or overtly, undertook before. The State here does not usurp a function, it creates one. It does what hitherto has been nobody's business.

To appreciate this point it is necessary to realize the essential distinction between the economic and the political order. The economic order, as such, has no central co-ordinating directing organ. It is an arena of competing and bargaining units which achieves the character of a system through the operation of those automatic forces summed up by the economists under the law of supply and demand. There is at any given moment one price for the same goods or service in the same market, not because anyone prescribes the price, but because the law of supply and demand is operative. There are established usages over a longer period because of the play of competition and custom. In appearance it is as though some authority had laid down a guiding principle, had determined wage-rates and prices, had regulated the relationships of the separate units. In actual operation these results come about automatically, directed by no human brain. To the classical economists this type of economic system seemed a beautiful and wonderful contrivance, and was reverenced as such, so that they resented the officious intrusion of Government into its admirable and beneficent working. The laws of the economic order were to them higher than the human regulations which merely perverted or disturbed their operation, and in their more reverent moods they ascribed these laws to Providence or the unseen divine hand.

Now in the simpler world of early capitalism such a characterization of the system presided over by the law of supply and demand was at least plausible. Governments were interfering in the wrong way, as the classical economists perceived, because they were attempting to rivet the tradition of feudalism on an order inspired by anti-traditional enterprise. Alive to the needs of the new order, the economists, with that partiality of vision which affects social scientists as well as the rest of humanity, saw its ideal rather than its real character. The beautiful automatism of the order, with its marginal balance of prices and costs, with its rewards proportioned to enterprise, with its meting out of equal recompense to equal toil, filled their horizon. The exploitations and miseries of the factory systems were ignored. When these could be tolerated no longer, the ensuing control by Government, the system of regulation which became known as social legislation—factory acts, health insurance acts, unemployment insurance acts, workmen's compensation acts and so forth—still left unimpaired the flywheel of the system. The grand equilibrium of the price-level still depended on a more universal law. The interactions of economic forces themselves still determined, with negligible exceptions, prices and costs, wages and interest-rates, rents and profits.

v. *The Practical Breakdown of the Principle of Economic Automatism.*

In short, at the opening of the twentieth century, the industrialized countries were still in a stage of capitalism, in which ostensibly, and for the most part actually, the greater inter-relationship of economic factors were not controlled directly by human wisdom or by human folly. This state of things was reinforced by the dominance, attained in the earlier part of the nineteenth century, of an international gold standard, which established an automatic equilibrium of prices for the range of goods that entered into world commerce. The system worked reasonably well for a time, but there were forces beneath the surface which at first merely disturbed and finally shook its stability. These disturbances were of two orders. Some were generated domestically, as in the growth of great corporate powers which erected areas of price rigidity, for steel, for oil, for transportation, for public utilities, so that the automatic forces of equilibrium could not longer establish a level to which these goods were subject. Others were generated internationally, as when, for example, the gold reserves of a country were diminished, or its discount rate raised, in consequence of an adverse balance of international payments. Such disturbing factors, present in the system from the first, but growing greater with the increasing complexity of advancing capitalism, reached a climax in the vast political upheavals of the war and the peace. And thus the demand for a new type of political regulation, for economic planning, impressed alike on the practices of Government and on the thoughts of men. No longer could they repose their old confidence either in automatic law or in the unseen hand.

Let me reiterate—for it is central to our argument—that what is new in the conception of a planned economy is precisely this, that men must collectively control these larger economic adjustments and interactions which hitherto had controlled themselves. In economic planning so understood, the State is not 'interfering' with the business of the manufacturer or the banker, of the corporation or the trade union. None of them, nor all of them together, ever undertook this business. It was nobody's business, save that of the god of automatism, or of the unseen hand. What the State is here boldly proposing is to enter into joint control with the automatic forces we call economic laws. The average entrepreneur or the average banker has quaintly assumed that any governmental 'interference' with his own particular business was at the same time an interference with formidable and eternal law, as though he were a vicegerent of the economic god. On the contrary, the State flings out its real challenge to the unseen hand when it refuses to accept the swaying equilibrium of economic forces; when it seeks to check the natural downward (or upward) movement of prices; when it seeks to increase the volume of employment beyond what the state of the market prescribes; when it undertakes to regulate the direction of the employment of capital; when it endeavours to divert resources from production to consumption, or *vice versa*; when it deliberately stimulates the scale of business operations by calculated appropriations for public works; when it manipulates the interest rate so as to discourage or to encourage saving or investment. Those are the hazardous operations of economic planning to which, in some degree, the logic of events or the misery of peoples has driven the Governments of our shaken Western civilization. These are the tentatives of that planned economy, the relation of which to the international order we must presently consider.

vi. *The Proper Function of Centralized Controls.*

Let us first, however, consider some of the consequences which flow from the fact that a planned economy, properly understood, does not as such usurp the initiative of private enterprise. A factory cannot be effectively run within its various departments unless the relation between them is properly organized. The central organization, instead of curbing the enterprise of the individual units, establishes conditions calculated to evoke it. This is true at least of the great successful corporations which have learned that bureaucracy is the death of all development or expansion. The ideal to which all intelligent organization tends is that all the parts shall be able to function more freely and fully because the whole is organized. That there is so much wrong-headed and depressing organization in the world makes it only the more necessary that the true role of organization should be emphasized. In a successful economic organization the central executive does precisely the kind of job which none of the departments could or would accomplish. The same principle is applicable to the State when it embarks on economic planning. It cannot be reasonably objected that it is then meddling with the preserves of private business. It may indeed be maintained that the task is beyond the competence of Governments, perhaps particularly of democratic Governments. Or it may still be maintained that the task is itself unnecessary, and that the unseen hand is still competent to direct and overrule into one sufficient system the myriad swarming activities of the economic life. The second is the crucial objection, for I take it that if we cannot delegate the task to Providence we must and can find some way of undertaking it ourselves.

vii. *The Nature, Necessity, and Limits of such Controls in our Present Civilization.*

It would take too long to show, what I hold to be the truth, that the age which indulges in stock exchanges and central banks and billion dollar corporations and interlocking directorates and cartels and international debts can no longer assign to Providence the stewardship of its economic affairs. I hold that national economic planning and the League of Nations have arisen out of precisely the same kind of necessity, that they belong to the same kind of world, and that therefore they belong together. But, lest my argument get out of bounds, I shall content myself with one illustration, to show how inevitably both the impulse and the need to seize the higher economic controls emerge as the machinery of living grows more complicated. Of all the automatic mechanisms of the pre-war world none was regarded as being more self-sufficient, more inviolable, more sacred, than the gold standard. Now the gold standard, when it works automatically, renders any country maintaining it subject to the impact on its price-level of international gold movements. When foreign exchanges move adversely, it must either let gold flow abroad, and in consequence restrict its internal credit, or it must restrict its internal credit so as to avoid the necessity of gold exports. This statement is an over-simplified way of putting the fact that under the automatic gold standard a country's credit policy, and in the longer run its price-level, were directly responsive to the conditions determining the demand and supply of foreign exchange. Now it came to prove distinctly inconvenient that the supply of funds for business activity should be thus at the mercy of the forces working on the exchange rates. And so the great central banks gradually learned to apply a steadying hand to a too sensitive mechanism by a deliberate control over gold movements. First it was practised by the Bank of England, then about the middle of the nineteenth century by the Bank of France, and at length by the Federal Reserve System. Before the war central banks were very modest indeed regarding either their desire or their ability to regulate or mitigate the working of the gold standard. But in the greater disturbances of the post-war period the necessity for control became so obvious and so imperative that no important country to-day, whether it is on or off the gold standard, permits the fluctuations of its gold supply to affect freely its price-level or the volume of its currency and credit. The very citadel of automatism has been surrendered.

Now as soon as a country deliberately regulates the supply of money or of credit it has already embarked on the difficult enterprise of a managed or planned economy. It has already accepted the concept of an economic equilibrium which is no longer the result of what the classical economists regarded as natural forces. It already seeks to attain some stability, some ordered relation between goods and prices, between debts and credits, between business funds and business activity, which will in a degree resist the disturbing effects of these so-called natural forces. With the memory of an unprecedented crisis behind it, and still subject to its obstinate consequences, the civilized world casts about not only for means of recovery but also for means of control which will render it less subject to such devastating crashes. In short, every country is making some attempt to regulate the economic mechanism, and as the mechanism has no governor of its own the task has inevitably fallen to the State.

This task, the concerted maintenance of an economic equilibrium, is one involving great difficulties and even hazards, but these are of a technical nature which I cannot dwell on here. Complicated though they are by political conditions, they are essentially problems of economic engineering which the ingenuity and experience of men can surely solve. A first lesson to be learned, however, is the limitation of the task to its proper scope, since in the name of economic planning some Governments have been carrying on dubious activities which are quite irrelevant to the project of a planned economy. May I be permitted to illustrate this point from the recent experience of the United States.

The Roosevelt administration, assuming office in the darkest days of the depression, was inevitably committed to the principle of a planned economy. Even conservative business was at length demanding such action, and its still more conservative ally, the banking fraternity, was powerless to save itself from impending ruin. Accordingly the Administration hastily but boldly improvised a series of measures designed to establish and maintain a new or restored economic equilibrium. It planned to reduce the gold value of the dollar and otherwise to raise the level of prices, to mitigate the disparity between the burden of debts, contracted at a very different price-level, and the current resources of the debtors, to supplement the shrunken demand for producers' goods by injecting the stimulus of vast public works, and so forth. We are not here concerned with the success or otherwise of these measures. It suffices that they belonged to the order of economic planning. Suddenly, in the midst of these feverish efforts, the N.R.A. came into being and presently filled the political horizon. Regulative codes were drawn up for hundreds of industries, for the most part in accordance with and through the co-operation of the particular interests associated with each industry. In a considerable number of instances it was forbidden to undercut an established price, or an open price policy, tending to the maintenance of a uniform price for all producers, was set up.

As these measures developed, considerations of national planning were submerged because each industry was considered by itself and made the object of separate regulation. That the aggregate of particular economic interests does not sum up into the national interest is an elementary economic truth. If each industry maintains a sheltered price, and thus indirectly limits its output, a situation is created within a country similar to that which high protection fosters in the greater international area. Fortunately, it is vastly more difficult to shelter industries against the whole within a country than it is to shelter countries against the whole within a world. The price-fixing policies of the N.R.A. have been proving unworkable, and a retreat is in progress. In the long run it seems likely that the whole price-fixing structure will dissolve, and that other features of the N.R.A., particularly the regulation of hours and minimum wages, will be embodied in a national scheme of social legislation.

I have taken this example to show that national economic planning is a quite different thing from the internal regulation of individual industries. I do not see any sign at present that the Roosevelt Administration is abandoning the principle of economic planning, though it is realizing more of the difficulties which attend its application. On the other hand I see definite signs that the administration is retiring from over-ambitious excursions into a type of regulation which, so far from being integral to the policy of economic planning, in reality impedes and distorts it. A planned economy is one in which the larger interactions of economic factors are made the objects of deliberate policy, so that some sort of equilibrium may be maintained between them and that the sharp disturbances, which make statistical charts look like a series of lightning flashes, and which are the cause of incalculable human suffering, may be reduced within tolerable limits. A planned economy may, of course, go very much further, may include, for example, schemes for the consistent development of national resources, may redistribute the national income on any principle that it approves—but the criterion of the planned economy, common alike to its capitalist and to its Socialist forms, is the maintenance of an equilibrium against the blind play of economic forces. It is an attempt to assure a greater stability, a more steady development, a less precarious order in a world subject, as it grows more complex, to the ever-more disturbing revolution of the economic cycle.

viii. *Economic Planning and National Self-containedness.*

How, then, does the introduction of economic planning accord with the conditions of an international order? The assumption is not infrequently made that if a country is to maintain some kind of economic equilibrium it must shut itself in from world influences, that a planned economy is a self-contained and even a self-sufficient economy. The road to stability through self-sufficiency is one which various countries have recently pursued, but that road leads back to the primitive earth. There are parts of Africa and of Asia that have not felt the shock of the world depression. They are self-contained, and the more self-contained they are the poorer they are, and the more subject to the vagaries of that power which is most completely beyond man's control, the power that sends storm or sunshine, rain or drought or blight. Self-containedness must not be confused with stability. Great countries can emulate on a higher level the self-sufficiency of these primitive communities. They can proudly make themselves independent of the resources of the world outside their frontiers. They can call on the assistance of a science that knows no frontiers to turn their own frontiers into Chinese walls. Great as the potency of science is, such countries are ironically applying those powers to make themselves indubitably poorer than they need otherwise be. For the prosperity of a country has always borne some relation to the extent of the area within which it could trade, or on the resources of which it could draw. There is no getting away from the fact that a self-contained economy is one which deliberately abjures the advantages of trade and of the natural resources which lie beyond its borders for the sake of an assumed security which never in the world's history has depended on self-containment. Economically considered, any scheme of national self-sufficiency is a grand plan for the limitation of productivity, and therefore for the artificial creation of comparative poverty. Next to modern warfare, it is the finest example of human intelligence in reverse, operating to reduce instead of to increase the fruits of intelligence.

ix. *National Economic Stability More Attainable Within an International Order.*

There is, however, another road to the comparative stabilization of a country's economy which does not involve national isolation. It is useful to remember that the depression from which we have been suffering was—or is—practically world-wide. In short, the conditions creating the economic crisis were themselves international in their causation no less than in their range. It may well be, then, that the solution of the problem also involves international action. It may be that while each country does wisely to set its internal affairs in order it can achieve at most a partial success until the international conditions of stability are assured. Indeed, this seems to me to be more than an hypothesis, I regard it as a certainty. Again, let us take an illustration from the monetary sphere. The international monetary system of pre-war days has broken down. Every country is seeking to control its own currency independently. Countries off the gold standard have even, at times, entered into a competitive struggle to reduce the gold exchange value of their respective monetary units, so as to gain an advantage in foreign trade. They have employed vast stabilization funds to offset the free movements of foreign exchange. They have limited trade in all sorts of ways, not merely on old protectionist grounds, but to safeguard their domestic policies from the disturbances caused by gold movements or exchange settlements in the absence of an efficient and balanced international system. In short, the endeavour of every country to maintain a domestic monetary and credit stability is rendered more precarious by the similar endeavour of all the rest, where there is no central co-ordinating system on which it can rely. This difficulty can be removed only when the world is intelligent enough not simply to return to the old automatic gold standard, but to set up a standard presided over by an international authority which alone can stabilize the value of gold. The Bank for International Settlements might develop, given the co-operation of the leading nations, into such an authority. This, however, is a subject which I cannot pursue. My point is that the control by each country of its monetary policy would be rendered more secure within, and not in isolation from, an international order.

x. *The Nemesis of National Self-containedness.*

No area which is narrower than the range within which the economic forces affecting it are operative can achieve efficient control in isolation. Autonomy is not isolation. An individual who isolates himself from his fellow-men is not thereby attaining autonomy: he is merely preventing himself from the exercise of autonomy. Nor does he gain stability thereby, for he becomes the victim of the delusions which isolation breeds. The only stability a man can acquire is the flexible control which enables him to adapt himself to the conditions of a changing world. And so it is with nations. Spiritually, if they shut themselves within their own assured culture—but which, of course, is never exclusively their own—their unventilated inbred dreams of grandeur become nightmares, first to the rest of the world, and finally to themselves. Economically, if they shut themselves within their own productivity, they are no less renouncing all that the greater world outside has to offer them, and they do not gain stability in recompense, for just as an isolated locality is more at the mercy of the indigenous forces that bring a plenteous harvest or a dearth, good times or bad times, so in its degree is an isolated nation. Economically, the world is more stable than any of its areas. The nearer we can get to world organization the nearer we approach the condition of economic stability.

A stable economy is an ideal which can never be wholly

attained. A complex civilization is inevitably a changeful civilization. Consequently, if we seek economic equilibrium, it must be a moving equilibrium, a flexible equilibrium. A planned economy must be a flexible economy. Its ideal must be the very antithesis of regimentation. It must operate like the governor of a mechanism, which allows the mechanism to function freely but prevents it from getting out of gear, or developing the excessive speed that leads to a breakdown. It is a quite false conception of economic planning which would suppress the automatic forces instead of keeping them within bounds. The ideal of a planned economy is not the feudal manor, nor its logical successor, the Marxist State. These systems do not admit the complex play of economic forces out of which Western industrial civilization has developed. They establish a kind of economic asceticism. Asceticism controls the evils of the flesh by denying the flesh. So these systems control the evils of competition and acquisitiveness by abolishing competition and acquisitiveness. They perform a major surgical operation on the economic body. But whole bodies have an advantage over those on which even the finest surgeons have exercised their skill. We are naturally unwilling to call in the economic surgeon, who unfortunately must remove certain other organs of freedom in cutting out the economic trouble, unless we are really convinced that the case is desperate.

xi. *Economic Planning and International Trade.*

Pardon the digression. What I started out to say was that the idea of a planned economy is one which allows the free decentralized functioning of the numerous parts which compose the system, but under centralized controls which prevent violent maladjustments developing between them. The desired flexibility cannot be attained if each part is specifically controlled, but only if the whole is generally controlled while each part remains free. Let me take an example from the sphere of international trade. One group of economic planners, which has been particularly vocal in the United States, holds that under a national policy trade between nations must take the form of *ad hoc* agreements for specific exchange of designated commodities. The United States, for example, would contract with France for the exchange of automobiles against wines, and with Japan for the exchange of cotton against silk, and so on in a series of bilateral or multilateral agreements. Here we have a splendid example of the way in which the ultra-modern reverts to the primitive. For this is, of course, the archaic and clumsy device of barter parading as a modern invention. People still think that methods which they would reject with contempt for the conduct of their private affairs are good enough for the conduct of public affairs, just as they complacently assign to nations stupidities of motive which, if exhibited by individuals, would render them fit subjects for a madhouse. While an occasional act of barter between nations may in the present state of international disorganization be a useful expedient, it needs no great economic intelligence to perceive that any extensive use of this principle would be exceedingly awkward and difficult, and would create a vast amount of international friction for a very small economic gain. The way to develop international trade is not through a series of huckstering deals in particular commodities, but by a revision of general tariff regulations. Governments can for the sake of internal stability take general measures to secure some balance of imports and exports, but what the particular imports and exports shall be must in the main depend on the play of economic forces.

The example I have just given reinforces our general conclusion that an international order is a condition of national stability, that genuine economic planning, instead of shutting itself out from an international system, can achieve its end only within such a system. Were the channels of world trade more free, nations would not be faced with a surplus of particular exportable goods while they suffer from a shortage of other goods. In this respect it would be easier for them to attain the equilibrium which is the prime object of economic planning. Were there a world monetary system, nations would not need to strive desperately to protect their currencies against the movement of foreign exchange, and they could trade with one another with far greater assurance, while capital would flow from country to country in accordance with the variant needs of lenders and borrowers. In short, the ideal of economic planning, that of a stable and flexible equilibrium of the national economy, could in general be more efficiently sought were another and greater ideal also in process of realization, that of an integrated and assured international order.

CHAPTER XI

FINANCIAL ASPECTS OF THE 'NEW DEAL' IN THE UNITED STATES IN SOME OF THEIR INTERNATIONAL IMPLICATIONS

by

DR. LELAND REX ROBINSON

President of the International Securities Corporation of America, and Lecturer on Finance, Columbia University

i. *The First and Second Post-war Economic Crises.*

THE economic upheaval which accompanied and immediately followed the World War affected the fortunes of different countries in various and often contrasted ways. The well-known fact that the network of commerce, industry, and finance enmeshing the peoples of all continents and climates had not prevented striking differences among them at any one time in their business fortunes and prospects seemed confirmed on a huge scale by those four years which cut a bloody gash across Europe. American business men and farmers knew the feverish character of the sudden prosperity which engulfed them, but they could not be expected to foresee how fictitious it would ultimately prove to be, nor to forego the opportunities for profitable penetration of South American markets, and for purveying of food and war materials, opened to them by the death-grapple of the belligerents. Regions in both hemispheres primarily producers of raw materials enjoyed unprecedented markets. On the other hand, among the belligerents the supreme necessities of war required the subordination of all ordinary economic activities. Labour forces of factory and field were decimated to supply the fighting fronts, and those agricultural and industrial pursuits which took on the character of a national emergency were carried on through increasing mechanization and an influx of women workers.

The unequal economic fortunes of war as between belligerents and non-belligerents, and among the belligerents themselves, were if anything accentuated in the immediate period of confusion, demobilization, and currency chaos in the years which followed the Armistice. For a time, indeed, it seemed to many Americans that the unnatural stimulus of war in commerce and manufacture might carry on indefinitely after the close of hostilities, so great were the ravages to be repaired, and so glowing were the hopes for a new heaven and earth 'fit for heroes to dwell in'.

The first great reaction following the war did, it is true, drive home what had been all but forgotten, namely, the common lot of humanity. However, even in the years 1920–3, when falling prices throughout the world accompanied acute embarrassment in raw material and industrial countries of every continent, but particularly in the period of partial recovery which followed in countries that had succeeded in maintaining confidence in their currencies, the differences in economic fortune from one nation to another were patent to all.

This is the factor which most distinguishes the present depression from the first post-war reaction in business and credit. For the present crisis, which is no more nor less than the secondary reaction following the titanic upheaval of 1914–18, has all the nations of the world in its grip.

It would be foolish to insist that there is literal truth, even to-day, in the lines of Lowell, that

> In the gain or loss of one race,
> All the rest have EQUAL claim;

but certainly no observer of world conditions can deny that this moral precept is now being demonstrated as never before in the history of mankind. Whether producer primarily of raw materials or fabricated products; whether on the Gold standard, the Silver standard, the Sterling standard, the Dollar standard, or any other form of managed money; whether large or small, near or far from the seat of the last war; whether former belligerent or neutral, the heavy hand of misfortune has been laid upon us all. Such limited measure of recovery as may have occurred in some countries has been in the face of almost negligible improvement in international trade, and the latter stands to-day at such shrunken proportions as would have seemed incredible in 1928.

Here, however, a very interesting fact may be noted, and this will also serve to set off the differences between the first and the second major crises following the World War. In the earlier period the great variations of economic fortune from country to country did not give rise to irrepressible demands for far-reaching reforms in the whole economic and social order. Except in Russia, the bases of private capitalism, though challenged on every hand, were not seriously undermined. The gospel of *laissez-faire*, subjected of course to various restraints, still offered the way to economic redemption. The old formulas and earlier habits of mind persisted.

In the present crisis of world affairs, however, the clearly established community of interest among all the peoples has been accompanied by the most amazing disparities in programmes for economic betterment. If the modest improvement which financial and production statistics of the League of Nations show for almost every country since the middle or third quarter of 1932 carries through in America and Europe, it will be used as the justification for a strange mixture of panaceas, in accordance with that ancient fallacy of *post hoc*, *ergo propter hoc.* In Italy the discipline of Fascismo will emerge as the established way of salvation; in Germany the *führer* principle of economic dictatorship will have won its spurs; in England democracy, not too unlike the old-fashioned model, will once more have demonstrated its capacity to 'muddle through'; in France, Cincinnatus will have returned to his plough, his mission accomplished, and the liberties of the people left intact; in the United States the 'New Deal' will be hailed by former friend and foe alike as able to combine recovery and reform without unduly cramping the style of either.

ii. *Remedies for Economic Discontent.*

It has been said that in Europe deep-seated economic discontent leads to a revolution, and in the United States to an experiment. Like many other generalizations this contains a grain of truth. It suggests the fact that agitation for reform on this side of the Atlantic finds its catch-calls and intellectual basis in the political *milieu*, and in America in the economic, or perhaps it would be more accurate to say in the financial. The daring new programme of the British Labour Party, political Socialism really in action; the working programme of co-operation between the French Socialists and Communists; the political reconstruction now under way in Italy with the new Corporations devouring the powers of the Chamber of Deputies—all these and other political programmes for economic reconstruction find their counterpart in the United States in the rallying-cry of the 'New Deal'. Under its banner are grouped strange allies, ranging from real conservatives, who recognize the necessity for certain moderate measures of financial or economic reform to rabid cranks and groups inimical to private capitalism, in its characteristic American forms. One and all, however, these adherents of the 'New Deal' instinctively think in terms of economic and financial interest, political panaceas playing an ancillary role.

Despite this basically economic, or financial, content of the 'New Deal' in the United States—as contrasted with the dominant political note in the slogans of 'Fascism', 'National Socialism', 'Communism', the 'Totalitarian State', and so on—it must be frankly admitted that economic as well as political slogans lend themselves to meaningless generalizations and to addle-headed thinking. Americans are as prone to pronounce with finality upon the most complicated financial and economic issues, regardless of their training and experience, as are Europeans to espouse or denounce different political conceptions with their fancied inevitable consequences in the life of the people. In a word, the 'New Deal' in the United States, like the more favoured brand of European political slogans, is loosely used in a way to conceal underlying similarities in purpose and programme as well as to exaggerate differences. Like 'Socialism', 'Communism', and 'Fascism', the 'New Deal' in the hands of its enthusiastic but uncritical protagonists has done as much to obfuscate thinking as to promote general intelligence. It is the way of all slogans to serve as convenient mental pegs upon which we hang our misconceptions and prejudices. What may be an inspiration for the statesman becomes a brain-trap for the unwary.

All of which is by way of pointing out that in giving some thought to the financial aspects of the so-called 'New Deal' in their international implications, we must separate its temporary, transitional, or purely accidental effects from its presumably permanent, logical, and constructive effects. We must remember that the 'New Deal' in the hands of its sober friends is something other than the 'New Deal' in the hands of its fanatical devotees. This is easier for the intelligent American to grasp than for the observer overseas, not only because the broad measures of permanent social policy tied in with the 'New Deal' are now emerging more clearly on the domestic front, but also because the dramatic repercussions of the 'New Deal' abroad have been in the form of unstable exchange, suggested price manipulattion, impracticable programmes for international co-operation in public works, and other schemes propounded at the abortive World Economic Conference and elsewhere, which must have seemed to a number of our European friends quixotic, or even pernicious at times.

iii. *Currency Doctoring and Credit Manipulation in the New Deal.*

The international impact of the 'New Deal' so far arises mainly from the frankly inflationary views which have been harboured within it, and which have permitted trial of certain monetary cure-alls mistakenly considered by some of its critics and friends alike as the very heart and core of the American experiment. It is natural that large numbers of people suffering from the collapse of business, credit, employment, and prices since 1928 should jump to the conclusion that the downward spiral can be arrested and the whole heartbreaking process reversed by the expedient of diluting the nation's monetary standard and forcing prices upward, if need be, by undermining the confidence of the people in their medium of exchange. 'The burnt child', says the old adage, 'runs from the fire.' This may explain the reluctance of gold-standard countries to depart from the orthodoxy of stable exchanges based upon one or another form of redemption in gold. With countries, as with the run of mortals, experience seems the only effective teacher; and large numbers of Americans, having never experienced the effects of rapidly depreciating currency, find plausible the extreme views of such leaders of the 'inflationary bloc' as Senator Thomas, of Oklahoma, who is reported to have said that the objective of certain legislation passed since the banking crisis of 1933 was to effect the transfer of $200,000,000,000 from the 'creditor' to the 'debtor' class by the deliberate cheapening of the dollar! The fact that the net creditor classes of the United States, in which must be included all savings bank depositors and life insurance policy holders, probably outnumber the net debtors by four or five to one does not seem to please the Senator, the naïvete of whose programme is only matched by its credulity.

In order to gain proper perspective on the 'New Deal', therefore, we must bear in mind that President Roosevelt has had from the first to contend with determined champions of change who envisaged the whole problem in terms of money-tinkering. They would have barred the way to the promised land of the 'New Deal' if liberal sops had not been thrown to Cerberus. The strident cry for 'cheaper money' reached its climax in the vote of the United States

Senate last year, in which a barely comfortable majority was mobilized against the restoration of bi-metallism at the ratio of sixteen to one for the free coinage of silver and gold, at a time when the market ratio was closer to the neighbourhood of seventy to one. The President shrewdly accepted permissive rather than mandatory inflationary powers, and proceeded to steer his course toward vital domestic reconstruction while placating from time to time the 'cheap money diehards'.

Whether it would have been advisable or financially possible to avoid leaving the gold standard in 1933, or, once having left it, to return to the old parity in 1934 became, therefore, an academic question in the minds of several of the President's advisers in view of the insistent demand for inflation in Congress and out of it, particularly in the Middle West, which could only have been countered by the President's throwing the whole of his enormous prestige behind the orthodox views of money and banking, and aligning himself with those 'changers of money' whose failures he had scored in his Inaugural Address, and whose leadership had dismally failed, in the minds of the people, with the complete collapse of the country's banking facilities in March 1933.

The gold standard having succumbed, the stage was set by the fall of 1933 for a practical trial of the theories of Professors Warren and Pearson. Opposed to those crude forms of inflation represented by bi-metallism at sixteen to one, or by issues of unbacked paper money, the President was much attracted to the elaborately documented thesis of Professor Warren, which purported to prove that price-levels are determined by supplies of gold, and that the world's troubles may be laid to the fall in prices since 1929—a phenomenon readily explained in terms of the high demand for the world's monetary gold following the low demand of the earlier post-war years. Granted this claim, the corollary readily followed that by a bidding up of the price of gold; that is, by making possible the creation of a larger volume of money on a given gold base, prices in the United States—and for that matter throughout the world—could be raised to any desired level. This level once reached the theories of Professor Irving Fisher, as well as those of Professors Warren and Pearson, gave plausibility to the idea that fluctuations from it in the general average could be controlled by changing the dollar's gold content, or by bidding up or down the price of gold in accordance with the fluctuations of index numbers.

In fact, it was believed by many Americans that some such scientific theory was being slyly and secretly applied by the British Government through its Exchange Equalization Fund. The diabolical cunning often attributed to our British cousins in Imperial affairs, behind their mask of 'muddling through', was here read into the gyrations of the Pound Sterling since its fall from grace in September 1931. It is apparently a human weakness to sense plots of one's enemies in events which prove embarrassing. In any event it was generally bruited about in the United States that instead of seeking its natural level the Pound had been deliberately forced down in the foreign exchanges for the purpose of raising prices, promoting exports at the expense of Uncle Sam, and very generally playing ducks and drakes with the hapless dollar, tied to its gold tether. The decision of the President to try the Warren plan, therefore, evoked a favourable response from many quarters: exporters, manufacturers of goods for export, agricultural interests, who hoped to force their products abroad through currency depreciation, speculators in commodities, and 'One Hundred Per Cent' patriots who rejoiced at last that the Dollar, freed from its golden anchor, could sail to join battle with the privateering Pound. Outright inflationists smiled deprecatingly. Mild medicine indeed! But let the President try it with their blessing. Bidding up the price of gold was at least a welcome step in the direction of cheapening the American medium of exchange. Allopathic doses of real currency dilution could come later.

The failure of the gold-buying programme to produce the desired effects need not be laboured here. Increasingly Americans are being impressed with the fact that this experiment, although it has driven up the prices (in depreciated American dollars) of goods exported and imported has had very little, if any, direct effect upon the physical volume of our foreign trade. If anything, in fact, the deliberate policy of driving down the Dollar in the international exchanges seems to have had an opposite effect than that intended upon American international commerce. Imports seem to have been encouraged, rather than otherwise, and exports discouraged in accordance with the well-known tendency for merchants to buy when prices are going up, and to withhold purchases when they are headed downward and the bottom is not in sight. At any rate the ability of any country to force its products upon consumers of other countries by exchange debasement is sadly impaired by the counter-measures in the power of other nations to apply; while apart from artificial restrictions in the form of tariffs, quotas, and exchange controls now weighing upon the movement of goods and services from country to country is the basic fact that imports and exports must go hand-in-hand at a time when the international flow of credits and capital has reached almost an historic low.

The domestic effects of the so-called Warren and Pearson plan of gold purchase at arbitrarily rising prices have been more debatable, perhaps. In any case, prices have advanced substantially within the United States, and it is easy for the constitutional money-tinkerer to credit depreciated exchanges and other inflationary moves, forgetting the effect of imported commodities in the index numbers, the so-called processing taxes and agricultural restrictions, and other forces, like the drought, operating in the direction of higher levels independently of any inflationary formulas.

The temporary stabilization of the dollar probably marked the end of definite experiments in internal price control through gold purchase at changing levels. It did not, however, end the demand for currency experimentation. With the apparent failure of the Warren formulas the floodgates of silver agitation were opened once more. The argument that something must 'be done for silver' received the hearty endorsement of a dozen or more United States Senators from sparsely populated metal-producing States. Service to their clients could thus be coupled, in the minds of these gentlemen, with the benefits of rising prices induced through further dilution of the money standard. In addition, it has been eloquently argued that by re-establishing silver as a basic money metal a vast increase of purchasing power would be released among the teeming millions of China and India.

So convinced have many Americans become that advances in the world price of silver would shower blessings upon the hordes of Asia that little attention has been paid to protests from Shanghai that further deflation would thus be forced upon China, which is an importer rather than a producer of the white metal, that her ability to export—and hence to import—would be curtailed with a raising of the exchange value of her currency, and that an embargo upon the export of silver might thus be forced. Inflation of the currency through silver purchase, and schemes for restoration of bi-metallism in modified form, or for substituting silver for gold in central bank and Government reserves, lend themselves to international discussion more readily than devices for paper-money inflation. Silver is a metal of considerable international importance. Bi-metallism was only abandoned in Europe some sixty years ago. Countries producing the metal, and others, like India, which though on the gold, or gold-exchange standard, have considerable hoards of silver, are vitally concerned with the programme of silver rehabilitation undertaken by the American Government. The questions may be stated, but not answered, as to what results the recent decree nationalizing the metal in the United States may have, as to the quantities which will be brought abroad in furtherance of the Congressional mandate to acquire silver until it replaces gold in 25 per cent of the monetary reserve, and as to whether this means the drainage of the world's current production to American monetary purposes for the next five or more years.

It was earlier mentioned that the international effects of the 'New Deal' dramatically forcing themselves upon the attention of other countries have been mainly in the sphere of money and exchange. Our friends abroad have witnessed the foundering of the World Economic Conference on the issue of the Dollar and the Pound. They have watched a unique experiment in internal price control through manipulation of exchange values in terms of the remaining gold currencies. They have stood by as huge quantities of their gold have flowed to England, and more recently to America, in neither of which countries it has been needed for credit expansion. They have heard with increasing wonder the rattling of the old bones of bi-metallism in the great Republic of the West. They have asked themselves why the United States Treasury should be committed to so vast a silver-purchase programme in the face of mounting prices for silver, which it is partly the purpose of this programme to stimulate. They have listened to pleas from over the Atlantic for world-wide efforts in the direction of lifting internal prices by public works expenditures at the same time that they have been pinched by the deflation forced through the pound, the yen, and the sinking dollar. And some of them have ended by dismissing the 'New Deal' with a sarcastic smile and a shrug of the shoulder.

This, however, is the beginning and not the end of the story. The 'New Deal' is not exclusively in the hands of its enthusiastic but fanatical and uncritical supporters. On the contrary, under the steadying leadership of the President it is now rapidly passing into the hands of its sober friends. From the plague of general panaceas it is now passing to the guidance of general plans. From money-tinkering it is now clearly entering the phase of fundamental reconstruction. Problems looming menacingly on the national horizon are now being tackled on many different fronts under the guidance of men of experience accustomed to grappling with hard facts. The cleavage is becoming more marked between those who had fondly hoped for a miracle through currency-doctoring and credit manipulation without more rigorous and far-reaching treatment, and those who, instead of spattering with inflationary buckshot charges, seek a clean rifle shot at scores of different targets. It is with the financial effects of the 'New Deal' in its more sober and fundamental directives that our friends abroad will be chiefly concerned in the years to come.

iv. *Alternating Attitudes Towards Foreign Countries.*

In order better to understand the international effects of the 'New Deal' in its more permanent and rational aspects we must look beyond the present period of almost studied American indifference in all that concerns co-operation for recovery among the nations. Despite her capacity for a substantial measure of self-containment the United States in the greater part of its history as a modern nation has been dependent upon, and in its economic development even dominated by international commerce and finance. Movement of goods to and from our shores has been as natural a part of our economic heritage as the air we breathed. In earlier years an incoming tide of capital goods, financed by loans from England and elsewhere, aided the development of our railroads and highways, our mines and factories, our public buildings and our commercial establishments. An outflow of foodstuffs and raw materials, as well as semi-fabricated and fabricated products paid the interest on these foreign loans and helped to reduce the principal. Our cotton and wheat belts did not spread over so vast an area merely to serve the requirements of domestic consumption. Over a long period of years the tendency for American imports to gravitate toward higher ratios of raw materials and semi-fabricated products and for our .exports to show mounting percentages of industrial products revealed in itself the spur to economic growth given by the international exchange of goods, services, and credits.

Neither of the two great American political parties, in fact, could be indifferent to the claims and necessities of foreign commerce. While 'protecting' the American manufacturer from the competition of 'cheaper made' foreign goods, and 'preserving the home market' for the farmer by high tariffs, the Republican Party has aggressively sought foreign outlets for the output of our mines, farms, and factories. The Democratic Party has been somewhat more logical in its approach, but none the less committed to the search for overseas outlets. The chief concern of the latter has, of course, been encouragement of such import of fabricated goods as would assure agriculturists—such as cotton and tobacco producers—reasonable prices for the things they must buy from the cities, and preserve their markets abroad by making it possible for foreigners to buy with the proceeds of their sales to us.

Speaking in financial terms, we may so interpret the international balance of payments as to make it, year by year, a barometer of American economic growth. Prior to the seventies the generally 'unfavourable' balance of trade was offset by foreign loans; in that decade the 'unfavourable' definitely changed to a year-by-year 'favourable' balance of trade, foreigners being enabled to offset their net debts on merchandise account by interest and amortization on their American loans, as well as by shipping and insurance services and the increasing remittances of immigrants lured to American shores. Net repayments of foreign loans reached an all-time high during the earlier years of the World War. Such a flow of foodstuffs and war materials as glutted the ports of the Allies prior to the entrance of the United States into the war would have been impossible without the British mobilization of hundreds of millions in pounds sterling of American loans to be pledged or sold for the necessary credits.

The continued expansion of American exports after the entry of the States into the war roughly marked the transition from a net debtor to a net creditor position among the nations, and reflected the billions of dollars lent to her late Allies by the United States Government. The distorted development of agriculture and of industries purveying war materials for export was continued after the war in the form of huge shipments made possible by billions of dollars of new American capital placed in foreign countries. The 'favourable' balance of trade which grew to such enormous proportions between 1914 and 1930 meant in the earlier years of the war the clearing of debts owed by Americans abroad; in the later years of the war and in the first few months following the Armistice it reflected the staggering totals of advances made by the United States Government; in the period preceding the collapse of world trade after 1930, it represented loans made by private American investors to foreign private and public borrowers, whose recklessness was often matched by the cupidity of the bankers and the gullible greed of creditors who were not content with a reasonable return on their money.

During all this time the American cotton-grower, the wheat farmer, the steel fabricator, the automobile manufacturer had come to rely upon foreign markets in a way vital to national economic health. A person enjoying perfect functioning of his digestive apparatus becomes alarmed and resentful when stomach disturbances set in. The people of the United States, having come to regard as their imprescriptible right a smooth working of the machinery of international credit, a continued ability of foreigners to pay both interest and amortization on their borrowings, and while doing this to buy more from the States than they sold, were destined to a rude awakening in 1931. We have shown as the result of this, I fear, some of the petulance of a spoiled child. Americans are given to over-optimistic pessimism.

The breakdown of international credit machinery from 1931 has awakened Americans to the fact that our own prosperity has had an intimate stake in the well-being of other nations. The effects in our foreign policies have varied with the time, the occasion, and the statesman involved. Prior to 1934, however, we have blown either hot or cold, and it is only within the last few months that the 'New Deal', with its emphasis primarily upon domestic problems and policies, has entered its present phase of indifference, an almost studied indifference as I earlier stated, to distinctly international problems.

The present almost exclusive American concern in things American, in the narrowest sense of the word, contrasts strangely with the alternating attitudes of bitter resentment and of missionary zeal toward foreign countries in the earlier years of the depression. The grand gesture of President Hoover in the moratorium proposed for all intergovernmental debt payments in 1931 was the occasion for a surprising demonstration of enthusiastic public approval. Keen disappointment and not a little hostile criticism was then directed against France for her failure at once to accept this dramatic proposal. The 'Credit Anstalt' failure, the crisis in Germany, and the abandonment of the gold standard by England as the result of her embarrassments on the Continent further proved to some impressionable Americans that the grave maladjustments of the American economic structure were due principally to the perfidy and financial maladies of other countries. The gentlemen's understanding in connection with the Lausanne Agreement that the scaling down of reparations should depend upon concessions from America added fuel to the flames; nor has the practical scrapping of reparations in the absence of any understanding with the United States served to mollify those who would seek the cause of our troubles abroad. European tariff, quota, and exchange restrictions served as a warning and an object-lesson to these super-patriots, who were ready to forget or overlook the leadership in high tariffs which the United States has so long exerted. Missionary zeal appears again, however, in our attitude toward foreign countries with the coming of President Roosevelt into power and for a few weeks after. In an attitude of universal benevolence, frank exchange of views and open-minded helpfulness, the nations of the world were to be led back to the path of prosperity by applying homely American remedies to complicated situations. The World Economic Conference of 1933 was the stage for this role of schoolmaster and miracle worker. Problems too difficult to be resolved at home were here to be grappled with in a meeting of the world's best brains, where brilliant and drastic remedies could be agreed upon. Again the phase of missionary zeal passed with the emergence of irreconcilable differences among the gold bloc, the sterling area, and the American monetary experimentalists. The President's earlier attitude of sympathetic concern for the possibilities of recovery through international action on a grand scale passed definitely into the discard with his message which gave the Conference its *coup de grâce*.

This incident, perhaps, as well as any other episode,

marks the transition to the present American phase of 'non-imperialistic nationalism' under which, to quote Professor Beard in his recent book on *The Idea of National Interest*, 'the principal avenue of escape from economic crisis lies, not in adjustments made at international conferences, not in outward thrusts of commercial power, but in the collaboration of domestic interests with a view to establishing the security which may come from integrated economic activities and a more efficient distribution of wealth or buying-power'. This is the reason why, as the 'New Deal' becomes more objective in its analysis and more concrete in its policies, it emphasizes matters of domestic import, and no longer assumes 'that outward thrusts of national power too strong to be controlled at home can be subdued at international conferences of diplomats representing Governments incapable of conquering at home the very forces whose impacts abroad they seek to master through treaties, agreements, and conversations'.

v. *Some Mutually Inconsistent Objectives.*

In its more concrete forms the 'New Deal' in America centres in the financial aspects of production rather than the economic aspects of consumption. We must look to ordinary business psychology for an explanation of this. Under private capitalism it is natural to visualize economic life in terms of physical production and from the acquisitive or pecuniary point of view. Given technical efficiency and productive capacity it follows as a corollary in the mental processes of most of us that adjustments of a purely financial character will suffice to bring us out of the night of depression into the sunlight of economic health again.

Hence the 'New Deal' as we now know it in America

may be defined as primarily directed toward the financial protection of producers of credit (i.e. bank depositors and investors), of agricultural producers, of producers of labour, and of producers of goods and services. This is not to overlook such broad-visioned projects as the integral development of the Tennessee Valley, a nation in miniature; afforestation on a national scale; assisted migration from impoverished regions to areas giving better promise of homestead subsistence; and the vast projects for social insurance which the Administration is apparently incubating. It is merely to emphasize that sponsors of the 'New Deal' have laboured under the conviction that these several thrusts in the direction of restoring financial solvency in the interest of production and producers would automatically bring back prosperity, and this despite the cross-purposes at which the 'New Deal' has been working in several sectors where violent attacks in different directions seem to have lacked the wise guidance of a general staff.

In efforts to protect bank depositors and investors much salutary legislation has been enacted for the regulation of security and commodity exchanges and in establishing higher standards of public responsibility among originators and distributors of new securities. 'Banker' has been since 1930 a term of reproach in the United States, and when one is dubbed an 'international banker' the obloquy is complete. It is not to be wondered at, then, that Acts designed to protect the people against the machinations of the bankers should have shown an almost savage severity in their earlier unamended form, and effectively militated against the issuance of new securities, even for refunding purposes. Recent amendments to the Securities Act, designed to bring it in spirit somewhat nearer the British Companies Acts, are loosening the flow of private credit once more, particularly toward municipal and public utility obligations. The fact remains, however, that the drastic character of the earlier legislation, particularly during the months when it stood unamended on the statute books, was a strong deterrent in the financing of capital goods industries, and therefore directly contributory to continuing unemployment. Blame attaching to the bankers for this sluggish flow of capital is only one of several factors which seem destined to postpone for an indefinite period the resumption of large-scale foreign lending on private account.

That part of the 'New Deal' directed toward the financial protection of agricultural producers aims to restore a 'natural' balance of purchasing power between city and country. This 'balance' is conceived in terms of general price ratios obtaining between products of the farm and products of the factory at an arbitrarily chosen earlier date; and the attempt to 'restore' it takes the form of forcing up agricultural prices faster than advances in the prices of the commodities which farmers must buy. Price-level being thus more important than quantity of products, or, rather, money in the farmer's pocket being more important than the amount of cotton or of foodstuffs which he sends to market, an elaborate system of crop restrictions is being built up, with provisions for compensating the producers by means of taxes paid by processors and consumers.

The danger that the farmer's pecuniary advantage, and that of the farmer's creditor, may be sacrificed to the rising prices of things the farmer has to buy is conceived as a necessary evil in the programme of protecting the city producers of labour. For here the 'New Deal', under the aegis of the National Reconstruction Act, aims at dividing the available work by restriction of hours and at the same time at increasing the money wage of every employed person by a more than proportionate increase in the hourly rates of pay. The wish that this stepping up in labour costs will not eventuate in higher prices of goods is father of the thought that such in fact may be the result when larger output corresponding to greater consumer demand reduces per unit costs. There is a bit of the Marxist analysis in all this—namely, that the cause of depression lies in the inability of labour, that is, the consuming public, to purchase the goods which it produces because of insufficient wage payments as well as the disproportionate amounts of the social product which it is believed drains off into rent, interest, and profits, and enhances demand for more capital goods, while it restricts demand for the ultimate consumers' wares.

Be this as it may, the Marxian thesis in even this modest guise could not gain consistent acceptance in the United States. The N.R.A. having increased costs of production, employers must be permitted certain liberties hitherto denied under the Anti-Trust Acts, and even permitted in many codes to raise prices by one or another form of agreement. The circle is thus completed. Relief to agriculturists suffering under burdens of mortgage indebtedness is sought rather in enhancing their money income than in scaling down their charges. Enhancement of their money income is to be obtained rather by increasing prices of their products than by better marketing, larger output, and higher quality. Higher prices of agricultural products necessitate higher money wages for factory workers. These in turn make their force felt in rising costs all around, and by lifting prices of fabricated and semi-fabricated goods come home to roost on the farmer's and wage-earner's doorstep. Granting this, however, it is felt that a net gain to the country arises from higher price-levels. Profits are multiplied in dollars, even though costs rise in the same ratios as prices, and the cheapening of money helps the farmer to pay his interest and taxes, and the debtor to meet his fixed charges.

vi. *Some Significant Results.*

It should not be inferred from this briefly critical summary of some mutually inconsistent objectives of the 'New Deal' that the series of measures and policies making it up have been barren of significant results. On the contrary there has been accomplished by ostensibly voluntary agreement between business men and the President a series of social gains which the inhibitions of the Federal Constitution and the conflicting claims of States' rights would otherwise have deferred for a generation. Child labour has been virtually abolished; great gains have been registered in the field of minimum wages; collective bargaining, grudgingly if at all admitted by many employers hitherto, has become a national issue; for the first time the nation as a whole has had to acknowledge and face its responsibility for the care of the unemployed and the cure of unemployment. If the attack upon our many-sided problems has been up to this time piecemeal, haphazard, dominated by pecuniary psychology rather than consumer interest; if it has caused for the time being the submergence of international interests, this may, we hope, prove but a temporary phase.

vii. *International Repercussions and the Outlook for the Future.*

In their international repercussions the financial aspects of the 'New Deal' may be described in terms of the urge toward higher domestic prices; the agitation for self-containment encouraged by resultant loss of export markets, and the curtailment of imports to protect an artificially high internal price-level; complete elimination, for the time being at least, of the American market for foreign capital; and the arbitrary policies of exchange depreciation coupled with the overhanging threat of further dollar devaluation which is suspended like the sword of Damocles over the market for international currencies.

There can be no doubt that the philosophy of self-containment has been embraced by many friends of the 'New Deal'. Added costs voluntarily incurred under the N.R.A. codes must be countered by higher prices charged to consumers; and these higher prices must not cause loss of markets to foreign manufacturers. Hence powers have been granted the President in several codes now governing various branches of industry to limit imports in a variety of effective ways. Higher prices insistently sought for agricultural products must necessarily greatly cut down foreign consumption of American wheat and foodstuffs. Hence processing taxes and payments to farmers for reducing production rest upon a basis of assumed needs for domestic purposes primarily. The elimination of New York as an important market for international capital cannot, of course, be attributed wholly to the 'New Deal'. The flow of new funds abroad had largely ceased by 1929, when the whirlpool of Wall Street speculation was drawing into its vortex an enormous amount of foreign capital and piling up a vast domestic inflation hidden, but by no means hindered by a fairly stable commodity price-level. In its emphasis upon internal problems and autonomous remedies, however, the 'New Deal' has necessarily increased the unpopularity and postponed the resumption of foreign lending, on both long and short term.

It may be well at this point to revert to the earlier mentioned legislation concerning origination and distribution of new securities. The rankling sense of grievance against bankers and brokers which has given birth to this stringent regulation of securities and commodities markets has been particularly marked against all those who have had to do with the extension of credit to the Governments and nationals of foreign countries. It is in vain that some financial writers point out the comparable, or even greater losses suffered by Americans in the equities and lower-grade bonds and mortgages originating in their own country. The stupendous defaults of Germany and other European borrowers, to say nothing of dramatic episodes in Latin America, are impressed too vividly upon the mind of 'the man in the street'. Nor is he without company among the elect. Anyone familiar with the slipshod methods followed by several American banking houses in picking up foreign business, and not unmindful of the high-powered house-to-house sales methods employed by the great distributing houses must recognize the urgent necessity for thoroughgoing reform. The 'New Deal' here has answered a crying need. It is to be expected that any revival of foreign lending, or any great progress in the refunding or scaling-down of foreign indebtedness, will be accompanied by a measure of co-operation among the banking houses concerned, with that delimitation of field, sense of professional responsibility, and absence of competitive profit-grubbing which marks the great issuing houses of London.

Some months ago a business associate of mine, charged with supervision of our foreign investments, reported to me the sale of a foreign holding of which we had long desired to clear our portfolios. This was a Finnish industrial bond guaranteed by a German company. We were finally able to liquidate it through sale to an investor resident in Italy, by the good offices of an Austrian broker operating in Switzerland, payment being effected partly in terms of pounds sterling upon delivery of the bonds in London, and partly in remittances from Egypt! The confusion in my mind resulting from an honest effort to understand all the details of this 'deal' has helped explain to me the instinctive mistrust which many folk in my country evince toward anything savouring of a foreign financial transaction. Little wonder that much is heard these days of the needs for capital nearer home, that there is much shaking of heads and wagging of tongues concerning the foreign competition which American investors have fostered by their losses. We need here only repeat that the 'New Deal' financial legislation, coupled with the great need for long-term capital among domestic industries which will become evident as soon as the private market for new securities revives, will probably postpone for some time an outward flow of new American capital. The revival of international trade will see London once again bearing its Atlas burden of long- and short-term international credits.

We do not need, however, to close on this negative note. In fact, the outlook is by no means discouraging for the evolution of helpful international policies. The stirring may now be felt of new forces gradually pushing us past the present dead-centre of almost studied indifference. A while back reference was made to American international balances of payments over the decades as illustrating the enormous importance of foreign trade and movements of capital to and from our shores in the growth of trade and industry in the United States. The situation may perhaps be summarized as follows. During the periods of rapid economic expansion of my country prior to the Great War, or perhaps it could be more accurately stated as prior to the turn of the century, the United States and its people accepted the role of borrower and the obligations of debtor among the nations. Until the mid-seventies 'unfavourable' American merchandise balances registered a willingness to receive foreign goods in the form of loans from abroad, and the 'favourable' merchandise balances from that time until the outbreak of the World War reflected the export of foodstuffs, cotton, and products of mine and factory in payment of interest and amortization on these foreign loans. A second phase may be distinguished, roughly dating from the outbreak of the World War to 1929, during which time the United States gladly embraced the role of lender among the nations without recognizing the duties or obligations of the creditor. We liquidated the greater part of our foreign indebtedness, and continued to export enormous quantities of foodstuffs raw materials, and fabricated goods on the basis of American capital lavishly and often foolishly afforded foreign borrowers. Our carelessness in lending can only be matched by our carelessness in collecting, a necessary corollary of exclusive tariff policies which placed the United States in the front ranks of highly protected countries at a time when its creditor position entitled the country to an 'unfavourable' balance of trade!

We are now as a nation in the third phase of our evolution *vis-à-vis* an intelligent and intelligible international financial policy. At present, we accept neither the position of lender nor the responsibilities of creditor. Like Pilate, we have washed our hands. But we have good reason to hope that this is a transitional attitude, and merely marks the passage to a fourth phase blessed by sober business sense in the refunding and scaling down of foreign debt to the real capacities of the debtor, in the careful provision of new business credits, and in the willingness to receive payment in the only ways in which payment can ever be rendered, by accepting in reason the goods and services which the people of other countries are prepared to furnish.

In fact, a hopeful view may be taken of the future by any internationalist who is at pains to look beyond the immediate somewhat opportunist, and certainly provisional, character of the 'New Deal'. He will note that the 'New Deal' is passing from generalization and panacea to a determined grappling with stubborn facts; and he will rightly gather from this that a rational and helpful view will in due course prevail in connection with foreign debts and credits despite any present indications to the contrary. He will await the inevitable rebirth of vigorous private initiative, without which real enterprise is wellnigh impossible, and which in the United States has been but temporarily eclipsed by an overdosage of governmental wet-nursing; from this will come a natural resumption of those innumerable business ties made among the people of different countries without political interference or nationalistic bias. He will watch with interest and confidence the passage from a narrowly financial to a broadly economic viewpoint, and await the certain result of this in expansion, first with Government and later with private credits, of trade with those countries best fitted to exchange their products with the United States. The flexible tariff powers recently granted the President may well serve in the promotion of those reciprocal trade agreements which will help protect too readily forgotten domestic consumers and restore a part of our lost exports without forgetting that we must buy and use if foreigners are to do likewise. If I read aright the signs of the times, the consumer viewpoint is rapidly gaining in America. It will be greatly encouraged if agreement can be reached among the United States, Great Britain, and Japan to put an end once and for all to the senseless depreciation of currencies which can only intensify trade rivalries while blinding us all to the mutual enrichment coming from freer international flow of goods and services.

Many are the prophets in the United States to-day of economic nationalism. This does not represent, however, the best thinking of the 'New Deal'. As a nation we shall not develop economic autonomy to its logical conclusion. Our position is too strongly entrenched as creditor, consumer, and exporter. The 'New Deal' in its international repercussions will prove to be neither poker nor solitaire. As the result of establishing more firmly a few wise bases of national policy it may be expected that our future international role will prove less quixotic, more sympathetically understanding, and therefore in the long run more governed by enlightened self-interest.

APPENDIX

CONTENTS OF PROBLEMS OF PEACE

(Eighth Series)

iii. The British Draft Convention
- (*a*) Security
- (*b*) Effectives
- (*c*) Land Material
- (*d*) Naval Material
- (*e*) Air Material
- (*f*) Chemical War
- (*g*) Permanent Disarmament Commission
- (*h*) Termination of the Convention
- (*i*) Expenditure
- (*j*) Arms Traffic and Manufacture

iv. A Policy.

CHAPTER IV

The Manufacture of Arms and the Arms Traffic. By Henri Rolin, Legal Adviser to the Belgian Ministry of Foreign Affairs.

i. The Fundamental Importance of Control
ii. Article 8 of the Covenant of the League
iii. Moral and Political Objections to Private Manufacture
iv. The Temporary Mixed Commission
v. The Convention of 1925
vi. The Work of the Council: Draft Convention of 1929
vii. The Disarmament Conference
viii. A Suggested Solution.

CHAPTER V

Public Opinion and the League of Nations. By E. J. Phelan, Chief of the Diplomatic Division of the International Labour Office.

i. The Nature of Public Opinion
ii. The Nature of the League
iii. Results and Failures
iv. Special Features of the Labour Conference
v. Public Opinion within the State
vi. The Indispensability of the Politician
vii. The Press and Public Opinion
viii. The Representation of Public Opinion at Geneva.

CHAPTER VI

Recent Territorial Disputes before the League of Nations. By Manley O. Hudson, Bemis Professor International Law, Harvard University.

i. The Changing Map of the World
ii. How are Changes to be Effected?
iii. The Method of Arbitration
iv. Effect of the Covenant
v. Present Methods of Settlement
vi. The Eastern Greenland Case
vii. The Leticia Dispute between Colombia and Peru
viii. The Chaco Controversy
ix. Conclusions.

CHAPTER VII

The Far East Dispute from the Point of View of the Small States. By Sean Lester, Permanent Delegate of the Irish Free State, Geneva.

i. The New Responsibility of the Small States
ii. Their Interest More than Academic
iii. League as Third Party to Disputes
iv. The Lytton Report Cleared the Way
v. The Balance Sheet is not yet Drawn Up
vi. Small States and the Future.

CHAPTER VIII

The Needs and Prospects of Modern China. By Sir John Hope Simpson, former Director-General of the National Flood Relief Commission in China.

i. The Revolution and the National Government
ii. The Kuo Min Tang
iii. The Needs and Prospects of Education
iv. The Relation of the Central and Provincial Governments
v. Lawlessness and its Cure
vi. Improvement of Position of Central Government
vii. The Future Economic Development
viii. Certain International Questions
ix. The Hope for China.

CHAPTER IX

The Gold Standard in International Relations. By Moritz J. Bonn, formerly Professor in the Handelshochschule, Berlin.

i. The Mechanism of the Gold Standard
ii. The Stability of Foreign Exchange
iii. Defects and Merits of the Gold Standard
iv. The Gold Standard and the Crisis
v. Controlled Currency and Price Stabilization
vi. Exchange Fluctuations.

CHAPTER X

International Aspects of American and Economic Policy. By Frank D. Graham, Professor of Economics, Princeton University.

i. European and American Economic Opinion
ii. Background of American Opinion
iii. Theory of the National Recovery Act
iv. Price-raising Policy and the Abandonment of Gold
v. The Breakdown at London
vi. National Character of Monetary Policy
vii. The Way of Reconciliation
viii. The Path for the Future
ix. The Gold Clause and its Repudiation
x. The Recovery Act and Commercial Policy
xi. International Character of Tariffs
xii. The Recovery Act and International Economic Co-operation.

CHAPTER XI

The World Monetary and Economic Conference. By Clarence K. Streit, Geneva Correspondent of the *New York Times*.

i. Was there Lack of Preparation?
ii. London's 'Forgotten Man'
iii. A Proposal: Political Experts
iv. The Three Who are to Blame

v. Who was Most to Blame?
vi. The Stabilization Hen-and-Egg
vii. Hull Makes Unanimity.

CHAPTER XII

Public Works and the World Crisis. By P. W. Martin, Research Division of the International Labour Office.
i. The Evolution of the Idea of Public Works as a Means of Dealing with Industrial Depression
ii. The Objections to Public Works as a Means of Dealing with Industrial Depressions
iii. The Difficulties to be Encountered in Using Public Works to Sustain Effective Demand
iv. The Attitude toward Public Works in the Various Countries
v. The International Co-ordination of Public Works
vi. Conclusion.

CHAPTER XIII

Recent American Legislation and its Effects on International Relations. By A. H. Feller, Instructor in the Law School, Harvard University
i. The Situation before 4 March, 1933
ii. Preservation of the Financial Structure
iii. Immediate Relief of Unemployment
iv. Measures for Raising the Price Level and Reducing the Burden of Private Debt
v. Currency Legislation
vi. The National Recovery Act
vii. Immediate Difficulties in the Application of the Programme.
viii. The Ultimate Objectives
ix. Domestic Problems of the Future
x. International Problems
(*a*) The World Economic Conference and the Change in American Ideology
(*b*) The Trend towards Economic Nationalism
(*c*) Other Factors in American Foreign Policy.

CHAPTER XIV

APPENDIX

CONTENTS OF PROBLEMS OF PEACE

(Seventh Series)

CHAPTER I

An Introductory Survey: 1931–2. By Dr. G. P. Gooch, Author of *History of Modern Europe, 1878–1919*, etc.

i. The Far East
ii. India and Siam
iii. The United States
iv. North-East Europe
v. The Balkans
vi. The Danubian Lands
vii. Western Europe
viii. Debts and Disarmament
ix. Conclusion.

CHAPTER II

The World Economic Crisis: Its Causes and Cure. By Sir George Paish, formerly Adviser to the Chancellor of the Exchequer and to the British Treasury on Financial and Economic Questions.

i. The Necessity of Action
ii. Economic Crises in the Past
iii. The Situation To-day
iv. The Approach of World Bankruptcy
v. Great Britain and the Gold Standard
vi. The Erection of Trade Barriers
vii. How to End the Crisis.

CHAPTER III

The League in Relation to the World Crisis. By William E. Rappard, Director of the Graduate Institute of International Studies, Geneva.

i. The Influence of the Crisis on the League
  (*a*) The Crisis and the Administrative Structure of the League
  (*b*) The Crisis and the Activities of the League
  (*c*) The Crisis and the Political Vitality of the League

ii. The Influence of the League on the Crisis
(*a*) The Assembly of 1930
(*b*) The Activities of the League after the 1930 Assembly
(*c*) The Assembly of 1931
(*d*) The Activities of the League after the 1931 Assembly
iii. Conclusions.

CHAPTER IV

The Results of the Lausanne Conference. By Dr. J. van Walre de Bordes, Member of the Financial Section of the Secretariat of the League of Nations.

i. The Origins of the Conference
ii. The Lausanne Convention
iii. The Agreement with Germany
iv. 'The Gentlemen's Agreement'
v. The Contents of the Agreement with Germany
vi. The Debts of the States to America
vii. Settlement with America
viii. The World Economic and Financial Conference.

CHAPTER V

Industrial and Social Aspects of the Economic Crisis. By E. J. Phelan, Chief of the Diplomatic Division of the International Labour Office.

i. The Real Nature of the Crisis
ii. A Crisis Mentality
iii. The International Labour Conference and the Crisis
iv. A Call to Action
v. The Decisions of the League
vi. The Claim of the International Labour Organization to Representation
vii. The Reduction of Unemployment by Shortening Hours of Work
viii. Conclusion.

CHAPTER VI

The Disarmament Resolution of July 1932. By W. Arnold-Forster. Author of *The Disarmament Conference*, etc.

i. Part I: Two General Principles
   (*a*) The General Case for Disarmament
   (*b*) The Hoover Proposals
   (*c*) Two Principles
ii. Part II: The Five Conclusions
iii. Part III: The Five Tasks
iv. Part IV: The Door Kept Open
v. Part V: The Truce Prolonged.

Appendix: The Text of the Resolution.

CHAPTER VII

European Unity. By William Martin, former Editor of the *Journal de Genève*.

i. Europe Defined
ii. Attempts at the International Organization of Europe
iii. The Two Europes
iv. The Economic Difficulties of Europe
v. The Analogy of the Pan-American Union
vi. Non-European Participation in European Affairs
vii. Why European Union is Irreconcilable with the League.

CHAPTER VIII

America's Participation in World Organization. By Manley O. Hudson, Bemis Professor of International Law, Harvard University.

i. American Psychology
ii. Pan-Americanism
iii. The United States and the Far East
iv. The United States and Europe
v. The World Court
vi. Membership of the League of Nations
vii. Secretary Stimson's Speech
viii. Conclusions.

CHAPTER IX

(A) The Indian Round Table Conference. By the Rt. Hon. H. B. Lees-Smith, Member of the Round Table Conference.

i. Diversity of Government, Race, Religion, and Caste
ii. Previous Governmental Reforms
iii. The Simon Report
iv. The First Round Table Conference
v. The Second Conference
vi. The Future.

(B) Comment by the Munshi Iswar Saran, former member of the Indian Legislative Assembly.

CHAPTER X

National Development and Reconstruction in the U.S.S.R. By Michael Farbman, Editor of the *Europe Year Book.*

i. The Changed Attitude toward Socialism
ii. International Effects of Russia's Constructive Effort
iii. Bolshevism not an Experiment
iv. The Advances and Retreats of Socialism
v. Agriculture as the Pivotal Problem
vi. The Mechanization of Agriculture
vii. The International Significance of the Agrarian Revolution.

CHAPTER XI

The Sino-Japanese Dispute: Impressions of an Eye-Witness. By Dr. Sherwood Eddy, Author of *The World's Danger Zone.*

i. The Japanese Case
ii. The Chinese Case
iii. The Japanese Advance in Manchuria
iv. The Manchurian 'Independence' Movement
v. 'Chaos' in China
vi. Communism in China
vii. Possible Courses of Action.

CHAPTER XII

Some Consequences of the Sino-Japanese Dispute. By Dr. G. P. Gooch, Author of *History of Modern Europe, 1887–1919*.

i. The Effect upon Japan's Friends
ii. Sympathy for China
iii. The Effect on the League
iv. The Effect on the Disarmament Conference
v. United States Co-operation with the League
vi. The Problem of Sanctions
vii. The Problem of Private Arms Manufacture
viii. The Welfare of China
ix. The Only Policy.

CHAPTER XIII

The Need for National and International Economic Planning. By Dr. C. Delisle Burns, Stevenson Lecturer in Citizenship, University of Glasgow.

i. No Lack of Plans
ii. Some Causes of Inaction
iii. Prejudice against 'Government Interference'
iv. The Fetish of Production
v. The 'Treasury Mind'
vi. The New Problem: 'Consumption'
vii. Changing Populations
viii. Competition for Markets
ix. A Plan to Meet the Common Needs of Ordinary Men.

APPENDIX

Conference for the Reduction and Limitation of Armaments: Text of the Resolution adopted by the General Commission on 22 July, 1932.

APPENDIX

CONTENTS OF PROBLEMS OF PEACE

(Sixth Series)

CHAPTER IV

The First General Disarmament Conference. By Henri Rolin, Legal Adviser to the Belgian Ministry of Foreign Affairs.

i. The Importance of the Conference
ii. The Necessity for Disarmament
 (*a*) The Problem before 1914
 (*b*) The Peace Treaties and the League.
iii. The Problem of Security
iv. The Need for International Control of Disarmament
v. The Draft Convention
vi. Some Practical Suggestions.

CHAPTER V

The Codification of International Law. By John J. Hearne, Legal Adviser to the Department of External Affairs, Dublin.

i. A New Chapter in International Law
ii. State Sovereignty
iii. The New International Order
iv. The Object of Codification
v. The Theoretical Reason for Codification
vi. Some Urgent Practical Reasons
vii. The League Method
viii. Codification to Include Amendment and the Making of New Laws
ix. Proposals for a Codification Committee
x. Conclusion.

CHAPTER VI

Europe and the World Community. By Alfred Zimmern, Montague Burton Professor of International Relations in the University of Oxford.

i. What is a Community?
ii. The Nature of a Future World Community
iii. Europe not a Unit
iv. A Myth or Economic Dictatorship
v. Danger of Large-scale Economic Blocs
vi. The Line of Progress.

CHAPTER VII

International Financial Relations. By Dr. Paul Leverkuehn, formerly Secretary of the German Embassy in Washington.

i. Pre-war International Financial Relations
ii. Some Misconceptions
iii. Security for Investments and for National Interests abroad present Different Problems
iv. British and American Policies
v. Germany's Pre-war Foreign Investments
vi. French Transactions before the War
vii. The Far East
viii. The Balkans
ix. The Extent of International Indebtedness To-day
x. Resulting Instability and Lack of Confidence
xi. The Separation of International Finance and Politics: Some Achievements of the League.

CHAPTER VIII

Labour and the World Community. By George A. Johnston, Chief of the Information Section of the Intelligence and Liaison Division of the International Labour Office.

i. Labour Class-conscious, Nation-conscious, and World-conscious
ii. The United Front
iii. The Philosophical Basis of Labour Organization
iv. Participation of Labour in the League of Nations and the International Labour Organization.

CHAPTER IX

The Theory of International Society. By Harold J. Laski, Professor of Political Science in the University of London.

i. A New Philosophy of Inter-State Relations
ii. Inadequate Foundations of International Law
iii. A New Basis
iv. The Political Prerequisites of International Society
v. The Issue before Us.

CHAPTER X

Russia and the World Community. By Dr. Sherwood Eddy, Secretary for Asia of the Young Men's Christian Association.

i. Ideals and Practice
ii. Russia and the League
iii. Russia not Organized for Military Aggression
iv. The Five-Year Plan
v. What is Communism?
vi. A Final Synthesis
vii. Note on Section ii.

CHAPTER XI

America and the World Community. By James W. Garner, Professor of International Law, University of Illinois.

i. The World Community
ii. America as a Member of the World Community
iii. Some Factors in the Development of American Foreign Policy
iv. A New Outlook
v. The United States and the League
vi. The Alternatives
vii. Leadership.

CHAPTER XII

The British Empire and the World Community. By E. J. Phelan, Chief of the Diplomatic Division of the International Labour Office.

i. Evolution in Opposite Directions
ii. The Terms 'Empire' and 'Commonwealth'
iii. Are the Dominions Members of the League?
iv. The Value to be Attached to the 1926 Report of the Imperial Conference
v. Implications of the *inter se* Doctrine
vi. Practical Difficulties to which the Doctrine may give Rise
vii. The Unity of the Commonwealth.

* * * *